ISBN 978-1-5285-2867-2
PIBN 10962544

1 MONTH OF
FREE
READING

at

www.ForgottenBooks.com

By purchasing this book you are eligible for one month membership to ForgottenBooks.com, giving you unlimited access to our entire collection of over 1,000,000 titles via our web site and mobile apps.

To claim your free month visit:

www.forgottenbooks.com/free962544

English
Français
Deutsche
Italiano
Español
Português

www.forgottenbooks.com

Mythology Photography **Fiction**
Fishing Christianity **Art** Cooking
Essays Buddhism Freemasonry
Medicine **Biology** Music **Ancient
Egypt** Evolution Carpentry Physics
Dance Geology **Mathematics** Fitness
Shakespeare **Folklore** Yoga Marketing
Confidence Immortality Biographies
Poetry **Psychology** Witchcraft
Electronics Chemistry History **Law**
Accounting **Philosophy** Anthropology
Alchemy Drama Quantum Mechanics
Atheism Sexual Health **Ancient History**
Entrepreneurship Languages Sport
Paleontology Needlework Islam
Metaphysics Investment Archaeology
Parenting Statistics Criminology
Motivational

American and English

CORPORATION CASES

A COLLECTION OF CORPORATION CASES, BOTH PRIVATE AND
MUNICIPAL (EXCEPTING RAILWAY CASES), DECIDED
IN THE COURTS OF LAST RESORT IN THE
UNITED STATES, ENGLAND,
AND CANADA

EDITED BY ADELBERT HAMILTON

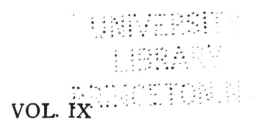

VOL. IX

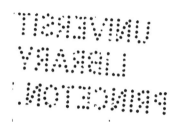

TABLE OF CASES REPORTED.

TABLE OF CASES REPORTED.

TOWN OF SUFFIELD

v.

TOWN OF EAST GRANBY.

(52 *Connecticut*, 175.)

The Statute (General Statutes, p. 88, sec. 3) provides for the appointment of a committee by the Superior Court in the case of disputed town lines, "to fix said disputed line and establish it by suitable monuments and report their doings to the court ;" and that, after the report is accepted by the court, and recorded on the records of both the towns, " said line so fixed and established shall forever thereafter be the true divisional line between the towns." *Held,* that the action of the committee, thus accepted and recorded, is final, and cannot be reviewed except for fraud or other improper or irregular conduct on the part of the committee.

APPLICATION to the Superior Court in Hartford County for the appointment of a committee of three to establish a disputed divisional line between the plaintiff and defendant towns, brought under Gen. Statutes, p. 88, sec. 3, which is given in full in the opinion. The committee was appointed, gave the notice required by the statute, heard the parties interested, fixed the divisional line and marked it by monuments, and made its report. The defendant town remonstrated against the acceptance of the report, the principal allegations of the remonstrance being as follows:

The defendant remonstrates against the acceptance of the report of the committee in the above-entitled cause, so far as it relates to the divisional line described in said report as a line " beginning at a granite monument at Sheldon's Corner, and thence running south, 25° 20' east, in a straight line to a granite monument at the northwest corner of ancient Windsor ; because—First. There was no evidence introduced before the committee proving or tending to prove that the divisional line, reported by them running from Sheldon's Corner to the northwest corner of ancient Windsor, was ever before the

9 Cor. Cas.--1

place of a line established to be a divisional line between the plaintiff and the defendant, or its predecessors in title, and the committee, in attempting to establish said line, have exceeded their power and jurisdiction. Second. That the following facts were proved before said committee, and found by them, no evidence to the contrary having been offered, namely : [The remonstrance here set forth the facts claimed with regard to the line claimed to be the true one.] And the remonstrants aver that it results as a conclusion of law from the facts above recited and found by the committee in the cause, that the true and only divisional line between the parties to this suit, from Sheldon's Corner southerly, is not the line reported by said committee, but the straight line hereinbefore described, drawn from said Sheldon's corner southerly to a heap of stones in the line between ancient Windsor and said Suffield, about forty-seven rods easterly from the southerly terminus of the line reported by said committee in this cause; and that said committee manifestly mistook the law in the premises, by reporting the line described in their report, and by not reporting the line above described in this remonstrance as the true divisional line between the parties to this suit. Also that said line reported by said committee is against the evidence in the trial before said committee. Third. That the committee have neglected to fix and establish the divisional line between the plaintiff and the defendant, and report their doings therein in respect to a considerable part of the line in dispute, namely, in respect to that part running from the southwest corner of Suffield to the northwest corner of the town of Windsor Locks, the same being a disputed divisional line between the plaintiff and the defendant. Wherefore the defendant prays the court to reject the report of said committee so far as the said report is herein and hereby remonstrated against, and to accept the same so far as it is not excepted to in this remonstrance, or otherwise dispose of the same as to law and justice may appertain.

The plaintiff town demurred to the remonstrance, and the court (Stoddard, J.) held the remonstrance insufficient, and accepted the report and ordered the same recorded. The defendant town appealed.

W. C. Case and *C. H. Clarke* for the appellant.

The committee cannot change or alter existing lines. Gorrill *v.* Whittier, 3 N. Hamp. 267; Lisbon *v.* Bowdoin, 53 Maine, 327; Bethel *v.* Albany, 65 id. 201; Freeman *v.* Kenney, 15 Pick. 46. What is the true line is matter of law. Doe *v.* Paine, 4 Hawks, 64; Hurley *v.* Morgan, 1 Dev. & Bat. 425 The construction of the statute is aided by the construction of that concerning the establishment of private boundaries. Gen. Statutes, p. 355, sec. 1. Perry *v.* Pratt, 31 Conn. 442; West Hartford Eccl. Soc. *v.* First Baptist Church, 35 id. 118. In Massachusetts, under similar authority, by a statute which required no report to the court by the committee, the court has reviewed the report and set it aside. Wrentham *v.* Norfolk, 114 Mass. 561. The statute in Maine does not require any acceptance of the report of the committee or other action of the court. Bethel *v.* Albany, 65 Maine, 202.

J. R. Buck and *A. F. Eggleston* for the appellees.

GRANGER, J—This is a proceeding under the following statute (Gen. Statutes, p. 88, sec. 3): "When the FACTS. selectmen of adjoining towns . . . shall not agree as to the place of the divisional line between their respective communities, the Superior Court, upon the application of either, shall appoint a committee of three to fix said disputed line, and establish it by suitable monuments, and report their doings to said court; and when said report shall have been accepted by said court, and, together with the record of acceptance, shall have been lodged for record in the records of both the communities interested therein, said line so fixed and established shall forever thereafter be the true divisional line between them; and said court may allow costs at its discretion." The act then proceeds to provide that the committee shall be sworn, that twenty days' notice of the time and place of their meeting shall be given in a mode prescribed, and that all parties interested shall have the right to be heard.

The determination of the present case depends on the construction to be given to this statute. It has stood upon our statute-book many years, but has never before been before the court for construction.

The committee in the present case, upon proper notice to, and hearing all parties interested, fixed a certain line as the divisional line between the plaintiff and defendant towns, and made its report to the court.   The defendant town remonstrated against the acceptance of the report upon the ground that the committee, upon the documentary and other evidence in the case, had erred in their conclusion as to the location of a part of the line, and that their decision was against the evidence in the case.   No fraud or other misconduct on the part of the committee is charged; the error is solely one of judgment.

The statute makes it the duty of the committee to " fix the disputed line and establish it by suitable monuments," and further provides that, after their report is accepted by the court and recorded upon the records of the two towns, " the line so fixed and established shall forever thereafter be the true divisional line between them."

We think it clear that the legislature intended that this action of the committee, thus accepted and recorded, should be final. Of course, if there has been fraud or other misconduct on the part of the committee, or irregularity in their proceedings, their report may be set aside on that ground. But nothing of the kind is claimed here. The case is entirely unlike that of a committee in chancery. There the committee is a mere arm of the court, and the judgment that is finally rendered is wholly the judgment of the court. The committee here is a special statutory tribunal, and the judgment is that of the committee rather than of the court. There is a reason why their action should be final in the fact that no title to land, or other private right of any kind, is affected by it.   The matter of town boundaries is one wholly for the discretion and within the power of the legislature, and it has full power to create a tribunal like the one in this case, for the establishment of disputed town lines, and to make their action final.   We are satisfied that it intended to do so here, and that it has made its intention plain in the language of the statute.

We advise that the remonstrance be overruled and the report of the committee accepted.

In this opinion the other judges concurred.

WHO MAY FIX MUNICIPAL BOUNDARIES.—The subject of municipal boundaries has been touched upon in three former cases in this series of reports : Willett *v.* Corporation of Belleville, 11 Tenn. 1; 2 Am. & Eng.

Corp. Cas. 248; deciding that courts of chancery in Tennessee are not authorized by statute to change the territorial limits of a municipal corporation. City of Topeka *v.* Gellett, Kansas, 1884; 5 Am. & Eng. Corp. Cas. 290; deciding that boundaries of municipality cannot be enlarged by municipal authorities so as to include for purposes of taxation property never laid out by its owners into blocks and streets, to which case was appended a note concerning the classification and powers of municipalities, and special legislation in reference thereto. And finally, City of Albia *v.* O'Hara, Iowa, 1884; 5 Am. & Eng. Corp. Cas. 326; a case defining corporate limits as including, for the purposes of a prosecution for violating a liquor ordinance, all the territory over which the city exercises jurisdiction for city purposes under claim of right.

To establish or change the boundaries of a municipality are acts in their nature legislative. Therefore power to perform them cannot constitutionally be delegated to the courts. City of Galesburg *v.* Hawkinson, 75 Ill. 152; S. P. People *v.* Nevada, 6 Cal. 143; *contra*, Keyser *v.* Trustees, etc., 16 Mo. 88. Nor can one settlement without the consent of another determine to enlarge its boundaries so as to include the latter. Thus in People *ex rel. v.* Bennett, 18 Am. Rep. 107; 29 Mich. 451; an attempt was made to incorporate as one, two village settlements separated by intervening farms; it was held that the statute was unconstitutional because it allowed the petitioners for incorporation to decide upon the extent of territory to be incorporated, and because the legislature had attempted to delegate legislative powers in this respect to private citizens instead of local bodies, boards, or officers, no notice, no hearing, and no right to a hearing being provided. In this case the court also declared that the question of the boundaries of an incorporated village belongs to policy rather than law, and is political and not judicial. The statute required that after the petition for incorporation was filed in the Circuit Court, a judge should appoint a time and place in the territory where an incorporation election should be held, after two weeks' notice posted by the clerk of the court. If the majority were in favor of incorporation, the judge was to enter an order declaring the incorporation, etc. It was held that an incorporation formed under the act could not be sustained.

But the legislature may create a tribunal to determine at least in a *quasi* judicial manner the desirability of enlarging boundaries by annexation, and to order such annexation if deemed desirable. Speaking of the statute, the court said : " It empowers the county commissioners to order the annexation of contiguous territory to a city or incorporated village upon the petition of the corporation, as provided. . . . The statute regards the municipal corporation, on the one hand, and the inhabitants of the territory proposed to be annexed, on the other, as adversary parties. It constitutes the board of county commissioners a tribunal to determine the question. Each has full opportunity to be heard. The commissioners may refuse to order the annexation if they deem it unreasonable or improper though the parties assent to the measure; and if they consider it reasonable and proper, they may order it upon petition of the corporation, without the consent and against the will of any other party;" and the court affirmed the constitutionality of this law. Powers *v.* Commissioners of Wood County, 8 Ohio St. 285. It is fair to say, however, that the precise point urged against the constitutionality of this statute was that it provided for annexation against the will of the parties. The point that it was a delegation of legislative duty does not appear to have been made. And a distinction is obvious between delegating such power to courts and delegating it to appropriate local bodies or boards, or officers—which latter kind of delegation appears to be sanctioned by respectable authority. Devore's Appeal, 56 Pa. St. 163; People *v.* Carpenter, 24 N. Y. 86; Osgood *v.* Clark, 26 N. H. 307.

In Indiana power is given to cities to enlarge their own boundaries over adjacent lands which have been legally platted of record; but over lands not so platted the power of annexation is exercised by other means. Mayor of Jeffersonville *v.* Weems, 5 Ind. 547; Elston *v.* Board of Trustees of Crawfordsville, 20 Ind. 272; Evansville *v.* Page, 23 Ind. 525.

In England, " if a place has no known or defined boundary, the law provides means for having the boundary ascertained, upon petition for that purpose, by a commission of inquiry, under direction of a Secretary of State formerly and now by a local government board, which is a body of large powers having supervision of such matters. When the boundaries are fixed, the process is as in other places. But if any number not less than one twentieth of the owners and rate-payers desire the whole or any part of the place to be excluded from the operation of the (Local Government) act, an inquiry is to be directed, and the matter is to be determined on its merits. These proceedings appear to be subject further to the supervision of the Queen's Bench by *certiorari*," per Mr. Justice Campbell in People *v.* Bennett, 18 Am. Rep. 113; 29 Mich. 451; citing Matlock Bath District, 2 Best & Sm. 542; Regina *v.* Northowram, L. R. 1 Q. B. 110; Regina *v.* Hardy, L. R. 4 Q. B. 117; Regina *v.* Local Government Board, L. R. 8 Q. B. 227.

The conclusions deducible from the authorities examined are these:

1. The legislature has the undoubted right to fix the boundaries of any municipal corporation it may create.

2. If it create such corporations by general act, it may delegate the power of defining the boundaries to any appropriate local board, body, or officer, but not to a court or to any citizen or number of citizens individually.

WASHINGTON

v.

THE STATE.

(75 *Alabama,* 582.)

The elective franchise is a privilege rather than a right, granted or denied on grounds of public policy, and is the subject of exclusive regulation by the State, limited only by the provisions of the Fifteenth Amendment to the Federal Constitution, which prohibits any discrimination on account of " race, color, or previous condition of servitude."

Section 3 of article viii. of the Constitution of 1875, denying the privilege of registering, voting, and holding office to those "who shall have been convicted of treason, embezzlement of public funds, malfeasance in office, larceny," etc., disqualifies from participation in the elective franchise all persons convicted of any one of the specified crimes prior to the adoption of the Constitution, as well as those thereafter convicted; and hence, a person convicted of larceny in 1871 may be convicted under the statute for voting at a general election held in August, 1884.

Section 3 of article viii. of Constitution, as thus construed, not taking away a legal right, nor imposing a legal burden, and requiring a conviction in the due course of judicial proceedings before disfranchisement, is neither an *ex post facto* law, nor a provision in the nature of a bill of attainder, within the meaning of the Federal Constitution.

APPEAL from Tuscaloosa Circuit Court.

Tried before Hon. S. H. Sprott.

The facts are sufficiently stated in the opinion.

Martin & Martin for appellant.

T. N. McClelland, Attorney-General, for the State.

SOMERVILLE, J.—The defendant is indicted for illegal voting at the general election held in August, 1884, and was convicted on the ground that he had voted while laboring under a constitutional disqualification, having been convicted of the crime of larceny in the year 1871. At the time of his conviction of the latter offence, he was not disqualified by this fact, the Constitution of 1868 being then in force.

Whether the present conviction for illegal voting was right or wrong depends upon the proper construction of section 3, article viii. of the Constitution of 1875, now the organic law of this State, which reads as follows: "The following classes shall not be permitted to register, vote, or hold office:

"First. Those who shall have been convicted of treason, embezzlement of public funds, malfeasance in office, larceny, bribery, or other crime punishable by imprisonment in the penitentiary.

"Second. Those who are idiots or insane."

The grade of larceny, whether grand or petit, is immaterial, GRADE OF LARCENY IMMATERIAL. as this section has been construed by us to embrace both classes of the offence, a conviction of either operating as a disfranchisement and disqualification of every voter coming within its provisions. Anderson *v.* The State, 72 Ala. 187.

The question for decision is, whether the section under consideration applies to convictions previous to the adoption of the Constitution, or whether it must be confined to those transpiring subsequently thereto. This is determined greatly by the policy and purpose of its provisions, and the nature of what, in common parlance, is called the right of political suffrage. It may be laid down as a sound proposition, using the language of Mr. Cooley, that "participation in the elective franchise is a privilege rather than a right, and it is granted or denied on grounds of general policy, the prevailing view being that it should be as general as possible, consistent with the public safety." Cooley's Con. Lim. (5th Ed.) 752 (*599). Mr. Story, without undertaking to say whether it has its foundation in natural right or not, says it "has always been treated in the practice of nations as a strictly civil right, derived from and regulated by each society according to its own free will and pleasure." 1 Story's Const. (4th Ed.) §§ 579-582. The SUFFRAGE IS A PRIVILEGE. weight of both reason and of authority, however, as we shall see, support the view that political suffrage is not an absolute or natural right, but is a privilege conventionally conferred upon the citizen by the sovereignty. There can be practically no such thing as universal suffrage, and it is believed that no such theory is recognized among any people. Some are necessarily excluded on the ground of infancy, and the privilege is infinitely varied among others, either upon the ground of public policy, or for reasons that seem arbitrary. No one can lawfully vote under any government of laws except those who are expressly authorized by

law. It is well settled, therefore, under our form of government, that the right is one conferred by constitutions and
statutes, and is the subject of exclusive regulation by the
State, limited only by the provisions of the Fifteenth Amendment to the Federal Constitution, which prohibits any discrimination on account of "race, color, or previous condition
of servitude." Cooley's Cons. Lim. (5th Ed.) *752 et seq.*;
McCreary on Elec. (2d Ed.) § 3; Brightley's Elec. Cases, 27;
Huber *v.* Reiley, 53 Penn. St. 112. The States MAY BE WITH-
having the power to confer or to withhold the right, HELD OR REGU-
LATED BY
in such manner as the people may deem best for STATES.
their welfare, it necessarily follows that they may confer it
upon such conditions or qualifications as they may see fit, subject only to the limitation above mentioned. As said in United
States *v.* Cruikshank, 92 U. S. (2 Otto), 542, "the right to vote
in the States comes from the States; but the right of exemption from political discrimination comes from the United
States." It is chiefly upon this theory that the exclusion of
females from the right of voting, although they are deemed
citizens, is justified in law, this not being necessarily a privilege or immunity of citizenship. Minor *v.* Happersett, 21
Wall. 162; Morse on Citizenship, § 3.

The right is also denied almost universally to idiots, insane
persons, and minors, upon the ground that they
lack the requisite judgment and discretion which IDIOTS, LUNA-
TICS AND MINORS
CANNOT VOTE.
fit them for its exercise. It has never been considered that any of these disqualifications were imposed as a
punishment, and no one has thought to view them as even in
the nature of a penalty. The same may be asserted as to the
exclusion of unnaturalized citizens who are disqualified on the
ground of alienage, and of paupers, to whom some States
deny the right upon principles of State policy. It is quite
common also to deny the right of suffrage, in the various
American States, to such as have been convicted NOR FELONS.
of infamous crimes. The manifest purpose is to preserve the
purity of the ballot-box, which is the only sure foundation of
republican liberty, and which needs protection against the
invasion of corruption, just as much as against that of ignor-
ance, incapacity, or tyranny. The evil infection of the one is
not more fatal than that of the other. The presumption is,
that one rendered infamous by conviction of felony, or other

base offence indicative of great moral turpitude, is unfit to exercise the privilege of suffrage, or to hold office, upon terms of equality with freemen who are clothed by the State with the toga of political citizenship. It is proper, therefore, that this class should be denied a right, the exercise of which might sometimes hazard the welfare of communities, if not that of the State itself, at least in close political contests. The exclusion must for this reason be adjudged a mere disqualification, imposed for protection, and not for punishment—withholding an honorable privilege, and not denying a personal right or attribute of personal liberty. Pomeroy on Cons. Law, § 535; Anderson *v.* Baker, 23 Md. 531; Blair *v.* Ridgely, 41 Mo. 63; *Ex parte* Stratton, 1 West Va. 305; Kring *v.* Missouri, 107 U. S. 221.

The clause of the Constitution which we are now consider-

PROHIBITION OF FELONS FROM VOTING NOT EX POST FACTO. ing cannot, for the foregoing reasons, be considered as either an *ex post facto* law, within the prohibition of section 10, article i. of the United States Constitution, or as in the nature of a bill of attainder. It is free from the latter objection, on the ground that it requires a conviction in the due course of judicial proceedings before disfranchisement is made to attach. 2 Story's Const. § 1344; Martin *v.* Snowden, 18 Gratt. (Va.) 100. It is not an *ex post facto* law, because it neither takes away a legal right, nor imposes any legal hurden, one of which is necessary to the infliction of a penalty. It merely withholds a constitutional privilege, which is grantable or revocable by the sovereign power of the State at pleasure. In this particular the case differs from that of *Ex parte* Garland, 4 Wall. 333, and Cummings *v.* The State of Missouri, Ib. 277, where a test-oath, obviously punitive in its nature, was held to be unconstitutional, so far as it was required as a prerequisite for the exercise of an ordinary calling, as that of an attorney at law or of a clergyman. The right to exercise these callings was a natural right, which was not conferred by government, but would exist without it, although the subject of legislative regulation. It was a valuable attribute of personal liberty in the nature of property, the deprivation of which was punitive in its character. Sedgw. on Stat. & Cons. Law (2d Ed., Pomeroy's), p. 558, note; Brightley's Elec. Cases, 97, note; McCreary on Elec. (2d Ed.) §§ 31, 32. Upon a like principle is based the ruling of the United States Supreme Court in another case, where a State statute was held void which excluded persons from the privilege of sustaining suits in the courts of the State, or from making application for rehearings, except upon condition of taking an expurgatory oath, that they had never engaged in hostile measures against the government. Pierce *v.* Carskadon, 16 Wall. 234. The fact that no one can exercise the elective franchise unless it is affirmatively and expressly conferred by the constitution or laws of a State, as Mr. Pomeroy observes, shows at once and of itself, "that the voter possesses a mere privilege; that the States have supreme control over this privilege; that taking it away, or, what is the same thing, refusing to confer it, does not impair a right, and cannot be regarded as a penalty or punishment. Pomeroy's Cons. Law, § 535.

We may further observe, what follows from the foregoing views, that there can be no such thing as a vested SUFFRAGE IS right in the elective franchise as against the State, NOT A VESTED RIGHT. or people, from which it was *ex gratia* derived; for, under our form of civil polity, all political power is inherent in the people, and "they have," in the language of the Constitution, "at all times an inalienable right to change their form of government, in such manner as they may deem expedient." Const. 1875, Art. 1, § 3.

These reasons induce us to the conclusion that the framers of the Constitution intended to disqualify from participation in the elective franchise all persons previously convicted of larceny, and other crimes specified, as well as those convicted subsequently to the date of the adoption of that instrument. They both alike come within the letter, as well as the spirit of its provisions touching the subject of suffrage and elections. The mischief to be remedied is not of greater magnitude in the one case than in the other. And as all the provisions of a constitution must go into effect as a whole, and at the time of its final adoption, unless otherwise declared, no reason appears to us why the operation of the one under consideration should be postponed by judicial construction.

We discover no error in the ruling of the Circuit Court, instructing the jury to find the defendant guilty if they believed the evidence ; and its judgment is affirmed.

CRIME AS A DISFRANCHISEMENT.—A conviction of petty larceny disqualifies a person from voting in Florida. State *ex rel.* Jordan *v.* Buckman, 18 Fla. 267. So also in Alabama and probably all the States. Anderson *v.* State, 72 Ala. 189. And the use of the word "other" before the generic term "crime punishable by imprisonment in the penitentiary" does not show that the particular kind of larceny which disqualifies is that larceny which is punished by imprisonment in the penitentiary. It includes petty larceny as well. Anderson *v.* State, 72 Ala. 187. In Oregon, Sawyer *v.* Walkinds, Deady, 245, the constitution (art. 2, sec. 3) declares that "the privilege of an elector shall be forfeited by any crime which is punishable in the penitentiary." The defendant was indicted for an assault with a deadly weapon, which by section 536 of the Oregon Criminal Code was made punishable by fine or imprisonment in the county jail or penitentiary, in the discretion of the court, and to which accusation he pleaded guilty and was sentenced to pay a fine of $200. Afterwards he voted for representative in congress. *Held*, (1) that "conviction" signified a proving or finding of guilt, without, however, including the sentence, (2) that a crime "is punishable" by imprisonment in the penitentiary when it may be so punished, and the fact that it is or may be otherwise punished does not change its grade or character in this respect; (3) that defendant's conviction forfeited his privilege as an elector. But a somewhat different view was taken in Nebraska in Gandy *v.* State, 10 Neb. 243, wherein the general rule of disfranchisement by conviction of felony was affirmed; but it was held that a conviction for conspiracy to violate a revenue law of the United States (sec. 5440 U. S. Rev. Stat.) is not a conviction of felony, but of a misdemeanor merely. And the court went further, holding that when the court in affixing the punishment for a given offence, is authorized in its discretion to consider it either as a felony or as a mere misdemeanor and treat it accordingly; the punishment which the court actually inflicts must determine the grade of the offence, especially when the consequence of conviction might deprive one of the right of suffrage. This was following the rule laid down in California in People *v.* Cornell, 16 Cal. 187—which rule the court declared "has the merit of being both just and humane." But this case was thoroughly considered by Judge Deady in Sawyer *v.* Walkinds, *supra*, and he refused to follow it.

Conviction of the crime is essential to work the forfeiture of the right to vote. This was decided in Huber *v.* Reilly, 53 Pa. St. 112, wherein it was held that a citizen drafted into the service of the United States, who had notice but refused to report and was registered as a deserter was nevertheless entitled to vote, unless he had been convicted of desertion by a court-martial.

But where the right to vote has been lost by crime, it will be restored by pardon. A pardon reaches both the punishment prescribed for the offence and the guilt of the offender. In the eye of the law the pardoned offender is as innocent as if he had never committed the offence. The pardon removes all penalties and disabilities, and restores the convict to all his civil rights, making him, as it were, a new man, and giving him a new credit and capacity. *Ex parte* Garland, 4 Wall. 333, 380; United

States v. Paddleford, 9 Wall. 531; United States v. Klein, 13 Wall. 128; Carlisle v. United States, 16 Wall. 147; Knote v. United States, 95 U. S. 149; Jones v. Board of Registers, 56 Miss. 768.

EX-POST-FACTO LAWS.—The point that a statute depriving a man of the right to vote merely takes a privilege from him and not a natural right, is by another line of cases brought out even more clearly than in the principal case. Those cases are the test-oath cases, arising under statutory provisions forfeiting the right to pursue an occupation or calling for failure to take a prescribed test-oath. In Missouri a statute declaring a forfeiture of office by curators of a college for failure to take a test-oath, was held void as *ex post facto*. State v. Adam, 44 Mo. 570; statutes requiring a test oath from attorneys as a condition of being allowed to practice were held void in *Ex parte* Garland, 4 Wall. 333; *In re* Murphy and Glover, 41 Mo. 339; State v. Heighland, 41 Mo. 388; but see Cohen v. Wright, 22 Cal. 293; *Ex parte* Yale, 24 Cal. 241; State v. Garesche, 36 Mo. 256. A similar statute as to clergymen was also held void. State v. Cummings, 4 Wall. 277; 36 Mo. 263.

Statutes requiring a test-oath as a condition of voting have been held both valid and invalid. Valid in Randolph v. Good, 3 W. Va. 551; State v. Neal, 42 Mo. 119. Void in Rison v. Farr, 24 Ark. 161. See also, Anderson v. Baker *et al.*, 23 Md. 531; Blair v. Ridgeley, 41 Mo. 63; State v. Staten, 6 Cold. (Tenn.) 248; Green v. Shumway, 39 N. Y. 418. Concerning the distinction between taking away legal rights and taking away legal privileges, Mr. Pomeroy very forcibly says : "Entirely agreeing with the decisions of the United States Court that the test-oath statutes were *ex-post-facto* laws when applied to the subject-matter of trades, professions, business, etc., and made a penalty for past crimes, we think there is a clear and broad distinction between such cases and those involving the right of suffrage. Of course, if the State constitution prescribes the qualifications of electors, and a statute demands other and antagonistic qualifications, it would violate the State constitution. But the question under discussion is concerned solely with the relations of State statutes or constitutions with the provision of the National Constitution, prohibiting the States to pass *ex-post-facto* laws. In order that a law should be *ex post facto* it must inflict some legal penalty, and thus must consist in taking away some legal right or imposing some legal burden. A State constitution which demands a test-oath of loyalty as a prerequisite of exercising the electoral franchise, does not take away a legal right or impose a legal burden, because no person in the State has any right to vote independent of the express provisions of the State constitution. The very constitution which contains the restriction is the source of all power, capacity, or right of voting; and if such constitution impose a test-oath as a qualification, it does the same in essence as when it imposes the age of twenty-one years, citizenship, or the male sex, as a prerequisite. In other words, as the subject of electoral capacity has been left to the States absolutely untrammelled, except by the provisions respecting race and color, any changes which the States may think best to make in defining the qualifications of voters, do not take away any right or impose any legal burden, and cannot therefore be *ex-post-facto* laws, however much they may apply to past acts and transactions." "Sedgwick on the Construction of Statute and Constitutional Law," page 558 (Pomeroy's note).

REYNOLDS

v.

SNOW.

(Advance Case, California Supreme Court. September 25, 1885.)

A ballot which does not conform to the requirements of section 1191 of the political code, as to length, and in other minor respects, cannot be counted.

The reason why a court of appeals declines, ordinarily, to interfere upon a conflict of evidence, is because the trial court has an advantage over the former, in that it can both hear the witness and observe his deportment, when before it and delivering his testimony. When, however, the findings of the trial court are entirely based upon documentary evidence, such as ballots cast at an election, photographic copies of which are before the appellate court, the reason of the rule fails, and with it the rule itself.

APPEAL from a judgment of the superior court of Stanislaus county, entered in favor of the plaintiff. The opinion states the facts.

Schell & Bond for the appellant.

Wright & Hazen for the respondent.

FOOTE, C.—A contest for the office of supervisor of district number one of Stanislaus county.

The bill of exceptions in the transcript should be considered by this court; the objections made to it by the respondent are not well taken. It appears by the official returns of the various election boards of the district, as canvassed by the board of supervisors of the county, that the appellant, William Snow, received three hundred and twenty-four, and the respondent, B. F. Reynolds, three hundred and twenty-three, votes. To the former the board awarded the certifi-

FACTS. cate of election and the office in dispute. The latter contested his right thereto, and prevailed in the contest. From that judgment Snow appealed. The court, upon a recount of the ballots, discovered that the contestant's exhibit number eight was one having the name of William Snow printed on it, and that of the office for which he was a candidate, but the paper on which it was printed was, when voted, only about eight and one half inches in length, and did not, in that and some other minor respects, conform to section 1191 of the political code, and ought not to be counted for Snow, as it had been. This conclusion of the court was correct.

That tribunal substantially found, also, that an election board had counted for Snow two ballots called plaintiff's exhibits two and three; that on them, and in the same line, were printed the following words and figures, viz., "23. Supervisor District No. 1, B. F. Reynolds." That the words "Supervisor District No. 1, B. F. Reynolds," had been distinctly and completely erased by several lead-pencil marks being drawn completely through said words, and each of them, and that upon one of said ballots had been written the words "Wm. Snow," and upon the other the word "Snow," and that these words were written opposite said figures 23, line and erasure.

That the words erased were still discernible and distinguishable, and that the voter intended by the erasure to strike from the ballots, and each of them, the name of the office of supervisor of said county, in and for said district, and that no such office remained designated upon said ballots, and that neither the board of election nor the court could ascertain that the voters intended to vote for said "Snow," and "Wm. Snow," respectively, for said office, and that it was not the intention of said voters to vote for any person for said office.

To this finding, upon a thorough inspection of those ballots, we cannot agree. In a case where there was FINDING RE-VERSED ON EVIDENCE. a conflict in the evidence, in the sense that witnesses in the presence of the court had sworn contrary to each other, as to facts, we should not feel warranted in entering our dissent; but where, as in this case, the ballots themselves were, on that point, the only evidence before the court, and as photographic copies of them are before us, it is clear that there was no such conflict in the evidence as should prevent us from exercising a judgment contrary to that of the learned judge below. The reason why a court of appeal declines, ordinarily, to interfere upon a conflict of evidence, is because the trial court has an advantage over the former, in that it can both hear the witness and observe his deport- ment when before it, and delivering his testimony.

In the present instance the reason fails, and with it the rule of action.

The persons writing " Snow," and " Wm. Snow," on ex- hibits two and three, intended to vote for William Snow for supervisor of district No. 1, Stanislaus county, and the board of election were right when they counted those ballots for him for said office. It became plain from an inspection of another of the ballots, by the court, that the board of election had erroneously counted for Reynolds one ballot, which was on its face unmistakably cast for Snow, and thereupon it was properly counted for Snow. The action of that tribunal, in taking from Snow a vote, upon evidence showing that Jarvis Whitehead, not being a legal voter, had voted for him in su- pervisor district No. 1, Stanislaus county, will not be re- viewed, as the evidence was conflicting, in the proper sense of that term.

The court found further that B. F. Reynolds received for the office in dispute three hundred and twenty-two, and Wil- liam Snow three hundred and twenty-one, legal votes.

From the foregoing, it appears that the finding should have been that B. F. Reynolds received three hundred and twenty- two, and Wm. Snow three hundred and twenty-three votes for the same.

The judgment should be reversed and cause remanded.

SEARLS, C., and BELCHER, C. C., concurred.

BY THE COURT.—For the reasons given in the foregoing opinion, the judgment is reversed and cause remanded.

REGULATION BY STATUTE OF THE SIZE AND FORM OF BALLOTS.—Sec- tion 1191 of the Political Code of California, which provides for the size, shape, and manner of printing ballots, etc., and that no ticket shall be used at any election that does not conform to such statutory requirements, and section 1208, which provides that any ballot which does not conform to the requirements of section 1191 must, with all its contents, be re- jected, were construed in the case of Kirk *v.* Rhodes, 46 Cal. 398.

In that case it was held that as to things over which the voters could have no control, such as the precise kind of paper on which the ballot was printed, and the exact mode of spacing and printing required by statute, and the exact size of the ballot, the statute was merely directory, and that a ballot cast by an elector in good faith, but not complying exactly with the statutory requirements as to matters over which the elector had no control, and where the defect in the ballot could not be detected by ordinary observation, should not be rejected. But that as to matters over which the elector had control the statute was mandatory, and that failure to comply with the statute rendered the ballot void. Thus the statute providing that ballots must not be so marked as to be capable of identification, if a ballot is so marked it should be rejected. Under this decision, if the ballot varies from the statutory requirement as to size in a small degree only it should not be rejected. But if the variation is so large as to be readily appreciable, the ballot, it would seem, should be rejected. In the principal case the ballot was only eight and one half inches long, the statutory requirement being twelve inches, or within half an inch of twelve inches, and it would seem that the variation was large enough to bring the case within the principle last laid down.

STATUTES PROHIBITING ANY MARK OR DEVICE ON BALLOTS.—It is held in Mississippi that a statute prohibiting any mark or device on ballots by which one ballot can be told from another, shall render the ballot void, rendered void a ballot containing distinguishing marks on its face which were not visible when the ballot was folded. The court say: "The legislature was trying to prevent multitudes from 'being voted,' and being guided by a mere device or mark by which they should distinguish the ballots they were to use in the process, without a knowledge of the names of the persons for whom their ballots were being cast." Oglesby *v.* Ligman, 58 Miss. 502, printers' dashes were held marks or devices within the statute, and to render ballots void. In Steele *v.* Calhoun, 61 Miss. 556, a mere dotted line across the face of the ticket was held a mark or device.

The laws of the State of Maine make certain requirements as to ballots, and require the officers presiding over the election to reject such ballots as do not conform to the requirements; but if a ballot that does not conform is received it must be counted. Revised Statutes of Maine, 1883, chapter 4, section 29, Answer to question nine by Governor Garcelon, 70 Me. 566.

9 Cor. Cas.—2

ATTORNEY-GENERAL

v.

BOARD OF COUNCILMEN OF THE CITY OF DETROIT.

(Advance Case, Michigan.   October 14, 1885.)

A statute requiring the common council of a city to appoint a Board of Commissioners, who are in turn to appoint for each election district in the city local registration boards, to be composed of members of the two leading political parties is unconstitutional, because (1) it removes the appointment of local registration boards from both the people and their representatives, the common council, and delegates it to a body of commissioners who are in no proper sense representatives of the people, and because (2) it makes political opinions and membership in politieal parties the test of the right to hold certain offices, and renders ineligible to such offices persons who are members of other than the two leading parties.

Mandamus.

CAMPBELL, J.—The attorney general applies for a *mandamus* Facts. to compel the respondents to take action upon certain nominations made by the mayor of Detroit of four persons, two being Republicans and two being Democrats, to act as a board of commissioners of registration and of election for the city of Detroit. Respondents refused to consider the nominations because they regarded the statute which provides for such board as unconstitutional and invalid. To an order to show cause they interpose that ground of defense. No other question is of much importance in the case. The necessity of an immediate decision, in order to allow time for the action of the city authorities in season for the coming election, made it impossible for the court to do more than announce its determination, on rendering judgment in favor of respondents, as any oral statement in brief form of the grounds of their action would have been liable to some misapprehension. It was therefore thought best that the members of the court should express their views more formally in writing. The statute in question purports to amend chapter 2 and some sections of chapter 3 of the charter of Detroit, as revised in 1883. Chapter 2, which refers to the registration of voters, is entirely superseded by the present act, as is also so much of chapter 3 as provided for the choice of inspectors of election. The new statute undertakes to provide a board of commissioners to appoint ward registers and inspectors, who are to perform the duties formerly imposed on the boards made up of aldermen and their appointees, and of persons elected by the voters. The board thus provided for is re-quired to be composed of four members holding office for four years, the first board being appointed for one, two, three, and four years respectively, so that one vacancy shall be filled each year. They are all to be resident electors of the city, and two members thereof to be from each of the two leading political parties of the said city. They are required two weeks before the time fixed by law for the meeting of boards of registration of voters, to appoint two qualified electors of each voting district, one from each of the two leading polit-ical parties of the said city, to act as registers and form a dis-trict board of registration. The various district boards sit-ting together are to constitute a city board of registration. The board of commissioners are to fill any district vacancies by persons of the same political party to which the absentee belongs. The commissioners are also required to appoint for each voting district two inspectors, one from each of the two political parties " represented in the common council of said city," the electors choosing a third. Vacancies in any board of inspectors are to be filled by *viva voce* vote of the electors, but each vacancy must be filled by a person of the same po-litical party as the absentee. The commissioners also appoint the various clerks of election, but have no immediate part in the work of registration by action or supervision.

The statute makes a number of new provisions upon the subject of registration and election, which were more or less discussed on the argument, but which would only be im-portant if the law were not held to be entirely invalid, as we deem it to be. These several provisions will not, therefore, be dwelt upon. The invalidity of the statute was chiefly based on the argument upon the illegality of creating a board with such powers as those conferred by the statute, and re-quired to be composed of equal numbers of two political par-ties appointed as such members, and ineligible without such party connection. Relator insists that the legislature, under its power to pass laws to preserve the purity of elections and guard against abuses of the elective franchise, has discretionary power over the metheds, and that, even if the partisan disqualification is improper, the court may treat it as not essential, and sustain the commission by allowing the selection of its members without any such test. Neither of these grounds is tenable, in our view of the Constitution,

In order to appreciate the bearing of the considerations presented on the case, it will be necessary to make some reference to the general elective system of the constitution itself. It is needless to explain that under that system the whole scheme of government, in every department, depends upon the action of the qualified voters in their electoral districts. All male citizens of lawful age, and some whose United States citizenship is incomplete, are entitled after a certain term of residence to vote in the townships or wards in which they reside. Every vote, for any purpose whatever, is required to be cast in such township or ward. The only exception is in case of soldiers in the field during the war. All legislation imposing restraint or conditions upon voting must conform to the other clauses and provisions of the constitution. No part of that instrument can be allowed to override or destroy any other part. It is also well settled that our Sta:e polity recognizes and perpetuates local government through various classes of municipal bodies, whose essential character must be respected, as fixed by usage and recognition when the constitution was adopted ; and any legislation for any purpose which disregards any fundamental and essential requisites of such bodies has always been regarded as invalid and unconstitutional. There is nothing in the constitution which permits the legislature, under the desire to purify elections, to impose any conditions which will destroy or seriously impede the enjoyment of the elective franchise. And as the right of voting is the same everywhere, it is obvious that the conditions regulating the manner of exercising it must be the same in substance everywhere. The machinery of the government differs in its details in cities, villages and townships, and of course in methods and officers to administer the election laws. But it cannot be lawful to create substantial or serious differences in the fundamental rights of citizens of different localities in the exercise of their voting franchises.

It is also a most important principle under our constitu-

GENERAL ELEC-
TIVE SYSTEM.

tional system that no one shall be affected in any of his legal and political rights by reason of his opinions on political subjects or other matters of individual conscience. The political right to freedom of belief and expression is asserted in the most distinct way, and applies to every privilege which the constitution confers. No one has ever supposed that any new condition could be added to those which the constitution has imposed on the right of suffrage, beyond such as are necessary to guard against double voting, or to prevent its exercise by those who are not legal voters. The only legitimate object of registration laws is to secure a correct list of actually qualified voters. Any attempt to inquire into the sentiments of the voters is not only an abuse, but one which it is the chief purpose of the ballot system to prevent. The ballot is a constitutional method which cannot be changed, and its perpetuation means the security to vote without any inquisition into the voter's opinions of men or measures; and it would be entirely meaningless if the voter's choice of candidates for any office must be made from any particular party or number of parties. But the constitution has made this more specific, (although this was hardly necessary,) by providing, after giving the form of an official oath, that "no other oath, declaration, or test shall be required as a qualification for any office or public trust."

It is manifest that any important function of government comes under one or the other of these heads of "office" or "public trust." The board of registration commissioners consists under this statute of persons holding permanent offices. The district registers, clerk, and inspectors perform functions connected with the most vital and important action of citizens in their capacity as choosers of the officers of government. The constitutional rule covers them all, literally as well as impliedly.

PARTY MEMBERSHIP CANNOT BE MADE THE TEST OF THE RIGHT TO HOLD AN OFFICE.

It was urged on the argument that if the term "test" can be held applicable to inquiries into party affiliation, it is equally applicable to those other qualifications often required for public service, such as education, scientific acquirements in surveyors and other specialists, legal knowledge in law officers, and the like. But this is not so. Not only is it evident from the other provisions in this clause that all the exemptions referred to are such as would be applicable in all sorts of offices, but the use of the word " test " is especially significant because its recognized legal meaning in our constitution is derived from the English test acts, all of which related to matters of opinion, and most of them to religious opinion. Such has been the general understanding of the framers of constitutions. If this were not so, and if the power of the legislature in imposing conditions of office is at the same time only restrained by express clauses applying in terms to officers and to no one else, it would not be difficult for any dominant party controlling the legislature to perpetuate its power until overthrown by revolution. But such discriminations are as repugnant to the rights of voters in selecting as to the rights of those chosen in assuming office, and this clause is but an additional assertion of a principle found in other parts of the constitution, expressed or clearly implied. In the case of People *v.* Hurlbut, 24 Mich. 44, it was not disputed by any of the judges who referred to the matter that it would not be lawful to confine the choice of officers to particular parties, although two of the judges thought that the provision in that particular case was capable of being eliminated from the statute. And it is claimed, in the present case, that the present law is declared and intended to be non-partisan, and that the board may be chosen without reference to this restriction of party membership.

It is altogether likely that the framers of the law were of opinion that the evils of partisan action, and the temptation to carry it to abusive extremes, would be lessened by requiring that one party should not monopolize the offices, but that two should share them. No one can doubt the advantage of impartiality in public action. But parties, however powerful and unavoidable they may be, and however inseperable from popular government, are not and cannot be recognized as having any legal authority as such. The law cannot regulate or fix their numbers, or compel or encourage adherence to them. Many good citizens form no permanent party ties, and when elections are close the effort of each party is to detach votes from the friends of the other. Where there are two parties larger than any other, the success of either is very often gained by coalition with a third one. In local matters party allegiance is not uncommonly laid aside for the time being, so that it cannot be said that any party is represented in the election. However well meant such a statute as that before us may be, it distinctly makes party adhesion a condition of office ; and not only so, but it puts all but the two favored parties beyond the possibility of representation, if the law is obeyed.

It is equally clear that this party representation is the essential purpose of the law, and that the other changes are merely subsidiary. There are some changes in detail, but the main purpose cannot be mistaken. The partisan qualifications are made emphatic in regard to all the offices. It is impossible for any candid person to read the act and believe that the real legislative design can be carried out. By leaving the councilmen and mayor at liberty to choose commissioners from a single party, or for the commissioners to appoint registers and inspectors, without distinction of party, at their pleasure, and it would need no great sagacity to see that if such unlimited power were vested in a body made up as this body might then be constituted, all of the old evils would remain, and would be made worse by the absence of any responsibility to the voters of the precincts.

In my judgment the creation of a board with such powers as are given to this board is quite as serious an DELEGATION BY COMMON COUNCIL infringement of the constitution as the partisan TO COMMISSION ERS. clauses, and much more dangerous. This board is made by the statute the repository of some of the most important powers of government. It has the entire control, directly or indirectly, of the elections on which all the departments of government depend. It has the appointment of officers who can deprive any man of his vote at any election, if they see fit to do so, without any adequate means of redress to save it. While it is unavoidable that a voter's rights at election must, in case of dispute, be disposed of summarily, it is all the more necessary that the tribunal which decides on so sacred a right should be made up in harmony with representative and popular institutions.

While boards are not uncommonly created for the more convenient management of the business interests of the municipalities, it is a principle universally settled in our system that all officers and functionaries exercising power of government and control over political action must derive their power and office either from the people directly, or from the agents or representatives of the people. The officers of towns and cities have always been so created. The discretion of a political body or functionary cannot be delegated indefinitely. Here the choice of ward officers is made, not by the people of the ward, nor by the chosen officers of the city, but by persons who are themselves appointees of a part of the city government. No doubt there are many ministerial powers which can be deputized. But a governing body cannot deputize others to perform the governing functions, and the legislature cannot authorize it to do so without destroying the character of the corporation which is required to be preserved.

It has always been held in this State that the municipalities which can be created by our legislature must be such in substantial character as they have heen heretofore known. Up to this time, and ever since elections were first held in Michigan, they have been not only localized in some municipal division, but regarded as municipal action, and supervised and managed by municipal officers, either directly elected, or else appointed by those who have been elected. Such a board as this, which is in no sense a mere agency of the city, is foreign to our system. If it can be created in a city, it can just as well be created in a county, or for the State. When the election ceases to be a municipal procedure, the whole foundation of municipal government drops out. And a municipality which is not managed by its own officers is not such a one as our constitution recognizes.

As the defects which have led to a refusal of a *mandamus* in this case invalidate the whole law, there is no occasion to consider anything else. In my opinion either of them is fatal.

CHAMPLIN and SHERWOOD, JJ., concurred.

MORSE, C. J.—The ostensible primary object of the law under consideration was to preserve the purity of elections and throw additional safeguards around the ballot-box. Such a law should be sustained, unless in plain violation of the letter or spirit of the constitution. Every good citizen, regardless of political belief or party action, ought to and does
FACTS. desire that the right of suffrage shall be amply protected against hinderance or obstruction to the legal voter, as

well as against the fraudulent exercise of the elective franchise. The security and permanency of good government
also depend upon it. We can take judicial knowledge, I
think, that political corruption exists, and that there has been,
and is liable to be, a dishonest depositing and an unfair counting of ballots. There is no doubt but legislation is needed to
protect and purify the exercise of this, one of the highest
privileges of the citizen. The constitutionality of this act,
which is in the form of an amendment to the charter of the
city of Detroit, was attacked upon the argument in this court
upon four grounds, namely: (1). That it is in conflict with
the provision of the constitution that "no law shall embrace
more than one object, which shall be expressed in its title."
(2). That it violates another provision of the constitution, to
wit: "No law shall be revised or altered or amended by reference to its title only; but the act revised, and the section or
sections of the act altered or amended, shall be re-enacted and
published at length." (3). The form of registration prescribed
is not in harmony with the constitutional qualifications of
electors in this State. (4). The act is wholly void because
of the political tests or qualifications of the registration and
inspection officers.

I am not satisfied that the first two objections are tenable.

As to the third objection, while I believe the form prescribed not applicable to our election laws, and one that would
do more harm than good, creating confusion instead of certainty, and having a tendency to hamper and perhaps to prevent the exercise of the elective privilege by the legal voter
in certain cases, and therefore unconstitutional; yet, under
the rule uniformly applied to statutes, it would not defeat the
operation of the remainder of the law, as I regard the form of
registration rather as an incident to than as the main principle
of the act.

The fourth objection to the law, it seems to me, is fatal.
The act provides in substance that the board of councilmen
of the city, upon the nomination of the mayor, shall **PARTY MEMBER-**
appoint a board of commissioners of registration and **SHIP CANNOT BE**
MADE TEST OF
election in and for the city of Detroit, who shall **OFFICE.**
consist of four resident electors, and whose term of office
shall be four years. This board of commissioners had placed
wholly in their hands the appointment of the district boards

of registration in every voting precinct in the city. They have also the absolute power of appointment of two of the three election inspectors in every voting district, leaving the electors the poor privilege of choosing the other upon the opening of the polls. Besides defining the powers of said boards of commissioners, registration, and election inspectors, the law prescribes the following qualifications of these officers as follows : " *First.* Said board" (of commissioners) " shall be strictly non-partisan in character, two members thereof to be from each of the two leading political parties in said city. *Second.* One of said registrars" (district board of registration) " to be from each of the two leading political parties in said city. *Third.* One inspector" (of elections) " so appointed to be from each of the two political parties represented in the common council of said city."

The law also provides that if any vacancy shall occur in the district registrars or election inspectors, such vacancy shall be filled from the same political party to which the absentee belongs. Section 1 of Article 7 of our constitution prescribes the qualifications of electors. It contains no. provision for a registration law ; and such a law can only be sustained and upheld under Section 1 of Article 7 of that instrument, which authorises the legislature to pass laws " to preserve the purity of elections and guard against abuses of the elective franchise." The legislature is utterly powerless to pass any act to hinder or abridge, in the exercise of the electoral right, any person who is an elector under the constitution, except the manifest intent and operations of the law be to protect the legal voters from fraud and abuse of the elective franchise. If a registration law, therefore, is constitutional, it must be so drawn as by its terms to proscribe no man because of his political belief ; and the officers whose duty it is to operate the machinery of registration and election, who sit in judgment upon the right of citizens to vote, cannot by law be restricted to any one or two political parties.

We must take judicial knowledge of the current undisputed history of our State and country, and act upon the assumption and the fact that there are to-day at least, in the State of Michigan and in the City of Detroit, four political parties, to wit, Republican, Democratic, National or **Greenback**, and Union or Prohibition. To confine the registration and election boards to men composed wholly of any one, two, or three of these parties would be a plain violation of the spirit of our constitution, and have a tendency to hamper and abridge the elective rights of those belonging to the political party or parties who, by law, would not and could not have any representation upon such boards.   But such a law is also in direct conflict with the plain letter of the constitution. Section 1, Article 18, of that instrument, after prescribing the form of the official oath of the members of the legislature and all officers, executive and judicial, concludes as follows : "And no other oath, declaration, or test shall be required as a qualification for any office or public trust."

In my opinion there can be no doubt but this law subjects the officers of registration and election in Detroit to a political test.   If the two leading parties in that city be Democratic and Republican, then any citizen who cannot, by reason of his political conscience, ally himself with one or the other of these parties is debarred by law of the right of holding one of these offices.   If the National and Prohibition parties should be the two leading ones, then the Republican or Democrat would be ostracized.   There can be in a true Republican government no political or religious test in holding office, the political and religious liberty of the citizen being at the foundation of Republican institutions.   If this law had provided in express terms that these various boards should be equally divided between Democrats and Republicans, its repugnance to the constitution would be plainly apparent to all. As it is, it accomplishes by indirect language the same result.

The opinion of Chief Justice Campbell in People *v.* Hurlbut, 24 Mich. 90-92, correctly applies the principle that no person can be prevented from holding office because of his political opinions.

Suppose the legislature should enact a law that the school officers of any city.or village in this State should be selected equally from the members of the two leading churches therein, making a religious test, would any one argue for a moment that such an act was constitutional?   And certainly the right of the citizen to his political opinions is and should be as zealously guarded as his right to his religious belief.

It is urged that the political proscription in this law is less than actually takes place without it; that those having the appointing power of registrars and inspectors under the old law do, in Detroit, as a matter of fact, appoint all these officers from one party instead of two, thus precluding still more citizens from these places. In answer it can be said that this is an abuse of power not sanctioned by the law, but permitted, if at all, by its silence, while this act before us puts the seal and stamp of approval upon the very abuse it seeks to cure, and makes it a requisite for these officers to be partisans of a certain name or designation, thus making this evil of partisan appointment a permanent feature of our State polity. For if the legislature has power to require that these offices shall be filled by members of two parties only, it is competent to pass a law thas they shall be holden only by the members of the leading party; and a partisan majority in the legislature might fix the political belief of every municipal officer in the State, taking from the people of the locality the right to have a government of a different political color than the legislature. The remedy is worse than the disease. It is not only political oppression, but a deprivation of a local self-government.

Suppose that in one or more election districts in the city of Detroit the Nationals and Prohibitionists combined were numerically stronger than the united Republicans and Democrats, though a minority in the whole city. Then, in these days of party coalition, it might be possible for the Democrats and Republicans, controlling the boards of registration and election in the city, and in these wards and districts, to combine against the other two parties in such districts. In such a case there would be naturally the same incentive to and opportunity for frauds and abuse as if all the registrars and inspectors belonged to one party, and it is therefore doubtful if the present law would in all cases have the effect desired.

Suppose, further, the two leading parties in Detroit to be, as they actually are, Democratic and Republican. The plurality of these dominant parties over the third party might be so small and trifling in the entire city that in two-thirds or even three-quarters of the wards in the city the third party might have a plurality of votes over either, and yet have no representation except one inspector upon any of these boards, and therefore liable to be subject to the same evils that we now deplore.

Again, the inspectors must be of the same political shade as the two leading parties in the common council; and it would not be an unusual thing to have the leading parties in the city not the same as the leading parties in the common council.

The argument might be elaborated further, but it is useless. In any way we turn this law, and apply it to the common every-day occurrence in political life and action at our elections, the more clearly does it appear that this act can have no other effect than a disfranchisement of a large body of the people from holding these offices, simply because they are politically for the time being in the minority in the whole city. And it should be remembered that all are liable to bear its ostracism. The changes and fluctuations in votes constantly going on often place the majority at the last election in the minority at the next, and they who wield the club of power under this law to-day may feel themselves its weight to-morrow.

I fully agree in the views so ably expressed by Justice Campbell in the leading opinion filed in this case. The nearer the officers are to the people over whom they have control the more easily and readily are reached the evils that result from political corruption, and the more speedy and certain the cure. The form of our State government presupposes that the people of each locality, each municipal district or political unit, are intelligent and virtuous enough to be fully capable of self-government, and the idea that the further removed the election officers are from the people the less we encourage fraud and the more nearly we attain virtue at the ballot-box, is not in harmony with the theory and spirit of our institutions. It matters not what legislation has heretofore been adopted in the same road with this law; it is our duty to deal with the encroachment brought before us and to remove it.

The writ of *mandamus* must be denied.

PARTY MEMBERSHIP AS A QUALIFICATION FOR OFFICE.—In Maryland it has been decided that a proviso of a statute declaring "that no Black Republican, or endorser or approver of the Helper Book" shall be appointed to any office under the board is unconstitutional, if it is to be understood that that class of persons are proscribed on account of their political or religious opinions, but the court refused to take judicial notice of who were meant by the proviso.   Mayor, etc., of Baltimore *v.* State, 15 Md. 379.

In Tennessee a statute requiring in cases where the venue had been changed that it should be changed back on affidavits of three unconditional Union men was unconstitutional and void.   Brown *v.* Haywood, 4 Heisk, 457.

DUTTEN

v.

VILLAGE OF HANOVER.

(42 *Ohio State*, 215.)

In *mandamus* in the court of common pleas to compel the council of an incorporated village to order an election on the question of a surrender of its municipal powers, under the provisions of the Revised Statutes, sections 1633 to 1647, the issue was whether the requisite number of qualified petitioners had petitioned the council therefor. *Held*, that this was an issue not of right triable by a jury, and either party might appeal from the judgment of the common pleas thereon.

Upon the presentation of a petition to the council for such an election, it is the duty of the council, before taking action thereon, to satisfy itself that it contains the requisite number of qualified petitioners, and for that purpose may refer the same to a committee to make the necessary examination.

While such petition is under consideration, and before action thereon by the council, signers thereof may withdraw their names from such petition, and if thereby the number of names is reduced below the requisite number, it is the duty of the council to refuse to order such election.

MOTION for leave to file petition in error to the District Court of Columbiana county.

This was a petition in the common pleas against the village council of Hanover, to compel that body to order an election as required by sections 1633 to 1647 of the Revised Statutes on the question of the surrender of its municipal powers.   It is alleged that on the 2d of October 1882, fifty-five electors of said village, which was more than a majority, petitioned the council to order such election, that this petition was referred to a committee, who reported the same back at the next regular meeting, with several names stricken off by the petitioners, at the solicitation of the committee, leaving less than fifty petitioners, and less than a majority of the electors, and thereupon the council refused to order such election.   The prayer is for a peremptory *mandamus* to compel the council to order such an election.

Issue was joined on the material allegations of the petition, and a trial had upon evidence. The common pleas adjudged in favor of said relator, and ordered such election to be held.

The defendant appealed to the district court.

A motion to dismiss the appeal was overruled, and exception taken.

On a trial the district court found that the number of electors required by the statute, had signed said petition before it was presented and referred to the committee, but that while the matter was in the hands of the committee, a number of signers, sufficient to reduce the petitioners to less than the required number, had, with the consent of the committee, withdrawn their names, so that at the next regular meeting of the council, when it refused to order the election, there were a less number of petitioners than required by statute.

There is nothing in the record to impeach the good faith of the council, or its committee to whom the petition was referred.

Clarke & McVicker for the motion.

J. W. & H. Morrison, contra.

JOHNSON, C. J.—The Revised Statutes, sections 1633 to 1647, provide the mode by which cities, villages, and hamlets may surrender their municipal powers. By section 1644, the number signing a petition for an election to be ordered, is prescribed in case of an incorporated village. By section 1635, it is made the duty of the council, when a petition is presented for such an election, to order such election, and fix the time for holding the same. **FACTS.**

Two questions are made on this motion for leave to file a petition in error: 1st, was the case one that could be appealed; and 2d, did the district court err in upholding the action of the village council in refusing to order an election?

1st. Was this case one for an appeal?

The issue made by the pleadings was of mixed law and fact. While it is the imperative duty of council (section 1635) to order an election, yet as an essential requisite to this duty, there must be a petition therefor, **PETITION MUST PRECEDE ORDER FOR ELECTION.** signed by a sufficient number of electors of the village.

In this case these petitioners must be electors, and this fact must be determined by the council. Before the council can be required to order an election, that fact must be made to appear. It is a condition precedent to making such order. On *mandamus* to compel the council to order an election, the court must be satisfied that it was the duty of the council to make the order. The issue was, therefore, as to this fact, was that a fact triable by a jury, as of right? The court might order a jury to try it under proper instruction; but was it bound to do so? For the purposes of this case, we assume, without deciding, that *mandamus* is the proper proceeding against the council for refusing the prayer of petitioners.

This proceeding can only be resorted to where there is not a plain and adequate remedy otherwise provided. Under our statute, the return to the alternative writ may be controverted. In this case it was controverted, and the question was, whether there was the required number of qualified petitioners. To determine this, the court must ascertain the number of electors in the village, the number of genuine signatures that were electors and the right of signers to withdraw their names.

To determine these questions in *mandamus*, neither party could demand a jury. Castle *v.* Lawlor, 47 Conn. 342; Chumasero *v.* Potts, 2 Montana, 242; High on Extra. Rem. § 30 c.

2d. Did the district court err in holding that persons who signed the petition, could withdraw their names therefrom before action had thereon?

We think not. When the petition was presented it was WITHDRAWAL OF NAMES FROM PETITION. the duty of the council to take proper steps to ascertain if the signatures were *bona fide*, and if it contained the requisite number who were electors? For that purpose the same might be referred to a committee and postpone action until time for such examination. Between the time the petition was presented and the next regular meeting, at which action was had thereon, several signers withdrew their names. This they had the right to do, the council not having acted thereon. Hayes *v.* Jones, 27 Ohio St. 218.

If the council had ordered the election, it may be that petitioners could not thereafter defeat an election, nor authorize the council to rescind its order, by withdrawal of their names. It was held, they could not do this in a road case, after the petition for a road had been acted on, and a report of the viewers made. Grinnell *v.* Adams, 34 Ohio St. 44.

Be this as it may, we think there was no error by the district court in holding that the action of the council in referring the petition to a committee until the next regular meeting, and in refusing to order the election on its then appearing that by voluntary withdrawals the number of petitioners had been reduced below the required number.

Motion overruled.

RIGHT TO TRIAL BY JURY IN PROCEEDINGS IN MANDAMUS.—High, Extraordinary Legal Remedies (2d Ed.), § 30 c., says : " The right of trial by jury in proceedings in *mandamus* is generally determined by constitutional or statutory enactments in the different States. In Connecticut it is held that the constitutional provision for jury trials has no application to proceedings in *mandamus,* and that when issues of fact are raised by the pleadings they are to be tried by the court without a jury. [Castle *v.* Lawlor, 47 Conn. 340.] And under the civil-practice act of Montana it is held that a proceeding in *mandamus* not being an ordinary action at common law, the relator is not entitled as a matter of right to a trial by jury, and that it rests in the sound discretion of the court to award such trial. [Chumasero *v.* Potts, 2 Mont. 242.] "

THE STATE *ex rel.*

v.

CONSTANTINE.

(42 *Ohio State*, 437.)

The election and the appointment of an officer, as authorized by section 27, article 2 of the constitution, are different and distinct modes of filling an office.

Where an office is filled by an election the election must conform to the requirements of the constitution, and each elector of the district is entitled to vote for a candidate for each office to be filled at the election.

A statute authorizing the election of four members of the police board at the same election, but which denies to an elector the right to vote for more than two members, is in conflict with article 5 of the constitution.

IN *quo warranto.* Reserved by the District Court of Clark county.

S. A. Bowman and *R. A. Harrison* for plaintiff.

No constitutional right of a voter can be abridged, added to, or altered by legislation. Monroe *v.* Collins, 17 Ohio St. 666, 686; Copin *v.* Foster, 12 Pick. 485, 488; Page *v.* Allen, 58 Pa. St. 338; Dills *v.* Kennedy, 49 Wis. 555.

The mode or manner of conducting an election is one thing, the election itself is another thing. State *v.* Adams, Brightly's Leading Cases on Elections, 286.

Charles W. Constantine for defendants.

McILVAINE, J.—This proceeding is prosecuted to oust de-
Facts.   fendants from the office of police commissioners of the city of Springfield, and wholly exclude them from the exercise of franchises, powers and authority, assumed to be conferred by the Act of April 21, 1884, entitled " An act to amend sections 1998, 2012, 2013, 2014, 2021 and 2022 of the Revised Statutes of Ohio."

Defendant Constantine, as mayor of the city of Springfield, and defendants Kinnane, Schneider, Fried and Conklin, who were elected to the office of police commissioners by the electors of the city of Springfield, in accordance with the terms of said statute, rely on its provisions as their sole authority for assuming to act as such board of police commissioners.

Section 1998, as amended by said act, reads as follows: " In cities of the first and second grades of the second class, and in cities of the third grade of the second class, having a population of nineteen thousand, and not exceeding twenty thousand, and in cities having a population of twenty thousand and not exceeding thirty thousand five hundred, by the last federal census, and that have not been advanced to a city of the second grade, second class, all powers and duties with respect to the appointment, regulation, government and control of the police shall be vested in and exercised by a board consisting of a mayor, who shall be president, and four commissioners, who shall be electors and freeholders of the city, and a majority shall constitute a quorum, and in cities of the third grade of the second class, having a population of nineteen thousand and not exceeding twenty thousand, and in cities having a population of twenty thousand and not exceeding thirty thousand five hundred, by the last federal census, and that have not been advanced to a city of the second grade, second class, said commissioners shall be elected by the people to serve for the term of two years, and until their successors are duly elected and qualified, the first election to be held within twenty days after the passage of this act; and thereafter said commissioners shall be elected at the annual municipal election, but no elector shall at any election vote for more than two persons for such commissioners, and any ballot containing the names of more than two persons for said office shall not be counted for any of the names thereon, and the four persons receiving the highest number of votes cast shall be declared elected; provided that in the case of said last-named cities the provisions of section nineteen hundred and ninety-nine of said revised statutes, which relate to the term of office of said commissioners, shall not apply, and all vacancies occurring during the term of said commissioners shall be filled as provided by said section nineteen hundred and ninety-nine; but in making such appointments the political complexion of the board shall not be changed, and in case any cities of the third grade of the second class, having a population of nineteen thousand and not exceeding twenty thousand, and any city having a population of twenty thousand and not exceeding thirty thousand five hundred by the last federal census, and that have not been advanced to a city of the second grade, second class, shall be changed in grade or class, the police board hereby provided for such cities and its powers and duties shall not be affected by such change; provided, that in said last-named cities the present police force shall continue in office only until a police force is appointed by said board and duly qualified."

It is admitted that the city of Springfield is embraced in the terms of this statute, but it is contended by the relator that the provision of the section that "no elector shall at any election vote for more than two persons for such commissioners, and any ballot containing the names of more than two persons for said office shall not be counted for any of the names thereon, and the four persons receiving the highest number of votes shall be declared elected" is in conflict with the constitution of the State, and an election held thereunder is therefore void.

HOW MANY VOTES ELECTOR MAY CAST.

Section 27, article 2 of the constitution, provides: "The election and appointment of all officers, and the filling of all vacancies not otherwise provided for by this constitution or the constitution of the United States, shall be made in such manner as may be directed by law ; but no appointing power shall be exercised by the general assembly except as prescribed in this constitution, and in election of United States senators ; and in these cases the vote shall be taken *viva voce.*"

That the defendants acting as a board of police commissioners, exercising the functions conferred by the Act of April 21, 1884, are officers, within the meaning of this provision of the constitution, is not controverted in this case. That they are such officers is made clear by the decision in State *v.* Kennon, 7 Ohio St. 546, and is not in conflict with Warnick *v.* State, 25 Ohio St. 21. This board is created by the statute, and the mode of filling it not being provided for by the constitution of this State or of the United States, it follows that it must be filled by election or appointment in such manner as may be directed by law. Two modes of filling an office are indicated by this clause in the constitution—by election and by appointment. The general assembly may choose either, and, having determined the mode, the manner of carrying it into execution is left to its discretion.

In the case before us the legislature, having created the office in question, determined that it should be filled by an election. The city of Springfield was made the election district, and the " electors" of this district were authorized to vote at the election. The first election was to have been held within twenty days after the passage of the act, and thereafter at the annual municipal election.

The qualifications of electors are not defined by this statute, but undoubtedly the legislature meant such QUALIFICATIONS OF ELECTORS. persons as had the qualifications required of electors by the constitution and general laws of the State, as we think it clear that the election for officers as authorized by this section of the constitution must be such an election as is held in conformity to the provisions of the constitution on that subject.

We have no doubt the filling of an office, not provided for APPOINTMENT. under the constitution of the State or the United States, may be referred to a body or class of persons who may or may not have the qualifications of electors, and the manner of ascertaining the sense of such body or class may be by taking a vote; but such mode of filling the office is not by an election as authorized by section 27, article 2, but by an appointment as therein authorized. Indeed, the manner of filling an office by appointment is unrestricted, save only that it cannot be by "an election," which is pointed out by the constitution as a different mode of filling an office.

The constitution does not provide in detail the manner of holding elections, leaving that to legislative discretion, but it does provide that all elections shall be by ballot, and, having prescribed the qualifications of an elector, provides that each elector "shall be entitled to vote at all elections." See constitution, article 5. By this article we have no doubt that each elector is entitled to vote for each officer, whose election is submitted to the electors, as well as on each question that is submitted. This implication fairly arises from the language of the constitution itself, but is made absolutely certain when viewed in the light of circumstances existing at the time of its adoption. No such thing as "minority representation" or "cumulative voting" was known in the policy of this State at the time of the adoption of this constitution in 1851. The right of each elector to vote for a candidate for each office to be filled at an election had never been doubted. No effort was made by the framers of the constitution to modify this right, and we think it was intended to continue and guarantee such right by the provision that each elector "shall be entitled to vote at all elections." Such right is denied by this statute, which provides for the election of four members of the board of police commissioners, but denies to any elector the right to vote for more than two persons for such commissioners.

The relator also claims that this statute is in conflict with section 1, article 13 of the constitution, which provides: "The general assembly shall pass no special act conferring corporate powers." In answer to this claim defendants rely on State v. Covington, 29 Ohio St. 111, which was approved in State v. Baughman, 39 Ohio St. 459.

This question has not been considered by this court, but, in order to avoid misunderstanding, it is deemed proper to say that the case referred to is not conclusive on the point made. In Covington's case, where the board of police commissioners was appointed by the governor, it was said that the board of

<small>CUMULATIVE VOTING.</small>

commissioners upon whom powers were conferred was not a corporation, and therefore the statute, though special, was not unconstitutional.

In the case before us it is claimed the power to hold an election was conferred upon the city of Springfield, a municipal corporation, and the act, being special, was prohibited. This is a very different question, but the solution of it is not deemed necessary by this court.

Judgment of ouster.

OKEY, J.—I concur in the judgment of ouster, but find it necessary to state separately the ground upon which I concur. The case involves the constitutionality of the act of April 9, 1884 (81 Ohio L. 121), so far as the same relates to " cities having a population of twenty thousand and not exceeding thirty-five thousand five hundred, by the last federal census, and that have not been advanced to a city of the second grade, second class." The relator insists that the act, so far as it applies to the cities above described, is invalid upon two grounds : first, that it violates the fifth article of the constitution, which relates to the elective franchise; and, second, that it violates the first section of the thirteenth article of the constitution, which provides, that "the general assembly shall pass no special act conferring corporate powers." These questions were very fully and ably argued orally and on briefs, and after the briefs were read and authorities cited were examined nothing remained to be done but for each judge to express his opinion. The court was unanimous in holding there should be judgment of ouster. I do not dissent from the view expressed in the opinion of McIlvaine, J., but I prefer to withhold the expression of an opinion upon that question until such opinion becomes necessary. I think the case will be properly decided when a correct answer is given to the question, whether the act, so far as its validity is involved in this case, is in conflict with the provision of the constitution inhibiting the granting of corporate powers by special act.

Not only is the fact found in the record that the words
SPECIAL ACT above quoted from the act apply to the city of
GRANTING COR-
PORATE POWER Springfield alone, but without such finding this
VOID.
court would take judicial notice that the words

never did and never can apply to any other municipal corporation than Springfield; and, consequently, the act, to that extent, is local and special. State *v.* Covington, 29 Ohio St. 102; McGill *v.* State, 34 Ohio St. 228, 258, 270; State *v.* Brewster, 39 Ohio St. 653; Devine *v.* Com. of Cook Co., 84 Ill. 590. And as the act assumes to confer upon the city of Springfield power to hold an election of its electors for public officers for the corporation, and exercise other important functions, it is too clear for argument that the act, in form, confers corporate power. State *v.* Mitchell, 31 Ohio St. 529. And the act being invalid, for the reason stated, so far as it authorizes the city of Springfield to hold a corporate election, and it being neither reasonable nor probable that the legislature would have made provisions with respect to Springfield unless the whole act could have effect with respect to that city, it follows that the whole act is void, so far as Springfield is concerned. State *v.* Sinks, *ante*, 345. So far from State *v.* Covington, *supra*, being opposed to this view, it will be found, on careful examination, that it strongly supports it. There the officers were not elected; they were appointed; and of course the appointment by the governor of officers for Cincinnati was an act done in pursuance of authority conferred upon him. In fact, no corporate power was conferred upon the city with respect to the selection of those officers; and, as the legality of their appointment was the only question involved, it was properly held in that case that art. 13, sect. 1 could not be successfully invoked to defeat their title, however clearly such constitutional provision might, in some other action or proceeding, be fatal to other parts of the act. The same remarks are applicable to State *v.* Baughman, 38 Ohio St. 455. Believing the position I have assumed to be impregnable, I am content to rely upon it.

CONSTITUTIONALITY OF STATUTES PROVIDING FOR MINORITY REPRESENTATION OR CUMULATIVE VOTING IN THE ELECTION OF PUBLIC OFFICERS.—It is believed that the opinion of McIlvaine, J., in the principal case is the first expression of judicial opinion on the constitutionality of statutory provisions for minority representation. The point was raised in two New York cases, People *v.* Crissey, 91 N. Y. 616, and Agenstein *v.* Kenney, 7 Am. & Eng. Corp. Cas. 677, but in both cases the court declined to pass upon it. In the latter case the court said, speaking of the constitutionality of minority representation: "The constitutional question which the plaintiff sought to raise by the commencement of this action is a very grave and

interesting one and should not be decided in any case unless properly presented and necessarily involved. It need not be decided in this case."
In the former case the court, referring to the discussion of the same constitutional point in the course of the argument by council, said : " We ought not to decide it. It has a possible importance beyond the issues involved. It touches the question of minority representation upon which has been founded very much legislation, and about which there is room for difference and debate."

The constitutional provision on which the court bases its decision in this case is contained in § 1 of Article V of the Ohio Constitution of 1851, entitled " Elective Franchise," and is to the effect that every duly qualified elector " shall be entitled to vote at all elections." The entire section reads as follows : " Every white male citizen of the United States of the age of twenty-one years who shall have been a resident of the State one year next preceding the election, and of the county, township, or ward, in which he resides, such time as may be provided by law, shall have the qualifications of an elector, and be entitled to vote at all elections."

It would seem that all that the section was intended to provide for was for the fixing of the qualification of electors, and if the last clause in the section was intended to guarantee any constitutional right to qualified electors, it was merely that of equality ; that is, that all qualified electors should have *equal rights* of voting at all elections and for all officers to be voted for. It would seem clear that it was not intended to prohibit minority representation and to give the right to each elector to vote for all officers to be elected. As the court remarks, the subject of minority representation was probably not known or thought of as a particular question at the time the Ohio constitution was framed (1851), and hence it is plain that the framers of that constitution did not intend to make any constitutional guaranty or provision in the nature of guaranty against it.

It is probable that the framers of the constitution contemplated that all officers to be voted for should be voted for by each elector, and that a plurality of votes should elect ; but is there anything in the constitution that amounts to a guaranty that the majority or plurality shall in every case have the absolute right to elect every officer to be voted for ? It would seem not. In certain cases the constitution contains express provisions as to the modes in which officers shall be elected. Thus § 3— of Article III provides that a plurality shall elect the executive officers of the State (Governor, Lieutenant-Governor, etc.). In the case of representatives, however, the constitution is not at all explicit ; § 2, Article II merely provides that they shall be elected by the electors in their respective districts. Under this provision it would seem that the legislature might by statute require that a majority vote or even a two-thirds vote was necessary to elect, and in case that the requisite number of votes were not attained by any candidate that the election might be thrown open to the house. Yet such legislation would have the effect of defeating the will of the majority in many cases, as where in a given district one party was in the predominance but not sufficiently so to elect their man, and in the house the opposite party was in the majority. The provisions of the constitution in relation to apportionment, Article XI, would seem to prohibit any minority representation in the case of representatives.

As to the validity of minority representation under the New York Constitution of 1881, the case is more difficult. § 1 of Article II, after fixing the qualifications of an elector, goes on to provide that he "shall be entitled to vote * * * for all officers that now are or hereafter may be elected by the people."

At the time this constitution was being framed the theory of minority representation had been in practical operation in the State of Illinois for several years under the provision of the constitution of 1870 [Article IV, §§ 7 & 8], and was well known to legislators as a practical system of representation. Moreover, the language of the constitution seems to be an almost express prohibition of minority representation. Still, even as to this constitutional provision, it would seem that it might be argued with much force that it intended to provide for equal rights of voting, rather than to prohibit minority representation. It is to be noticed that the system of minority representation provided for by §§ 7 & 8, Article IV of the Illinois Constitution of 1870 is different from that adopted by the statute held unconstitutional in the principal case. §§ 7 & 8, Article IV of the Illinois Constitution provide that three representatives shall be elected in each district, and that: "In all elections of representatives aforesaid each qualified voter may cast as many votes for one candidate as there are representatives to be elected, or may distribute the same, or equal parts thereof, among the candidates, as he shall see fit; and the candidate highest in votes shall be declared elected." In the statute in question in the principal case each voter was entitled to vote for only two of a board of officers, and the statute was held unconstitutional as infringing on the right of voters to vote for *all* officers to be elected. But a provision similar to that of the Illinois Constitution would not come under this objection, as each member would be entitled to vote for all the members of the board if he chose. Yet of course the purpose and result of provisions like that in the statute in question and of those like that in the Illinois Constitution are identical, *i.e.*, to give representation to the minority.

CUMULATIVE VOTING IN PRIVATE CORPORATIONS.—It is provided by several State constitutions that in the election of directors, etc. of a private corporation the voting power of each stockholder shall be the number of shares he owns multiplied by the number of directors to be elected, and that he may divide this power among as many candidates greater than the whole number to be elected and in such proportions as he shall see fit. Such a provision is contained in the following State constitutions: Illinois (1870), Article XI, § 3; Pennsylvania, Article XVI, § 4; West Virginia (1872), Article XI, § 4; Nebraska (1875), Article XI; Miscellaneous Corporations, § 5; Missouri (1875), Article XIII, § 6; California, Article XII, § 12.

It is held that such constitutional provisions are unconstitutional as impairing the obligation of contract and infringing on vested rights, as far as they concern corporations chartered before the adoption of the constitution. In the case of Hays *v.* Commonwealth of Pennsylvania, 82 Pa. St. 518, it was held that the constitutional provision allowing cumulative voting [Constitution of Pennsylvania, 1874, Article XVI, § 4,] if it applied to existing corporations was void, as within the constitutional inhibition against impairing the obligation of contract. The court says: "Now, whilst it cannot be said that this would not be an alteration in the terms of the charter, it is nevertheless urged that it is a mere regulation of the right of suffrage in corporations, but affects the vested rights of no one. But if it be not a vested right in those who own a major part of the stock of the corporation to elect, if they see proper, every member of the board of directors, I would like to know what a vested right means?" The case of The State *v.* Greer, 78 Mo., 188, is a similar decision as to the constitutional provision of the State of Missouri, providing for cumulative voting in private corporations, Constitution of Missouri (1875), Article XII, § 6.

BREDIN'S APPEAL AND GREER'S APPEAL.

(Advance Case, Pennsylvania. October 5, 1885.)

Under Pennsylvania Constitution, art. V. sec. 5, which provides that "whenever a county shall contain forty thousand inhabitants it shall constitute a separate judicial district, and shall elect one judge learned in the law," and that counties containing less population "may be attached to contiguous districts," the right of voting for judge extends to the inhabitants (qualified to vote) of all the counties of which a district is composed; to a small county which has been attached to the district by the Legislature, as well as to the large one entitled by population to be a district.

APPEALS from decrees of the Court of Common Pleas of Butler County.

The facts, and the section of the constitution on which the case turned, are stated in the opinion.

James Bredin, G. A. Jenks and *J. T. Britain,* for appellants.

S. W. Dana, D. B. Kurtz, Chas. McCandless and *John M. Thompson,* for appellees.

MERCUR, C. J.—These appeals were argued together. They FACTS. are from the same decree. They present the same question. The contention arises under the act of 7th August, 1883. It provides for the formation of the judicial districts of the commonwealth; how each shall be numbered, composed and designated, and the number of judges each shall have. Section 1, *inter alia,* declares, "the seventeenth district (shall be composed) of the County of Butler, to which the County of Lawrence is hereby attached, and shall have two judges learned in the law, and the additional law judge shall reside at New Castle, in Lawrence County."

Section 2 declares, " In all cases where a county is or shall be attached to an adjoining district the qualified voters of such county shall be entitled to vote for the president judge, and an additional law judge when provided for."

At the general election held in November, 1884, for the election of two judges learned in the law, for the 17th judicial district, the appellants, and John McMichael and Aaron L. Hazen, and another, were candidates.   The qualified electors of each of said counties met at their respective legal places for holding elections, and voted for two judges, and the votes cast in each county were counted and ascertained at the county-seat thereof.   A return judge was appointed according to the requirements of the statute in each county, to meet a similar officer appointed by the other county.

These two met at the county-seat of Butler County, at the time designated by statute, and cast up the votes of both counties and, on a correct computation thereof, found that John McMichael and Aaron L. Hazen had received the highest number of votes, and issued certificates to them accordingly.

The appellants attack the constitutional validity of the act of 1883 in permitting the qualified voters of the County of Lawrence to vote for law judges; and they claim that the votes cast in that county were improperly counted.

If this view be correct, then appellants were duly elected and entitled to receive the certificates accordingly.

The tribunal authorized by law to decide such a contest decided adversely to the claim of the appellants, and the commissions have been issued to the other candidates named.

The appellants rest their case on article V, section 5 of the constitution, which declares : " Whenever a county shall contain forty thousand inhabitants it shall constitute a separate judicial district, and shall elect one judge learned in the law; and the General Assembly shall provide for additional judges as the business of the said districts may require. Counties containing a population of less than is sufficient to constitute separate districts shall be formed into convenient single districts, or, if necessary, may be attached to contiguous districts, as the General Assembly may provide."

As the United States decennial census of 1880 showed, the

County of Butler contained more than fifty thousand inhabitants; the appellants claim that it alone thereby became entitled to become a separate judicial district, and that the electors thereof only could participate in the election of judges learned in the law, assigned to said district; in other words, although the County of Lawrence was legally united, annexed or attached in the formation of the district, yet the qualified electors thereof are, by the constitution, denied all right to vote for the judges who, for a full term of ten years, are to preside in the courts of their county.

A proposition so startling as this, and one affirming such an unequal and unjust discrimination against all the legal voters of a county, ought not to be assented to, unless its correctness be already established.

The section of the constitution relied on was before us for CONSTRUCTION OF CONSTITUTION- AL PROVISION AS TO JUDICIAL ELECTORAL DISTRICT. construction in the case of Commonwealth *v.* Harding, 87 Pa. St. (6 Norris), 343. It was carefully considered and construction given thereto. It was held that this section did not, of itself, constitute a separate district when a county attains the number of inhabitants specified; but it indicates the basis on which, at the proper time and in the proper manner, judicial districts may be created by the Legislature. The unreasonable and mischievous effects of any other construction are well stated in the able opinion of Mr. Chief Justice Agnew. The correctness of this construction has since been affirmed and approved by this court, in a distinct manner, in Commonwealth *v.* Handley, Pittsburg Legal Journal of December 24, 1884, and in Petition of Cahill, Slevin and McVay, not yet reported.

That the section of the constitution cited was not intended LEGISLATIVE AC- TION REQUIRED. to execute itself in the formation of judicial districts, but requires legislative action, is clearly shown by section 14 of the schedule.

It declares: "The General Assembly shall, at the next succeeding session after each decennial census, and not oftener, designate the several judicial districts ás required by the constitution." Thus not only is the whole power of designating judicial districts given to the Legislature, but it can be exercised only after each decennial census. Although a county forming part of another district may, in fact, for many years, have the population stated as sufficient to constitute a separate judicial district, yet it must bide its time and wait the action of the General Assembly.

In seeking for the true meaning and proper construction of section 5, article V, we must consider other portions of the constitution, and so interpret the different parts as to produce harmony between them and give a just and reasonable effect to the whole.

Section 15 of the same article declares : "All judges required to be learned in the law, except the judges of the Supreme Court, shall be elected by the qualified electors of the respective districts over which they are to preside, and shall hold their offices for the period of ten years, if they shall so long behave themselves well."

Who are qualified electors? Section 1, article VIII answers this question. "Every male citizen twenty-one years QUALIFIED ELEC-TORS DEFINED. of age, possessing the following qualifications, shall be entitled to vote at all elections." The qualifications following refer only to citizenship, duration of residence and the payment of taxes. If, then, persons possessing these qualifications are entitled to vote at all elections, and judges learned in the law shall be elected by the qualified electors of the respective districts over which they are to preside, it must be conceded that these sections intend to give and do give to the electors of the County of Lawrence the right to vote for their judges, unless that county is not within the 17th judicial district over which said judges are to preside.

This conclusion is supported by Calvin v. Beaver, 94 Pa. St. (13 Norris) 388.

Two things are indisputable. One is, that the law judges of the 17th district do preside over and in the County of Lawrence. The other is that the county is not in any other judicial district. No judges, other than those of the 17th district, are authorized to preside there. All writs issued from the several courts of record of the County of Lawrence must be tested in the name of the president judge of the district. The commissions issue to these judges, as judges of the 17th judicial district. If the County of Lawrence is not within the district of these judges, then the president judge thereof has no power to call upon the president or law judge of any other district to hold a term of court therein. The electors of the County of Lawrence are either within the 17th district, with the right to vote in the election of judges learned in the law.

to preside there, or else they are outside of that district and in no other, and legally have no such judge to preside in the courts of their county.   Such a result would not only be repugnant to the whole scope and spirit of the constitution relating to courts, but would destroy that uniformity in the organization and operations of courts of equal grade which it expressly declares shall be preserved.   This section 26 of article V, *inter alia*, declares : " All laws relating to courts shall be general and of uniform operation, and the organization, jurisdiction and powers of all courts of the same class or grade, so far as regulated by law, and the force and effect of the process and judgments of such courts shall be uniform."

The construction claimed by the appellants for section 5 denies to one county that uniform organization and operation which the constitution declares shall be enjoyed by all the counties, and which no law shall impair.

The authority given by law to the presiding judge constitutes an essential part of the organization of the court, and fixes a limit to its operations.   This, however, is only one view of the case.   It has another side—that side is the people. Uniformity in the organization and operations of a court is not for the exclusive convenience of the judge who administers the laws, but its main purpose is for the benefit of the people of every county, whose rights might be injuriously affected by an absence of this uniformity.

We cannot assent to the view of the appellants.   It is in clear conflict with too many parts of the constitution.   It strikes down those equal rights and valuable privileges which are so highly prized by our people, and which the constitution was intended to secure, and we think does secure.

We are not unmindful of the case of Commonwealth *v.* Dumbold, 1 Outerbridge 293.   It was twice argued and each time decided differently, the last time by a bare majority of the judges of this court.

It stands, however, as authority, that under the legislation then existing the County of Fayette was not entitled to elect associate judges.

The question as to the right of the qualified electors of the county attached to vote was not before us for decision and was not decided.

ELECTORS HELD ENTITLED TO VOTE FOR JUDGE.   We are therefore unanimously of the opinion that the qualified electors of the County of Lawrence were entitled to vote for judges learned in the law at the election held on the 4th day of November, 1884, and that John McMichael and Aaron L. Hazen received the greatest number of legal votes, and are entitled to the office to which each was elected.

It is further ordered that this decision be certified to the secretary of the commonwealth, decree affirmed, and the appeal in each case is dismissed at the costs of the respective appellant therein.

PEOPLE *ex rel.* LEVERSON
v.
THOMPSON, Secretary, etc.

(*Advance Case, California, in Bank. October* 30, 1885.)

Conceding that the act of March 13, 1883, entitled "An act to divide the State of California into congressional districts" was invalid, because of non-compliance by the legislature with certain formalities required by the constitution, still the petitioners are not entitled to a mandate directing the Secretary of State to certify to the Governor that two of them were duly elected congressmen-at-large, and that each of the others was elected a member of the House of Representatives, in a congressional district created by the act of March 30, 1872, because the electors throughout the State did not vote for two members of congress-at-large, nor did the electors within the limits of each of the congressional districts, as prescribed by the act of 1872, vote for a member of congress to represent the people of such district.

Notice, by proclamation, of an election, is necessary whenever the voters are not bound by law to take notice of the time of the election, and of the officers then to be chosen.   And, conceding that when a term of office is to expire at a certain date after a general election, the electors take notice the office is to be filled at such general election, still, where a vacancy has occurred, by reason of death or resignation, the voters are not bound to take notice of such vacancy, and the casting of votes for a candidate fo fill the vacancy does not constitute an election.

The electors throughout the State were not bound to know, under penalty of disfranchisement, that the Statute of 1883, regular in form, certified to have been properly passed by the appropriate officers, published as other statutes are published, approved by the Governor, and by him acted upon when he issued his proclamation for a general election, held on November 4, 1884, was void because of matters not appearing on the face of the statute, but which could be ascertained only by an examination of the journal of the two houses of the legislature, or that the law of 1872 was still in full force and operation.

Amendments to bills pending before the legislature need not be read three times, per Ross, J.

THIS is an application for a writ of mandate, compelling the Secretary of State to compare and certify the votes cast at the last congressional election, in accordance with the law in force in this State prior to the thirteenth day of March, 1883.

It is claimed by petitioner that at the election for representatives in Congress, held on the fourth day of November, 1884, there were to be elected four representatives, under the act of March 30, 1872, entitled "An act to divide the State of California into congressional districts," and two representatives at large, under an act of Congress, entitled "An act making apportionment of representatives in Congress among the several States, under the tenth census," approved February, 1882, and that the votes cast at such election should be compared and estimated in accordance with said acts.   In order to sustain this claim the act of the legislature of March 13, 1883, entitled "An act to divide the State of California into congressional districts, under which said election was held and the votes cast thereat compared and estimated, is sought to be declared null and void.   This act is attacked, not as to its matter, but as to the mode of its passage, and the journals of the legislature are resorted to in order to sustain this attack.

Petitioner claims that this act was not passed in accordance with Section 15, Article IV of the constitution, requiring that every bill shall be read on three several days in each house, because the amendments made to the bill during its passage were not read on three several days in each house, and further, because the bill, with the amendments thereto, was not printed for the use of the members on its final passage, and he produces the journals and other testimony to sustain this point.

E. C. Marshall, Attorney-General, *M. R. Leverson* and *George W. Chamberlain* for the petitioner.

Horace G. Platt, amicus curiæ, for the respondent.

McKINSTRY, J.—The petitioners are not entitled to a mandate directing the Secretary of State to certify to the Governor that two of them were duly elected congressmen-at-large, and that each of the others was elected a member of the House of Representatives, in a congressional district created by the act of the legislature in 1872.

If it should be conceded that the act of 1883 is invalid, because of non-compliance by the legislature with certain formalities required by the constitution, yet, as appears from the petition and facts, of which we take judicial notice, the electors throughout the State did not vote for two members of Congress at large, nor did the electors within the limit of each of the congressional districts, as prescribed by the act of 1872, vote for a member of Congress to represent the people of such district.

Notice to the electors lies at the foundation of any popular system of government. It has sometimes been held NOTICE TO ELEC- that the existence of a law fixing the time of an TORS DISCUSSED. election, and the offices to be filled, is of itself notice. It may be conceded that when a term of office is to expire at a certain date after a general election, no other election to intervene, the electors take notice the office is to be filled at such general election. Some decisions have gone so far. But it is well settled that when a vacancy has occurred by reason of death or resignation the voters are not bound to take notice of such vacancy, and the casting of votes for a candidate or candidates to fill the vacancy does not constitute an election. The facts of the present case bring it within the principle of the decisions which hold that, in cases of special elections to fill a vacancy, a proclamation is necessary, even although the special election be held at the same time as a general election. The principle is that a notice by proclamation is necessary whenever the voters are not bound by law to take notice of the time of the election and of the officers then to be chosen.

The contrary not being averred in the petition, it must be presumed that the Governor, who had approved the act of 1883, issued his proclamation for the election of a member of Congress in each of the districts defined by that act.

The general rule is that all are bound to know the law. But the recognition of this general rule does not compel KNOWLEDGE OF us to hold that the elector, as matter of fact, knew UNCONSTITUTION-ALITY OF LAW IS that the act of 1883 was of no force or effect. It NOT PRESUMED. does not compel us to hold that, as a matter of law, the electors throughout the State were bound to know, under penalty of disfranchisement, that a statute regular in form, certified

9 Cor. Cas.—4

to have been properly passed bý the appropriate officers, published as other statutes are published, approved by the Governor, and by him acted under when he issued his proclamation, was void, because of matters not appearing on the face of the statute, but which could be ascertained only by an examination of the journals of the two houses of the legislature; that, thus taking notice of the invalidity of the act of 1883, the electors were bound to know that the law of 1872 was still in full force and operation.

That the electors did not know all it is claimed they ought to have known is apparent from the matters set forth in the petition, and from the fact that the petitioners have found it necessary to ask that the Secretary of State be prohibited from estimating the votes cast for members of the House of Representatives of the United States in the respective districts created, or attempted to be created, by the act of 1883.

Courts of justice in this State take judicial notice, perhaps, of the contents of the journals of the JUDICIAL NOTICE OF JOURNALS OF LEGISLATURE. two houses of the legislature; the citizens at large are not required to take legal notice of the entries in the journals. The people had not actually been notified of such entries when the election was held. They had before them (let us assume) the statute of 1883, approved by the Governor and published as statutes are required to be published, and the Governor's proclamation. We are asked to decide that all the voters should have inquired whether the statute was invalid by reason of matters of which they had not been notified; that the duty was imposed upon them to make investigation into the history in the legislature of the bill for the act of 1883; to consider questions as to the validity of the law arising out of the proceedings in the legislature which preceded its final passage; to determine such questions correctly, or as petitioners claim they should be determined (questions, it may be, difficult of solution by the courts, with the aid of counsel learned in the law), and then to vote for officers not mentioned in the Governor's proclamation, in districts not defined in the law so as aforesaid to be mentally determined to be invalid, and not recognized as continuing in existence by the executive or other officers of the State. Thus to decide would be a formal acknowledgment by this court of results which cannot be treated as an intelligent and binding expression of the voice of the people, and which are entirely beyond any consequence legitimately derivative from the maxim that all are supposed to know the law.

Whether anybody else was or was not elected to the House of Representatives of the United States at the general election, we are quite certain that the petitioners were not.

Writ denied and petition dismissed.

McKee, J., Thornton, J., and Morrison, C. J., concurred.

Ross, J., concurring : I concur in the main in the views expressed by Mr. Justice McKinstry. I wish to add that, in my opinion, the act of 1883 is a constitutional and valid law.

Section 15 of Article IV of the present constitution provides : " No law shall be passed except by bill. Nor shall any bill be put upon its final passage until the same, with the amendments thereto, shall have been printed for the use of the members, nor shall any bill become a law unless the same be read on three several days in each house, unless, in case of urgency, two-thirds of the house where such bill may be pending shall, by a vote of ayes and noes, dispense with this provision. Any bill may originate in either house, but may be amended or rejected by the other, and on the final passage of all bills they shall be read at length, and the vote shall be by yeas and nays upon each bill separately, and shall be entered on the journal ; and no bill shall become a law without a concurrence of a majority of the members elected to each house."

It is earnestly insisted by the petitioners for the writ that under this provision of the constitution it is requisite to the validity of a bill that each and every READING OF amendment thereto should have been read on three AMENDMENTS IN LEGISLATURE. several days in each house. It is very certain that the constitution does not so provide in terms. The provision with respect to the passage of bills is extremely explicit. Express authority is given for the amendment of any bill in either house, and it is expressly declared that no bill shall be put upon its final passage until the same, with the amendments. thereto, shall have been printed for the use of the members. If it had been intended to provide that, except in case of ur-

gency, no bill shall become a law unless the same, with the
amendments thereto, be read on three several days in each
house, it would have been an easy matter to have said so.
The insertion of the words " with the amendments thereto"
in the first clause and their omission from the second, is, to my
mind, very strong evidence that the clause from which they
were omitted was not intended to apply to them.

In Miller *v.* the State, 3 Ohio St. 479, it appeared that a bill
originally introduced in the senate, after being read twice, and
on different days, was committed to a select committee, who
reported it back with one amendment, to wit: " Strike out
all after the enacting clause and insert a new bill;" that on a
subsequent day, April 12th, this amendment, after being
itself amended, was agreed to, and the bill, as amended,
ordered to be engrossed and read a third time to-morrow ;
that on the morrow, April 13th, it was " read the third time"
and passed, and, having afterward passed the house, and been
duly enrolled, was signed by the presiding officers of the two
houses, filed in the proper office, and published among the
laws. The constitution of the State then provided that
" every bill shall be fully and distinctly read on three
different days, unless, in case of urgency, three-fourths of the
house in which it shall be pending shall dispense with this
rule."

In that case it was claimed, as it is claimed here, that the
amendment was in fact a 'new bill,' and that it was only read
once, and therefore invalid under the constitutional provision quoted. In the course of the opinion the court,
speaking through Judge Thurman, said : " But, for argument's
sake, let it be admitted that the bill as amended was read
but once in the senate ; is the act for that reason void ?
That, counting the two readings before the amendment and
the final reading, the bill was read three times, is conceded,
for these readings are shown by the journal, and it is also
conceded that in general three readings of an amendment are
not necessary. But inasmuch as the amendment in this case
is styled in the journal a ' new bill,' it is said that three readings were necessary. Why necessary ? The amendment
was none the less an amendment because of the name given
it. It is not unusual in parliamentary proceedings to amend
a bill upon striking out all after the enacting clause and in-

serting a new bill. Jefferson's Manual, Sec. 5. When the subject or proposition of the bill is thereby wholly changed it would seem to be proper to read the amended bill three times, and on different days ; but when there is no such vital alteration three readings of the amendment are not required."

What is here said by the learned judge covers both points made by the petitioners, for, apart from their claim that every amendment must be read in each house on three several days, it is contended that the purported amendment to the bill in question was in fact no amendment, but a new bill. The original bill was one to divide the State of California into congressional districts, and the amendment adopted did but change the lines of the districts as fixed in the original bill. "The subject or proposition of the bill" was not at all changed. When that is done the bill as amended should undoubtedly, as observed by Judge Thurman, be read on three several days, for it then becomes in effect a new bill, but not so when there is no such vital alteration.

In the case of The People *v.* Wallace, 70 Ill., 680, the Supreme Court of that State held that the constitutional provision of the State requiring bills to be read on three several days before their passage did not apply to amendments, the court saying : " It is also objected that the tenth section of the act was not constitutionally adopted, because it was engrafted as an amendment whilst the bill was being considered, and was not read on three several days in the house adopting it as an amendment. We are clearly of opinion that the requirement does not apply to an amendment, and the objection cannot prevail." See, also, McCulloch *v.* The State, 11 Ind. 434–5. Nothing here said conflicts with the decision in Weil *v.* Kenfield, 54 Cal. 111, of the correctness of which I have no question.

MYRICK, J.—For the reasons given in the opinion of Mr. Justice Ross, I am of opinion that the act of 1883 is constitutional and valid. I therefore concur in the judgment.

INGLIS

v.

SHEPHERD.

(*Advance Case, California.   September* 24, 1885.)

A candidate for the office of supervisor for the first district of a county is entitled to have counted for him ballots which, on their face, showed that he was voted for as supervisor for the second district, when it appears, from all the circumstances of the case, that such ballots were intended for him.

APPEAL from a judgment of the Superior Court of San Joaquin County, entered in favor of the plaintiff. The opinion states the facts.

J. H. & J. E. Budd for the appellant.

Campbell & Hosmer and *Smith & Keniston* for the respondent.

FOOTE, C.—Wm. Inglis contested D. C. Shepherd's election as supervisor for the first district of San Joaquin County.

The court below gave judgment in favor of the contestant, and respondent appeals therefrom.

The question determining the contention was this: **Was,** or WHAT BALLOTS TO BE COUNTED. not, Inglis entitled to have counted for him, as supervisor for the first district of San Joaquin County, sixty-seven ballots, which, on their face, showed that he was voted for as supervisor for the second district of said county? The evidence admitted by the court, and which, under the circumstances of this case, is permissible, was that at the time no other person named William Inglis, except the contestant and his minor son, resided in said county; that contestant was the only person of that name running as a candidate for the office of supervisor of said first district; and that he lived in said district, and that he was the only candidate of his party therein for said office. The board of election all knew those facts. His name, together with the name of the office and the number of the district, were properly printed on the great majority of the ballots voted for him, as issued by the printer employed by his party managers to attend to the matter. By some mistake of that printer the figure 2 became substituted for the figure 1 on said sixty-seven ballots, and others placed on tables convenient for the use of voters. Some time during the day of election this mistake was discovered, and, as far as possible, the misleading ballots were destroyed. Before this mistake was discovered those sixty-seven ballots were voted at the proper precinct of the district in which contestant was such candidate. And nearly half of them were counted for him by the proper election board, but they refused to count for him some thirty-six of them. Those sixty-seven ballots, with one or two exceptions, were what are called "straight tickets."

Thus it appears that the voters casting the disputed ballots intended to vote for William Inglis for supervisor of the first district of said county, and, no fault resting on them, we do not perceive the propriety of permitting the carelessness or mistake of a printer to defeat that intention.

The judgment of the court below should be affirmed.

SEARLS, C., and BELCHER, C. C., concurred.

By the COURT.—For the reasons given in the foregoing opinion the judgment is affirmed.

THE PAROL EVIDENCE RULE AS APPLICABLE TO BALLOTS.—Ballots come within the rule which prohibits the admission of extrinsic evidence to contradict or govern the meaning of written or documentary evidence. But, as in the case of other written evidence, this meaning, if doubtful or ambiguous, may be explained by extrinsic evidence. Thus, when the name of a candidate for district-attorney was George B. Ely, and ballots were cast bearing the name George B. Ela and Ely Ely and Ely, it was held that evidence that there was no lawyer in the district named George B. Ely, and that there was no lawyer in the district having the surname Ely except George B. Ely, was admissible, as tending to show that the votes were intended for George B. Ely. Carpenter *v.* Ely, 4 Wis. 420.

So it was held that extrinsic evidence would be admitted to prove that votes cast for Alvin J. Willoughby were intended for Alvin L. Willoughby, State of Connecticut *v.* Gates, 43 Conn. 533.

That extrinsic evidence is admissible to explain initials has been almost universally held. The State *v.* Griffen, 5 Neb. 161; People *v.* Ferguson, 8 Cow. 102; People *v.* Seaman, 6 Denio, 409; Lee *v.* Rainey, House of Rep. 44th Congress; McKenzie *v.* Beaxton, House of Rep. 42d Congress; McCrary on Elections, §§ 395 *et seq.;* State *v.* Foster, 38 Ohio St. 599.

In Michigan it was held in an early case that a ballot cast for a candidate giving his last name in fall, but only the initials of his first name, could not be shown by extrinsic evidence to have been intended for such candidate, and could not have been counted for him. The People *v.* Tisdale, 1 Dougl. 59. In a later case the court, though of the opinion that this doctrine of the case was unsound, yet considered it too well established to be changed except by legislative action.   People *v.* Cicott, 16 Mich. 283.   The Chief-Justice (Judge Cooley) was of the opinion that the case of People *v.* Tisdale should be overruled.

In this case (People *v.* Cicott) Judge Cooley suggests the following rule as to when extrinsic evidence is admissible to explain a defective or ambiguous ballot : " The true rule on the subject I conceive to be this : Evidence of such facts as may be called the circumstances surrounding the election, such as, who were the candidates brought forward by the nominating conventions ; whether other persons of the same name resided in the district from which the office was to be filled, and if so, whether they were eligible to the office, and were publicly named for it, and the like, is always admissible for the purpose of aiding in the application of any ballot which has been cast, and where the intent of the voter, as expressed by his ballot, when considered in the light of such surrounding circumstances, is not doubtful, the ballot should be counted and allowed for the person intended.   This rule is just and easy of application, and it has the merit of harmonizing with the rules applied to other written instruments, which I think is no slight recommendation."   See also Cooley Constit. Sims, 768.

That extrinsic evidence was admissible to prove that a vote cast for Benjamin Wall was intended for Benjamin Wall, Jun,, there being a father and son of that name, was held in People *v.* Cook, 14 Barb. 259 ; affirmed in 8 N. Y. 67.

Extrinsic evidence is not admissible to contradict the plain terms of a ballot nor to change its meaning.   Thus, a vote for " Pence " cannot be shown to have heen intended for " Spence."   Cooley Constit. (5th Ed.) p. 768, note 1.

The amount of extrinsic evidence necessary to show for whom a given vote was intended to be cast will, of course, depend on the degree of defectiveness or uncertainty of the ballot.   In every case a certain knowledge of extrinsic facts is necessary to identify the person voted for.   People *v.* Cicott, 15 Mich. 283–319.   It would seem that when a ballot gives the last name of the candidate correctly and correct initials very slight evidence is necessary to explain the uncertainty. Falkington *v.* Turner, 71 Ill. 234.

EVIDENCE OF VOTERS AS TO WHOM THEY INTENDED TO VOTE FOR.— The testimony of a voter as to whom he intended to vote for is not competent to explain an uncertain or ambiguous ballot, unless in case of a latent ambiguity.   State *v.* Cooley Constit. Lim (5th Ed.) 768.   But see People *v.* Pease, 27 N. Y. 45 ; McKinnon *v.* Mulzacher, 5 Am. & Engl. Corp. Cas. 492.

In Beardstown *v.* Virginia, 76 Ill. 34, it was held that declarations of a voter as to how he intended to vote are not admissible to show how he did vote.   See also People *v.* Saxton, 22 N. Y. 309.

When several persons are to be elected to an office, and a voter places upon his ballot more names than there are persons to be elected, it is held that the ballot is wholly void and must be thrown out.   People *v.* Loomis, 8 Wend. 396.

And extrinsic evidence is not admissible to show that the voter intended to erase certain names and leave only the number that were to be voted for. People *v.* Seaman, 5 Den. 409.

ATTORNEY-GENERAL
v.
CROCKER *et al.*

(138 *Massachusetts*, 214.)

The authority of tellers appointed to aid in checking the names of voters and in assorting and counting the votes cast at a town meeting, in accordance with the St. of 1883, c. 229, does not cease with the resignation of the moderator who appointed them, before they have reported the result of the votes.

The record of a town meeting showed that a moderator was chosen with the use of the check-list; that a vote was then passed that the check-list be used in the election of town officers and upon the question of granting licenses, and no other, without a vote of at least one-half the meeting; that the moderator resigned; and that another person was elected moderator, and acted as such. *Held*, that whether the record showed that this person was elected by ballot and by the use of the check-list or not, it sufficiently showed that he was a moderator *de facto.*

At a town meeting, after the votes for town officers had been cast, but before the result was announced, the moderator and clerk resigned their offices. The selectmen, who were not present at the meeting, appointed in writing, C. town-clerk *pro tempore.* C. appeared and was duly sworn, and made a record of his appointment and qualification and of the subsequent doings of the meeting, which included the election of a moderator, the announcement of the vote for town officers, the declaration of the persons elected, the vote to adjourn the meeting, and the resignation of C. as clerk *pro tempore. Held*, on an information by the attorney-general in the nature of a *quo warranto* against the persons elected, that C. was a town-clerk *de facto* at the meeting, although the selectmen had no authority, under the Pub. Sts. c. 27, §§ 80, 97, 98, to appoint a clerk at that time, and notwithstanding one voter protested against the validity of the election; that his record was admissible in evidence; and that the officers elected were entitled to their offices.

W. S. B. Hopkins for relators.

W. Gasters and *D. W. Bond* for respondents.

W. ALLEN, J.—This is an information in the nature of a *quo warranto* to try the title of the respondents, re-   FACTS. spectively, to the offices of town-clerk and selectmen of the

town of Montague, which, it is alleged, they have usurped.
The facts, as they appear from the report of the single justice
of this court who heard the cases, are as follows:

At the annual town meeting on March 3, 1884, a moderator
was duly chosen and tellers were duly appointed by him to
aid in checking the names of the voters and in assorting and
counting the votes, according to the St. of 1883, c. 229. After
the votes for town officers, including the town-clerk, were all
cast, and after they were assorted and counted by the tellers,
and while they were putting the results into form for announcement to the meeting, the moderator and clerk resigned
their offices. No question is made that their resignations
created legal vacancies in their offices, and we have not considered the effect in that respect. After their resignations,
other persons acted as moderator and clerk; it was voted to
hear the report of the tellers, and they reported the votes,
which showed the election of the respondents and other officers; and the votes were announced, and the officers declared
elected.

The principal objection to the title of the respondents to
their offices is, that the proceedings of the meeting after the
resignation of the moderator and clerk were illegal and void,
because their successors were not legally chosen.

Another objection is, that the authority of the tellers
CESSATION OF ceased with that of the moderator who appointed
TELLER'S AU-
THORITY. them. But they were appointed to assist the moderator officially, and not personally, and their authority would
survive a change in the person of the moderator. They continued to be lawful tellers.

It is also objected that the record does not show that the
check-list was used in the choice of the second moderator, or
that he was chosen by ballot, but only states that he was
USE OF CHECK- elected. After the first moderator had been twice
LIST IN VOTING. chosen, the second time with the use of the check-
list, the admitted record shows that it was " voted that the
check list be used in the election of town officers, and upon
the question of granting licenses, and no other, without a
vote of at least one-half the meeting." There is no other
record of the use of the check-list. Its use was as necessary
to the election of the selectmen and town-clerk as of a moderator. Pub. Sts. c. 27, § 80; c. 7, § 9. In Andrews *v.* Boyls-

ton, 110 Mass. 214, a record, " Voted, to re-establish the school-district system," was held insufficient, the statute requiring the votes of two-thirds of all the legal voters present and voting. The court say, "The form of expression is that which is ordinarily used in setting forth the vote of a mere majority ; and there is nothing on the face of the record to indicate that either the officers or the voters had their attention called to the fact the law required a two-thirds vote." See also Morrison *v.* Lawrence, 98 Mass. 219 ; Judd *v.* Thompson, 125 Mass. 553. In the case at bar, the matter concerns the mode of voting, and not the essentials of the vote ; and the admitted record shows that the meeting intended to use the check-list, and that the fact that it was required was in the minds of the voters. We are inclined to the opinion that the record, if competent, shows that the second moderator was an officer *de jure*. See Howard *v.* Proctor, 7 Gray, 128. We do not decide this, because the reasons which render the record competent show that the moderator was a good officer *de facto*, if not one *de jure*.

The principal question relates to the town-clerk. A moderator and clerk are essential to a town meeting APPOINTMENT OF for the choice of town officers, and there cannot be TOWN CLERK. a record without a clerk. In the absence of a moderator, and for the choice of one, the clerk presides, and, in his absence, the selectmen. Pub. Sts. c. 27, §§ 58, 59. At that meeting, the clerk to be chosen was voted for with the selectmen and other officers, and the vote had not been declared when the moderator and clerk resigned, and their offices are assumed to have become vacant. The selectmen appear not to have been present. After several hours one of the selectmen came into the meeting and read a paper signed by the selectmen as follows: "Montague, March 3, 1884. William O. Crocker is hereby appointed town-clerk *pro tempore*, in place of J. H. Root, resigned." Said Crocker was duly sworn, and made a record in the book of town records of his appointment and of the subsequent doings of the meeting, the last entry, made after that of the vote to adjourn, being of his own resignation as clerk *pro tempore*. This record is sufficient, if competent, to show that the respondents were duly elected. On March 6, a town-clerk was duly appointed by the selectmen and sworn, who.

on March 8 administered the oath of office to the respondents, and made a record thereof. No objection is made that
the respondents were not duly qualified, if elected; and the
question is whether the record made by William O. Crocker,
as clerk, is competent,—in other words, whether the act of
the meeting in receiving the report of the tellers and declaring the election of the respondents was invalid for want of
officers, and incapable of proof for want of a record. The
former clerk completed the record to and including his own
resignation. What is contained in the disputed record is the
appointment and qualification of the clerk *pro tempore;* the
election of a moderator; the vote to hear the report of the
tellers, and their report that the vote was announced and the
election declared ; that one voter protested as to the validity
of their election: and the vote to adjourn to March 10.

That William O. Crocker had no lawful authority to act as
DE-FACTO TOWN town-clerk at the meeting is clear. Section 80 of
CLERK.   the Pub. Sts. c. 27 provides that the election of
town-clerks shall be by written ballots. Section 97 provides
that when there is a vacancy in the office of town-clerk at a
town meeting, or when he is not present, the voters present
shall elect a clerk *pro tempore* in the same manner as town-
clerks are chosen, who shall be sworn to discharge the duties
of said office at said meeting. Section 98 provides that when
other duties than those mentioned in the preceding section
are required to be performed by a town-clerk, and there is a
vacancy in the office, or the clerk is prevented from performing such duties, the selectmen may in writing appoint a clerk
for the performance thereof, who shall be sworn, and shall
make a record of his appointment. The selectmen had no
authority to appoint a clerk for the town meeting, and the
appointment made by them gave the appointee no authority
to act as such. But this is not a proceeding against him to
test his title to the office, but one in which the rights of third
persons and of the public, acquired by virtue of his official
acts, are concerned, as to whom the official acts of a public
officer *de facto* are as valid as if he held the office *de jure.*
There can be no doubt that the principle applies to the office
of town-clerk. Suppose a town-clerk to be regularly elected
and qualified, except that the check-list was not used, and to
exercise the functions of the office during the year for which

he was so elected. He would at no time have been lawfully the town-clerk, or able to maintain his own right to the office; but his official acts, whether in recording the doings of town meetings, or in the performance of other duties of the office, would be as valid, as to all other parties, as if he had been town-clerk *de jure.* The illustration shows the reasons of public policy and of private justice upon which the rule is founded. It applies to a town-clerk as presiding and record- ing officer of a town meeting, and the question upon which the competency and sufficiency of the record we are considering depends is whether William O. Crocker was, when so acting, town-clerk *de facto.*

An officer *de facto* may be said to be one who assumes the functions of an officer under color of title of the office. The definition cited and approved in Petersilea *v.* Stone, 119 Mass. 465, and sustained by the decision in that case and by the au- thorities cited in the opinion, is, " One who has the reputation of being the officer he assumes to be, and yet is not a good officer in point of law." These are very general statements, and afford only a starting-point for the consideration of par- ticular cases. What is color of office, and what facts show that one assumes and is reputed to hold a particular office, are left open questions, and perhaps no statement of them can be found sufficiently comprehensive and particular to be applica- ble to the circumstances of every case which may arise.

The relators contend that, upon the facts of this case, there was neither an assumption of the office under color of title, nor a reputation of holding it, within the meaning of the law. That William O. Crocker assumed to have been duly appointed town-clerk, and that he took the oath and performed the duties of the office under a claim of title to it, cannot be questioned. The relators con- tend that this is not sufficient, unless the office is assumed under color of an election or appointment by some body or person authorized to elect or appoint to the office. No deci- sion is cited in support of this position, though some defini- tions of the term officer *de facto,* made as applicable to par- ticular facts, may seem to favor it. The authorities to the contrary are numerous and decisive. Among them are Fowler *v.* Bebee, 9 Mass. 231, and Petersilea *v.* Stone, *ubi supra,* the latter of which is directly in point. The question is discussed.

COLOR OF TITLE NOT NECESSARY TO DE-FACTO OF-FICER.

and the cases bearing upon it fully cited, in the elaborate and able opinion by Chief Justice Butler in State *v.* Caroll, 38 Conn. 449.

It is further contended that, because the office was claimed DE FACTO OFFI- under the selectmen, who had no authority to ap- CER. ASSUMP- TION OF OFFICE. point to it, and the claim was made, and the acts under it performed, in the presence of and in relation to the body which had the rightful power of electing to the office, such acts cannot show either an assumption of the office, or a reputation of holding it, and are insufficient to prove that the person performing them was an officer *de facto*. The presence and conduct of the person authorized to appoint to an office, when another person acts as holding the office under a stranger, may be evidence, but cannot be conclusive upon the public or upon third persons. Such evidence may tend to prove that the assumption is a pretence, and that the pretender is reputed not to be an officer; or it may be such as to tend strongly to prove an assumption as of right, and a reputation of holding the office. If it showed assent or acquiescence of the body which had the right of appointment, it would have that effect; if it showed dissent or opposition, it would not be conclusive the other way. The protest made by a single voter, after the respondents were declared elected, "as to the legality of their election," is certainly not conclusive that William O. Crocker was not reputed to be town-clerk. The protest was not against the appointment of the clerk *pro tempore*, but the election of the regular town officers, and it does not show whether it was upon the ground still insisted on, that the tellers had no authority to act under another moderator than the one who appointed them, or for some other reason. Had the reason of the protest been the invalidity of the appointment of the clerk, it wonld properly and probably have been made when he assumed the office. The acquiescence of the voter until the election of officers was declared, and the confining of the protest to the election of those officers, with the consideration that there was an obvious fact which has been supposed to render their election illegal, and which had no connection with the validity of the appointment or acts of the clerk *pro tempore*, indicate that the effect of the protest, whatever that may be, should be expended upon the election of the officers to which it referred; and it is admitted in the argument for the relators that they are officers *de facto*, whose acts as such are valid.

It makes no difference whether the appointment by the selectmen is construed as an appointment of clerk of the town meeting, in which case it would be void, or as an appointment, which they had the power to make, to perform the other duties of the town-clerk, in which case it would not purport to authorize the appointee to act as clerk at a town meeting. It appears clearly from the facts that he assumed the office of clerk of the town meeting under color of the appointment, and whether he did it under an illegal appointment from the selectmen, or by an illegal assumption of power under a legal appointment, is immaterial.

The facts show that William O. Crocker, claiming a due appointment, assumed the office of clerk of the town meeting; that he was duly sworn as such, and made a record of his appointment and qualification; that he presided at the choice of moderator, and performed the duties of clerk until the adjournment of the meeting; that the meeting acquiesced in his assumption, and treated him as its lawful officer; and that no objection or suggestion that he was not the lawful officer was made by any individual while he assumed to hold the office,—unless the protest, which has been considered, of a single voter, just at the adjournment of the meeting, to other action of the meeting could be so considered. Upon these facts, without considering the further facts urged by the respondents,—that the person who protested, subsequently, under an appointment as town-clerk from the selectmen, administered the oath of office to the respondents against whose election he had protested, and that at the adjournment of the same meeting the record in question was read and approved,—it is clear that William O. Crocker was reputed to be town-clerk at the meeting, and was clerk *de facto*.

The question concerns the public; there are no contestants to the offices held by these respondents, and there was none to the office assumed by William O. Crocker. It is a question of public policy in regard to the validity of the doings of a town meeting as to persons claiming rights by virtue of them. The facts are extraordinary. An annual town meeting, after being fully organized, was deprived of its moderator and clerk. The selectmen were not present. The necessary business of the meeting could not be proceeded with until after a moderator and clerk should be chosen, and that could be regularly done only by ballot, with the use of the check list. No one but the selectmen was authorized to receive ballots or use the check list, and the meeting, even if it could act, had no power to compel their presence. Under these circumstances, if a person appointed by the general voice of the voters present for the purpose had assumed to act as moderator while a clerk was chosen and qualified in due form, we are not prepared to say that his acts would not have been valid as acts of a moderator *de facto*, although he and every voter present should have known that he was not legally elected, and was not a good officer in point of law. But this case presents no such question. After the proceedings of the meeting had been suspended for several hours, a person appeared showing an appointment which he claimed made him lawful clerk, and assumed the office and performed its duties with general assent. There is no reason to doubt that he was universally reputed to be, not only acting, but legal clerk. But if all opposed to carrying on the meeting had opposed and protested against his appointment, the meeting still accepting him as clerk, we think he would have been clerk *de facto*.

Public necessity and policy require that the acts of an actual incumbent of a public office, in the performance of its duties, shall be held valid, although the incumbent should not have a legal right to the office, and though his right should be questioned and disputed. A single illustration will suffice. The act establishing the County of Hampden was passed in February, 1812, to take effect on the 1st day of the next August. In May, Governor Gerry, whose term expired on the last Wednesday of that month, appointed the officers for the expected county, including the judge of probate and the sheriff. The Governor had no more authority to make these appointments than the selectmen in the case at bar had to appoint the clerk of the town meeting, and they were void. Commonwealth *v.* Fowler, 10 Mass. 290. The acts of the officers and of their deputies were valid, as acts of officers *de facto*. Fowler *v.* Bebee, *ubi supra*. As these appointments were made a short time before the expiration of the term of office of the Governor, and as he was of a different political party from that ·of the incoming Governor, who alone had power to make the appointments, it was natural that the authority to make the appointments should be questioned, and that all the facts showing them to be invalid should be generally known and discussed, and the right of the incumbents to their offices denied by a large portion of the public. That this was so may be inferred from the fact that the information against the judge of probate was filed in accordance with a vote of the House of Representatives. It cannot be argued that such facts, if they existed, made the acts of the actual incumbents invalid, nor that the fact that acts were performed in the presence of the Governor, who had the power of appointment, could make any difference in their validity. Had Governor Strong offered himself to the acting judge of probate as attesting witness to a will, the oath administered to him would unquestionably have been legal, and so would the probate of a will admitted by the usurping judge in the presence and against the protest of the Governor.

The public and parties, having rights depending upon official acts, are not so much concerned with the title to an office as they are that the duties of the office shall be performed, and the rights depending upon their performance secured and protected ; and when they find an actual incumbent of an office performing its duties, they have a right to rely upon his acts as done by virtue of the office.

Information dismissed.

STATE *ex rel.* ATTORNEY-GENERAL

v.

HORTON *et al.*

(*Advance Case Nevada. October* 12, 1885.)

A judge of an election for school trustees has no power to administer the official oath of office to the elected school trustees. The only oath which he can administer is the one prescribed in the statute of 1885, section 9, to a voter when challenged.

A statute requiring the official oath of a public officer to be endorsed on his certificate of appointment is sufficiently complied with if such oath be attached to the certificate.

Application for *quo warranto*. The opinion states the facts.
R. M. Clarke and *J. D. Torreyson* for the relator.
A. C. Ellis for the respondents.

HAWLEY, J.—This is a proceeding in the nature of a *quo*
FACTS. *warranto*, to determine whether the respondents
have wrongfully and unlawfully introduced themselves into,
and usurped, the offices of school trustees of Empire school
district in Ormsby County.

The material facts, as presented by the pleadings and proofs,
are that the number of census children in Empire school district is less than four hundred; that at the general election in
November, 1882, W. J. Smyth was elected school trustee in
said district for the term of four years from and after January 1, 1883; that at the general election in 1884, J. P. Woodbury and John Christiansen were elected trustees,—the former
for a term of four years, and the latter for two years; that
said parties qualified by taking the regular oath of office before an officer authorized to administer oaths, and that their
oaths of office were endorsed upon their certificates of elections; that on the second Saturday of May, 1885, at an election
held, pursuant to the provisions of the supplemental school
act approved March 12, 1885, Stat. 1885, 111, the respondents, Horace A. Bowley, George Horton, and A. D. Smith,
were elected school trustees in said district for the respective
terms of one, two, and three years from the first day of September, A.D. 1885; that they received their certificates of
election on the ninth of May, and the oath of office was administered to them by one of the judges of the school election; that on the third day of September, A.D. 1885, S. H.
Wright, county superintendent of schools in Ormsby County,
believing that a vacancy existed, appointed J. P. Woodbury,
W. J. Smyth, and John Christiansen school trustees of said
school district; that on the fifth of September, 1885, W. J.
Smyth and John Christiansen signed and subscribed the
official oath, and it was sworn to before a justice of the peace;
that on the twelfth day of September, 1885, J. P. Woodbury
qualified by taking the official oath before a notary public;
that the respective oaths of office were attached to their
certificates of appointment; that, subsequently, on the twenty-
first of September, 1885, after the information in this case had

been filed with the clerk of this court, Horace A. Bowley and A. D. Smith went before a notary public and had the official oath administered to them and annexed to a paper containing what purported to be a copy of their certificates of election.

Counsel for the respective parties discussed the question of the construction and constitutionality of the supplemental school act; but it is unnecessary for us to consider either of these questions in deciding this case. The judges of the election had no authority to administer the official oath of office to the elected school trustees. The only oath which a judge of election could administer is the one, prescribed in the statute, to a voter when challenged. Stat. 1885, 113, sec. 9.

JUDGE OF ELECTION CANNOT ADMINISTER OATH.

If the supplemental school act is unconstitutional, the respondents would have no right whatever to the offices of school trustees, and Woodbury, Smyth, and Christiansen would be entitled to the offices by virtue of their election and qualification under the old law. If the supplemental act is constitutional, respondents would not be benefited thereby, because they failed to qualify as required by law, and Woodbury, Smyth, and Christiansen would be entitled to the offices by virtue of their appointment. The question whether S. H. Wright qualified as superintendent of schools, according to the provisions of the statute, cannot be inquired into in this proceeding. It was enough to show that he was elected and entered upon the duties of this office, and that he has ever since been exercising the duties thereof.

OFFICIAL OATH. INDORSEMENT.

The objections made to the effect that the official oaths of Woodbury, Smyth, and Christiansen were attached to, instead of being endorsed upon, the back of their certificates of appointment, or endorsed on the face, instead of the back, of their certificates of election, are without merit. Brown *v.* Foster, 2 Met. 155.

The respondents having failed to show any legal right to the offices of school trustees, a judgment of ouster must be entered against them, with costs. It is so ordered.

LEONARD, J., concurring. I concur in the judgment.

STATE *ex rel.* JAMES H. LIBBEY

v.

JAMES H. MEGIN.

(*Advance Case, New Hampshire.* *July* 31, 1885.)

In *quo warranto* to determine the right to an elective office the record of the declared election is not conclusive.

A person declared elected and inducted into office is a *de facto* officer, though not lawfully elected.

INFORMATION, in the nature of a *quo warranto*, filed by the attorney-general at the relation of James H. Libbey to determine the right of the defendant to the office of prudential committee of School District No. 2 in Hooksett. Facts found by a referee.

The record of the school meeting held March 7, 1885, shows that the defendant had a plurality of votes and was elected. Upon evidence tending to show how individuals voted, received subject to the defendant's exception, and upon other evidence, it was found that the relator had a plurality of votes and was elected. The defendant assumed the duties of the office, and about April 1st hired a competent teacher for the year at a stipulated salary. The relator and the defendant are equally suitable to fill the office.

Chase & Streeter for plaintiff.

Osgood & Prescott for defendant.

CARPENTER, J.—Upon the question which of the parties received a plurality of votes for the office, the record

RECORD OF VOTE AS EVIDENCE.

of the declared vote is, in this suit, merely evidence. If the record of the declaration of the moderator in the case of town and school district officers and of the canvassing board appointed by law in the case of other officers were conclusive, this proceeding could never be maintained to test the right to an elective office. It cannot be instituted until possession of the office is taken (Osgood *v.* Jones, 60 N. H. 282), and no one can take possession until his election is declared. The exception to the reception of evidence outside the record must be overruled.   People *v.* Vail, 20 Wend. 12.

Whether there may be cases in which the law does not require an information to be issued or the writ to be granted, although it appears that the defendant is not entitled to the office, as where a determination of the proceedings cannot be reached until after the expiration of the term of office, or where greater public mischief would be done by granting than by refusing the writ (People *v.* Sweeting, 2 Johns. 185; People *v.* Loomis, 8 Wend. 396; Commonwealth *v.* Athearn, 3 Mass. 285; Howard *v.* Gage, 6 Mass. 462; State *v.* Jacobs, 17 Ohio 143; State *v.* Schnierie, 5 Rich. (S. C.), 299; King *v.* Parry, 6 Ad. & E. 810; State *v.* Mead, 56 Vt. 353; State *v.* Tolan, 33 N. J. 195; Commonwealth *v.* Jones, 12 Pa. St. 365), is a question not necessary to be considered. No sufficient reason here appears why the defendant should not be removed. He was not and the relator was lawfully elected; a part only of the term of office has expired, and no CONTRACT OF DE-FACTO OFFICER. public mischief can result from the removal. By virtue of his declared election and induction into the office, the defendant became, and, until judgment rendered, will remain, a *de facto* officer. His official acts are valid. His contract with the teacher, if made in good faith by both parties, will have the same force and validity as if the judgment in this case were for the defendant. The prudential committee is charged with various duties besides the employment of teachers (Gen. Laws, ch. 86, s. 27; ch. 87, s. 14; ch. 88, s. 15; ch. 91, ss. 1 and 2), all of which may as well be performed during the remainder of the term by the relator as by the defendant, both being equally competent. No more inconvenience can result to the district from granting the information than is met in the ordinary case of the death, resignation, or removal of the committee and the election or appointment of another.

Information granted.

All concurred.

PROOF OF OFFICIAL CHARACTER—DE FACTO OFFICERS.—When an officer's official character is in issue he need not prove that the appointing power was *de jure*. Stevens *v.* Newcomb, 4 Den. 437. If he produces a record of his appointment issued by an authority having apparent jurisdiction, this is conclusive. State *ex rel.* Leonard *v.* Sweet, 27 La. Ann.

541 ; Wood *v.* Peake, 8 Johns. 69. And parol evidence is sufficient to prove
the appointment where there is no writing, and none is required by law.
Hoke *v.* Field, 10 Bush (Ky.) 144. In regard to proof of official character
where an official is trying to justify an official act complained of, three
rules are formulated : (1) He must aver and prove that he was legally an
officer duly elected or appointed, and qualified to act. Conover *v.* Devlin.
15 How. Pr. 478 ; Green *v.* Burke, 23 Wend. 490; Blake *v.* Sturtevant, 12
N. H. 567 ; Cummings *v.* Clarke, 15 Vt. 653 ; Colburn *v.* Ellis, 5 Mass.
427. (2) That he must at least show color of election or appointment from competent authority. State *v.* Carroll, 38 Conn. 449; 9 Am.
Rep. 409, and that this is *prima facie* sufficient for the protection of an
officer *de facto.* Willis *v.* Sproule, 13 Kan. 257. (3) That he may *prima
facie* establish his official character by proof of general reputation, and
that he acted as such officer (Colton *v.* Beardsley, 38 Barb. 29) in other
matters besides those in question. Hutchings *v.* Van Bokkelen, 34 Me.
126. See generally " Abbott's Trial Evidence," 201.

In State *v.* Carroll, *supra,* a very thoroughly considered case, an officer
de facto is defined, and the rules governing his conduct are formulated, as
follows: An officer *de facto* is one whose acts, though not those of a lawful
officer, the law, upon principles of policy and justice, will hold valid, so far
as they involve the interests of the public and third persons where the
duties of the office were exercised, (1) Without a known appointment or
election, but under such circumstances of reputation or acquiescence as
were calculated to induce people, without inquiry, to submit to or invoke
his action, supposing him to be the officer he assumed to be. (2) Under
color of a known and valid appointment or election, but where the officer
has failed to conform to some precedent, requirement, or condition, as to
take an oath, give a bond, or the like. (3) Under color of a known election
or appointment, void, because the officer was not eligible, or because there
was some want of power in the electing or appointing body, or by reason
of some defect or irregularity in its exercise, such ineligibility, want of
power, or defect being unknown to the public. (4) Under color of an
election or appointment by or pursuant to a public, unconstitutional law
before the same is adjudged to be such. See also Laver *v.* McGlachlin, 28
Wis. 364.

MILFORD

v.

GREENBUSH.

(Advance Case, Maine. May 4, 1885.)

Copies of a town's voting-lists, voluntarily and not officially made by the town-clerk, who had since died, are inadmissible as evidence of such lists.

A town assessor's books purporting to show whose taxes have been abated during certain years are not admissible to show that one who is not named therein has paid his taxes.

Appendices to a State adjutant-general's report, printed by the State printer, are admissible to prove returns made to such adjutant-general.

Davis & Bailey for plaintiff.

C. P. Stetson and *J. A. Blanchard* for defendant.

EMERY, J.—I. The voting-lists of the town were shown to be lost, and the plaintiffs offered in their stead what they alleged to be copies of those lists. These alleged copies were found apparently recorded from year to year upon the book of the town records, and in handwriting of the successive clerks of the town. Proof that they were, in fact, copies of the originals was essential to their admission in evidence. It was no part of the duty of the town-clerk to copy such lists upon the town records. Such work would have been purely voluntary and unauthorized. Hence the alleged copies were not admissible as official copies or records. The plaintiffs do not contend that they were.

As to the alleged copy of the list for the year 1869, the plaintiffs were able to prove, and did prove, it to be a copy by the testimony of the man who made it, and it was admitted as a copy. As to the other alleged copies, there was no evidence from any one who could say that he made them, or saw them made, or had compared them with the originals, or that they were according to his recollection of the originals. Evidence that the man who made the writings was dead was no proof that he made true copies. The fact that he was town-clerk at the ·time, and had interjected these unauthorized writings into the town records, gave them no evidential value. The plaintiffs simply found some writings in the handwriting of one deceased, which they believed to be copies of the papers lost, but which they were unable to prove to be copies. Their only witness was dead. It was their misfortune.

The authorities cited by the plaintiffs' counsel are not applicable. This is not a question of the admissibility of a record, or of an entry, where the maker is dead. It is a question of the sufficiency of evidence that a certain writing was a copy of a lost document. We think the evidence was not sufficient.

II. Upon the issue whether the pauper had paid any tax assessed against him for several years in the defendant town, the plaintiffs offered the assessors' books of the defendant town, containing what purported to be a list of the abatements for those years, in which the name of the pauper did not appear. We think it was incompetent. The assessors have nothing to do with the collection of the taxes. The collector's accounts might afford evidence upon that issue, but the assessors' list of abatements does not. *Non constat* that every tax is paid or abated. The collector often fails to collect where there is no abatement. His own neglect, the insufficiency of his warrant, the property of the person taxed, may be the cause of non-collection.

III. The pauper was a private in a Maine regiment during the war of the rebellion. The captain of his company made, in each of the years of 1861 and 1862, an official return to the State adjutant-general of the members of his company, with dates, places of residence and enlistment, etc. That these returns, or duly proved copies of them, might be evidence of any fact properly stated therein, the plaintiffs do not now dispute; but they contend that what were offered as copies were not admissible as such without further proof. The offered papers were the printed reports of the adjutant-general for those years, with the usual accompanying appendices, in which appear what purport to be copies of all such returns from all the Maine regiments. The reports, with the appendices, were made to the governor, and, we may assume, were by him laid before the legislature. The printed books purport to be printed by the State printer under legislative authority. The real value of the reports was in the appendices; all else was merely general statement and comment. The actual and desired facts and data, to promulgate which the reports were made and printed, were in the annexed papers. These were, in effect, a part of the reports.

Being printed by the official printer, under official supervision, they are presumably compared and correct copies of the originals. They have become *prima facie* copies, and we think are within the principle admitting printed public documents in evidence as copies of the original documents. King *v.* Holt, 5 Term R. 436; Radcliff *v.* United Insurance Co., 7 Johns. 38; Bryan *v.* Forsyth, 19 How. 338; Watkins *v.* Holman; 16 Pet. 58; Whiton *v.* Albany Insurance Co., 109 Mass. 30.

The legislature has not suspended the use of these printed copies of the records and files in the adjutant-general's office as evidence. Section 113 of chapter 82, Rev. Stat., referred to by the plaintiffs' counsel, does not specify any mode of making or proving copies of such papers. It does not require that all copies used in evidence shall be certified by the adjutant-general. It only provides that certain particular facts may be certified by the adjutant-general as found upon the records, without the whole record being copied. There is no prohibition against using a full copy, if a party desires it.

Exceptions overruled.

PETERS, C. J., DANFORTH, VIRGIN, FOSTER, and HASKELL, JJ., concurred.

PEOPLE *ex rel.* SWIFT
v.
POLICE COMMISSIONERS.

(Advance Case, New York. June 26, 1885.)

A rule of the police department of New York provided that in case testimony upon complaints made against any member of the police force should be heard by less than three commissioners, it should be "laid before and examined by the several commissioners before judgment thereon." *Held*, where the evidence was heard by one commissioner, that it was sufficient to lay it before three of the commissioners at a regular meeting of their board. Three of them forming a majority of the board, and as

such authorized to act in its name, the concurrence of the fourth commissioner was held unnecessary.

APPEAL from an order of the general term affirming the
proceedings of the Board of Police Commissioners of New
York in dismissing the relator from the police force. The
facts are stated in the opinion.

D. C. Calvin for appellant.

D. J. Dean for respondent.

EARL, J.—The police department was authorized to make
FACTS.   rules for the government and discipline of the department, and one of the rules provided that in case testimony
upon complaints made against any member of the police force
should be heard by less than three commissioners, it should
be "laid before and examined by the several commissioners
before judgment thereon." In this case the evidence was
taken before one of the commissioners, and thereafter at a
regular meeting of the board, when three only of the four
commissioners were present, it was presented to and considered by them, and they adopted a resolution that the
charges against the relator were true, and that he be removed
from the police force. This decision was affirmed at general
term, and the relator has appealed to this court, and claims
that his removal from the police force was without jurisdiction, and wholly void, because the evidence was not considered and action thereon taken by all the commissioners.
He claims that the rule of the police department referred to
required that the evidence should be laid before and examined by the several commissioners, to wit: All the commissioners. It was held by the general term that
MAJORITY OF
POLICE BOARD it was sufficient to answer the requirement of this
MAY PASS ON
CHARGE AGAINST rule that the evidence was laid before and ex-
POLICE OFFICER.
amined by the several commissioners constituting
the board at a regular meeting thereof, and we are constrained to adopt that construction. We can perceive no
reason for supposing that it was intended by the rule to
deprive the board at any of its regular meetings of jurisdiction to act upon such evidence, or that it was intended
that all the commissioners should severally examine the evidence while a majority of them, at any regular meeting, were
vested with power by the statute to perform any act within

the jurisdiction of the board. We think the language of the rule is satisfied with the construction given at the general term, and that the interpretation of the rule by the board which made it, as evidenced by its practice thereunder, should have some weight.

It is also claimed by the learned counsel for the relator that as the Board of Police Commissioners consisted of four members, it was necessary that they should all be present at a meeting in order to give jurisdiction for any action whatever under section 27, 2 R. S. 555, which provides that "whenever any power, duty, or authority is confided by law to three or more persons, and whenever three or more persons or officers are authorized or required by law to perform any act, such act may be done, and such power, authority, or duty may be exercised and performed by a majority of such persons or officers upon a meeting of all the persons or officers so entrusted or empowered, unless special provision is otherwise made." But that section was amended by chapter 321 of the Laws of 1874, so as to authorize action by a majority at a meeting properly held, of which all have had notice. It is also specially provided in the Consolidation Act—chapter 410 of the Laws of 1882, section 46—that "a majority of the members of a board in any department of the city government, and also of the board for the revision and correction of assessments, shall constitute a quorum to fully perform and discharge any act or duty authorized, possessed by, or imposed upon any department or any board aforesaid, and with the same legal effect as if any member of any such board aforesaid had been present, except as herein otherwise specially provided." And there is no special provision requiring all the police commissioners to be present upon the trial of any member of the force upon any charges presented against him. Therefore, it was competent for the three commissioners constituting a majority of the whole board, at any regular meeting, to take action upon the complaint made against the relator and the evidence relating thereto.

We have carefully considered the evidence, and find it sufficient to justify the action of the commissioners, and we cannot, therefore, interfere with their determination.

The order should be affirmed, with costs.

All concur.

PEOPLE *ex rel.* KENT

v.

BOARD OF FIRE COMMISSIONERS OF NEW YORK CITY.

(*Advance Case, New York. October* 6, 1885.)

On a common-law *certiorari* to review the judicial action of boards, commissioners, or inferior officers, the court was limited to the question of jurisdiction. By statute the court is authorized to look into the proceedings to see whether any rule of law has been violated, or whether there is an absence of evidence to support the adjudication. But questions of fact arising upon conflicting evidence, or matters of judgment or discretion, are not reviewable on *certiorari*. Therefore, *held* that the General Term of the New York Supreme Court would not review the discretion of the Board of Fire Commissioners of New York City in respect to punishing a police-officer for neglect of duty, and impose a milder punishment than the one imposed by the commissioners.

D. J. Dean for the Board of Fire Commissioners.

Wm. King Hall for the people.

ANDREWS, J.—The relator was duly charged with having FACTS. been under the influence of liquor, while engaged in the performance of official duty at the Star Theatre, to such an extent as to render him unable to perform the duty for which he was detailed. The charge was publicly examined by the commissioners, upon notice to the relator, and in his presence. The testimony tended to sustain it. The relator admitted that he drank a glass of liquor before going to the theatre, but claimed that he did it because he was unwell. There was some conflict as to the extent of the intoxication.

It is not claimed that illegal evidence was admitted, or that any rule of law was violated, by the commissioners in the course of the proceedings. The proceedings, trial, and judgment were in all respects regular, and the commissioners, in dismissing the relator, kept within their jurisdiction. The intoxication of a policeman while on duty, to an extent sufficient to interfere with its performance, is a violation of the rules of the department, and the statute makes the violation by a member of the force of such rules, or neglect of duty,

or conduct injurious to the public welfare, or any conduct
unbecoming an officer, punishable by the board, by reprimand,
forfeiture of pay for a period not exceeding ten days, or dismissal from the force.   There was no question either of jurisdiction, procedure, or evidence upon which the general term
could interfere with the decision of the commissioners.   It,
however, modified the sentence by substituting, in place of
dismissal from the force (the punishment imposed by the
commissioners), suspension from duty without pay for the
period of six months.   The only question is whether the general term had power to review the discretion of the commissioners in respect to the punishment, and impose a milder
punishment upon its view of the circumstances and gravity
of the offence.

It is clear that no power was vested in the general term to
review the discretion of the commissioners, unless given by
section 2141 of the Code of Civil Procedure.   It REVIEW ON CER-
was originally held in this State that, on a common- TIORARI
law *certiorari* to review the judicial action of boards, commissioners, or inferior officers, the court was limited to the ques
tion of jurisdiction.   The scope of the proceeding was subsequently enlarged, and it came to be held that the court
would look into the proceedings to see whether any rule of
law had been violated, or whether there was an absence of
evidence to support the adjudication.   People *v.* Board Police,
39 N. Y. 506; People *v.* Same, 72 N. Y. 416; People *v.* Board
Fire Com'rs, 82 N. Y. 358.

But questions of fact arising on conflicting evidence, or
matters of judgment or discretion, were held not to be reviewable.   People *v.* Board Police, 69 N. Y. 408.   This was the
state of the law when section 2141 of the Code was enacted.
It is contained in the article relating to the writ of *certiorari*,
and is as follows: " The court, on the hearing, may make a
final order annulling or confirming, wholly or partly, or
modifying, the determination reviewed, as to any or all the parties."   This section, considered alone, would justify the action
of the general term, and subject the adjudication of inferior
jurisdictions to the supervisory power of the court, whether
resting in discretion or depending upon legal principles.   If
this was intended, the section greatly enlarges the scope of
the writ, and vests in the court a jurisdiction which it never

before possessed. But, reading section 2141 in connection with section 2140, which defines the questions which may be determined by the court, it seems quite clear that section 2141 is an auxiliary section, enacted merely to complete and supplement the jurisdiction conferred by the previous section, and to remove a doubt which might be entertained in view of the prior decisions as to the power of the court on *certiorari* to correct an erroneous adjudication, instead of reversing it absolutely. Reading the two sections together, the result is that section 2140 regulates the jurisdiction of the court in respect to the questions to be reviewed, and section 2141 the mode in which its determination may be declared and its judgment made effectual. The latter section was not, we think, intended to confer jurisdiction over subjects other than those embraced in section 2140, or to change the settled policy of the law that the determination of inferior jurisdiction in matters confided to their discretion is not reviewable on *certiorari*.

The order of the general term should therefore be reversed, and that of the commissioners confirmed.

All concur.

CERTIORARI. WHEN IT WILL LIE.—It is well settled that courts of superior jurisdiction will on *certiorari* review the proceedings of special jurisdictions or officers. Groenvelt *v*. Burwell, 1 Ld. Raym. 454, 469; Rex *v*. Inhabitants, 1 Ld. Raym. 580; Parks *v*. Boston, 8 Pick. 218; Wood *v*. Peake, 8 John. 68; Wildy *v*. Washburn, 16 John. 49.

When a new jurisdiction is created by statute, it is held, in the absence of any statutory provision, that courts of general superior jurisdiction may review the proceedings of the officers or body exercising such jurisdiction. Boston *v*. Parks, 8 Pick. 218; Miller *v*. Trustees of School, 88 Ill. 26; Ewing *v*. City of St. Louis, 5 Wall. 413; Dorchester *v*. Wentworth, 11 Fost. 451; Dwight *v*. City Council of Springfield, 4 Gray, 107; 2 Dill. Mun. Corp. §925.

Even where it is expressly provided by statute that the proceedings of the inferior tribunal shall be "final and conclusive," or "without appeal," it is held that there is a right to review its proceedings by writ of *certiorari*. Thus, in *certiorari* from the decision of a justice of the peace under the "Conventicle act," which provided "that no other court whatsoever shall intermeddle with any cause or causes of appeal upon this act, but they shall be finally determined in the quarter-sessions only," it was held that the writ would lie. Rex *v*. Morely, 2 Burr. 1040. See also Lawton *v*. Commissioners of Cambridge, 2 Caines, 179; *Ex parte* Heath, 3 Hill, 42, 52.

At common law the writ of *certiorari* would not lie unless the act to be reviewed were a judicial act as distinguished from a ministerial or legislative act. People *v.* Mayor, etc., of New York, 2 Hill, 9; In the matter of Mount Morris Square, 2 Hill, 14–21.

In New Jersey, however, it is held that all acts of a municipal corporation, whether judicial, ministerial or legislative, can be reviewed on *certiorari.* Camdem *v.* Mulford, 2 Dutch. 49; Canon *v.* Martin, 2 Dutch. 594; Morris Canal Co. *v.* Jersey City, 1 Beasley, 252; Holmes *v.* Jersey City, 1 Beasley, 299.

And in other States the courts are liberal in construing acts to be judicial. Thus the mayor and aldermen of the town of Boston, being empowered to lay out or widen a street " whenever in their opinion the safety or convenience of the inhabitants of said town shall require it," it was held that the power thus conferred was a judicial one, and that its exercise could be reviewed on *certiorari.* Parks *v.* Boston, 8 Pick. 218; Dwight *v.* Springfield, 4 Gray, 107; Stone *v.* Boston, 2 Metc. 220.

CERTIORARI. WHAT QUESTIONS MAY BE GONE INTO.—2 Dillon, Mun. Corp. (3d ed.) § 928, states the law on this subject as follows: " Although there is some contrariety of opinion as to just what the writ removes, and as to whether the evidence, if certified, can be considered at all, the more liberal and better view is that the revisory court may not only inquire into the jurisdiction of the inferior tribunal, but into errors of law occurring in the course of the proceedings and affecting the merits of the case, and may also examine the evidence embodied in the return, " not to determine whether the probabilities preponderate one way or the other, but simply to determine whether the evidence is such that it will justify the finding as a legitimate finding from the facts proved, whether that inference would or would not have been drawn by the superior tribunal." Milwaukee Iron Co. *v.* Schubel, 29 Wis. 444.

In certain States, however, it is held that the only questions that can be gone into are those of jurisdiction ; that is, " whether the inferior jurisdiction has pursued the powers and conformed to the requirements of the law under which it professes to act." 2 Dill. Mun. Corp. (3d ed.) § 928 n. 1. Parks *v.* Boston, 8 Pick. 218; People, etc., *v.* Mayor, etc., of New York, 2 Hill, 9; *In re* Mount Morris Square, 2 Hill, 14; Stone *v.* Mayor, etc., 15 Wend. 157, 167; Locke *v.* Lexington, 122 Mass. 290.

STATE *ex rel.* ATTORNEY-GENERAL

v.

LAUGHTON.

(Advance Case, Nevada. October 23, 1885.)

Making a person an *ex-officio* officer, by virtue of his holding another office, does not merge the two offices into one.

The failure of the lieutenant-governor to give the bond required by statute, as *ex-officio* State librarian, does not create a vacancy in the office of lieutenant-governor.

There is nothing in the constitution of Nevada prohibiting he same person from holding the office of lieutenant-governor and the office of State librarian. Such being the case, the legislature had power to create the last-named office, and make the lieutenant-governor *ex-officio* State librarian, and to impose reasonable conditions precedent to the holding of the legislative office. It had power to require the giving of a bond to se- cure a faithful discharge of the duties of that office, and to provide that such bond should be kept good; and in case of failure so to do, that the office should become vacant.

The act of February 17, 1883, making the lieutenant-governor *ex-officio* State librarian, and the act of March 1, 1883, requiring the *ex-officio* State librarian to give a bond, must be construed together with the provisions of the general statutes declaring under what circumstances an office shall become vacant, providing for the release from liability of any surety, and prescribing the result of a failure to file a new or additional bond, within the time stated, after the filing by a surety of a legal statement in the office of the Governor or Secretary of State, and the service of a legal notice upon the officer.

Under such section a surety desiring to be released from an official bond must file with the Governor, or with the Secretary of State, a statement in writing, duly subscribed by him, or some one in his behalf, setting forth the name of the office of the person for whom he is surety, the amount for which he is liable as such, and his desire to be released from further lia- bility on account thereof, and a notice containing the objects of such state- ment must be served personally on the officer. *Held,* that such notice and statement need not be contained in two separate papers; that the notice need not state the time when, nor the place where, the statement was filed; that the statement and notice in the present case were sufficient, and that the latter was personally served on the respondent.

APPLICATION for *quo warranto.* The opinion states the facts.

R. M. Clarke for the relator.

A. C. Ellis for the respondent.

LEONARD, J.—This is a proceeding to determine the right FACTS. of respondent (1) to hold the office of lieutenant- governor, and (2) to hold the office of State librarian.

At the general election for State officers in November, 1882, respondent was elected lieutenant-gcvernor. He after- wards qualified according to law, and he entered upon the duties of said office on the first Monday in January, 1883. On the 17th of February, 1883, an act was passed, to take effect March 2, 1883, which provides, among other things, that the lieutenant-governor shall be *ex-officio* State librarian. Stats. 1883, 41. On the 1st of March, 1883, an act was passed (to take effect immediately), which provides that, " before entering upon the duties of the office (State librarian), the lieutenant-governor, as *ex-officio* State librarian, shall execute an official bond in the sum of one thousand dollars, with sureties to be approved by the Governor, conditioned for the faithful discharge of his duties, and delivery over to his successor of all the books and other property belonging to the State librarian." . . . Respondent gave the required bond, with J. R. King and D. L. Bliss as sureties, each in the sum of one thousand dollars, and entered upon the discharge of the duties of State librarian.

Section 2633 of the compiled laws provides that " every office shall become vacant upon the occurring of either of the following events before the expiration of the term of office : . . . Fifth. A refusal or neglect of the person elected or appointed to take the oath of office, as prescribed in section 22 of this act ; or when a bond is required by law, his refusal or neglect to give such bond within the time prescribed by law." . . .

By sections 2929, 2930, 2931, it is provided that "any surety on the official bond of any State . . . officer, or on the bond or undertaking of any person, where, by law, a bond or undertaking is required, may be released from all liability thereon, accruing from and after proper proceedings had therefor, as provided in this act."

" Any surety desiring to be released from liability on the bond of any State officer shall file with the Governor or Secretary of State a statement in writing, duly subscribed by himself, or some one in his behalf, setting forth the name and office of the person for whom he is surety, the amount for which he is liable as such, and his desire to be released on account thereof. A notice containing the objects of such statement shall be served personally on the officer." . . .

" If any officer . . . shall fail within ten days from the date of a personal service . . . to file a new or additional bond or undertaking, the office or appointment of the person or officer so failing shall become vacant, and such officer or person shall forfeit his office or appointment, and the same shall be filled as in other cases of vacancy, and in manner as provided by law, and the person applying to be released from liability on such bond or undertaking shall not be holden or liable there-

on, after the date herein provided for the vacating and forfeiting of such office or appointment."

On July 31, 1885, D. L. Bliss, one of the sureties named,
filed in the office of the Governor and of the Secretary of
State the following document, in writing :

"CARSON CITY, July 31, 1885.

" Hon. Chas. E. Laughton, Carson, Nev.

" SIR,—You are hereby notified that I, as surety for the sum
of one thousand dollars ($1000) upon your official bond as *ex-
officio* State librarian of the State of Nevada, desire to be released from further liability on account thereof, and to withdraw and be discharged from said bond.

" D. L. BLISS."

It is claimed by plaintiff that an exact copy of this paper
was served personally on respondent, at his office in Carson,
July 31, 1885. Respondent denies the service. Its validity
will be considered further on. Respondent has not filed a new
or additional bond.

On September 4, 1885, the Governor filed in the office of
Secretary of State his written proclamation declaring the
office of State librarian vacant.

1. There is no vacancy in the office of lieutenant-governor,

FAILURE TO FILE
BOND: VACANCY.
MERGER OF OF-
FICES.
by reason of respondent's failure to file a new or
additional bond. It is claimed and conceded by
both sides that the office of lieutenant-governor
and the office of State librarian are separate and distinct.
Making a person an *ex-officio* officer, by virtue of his holding
another office, does not merge the two into one. People *v.*
Edwards, 9 Cal. 286; People *v.* Love, 25 Cal. 520; Lathrop *v.*
Brittain, 30 Cal. 680; People *v.* Ross, 38 Cal. 76; Territory
of Wyoming *v.* Ritter, 1 Wy. 333; Denver *v.* Hobart, 10 Nev.
31.

It is true, the lieutenant-governor is required to give the
bond, because the lieutenant-governor and librarian are one
person; but he gives it for the *ex-officio* office, not the principal one. The sureties are not, and were not, intended to be
liable for any malfeasance outside of the *ex-officio* office. We
cannot say in this proceeding that respondent's right to hold
the office of lieutenant-governor, and enjoy the emoluments
thereof, depends upon a faithful discharge of the duties of

State librarian, or upon his compliance with the statute concerning the bond required of him as librarian. We cannot pronounce the office of lieutenant-governor vacant, unless respondent has done something, or failed to do something, which the law declares shall produce a vacancy therein.

The fault here charged is failure to give the bond required as State librarian. For that fault, if it exists, the only penalty that can follow in this proceeding is, at most, to declare that the office in which the bond is required was, by such failure, vacated and forfeited.

2. Did the office of State librarian become vacant in law by reason of a failure on the part of respondent to file HOLDING TWO a new or additional bond, within the time pre- OFFICES. scribed, after the filing by D. L. Bliss, in the office of the Governor or Secretary of State, of a legal statement, and after personal service of a legal notice?

There is nothing in the constitution of this State prohibiting respondent from holding the office of lieutenant-governor and the office of State librarian. Crossman *v.* Nightingill, 1 Nev. 326. Such being the case, the legislature had power to create the last-named office, and make the lieutenant-governor *ex-officio* State librarian. If the legislature had the powers mentioned, it must follow that it had authority, also, to impose reasonable conditions precedent to the holding of the legislative office. It had power to require the giving of a bond to secure a faithful discharge of the duties of that office. It could provide that such bond should be kept good, and, in case of failure to do so, that the office should become vacant.

When the statute of February 17, 1883, making the lieutenant-governor *ex-officio* State librarian, and the statute of March, 1883, requiring the lieutenant- FILING BOND ESSENTIAL TO OFFICE-HOLDING. governor, as *ex-officio* State librarian, to give a bond, were passed, they were general statutes declaring under what circumstances all offices should become vacant, providing for the release from liability of any surety, and prescribing the result of a failure to file a new or additional bond within the time stated, after the filing by a surety of a legal statement in the office of the Governor or Secretary of State, and the service of a legal notice upon the officer.

These different statutes must be construed together, and in

RELEASE OF such a manner, if possible, as to carry out the legis-
SURETY ON OFFI-
CIAL BOND. lative intent. When the statute requiring the
lieutenant-governor, as *ex-officio* State librarian, to give a bond
was passed, it was the law of this State that any or all of respondent's sureties might be released from liability by doing
certain things, and that a failure of respondent to file a new
or additional bond would render the office of State librarian
vacant. The legislature knew the law, and, with such knowledge, required the bond. In view of the then existing law,
can it be said that the legislature intended to say respondent
might give a bond or not, according to his caprice or whim?
Were they acting a legislative farce when they provided
that he should secure the State in the faithful discharge of
the duties of this most important office? We have no right
to think so, and in our opinion the natural construction of the
different statutes referred to will not only relieve the legislature of a farcical intent, but it will also render operative
and beneficial all the statutes touching the subject in hand.

Sections 2633, 2929, 2930, and 2931 are not repugnant to
section 5 of the act of March 1, 1883. It is said to be so, because the last-named law declares that the lieutenant-governor
shall be *ex-officio* State librarian at all events, and permits no
other person to fill the office or perform its duties, and, consequently, it is claimed that the requirement of a bond is a
mere directory provision which may be disregarded with impunity by respondent, except so far as he might be amenable
to the criminal laws of the State. It is true the legislature
declared that the lieutenant-governor should be *ex-officio* State
librarian, but it was also declared that before entering upon
the duties of the office the lieutenant-governor, as *ex-officio*
State librarian, should execute a bond. The first provision
was intended to be dependent upon the last. It was not intended that the lieutenant-governor should hold the *ex-officio*
office without keeping good his bond.

Suppose the legislature had created the office of State librarian and declared that a certain person named in the
statute should hold the office until the next general election,
but had provided that he should execute an official bond
with sureties before entering upon the duties of the office.
Can it be doubted that in such case the person named would
have been obliged to file his bond and keep it good, and that,

in case of failure to do so, there would have been a vacancy, which, under section 8 of article 5 of the constitution, it would have been the governor's duty to fill? We think not; and yet it would have been as true in that case that the person named was intended to be State librarian, at all events, as it is now that the lieutenant-governor shall be.

In 1869, "An act to create the county of White Pine, and provide for its orgnization," was passed by the legislature. It provided, among other things, that certain named persons should be the officers of the county, until the next general election. M. W. Kales was made county treasurer. By the act itself, no bonds were required. Stat. 1869, 108. But, by the general law relating to county treasurers, each county treasurer, before entering upon the duties of his office, was required to take an official oath and give a bond. The same was true of other officers. Unquestionably, their tenure of office depended upon a compliance with the general law governing qualification, and yet the act creating the county declared that they should be the county officers until the next general election. If the treasurer had said: " I will hold my office without taking any oath or filing any bond, because the latest statute upon the subject declares that I shall be treasurer at all events, and permits no other person to fill the office or perform its duties," he would have found out its error.

The case of The People *v.* Sanderson, 30 Cal. 160, is cited as authority in support of the claim that there is no vacancy in the office of State librarian, even conceding that the statement filed and the notice, together with the service thereof upon respondent, were sufficient in law. We quote from the opinion ;

"The next question is, was there a vacancy in the board of trustees of the State library to be filled at the time of the appointment of the relator by the governor? The act provides that the State library shall be under the direction and control of a board of trustees, to consist of five members, as therein provided. It next provides that the governor and the chief justice of the supreme court shall be *ex-officio* members of the board. This designation is not of an individul or individuals by name, but of certain officers who, by reason of their character as officers, are declared by the act to be members of the board. The appellant in this case could not, under the act, hold the position of trustee, except in his character of chief justice of the supreme court. As a trustee, he has no power to resign unless he resigns the office on which it depends. There can be no vacancy of the place in the board of trustees so long as there is a chief justice and no person other than that functionary can fill it, because the statute makes no provision for an incumbent of the place designed to be occupied in the board by the chief justice other than the person who may for the time be invested with the superior office. The relator cannot fill the place intended by the act to be filled by the chief justice as such, because he does not possess the official character, which is essentially a condition precedent to his capacity and power to hold the place alleged, on his part, to have been vacant by constitutional consequence when he was appointed to it by the governor. The legislature, by the act, evidently intended that the board of trustees should consist of five members, and it is quite as evident that it was intended one of them should be the chief justice of the supreme court, and no other person ; but as the chief justice was, at the time, and from thence hitherto has been, constitutionally incompetent to perform the duties of trustee, the act as to him, and the place to be filled by him, was and is inoperative and void. The conclusion to which we have come on this point is, that there was no place in the board of trustees to be filled at the time the relator was appointed, as set forth in the information, and that the appointment of the relator trustee was without authority and void."

We cannot agree with many of the conclusions expressed above. In our opinion, under the statutes of California, similar to ours, there was a vacancy in the board, which it was the duty of the legislature, if in session, to fill; and if it was not in session, that duty devolved upon the governor.

It was decided by the court in that case that the chief justice, by reason of his judicial position, could not, under the constitution, exercise the functions and duties of trustee of the State library. In other words, it was, in effect, decided that one of the persons or officers named in the act who should constitute the board, in part, was incompetent. The legislative appointment, as to that officer, was null. It was as though it had not been made. But that fact did not make the

board consist of four instead of five. It still remained true
that the board should consist of five members. Why disregard that provision of the statute, simply because, by reason
of a mistaken idea of the constitution, the legislature had
done a void act?

The statute of California, Wood's Digest, article 2871, provided that "every office shall become vacant upon the happening of either of the following events before the expiration
of the term of such office. . . . . 8. The decision of a competent tribunal declaring the election or appointment void or
the office vacant." And the second section of the statute
creating the board provided that "In case of a vacancy, for
any cause, in the board of trustees, the legislature shall elect,
on joint ballot, to fill such vacancy. If a vacancy occur when
the legislature be not in session, the governor shall have
power to fill such vacancy until the ensuing session of the
legislature."

It seems to us that when the supreme court, a competent
tribunal, declared the appointment of the chief justice void
for constitutional reasons, the board, still consisting of five
members, was but four-fifths full, and that as to the other
fifth there was a vacancy, which could have been filled by the
proper appointing power.

3. It is urged by counsel for respondent that the document
filed with the governor and in the office of the
Secretary of State, and the notice claimed to have NOTICE OF SURETY TO RELEASE HIM ON BOND.
been served personally upon respondent, were in-
sufficient in law. It is undoubtedly true that, in order to be
released from future liability, a surety must proceed, in substance, according to the requirements of section 2930, compiled laws. Did Mr. Bliss do so in this case?

It is provided by section 2921, compiled laws, that official
bonds of all State officers, except that of the Secretary of
State, shall be approved by the governor and filed in the
office of Secretary of State. Such were the requirements in
relation to the bond in question. Stat. 1883, 102, sec. 5. Section 2930, compiled laws, provides that sureties desiring to
to be released from bonds of State officers shall file with the
governor who approved them, or with the Secretary of State,
in whose custody they are kept, "a statement in writing, duly
subscribed by himself, or some one in his behalf, setting forth

the name and the office of the person for whom he is surety, the amount for which he is liable as such, and his desire to be released from further liability on account thereof;" and "a notice containing the objects of such statement shall be served personally on the officer." . . .

By sections 2929, 2930, 2931, the legislature intended to accomplish three things : First, to enable an unwilling surety to absolve himself from future liability ; second, to protect the State by giving it notice, through its proper officers, of the desire and intention of the surety to be released ; and, third, to give the officer time, after receiving notice, to make good his bond and thus escape the penalty of forfeiture. A compliance with the statute sufficiently strict to accomplish the objects intended should be required.

From the written document filed with the Governor and Secretary of State, it cannot be doubted that each of those officers was informed that Mr. Bliss was surety for respondent on his official bond, as *ex-officio* State librarian, in the sum of one thousand dollars, and that he desired to be released from further liability on account thereof. Those facts, and no others, could be gathered from the paper. It is said that the statute contemplates a statement and notice,—two different papers, each performing a distinct office, differing in form and substance. That they may be different is true, but that they must be so is incorrect. If each contains all that is required to be put in both, neither becomes invalid because something is inserted therein which might have been left out.

A written statement is a series of facts or particulars expressed on paper. The one filed in this case is in the form of a notice addressed to respondent, but it is a statement still. It is a writing informing any one who reads it, of all the facts required by the statute to be inserted in a statement, and is sufficient to accomplish all the purposes intended. It is said that the notice should contain the substance of the statement, and also, the time when and place where the statement was filed. This notice does contain the entire contents of the statement filed. It is a true copy of the statement. But it need not inform respondent of the time and place of filing,— first, because the statute does not require it ; and, second, because such notification would be useless and accomplish no useful end. Any officer must be presumed to know the law.

He knows that a surety who wishes to be released from his bond must file a statement in one of two places, and serve a notice upon him. When he receives the notice, he may and should seek the proper depository of the statement and there ascertain its contents, if one has been filed, and, if it has not, the notice goes for nought. If it has been filed, it is his duty to proceed according to law and file a new bond. The "objects of the statement" must be inserted in the notice. In other words, the surety, by the notice, must inform the officer what induces him to take action in the premises,—what he intends to accomplish. But he need not use the exact language of the statute and say, "I have filed a statement in the office of the Governor, and my object in so doing is to be released from your bond." It is enough if he states the objects without specifying them as such. It is plain that the object of Mr. Bliss in making his statement, in all that he did, was to be released as surety. That object only is contained in the notice. We think the written notice is sufficient in form and substance.

4. But one other question remains for consideration: Was the notice served on respondent personally on July 31, 1885? After careful examination of all the evidence introduced in the case, including surrounding circumstances, we are satisfied that it was.

It follows from the foregoing that respondent is not entitled to hold and enjoy the office of State librarian of the State of Nevada, and as to that office a judgment of ouster must be entered against him, with costs.

It is ordered.

FORFEITURE OF OFFICE BY REASON OF FAILURE TO FILE OFFICIAL BOND. NOT A FORFEITURE, BUT A CAUSE OF FORFEITURE.—Failure on the part of a person duly elected or appointed to a given office to file the official bond required of incumbent within the time prescribed by statute does not of itself and *ipso facto* vacate the office. The office is not vacated in such case until a vacancy has been declared in the proper manner and by the proper officers. Kottman *v.* Ayer, 3 Strob. (S. C.), 92, 94; People *v.* Hapson, 1 Denio (N. Y.), 574; Weeks *v.* Ellis, 2 Barb. (N.Y.), 320; Cronin *v.* Gundy, 16 Hun (N. Y.), 520. Even where the statute provides that if the person elected or appointed fails to file his bond within the time prescribed "he vacates his office," it is held that a failure so to do is a cause of forfeiture, but does not *ipso facto* work a forfeiture. Sprowl *v.* Lawrence, 33 Ala. 674. But see Beebe *v.* Robinson, 52 Ala. 66, 71.

So when the statute declared that upon failure to file a bond within the prescribed time "his office shall be deemed absolutely vacant, and shall be filled by election or appointment, as heretofore provided." State *v.*

Toomer, 7 Rich (S. C.), 216; Treasurer *v.* Stevens, 2 McCord (S. C.), 107, 216. See also Crawford *v.* Howard, 9 Ga. 314.

WAIVER OF FORFEITURE.—It was held in State *v.* Toomer, *supra*, that the State could waive the cause of forfeiture arising from a failure to file a bond within the prescribed time, and that an acceptance of a bond by the proper officer after the prescribed time had elapsed amounted to such a waiver on the part of the State.

The question of forfeiture of office by reason of failure to file bond is said to be analogous to that which arises when corporations do some act which it is provided by their charter shall amount to a forfeiture of their vested rights. Sprowl *v.* Lawrence, 33 Ala. 674, 690; Foote *v.* Stiles, 57 N. Y. 399.

In Foote *v.* Stiles, 57 N. Y. 399, it was held that a statute providing that if any person should execute the duties of an office without having taken the oath of office and filed a bond, if required by law to do so, he should "forfeit the office." was not intended to work an *ipso facto* forfeiture in case its terms were disobeyed, but merely to authorize the declaring of a forfeiture. The court says : " It is plain that the failure to file the bond is a cause of forfeiture. The office in that case does not become *ipso facto* vacant, but there must be a direct judicial or other authorized proceeding on the part of the proper authority to enforce the forfeiture. The act resembles a cause of forfeiture of a franchise or corporate charter, which is only enforceable by a proceeding in the nature of a *quo warranto.*"

FAILURE TO FILE BOND MAY BY PROVISION OF STATUTE CREATE IPSO FACTO A VACANCY.—Where the statute provided that an office should become vacant upon the happening of certain events, one of which was the death of the incumbent and another his failure to file his official bond within the prescribed time, it was held that the statute created a vacancy on the failure to file a bond within the prescribed time, and that no declaration of forfeiture or vacancy was necessary. People *v.* Taylor, 57 Cal. 620.

FILING BOND A CONDITION PRECEDENT—CONSTITUTIONAL LAW.— Where the constitution has created certain offices and prescribed the qualifications to be required of incumbents it seems that the legislature cannot by statute make the filing of a bond a condition precedent to the entering upon said office, that is, where the constitution says nothing about the filing of a bond. Such a statute would in effect create a new qualification in addition to those of the constitution and hence would be unconstitutional. Cooley, Const. Lims. (5th ed.), 78; Sprowl *v.* Lawrence, 33 Ala. 674, 689.

But a statute providing for a forfeiture of the office in such a case would not be unconstitutional. Sprowl *v.* Lawrence, *supra* ; Hyde *v.* State *ex rel.* 52 Miss. 665.

TIME WHEN COMPENSATION BEGINS.—When it is provided that the officer must qualify by taking the oath of office, filing a bond, etc., before entering upon the duties of his office, such officer cannot legally act in his official capacity before qualifying. Rounds *v.* Mansfield, 38 Me. 586; Rounds *v.* Bangor, 46 Me. 541. And his salary will not begin to run until then. Jump *v.* Spence, 28 Md. 1.

CHOWNING

v.

BOGER.

(Advance Case, Texas. 1885.)

The resignation of a regular sheriff of a county creates a vacancy *eo instanti*, which vacancy the Commissioners' Court alone has authority to fill, and the person so appointed becomes *ipso facto* sheriff .

A *de jure* officer is one who has the legal title ; a *de facto*, one who has a colorable title accompanied by possession or incumbency. See case in which the *de jure* officer is entitled to fees from the date of his appointment, as against one who was appointed by the district judge.

APPEAL from Wichita County.

WHITE, P. J.—This case originated in Wilbarger County, and the venue was changed to Wichita County.

One T. L. Stewart was the regularly elected and qualified sheriff of Wilbarger County. On account of cer- FACTS. tain proceedings instituted against him in the District Court for malfeasance in office, the district judge temporarily suspended him from his office and appointed A. T. Boger, appellee, as sheriff *pro tem.* to exercise the duties of said office until the next, the March term, of the District Court of Wilbarger County, at which term the proceedings against Stewart were to be heard. Boger qualified and entered upon the duties of the office. Meantime Stewart, the old sheriff, perhaps not desiring any further investigation as to his official conduct, resigned his office as sheriff, and the Commissioners' Court of Wilbarger County, believing that Stewart's resignation created an actual and absolute vacancy in the office, on December 31, 1883, appointed H. Chowning, appellant, sheriff of Wilbarger County, and he qualified by giving bond as sheriff and tax-collector. Boger, the district judge's appointee, refused to surrender the office, but continued to, and did, exercise the functions of said office until the next March term of the District Court, to which he had been appointed. Chowning, as soon as Boger refused to yield the office to him, instituted proceedings in the nature of a *quo warranto* against him. At the March term the *quo warranto*

proceedings were dismissed by Chowning. The district
judge, in the case of The State v. Stewart, declared the office
still vacant, legalized the acts of Boger by virtue of his appointment, and rendered judgment awarding him all the fees,
perquisites, and emoluments of the office of sheriff for the
time he had served and until a sheriff was legally appointed
and qualified.

Appellant Chowning then resigned as sheriff, and on the
eleventh day of June following, brought this suit against
Boger for $730.76, which he claimed to be due him for fees,
emoluments, and perquisites for the said office of sheriff from
the date of his appointment by the Commissioners' Court,
December 31, 1883, to March 25, 1884, the date of his resignation, alleging that said fees were unlawfully withheld from
him and had been illegally appropriated by defendant,
Boger.

The case was tried by the judge without a jury, and he
rendered judgment for defendant Boger, and Chowning appeals to this court.

The first question for our decision is, Was the office of
Resignation vacates office. sheriff made vacant by the resignation of the regular sheriff, Stewart? In Byars v. Crisp (5 Texas
Law Review, 586) it was held that a voluntary peremptory
resignation of an office, if accepted, created *eo instanti* a vacancy in the office, and in that case, which was with reference to the resignation of the county judge, it was also held
that a special judge could not be elected to hold a term of
the court on account of the vacancy thus created, but that
said vacancy could only be filled by appointment by the
Commissioners' Court of the county until the next general
election in accordance with article 1137, Revised Statutes.

With regard to sheriffs our statute provides: "Should a
vacancy occur in the office of sheriff the Commissioners'
Court of the county shall fill such vacancy by appointment,
and the person appointed, after qualifying in the manner provided by law for persons elected to said office, shall discharge
the duties of sheriff for the unexpired term and until the election and qualification of his successor." Rev. Stats., art.
4515.

In so far, then, as Stewart was concerned, if he can be
legitimately considered as the regular sheriff of the county at

the date of his resignation, his resignation created a vacancy *eo instanti* which the Commissioners' Court could fill, and alone had the authority to fill, and their appointee would *ipso facto* become sheriff.

This renders necessary an answer to the second question which is, Was Stewart the sheriff of the county when he resigned? That he was sheriff *de jure* cannot be questioned. But he was not sheriff *de facto*. He had been legally suspended from his office by the district judge pending legal proceedings against him for removal from his office, and the district judge, by virtue of express authority of the statute, had suspended him and appointed, "for the time being, another person to discharge the duties of the office." Rev. Stats., art. 3409. This other person was the appellee, Boger, who, at the time of Stewart's resignation, was sheriff *de facto*. Stewart's resignation did not create a vacancy in the *de facto*, but in the *de jure* office. Suppose Stewart, the *de jure* officer, had never resigned, and that he had come clear, on a trial, of the charges against him, could he have sued and recovered the fees of office which had been collected and received by the *de facto* sheriff, Boger, for services rendered by the latter whilst exercising the functions of the office? If Stewart could not have had a cause of action and right of recovery under such circumstances, then it is clear that Chowning, his successor, who was also only a *de jure* officer, could have no further or greater right; but if Stewart could, Chowning also could, for he was *de jure* after Stewart's resignation, and his appointment to the same extent as Stewart was.

Let us see what the rules of law are as to the rights of a *de jure* as against a *de·facto* officer in a contest for the salary or fees of office which have been received by the latter.

A *de jure* officer is one who has the legal title; a *de facto* one who has a colorable title accompanied by possession or incumbency. It is the settled doctrine in New York "that the right to the salary and emoluments of a public office attach to the true and not the mere colorable title; . . . that actual incumbency merely gives us right to the salary or compensation. 1 Denio, 579; 46 N. Y., 382; 30 Barb. 193; 6 Abb. Prac., 296; see also 1 Taunt, 112; 42 N. H. 56; 7 Sergt.

(marginal note: DE JURE SHERIFF WHO IS SUSPENDED IS NOT SHERIFF DE FACTO.*)*

(marginal note: DE FACTO AND DE JURE OFFICERS DEFINED. THEIR RIGHTS.*)*

and Rawle, 392. . . . The principle is that the right follows
the true title, and the courts will not aid the intruder by permitting him to recover the compensation which rightfully
belongs to another. That an officer merely *de facto* has no
right to the compensation of the office also clearly appears
from the consideration that if he obtains it he is liable on an
action for money had and received by the officer *de jure* to
recover it. Harwood *v.* Wood, 2 Lev. 245 ; Glosbeck *v.*
Lyons, 20 Ind. 1 ; Dolan *v.* Mayor, 68 N. Y. Ct. App. 274.

In Dorsey *v.* Smith, 28 Cal. 21, it is held : " When the question as to who is the legal successor of an officer is in litigation
upon a point of law, the officer is bound to know who his
successor is, and if the legal successor qualifies and demands
the office, and the incumbent refuses to deliver it up upon
the termination of the litigation, he becomes a trespasser *ab
initio.* One having the legal right to an office, but not in possession of the same, is entitled to the salary for the term for
which he was elected, and the payment of the salary to one
in possession of the office without title will not prevent the
one having the title from recovering the salary."

In the case of Mayfield *v.* Moore, which was an action to
recover fees received by a *de facto* sheriff and collector of
taxes, the Supreme Court of Illinois says : " We also find that
the authorities have gone still further, and held that where
a person has usurped an office belonging to another, and received the accustomed fees of the office, money had and
received will lie at the suit of the person entitled to the
office against the intruder. Aris *v.* Strekely, 2 Md. 260; 1
Sel. *Nisi Pri.* 68.

" The same rule was announced and enforced in the case
of Croskie *v.* Hurley (1 Alcock *v.* Napier, 431). In this last
case there was a contest as to the title to the office, and the
person recovering the title to it sued the other who had
acted, and recovered the fees and emoluments received while
in possession and exercising the duties of the place. The
same rule has been adopted in this country, and seems to be
based in common-law rules.

" It is said by Blackstone, in his Commentaries (vol. 2, p.
36), that officers have a right to exercise a public or private
employment, and to take the fees and emoluments thereunto
belonging, and are also incorporeal hereditaments, whether

public, as those of magistrates, or private, as bailiffs, receivers, or the like ; for a man may have an estate in them, either to him and his heirs or for a term of years, or during pleasure only, save only that offices of public trust cannot be granted for a term of years, especially if they concern the administration of justice, for then they perhaps might vest in executors or administrators. Thus it is seen that the right to the fees and emoluments is stated to be coextensive with the office. This is undoubtedly correct, as it is analogous to every other thing capable of ownership. No principle of law can be clearer than that the owner of lands or chattels is entitled to the products, increase, or fruits flowing from them. The fees of an office are incident to it as fully as are the rents and profits of lands, the increase of cattle, or the interest on bonds or other securities.

" A person owning any of those things is, by virtue of such ownership, equally entitled to the issues and profits thereof as to the things itself. If, then, appellant was the owner of and held the title to the office of sheriff, he was as clearly invested with the right to receive the fees and emoluments. They were incident to and as clearly connected with the office as are rents 'and profits to real estate, or interest to bonds, and such like securities. See Glascock *v.* Lyons, 20 Ind. 1 ; Petit *v.* Rosseau, 15 La. 239 ; Daney *v.* Smith, 28 Cal. 21, and The People *v.* Tiernan, 30 Barb. 193. We think that, on both reason and authority, appellant is entitled to recover the fees and emoluments arising from the office while it was held by appellee. 53 Ill. p. 429.

From these authorities we are of the opinion that appellant Chowning, was, as *de jure* sheriff of Wilbarger County, entitled to his cause of action and judg- RIGHT OF DE JURE OFFICERS TO FEES. ment for fees of the office from the date of his appointment by the Commissioners' Court. But, inasmuch as appellee, Boger, had been legally appointed, and was acting in apparent right, and without any fraud in the premises, he should only be required to account for the fees and emoluments of the office received by him after deducting reasonable expenses and in earning them. This being an equitable action, it should be governed by the same rules that would obtain had this been a bill for an account, instead of an action for money had and received. He should have only a

reasonable allowance for the necessary expenses in earning
them. Had he intruded into the office without pretence of
legal right, a different rule would apply." Mayfield *v.* Moore,
supra.

The judgment of the court below is reversed and the case
remanded for a new trial, in accordance with the principles
herein announced.

Reversed and remanded.

For a full note on the subject of compensation as between *de facto* and
de jure officers, see note to Beard *v.* City of Decatur, 7 Am. & Eng. Corp.
Cas. 145.

DIBBLE

v.

MERRIMAN *et al.*

(*Advance Case, Connecticut. July* 16, 1884.)

The State Constitution (art. 10, sec. 2) provides that "each town shall
annually elect selectmen and such officers of local police as the laws may
prescribe." *Held*, that tax-assessors are not officers of local police, and
that therefore an act providing for their election for a term of three years
is not unconstitutional.

APPLICATION to a judge of the Superior Court for a certificate of election as a tax-assessor and for a mandamus.
Facts found and case reserved for advice. The case is
sufficiently stated in the opinion.

A. H. Robertson and *H. L. Hotchkiss* for the plaintiff.

W. J. Mills and *W. H. Law*, with whom was *H. Dailey*, for
the defendants.

PARK, C. J.—In the year 1879 the legislature passed an act
FACTS.   providing that "assessors of the towns of Hartford,
Bridgeport, and New Haven shall hereafter hold office for
the term of three years from the first Monday of June succeeding their election." Pub. Acts of 1879, p. 381. Under
this statute the town of New Haven, at the annual town
meeting in the month of December, 1882, elected the defendants and other assessors for the term of three years from the

first Monday of June then next following. At the annual town meeting of New Haven in the month of December, 1883, such proceedings were had that the plaintiff and others would have been assessors of the town from the first Monday of the following month of June, if at that time there would be vacancies in the office.

The plaintiff claims that the statute of 1879 extending the term of office of assessors for a longer period than one year is in conflict with the provision of the constitution of the State which provides that "each town shall annually elect selectmen and such officers of local police as the law may prescribe," and is consequently void. The claim is, that assessors are officers of local police, and so come within the constitutional requirement of annual elections, and hence that there were vacancies in the office of assessors on the first Monday of June, 1884, which the plaintiff and others were elected to fill.

The plaintiff's conclusion would be correct if the act of 1879 is unconstitutional; and this depends upon the question whether assessors are "officers of local police" within the meaning of the constitution.

Webster defines the word "police" as follows: "The government of a city or town; the administration of ASSESSORS ARE the laws and regulations of a city or incorporated NOT LOCAL POLICE. town or borough." The question, then, is, do the duties of assessors pertain to the government of a town, or to the administration of the laws and regulations therein?

Clearly assessors have nothing to do with the performance of such duties as these. Their duties are confined wholly to the proceedings provided by law for the assessment of taxes, and these proceedings lie wholly outside of what may be called the "local police" of a town.

We think it is clear that assessors are not officers of local police of a town within the meaning of the constitution, and that therefore the act of 1879 is constitutional and valid.

The view we have taken of this question renders it unnecessary to consider the other questions raised in the case.

We advise judgment for the defendants.

In this opinion the other judges concurred.

9 Cor. Cas.—7

THE STATE *ex rel.* HORD, Attorney-General,

v.

THE BOARD OF COMMISSIONERS OF WASHINGTON COUNTY.

(101 *Indiana*, 69.)

Under section 1 of article 7 of our State Constitution of 1851 (section 161, R. S. 1881), it was competent for the General Assembly to provide by law that the board of commissioners of each county should constitute a court of inferior jurisdiction, and to clothe such court, as has been done, with original jurisdiction and judicial power over claims and accounts against the corporate county, and other matters of local interest, providing for appeals from its decisions to courts of superior jurisdiction.

Under sections 5758, 5759, and 5760, R. S. 1881, in force since May 31, 1879, the board of commissioners of the county has exclusive original jurisdiction of any claim against such county; and the decision of such board either for or against such claim, if not appealed from as provided by law, is final and conclusive, and the adjudication may be pleaded in bar of another suit on such claim.

FROM Washington Circuit Court.

F. T. Hord, Attorney-General, for appellant.

S. B. Voyles and *L. C. Embree* for apellee.

HOWK, J.—On the 5th day of June, 1884, the State of Indiana, by the Hon. Francis T. Hord, its attorney-general, presented to and filed with the appellee, for allowance, three separate demands, each containing "a detailed statement of the items and dates of charge," against such appellee. Of these demands the first was for the aggregate sum of $1,282.96, the second was for the aggregate sum of $1,617.53, and the third was for the aggregate sum of $146. The county board refused to allow the demands, or any part thereof, and adjudged that the appellant take nothing thereby, and that the relator "pay all costs herein." From this judgment of the county board the State, by its attorney-general, appealed to the Circuit Court of Washington County. There the appellee by its counsel appeared and answered, in four paragraphs, the appellant's cause of action. Of these paragraphs of answer the first was a general denial, and was subsequently withdrawn; to the second paragraph the appellant's demurrer was sustained by the court, and to the third and fourth paragraphs of answer, the appellant's demurrers for the alleged insufficiency of the facts therein were overruled by the court. The appellant refused to reply to the third and fourth paragraphs of answer, and thereupon it was adjudged that the appellant take nothing by its suit, and that appellee recover of the relator its costs herein.

The overruling of its demurrers to the third and fourth paragraphs of appellee's answer are the only errors assigned here by the appellant.

In the third paragraph of its answer, the appellee alleged that Daniel P. Baldwin, Esq., was the immediate predecessor of the relator, as attorney-general of the State of Indiana, and on June 6, 1882, the appellant, upon the relation of said Baldwin, as its attorney-general, presented and filed the same claims and demands, now in suit, before the board of commissioners of Washington County; that upon such demands and items an issue was made on the day last named before such board, in regular session; that, by the consideration of such board, such items and demands were then tried and refused, and judgment was then rendered by such board, that the appellant take nothing by its suit, and that the relator, Baldwin, should pay the costs therein; that from such judgment no appeal was ever successfully taken, and such judgment was still in force; and that in the determination of the matters involved in such former suit, the matters and demands now in suit were fully and finally adjudicated and settled. Wherefore, etc.

In the fourth paragraph of its answer the appellee alleged that, on December 4, 1883, appellant, upon the relation of Francis T. Hord, Esq., its attorney-general, presented and filed the same claims, items, and demands, now in suit, before the board of commissioners of Washington County for allowance and payment; that on such claims, items, and demands an issue was formed on the day last named before such board in regular session; that, after trial and hearing, such board rendered judgment of record, which stood unappealed from and unreserved, that the appellant take nothing by its suit, and that the relator pay the costs therein; and that upon such hearing of said cause, on the day last named, the same claims, items, and demands now in suit were fully and finally considered, adjudicated, and set at rest. Wherefore, etc.

The only objections which can be urged, with any degree of plausibility, to these paragraphs of answer are, that under the laws of this State a board of county commissioners is not a court, or that, if a court, it cannot sit in judgment upon a claim against the county, because, in its corporate capacity, the board is the county. Both these objections are strenuously urged upon our consideration in the case in hand, and have been ably and elaborately discussed by the learned attorney-general in his exhaustive brief of this cause. It seems to us too late to claim that the board of commissioners of a county is not, in this State, a court. In section 1 of article 7 of the Constitution of 1851 (section 161, R. S. 1881), it is declared that the judicial power of the State shall be vested in a supreme court, in circuit courts, and in such inferior courts as the General Assembly may establish." On March 14, 1881, this section was amended by omitting the word "inferior," where it occurs, and by substituting in its place the word "other." In the first session of the General Assembly, after the adoption of the Constitution of 1851, largely composed of members of the convention which framed the Constitution, provision was made by law for the organization in each county of a board of commissioners of the county, and by that and other laws, then and since passed, such boards have been clothed with original jurisdiction and judicial power over a large class of cases materially affecting the local interests of the people, so that they have become the most important courts of inferior jurisdiction in the State. Especially was the board of commissioners clothed with jurisdiction to hear and decide upon all claims and accounts chargeable against its county; and from the decisions of such board upon any such claims, provision was made by law for appeals to the Circuit Court of the proper county. Sections 5771 and 5782, R. S. 1871. It is true that under section 5771, if a claim was disallowed, in whole or in part, the claimant might appeal, or, at his option, bring an action against the county. Jameson *v.* Board, etc., 64 Ind. 524, and cases cited.

This provision of section 5771, however, was repealed by necessary implication, by "An act regulating the presentation of claims against counties in the State of Indiana before the board of county commissioners, and the adjudication of the

(margin note: COUNTY COMMISSIONERS ARE A COURT.)

same," approved March 29, 1879. This act took effect on the 31st day of May, 1879, and is still the law of this State. Sections 5758, 5759, 5760, and 5769, R. S. 1881. Section 5758 provides, in effect, that every claim against a county must be presented to its board of commissioners. Section 5759 requires the county commissioners to examine into the merits of all claims so presented, and, in their discretion, to allow any claim in whole or in part, if they find it to be just and owing. Section 5769 provides that any person or corporation, feeling aggrieved by any decision of the board of county commissioners upon any such claim, may appeal to the Circuit Court of such county, as provided in section 5773, in force since May 6, 1853. And section 5760 provides that no court shall have original jurisdiction of any claim against any county in this State, in any manner, except as provided for in the above entitled act of March 29, 1879.

In Pfaff *v.* State *ex rel.*, 94 Ind. 529, it was held by this court, and correctly so, we think, that under the provisions of the aforesaid sections 5758, 5759, 5760, and 5769, R. S. 1881, the board of commis-

MAY AUDIT CLAIMS AGAINST COUNTY.

sioners of each county has exclusive original jurisdiction of every legal claim against such county; that every such claim must be presented to such board for allowance, and that no other court can acquire jurisdiction of the claim except by appeal from the judgment of the county board. From the earliest organization of the board of county commissioners, this court has always considered such board a court of inferior or limited jurisdiction, and has uniformly held that the decisions and judgments of such board, in causes or proceedings whereof it had jurisdiction, however erroneous they might be, were not void, and were not the subjects of collateral attack. In Snelson *v.* State *ex rel.*, 16 Ind. 29, it was argued by the appellee that certain judgments of the county board, allowing claims against the county,

REVIEW OF DECISIONS.

were void for want of jurisdiction, because the claims so allowed were not chargeable against the county. In answering this argument the court said: "But whose province and duty was it to judge whether the accounts were chargeable against the county? Clearly that of the board. If they decided that question wrongly, they committed an error of judgment, but did not usurp an unconferred jurisdiction.

If the account was properly chargeable against the county, it is clear that the action of the board would be conclusive, unless appealed from. Now, the argument . . . proves too much. It proves that when the board decides correctly upon the liability of the county, the decision is conclusive; but when it errs in that respect, its decision is a nullity, and not merely erroneous; that the board has jurisdiction to decide right, but no jurisdiction to decide wrong."

In Board, etc. *v.* Gregory, 42 Ind. 32, the court said : "We have, after much reflection and upon mature consideration, reached the conclusion that the board of commissioners, in acting upon claims against the county, act in a judicial capacity, and that their decisions are conclusive and binding alike upon the county and the claimant, unless appealed from or an independent action is brought against the county where the claim is disallowed." Of course, as we have seen, under the statute now in force an "independent action" is no longer allowable, but the only remedy of the claimant, where his claim is disallowed, is now an appeal to the circuit court of the county. Section 5769, R. S. 1881. If no such appeal is taken the decision of the county board disallowing his claim is now conclusive and binding against the claimant. But we need not extend this opinion in the citation of authorities for the purpose of showing that in this State, under its constitution and laws, the board of commissioners of a county is a court of inferior or limited jurisdiction. See Ind. R. *passim.*

We are of opinion, also, that the former adjudications of the claims now in suit, pleaded by the appellee in bar of the COUNTY COMMISSIONERS MAY BE MEMBERS OF COUNTY CORPORATION. present suit, were not void by reason of the fact that the same men who constituted the court also constituted, in their corporate capacity, the corporation county. If the appellant felt itself aggrieved by either of the adjudications, it had as full and complete a remedy as any other suitor, by an appeal to the circuit court of the county and by change of venue from the county. Not having taken an appeal from either of the former adjudications of its claim within the time limited by law, the State of Indiana, like any other claimant, must be held, we think, to be concluded and bound by such former judgments. When the State becomes a suitor in any of the courts, it is as much bound by the laws of the land, by the rules of pleading and practice, and by the decisions and judgments of the courts, inferior or superior, as any other suitor.

We conclude, therefore, that the court committed no error in overruling the demurrers to the third and fourth paragraphs of answer.

The judgment is affirmed, with costs.

COUNTY COMMISSIONERS AS A COURT—CANNOT ACT JUDICIALLY.— County commissioners are not judges within the meaning of the constitution of Connecticut, article 5, section 1, providing that no judge shall be capable of holding his office after he arrives at the age of seventy years. Betts *v.* New Hartford, 25 Conn. 180. Nor where they are authorized to assess damages for removing a town site have they jurisdiction to try the question of title to land. Strange *v.* Bell, 11 Ga. 103. Nor have they power as a court to require a sheriff to execute a new bond when a prior bond shall become insufficient, and to declare the office vacant in case of failure to file such new bond. Ruckles *v.* State, 1 Oreg. 347; Wren *v.* Fargo, 2 Oreg. 19.

County commissioners having no judicial powers cannot review the certificate of probable cause in event of which costs may, under Mont. Crim. Prac. Act, section 410, be paid by the county. Hedges *v.* Lewis & Clarke Co. Com., 4 Mont. 280. And in Montana it is also held that the discretionary power of county boards in allowance of claims against the county must be controlled by legal considerations, and is always subject to review by the courts. Davis *v.* Lewis & Clarke Co. Com., 4 Mont. 292. In Georgia the statute does not confer judicial powers on the commissioners, save as to roads. Cox *v.* Whitfield Co. Com., 65 Ga. 741.

They may summon a sheriff to renew his bond or declare a vacancy in his office. People *v.* Green, 75 N. C. 329. But they cannot suspend an attorney from practice before them, although they may fine him for contempt. Cass County Commissioners *v.* Logansport & R. C. R. Co., 88 Ind. 199. Nor in New York have they any jurisdiction over the railroad commissioners. Hence disobedience to a subpœna of the board of commissioners to attend an investigation by it to ascertain who are the railroad commissioners of a town was no contempt. *Re* Bradner, 87 N. Y. 171. See also Faulkner *v.* Morey, 22 Hun (N. Y.), 379.

MAY ACT JUDICIALLY.—In some States, of which Indiana is a noteworthy example, the board of county commissioners is a court of record. State *v.* Connor, 5 Blackf. (Ind.) 325; Board of Commissioners of La Grange County *v.* Cutler, 7 Ind. 6. But they have only a limited statutory, special jurisdiction, and on the face of their proceedings the facts constituting their jurisdiction must appear. Rosenthal *v.* Madison R. R. Co., 10 Ind. 359; Fayette County *v.* Chitwood. 8 Ind. 504. And their acts can be proved only by the record. State *v.* Connor, 5 Blackf. (Ind.) 325; Board of Commissioners of La Grange County *v.* Cutler, 7 Ind. 6. In Nevada the authority of county commissioners to act judicially to determine whether the number of qualified electors have petitioned for an election has been affirmed. Hetzel *v.* Board of Commissioners, 8 Nev. 309.

They have jurisdiction of a claim by a physician for services rendered at a *post-mortem* examination made at the direction of the coroner, and it is not material that the claim is not presented before them in the form of a suit at law. Gaston *v.* Commissioners of Marion County, 3 Ind. 497. In Massachusetts, where they have jurisdiction, a final determination of business at which opposing parties appear is erroneous unless all of the three commissioners present have heard the evidence. Joslyn *v.* County Commissioners, 15 Gray, 567. And in ordering the raising or lowering of a turnpike they must make a specific, not an alternative, order. Roxbury *v.* Boston, etc., R. R. Co., 6 Cush. 424.

APPEAL FROM DECISIONS OF COMMISSIONERS.—In Indiana the decision of the Circuit Court or Court of Common Pleas upon an appeal from the action of the board of county commissioners in granting or refusing a license to sell intoxicating liquor is final. Brown *et al. v.* Porter, 37 Ind. 206. But see Cox *v.* Lindley, 80 Ind. 327. The members of the board are held to have notice of an appeal from it, and hence need not be served with summons. Cass County Commissioners *v.* Adams, 76 Ind. 504. In Idaho it is held that on appeal from a decision of county commissioners, the county cannot be made a party to the proceedings. It can be proceeded against only in the manner provided by law. Gorman *v.* Boise County Commissioners, 1 Idaho (N. S.) 627.

In the matter of appeal a distinction is to be remembered between those acts of the commissioners which involve legal rights and those which involve merely the discretion of the commissioners, the former being appealable often, while the latter are never reviewed, except, perhaps, in the instance of manifest abuse of power, There is no statute in Indiana which authorizes an appeal from the action of the board of commissioners upon a matter involving no question of legal right, but simply a matter for the discretion of the board. Sims *v.* Board of Commissioners, 39 Ind. 40; Board of Commissioners *v.* Elliott, 39 Ind. 191. See Long *v.* Commissioners of Richmond, 76 N. C. 273. No appeal lies from a decision of county commissioners upon an application of a turnpike company for leave to construct its road along a public highway. Dudley *v.* Blountsville, etc., Turnpike Co., 39 Ind. 288. It may be doubted, too, whether an appeal will lie from a "decision" of county commissioners to issue bonds. In the case of O'Boyle *v.* Shannon, 80 Ind. 159, an appeal from an order of the board of county commissioners to sell railroad stock belonging to the county was dismissed. The court said that "this discretionary power of county commissioners over property of their respective counties has been held to be analogous to the legislative power possessed by many municipal bodies, and is distinguishable from the judicial or *quasi* judicial powers conferred upon such commissioners. Hanna *v.* Board, 29 Ind. 170. It follows, therefore, that the order of sale from which an appeal was prayed in this case was not a "decision" within the meaning of the statute authorizing appeals in a large class of cases." See also Hamrick *v.* Rouse, 17 Ga. 56.

RECORDS—AMENDMENT—IMPEACHMENT.—The board of county commissioners in Massachusetts has the same discretionary power as any court to amend its records upon new evidence. Framingham Water Power Co. *v.* Commissioners, 112 Mass. 206; Gloucester *v.* Commissioners of Essex, 116 Mass. 517. But they cannot set aside decisions after the close of the term in which they were rendered. 88 Ind. 199. And their records cannot be impeached collaterally. Brewer *v.* Boston, etc., R. R. Co., 113 Mass. 52; Cicero *v.* Williamson, 91 Ind. 541; Argo *v.* Barthand, 80 Ind. 63.

CHRISTY

v.

COMMISSIONERS OF ASHTABULA COUNTY.

(41 *Ohio St.* 711.)

Under section 20, Revised Statutes, the board of county commissioners of any county in Ohio may take and hold any property devised or bequeathed to it, or to its members, for any lawful public purpose recognized by statute, in which the tax-payers of the whole county are interested.

Although the actual disbursement of the school fund is by statute committed to township, city, and village boards of education, the maintenance of schools in such a lawful public purpose in which all the people of the county are interested.

A testator devised and bequeathed the residue of his property "to the County of Ashtabula in the State of Ohio, for educational purposes, to be under the full control of said commissioners, to use and expend, as seems best in their judgment, to promote and advance the cause of education in said County of Ashtabula." *Held:*

The residue was devised and bequeathed to the board of county commissioners of Ashtabula County.

That board is competent to take and hold it; and may authorize its expenditure by the respective boards of education within said county, for such legal educational purposes and in such proportions as the board of county commissioners shall deem best to promote and advance the cause of education in the county.

Under existing statutes said county commissioners, in case an orphan-asylum or children's home for the county be established, may themselves expend money of this devise and legacy in furnishing a room, books, etc., for a school therein, and may set apart another portion for disbursement in support of said school by the proper board of education.

Being competent to take, hold, and administer this devise and legacy, said commissioners may exercise, in the disbursement of said fund, such additional powers as the general assembly of the State shall see fit to

grant; but no statute passed after the decease of the testator can authorize them to do any act not beforehand assented to by him under a proper
construction of the will.

ERROR reserved in the District Court of Ashtabula
County.

On the 12th day of November, A.D. 1880, James Christy
died testate in Ashtabula County. He left no issue of his
body, no adopted child, and no legal representative of any
such issue or child. On the 18th day of December, 1880, his
will was duly admitted to probate. It contained the following clause. "Fifth—The balance or residue of my property, both real and personal, I will, devise, and bequeath to
the County of Ashtabula, in the State of Ohio, for educational
purposes, to be under the full control of said commissioners,
to use and expend, as seems best in their judgment, to promote and advance the cause of education in said County of
Ashtabula."

Some of the heirs-at-law of the testator, by writing, requested the executor to begin an action in Ashtabula Common
Pleas "asking its direction and judgment as to the just
effect of said will in the disposition of said residue of said
estate, and as to his duty in the distribution thereof." Thirty
days having elapsed without action by the executor, said
heirs-at-law began suit against the executor and the county
commissioners of Ashtabula County asking the court to construe the will and direct a proper distribution of said "residue." The other heirs-at-law were made defendants, but by
answer they adopted the prayer of the petition. The Common Pleas held that the residue passed to the commissioners,
and directed the executor to distribute it to them. A petition
in error was filed by the heirs in the district court, and that
court reserved the case for decision here.

George M. Tuttle and *F. E. Hutchins* for plaintiff in error.
Theodore Hall and *Boynton & Hale* for defendants in error.

GRANGER, C. J.—Section 20, Revised Statutes, reads thus:
"The State county, commissioners, township trustees,
boards or officers of municipal corporations, and the boards
of directors, trustees or other officers of any of the benevolent, educational, penal, or reformatory institutions wholly or
in part under control of the State, and any of said munici-

palities or institutions, shall be capable of receiving by, gift, devise, or bequest, moneys, lands, or other property for their benefit or the benefit of any of those under their charge, and to hold and apply the same according to the terms and conditions of the gift, devise, or bequest; but this section shall not be held to affect or change the statutory provisions as to devises or bequests for such purposes.

It seems to us that the words "commissioners of the" were intended to precede the word "Ashtabula" STATUTE CON. in the second line of the fifth clause of the will. STRUED AS TO DEVISE TO The subsequent words "to be under the full con- COUNTY COMMIS- SIONERS. trol of said commissioners" indicate that the writer supposed that they had previously been named or referred to. Be that as it may, the fair construction of the clause as a whole makes it a devise and bequest to the county commissioners for the county. See WELSH, J., in Carder *v.* Commissioners, 16 Ohio St., 369. Could they take, hold, and administer?

Section 20, quoted above, took the place of section 1 of the act of February 11, 1869 (66 Ohio Laws, 8); section 20, of the act of March 1, 1877 (74 Ohio Laws, 38); and section 1 of the act of March 7, 1878 (75 Ohio Laws, 42). The last-named act related to trustees of any of the benevolent, educational, penal, and reformatory institutions of the State, and authorized them to take "for the benefit of any of such institutions, or of any of the inmates of the same." The revisers evidently intended a section sufficiently comprehensive to furnish a representative for the people of the State in each of their subdivisions, as well as in their aggregate, capable of taking, holding, and administering any property that any testator might choose to devise or bequeath for the benefit of that aggregate, or of any of its recognized parts, to be used for any purpose recognized by the statutes controlling the beneficiary. Primarily the subdivisions are counties and townships; secondarily, cities, villages, and hamlets; thirdly, collections of individuals segregated from home-dwelling people by physical or mental defect or infirmity, or by affliction, poverty or crime. These last inhabit what are referred to as "institutions." In every case the actual beneficiaries are the people, or some definite portion of them recognized as such by legislation. The only designated representative of that part of the people of the State which in-

habits and constitutes a county, is the board of county commissioners. That board has no " charge " of persons. It has
charge of certain county property and manages such business
of the county (that is, of that fragment of the State population
which dwells within the county lines) as has been committed to it by statute. The persons whose interests are
under the charge of these commissioners are the people of the
county. But while the boards controlling the " institutions " before referred to have in charge the individuals who
are inmates, the board of county commissioners does not
represent the several interests of the persons who inhabit the
county. It does represent many property interests of those
persons as an aggregate. As an aggregate those people
in a corporate capacity, own buildings such as court-house,
jail, etc., and the ground under and appurtenant thereto;
roads of divers kinds; bridges; stocks in certain corporations; moneys raised by taxation, etc. These are named as
examples, not as an attempted enumeration of all.

Section 3956 directs the Auditor of State to apportion the
State common-school fund to the several counties of the State
COMMISSIONERS' semi-annually. Thus, the county, as a county, own
DUTY AS TO
SCHOOL FUNDS, the portion so assigned to it. As it is payable to
ETC.   the treasurer; apportioned to the townships by the
county auditor, and paid out under direction of the several
boards of education within the county, no part of this fund is
directly controlled by the commissioners. But it is their
duty, each September, to count all the funds in the treasury,
examine and compare books and vouchers, and remove a
treasurer who has embezzled any of the funds. Moreover,
they are expressly required, when called upon (see 3969), to
so far examine into the action of the several boards of education as to see whether or not they provide funds enough to
give to all the youth of school age in each district sufficient
school privilege; that in each district a school shall be continued for at least six months in the year, or that each school
shall have an equitable share of school advantages as required
by the statutes relating thereto; and if any school board fails
to so provide, the commissioners make the needed levy.
Under section 4010, they must, under the circumstances
therein named, provide the necessary school room or rooms,

furniture, apparatus, and books for the school in any infirmary, children's home, or orphan-asylum belonging to the county.

It seems to us that the county, in its corporate capacity, is the owner of the money that supports the COUNTY IS OWN-schools within the county. Its auditor divides that ER OF SCHOOL MONEY. money amongst the townships before it is expended, but that fact does not affect the county ownership of the fund so long as it remains in the county treasury. This ownership is in trust for the county school system, as regulated by statute. By its legislation the State has made the county the trustee and custodian of the school fund for all the schools within the county lines, while the people of each school district manage its school through a board chosen by themselves. This board calls upon the county for the share of the money in its charge, which that portion of its people have a right to expend. Moreover, the county maintains and furnishes the school in its infirmary, its children's home, and its orphan-asylum. So, as already stated, we think that section 20 intended to create a representative of the people of the county, —capable of taking, holding, and administering money or property that could, under the terms of the will, be used for any purpose for which said quasi-corporation aggregate might lawfully hold or expend money. Section 3964 seems to contemplate the possible presence in the county treasury of money for schools other than the county's share of the moneys apportioned by the State auditor, or raised by taxation. After providing for these last-named moneys, it concludes with a provision that "all other money in the county treasury for the support of common schools . . . shall be apportioned annually in the same manner as the State common school fund."

If, then, this so-called corporation aggregate, the county, may hold and expend any funds for schools within COUNTY MAY its territory, its designated representative may TAKE BY DEVISE FOR EDUCATION-take and hold any devise or bequest therefor, un- AL PURPOSES. less the will requires its expenditure in an unlawful manner or for an unlawful purpose.

This will designates the purposes as "educational," and prescribes, as the manner, "to use and expend as seems best in their judgment to promote and advance the cause of education in said county." The purpose is the identical one for which our school tax is collected. No word in the will requires an unlawful act. The commissioners can pay into the county school fund so much as they deem best. The auditor will apportion this under section 3964. They may apply part of it to furnish the room, furniture, apparatus, and books under section 4010. If they find that any board of education has failed to provide the funds required by section 3969, they may use part of it instead of making a levy.

It is urged that the clause does not sufficiently define its object; also, that unless the commissioners can COUNTY COMMIS-SIONERS' CON-TROL OF DEVISE IS LIMITED TO THEIR CHARTER PURPOSES. legally exercise the wide discretion allowed by the terms of the will the actual intent of the testator cannot be carried out; that he would not have made the devise and bequest if he had supposed that the discretion of the commissioners would be limited to the sphere of their statutory powers.

These claims can best be considered together. The presumption must be that the testator knew the law. When he selected public officers, whose powers were granted by statute, to administer his bounty for a public purpose, in law he knew the limitations of their powers, although in fact he may have been ignorant of them. Whether actually ignorant of those limitations or not, the testator used well-chosen words. They convey his consent that the commissioners may freely exercise their discretion. Hence, no matter how largely the legislature of the State may add to the power of county commissioners in educational matters, the terms of the will permit the board to exercise those powers according to their discretion—" as seems best in their judgment to promote and advance the cause of education in said county."

In Carder *v.* Commissioners, 16 Ohio St. 353, the devise was to the County of Fayette. No object was named. The court held it good; that the property could be used for any purpose for which a county could lawfully hold property. The will of James Christy is more definite. If a county can hold and distribute or expend any funds for educational purposes within its own bounds, the case cited is in point, and supports the judgment of Ashtabula Common Pleas.

That a county, under the statutes in force in 1880, could so hold, distribute, and expend some funds we have already shown. While it may not be material to show that such funds could be held, distributed, or expended by the commissioners, section 4010 expressly directs such expenditure by them.

Unless under section 20 the commissioners can take and hold for every purpose for which a county can hold, own, or expend, counties are left unrepresented in the subject-matter of said section as to important interests. It is true that each board of education is competent to take a devise or legacy for its schools, but that does not supply representation for the educational interests of the people of the county. If this will had named the school boards of Ashtabula County as devisees and legatees, infinite difficulty and embarrassment in administration would result. We cannot think that the legislative body intended that the testator's bounty should either be given to the whole State or limited to a school district. As we read it, county commissioners may take and hold title to anything that a county may hold or own, although in the actual custody or expenditure the county must, under some statute, act by an officer or officers other than its commissioners. Section 20 clothes that board with power to take and hold, and transmit to the proper custody, the subject of the devise and legacy. In so far as the actual expenditure of the Christy residue must, under the statutes, be made by boards of education, such expenditure is within the county for educational purposes. The will, in effect, directs the commissioners to determine what schools and in what sums the residue shall be apportioned. Section 20 gives them power to receive from the executor. Other statutes make it their duty to place county money, that comes to their custody, in the treasury. Moneys so placed, designated as for expenditure in special school districts, the auditor must credit to those districts, and the proper school board is charged with the actual expenditure.

Under the terms of this will we think the legislature may add to the powers of the commissioners in educational matters, and the board can use such powers as far as the terms of the will permit.

The judgment of the Common Pleas is affirmed.

NASH and MARTIN, JJ., dissented.

NASH, J.—I am unable to concur in the conclusion that the

commissioners of Ashtabula County have capacity to take and hold the real and personal property attempted to be given by James Christy in his will to the County of Ashtabula "for educational purposes, to be under the full control of said commissioners to use and expend as seems best in their judgment to promote and advance the cause of education in said County of Ashtabula." This proposition is not sound unless "the cause of education" is one of the objects committed to the care of county commissioners.

In the case of Carder *v.* Commissioners of Fayette County, 16 Ohio St. 353, it was held that a county can take property by devise, and when the devise is made to the county by name, without limiting the uses of the property, it vests in the board of commissioners for the use of the county, and may be appropriated by them to any and all authorized county purposes. These are the support of the poor, the maintenance of local government, the establishment and repair of roads and bridges, and perhaps other purposes. But the cause of education is not one of these. For this the State is divided into school districts, styled respectively city districts of the first class, city districts of the second class, village districts, special districts, and township districts (section 3885, Rev. Stats.), and each district is provided with a board of education. These boards are bodies politic and corporate, capable of suing, and being sued, contracting and being contracted with ; acquiring, holding, possessing, and disposing of property, both real and personal ; and taking and holding in trust for the use and benefit of such districts any grant or devise of land, and any donation or bequest of money or other personal property, and of exercising such other powers as have been conferred by the general assembly. Section 3971, Rev. Stats. For the support of the schools under their charge, money is provided by the State, and also by the boards themselves, by annual levies, which it is their duty to make. The money thus provided is expended under their direction. Full provision is thus made for the proper promotion of the educational interests of a county by bodies corporate, independent of the county commissioners.

Section 3969 Rev. Stats. gives to county commissioners power to do certain things in case any board of education fails to perform its duty. They acquire jurisdiction only where there has been a neglect, and then only over the district where the omission occurred. In such case they care not for the educational interests of the county, but have temporary control of this interest in a small subdivision of the county.

By section 4010 Rev. Stats., the board of any school district in which a children's home or orphans' asylum or a county infirmary is located, is required, when requested by the trustees of such children's home or orphans' asylum, or by the directors of such infirmary, to create a separate school therein, so as to afford to the children therein the advantages of a common-school education. All that the county commissioners are required to do in such case at the expense of the funds under their control, is to furnish a room or rooms for the school. The money necessary for the support of such school comes from the funds of the school district, or from the funds of the institution, and the furniture, apparatus, and books for the school, although furnished, in the first instance, by the county commissioners, must be paid for out of the funds of the institution. The exceptional cases wherein the county commissioners have a remote and comparatively unimportant connection with schools do not make "the cause of education" one of the objects of their official care.

Section 20 Rev. Stats. does not authorize county commissioners to receive bequests for educational purposes. It reads as follows: "The State, county commissioners, township trustees, the councils, boards or officers of municipal corporations, and the boards of directors, trustees, or other officers of any of the benevolent, educational, penal, or reformatory institutions, wholly or in part under the control of the State, and any of said municipalities or institutions, shall be capable of receiving. by gift, devise, or bequest, moneys, lands, or other property, for their benefit or the benefit of any of those under their charge, and to hold and apply the same according to the terms and conditions of the gift, devise, or bequest; but this section shall not be held to affect or change the statutory provisions as to devises or bequests for such purposes."

This section does not enlarge the powers possessed by county commissioners when the case of Carder *v.* Commissioners, before referred to, was decided. It is contended that the words " or the benefit of any of those under their charge,"

9 Cor. Cas.—9

contained in section 20, have extended their power of receiving bequests. The commissioners have certain business interests and property of the county in their keeping, but they do not have persons under their charge. The commissioners who codified our laws made this section comprehensive in conferring the power to receive bequests upon the State, county commissioners, township trustees, the councils and boards or officers of municipal corporations, and the boards of directors, trustees, or other officers of any of the benevolent, educational, penal, or reformatory institutions, wholly or in part under the control of the State, and of any such municipality. To do this they were compelled to use language which would apply to some of the bodies or official boards named, but not to others. The directors, trustees, and officers of the benevolent, educational, penal, and reformatory institutions of this State, and of municipalities and counties, have persons wholly or in part under their charge, but county commissioners do not. Hence I think that the words of section 20 applicable to county commissioners are these: "County commissioners shall be capable of receiving, by gift, devise, or bequest, moneys, lands, or other property for their benefit "— for the benefit of the objects under their control—" and to hold and apply the same," etc.

An examination of the law relating to orphans' homes shows that county commissioners have a much nearer relation to these benevolent institutions than they have to the educational interests of a county. If the General Assembly intended that section 20 should have the broad application which is now sought to be given to it, it was an unnecessary labor for them to place section 923 Rev. Stats. in the statutes, and give again to the commissioners of the several counties power to receive bequests for the purpose of a site and erection of an orphan-asylum thereon, and to maintain the same.

DEVISES TO MUNICIPAL CORPORATIONS GENERALLY AT COMMON LAW.—At common law a corporation may take real or personal property by devise or bequest. The present rule as to devises to municipalities is thus laid down by Judge Dillon : " Municipal and public corporations may be the objects of public and private bounty. This is reasonable and just. They are in law clothed wtih the power of individuality. They are placed by law under various obligations and duties. Legacies of personal property, devises of real property, and gifts of either species of property directly to the corporation, and for its own use and benefit, intended to and which have the effect to ease them of their obligations or lighten the burdens of their citizens, are valid in law, in the absence of disabling or restraining statutes. Thus a conveyance of land to a town or other public corporation for benevolent or public purposes, as for a site for a school house, city or town house and the like, is based upon a sufficient consideration, and such conveyances are liberally construed in support of the object named." 2 Dill. Mun. Corp. § 566.

INSTANCES.—Examples of the above rule are, amongst others, the following : A school district may take a fund bequeathed it to be invested in a library. Maynard *v.* Woodard, 36 Mich. 423. A town may take a bequest for a high school. Hathaway *v.* Sackett, 32 Mich. 97. County commissioners may take a bequest for orphan poor and other destitute persons in such county. Board of Comr's *v.* Rogers, 55 Ind. 297 ; Craig *v.* Secrist, 54 Ind. 419. Redfield lays down the rule for New York State very broadly. "So, also, real and personal estates may be granted to the corporation of any city or village of this State (New York), in trust, for any purpose of education or the diffusion of knowledge, or for the relief of distress, or for parks, gardens, or other ornamental grounds, or grounds for the purpose of military parades and exercise, or health and recreation, within or near such city or village. And property may also be granted to superintendents or common schools of any town, and to trustees of school districts in trust for the benefit of the common schools of the town, or of the schools of the district." Redfield's Surrogate Law and Practice, 190. See also Adams *v.* Perry, 43 N. Y. 487; Yates *v.* Yates, 9 Barb. 324. And this appears to be the law throughout the United States. 2 Dill. Mun. Corp. § 566.

Bequest to county "for the benefit of public schools" is not void for uncertainty. Bell County *v.* Alexander, 22 Tex. 350. But a bequest to "school commissioners" was held void because they were not a corporate body. Janey's Executors *v.* Latine, 4 Leigh. (Va.) 327.

Bequest "to the orphans" of a municipality was sustained, Succession of, etc. 2 Rob. (La.) 438, and in Richmond *v.* State, 5 Ind. 334, a devise of real property "to be forever appropriated to the education of children of this town" was sustained.

A will by which the testator devised "one third of all his property, real and personal, to the City of St. Louis in trust, to be and constitute a fund to furnish relief to all poor emigrants and travellers coming to St. Louis on their way *bona fide* to settle in the West," was sustained in Chambers *v.* St. Louis, 29 Mo. 543.

A bequest to Philadelphia to buy ground on which to build a hospital and maintain the same was held valid. Mayor of Philadelphia *v.* Elliott, 3 Rawle (Pa.), 170.

Bequest "to the citizens of W. to purchase a fire-engine" was sustained as a charitable gift—the name being considered immaterial. Wright *v.* Linn, 9 Barr (Pa.), 433; *vide* Kirk *v.* King, 3 Barr (Pa.), 436; and 6 Barr (Pa.), 31.

A devise to a town or parish to maintain schools is valid. First Parish in Sutton *v.* Cole, 3 Pick. 232.

A devise to a town of land, "all the interest thereof to be laid out in re-pairing highways and bridges yearly, and not to be expended for any other use, is a devise for a public and charitable use, and is valid under the statute relating to lands given for public use." Town of Hamden *v.* Rice, 24 Conn. 349.

A town may also be made the beneficiary of a bequest in trust. Brown *v.* Brown, 7 Ore. 285.

A legacy to a town to erect a town house for transacting town business is valid as a charitable bequest. Coggeshall *v.* Pelton, 7 John. Ch. 292; citing Attorney-General *v.* Clarke, Amb. 422 ; Jones *v.* Williams, Amb. 651.

A town may receive by bequest a sum of money the income of which is to be invested yearly in the purchase and display of United States flags. And although a forfeiture be provided for in case the town should omit to fulfil the condition, the town may without risk of forfeiture expend a reasonable portion of the income of the fund to buy and erect flag-staffs, ropes, halliards, and other necessary paraphernalia. Sargent *v.* Cornish, 54 N. H. 18.

Grants to support bridges and highways were held not to be within the statutes of mortmain of Henry VIII., because of their public and chari-table character. Porter's Case, 1 Coke, 26; to which case Lord Coke added this note: "That any man at this day may give lands, tenements, and hereditaments to any person, etc., for the finding of a preacher, mainten-ance of a school, relief and comfort of maimed soldiers, sustenance of poor people, reparation of churches, bridges, and highways, for education and preferment of orphans," etc.

In the McDonough will case (Executors of McDonough *v.* Murdock, 15 How. 367) the subject of bequests to municipalities was exhaustively con-sidered both by counsel and by the United States Supreme Court, and the civil and common systems of jurisprudence were compared upon the points involved. The case was this: McDonough, a citizen of Louisiana, made a will in which, after bequeathing certain legacies not involved in the present controversy, he gave, willed, and bequeathed all the rest, residue, and remainder of his property to the corporations of the cities of New Orleans and Baltimore forever, one-half to each for the education of the poor in those cities. The estate was to be converted into real property, and managed by six agents, three to be appointed by each city. No alienation of this general estate was ever to take place, under penalty of forfeiture, when the States of Maryland and Louisiana were to become his residuary devisees for the purpose of educating the poor of those States. It was *held*, that although there is a complexity in the plan by which the testator proposed to effect his purpose, yet his intention is clear to make the cities his legatees; and his directions about the agency are merely sub-sidiary to the general objects of his will, and, whether legal and prac-ticable or otherwise, can exert no influence over the question of its validity. That the City of New Orleans, being a corporation established by law, has a right to receive a legacy for the purpose of exercising the powers which have been granted to it, and amongst these powers and duties is that of establishing public schools for gratuitous education. (This ruling was followed in Perin *v.* Carey, 24 How. 465.) That the testator might define the use and destination of his legacy. That the conditions attached to the legacy, the prohibition to alienate or to divide the estate, or to separate in its management the interests of the cities, or their care and control, or to deviate from the testator's scheme, do not invalidate the bequest, because the Louisiana Code provides that " in all dispositions *inter vivos* and *mortis causa*, impossible conditions, those which are contrary to the laws or to morals, are reputed not written." That the City of Baltimore is entitled to receive this legacy under the laws of Maryland, and the laws of Louisiana do not forbid it. The provision in the Louisiana Code, that "donations may be made in favor of a stranger, when the laws of his country do not prohibit similar dispositions in favor of a citizen of this State," does not probably apply to citizens or corporations of the Union. And in case of failure of the devise to the cities, the limitation over to the States would have been operative.

EXCEPTIONS TO GENERAL RULE.—But it is decided that the United States cannot take property by devise for the purposes of a general charity. ' The government," says Mr. Redfield, " exists under grants of power, express or implied, in a written constitution, and the functions of all the departments are definitely limited and arranged, and it is not within its express or implied power to administer a charity." Redfield's Law and Prac. of Sur. Courts, 196, citing Levy *v.* Levy, 33 N. Y. 97 ; rev'g 40 Barb. 585; Matter of Fox, 52 N. Y. 530; rev'g 63 Barb. 157. In Chapman *v.* School District, Deady 139, the City of Portland, Oregon, was decided not to be successor to trustees elected to erect a school and meeting-house. The facts were these : When the City of Portland, Oregon, was a settlement of not more than 100 persons living in ten or twelve houses, some of the residents of the place and neighborhood agreed to contribute money to build a school and meeting-house for their own use and to be managed by such persons as a majority of the contributors chose. Three trustees were selected and authorized to buy a lot and provide for the erection of a building thereupon. To these " trustees of the school and town meeting-house of Portland, and their successors in office," a bond for a deed to a lot was executed, upon condition that such lot was to be held by the trustees for school or meeting-house purposes, exclusive of any restrictions of any school law. *Held,* that the trustees or corporation intended by the bond were a private corporation to which neither the school district No. 1 of Multonomah, nor the City of Portland, were successors, nor authorized to administer the trust.

And the United States Supreme Court in United States *v.* Fox, 94 U. S. 315, affirming same case in 52 N. Y. 530, *held,* a devise of land in New York to the United States for the purpose of assisting to discharge the debt contracted by the war to suppress the Rebellion was invalid. But this was solely because by the law of New York none but a natural person or corporation created by that State with authority to take by devise, could be a devisee of lands in that State. Where not prohibited by statute, a devise or bequest for such a purpose is a good charitable gift.

Russell *v.* Allen, 107 U. S. 163; Nightingale *v.* Goulburn, 5 Hare, 484; 2 Phil. 594; Dickson *v.* United States, 125 Mass. 311.

And Judge Dillon says: " But municipal corporations cannot hold lands in trust for any object or matter foreign to the purpose for which they are created and in which they have no interest." 2 Dill, Mun. Corp. § 573, citing Plowd. 103; 1 Kydon Corp. 72; Howe, *in re* 1 Paige (N. Y.), 214; Trustees *v.* Peaslee, 15 N. H. 317; Farmers' Loan, etc., Co. *v.* Carroll, 5 Barb. 613; Hornbeck *v.* Westbrook, 9 Johns. 73; North Hempstead *v.* Hempstead, 2 Wend. 109; Coggeshall *v.* Pelton, 7 John. Ch. 292; Sloan *v.* McConahy, 4 Ohio, 157; Trustees *v.* Peaslee, 15 N. H. 317, holding that authority to establish an institution "for the instruction of youth" cannot become a trustee of funds and an income to be paid for the support of missionaries.

LEGISLATIVE CONTROL OVER DEVISES TO MUNICIPALITIES.—But while a municipal corporation may take property in trust for charitable purposes, the legislature may divest it of control over such property and put it in charge of other trustees. This is decided in Philadelphia *v.* Fox, 64 Pa. St. 169, a case wherein the legislature took away from Philadelphia the power to administer the trusts created by Mr. Girard's will, and conferred it upon a new independent board of trustees not appointed by the city. In this case the opinion was written by Mr. Justice Sharswood, and is well worth careful perusal. See in this connection Vidal *v.* Girard Executors, 2 How. 127.

Where there is a valid devise to a corporation in trust for certain charitable purposes, unaffected by any question as to its validity because of superstition, the sovereign may interfere to enforce the execution of the trust, either by changing the administrator if the corporation be dissolved or, if not, by modifying or enlarging its franchises, provided the trust be not perverted and no wrong be done to the beneficiaries. Where the trustee is a corporation, no modification of its franchises or change in its name, while its identity remains, can affect its right to hold property devised to it for any purpose, nor can a valid vested estate in trust lapse or become forfeited by any misconduct in the trustee or inability in the corporation to execute it, if such existed. Charity never fails; and it is the right as well as the duty of the sovereign by its courts and public officers, as also by legislation if needed, to have the charity properly administered. Girard *v.* Philadelphia, 4 Phil. 413. And where property is vested in a municipality in trust, heirs of the testator have no right to interfere by bill *quia timet*, because they anticipate future perversions of the charity by the corruption or folly of the municipal corporation, and the moral impossibility of its just administration. Girard *v.* Philadelphia, 4 Phila. 413. See also Girard *v.* Phila., 7 Wall. 1.

STATE OF OHIO *ex rel.* MANIX

v.

TURPEN, Auditor, etc.

(Advance Case, Ohio. June 9, 1885.)

The provisions of section 877 R. S. requiring county commissioners to publish notice of their intention to purchase any lands or erect any building do not apply to proceedings under section 929 *et seq.* for the purchase of lands for a children's home.

Where the commissioners of a county have, in conformity with the requirement of section 929 R. S., formally accepted a proposition for the sale and conveyance of lands, for the erection thereon of a children's home, accepted a duly executed deed therefor, delivered the same to the recorder for record, taken possession of the land, allowed the purchase-price, and ordered the county auditor to draw his warrant on the county treasurer for the amount of it, they have no power, in the absence of fraud, imposition, or failure of consideration, to rescind such order and direct the auditor to withhold his warrant for the sum so allowed.

The adoption by the commissioners, in such case, of a resolution in form rescinding their former action, and directing the auditor to withhold his warrant, furnishes no excuse to such auditor for his refusal to draw his warrant on the treasury in obedience to the original order.

A writ of *mandamus* is a proper remedy in such case to compel the auditor of the county to draw his warrant in favor of the grantor of the land for the amount of the purchase-price as allowed by the commissioners.

The right to a writ of *mandamus* to enforce the performance of an official act by a public officer depends upon his legal duty, and not upon his doubts; and where his duty is clear, its performance will not be excused by his doubts concerning it, however strong or honest they may be.

THIS is a proceeding in *mandamus* to compel the auditor of Darke County to issue his warrant upon the treasury of that county in favor of the relator for the sum of $13,898.90, to pay for a site purchased from him by the commissioners of that county for a children's home. The commissioners having taken the necessary steps therefor, a proposition to establish a children's home, and to raise by taxation the sum of $25,000 for the purchase of a site and the erection thereon of suitable buildings, was adopted by the electors of Darke County at the April election, 1882. The tax was levied, and the entire amount was collected before the commencement of this proceeding.

On November 8, 1883, a proposition of the relator to sell about one hundred and twenty acres of his farm at $115 per

acre was accepted by the commissioners, and the further consideration of the proposition was postponed to November
28, 1883, when the commissioners resolved to purchase
120⁸⁸⁄₁₀₀ acres of his farm at $115 per acre, and that the same
should be used as a site for the home. It was further "ordered that, on presentation of a deed for said lands by said
George W. Manix, the auditor of said county issue an
order on the county treasurer for said purchase-money of
$13,898.90." A deed duly executed was thereupon delivered by
Manix to the commissioners, who accepted it in open session,
and caused it to be left for record on the same day with the
recorder of the county, who soon thereafter recorded it.
Upon the delivery and acceptance of the deed, a further
order was made reciting these facts, and directing the auditor
to draw his warrant on the treasury for the agreed purchase-
price of the farm. By arrangement between the commissioners and the relator, the latter was to remain upon ,and
care for the land so purchased until the commissioners should
require actual possession of it, when it was to be wholly sur-
rendered to the latter.

No notice such as is required by section 877 R. S. was
given by the commissioners of their intention to make the
purchase. On the 3d of December, 1883, and after the transactions above recited, one member of the board of commissioners retired, upon the expiration of his term of office, and
his successor was qualified, and entered upon the duties of his
office. On the 15th of December, 1883, the board of commissioners, as then constituted, adopted a resolution, in form rescinding and for the purpose of rescinding the resolutions of
November 28th, purchasing the farm, locating the site, and
ordering the auditor to draw his warrant. On the 28th of
November, 1883, after the commissioners had ordered the
auditor to issue his warrant, as above stated, legal proceedings were commenced to enjoin the issuing thereof, which
were pending until the May Term of the District Court of
Darke County, 1884, when they were finally dismissed.
After such dismissal the relator demanded of the defendant
that he issue his warrant, acording to the order of the commissioners, which was refused. In August, and again on the
4th of September, 1884, the relator notified the defendant
that, on the 9th of September, 1884, he would apply for an

alternative writ herein, and on the 10th of that month such writ was allowed and issued. On the 9th of September, 1884, the commissioners purchased another tract of land as a site for a children's home, for which they paid the money in December, 1884.

The issues joined were tried upon the pleadings and evidence, and the facts admitted or found by the court, so far as they are considered in the opinion, are stated above. The defendant maintained : 1, that the failure to give the notice required by section 877 R. S. was fatal to the validity of the proceedings of the commissioners ; 2, that the commissioners had full power to pass the rescinding resolutions of December 15, 1883, and abandon the contract ; 3, that the relator is not entitled to this extraordinary writ of *mandamus,* but has an adequate remedy at law.

H. J. Booth, George B. Okey, Anderson & Chenoweth, and *M. T. Allen* for relator.

J. Riley Knox and *D. C. Meeker* for defendant.

OWEN, J.—1. The commissioners proceeded under section 929 R. S. This and the following sections to 950, inclusive, provide a complete scheme for the organization, management, and support of children's homes. The requirement of section 929, that, before the submission of the question of the purchase of a site and the erection of buidings to the electors of the county, notice of such election shall be published four weeks in two or more newspapers of the county, was complied with. Section 877 R. S. provides that " before the county commissioners purchase any lands or erect any building or bridge the expense of which exceeds \$1000, they shall publish and circulate hand-bills, and publish in one or more newspapers of the county, notice of their intention to make such purchase, erect such building or bridge, and the location of the same, for at least four consecutive weeks prior to the time that such purchase, building, or location is made ; and they shall hear all petitions for and remonstrances against such proposed purchase, location, or improvement. 68 Ohio L. 103, sec. 19; 63 Ohio L. 32, sec. 2."

The defendant maintains that the failure to comply with the requirements of this section is fatal to the validity of the action of the commissioners, and a complete answer to the

petition of the relator. It is conceded that the provisions
embodied in this section by the revision of 1880 were originally limited to the purchase of lands for and the erection
thereon of court-houses, jails, and county infirmaries, and the
building of bridges. The act, of which these provisions were
a part, related to this subject alone. The only change effected by the revision is, that the words "as provided by this
act," which originally occurred between the words "bridge"
and "the éxpenses," are omitted. It is contended that the
codifying commissioners intended, by the omission of these
words from the new section 877, to enlarge its operation.
No such requirement of notice as is now found in this section was to be found in any of the provisions relating to
children's homes prior to the revision of 1880. In Allen *v.*
Russell, 39 Ohio St. 337, it is said: "Where all the general
statutes of a State, or all on a particular subject, are revised
and consolidated, there is a strong presumption that the same
construction which the statutes received, or, if their interpretation had been called for, would certainly have received,
before revision and consolidation, should be applied to the
enactment in its revised and consolidated form, although the
language may have been changed."

In Comrs. *v.* Board of Public Works, 39 Ohio, 632, it is
said: "Particular and positive provisions of a prior act are
not affected by a subsequent statute in general terms, and not
expressly contradicting the provisions of the prior act, unless
such intention is clear." As the chapter in which section 877 is
found was a compilation and consolidation of numerous acts,
the retention of the words "as required by this act" would
have been an absurdity. Their omission is accounted for
upon other grounds than that of an intention to extend the
application of the requirements of this section to subjects not
originally within its operation. There is no warrant for the
conclusion that, by the mere omission of these words, it was
intended to apply section 877 to the provisions relating to
children's homes, which have been brought into the revision
also, without substantial change from their original form.

2. Was the auditor excused from issuing his warrant by the
COMMISSIONERS resolution of December 15, in form rescinding the
CANNOT RESCIND
ORDER OF PAY- former order directing him to issue his warrant for
MENT OF PUR-
CHASE PRICE the agreed purchase-price of the farm? That the

power of the commissioners to make and execute the contract for the purchase of the land of the relator was ample is unquestioned. No considerations of public policy, fraud, or abuse of discretion are shown to have intervened to impair or qualify this power. Before the attempted rescission of their former action by the commissioners, the proposition of the relator to sell his land had been accepted. The deed was duly executed and delivered, accepted by the commissioners, and by them delivered to the recorder to be recorded. Substantially and practically, possession had been delivered to and accepted by the commissioners. They had ordered the auditor to draw his warrant upon the treasurer for the amount of the purchase-money. When this order was made, the power of the commissioners over the public funds was exhausted. In fact, everything which either party to the contract could do toward its execution was accomplished. The right of the relator to his purchase-money was then complete. It was a right growing out of a contract which the other contracting party had abundant authority to make. It was unaffected by any considerations of fraud, imposition, or failure of consideration. It was not in the power of the commissioners, by any act of theirs, to divest him of the right which had so vested in the relator, or to impair any of the contract rights or obligations which flowed from the transaction. This is practically conceded; but it is maintained that the order directing the auditor to withhold his warrant impairs no contract right of the relator, but simply affects his remedy.

This position is untenable. The order of the commissioners directing the Auditor to draw his warrant on the treasurer in favor of the relator was the only means by which they could fully perform and execute the contract on their part. By this act their power over the subject of the contract was expended and the rights of the relator fixed. To recall or rescind their action in this behalf would be a substantial and serious interference with a most important contract right of the relator.

A statute of Indiana authorized the county commissioners to purchase a "tract of land" for an asylum for the poor. The board provided one tract and then undertook to purchase another. It was held that "when the board have acted, and provided a farm for the occupancy of the poor of the county, their legislative power on that snbject is exhausted." Hanna *v.* Commissioners Putnam Co., 29 Ind. 170; see, in support of the same general principle, Nelson *v.* Milford, 7 Pick. 18; Hall *v.* Holden, 116 Mass. 172; New Orleans *v.* Church of St Louis, 11 La. Ann. 244; Appeal of Comrs., 57 Pa. St. 452; · Western Sav. Fund Soc. *v.* Philadelphia, 31 Pa. St. 175; Indianapolis *v.* Indianapolis Gas-light & Coke Co., 66 Ind. 396; State *v.* Board of Education, 35 Ohio St. 368; State *v.* Hastings, 15 Wis. 75.

The case of *Ex parte* Black, 1 Ohio St. 36, is relied upon by the defendant as authority establishing the power of the commissioners to rescind their action ordering the auditor to issue his warrant in favor of the relator. The distinction between that case and the case at bar will be found, upon a thoughtful examination, to be marked. The commissioners of Hamilton County had, in pursuance of a special act author-izing it, entered into a contract with Milton H. and Alfred M. Cook, partners, for the erection of public buildings for the use of the county. After the Cooks had made substantial progress with the work, two of the commissioners, acting for the board, and without the assent of the third, ordered all work suspended. Black, the relator, who was the third com-missioner, applied to this court for a writ of *mandamus* to compel the board of commissioners to proceed with the work. The Cooks were not complaining. The writ was re-fused. Thurman, J., said: "Let the validity of the contract be assumed for present purposes; what claim does it give the relator to the writ he seeks? If any individual right has been violated by its breach, it is the right of the Cooks, and they ask for no *mandamus.* Were they to do so, it would possibly be a sufficient answer to say that they have no right, under the contract, to any specific thing; that their whole compensation is to be in money; and that an action at law would afford them a plain and adequate mode of redress. But it is unnecessary to say what we would do were they the relators. It is sufficient that Black has no right to prosecute for them. . . . But it is said that this is to repudiate a con-tract by the commissioners. It is not so. It is only to say that *mandamus* is not the proper remedy." Why *mandamus* was not the proper remedy in that case will be considered in another part of this opinion. The case is strong authority for the proposition that, in the present case, the contract rights of the relator must be faithfully and fully respected. That the rights of the Cooks under the contract could be impaired by the action of the commissioners is expressly repudiated. In that case the contract was but part executed. In that case at bar, each party had done all that was in his power to perform it.

If we concede the right and power of the commissioners to change or modify their established plan for the erection of a home, still, as the contract with Manix was within their authority, and was fully performed, the title to the land, which is admitted to be good, became vested in the county, and they were clothed with abundant capacity to convey it to any person, and appropriate its proceeds to the purposes of a home. Taylor *v.* Bingford, 37 Ohio St. 262.

But no facts have been made to appear upon this hearing which justified the commissioners in the attempt to revoke or rescind the acts which they had done in performance of their contract.

In State *v.* Commissioners Henry Co., 31 Ohio St. 211, the defendants, under the authority of a special act, levied and collected part of the taxes necessary for the building of a bridge. They then abandoned the purpose of building the bridge, and declined to make further levies. It was held that they will not be compelled by *mandamus*, at the suit of tax-payers, to build the bridge or make further levies for that purpose. The soundness of this case, and of *Ex parte* Black, *supra*, are unquestioned. But let it be supposed that, in either case, a contractor had performed his contract and the commissioners had allowed him his stipulated compensation, and directed the auditor to draw his warrant therefor. Would it be claimed that the power to suspend or abandon the prosecution of the work involved the right to rescind or revoke their allowance to the contractor and direction to the auditor? Surely, a proposition so at war with the inviolability of contract obligations will not be seriously contended for. If we are right in this conclusion, it follows that the commissioners could not impair the plaintiff's rights by the purchase of other lands for the purposes of a home.

3. Is *mandamus* the proper remedy? In *Ex parte* Black,

it is very clear that *mandamus* would not lie in favor of the Cooks. Their claim was one for money and the amount was unascertained. If their claim had been ascertained by a judgment of court or allowance of the commissioners, it would have become the plain duty of the auditor to issue his warrant for the amount, and upon his refusal *mandamus* would have been the appropriate remedy to compel him. Section 1024 R. S.

Commissioners Putnam Co. *v.* Auditor Allen Co., 1 Ohio St. 322, is relied upon to sustain the position of defendant. In that case it was held that "*mandamus* will not lie to compel the auditor of a county to draw an order on the county treasurer where the auditor has not the right to fix the amount to be drawn for, unless snch amount has been ascertained and liquidated." Caldwell, J., says: "If the amount were fixed in the mode contemplated in the statute, or if it were liquidated by judgment, *mandamus* would be the proper remedy to compel the auditor to perform the ministerial act of drawing the order; but until the amount is thus liquidated, we think the auditor cannot be compelled to act; the time for his action has not arrived."

It seems very clear that if an action of law would lie against the county for the agreed purchase price of the land, the only effect of such a proceeding would be to fix or determine the amount to which the relator is entitled. This has already been accomplished. After such a judgment, it would still remain for the auditor to draw his warrant for the amount of it. Upon his refusal, *mandamus* would clearly lie to compel his action. Such a proceeding would seem vain and idle. If the relator should invoke the remedy of specific performance, the commissioners could answer that they had already fully performed the contract on their part; and such answer would be abundantly sustained by the facts.

The defendant urges that another remedy for the relator is to apply for an order against the board of commissioners to vacate the entry of December 15. If this entry was authorized, it is not easy to see how a court could order its vacation. If, on the other hand, it was unauthorized, it furnishes no excuse to the auditor for his refusal to obey the command of the first order. It is not enough that the auditor may honestly entertain doubts concerning the propriety of the original order, or the effect of the order of rescission. The right to a writ of *mandamus* to enforce the performance of an official act by a public officer depends upon his legal duty, and not upon his doubts. Ryan *v.* Hoffman, 26 Ohio St. 109.

If his duty is clear, its performance will not be excused by his doubts concerning it, however strong or honest they may be. It is not doubted that it is competent for an auditor to defend against an application for *mandamus* to compel him to issue his warrant on the treasurer, upon an allowance and order of the commissioners, by showing that the order was wholly unauthorized, and that the commissioners had no authority to make it. State *v.* Yeatman, 22 Ohio St. 546.

It is enough to say that in the present case no fact is shown which impeaches the original order of the commissioners, or excuses the auditor from obeying its command. His duty to draw his warrant in favor of the relator is clear. That *mandamus* is the proper remedy to compel the performance of that duty is abundantly established by authority. Commissioners Putnam Co. *v.* Auditor Allen Co., *supra;* Ryan *v.* Hoffman, *supra;* Smith *v.* Commissioners, 9 Ohio, 26; State *v.* Burgoyne, 7 Ohio St. 153; Commissioners *v.* Hunt, 33 Ohio St. 169; State *v.* Board Ed., 35 Ohio St. 368; State *v.* Wilson, 17 Wis., 687, 694; State *v.* Auditor Delaware Co., 39 Ind. 272.

"The drawing of a warrant for the payment of a demand or claim which had been duly audited and allowed by the proper authority is regarded as a duty of a purely ministerial nature, and hence properly falling within the scope of *mandamus.* And wherever the demand has been definitely ascertained as prescribed by law, and the duty is plainly incumbent by law upon a particular officer of drawing his warrant upon the treasury for the amount due, a refusal to perform this duty will warrant the interposition of the courts by *mandamus.*" High, Extr. Legal Rem., sec. 104.

4. Other defences were relied upon by the defendant, but as they rested upon averments of fact, which the proofs failed to establish, they are not considered in this opinion.

Peremptory writ awarded.

McILVAINE, C. J., dissenting.—For my present purpose, in

dissenting from the judgment of the court, I will concede the facts to be as claimed by the relator, which is conceding more, I think, than the testimony shows. The case may, therefore, be stated thus: The board of commissioners of Darke County purchased of the relator a farm for the use of the county, as it was authorized to do. The relator executed and delivered to the commissioners in due form a deed of conveyance therefor. The board of commissioners accepted the deed, and thereupon directed the auditor of the county to draw a warrant in favor of the relator on the treasurer of the county for the amount of the purchase-money. Before the warrant was drawn by the auditor, the board of commissioners assumed to revoke the authority of the auditor to draw it. After the authority to draw a warrant was revoked and the revocation was entered on the journal of the commissioners, the auditor, on demand, refused to draw the warrant in favor of relator, and thereupon this proceeding was commenced to compel the auditor by *mandamus* to draw the warrant.

It is conceded that the auditor, without authority from the commissioners, has no power to draw the warrant. It therefore follows that a controlling question in this case is as to the power of the commissioners to revoke the authority of the auditor to draw the warrant. That it has been revoked, if the board of commissioners had the power of revocation, is not disputed. It is true that, between the date that the order to draw was given to the auditor and the date that it was revoked, the term of office of one of the commissioners had expired and his successor had been qualified; but it appears to me so palpably plain that the power of the board was not thereby controlled that the fact has received all the attention it deserves in the mere statement of it.

As to the powers of the commissioners to revoke the order granting authority to the auditor to draw a warrant on the treasury, although it is not given in express terms by the statute, it is, nevertheless, necessarily implied from the nature of the powers granted, the power to purchase. Let us suppose that, after the order on the auditor to draw, as in this case, the board of commissioners had discovered that the relators title was worthless, or that the premises were subject to liens; who could doubt the power or propriety of the purchaser to stop the payment of the purchase-money? If the purchaser were a natural person, surely no one would doubt the power. Every reason for its implied existence is present when the purchaser is a public agent, using public funds in making the purchase. In such case the existence of the power is essential to prevent public loss. I admit that the exercise of such power may be abused, but this admission does not imply that the power does not exist. But I do deny that the auditor is the judge to determine whether the power is properly or improperly used in any given case.

If the power of revocation in this case has been improperly used by the board of commissioners, the courts are open to redress, in the due and ordinary course of law, any wrong which the relator has suffered. But, to my mind, a plain duty under the law does not rest upon the auditor to draw his warrant upon the treasurer for the payment of the purchase-money which may or may not be due the relator; and unless the duty of the auditor to do so be plain, this proceeding should be dismissed.

I also wish to express my unqualified dissent to the proposition that the right of the relator to demand and receive the purchase price of this sale is *res adjudicata;* that the order of the commissioners upon the auditor to draw a warrant on the treasurer therefor, in favor of the relator, has the force and effect of a judgment at law, which cannot be collaterally impeached or modified by the commissioners after the term at which it is made. I deny that the order of the board of commissioners has any such force and effect. Instead of acting judicially in the matter, it was simply acting as a contracting party, not in making but in executing the contract. And the order of revocation was not a rescission of the contract, but a refusal to execute it. If the right of the auditor to pass on grounds of revocation did not exist, the grounds upon which the revocation was made are immaterial in this action.

JOHNSON, J., also dissented.

9 Cor. Cas.—9

BALLARD, Petitioner,

v.

STATE OF OHIO.

(*Advance Case, Ohio.   June* 16, 1885.)

In determining the power of the marshal of a municipal corporation to arrest without warrant, section 1849 of the Revised Statutes, which makes it the duty of that officer to arrest any person "in the act of committing any offence," etc., and section 7129 of same statutes, which makes it the duty of certain officers named, including such marshal, "to arrest and detain any person found violating any law," etc., relate to the performance of the same duty, and should be construed together to determine the extent of such power.

Under a proper construction of these sections, a marshal of a municipal corporation is authorized, without warrant, to arrest a person found on the public streets of the corporation carrying concealed weapons contrary to law, although he had no previous personal knowledge of the fact, if he acted *bona fide*, and upon such information as induces an honest belief that the person arrested is in the act of violating the law.

MOTION for leave to file petition in error to the Court of Common Pleas of Greene County. A great number of errors are assigned, all of which have been passed upon by the court, but only one is reserved for report. The indictment was for murder in the first degree, in killing one John T. Van Doren, Marshal of the town of Wilmington, Clinton County, and, on change of venue, the accused was convicted and sentenced for manslaughter in Greene County. Van Doren, as marshal, was in the act of arresting Ballard for carrying concealed weapons, when he was shot by the latter. The marshal had no warrant. There was resistance by Ballard, and a struggle, during which, by the discharge of Ballard's pistol, Van Doren was killed. Whether the arrest without warrant was authorized, and under what circumstances one thus arrested may defend himself, were questions directly involved by the evidence. Upon these questions the court charged as follows:

" In reference to the lawfulness or unlawfulness of the alleged arrest or attempt to arrest, I say to the jury that, by the laws of Ohio, the marshal of a village is bound to arrest any person in the act of committing any offence against the laws of the State, and forthwith bring such person before the mayor or other competent authority for examination or trial. According to the literal reading of the statute, the lawfulness of the arrest depends upon one thing alone,—namely, the fact that the person arrested is, at the time of the arrest, in the act of violating a law of the State,—and it is claimed by the State that the belief, or the knowledge, or the suspicion of the officer making the arrest as to the guilt or innocence of the party arrested does not affect the question, and is immaterial.

" The State admits that deceased had no warrant for the arrest of defendant, and no claim is made that defendant was committing or had committed a felony. It is claimed by the State that at the time of the alleged arrest deceased was marshal of the village of Wilmington, in Clinton County, Ohio; that the defendant was going about the streets of said village with a pistol concealed upon or about his person; that he was carrying such pistol unlawfully ; that is to say, he was engaged in no lawful business, calling, or employment ; and the circumstances in which he was placed were not such as would justify a prudent man in carrying a pistol for the defence of his person, property, or family ; and that deceased, learning of this, attempted to disarm him first, and, failing in that, put him under arrest for carrying such weapon concealed upon or about his person ; and, having so put him under arrest, was proceeding to take him before the proper officer for such legal proceedings as might be warranted by law, when the homicide occurred. If the jury are satisfied that these facts are proven, then the arrest was lawful, and defendant ought quietly to have submitted to it.

" The point is made by the defence that unless the officer has absolute knowledge that an offence is being committed against the laws of the State, he has no right to arrest without a warrant · for a misdemeanor. This claim is not tenable. If the person arrested is, as a matter of fact, in the act of committing such offence at the time of the arrest, and the officer has information or knowledge which induces him to reasonably believe, and at the time of the arrest he does believe, that such offence is being committed, and the arrest is made on that account, this is sufficient.

"The charge in the Weymouth case has been read as to this point, and referred to in your hearing, in which the judge told the jury, very correctly, that the officer must have personal knowledge of the offence and the offender. This, as I say, was good law for that case, because in that case the claim was not made, as it is here, that, as a matter of fact, the defendant at the time of the arrest was committing any offence; nor was there any evidence, as I understand the case, to support such claim.

"The State there claimed that the accused had been violating an ordinance of the village of Cedarville, but the officer was not present during the commission of the unlawful act, and it was fully completed before the alleged arrest was made. If the officer has no knowledge or information as to the commission of the offence, I say to the jury the arrest would be unlawful, even though the party arrested were, at the very time of the arrest, in the act of committing the offence·for which he was arrested.

"The State claims that if an officer, at a venture, without any information, knowledge, or suspicion on the subject, arrests a man without a warrant for unlawfully carrying a pistol concealed on his person, and it truns out, as matter of fact, that the party arrested is, at the time of the arrest, committing the offence for which he is arrested, the officer is protected, and the arrest is lawful. This claim, I say to the jury, cannot be allowed. In such case, to make the arrest lawful, the officer should believe that the party arrested is guilty of the offence for which the arrest is made, and the belief should be based on such facts or such information, or both, as might reasonably induce such belief."

Counsel for defendant excepted to this charge on the ground that it did not correctly state the law of arrest without warrant, nor the right of the person arrested to defend himself in such a case.

C. H. Blackburn and *Smith & Savage* for the motion.

James Lawrence, Attorney-General, *contra*.

JOHNSON, J.—By section 7129 R. S., "a sheriff, deputy-sheriff, constable, marshal, or deputy-marshal, watchman, or police-officer shall arrest and detain any person found violating any law of this State, or any legal ordinance of any city or village, until a legal warrant can be obtained." By section 1847 the marshal of municipal corporations is the chief ministerial officer of the corporation. By section 1848 he is to exceute all writs and processes, etc. By section 1849 he is to arrest all disorderly persons in the corporation; suppress all riots, disturbances, and breaches of the peace; pursue and arrest any person fleeing from justice in any part of the State; arrest any person in the act of committing any offence against the laws of the State or ordinances of the corporation, and forthwith bring such person before the mayor or other competent authority for examination or trial.

These two sections, 1849 and 7129, provide what a marshal of a municipal corporation may do as a conservator of the peace without a warrant. Section 1849 is the same as section 142 of the Municipal Code of 1869, 66 Ohio L. 173, where the authority extends to the arrest of any person " in the act of committing an offence," etc. Section 7129 is copied from 66 Ohio L. 291, section 21 of the Code of Criminal Procedure, where the words are, " any person found violating," etc.

Section 1849 is the primary source of a marshal's authority, and if there was any substantial difference in the words " in the act of committing any offence" and " found violating any law," as found in section 7129, the former would be adopted, if necessary to protect the officer. But we think there is no substantial difference. Under either the citizen is protected from arrest without warrant to the same degree as in the other. Both equally enlarge the power to arrest without warrant, in cases of misdemeanors, from what it was at common law. There a constable had original and inherent power to arrest for breach of the peace, or for felony actually committed, etc., or in the act of committing ·treason or felony, etc. 4 Bl. Com. *292; Hale, P. C., 587; 1 Bish. Crim. Proc. 167, 168. Section 1849 is, in legal effect, the adoption of the common-law rule as to arrests by sheriffs and constables without warrant, made applicable to other crimes than treason, felony, or breach of the peace.

With respect to the charge given, there was evidence tending to show that the deceased was marshal of the town of Wilmington, and known to Ballard to be such at the time of the attempted arrest and shooting; that Ballard was on the streets of the town carrying concealed weapons contrary to

law ; that he discharged the pistol, killing the marshal, while
he was engaged in resisting the arrest.   In making the arrest
for carrying such weapons, the marshal acted on information
and belief, and not from actual personal knowledge of the
facts.   This information, which proved to be true, was based
upon such statements of fact and from such sources as would
warrant a prudent man in acting.

Under these circumstances we think the officer was in the
performance of official duty.   This does not authorize such
ARREST BY an arrest without warrant, on a mere venture, with-
MARSHAL WITH-
OUT WARRANT. out knowledge or reliable information, though, in
fact, as afterwards discovered, concealed weapons were found.
The accused was "in the act of committing an offence" within the purview of section 1849, and "was found violating a
law of the State" within the terms of section 7129.   The accused was committing a concealed crime, not one open to
view, and hence the greater necessity of acting on knowledge
or information.   Good faith, an honest belief, based upon reliable information, which proves to be true, is all the law requires.   We need not inquire what is the law if the information is false and the party is innocent, as that question is not
before us.   Even in such a case, where the official character
of the officer, as well as the reason for the arrest, is known
to the party arrested, it would be no defence to a charge of
manslaughter if he purposely took the life of the officer to
prevent his arrest. In such a case it would rather be his duty
to yield obedience to the efforts of the officer, trusting to the
law for his redress, when there is no apparent danger to life
or of great bodily harm.

Upon a careful consideration of the charge of the court
upon this point, we think there is no error.

Motion overruled.

STATE *ex rel.* CUNNINGHAM, Plaintiff,

v.

RAY.

(*Advance Case, New Hampshire. July* 31, 1885.)

A statute which authorizes a justice of the peace to commit to the industrial school a minor under the age of seventeen years, upon a complaint charging a crime with respect to which the jurisdiction of the justice only extends to requiring the accused to recognize with sureties for his appearance at court, is in conflict with art. 15 of the Bill of Rights.

Where minors under sixteen years of age are brought before a justice of the peace upon a complaint charging them with burglary, a crime punishable by imprisonment in the State prison for a term of years, an order requiring them to recognize for their appearance before the Supreme Court exhausts the authority of the justice, and a further order committing them to the industrial school till respectively attaining their majority is null and void.

Habeas Corpus. The relator is father of John Cunningham, aged sixteen years, and of Eddie Cunningham, aged thirteen years, who were arraigned upon a complaint for burglary before a justice of the peace, June 10, 1884, and pleaded not guilty. After an examination, the justice ordered them to recognize in the sum of $100 each, with sureties, for their appearance at the October Term of this court, but immediately thereafter, upon the application of the State's counsel, under ch. 287, § 14, and without the consent of said minors or their friends, the justice revoked the order to recognize, refused to take bail, and sentenced John to the industrial school for two years, and Eddie for three years, and issued a *mittimus* for their commitment, which was executed June 12.

At this term, Ray, as superintendent of the industrial school, having produced them before the court on a writ of *habeas corpus* issued upon the relator's petition, a hearing was had and they were discharged, on the ground that the justice had no jurisdiction to impose the sentence aforesaid, and the defendant excepted.

Hoskins & Stoddard for plaintiff.

E. P. Dole for defendant.

SMITH, J.—"When any minor under the age of seventeen years, charged with any offence punishable by imprisonment FROM.   otherwise than for life, shall be convicted and sentenced accordingly, or shall be ordered to recognize for his appearance at the Supreme Court, the court or justice, upon application of such minor, his friends, or the State's counsel, may order that, instead of such imprisonment or recognizance, the said minor may be sent and kept employed and instructed at the reform school for such term, not less than one year, nor extending beyond the age of twenty one years, as said court shall judge most for his true interest and benefit, provided he shall conduct himself according to the regulations of said school; and a copy of such order shall be sufficient authority for his commitment and detention at such school," G. L. c. 287, s. 14. By Laws 1881, c. 37, the name of the institution was changed to the industrial school. Under the authority of this statute, the relator's minor sons, one of the age of thirteen and the other of the age of sixteen years, had been sent to the industrial school for the terms of three and two years respectively, neither having been convicted of any crime or offence. They were brought before a justice of the peace upon a complaint charging them with having committed the crime of burglary,—a crime of the gravest character and punishable by imprisonment in the State prison for a long term of years. The crime was one which the magistrate had not jurisdiction to determine, but only to inquire if just cause appeared to hold the accused to answer at the Supreme Court. They were heard upon no other charge than that set out in the complaint, and were not in law required to defend against any other. An order was made requiring them to recognize for their appearance before the Supreme Court. So far the justice had jurisdiction. At this stage of the proceedings, the counsel for the State moved for an order that the accused be sent to the industrial school, and the justice, declining the offer of the accused to recognize agreeably to the order then just made by him, issued an order committing them to the school for the terms above mentioned. The commitment was not for the purpose of securing their appearance at the Supreme Court, for the shortest term for which they might be sent to the school would extend much beyond the next term of the Supreme Court. If they were committed as a punishment for having committed the crime of burglary., they have never been tried or convicted of that crime by the judgment of their peers. Article 15 of the Bill of Rights provides that "no subject shall be arrested, imprisoned, despoiled, or deprived of his property, immunities, or privileges, put out of the protection of the law, exiled, or deprived of his life, liberty, or estate, but by the judgment of his peers or the law of the land." This clause in our Constitution is a translation from Magna Charta, and dates from 1215. Its meaning has become fixed and well determined, "and asserts the right of every citizen to be secure from all arrests not warranted by law." Mayo *v.* Wilson, 1 N. H. 53, 57.

It guarantees the right of trial by jury in all cases where the right existed at common law in this State at the adoption of the Constitution. That a person charged with having committed the crime of burglary is entitled to a jury trial has never been questioned. As the justice only had jurisdiction to inquire and not to convict, the accused have had no trial. Provision is, and ever since the adoption of the Constitution has been, made by statute for a trial by jury of every crime indictable by a grand jury, and of every offence where an appeal is taken from the judgment of a justice or police court. Final judgment cannot be enforced for the commission of any police offence, however trivial, until the appellant has been convicted by a jury of his peers. If the relator's sons were sent to the industrial school for some other crime or offence, it was one of which they have never been convicted, and in violation of article 15 of the Bill of Rights, which provides that "no subject shall be held to answer for any crime or offence until the same is fully and plainly, substantially and formally described to him, or be compelled to accuse or furnish evidence against himself. And every subject shall have a right to produce all proofs that may be favorable to himself, to meet the witnesses against him face to face, and to be fully heard in his defence by himself and counsel."

But the commitment and detention of the relator's sons is justified by the respondent upon the ground that the industrial school is not a prison; that the order COMMITMENT TO INDUSTRIAL SCHOOL ILLEGAL of commitment was not a sentence; and that their detention is not a punishment. The contention is that the industrial school is a part of the school system of the State, and that the State as *parens patriæ* may detain in the school such scholars as may need its discipline. If it is a privilege to be admitted a member of the school, it is a privilege limited to " offenders against the law." At no time since its institution in 1855 have its doors been open to the admission of any other class of scholars. Its advantages have not been offered to every minor under the age of seventeen years who might CHARACTER OF desire to enter, or whose parents or guardian might INDUSTRIAL SCHOOL. seek to place him there. The relator's sons were sent to the school, either because they had committed some crime or offence, or because the justice judged it to be for their "interest and benefit" to be placed there. For whichever of these causes they were committed, the commitment was illegal. As already remarked, they have never been convicted of the crime of burglary, and they have not been tried or had any opportunity to defend against any other charge. If the order for their commitment was made because the justice judged it to be for their " interest and benefit," the answer is that he had no authority by statute to commit them for that cause. Whenever a court or a justice may send a minor to the school, he may fix the term during which he may be kept at the school at not less than one year nor extending beyond the age of twenty-one years, as the court or justice "shall judge most for his true interest and benefit." The limit of his stay or confinement in the school is determined by the consideration of what shall be " most for his true interest and benefit;" but the statute does not confer upon the court or justice the power to send a minor to the school solely for the reason that the court or justice may be of opinion that it may be for the interest or benefit of the minor to be sent there. The original name of the school " House of Reformation for Juvenile and Female Offenders against the Laws," Laws 1855, c. 1660, indicated the character of the institution. The act provided that any boy under the age of eighteen years, or any female of any age, " convicted of any offence known to the laws of this State, or punishable by imprisonment, other than such as may be punished by imprisonment for life," might be sentenced to the house of reformation. *Ib.*, s. 4. At no period in its history could a person become an inmate of the institution, unless, being within the prescribed age, he or she had been convicted of a crime or offence. The only exception is the unconstitutional provision inserted in the revision of 1867 (Gen. Stats. c. 2, s. 14 ; G. L. c. 287, s. 14) authorizing a justice to send to the school a minor less than seventeen years of age whom he shall have ordered to recognize for his appearance at the Supreme Court. We cannot ignore the fact that in the public estimation the school has always been regarded as a *quasi* penal institution, and the detention of its inmates or scholars as involuntary and constrained. The great purpose of the institution was the separation of youthful offenders from hardened criminals of mature years, in the hope of their ultimate reformation, and of their becoming useful citizens. But the fact cannot be overlooked that the detention of the inmates is regarded to some extent as a punishment, with more or less of disgrace attached on that account. If the order committing a minor to the school is commitment to school is a sentence. not a sentence, but the substitute for a sentence, as claimed by the respondent, what is a substitute for a sentence but a sentence in and of itself? It is worthy of remark that the legislature has not undertaken to authorize the commitment of a minor to the industrial school upon the mere presentment of the grand jury.

In this case, the relator, the natural guardian of his sons, has been deprived of their care, nurture, education, and custody, against his consent, and without any trial or hearing to which he was a party, upon the ground, and deprives children of parent's care. only ground, that the justice found there was just cause to require them to appear at the Supreme Court to answer further. If he is not a suitable person to have the care and education of his children, that fact has not been found, nor does it appear that their education has been neglected. But how far he is entitled to be heard upon that question we do not decide. We have only alluded to the matter as showing what consequences may flow from the unlawful commitment of a minor to this school. Where the commitment is lawful the loss by the parent of his custody of his child follows as one of the incidents for which there is no remedy, and perhaps in many instances, because of his unfitness, there ought to be none.

It is further deserving of consideration that the children cannot plead autrefois convict. relator's sons, if indicted for the crime of which they were charged before the justice, cannot plead *autrefois convict*, although they may remain at the school the full term for which they were sentenced ; and if their detention at the school is a punishment, they are liable to be punished twice for the same offence, in violation of the fundamental maxim, " *Nemo debet bis puniri*," etc.   Broom, Legal Max. 348. In coming to this conclusion, we have not overlooked the decisions in other States.   Milwaukee Industrial School *v.* Supervisor Milwaukee County, 40 Wis. 328; s. c., 22 Am. Rep. 702 ; M'Lean Co. *v.* Humphreys, 104 Ill. 378 ; Petition of Ferrier, 103 Ill. 367 ; s. c., 42 Am. Rep. 10 ; Roth *v.* House of Refuge, 31 Md. 329 ; *Ex parte* Crouse, 4 Whart. (Pa.) 9.

In these cases the detention of abandoned, or dependent, depraved children in houses of refuge or in industrial or reform schools is upheld upon the ground that the power of magistrates and county courts to commit, and of such institutions to detain such children, is " of the same character of the jurisdiction exercised by the Court of Chancery over the persons and property of infants, having foundation in the prerogative of the Crown, flowing from its general power and duty as *parens patriæ* to protect those who have no other lawful protector; 2 Story Eq. Jur. 1333" (Sheldon, J., in Petition of Ferrier, *supra*), or, as stated in *Ex parte* Crouse, *supra*, " May not the natural parents, when unequal to the task of education, or unworthy of it, be superseded by the *parens patriæ*, or common guardian of the community ?"   As to the soundness of the reasons given in these cases, we have nothing to say.   No one of them is an authority for the commitment of a minor charged with the commission of a crime to such an institution without some kind of a trial and conviction.

The People *v.* Turner, 55 Ill. 280, was an application by the father for a writ of *habeas corpus* for the discharge from a reform school of his minor son.   A statute of Illinois authorized the commitment to a reform school of children between six and sixteen years of age, who are " vagrants, or destitute of proper parental care, or are growing up in mendicancy, idleness, or vice," " to remain until reformed, or until the age of twenty-one years."   The relator's son, committed to the school under this statute, was discharged, the commitment being held not to have been for any criminal offence, and the statute was declared unconstitu-

AUTHORITIES REVIEWED.

tional. His confinement was held to be imprisonment without due process of law. Thornton, J., said : " Such a restraint
upon natural liberty is tyranny and oppression. . . . If a
father confined or imprisoned his child for one year, the
majesty of the law would frown upon the unnatural act, and
every tender mother and kind father would rise up in arms
against such monstrous inhumanity. Can the State, as *parens
patriæ*, exceed the power of the natural parent, except in punishing crime ?"

In Commonwealth *v.* Horregan, 127 Mass. 450, it was held
that certain statutes relating to juvenile offenders, so far as
they purport to give inferior tribunals jurisdiction of offences
punishable by infamous punishment, are unconstitutional.

A statute of Ohio authorizing the grand jury, where a
minor under the age of sixteen years is charged with crime,
and the charge appears to be supported by evidence sufficient
to put the accused upon trial, instead of finding an indictment to return to the court that the accused is a suitable
person to be committed to the house of refuge, directed the
court thereupon to order his commitment without trial by
jury. The statute was declared constitutional. Prescott *v.*
State, 19 Ohio St. 184 ; s. c., 2 Am. Rep. 388.

The decision is put upon the ground that the case " is neither a criminal prosecution nor a proceeding according to the
course of the common law, in which the right to a trial by
jury is guaranteed. The proceeding is purely statutory, and
the commitment, in cases like the present, is not designed as
a punishment for crime, but to place minors of the description and for the causes specified in the statute under the
guardianship of the public authorities named, for proper care
and discipline, until they are reformed or arrive at the age
of majority. The institution to which they are committed is
a school, not a prison ; nor is the character of their detention
affected by the fact that it is also a place where juvenile con-
victs may be sent, who would otherwise be condemned to
confinement in the common jail or penitentiary." The statute
further provided that in case the cause for the child's detention shall be inquired into by a proceeding in *habeas corpus*, it
shall be a sufficient return to the writ that he was committed
to the guardianship of the directors of the school, and that
the period for his discharge had not arrived. It is intimated,

in the opinion of the court, that it is questionable whether this provision can operate to restrict the power of the court, invested by the constitution with jurisdiction in *habeas corpus*, from inquiring fully into the cause of the detention of a person restrained of his liberty.

With due respect for the learned court who pronounced this opinion, we are not convinced of the soundness of the reasoning or conclusion. The proceedings by which the accused was adjudged a suitable person to be committed to the house of refuge were conducted in secret, without his knowledge or consent, or that of his parent or guardian, with no opportunity to be represented by counsel, to be confronted with and cross-examine the witnesses for the prosecution, or to produce witnesses in his own behalf. The liberty of the minor during the term of his minority, which might be for a period of many years, was made to depend upon the deliberations of a secret tribunal. A judgment rendered upon such an *ex parte* hearing is as little calculated to command the respect of the community as the proceedings of the ancient court of the Star-Chamber. And so far as the other cases cited are like the Ohio case in legal effect, we cannot follow them. Whether what has been called a trial in other jurisdictions in cases of this class is a trial within the meaning of our Constitution, and whether on any other ground than that of a charge of crime the legislature can authorize minors or persons of age to be committed to the industrial school without a trial by jury, if it were claimed, and without the consent of parent or other guardian, are questions on which we give no opinion. Persons poor and standing in need of relief may and must be cared for by the overseers of the poor, and may be sent to the almshouse for support; but their detention cannot be regarded as involuntary. They are in no sense deprived of their liberty without the judgment of their peers or against the law of the land. They are neither criminals nor charged with the commission of crime, and this provision of the Constitution was not understood by its framers as restricting the power of the legislature to provide for the relief of the worthy poor. So children of profligate parents, or of vicious surroundings, may be taken from the custody of their natural guardians and committed to the guardianship of those who will properly care for their moral, intellectual, and physical welfare. Prim *v.* Foote, *supra*, 52.

But this is a power exercised by the State as *parens patriæ*, in the welfare and interest of its citizens. 2 Story, Eq. Jr. s. 1333.

The common-law principle of reasonable necessity has an extensive constitutional operation (Aldrich *v.* Wright, 53 N. H. 398, 399, 400; Haley *v.* Colcord, 59 N. H. 7, 8; Hopkins *v.* Dickson, 59 N. H. 235; Johnson *v.* Perry, 56 Vt. 703; State *v.* Morgan, 59 N. H. 322, 325); and in many cases authorizes the restraint of an insane person (Colby *v.* Jackson, 12 N. H. 526; Davis *v.* Merrill, 47 N. H. 208; O'Connor *v.* Bucklin, 59 N. H. 589, 591; Kelleber *v.* Putnam, 60 N. H. 30; Hinchman *v.* Richie, Bright (Pa.), 143; Fletcher *v.* Fletcher, 1 E. & E. 420; Bushnell, Insanity, ss. 19, 24); even when he is committed to an asylum upon a defective process. Shuttleworth's Case, 9 A. &. E. (N. S.) 651.

But a magistrate's power to commit to the industrial school, for detention during minority, every person under the age of seventeen years charged with **MAGISTRATE'S COMMITMENT TO SCHOOL ILLEGAL.** but not convicted of an offence punishable with imprisonment otherwise than for life, on the ground of the "true interest and benefit" of the accused, does not come within any constitutional idea of reasonable necessity that has prevailed in this State. For his interest and benefit, the magistrate might as well be authorized to send him to the State prison as to the industrial school, or any other penal institution.

We are of opinion that so much of s. 14, c. 287, G. L., as authorizes a justice of the peace to commit to the industrial school a minor under the age of seventeen years, upon a complaint charging him with the commission of a crime, of which the justice has jurisdiction only to require him to recognize for his appearance at the Supreme Court, on the motion of the State's attorney, and without the consent of any person authorized to bind the magistrate by consent, is in violation of article 15 of the Bill of Rights.

Exceptions overruled.

BLODGETT, J., did not sit; the others concurred.

MILLER, Adm'r,

v.

WHITE RIVER SCHOOL TOWNSHIP.

(101 *Indiana,* 503.)

A demurrer to a reply in substantial compliance with the provisions of section 357 R. S. 1881 is sufficient both in form and substance, and is not rendered defective by the introduction of other matter, which may be properly regarded as surplusage.

The trustee of a school corporation has power to contract a debt in the name of and binding upon such corporation, in the purchase of necessary furniture, apparatus, and other supplies of its schools, and to execute in the name of his corporation a valid and binding certificate of indebtedness or note for the amount of such debt; and such certificate or note will constitute *prima facie* a good cause of action against such corporation.

Such a certificate or note is not rendered invalid by the trustee's failure to comply with the provisions of sections 6006 and 6007 R. S. 1881, as those sections of the statute have no application to the ordinary debts of a school corporation incurred by the trustee for the usual and necessary furniture, apparatus, and other supplies of its common schools.

Ordinarily, it is the duty of the trial court, when requested by either party, to instruct the jury, if they render a general verdict, to find specially upon particular questions of fact, in answer to written interrogatories within the scope of the issues, and it is error to refuse such an instruction, or to submit to the jury such interrogatories.

Where the court, in the discharge of its duty, and without invading the province of the jury, may properly instruct them to return their verdict for either party, the error of the court in refusing to submit interrogatories to the jury, at the request of the other party, is at most a harmless error.

Where the complaint states a good cause of action, and issue is joined upon a special or affirmative paragraph of answer, which states no defence whatever to plaintiff's action, and where the allegations of such paragraph of answer are admitted to be true on the trial, it is error for the court to instruct the jury, upon such immaterial issue, to return a verdict for the defendant.

FROM Gibson Circuit Court.

L. C. Embree and *W. D. Robinson* for appellant.

J. E. McCullough and *J. H. Miller* for appellee.

HOWK, J.—This action was brought by the appellant, as FACTS.   the administrator of one John Miller, deceased, against the appellee, upon a certificate of indebtedness, executed by the trustee of White River township, of which certificate the following is a copy :

" STATE OF INDIANA, COUNTY OF GIBSON :
     " *Trustee's Office, White River Tp.*, *Nov.* 23, 1881.
   " This is to certify that there is now due from this township to H. L. Kimberlin & Co. one hundred and seventy-five dollars for part five of the McBride Tellurians bought for the use of this township, and payable out of the special school funds at the People's Bank at Princeton, Indiana, on the 1st day of June, 1883, with interest at eight per cent, and eight per cent on the amount after maturity till paid.
     (Signed)   " WILLIAM F. HUDELSON,
          " School Trustee of White River Township."

The appellant alleged in his complaint that before the maturity of such certificate of indebtedness, it was endorsed in writing to his decedent, John Miller, by the payees thereof, and that it was past due and wholly unpaid. Wherefore, etc.

The cause was put at issue and tried by a jury, and a verdict was returned for the appellee, the defendant below; and, over the appellant's motion for a new trial, judgment was rendered against him for the appellee's costs.

In this court, the first error assigned by the appellant is that the circuit court erred in sustaining the demurrer to the second and third paragraphs of his reply. In discussing this alleged error, the appellant's counsel do not claim that either the second or third reply stated facts sufficient to constitute a good reply, but they say : " We desire to question the form and sufficiency of the demurrer," and they conclude that it " is insufficient both in form and substance." The demurrer thus called in question reads as follows:

" The defendant demurs separately to the second and third paragraphs of reply, for the reason that neither of SUFFICIENCY OF said paragraphs states facts sufficient to constitute DEMURRER. SURPLUSAGE. a reply, or avoidance of the facts stated in the paragraphs of answer to which said paragraphs of reply are respectively pleaded."

In section 357 R. S. 1881, it is provided as follows: " The defendant may demur to any paragraph of the reply, on the ground that the facts stated therein are not sufficient to avoid

the paragraph of answer," etc. It is apparent that the demurrer objected to in this case is in substantial compliance
with the requirements of the statute, and it is sufficient, we
think, " both in form and substance." It is true, perhaps, that
there is some surplusage in such demurrer, but it is equally
true, as to any pleading, that "surplusage does not vitiate
that which is good." Mires *v.* Alley, 51 Ind. 507; Owen *v.*
Phillips, 73 Ind. 284; Morris *v.* Stern, 80 Ind. 227.

The only other error assigned by appellant is the over-·
ruling of his motion for a new trial. Under this error, the
first question discussed by his counsel is thus stated in their
brief: "Did the lower court err in refusing to submit to the
jury the interrogatories propounded by appellant?" Before
considering this question, it is proper that we should state,
more fully than we have done, the issues in the cause which
were submitted to the jury for trial. We have already stated
the appellant's cause of action.

The appellee originally answered in four special or affirm-
Answer.   ative paragraphs. In the first paragraph, it was
alleged that the written instrument sued upon was made and
executed without any consideration whatever therefor.

In the second paragraph of its answer, the appellee alleged
that, on the 23d day of November, 1881, H. L. Kimberlin
& Co. agreed and contracted with appellee to deliver to him,
within a reasonable time after that date, five of McBride's
Tellurians; that the written instrument sued upon was executed in part consideration of such contract, and upon no
other consideration whatever; and that H. L. Kimberlin &
Co. wholly failed and neglected to deliver such Tellurians,
or any of them, to the appellee within such reasonable time,
or to deliver them at all; wherefore the consideration of
such written instrument had wholly failed.

In the third paragraph of answer, after stating the consideration of the written instrument sued upon substantially as
the same was stated in the preceding paragraph, it was alleged
that the Tellurians were to be delivered to appellee by H. L.
Kimberlin & Co. within, to wit, three months from the date
of the contract; that H. L. Kimberlin & Co. wholly failed
and neglected to deliver to the appellee such Tellurians
within such time; that thereupon appellee elected to rescind
such contract and so notified H. L. Kimberlin & Co., and

that the Tellurians had not, nor had either of them, ever been delivered by H. L. Kimberlin & Co., or by any one in their behalf, or been accepted or received by the appellee.

In the fourth paragraph of answer, the consideration of the written instrument sued upon is stated substantially as it was stated in the second paragraph ; and it was then averred that at the time of making such contract and of executing such instrument there was an outstanding indebtedness against the appellee, and chargeable against its special school fund, in the amount of $6000, and greatly exceeding in, to wit, the sum of $4500, the aggregate amount then on hand belonging to such fund, together with the amount to be derived from the tax assessed against such township for that year in favor of such fund ; and that such contract was made with H. L. Kimberlin & Co., and such indebtedness to them was attempted to be contracted by such trustee, without his having procured any order from the board of commissioners of Gibson County authorizing such trustee to contract any such indebtedness, or without his having presented any petition to such board for such an order or having given notice of any such petition.

Upon the foregoing paragraphs of answer the appellant joined issue by his reply in general denial.

Afterwards the appellee filed its fifth paragraph of answer, verified by the oath of its then trustee, wherein it was averred that the written instrument sued upon was never executed by the appellee, nor by its trustee, nor by any other person authorized to execute the same on its behalf; and that at the time William F. Hudelson signed such instrument, if at all, he was not the trustee of such appellee.

With this statement of the issues in the cause, we come now to the consideration of the first question presented by the appellant's counsel in argument, under the alleged error of the court in overruling the motion for a new trial, namely: Did the court err in refusing to submit to the jury the appellant's interrogatories? The record shows that, at the proper time, the appellant submitted to the court SUBMISSION OF INTERROG- ATORIES TO JURY a number of written interrogatories, and requested the court to instruct the jury to answer the same and to find specially upon the several questions of fact stated therein, in case they should return a general verdict ; that the court re-

fused to submit such interrogatories to the jury and to instruct them as requested ; and that to this action and ruling
of the court the appellant at the time excepted.   We need
not set out these interrogatories : it will suffice to say that
they seem to us to have been within the scope of the issues
in the cause.   No objection was made below, and none is
made here, to either the form or substance of the interrogatories.   In section 546 R. S. 1881, it is provided that in all
cases, when requested by either party, the court shall instruct
the jury, if they render a general verdict, to find specially
upon particular questions of fact, to be stated in writing.   In
Campbell *v.* Frankem, 65 Ind. 591, the court said : " It is the
right of a party to have the jury find upon facts which fall
within the scope of the issues in the case. . . . The court
may control the form of interrogatories, and judge of their
propriety, but, when properly asked for, it is error to reject
them."

In discussing the question we are now considering, the appellee's learned counsel do not claim, as we understand their
argument, that the appellant's interrogatories to the jury
were defective either in form or substance, or that they were
not within the scope of the issues in the case.   Counsel say
that the appellant was not injured by the court's refusal to
submit his interrogatories to the jury, because the court instructed the jury that "under the issues, evidence, and admissions in the case, it is the duty of the jury to find for the
defendant," unless this court should be of the opinion that
such instruction was erroneous.   In other words, the appellee's counsel virtually concede that the trial court erred in its
refusal to submit the appellant's interrogatories to the jury,
unless the case was one in which the court, without invading
the province of the jury, and simply in the discharge of its
own duty, had properly instructed them to return their verdict for the appellee.   If the court's instruction above quoted
was right and properly given, then the error of the court, if
such it were, in refusing to submit the appellant's interrogatories to the jury, was at most a harmless error ; and for such
an error this court will not reverse a judgment.

This view of the question under consideration seems to us
to be the correct one, and it is in harmony with the decision
of this court in McClaren *v.* Indianapolis, etc., R. R. Co., 83 Ind.

319. In that case the court said : "Where the interrogatories are entirely unnecesary, as where, under the evidence,
there is no cause of action, and the court is, therefore, authorized to direct a verdict for the defendant, there the withdrawal of the interrogatories, which, in such a case, should
not have been submitted to the jury, is not error." So that
the proper decision of the question we are now considering
depends upon the answer which must be given to this further question, namely, Did the trial court err in instructing
the jury that, " under the issues, evidence, and admissions in
the case, it is the duty of the jury to find for the defendant?"

Of course, there are cases in which the trial court, of its
own motion and without any invasion of the prov-
ince of the jury, may properly instruct the jury to   INSTRUCTING
return their verdict for the one or the other party.   JURY TO FIND
                                                       VERDICT.
Dodge *v.* Gaylord, 53 Ind. 365 ; Moss *v.* Witness Printing Co.,
64 Ind. 125 ; American Ins. Co. *v.* Butler, 70 Ind. 1.   Where
issue is joined on the plaintiff's complaint by an answer in
general denial merely, and evidence is introduced which tends
to sustain the material averments of the complaint, it would
certainly be error for the court to direct a verdict for the defendant ; for, in such case, the sufficiency or insufficiency of
the evidence is a question for the jury, and the plaintiff has
the right to claim a verdict, either for or against him, unin-
fluenced by the court's opinion in relation to the evidence.
Adams *v.* Kennedy, 90 Ind. 318.   In the case in hand, however,
all the paragraphs of appellee's answer, except the fifth,
which is not sustained by any evidence, were special paragraphs wherein the appellee pleaded affirmative facts in bar
of the action.   To these special or affirmative paragraphs the
appellant replied by a general denial, and as to each of them
the appellee, of course, had the burden of the issue.   If a
special or affirmative paragraph of answer states a good defence, in bar of the action, and is sustained by sufficient legal
evidence, without any conflict therein, we think the court
may properly instruct the jury to return a verdict for the defendant without any invasion of the province of the jury, even
though the plaintiff's evidence may have made a *prima facie*
case in his behalf.   But where issue is joined upon a special
or affirmative paragraph of answer which states no defence
whatever to plaintiff's action, and would have been held bad

on demurrer, then, although upon the trial the facts stated in such paragraph are proved to be true ·by an abundance of uncontradicted evidence, it would be error for the court to instruct the jury, upon such issue, to return a verdict for the defendant. This is settled, we think, by the decisions of this court. Western Union Tel. Co. *v.* Fenton, 52 Ind. 1 ; Dorman *v.* State, 56 Ind. 454 ; McCloskey *v.* Indianapolis, etc., Union, 67 Ind. 86 (33 Am. R. 76).

In the case in hand, it is claimed on behalf of the appellee that the fourth paragraph of its answer, the substance of which we have already given, stated a good defence in bar of the appellant's action, and that it was abundantly sustained, POWER OF without contradiction, by the admissions of the ap-
SCHOOL TRUSTEE pellant as evidence on the trial. We are of opin-
TO CONTRACT
DEBTS. ion, however, that the fourth paragraph of answer stated no defence whatever to the appellant's action. It is manifest that the paragraph was prepared upon the supposition of the pleader that the contract for the Tellurians, mentioned in the complaint, was void because the appellee's trustee had not complied with the provisions of sections 6006 and 6007 R. S. 1881 before making such contract. We think, however, that those sections of the statute can have no application to the ordinary debts incurred by the trustee for furniture, apparatus, and other supplies for the schools of his township, such as the debt in suit for the Tellurians. Besides, the sections of the statute did not enlarge, but were intended to limit, the power of the trustee to contract debts in the name of and binding upon his township. This is shown by the phraseology of the sections, and by the title of the act from which the sections are taken. The title of such act is, " An act to limit the power of township trustees in incurring debts," etc. Acts 1875, Reg. Sess., p. 162.

This court has repeatedly held that notes executed by a township trustee for borrowed money did not evidence debts of the township unless it was shown that the money borrowed had been used for the legitimate purposes of the township. Wallis *v.* Johnson School Tp., 75 Ind. 368 ; Pine Civil Tp. *v.* Huber, etc., Co., 83 Ind. 121 ; Reeve School Tp. *v.* Dodson, 98 Ind. 497.

If, therefore, it were conceded that the fourth paragraph of answer stated a good defence to this action, we would be bound to hold that it was not sustained by sufficient evidence. For, while it was shown by the appellant's admissions on the trial, that certain notes had been executed by the trustee, Hudelson, for borrowed money, which notes were yet unpaid, still it was not shown in any manner by the appellee, who had the burden of the issue, that the money so borrowed had been used for the township. It is clear, therefore, that, under the decisions of this court, the appellee failed to show the existing outstanding indebtedness of the township, alleged in its fourth paragraph of answer.

Our conclusion is that the court erred in instructing the jury to return a verdict for the appellee, and in refusing to submit appellant's interrogatories to the jury trying the cause.

Other questions are discussed by counsel, but, as they may not arise on a new trial of the case, we need not now consider them. Appellee's counsel suggest, in argument, that the complaint is bad, and that, for this cause, the judgment below should be affirmed. The sufficiency of the complaint was not called in question below, nor is it questioned here by any assignment of error or cross error. Therefore, the question suggested is not presented for our decision. Besides, the evidence in the record fully supplied, or tended to supply, any defect in the complaint as the question is now presented.

For the reasons heretofore given, we are of opinion that the court erred in overruling the appellant's motion for a new trial.

The judgment is reversed, with costs, and the cause is remanded with instructions to sustain the motion for a new trial, and for further proceedings not inconsistent with this opinion.

STATE *ex rel.* GRAHAM

v.

BABCOCK.

(Advance Case, Nebraska.   September 29, 1885.)

Where the State constitution provides that "no money shall be drawn
from the treasury except in pursuance of a specific appropriation made
by law," *held* that the auditor of public accounts has no authority to
draw a warrant on the State treasury in favor of county treasurers for
commissions on money collected by them and paid into the treasury,
though it was customary for treasurers to deduct their commissions before paying money collected into the State treasury.

MANDAMUS.

Charles O. Whedon for relator.

The Attorney-General for respondent.

REESE, J.—This is an application to this court, in the exer-
ꜰᴀᴄᴛꜱ.   cise of its original jurisdiction, for a writ of *man-*
damus to compel the auditor of public accounts to issue his
warrant on the State treasury for a sum of money which the
relator claims is due him as commission or fees for collecting
moneys due the State as proceeds from the sale and leasing
of school lands.

The relator alleges that he collected the moneys referred
to, and paid them over to the State treasurer, without deducting therefrom his commission for making the collection.   It
is alleged that it is the custom for county treasurers not to
deduct their commissions from the money they collect for the
State, but to pay it all to the State treasurer, and then to receive from the auditor a warrant for the amount of commissions to which such treasurer may be entitled; that he has
demanded from the auditor a warrant for the amount of commissions due him, but that the auditor has refused to issue it.

It is claimed that under the provisions of section 164, c. 77,
ᴄᴏᴍᴍɪꜱꜱɪᴏɴꜱ ᴛᴏ Comp. St., he is entitled to this warrant as for
ᴄᴏᴜɴᴛʏ ᴛʀᴇᴀꜱ-
ᴜʀᴇʀ.   money which he has overpaid.   This section provides that "if any county treasurer shall have paid, or may
hereafter pay, into the State treasury any greater sum or
sums of money than are legally and justly due from such collector, after deducting abatements and commissions, the audi-

tor shall issue his warrant for the amount so overpaid, which shall be paid out of the fund or funds so overpaid on said warrant." This section would seem to give the auditor the authority contended for by the relator; but we must hold that it does not. Section 22 of article 3, entitled "Legislation," of the constitution of this State provides, among other things, that "no money shall be drawn from the treasury except in pursuance of a specific appropriation made by law, and on the presentation of a warrant issued by the auditor thereon." . . . This section must be treated as, and is, a complete denial of the right or power of the auditor to draw his warrant on the treasury for any sum of money for any purpose except in pursuance of an appropriation made by law. The money is conceded to be in the treasury. It must remain there until drawn out "in pursuance of a specific appropriation" giving authority therefor.

In so far as the section of the revenue law above quoted is in conflict with the provision of the constitution, if at all, it is void; but as the two sections must be construed together, and if possible harmonized, it may be said that there is nothing in the section requiring the warrant to issue without an appropriation being first made, and that there is no conflict. However that may be, it is clear the auditor cannot legally draw the required warrant.

The other questions discussed by counsel need not be noticed, as, in our view, the writ cannot issue, and is therefore denied.

SCHEERER

v.

EDGAR, Auditor, etc.

(Advance Case, California, in Banc. August 26, 1885.)

A county auditor who appeals a *mandamus* proceeding against him acts in his official capacity, and need not be required to give an appeal bond.

APPEAL from Superior Court of San Francisco. Hearing on motion to dismiss appeal.

John Lord Love for appellant.

E. A. & Geo. E. Lawrence for respondent.

Ross, J.—This is an appeal taken by the defendant from a judgment of the superior court directing a writ of mandate to issue compelling the defendant, as auditor of the city and county of San Francisco, to issue to the plaintiff a warrant upon the treasurer of the city and county for the payment of a certain sum of money. The court below, by an order made, dispensed with an undertaking on appeal on the part of the appellant, by virtue of that portion of section 946 of the Code of Civil Procedure which provides that "the court below may, in its discretion, dispense with or limit the security required by this chapter, when the appellant is an executor, administrator, trustee, or other person acting in another's right."

In taking the appeal the defendant was not acting in his individual capacity, for in that capacity he was not a party to the proceeding. He was proceeded against in his official capacity as auditor; it was against him as auditor that the judgment went in the court below, and in that capacity only could he appeal. He was not acting, therefore, in his own individual right, but in that of the city and county. The case, therefore, falls within the provision of the Code of Procedure cited, and the motion to dismiss the appeal is therefore denied.

We concur: McKinstry, J.; Morrison, C. J.; Thornton, J.; Myrick, J.; McKee, J.

THE STATE

v.

M. T. POLK *et al.*

(14 *Lea (Tennessee)*, 1.)

The bond which the statute requires the treasurer of the State to give is a joint and several bond, each obligor becoming bound for the entire penalty.

But if the treasurer execute a bond, which is accepted, binding each of the sureties for only an aliquot part of the penalty, the sureties cannot be held liable beyond the terms of the contract.

If the treasurer execute a bond more than a year after the commencement of his term of office, which is accepted, containing no words of relation, the sureties will only be liable for such funds as the treasurer then had in his hands, and such as were afterwards received by him during the time he continues in the discharge of the duties of the office.

FROM Davidson. Appeal from the Chancery Court at Nashville. A. G. MERRITT, Chancellor.

Attorney-General Lea and *Vertrees & Vertrees* for the State.

Colyar, Marks & Childress, Demoss & Malone, John Rhum, N. N. Cox, Webster & Taylor, and *McDowell* for defendants.

COOPER, J.—Bill filed May 12, 1883, by the State against M. T. Polk, late treasurer of the State, and the ꜰᴀᴄᴛꜱ. sureties on his official bond of May 20, 1882, for the recovery of such moneys as might be found due from the defendants severally to the State, by reason of the failure of M. T. Polk to properly account for and pay over to his successor in office funds which came to his hands in his official capacity as treasurer. Polk died pending the litigation, and the suit has been revived against W. L. Granberry as the administrator of his estate. Upon final hearing, the Chancellor rendered a decree in favor of the State against Granberry, as administrator, for $419,768.45, being the full amount of Polk's defalcation, with interest. But he found that the State was only entitled to recover from the sureties the sum of $39,111.82, and that the sureties had paid this sum to the State in the new issue of the Bank of Tennessee. He therefore gave a decree against the defendants for the costs, and the State appealed.

M. T. Polk was elected treasurer of the State for three successive terms of two years each, continuing in office from February 7, 1877, to January 5, 1883, when he absconded and left the State. He was elected in January, 1877, 1879, and 1881, on the last occasion for a term of two years, beginning January 15, 1881. The only bond given by him after this last election was executed by him and the defendants, his sureties, on May 20, 1882. It is agreed that Polk's defalcation, between the date of his last election and May 20, 1882, amounted to more than $100,000, exclusive of certain United States bonds and coupons amounting to $84,287.50. And it is also agreed that the defalcation after May 20, 1882, after allowing certain specified credits and calculating interest, amounted to $39,111.82, which has been paid by the sureties mentioned in the agreed statement of facts, in the new issue of the Bank of Tennessee.

The bond of May 20, 1882, is in the words and figures following, to wit:

STATE OF TENNESSEE,   NASHVILLE, TENNESSEE,
DAVIDSON COUNTY.   MAY 20, 1882.

Know all men, by these presents, that Marshall T. Polk, as principal, is held and firmly bound to the State of Tennessee in the penal sum of one hundred thousand dollars ($100,000), and that W. M. Duncan, James K. Polk, R. P. Cole. A. R. Duncan, W. Morrow, J. E. R. Carpenter, A. S. Horsley, Max Sax, F. T. P. Allison, and Will Polk, as sureties for the said Marshall T. Polk, are bound, severally, to the State of Tennessee each in the penal sum of ten thousand dollars, and no further, to the payment of which the parties aforesaid bind themselves, their heirs, executors, and assigns as aforesaid. The conditions of this obligation are, that if the said Marshall T. Polk shall perform all the duties enjoined on him by law to be performed, and shall faithfully account for and pay over all money which shall be received from time to time as treasurer of Tennessee, and shall deliver safely to his successor in office all books, vouchers, accounts, and effects whatever, and all moneys which shall soon come into his hands as treasurer aforesaid, then this obligation shall be null and void, otherwise to remain in full force and effect, binding said Marshall T. Polk in the full amount, and each surety to the extent of ten thousand dollars, and no further.

By the Code, section 222, the treasurer of the State is elected by a joint vote of both houses of the General Assembly, and holds his office for the term of two years, and until his successor is elected and qualified. By section 224 he is required to enter into bond, with ten or more sureties, in the sum of one hundred thousand dollars, payable to the State of Tennessee, and conditioned as set out in the bond of May 20, 1882. The bond is required to be acknowledged before a judicial officer, by whom its acknowledgment and sufficiency are to be certified, and the treasurer is thereupon to take a prescribed oath of office. The bond in controversy was acknowledged and certified, and the treasurer then took the oath of office.

The bond which the statute requires the treasurer to give STATE TREA-SURER'S BOND HELD JOINT AND SEVERAL. is manifestly a joint and several bond by the treasurer and his sureties, each becoming bound for the

entire penalty of the bond. This has been the general requirement of all official bonds in this State, and the uniform
practice under our statutes. The bond before us does not,
therefore, comply with the law. It undertakes in express
terms to limit the liability of each surety to an aliquot part of
the penalty, instead of extending the liability to the whole
penalty, as it should have done. Upon common-law principles
it is clear that the surety cannot be held bound beyond the
terms of the bond, for the obvious reason that per- <small>LIABILITY OF</small>
sons can only be held liable by the contract which <small>SURETIES AT COMMON LAW AND UNDER STA-</small>
they have actually entered into. Nichol *v.* Mc- <small>TUTES.</small>
Combs, 2 Yer. 83 ; United States *v.* Knight, 14 Pet. 301, 314.
An express statute has in one instance been held to extend
the liability of the principal and sureties on a bond beyond its
terms. Ogg *v.* Leinart, 1 Heis. 40. But there is no such
statutory provision in relation to bonds of the character of
the bond before us. By the Code, section 773, it is provided
that whenever any officer, required by law to give an official
bond, acts under a bond which is not in the penalty, payable
or conditioned as prescribed by law, or is otherwise defective,
such bond is not void, but stands in the place of the official
bond, subject, on its condition being broken, to all the remedies which the person aggrieved might have mantained on the
official bond of such officer, executed, approved, and filed according to law. So, also, by section 774, if any officer who is
required by law, or in the course of judicial proceedings, to
give bond for the performance of an act or the discharge of
duty receives money or property upon the faith of such bond,
he and his sureties are estopped to deny the validity of the
bond, or the legality of the proceeding under which the
money or property was obtained. But the first of these sections simply gives the same remedy, by motion or action, on
the irregular bond as if it had been entirely regular, "on its
condition being broken," without extending the relief beyond
the terms of the bond. And the other section is only in affirmance of the common-law principle of estoppel, when
money has been received on the faith of the bond, so as to
hold the parties to its terms. McLean *v.* State, 8 Heis. 22,
255 ; Galbraith *v.* Gaines, 10 Lea, 568, 574. These sections
do preclude the defendants, as is conceded by their learned
counsel, from insisting that the bond is void for irregularity

or that it is not subject to the same remedies as a regular statutory bond. But we are unable to see any ground upon which the sureties to the bond can be held liable beyond the terms of their contract as plainly expressed on its face.

The only other question is, whether the bond is only binding TIME COVERED on the sureties from the date of its execution, or re- BY BOND OF lates back to the beginning of the treasurer's term TREASURER. of office under the last election. In the former case, the liability of the sureties will be limited to the sum with which they were found chargeable by the chancellor. In the latter event, they will be liable to the extent of their respective obligations for the defalcations of the treasurer between the commencement of his last term of office and the date of the execution of the bond. This defalcation, it is agreed, as we have seen, amounted to over one hundred thousand dollars.

There can be no doubt, under our decisions, that where an officer has been re-elected to office, and either has in hand or receives, after he has qualified by giving bond, money belonging to the office, which he actually received or would have been authorized to receive during his previous term. the sureties on the new bond would be liable therefor. Yoakley *v.* King, 10 Lea, 67; State *ex rel. v.* Cole, 13 Lea, 367. It is equally true that the sureties on the new bond would not be liable for an actual defalcation committed during the previous term. State *ex rel. v.* Orr, 12 Lea, 725; Cox *v.* Hill, 5 Lea, 147. The common-law rule is, moreover, that the obligation of the sureties of a public officer for the faithful appropriation of money which he collected before they executed the bond can only exist when the money was in his hands as the bailee of the government at the time of the execution of the bond, unless the bond be retrospective in its terms. A previous wrongful appropriation of the money would convert his relation of bailee into that of defaulter. Farrar *v.* United States, 5 Pet. 373; United States *v.* Boyd, 15 Pet. 187; Board of Education *v.* Fonda, 77 N. Y. 350. Unless, therefore, our statutes regulating the execution of official bonds changes the rule, the sureties in the present case would only be liable for funds held by their principal as bailee at the date of their bond, or received afterwards; for there is nothing in the language of the bond of a retrospective character, and calling the attention of the sureties to the fact that they were binding themselves for the past as well as the future acts of their principal during his last official term. The statutes most certainly contemplate a qualification of the officer by the execution of an official bond before entering upon the discharge of his duties. But if he neglects to comply with the law, and the proper officers fail to compel him, or afterwards fail to take a bond stipulating to cover the past as well as the future, it is impossible to see how the sureties can be held liable beyond the terms of their bond. The Code, section 771, does provide that every official bond executed under the Code is obligatory on the principal and sureties thereon for any breach of the condition during the time the officer continues in office, or in the discharge of any of the duties of such office. But the object of this provision seems to be to extend the liability beyond the term, so long as the officer is in the discharge of any of the duties of the office —the constitution and statute continuing him in office until his successor is elected and qualified. And the liability is "for any breach of the condition" of the bond, bringing us back to the construction of its terms.

There is no error in the decree of the chancellor, and it must be affirmed, with costs.

BRIGGS

v.

HINTON *et al.*

(14 *Lea, Tennessee*, 233.)

Sureties on the official bond of a sheriff, against whom judgment has been rendered for default of sheriff, the sheriff alone appealing to the Supreme Court, are not in the jurisdiction of the latter court, and it can render no judgment against the sureties not appealing.

The surety in such case, though not bound by the Supreme Court judgment, is bound by the judgment below for the same original liability, and his payment of Supreme Court judgment without execution to the amount of the judgment below, is not an officious payment.

On the payment by the surety of the debt, he becomes entitled to the rights of the creditor in the appeal bond, and the sureties in the appeal bond are liable before the sureties on the official bond.

The surety on sheriff's bond, who pays a judgment against him and the

sheriff, for the default of a deputy sheriff, is entitled to have the bondsmen on the deputy sheriff's bond to the sheriff held liable.

A surety cannot hold his co-sureties liable for any payment made by
him which he was not bound to pay.

FROM Davidson.

APPEAL from the Chancery Court at Nashville. A. G.
MERRITT, Ch.

J. C. & J. M. Gaut for Briggs.
Demoss & Malone for Mrs. Stewart.
Robt. L. Morris for Tally heirs.
Nathaniel Baxter for Mrs. Horne.

DEADERICK, C. J.—On November 28, 1873, complainant
FACTS.   filed his bill in the chancery court at Nashville
against defendants, alleging that at the April term, 1862, of
the county court of said county, the complainant and M. S.
Stewart, with others not made defendants because insolvent,
became securities upon the official bond of defendant, Hinton,
who was qualified as sheriff of said county ; that said Hinton
afterwards appointed one Thomas Hobson as one of his deputies, and took from him an official bond in the penalty of
$10,000, for the faithful performance of his duties as deputy
sheriff, with Nicholas Hobson and Reuben Tally as his sureties ; that said deputy afterwards received for collection an
execution for $1,191.40, in favor of one Franklin against one
McKay, upon which said deputy made an insufficient return,
and thereupon, upon motion, judgment was rendered in favor
of Franklin, on April 17, 1868, for $1,503 and costs, against
Hinton and his sureties on his sheriff's bond in the circuit
court of said county ; that said Hinton consented to an appeal
by said N. and Thomas Hobson giving bond and security for
appeal, which they did, defendant, Narcissa Horne, becoming
security on said appeal bond.   By an amendment it is charged,
that Hinton alone appealed, and that none of the securities on
his official bond appealed, and a copy of said appeal bond is
exhibited with the amended bill.   The bill then alleges that
the other securities knew nothing of the appeal, and never
authorized the same or signed the bond therefor, and complainant insists that he was not liable on the judgment rendered on said appeal by the Supreme Court, as he did not
appeal from the judgment of the circuit court against him.

It is further alleged, that on December 16, 1872, judgment was rendered against all the defendants below by the Supreme Court, and against the parties to the bond for appeal for the whole amount of the judgment below, and that he, the complainant, has paid the same, amounting to $2,234.50.

It is further alleged, that Hinton, on March 28, 1870, took a judgment over on Thomas Hobson's bond against him and Nicholas Hobson, for $1,688.52, and that Reuben Tally, also a surety on Thomas Hobson's bond, was then dead, and no judgment was taken against him. Said Tally's heirs are made defendants to this bill.

Complainant insists he has the right to be reimbursed for payment of said judgment, by the parties who appealed and signed the appeal bond, Mrs. Horne being surety thereon is first liable, and to contribution by Mrs. Stewart, if not thus reimbursed, she being the administratrix of her late husband, M. S. Stewart, deceased, who was the only other solvent surety, beside complainant, of said Hinton.

A second amended bill was filed by complainant, making the administrator *de bonis non* of the estates of E. A. Horne and Reuben Tally defendants, the complainant claiming that he is entitled to be substituted to the rights of Hinton in the bond of Thomas Hobson, his deputy, who made the insufficient return, and that said Horne's and Tally's estates are solvent, and they are the only solvent sureties of said Thomas Hobson.

Answers were filed by Mrs. Horne, the administratrix of Horne, Tally, and Mrs. Stewart, the heirs-at-law of Tally and Stewart, and by Hobson and wife, raising questions presented in the report of the Referees.

The chancellor decreed that Hinton alone appealed from the judgment of the circuit court against him and his sureties on his official bond, without the knowledge of said sureties, and gave as sureties for the appeal N. Hobson and Narcissa Horne, in the sum of $3,006.22; that the judgment of the circuit court was affirmed by the Supreme Court, December 16, 1872, and was so entered as to include the sureties of both the appeal bond and official bond; that neither complainant nor M. L. Stewart knew of or consented to the appeal, nor was either of them on the appeal bond, and neither had

9 Cor. Cas.—11

knowledge of the suit until after the affirmance aforesaid, and that said judgment was paid by complainant.

The court further adjudged that the Supreme Court had no jurisdiction of complainant or of Stewart, and that the judgment against them was void. His Honor further held that the payment of the judgment by the complainant was officious as to Stewart, and that he had no right to call upon his estate for contribution; that the payment as to defendant, Horne, was a ratification of the appeal by complainant, and he is not entitled to recover against her; and that the second clause of the demurrer of Tally's heirs should be sustained; and the chancellor dismissed the bill as to Mrs. Stewart, Mrs. Horne, and Tally's heirs. But he rendered a decree in favor of complainant against Gannaway, the administrator of Tally, for the sum of $3,210, to be paid out of the personal assets of said estate, but as it appeared, no such assets had come, or would come to his hands, complainant was allowed to proceed to subject the property that had passed to the heirs. The chancellor also rendered a decree in favor of the complainant against Hinton, the sheriff, and Hobson, his deputy, for the sum of $3,210.

Complainant appealed from so much of the decree as refused him relief against Mrs. Horne and Mrs. Stewart as administratrix, and has also filed the record for writ of error.

The Referees find that it is satisfactorily shown that Hinton NO JUDGMENT alone appealed, and that Nicholas Hobson pro-AGAINST PARTIES NOT APPEALING. cured Mrs. Horne to join him in becoming surety on the appeal bond. Nicholas Hobson, and Mrs. Horne's husband, then dead, were sureties to Hinton on the deputy sheriff's bond, and the complainant and Stewart took no appeal; this is also apparent from the bond itself, as it purports to be the bond of Hinton, N. Hobson, and Mrs. Horne. And in this conclusion we think they are correct. The complainant and Mrs. Stewart not having in fact appealed, this court had no jurisdiction to render any judgment against them, and the fact that they did not appeal may be shown either by the record or by proof *aliunde:* 8 Hum. 489; 12 Heis. 303; 18 Wall. 466.

But although complainant was not bound by the Supreme Court judgment, he was bound by another judgment for the same original liability, upon which an execution might have issued, and would have issued, if he had not paid the amount demanded.

The Referees also find that when complainant paid the debt to Franklin he became entitled to the rights of Franklin in the appeal bond, and the sureties in the appeal bond, by the judgment of the Supreme Court, were liable for the debt before the sureties on the official bond; that the obligors in the bond of the deputy are next liable, and next the solvent sureties on the sheriff's official bond. They, therefore, recommended a reversal of the decree.

To this report Mrs. Horne and Tally's heirs except.

Mrs. Horne's first and second exceptions go to so much of the report as finds that she was surety on the appeal bond for Hinton only, and not for complainant, and in admitting parol evidence to contradict the recitals of the bond, that all the sureties on the official bond appealed.

The judgment of the circuit court was rendered against the sheriff and his sureties, and the record recites the defendants except, and *they* also pray an appeal, etc., which is granted, bond and security having been given according to law. The bond for appeal recites: "We, Jas. M. Hinton, N. Hobson, and Narcissa H. Horne" are held, etc.

The condition is: "James M. Hinton *et als.* have prayed," etc., "if said James M. Hinton *et als.* shall well and truly prosecute said appeal," etc. This bond is signed James M. Hinton, N. Hobson, Narcissa Horne. It is in legal effect the bond of Hinton. He cannot bind his sureties by his bond. His recital of "James M. Hinton *et als* have appealed," cannot be construed as imposing any obligations on persons who did not appeal or sign the bond. He is principal, and they sureties in the judgment appealed from, having different rights in respect to it. So that on its face the bond does not purport to be the bond of complainants, and, besides, the evidence is full and clear that neither the complainant nor the said Stewart had any knowledge that such an appeal was taken. That the fact that they did not appeal may be shown by parol evidence, even where a bond recites otherwise, we think is well settled in Tennessee. But in this case we think the bond itself shows upon its face that complainant and Stewart did not appeal.

Third.   It is said that the Referees erred in reporting that
SURETIES — CON- a surety who becomes bound in the course of legal
TRIBUTION — SUB-
ROGATION.   proceedings for the principal is not a co-surety of
the original surety for the debt.   They are both bound to the
creditor of the principal, but as between themselves it is held
that one who becomes surety, in the course of legal proceedings against the principal, has no right of contribution against
the original surety for the debt, but on the contrary the latter
has the right to be subrogated to the creditor's right against .
him: 4 Sneed, 191; 1 Lea, 612; 8 Hum. 489.   And this is
what the Referees correctly held.

Fourth.   It is next objected that the Referees erred in re-
PAYMENT   OF porting that Briggs, by paying the Supreme Court
JUDGMENT — ES-
TOPPEL.   judgment, was not estopped from impeaching it as
a valid judgment against himself.

As stated, the judgment of the Supreme Court was an affirmance of the judgment of the circuit court.   Both judgments were upon the same cause of action.   That of the circuit court was in force against complainant; an execution
might issue against him upon it.   He admitted his liability,
and was not bound to await the issuance of an execution.
The payment of the Supreme Court judgment was a satisfaction of the other and a discharge of the whole claim of the
creditor, and entitled complainant to all the creditor's rights
against those who were first or jointly bound with him.

Fifth.   It is also objected that the Referees did not report
JUDGMENT QUES- that the bond was illegally required to cover the
TIONING COLLAT-
ERALLY.   debt, etc., when it should have been for costs and
damages only.

However this may be, the court had jurisdistion of the persons of the principal and his sureties on the appeal bond, and
of the subject matter; and the validity of the judgment, even
if erroneous, cannot be questioned in this proceeding.

Sixth.   Hobson's bond, it is objected, did not cover the
time at which his default occurred.

The bond does bear date, whether by clerical mistake
TIME COVERED or otherwise, of a later period than the time of the
BY BOND.   default.   But all the parties in the cause recognize
it as subsisting and in force before the default, and it is so repeatedly stated to be during the progress of the cause below,
and there being no contest of this fact below, nor exception

to parol evidence going to show it, we assume it to be as accepted and treated, a bond covering the default in question.

We think, therefore, that the exceptions of defendant, Horne, are not well taken, and they will be overruled.

The heirs of Reuben Tally except to the report of referees, because, they say, that they are not properly joined in the bill.

Tally's heirs were first made parties to the bill; thereupon they demurred, and insisted the suit could not be maintained against them without having an administrator of said Tally's estate. An amended bill was filed making the administrator a party, and praying to have complainant's rights against said administrator adjudged, and insisting that, having paid Hinton's debt, he is entitled to be substituted to his rights against the estates and administrators of Tally and Horne on the bond of Thomas Hobson, said Tally and Horne being securities thereon.

The original and amended bills pray to have a decree against the administrators, and if necessary against the heirs for lands descended. All the parties are before the court, and complainant is entitled to have Thomas Hobson's, the defaulting deputy's, bondsmen held liable for the default *as* reported by the referees, and the exception is not well taken.

The referees report that Mrs. Stewart, as administratrix and Stewart's estate will be liable for one-half of the amount paid by complainant, which may not be realized from Mrs. Horne as surety on appeal, or from the sureties on Thomas Hobson's bond, the estate of Stewart and complainant being the only solvent sureties of Hinton.

The result is, that the exceptions to the report of the referees are overruled, and said report is in all respects confirmed, except that complainant's re- _{Report sub-tained.} covery must be limited to the amount of the judgment of the circuit court and interest thereon, and the costs of that suit, this being the extent of his liability. And any payment made by him in excess of this sum he was not legally bound to pay, and cannot hold defendants liable for.

· The costs of this court and of the chancery court will be paid by defendants.

Upon a petition to rehear, DEADERICK, C. J., said:

Complainant, Briggs, has presented a petition for rehear-
ᴘᴀᴄᴛ&.   ing as to one point. In the opinion heretofore
delivered, it is held that complainant did not appeal from the
judgment of the circuit court, and was legally bound to pay
only the amount of said judgment and costs thereon, and
that this was the extent to which he had a right to a decree
against any of the defendants, notwithstanding he paid the
full amount of the Supreme Court judgment, which was for
a larger amount than the judgment of the circuit court.

It is insisted that in order to entitle himself to substitution
ᴀᴜʙᴋᴏᴏᴀᴛɪᴏɴ   to the rights of Franklin, the creditor, against Mrs.
ᴏᴠ ᴡʜᴏ'ᴇ ᴅᴇʙᴛ Horne, the surety in the appeal bond, and others
ʙʏ ᴀᴜʀᴇᴛʏ ᴺᴼᵀ
ɴᴇᴄᴇᴀᴀᴀʀʏ.   bound with him, complainant was compelled to
pay the whole amount of said Supreme Court judgment before subrogation can take place. And section 262, Brandt on
Surety, is cited in support of this proposition. That section
does say that, as a general rule, subrogation cannot be enforced until the whole debt is paid to the creditor, nor can
there be an assignment of an entire debt to a surety, by operation of law, where the surety had paid but a part, and
still owes a balance to the creditor ; nor an assignment *pro
tanto*, the effect of which would be to give distinct interests
in the same debt to creditor and surety. In this section it is
said : " It would not subserve the ends of justice to consider
the assignment of an entire debt to a surety as effected, by
operation of law, where he had paid but a part of it, and
still owed a balance to the creditor." A surety is entitled to
be subrogated to the amount of his own indebtedness, which
he has paid, although it may be less than the whole indebtedness of said co-surety, subject to the creditor's right, and not
in hostility to it, and the rule that he can't have subrogation
until the whole debt is paid assumes that he is liable for the
whole debt, which is obviously correct, for he should not be
allowed to pay part and take the benefit of the whole.

It is argued that the complainant was compelled to pay to
the creditor the whole debt before subrogation could be enforced. But does it follow that, when he thus pays more
than the creditor had any legal right to claim of him, he
can compel the other surety to account to him for it? A
surety ordinarily has no greater rights against a co-surety

than the creditor has against them both. Brandt on Sur., sec. 232.

The amount paid by complainant was in excess of the judgment in the circuit court; and to the amount PAYMENT IN EX-of this excess was a payment of a sum due from CESS OF JUDG-MENT. VOLUN-defendants in the Supreme Court judgment, for TARY CONTRIBU-TION.

which the complainant was not liable, and was therefore to that extent the voluntary and officious payment of the debt of another, for which he cannot have contribution from other sureties for same debt.

The decree heretofore directed to be entered will in this respect remain undisturbed, and complainant's petition for rehearing will be dismissed, as the exceptions filed by Mrs. Horne to holding her liable for any part of the judgment may be allowed so far as valid in part, though not allowed to the extent claimed.

Mrs. Horne has also presented a petition to rehear, and insists that her sixth exception was improperly dis-TIME COVERED allowed. That exception we gather from the BY BOND.

opinion delivered in this cause, the exceptions themselves not now being with the record, that Hobson's bond did not cover the date at which the default occurred. This has reference to Thomas Hobson's bond to Hinton, made an exhibit to Hinton's deposition, and bearing date April 1, 1864.

This bond is signed by Thomas Hobson, Reuben Tally, E. A. Horne, E. P. Fort, and N. Hobson, and has a one-dollar United States revenue-stamp attached. Hinton does state that the above named parties were sureties of Thomas Hobson at the time of rendition of the judgment in the circuit court against him and his sureties, and exhibits the bond as stated, and said bond was assumed by the referees and by this court, in the opinion, to be the bond under which the default occurred. But a more careful examination of the record satisfies us that this was a mistake.

Complainant in his bill alleges that " on the 10th of April, 1862, said Hinton appointed Thomas Hobson one of his deputies, and took from him a bond, in the penalty of ten thousand dollars, for the faithful performance of his duties as deputy-sheriff, with Nicholas Hobson and Reuben Tally, now deceased, as his sureties." The bill then alleges that on June 2, 1862, a *venditioni exponas* was issued from the circuit

court of Davidson County, and placed in the hands of said
Thomas Hobson, who made an insufficient return thereon, for
which judgment was rendered against Hinton and his sureties in favor of William Franklin.

Again, it is alleged in the bill that in 1870 Hinton took judgment over against Thomas Hobson and Nicholas Hobson, his
sureties, for $1688.52, and costs ($5.90), and that Reuben Tally,
the other surety, was dead. These averments and specifications satisfy us that the facts charged were ascertained upon
inspection of the record, and that the bond under which the
default occurred was the bond for $10,000, dated April 1, 1862,
and to which N. Hobson and Tally were the only sureties.
That Hinton obtained judgment on this bond, and having the
other bond in his possession with Hobson, Tally, Horne and
Fort, dated April 1, 1864, for $20,000, executed during his sec-
ond term of office, he exhibited that with his deposition.
Another circumstance to show this bond was executed after
April 10, 1862, is that a United States revenue-stamp was
attached to it, such stamps not being in use here at the
alleged date of the first bond.

The decree will be accordingly so modified as to declare
that Horne was not one of Thomas Hobson's sureties at the
time of his default. In all other respects the former opinion
of the court will be adhered to, and the petition to rehear
filed.

SUBROGATION BETWEEN A SURETY ON A BOND TO STAY LEGAL PRO-
CEEDINGS AND A SURETY ON THE ORIGINAL DEBT. APPEAL BOND.—
The rule stated in the principal case—that a surety in a joint obligation on
which a judgment is had, from which judgment an appeal is taken by the
principal debtor, has a right of subrogation against the sureties on the
appeal bond to compel them to pay the entire judgment—is supported by
the authorities. Mitchell *v.* DeWitt, 25 Tex. 180; Jamison *v.* Garnett, 10
Bush (Ky.), 221.

BAIL BOND.—Similarly, it is held that, as between a surety and a bail
for the principal debtor, the bail should bear the burden of paying the
debt. Parsons *v.* Briddock, 2 Vern. 608 (approved in Wright *v.* Morley, 11
Ves. 12, 22, and Tennessee Hospital *v.* Fuqua, 1 Lea (Tenn.), 608, 612); W.
& T. Lead. Cas. in Eq. [3d Am. ed.] 158. And, conversely, that the bail
has no right of subrogation against the surety for the principal debt.
Smith *v.* Bing, 3 Ohio, 33.

INJUNCTION BOND.—The same principle applies in cases where judgment on the debt is enjoined by the principal debtor, and a bond to secure
the payment of the judgment is given; in such a case, if the surety has to

pay the judgment he may have recourse in equity against the surety in the injunction bond. Coles *v.* Anderson, 8 Hum. (Tenn.) 489. See also Brandenburg *v.* Flynn, 12 B. Mon. (Ky.) 397 ; Bohannon *v.* Combs, 12 B. Mon. (Ky.) 563, 577 ; Daniel *v.* Joyner, 3 Ired. (N. C.) Eq. 513 ; Douglass *v.* Fagg, 8 Leigh (Va.), 588, 599, 603. But, *contra*, see Semmes *v.* Naylor, 12 Gill & John (Md.), 358.

Similarly, sureties in instruments given to procure a stay of execution against the principal debtor, on a judgment, may be compelled by a surety for the original indebtedness who has paid, to reimburse him for such payment. Burns *v.* Huntingdon Bank, 1 Pen. & Watts. (Pa.) 395 ; Pott *v.* Nathans, 1 Watts & Serg. (Pa.) 155 ; Chaffin *v.* Campbell, 4 Sneed, Tenn. 184 ; Stout *v.* Vause, 1 Rob. (Va.) 169, 180.

BONDS GIVEN TO RELEASE THE PERSON OR PROPERTY OF THE PRINCIPAL DEBTOR FROM EXECUTION. — Where the person of a debtor, or enough of his property to satisfy the debt, has been taken in execution, such a taking in execution extinguishes the judgment, and consequently releases the sureties. Hence, if a bond with sureties is given to release the execution, such a bond takes the place of the person or property taken in execution, and is in no sense security for the judgment which has been extinguished. As a matter of course, then, the sureties have no recourse against the sureties in the original judgment. Knox *v.* Vallandingham, 13 Sm. & Mar. Miss. 526 ; see Givens *v.* Nelson, 10 Leigh (Va.), 382. The principle above stated is strikingly illustrated in Langford *v.* Perrin, 5 Leigh (Va), 600. In that case judgment was recovered on a bond against A and B, sureties, and D, the principal, but not against C, a surety : the judgment was levied on the property of D, who proceeded to give a forthcoming bond in which A, B, and X joined as sureties. A was compelled to pay a part of this bond and X the rest. It was held, first, that A had no right to enforce contribution against C, and, second, that A, B, and X were co-sureties, and hence that X could only enforce contribution against A and B, and could not compel them to reimburse him for all that he paid. President Tucker, in the course of his able separate opinion, states the principle of the case with great clearness and force : " By the levy of the execution on the property of the principal debtor, D, C, who was the surety in the original bond, was relieved of his responsibility. Clerk *v.* Withers, 1 Salk. 322 ; Cooper *v.* Chitty, 1 Burr. 34, cited by Roane, J., in Lusk *v.* Ramsay, 3 Munf. Va. 441. Had the property been permitted to remain in the hands of the officer and at his risk, C would have been discharged of the debt by the proceeds of the sale, unless they fell short of the demand. Others, however, intromitted : they became sureties,—not for the original debt, but for the return of the property upon the day of the sale,—and thus instrumental in withdrawing the property from the officer's control, and replacing it in the hands of the debtor, upon his engagement to deliver it up for sale. He has failed in his engagement ; he has forfeited his bond. Who ought to be responsible ? Not C, who had been absolved by the levy, but the sureties in the forthcoming bond, who, by their interference, have given a new credit to D and have enabled him to get back and to eloign the property which but for their interference would have paid the debt."

As to the question of the right of subrogation between X and A and B, he proceeds : " And, in like manner, we readily admit that the surety for a principal debtor may stand in the relation of principal to a supplemental surety, when that was the obvious meaning of the undertaking. Here, however, the forthcoming bond is a distinct and independent engagement ; not constituting part of, or being a supplement to, the original bond or contract, but binding the parties to the performance of a different act, who accordingly engage with each other upon new and different terms." Again, further on, he proceeds ι " In truth, A, B, and X are all chargeable for the breach of the forthcoming bond, not for the payment of the original debt ; for that had, in effect, been discharged by a sufficient levy." From these premises he reasons that A, B, and X, joining the new obligation of the forthcoming bond at the same time, were co-sureties.

PRINCIPLE ON WHICH A SURETY IN AN APPEAL BOND, ETC., IS HELD LIABLE TO REIMBURSE A SURETY OF THE ORIGINAL DEBT.—The cases relating to the right of subrogation of a surety against the surety in an appeal bond, etc., executed on behalf of the principal debtor, go on different grounds from those just stated in relation to forthcoming bonds, etc. The principle of these cases is variously stated. In Parsons *v.* Briddock, 2 Vern. 608 (a bail bond case), the Lord Chancellor (Lord Cowper) says: " The bail stands in the place of the principal, and cannot be relieved on any other terms than on payment of principal, interest, and costs, and the sureties in the original bond are not to be contributory." In Burns *v.* Huntingdon Bank, 1 Pen. and Watts (Pa.), 395 (bond given to stay execution), the court say: " and although both parties stood in the relation of surety towards the principal, they nevertheless stood in unequal equity between themselves, because the bail had so identified himself with the principal as not to be distinguished from him. Nor ought they to be distinguished here, inasmuch as they interposed to procure a personal advantage to the principal, and to the detriment of the surety, who might perhaps have been exonerated had the proceedings not been stayed against the principal, and in this respect the case is rather stronger than Parsons *v.* Briddock." This reasoning was approved in Pott *v.* Nathans, 1 W. & Serg. (Pa.) 155; Mitchell *v.* DeWitt, 25 Tex. 180 (case of appeal bond); Kellar *v.* Williams, 10 Bush (Ky), 216 (appeal bond) ; Douglass *v.* Fagg, 8 Leigh (Va.), 588, 599, 603 (injunction bond) ; White. & Tudor, L. C. in Eq. (3d Am. ed.).

It must be borne in mind that, in general, sureties for the same indebtedness, though by different instruments, executed at different times, are co-sureties and entitled to contribution from one another. Craythorne *v.* Swinburne, 14 Ves. 160 ; Dering *v.* Earl of Winchelsea, 1 Cox, 318. But it may also happen that as between several sureties some of them bear the relation of principals to the rest, and extrinsic evidence is admissible to show that such is the fact. Craythorne *v.* Swinburne, 14 Ves. 160. In the like manner, it is conceived that where there is personal security and the security of things [such as a pledge, mortgage, etc.] for the same debt, the personal security may be a principal debtor as to the "real" security, or *vice versa.* In Parsons *v.* Briddock, 2 Vern. 608, the arrest of the principal debtor gave the creditor a lien against the body of such debtor for the security of his debt. As between this security and the surety for the debt, it is plain that the former was the principal. Now, the bail bond was given in the place of this lien against the body of the debtor, and hence it also sustained the relation of principal to the personal surety for the debt.

This, it is conceived, is the explanation of the case of Parsons *v.* Briddock. Whether the same principle applies to the case of a surety on an appeal or injunction bond is perhaps doubtful. If the judgment against the principal debtor, although it merges the debt, can be regarded as a *security* for the debt, then the explanation of the case of Parsons *v.* Briddock, *supra,* would apply.

STATE
v.
NEVIN.

(Advance Case, Nevada. July 25, 1885.)

Public officers who are intrusted with public funds and required to give bonds for the faithful discharge of their official duties are not mere bailees of the money, to be exonerated by the exercise of ordinary care and diligence. Their liability is fixed by their bond, and the fact that the money is stolen from them without any fault or negligence on their part does not release them from liability on their official bonds.

APPEAL from a judgment of the district court of the first judicial district, Storey County, entered in favor of the plaintiff. The opinion states the facts.

W. E. F. Deal and *William Woodburn*, for ap, llant.

W. H. Davenport, attorney-general, and *J. A. Stephens*, district-attorney, for respondent.

HAWLEY, J.—This action was brought against the county treasurer of Storey County, and the sureties upon FACTS. his official bonds, to recover an amount of money admitted to be deficient in the accounts of the county treasurer. The answer alleges that the money was forcibly taken by robbers from the treasurer and carried away by irresistible force "without any fault or negligence, or want of reasonable care or diligence, in the preservation and care of said sum of money, so that said sum of money was entirely lost to the treasury of said county, and no part thereof has ever been recovered." The district court sustained a demurrer which was interposed to this answer, upon the ground that the facts stated did not constitute any defence to the cause of action.

Was this ruling of the court correct?

The condition named in the official bonds " is such that if the above-bounden, Dennis Nevin, shall well and truly and faithfully perform and execute the duties of treasurer of the County of Storey, now required of him by law, and shall well, truly, and faithfully execute and perform all the duties of such office of treasurer required by any law to be enacted subsequently to the execution of this bond, then this obligation to be void and of no effect, otherwise to be and remain in full force and effect."

Appellant insists that his responsibility under this contract is simply that which the common law imposes upon a bailee for hire; that he is not in any sense an insurer of the moneys in his custody, and should not be held responsible for the money that was stolen from him, and taken by the use of irresistible force without any negligence or fault or want of care on his part.

The great weight of the authorities upon this subject is PUBLIC OFFICERS adverse to the views contended for by appellant. NOT BAILEES, BUT ARE LIABLE The general rule upon this subject is to the effect FOR MONEY STOLEN. that public officers who are intrusted with public funds and required to give bonds for the faithful discharge of their official duties are not mere bailees of the money, to be exonerated by the exercise of ordinary care and diligence; that their liability is fixed by their bond; and that the fact that money is stolen from them without any fault or negligence upon their part does not release them from liability on their official bonds.

Recognizing the almost universality of this rule, appellant AUTHORITIES. contends that the decisions against him are founded upon the peculiar wording of the bonds, or provisions of the statute, to the effect that the officer shall safely keep and pay over all moneys coming into his hands. It is true that in United States *v.* Prescott, 3 How. 588; Com. *v.* Comly, 3

Penn. St. 374; State *v.* Harper, 6 Ohio St. 610; Inhabitants of Hancock *v.* Hazzard, 12 Cush. 112, and other cases, considerable stress is placed upon this language in the bond. Thus, in United States *v.* Prescott, the court said: "The condition of the bond has been broken, as the defendant, Prescott, failed to pay over the money received by him, when required to do so; and the question is, whether he shall be exonerated from the condition of his bond, on the ground that the money had been stolen from him? The objection to this defence is, that it is not within the condition of the bond, and this would seem to be conclusive. The contract was entered into on his part, and there is no allegation of failure on the part of the government; how, then, can Prescott be discharged from his bond? He knew the extent of his obligation when he entered into it, and he has realized the fruits of his obligation by the enjoyment of the office. Shall he be discharged from liability, contrary to his own express undertaking? There is no principle upon which such a defence can be sustained. The obligation to keep safely the public money is absolute, without any condition, express or implied; and nothing but the payment of it, when required, can discharge the bond." But there are an equal or greater number of cases like Muzzy *v.* Shattuck, 1 Denio, 233; District Township *v.* Morton, 37 Iowa, 550; Inhabitants *v.* McEachron, 33 N. J. L. 340; Boyden *v.* United States, 13 Wall. 17, and State *v.* Moore, 12 Fed. Rep. 740, where the condition of the bond, like the one under consideration here, was for the faithful performance of the official duties, and the conclusions of the courts are substantially the same as announced in United States *v.* Prescott.

It is apparent that a bond requiring a faithful performance of official duty is as binding upon the principal and his sureties as if all the statutory duties of the officer were inserted in the bond.

In Indiana, the statutory conditions in the bond are the same as required by the laws of this State.

In Halbert *v.* State, 22 Ind. 130, the treasurer's bond was, however, conditioned not only for the faithful performance of his duties as the statute required, but also that he should "pay over all moneys according to law that might come into his hands as such treasurer." The court said: "It is objected that the latter branch of the condition was unathorized by law, and therefore of no effect. But if the condition for the faithful performance of his duties includes the paying over, according to law, of all moneys that might come into his hands as such treasurer, nothing is added to the legal effect of the bond by the latter branch of the condition. An examination of the various statutes bearing on the question shows clearly enough that one of the duties of a county treasurer is to pay over according to law all moneys that come into his hands as such treasurer; hence we shall consider the case as if the bond had been conditioned simply for the faithful performance of the duties of the office."

In Boyden *v.* United States, 13 Wall. 24, the court, referring to United States *v.* Prescott, said : " The condition of the receiver's bond in that case, it is true, was that the receiver should pay promptly when orders for payment should be received, while the bond in the case before us is conditioned that Boyden, the receiver, had truly executed and discharged, and should continue truly and faithfully to execute and discharge, all the duties of said office according to law. But the acts of Congress respecting receivers made it their duty to pay the public money received by them when ordered by the Treasury Department. . . . The bond therefore was an absolute obligation to pay the money, and differing not at all, in legal effect, from the bond in Prescott's case."

What are the duties of a county treasurer under the statutes of this State?

In addition to requiring an oath and an official bond, it is, DUTIES OF COUNTY TREAS- URER. among other things, provided that the county treasurer "shall receive all moneys due and accruing to his county, and disburse the same, in the proper orders issued and attested by the county auditor." 2 Comp. L. 2981.

[Other statutory duties omitted.]

Under these provisions, is it not manifest that it is the duty of county treasurers to safely keep the public money and pay it out only as provided by law? The fact that the county treasurer is required "to receive money, and enter it in his cash-book, implies, without any other special regulation, that he is to keep it, and, being required to keep it, it follows that he is to keep it safely. This is one of the duties

of his office he has undertaken faithfully to discharge."
Thompson *v.* Trustees, 30 Ill. 101.

Unless he safely keeps it, he could not exhibit it to the
commissioners, as required by law, and it could not be
counted.   Neither could he deliver it to his successor in
office.   The duty to safely keep the money is made absolutely clear by the provisions of the statute already quoted
and referred to.   But there are also other provisions which
are equally as strong and cogent.   If any officer charged
with the safe-keeping of public money converts the same to
his own use, or loans any portion of such money, he shall be
guilty of embezzlement.   Stat. 1881, 82; Stat. 1883, 96.

Could a county treasurer who converts the money to his
own use claim that he is not an officer who is charged with
the safe-keeping of the public money?   It would be a stigma
upon the law and a disgrace to the judiciary to say that he
could successfully maintain such a defence.   The statutes of
this State in relation to the duties of county treasurers are
almost identical with those of Indiana.

The Supreme Court of that State, in Halbert *v.* State,
supra, after quoting the statutory provisions, said : " By these
various provisions it is clearly seen that it is the duty of a
county treasurer to pay over the funds in his hands according
to law, which may be upon orders drawn upon him by the
auditor, or to his successor in office, and a failure to make
such payment constitutes a breach in his bond, conditioned
for the faithful performance of his duties ;" and declare that
the fact that the money was stolen from the treasurer without his fault did not " relieve him from the necessity of discharging the obligation imposed upon him by his bond." This
decision was followed in the subsequent cases of Morbeck *v.*
State, 28 Ind. 86; Rock *v.* Stinger, 36 Id. 348 ; and Linville *v.*
Leininger, 72 Id. 494.

In Iowa, where the statute is not as strong as in this State,
the same doctrine is held and applied to an officer upon a
bond conditioned for the performance of his duties " to the
best of his ability."   District Township *v.* Smith, 39 Iowa,
9; s. c., 18 Am. Rep. 39.

The statutes of this State are more stringent than the
statute of Ohio, except in relation to the conditions of the
bond.

In State *v.* Harper, 6 Ohio St. 610, the court said: "By accepting the office, the treasurer assumes upon himself the duty of receiving and safely keeping the public money, and of paying it out according to law. His bond is a contract that he will not fail, upon any account, to do those acts. It is, in effect, an insurance against the delinquencies of himself, and against the faults and wrongs of others in regard to the trust placed in his hands. He voluntarily takes upon himself the risks incident to the office and to the custody and disbursement of the money. Hence it is not a sufficient answer, when sued for a balance found to have passed into his hands, to say that it was stolen from him ; for even if the larceny of the money be shown to be without his fault, still by the terms of the law and of his contract he is bound to make good any deficiency which may occur in the funds which came under his charge."

We deem it unnecessary, upon this branch of the case, to specially refer to the numerous other authorities where the same doctrines are announced, as it is absolutely clear, from those already cited, that the distinction sought to be maintained by appellant that the conditions of the bond and the provisions of the statute of this State should be construed differently from the construction given in the decided cases cannot be maintained.

In many of the cases the courts have given an additional reason for their conclusions that a public officer cannot set up the defence of a robbery of the public funds in his possession. Thus, in United States *v.* Prescott, *supra,* Justice McLean, in delivering the opinion of the court, said: "The liability of the defendant, Prescott, arises out of his official bond, and principles founded upon public policy." After discussing Prescott's liability upon the bond, he adds: "Public policy requires that every depositary of the public money should be held to a strict accountability. Not only that he should exercise the highest degree of vigilance, but that he should keep safely the moneys which come to his hands. Any relaxation of this condition would open a door to frauds, which might be practised with impunity. A depositary would have nothing more to do than to lay his plans and arrange his proofs, so as to establish his loss, without laches on his part. Let such a principle be applied to our postmasters, collectors of the customs, receivers of public moneys, and others who receive more or less of the public funds, and what losses might not be anticipated by the public?"

In Com. *v.* Comly, *supra*, Gibson, C. J., in delivering the opinion of the court, said : "The opinion of the court in the case of United States *v.* Prescott is founded on sound policy and sound law. . . . The keepers of the public moneys, or their sponsors, are to be held strictly to the contract, for if they were to be let off on shallow pretences, delinquencies, which are fearfully frequent already, would be incessant." To the same effect are the decisions in District Township *v.* Morton, 37 Iowa, 553 ; United States *v.* Watts, 1 New Mex. 562 ; Commissioners of Jeff. Co. *v.* Lineberger, 3 Mon. 241.

The only defence recognized by any of the authorities in the United States at the present time, with the exception of Cumberland County *v.* Pennell, 69 Me. 357 ; s. c., 31 Am. Rep. 284, for the failure of a public officer charged with safe-keeping of the public funds to pay over the same, is where he is prevented from doing so by the act of God or the public enemy, without any neglect or fault on his part. We say the Maine case stands alone in its opposition to what it is pleased to term the new-born policy of the law. In that case some reliance seems to have been placed upon the case of Albany *v.* Dorr, 25 Wend. 440 ; but the principles of that case were repudiated in Muzzy *v.* Shattuck, *supra*, and hence we are authorized to say that the case in Maine in unsustained by any other recognized authority in any of the courts of the United States, Federal or State.

In United States *v.* Thomas, 15 Wall. 341, it was held that the act of a public enemy in forcibly seizing or destroying property in the hands of a public officer, against his will, and without his fault, is a discharge of his obligation to keep such property safely, and of his official bond, given to secure the faithful performance of that duty, and to have the property forthcoming when required.

Bradley, J., in delivering the opinion of the court, questions the correctness of some of the extreme views stated in some of the authorities referred to, and claims that broader language was used than was necessary where the defence set up was that the money was stolen, and says that "a much more limited responsibility" than was indicated in the lan-

9 Cor. Cas.—12

guage in Prescott's case " would have sufficed to render that
defence nugatory." But there is no declaration of any legal
principle contained in this opinion that would justify a court
in permitting such a defence as was sought to be interposed
in this case. It is said that public officers are bailees, "but
they are special bailees, subject to special obligations. It is
evident that the ordinary laws of bailment cannot be invoked
to determine the degree of their responsibility."

In United States *v.* Humason, 6 Sawy, 201, the court permitted the defence that the officer with the money was on a
steamship which was lost at sea, and the officer drowned and
the money lost in the Pacific Ocean. The doctrines announced
in that case are similar to the case of United States *v.*
Thomas, and do not in any manner militate against the general views we have expressed.

In State *v.* Moore, the defendant, who was county treasurer,
answered that he ought not to be held upon his bond because
Mississippi County " being overrun with tramps, thieves, robbers, public enemies, the money could not be safely kept in
said county," and that for the purpose of keeping it safely he
deposited to his credit, as treasurer, in a bank in St. Louis,
which failed, whereby the money was wholly lost. The court
said: "Such an answer as this, we think, is insufficient to
shield defendant from liability in any view which can be taken
of the case. If the obligation assumed by defendant in his
bond to deliver over to his successor in office all money belonging to the county can only be met or discharged by making such delivery or payment, it is clear that the facts set up
in the answer, and admitted to be true, constitute no defence.
That the above rule is a correct one, governing in such cases,
is established by the following authorities" (citing State *v.*
Powell, 67 Mo. 395, and the various decisions of the Supreme
Court of the United States). " If, on the other hand, under
the rule laid down in the case of United States *v.* Thomas, 15
Wall. 337, defendant is to be regarded as a bailee and exempt
from liability to pay when the loss is occasioned by the act of
God or a public enemy, he would still be liable under the
facts stated in the answer, because they show that the loss was
not occasioned in either of these ways. The tramps, thieves,
and robbers who, it is alleged, overrun Mississippi County,
while they are enemies to the peace and safety of the public

and social order, they are not public enemies in the legal sense of these words. By enemies is to be understood public enemies, with whom the nation is itself at open war; and not merely robbers, thieves, and other private depredators, however much they may be deemed, in a moral sense, at war with society. Losses, therefore, which are occasioned by robbery on the highway or by depredations of mobs, rioters, insurgents, and other felons are not deemed losses by enemies within the meaning of the exception." 12 Fed. Rep. 790.

The action of the district court in sustaining the demurrer to the answer was correct.

The other positions taken by appellant relative to the time when the cause of action could be commenced are wholly untenable. Having admitted the defalcation and claimed the right to interpose the defence inserted in his answer, the State was not compelled to wait until the close of the appellant's term of office before commencing an action upon his bond.

The judgment of the district court is affirmed.

[See 40 Am. Rep. 675 as to meaning of " faithfully" in such bond. See State *v.* Chadwick, 10 Oregon, 465.—ED.]

INHABITANTS OF MACHIASPORT *v.* SMALL and others.

(77 *Maine,* 109.)

In debt upon a collector's bond, before the defendant is put to proof of a plea of performance, the plaintiff must show, either that the collector has been clothed with legal authority to collect taxes, or that he actually did collect them.

When such authority is shown, or the collector has been proved to have collected taxes, the burden under such plea rests upon the defendants to prove that the collector has performed the condition of his bond, by having faithfully performed all the duties of his office, or by having legally disposed of the taxes which he is shown to have collected.

In such action, on such issue, if the defendant fails to support the plea, the penalty of the bond is forfeit, and judgment should be entered therefor.

After judgment for the penalty of a bond of defeasance, on motion of the defendant, the penalty thereof may be chancered as the equitable rights of the parties may reqnire, and execution should issue for the sum fixed by the court.

To reach this result the court may send the cause to an auditor to hear the parties and report the facts to the court.

When the penalty of a bond of defeasance is sued for, and breaches are not assigned in the declaration, the defendant may have oyer of the bond, and if it have a condition, the court on motion will order the plaintiff to assign the breaches upon which he relies, and the defendant may interpose his defence by way of brief statement under the general issue.

Two assessors are not authorized to assess a tax when a third assessor has not been qualified.

An assessor's warrant failing to show what year's State tax was included in the assessment, and the precise date of the town meeting at which the town tax was voted, and when the collector should account to the State and county treasurers respectively for the State and county taxes, and authorizing a distress immediately, without waiting twelve days, and not authorizing the arrest of a taxpayer if he is possessed of "tools, implements, and articles of furniture which are by law exempt from attachment for debt," is invalid.

ON report.
Debt upon a tax collector's bond.
The facts are stated in the opinion.
John C. Talbot for plaintiffs.
McNichol & Sargent for defendants.

HASKELL, J.—Debt upon the bond of a collector of taxes
FACTS.   for the town of Machiasport, conditioned for the faithful performance of his duty for the year 1876.

The plea was *non est factum* with a brief statement of performance.

The plaintiffs read in evidence the bond, the record of the assessment of the tax for the year 1876, the commitment of the same to the collector, and the warrant to him for the collection of the tax. It was admitted that defendant Small was collector of taxes for the plaintiffs for that year, There was no other evidence showing a breach of the bond. The case comes forward on report.

Had the taxes been legally assessed, and the commitment
DEBT ON BOND. and warrant been in legal form, the collector
BURDEN OF would have been chargeable under his bond for the
PROOF. taxes so committed to him for collection, Inh'b'ts of Trescott *v.* Moan, 50 Maine, 347; and the plaintiffs would have made out a *prima facie* case. The burden would then have rested upon the collector to substantiate his plea of performance by showing a faithful discharge of the duties of his office. This he is not required to do, until the plaintiffs have shown him

legally bound to perform those duties. The law did not require him to execute a precept that could afford him no protection, nor to collect a tax illegally assessed. Until he is shown to be legally bound to perform official duty, he is not called upon to justify its performance. Under a plea of performance to a suit upon an official bond, the defendant is not required to justify, until he is shown to be legally bound to perform faithfully some particular duty, or to be chargeable with some particular property. In this case, the defendant Small is not chargeable with the collection of any tax, until he is shown legally bound to collect it,—that is, until he has been provided with a sufficient precept, giving him lawful authority so to do.

Much confusion has arisen as to when proof is required to support a plea of performance to a suit upon a PLEA OF PER-FORMANCE ON bond. This is largely due to the relaxation of the BOND. PROOF common law rules and methods of pleading. When a special plea of performance is interposed in such cases, the plaintiff is required to make replication assigning the breach relied upon, and if the bond is for the performance of covenants and agreements, several breaches may be assigned, and the jury must assess the damages when on issue framed to them they find the condition broken. R. S. c. 82, §§ 20, 32.

After replication the defendant must either demur or rejoin; and if the rejoinder is a traverse, then on issue taken the burden rests upon the plaintiff to prove the breaches assigned, and if the bond be one for the performance of covenants and agreements, to prove the damages. Philbrook *v.* Burgess, 52 Maine, 271; McGrogory *v.* Prescott, 5 Cush. 67; see Bailey *v.* Rogers, 1 Maine, 186; but if the rejoinder is an affirmative plea supporting a plea of performance, the burden rests upon the defendant to maintain the truth of his plea, unless the bond is conditioned for the performance of covenants and agreements, when the burden rests upon the plaintiff to prove both the breach of it and his damages. Philbrook *v.* Burgess, *supra*, and case cited.

So when performance is pleaded by brief statement to a suit upon a bond, if it be conditioned for the performance of covenants and agreements, the burden rests upon the plaintiff to prove its breach and damages; but if the bond is simply a bond of defeasance, then the burden is upon the defendant to prove performance as alleged in his brief statement, and the issue is for the jury to find whether the condition has been broken, and if they find that it has, then judgment goes for the penalty of the bond, and on motion that the penalty be chancered as the equitable rights of the parties may require, the court, with the aid of necessary auditing officers, fixes the amount for which execution should issue.

The bond in this case is of the latter class. It is conditioned to be void upon the faithful performance of official duty. If it is suggested that no further proof is required under the rule above stated than for the plaintiffs to read in evidence their bond, a sufficient reply is, that the bond when so put in evidence shows an official duty upon the performance of which the bond is to be void. The law does not cast that duty upon the colleetor until the plaintiffs show him legally chargeable therewith. That is, until a condition of things appears upon which the bond becomes effective, the defendant has no performance required of him. So if the plaintiffs are unable to charge the defendant Small with a legal duty to perform, for want of a legal tax, a legal commitment, or a legal warrant to collect the tax, they must prove that he actually received taxes,—that is, money,—touching which the bond can operate, and then he is put to proof of his plea of performance. If he fails upon the issue, the penalty of the bond is forfeit, and the court will award execution for the actual damages sustained. Philbrook *v.* Burgess, *supra ;* Clifford *v.* Kimball, 39 Maine, 413. The same burden would rest upon the plaintiffs if the issue had been reached after a special plea of performance, for in that method of procedure, after plea of *omnia performavit* the plaintiffs would reply, either a legal tax, a legal commitment, and a sufficient warrant, or that the collector received certain moneys in the discharge of his office for which he had not accounted ; and then, if the defendants denied either the sufficiency of the tax, or of the commitment, or of the warrant, or that any such documents existed, or that the collector received the moneys specified, it would be a negative plea, either raising an issue of law, or fact, which the plaintiffs must sustain and prove ; but if the defendants confessed these issues, and rejoined that the collector had performed his duty under his warrant, or had accounted for the moneys with which the plaintiffs had charged him, then they would have tendered an affirmative plea, and if the plaintiffs took issue thereon, the burden would rest upon the defendants to prove performance. So in suit upon a bond . of defeasance, where the penalty is sued for, if breaches are not assigned in the declaration, the defendant may have oyer of the bond and an order from the court that the plaintiff specify the breaches upon which he relies, and then the defendant by way of brief statement can state his defence, showing how many of the affirmative facts alleged by the plaintiff he denies, and how far he takes upon himself the burden of proving his own performance of the conditions of his bond. This latter method is one that has been adopted in some of the important causes of this nature recently tried in this State.

The assessment, commitment, and warrant in this case appear to be signed by only two assesssors. It does not appear that the plaintiffs elected or had another assessor duly qualified to act during the year 1876. "Two assessors are not authorized to assess a tax when they alone have been qualified." Inhabitants of Williamsburg *v.* Lord, 51 Maine, 599. Nor can they issue a warrant, Sanfason *v.* Martin, 55 Maine, 110. The warrant fails to show what year's State tax was included in the assessment; also, the precise date of the town meeting at which the town tax was voted; also, when the collector should account to the State and county treasurers for the State and county taxes respectively. It authorizes the arrest of taxpayers for want of property whereon to make distress immediately, without waiting twelve days as required by statute. Nor does it authorize the arrest of any taxpayer if he is possessed of "tools, implements, and articles of furniture, which are by law exempt from attachment for debt." It is so unsound, that a discussion of its merits would be idle. Inhabitants of Orneville *v.* Pearson *et als.* 61 Maine, 552; Pearson *v.* Canney, 64 Maine, 188; Inh'b'ts of Harpswell *v.* Orr, 69 Maine, 333.

The plaintiffs have failed to make out a *prima facie* case from the insufficient authority with which they clothed their collector to perform his duty, and he is chargeable under his bond only for the taxes which he has actually received, and for which he has failed to account.

The agreement of the parties does not stipulate what disposition shall be made of the case under the conclusions of this opinion, therefore to afford complete justice to both parties it is ordered, that

The action stands for trial.

PETERS, C. J., DANFORTH, VIRGIN, EMERY, and FOSTER, JJ., concurred.

STATE

v.

STEVENS.

(Advance Case, Indiana. September 17, 1885.)

§ 6031 of Revised Statutes of 1881 of Indiana provides that any officer who shall take any fee other than is allowed by the provisions of the act shall be deemed guilty of a misdemeanor, and on conviction thereof shall be fined, not exceeding $100, and shall be liable on his official bond to the party injured for five times the illegal fees taken, and the same may be recovered in the circuit court. In a suit on an official bond to recover five times the illegal fee charged, it was held that the clause of the statute authorizing such recovery was not unconstitutional as putting a person in jeopardy twice for the same offence.

Koerner *v.* Oberle, 56 Ind. 284, holding that the constitutional inhibition just referred to prevented the recovery of primitive damages for an illegal act punishable as a crime, approved and distinguished on the grounds—(1) that the clause in question was rather intended as a compensation for the person injured than as a penalty pure and simple, and (2) that each part of § 6031 provided but a part of the punishment of the crime; that the fine imposed was but a part of the penalty, the other part being the payment of five times the illegal charge.

Held, that said § 6031 of Rev. Statutes, 1881, applies to bonds executed before it was enacted.

Averments of declaration as to the illegal charge having been made by defendant in his official capacity held sufficient.

An action brought under § 6031 on an official bond of a clerk of court to recover for an illegal fee taxed as costs does not attack the judgment collaterally.

Such an action is an action on an official bond, and comes under the provision of the Statute of Limitations in regard to official bonds, and not those relating to the recovery of a penalty.

APPEAL from Decatur circuit court.

John S. Scobey for appellant.

Miller & Gavin for appellees.

MITCHELL, C. J.—The relator brought this suit on the official bond of Stevens, who was formerly clerk   ꜰᴀᴄᴛꜱ. of the Decatur circuit court. The action was based on section 6031 Rev. St. 1881. This section enacts that "any officer who shall charge, demand, or take any fee for any official act done or performed under the provisions of this act other than as is herein allowed and provided for shall be deemed guilty of a misdemeanor, and on conviction thereof shall be fined in any sum not exceeding one hundred dollars, and shall be liable on his official bond to the party injured for five times the illegal fees charged, demanded, or taken, and the same may be recovered, with costs, in the circuit court."

It is charged that the defendant Stevens, having been elected and qualified as clerk, took upon himself the duties of that office on the first day of November, 1875, and continued therein until the expiration of his term; that on the sixth day of February, 1877, a civil suit was commenced against the relator in the Decatur circuit court, which continued pending until the third day of July, 1879, when it was dismissed, at his costs; that upon the dismissal of the suit Stevens made up and taxed the costs for his services as clerk on the fee-books of the court, and that of the costs so taxed there was included in various specified items the sum of $20 in excess of his legal charges, which, on the twenty-ninth day of May, 1882, he demanded of the relator, and for which he issued a fee-bill on the fifth day of June, 1882. The relator prays judgment for $100, being five times the amount of the fees alleged to have been illegally charged and demanded. The court below sustained a general demurrer to the complaint, and the case comes here on this ruling.

It is argued by the learned counsel for the appellees that so much of the statute as authorizes the recovery of five times the illegal fees charged, in a suit by the orig-   ʀᴇᴄᴏᴠᴇʀʏ ᴏꜰ ꜰɪᴠᴇ ᴛɪᴍᴇꜱ ɪʟ- inal party on the official bond of the officer, is un-   ʟᴇɢᴀʟ ꜰᴇᴇꜱ ᴄʜᴀʀɢᴇᴅ.— constitutional, as being within the prohibition of   ᴛᴡɪᴄᴇ ɪɴ ᴊᴇᴏᴘ-ᴀʀᴅʏ. that part of the bill of rights which declares that "no person shall be put in jeopardy twice for the same offence." The extent of the argument on this point is the statement of the proposition by counsel for the appellees, and the citation in its support of Koerner *v.* Oberly, 56 Ind. 284.

In the appellant's brief we find no allusion to the question.

This leads us to conclude that the ruling below must have turned upon some other point. As the question is presented for decision, it would have been a source of satisfaction to the court if the learned counsel on both sides had favored us with such argument of it as their learning and ability led us to expect. Whatever may be said of the case above cited, we do not think it controls the decision of the one before us. That was a suit brought by a wife to recover damages for an unlawful sale of intoxicating liquor to her husband, who was in the habit of becoming intoxicated. Section 12, Acts 1873, p. 151, gave a right of action against any person so offending in favor of any person who should be injured thereby in person, property, or means of support. It authorized a recovery by any person so injured of all damages which might be sustained, "and for exemplary damages." The same act made it a misdemeanor for any person to sell intoxicating liquor to a person in the habit of becoming intoxicated, and provided a penalty, to be enforced by indictment or otherwise. It was held, in the case relied on, that, in so far as section 12 attempted to authorize the recovery of exemplary damages by the injured person, it was in conflict with the provision in the bill of rights above quoted, and therefore inoperative and void. It has been the settled rule of decision in this State since the case of Taber *v.* Hutson, 5 Ind. 322, that in all that class of torts for which, in 'addition to the .civil remedy allowed to the injured party, the wrong-doer was amenable to criminal punishment, exemplary or punitory damages could not be recovered in a civil action; while in the class not rising to the degree of criminality the injured party might, where the element of fraud, malice, gross negligence, or oppression mingled in the controversy, in addition to full compensation for all other damages, recover what is termed exemplary or punitive damages. Lytton *v.* Baird, 95 Ind. 349; Stewart *v.* Maddox, 63 Ind. 51, and cases cited.

As defined, compensatory damages are held to include, not

COMPENSATORY AND EXEMPLARY DAMAGES DEFINED. only such pecuniary loss or injury in a given case as is capable of approximately accurate calculation, but, in addition thereto, such a sum as may be supposed adequate to compensate "for injury to business or profession, reputation or social position, and for physical suffering,—as bodily pain, permanent disfiguration, etc.,—and for mental trouble,—as anguish of mind, sense of shame or humiliation, loss of honor, etc.,—all of which are considered compensatory, and not exemplary or punitive, damages." Exemplary or punitive damages, the terms exemplary and punitive being synonymous, are damages allowed as a punishment, or by way of example to deter others from the like offences, for torts committed with accompanying fraud, malice, or oppression. The rule of decision defining the class of cases in which exemplary damages would, and that in which such damages would not, be allowed rests wholly on judicial construction, and except in the case of Koerner *v.* Oberly, *supra*, and Schafer *v.* Smith, 63 Ind. 226, which involved the same statute and followed the first-named case, none of the cases in which the rule is declared and applied involve any question of legislative power.

Previous to the decision in the Koerner case the court seemed to regard the constitutional provision re- EXEMPLARY DAMAGES WHERE DEFENDANT IS PUNISHABLE CRIMINALLY. ferred to as an obstacle against its power to allow, or at least against the policy of allowing, exemplary damages in the class of cases where the defendant was also subject to criminal punishment. While the question of power was not in any case, so far as we know, directly determined, the prevailing rule was adopted by the court as being in consonance with the spirit of both the constitutional provision and the ancient common-law maxim, and as a safe middle ground in a controversy with which courts and lawyers are familiar. In Koerner *v.* Oberly it was distinctly ruled that the legislature was prohibited by the constitution from authorizing the infliction of exemplary damages for a wrong which was also punishable as a crime.

Whatever may be thought of the rule so far as it rests on judicial construction, in the opinion of the writer it is not that part of it which denies the infliction of punitory damages in some cases which is open to criticism, so much as that which permits it in any civil case. The assumption that the Penal Code should be supplemented by judicial legislation so as to allow damages to the injured party by way of punishment of the wrong-doer, in cases where none is inflicted by legislative enactment, is, as it would seem, much less defensible than the denial either to the courts or legislature of the right to add unlimited damages as a punishment in civil cases where a prescribed punishment is already attached to the offence. Whether the provision that "no person shall be twice put in jeopardy for the same offence" has technical application to the infliction of punishment by way of exemplary damages in civil cases, so as to prohibit it, has been the subject of much learned discussion. In Taber *v.* Hutson, *supra*, after suggesting that to allow exemplary damages might expose the defendant to double punishment in violation of the spirit of the bill of rights, it was said that "though that provision may not relate to remedies secured by civil proceedings, still it seems to illustrate a fundamental principle inculcated by every well-regulated system of government, viz., that each violation of the law should be certainly followed by one appropriate punishment and no more." In the case of Brown *v.* Swineford, 44 Wis. 282, Ryan, C. J., impliedly admitting that the rule which allowed exemplary damages in such cases was against the spirit of the maxim that no one should be twice vexed for the same offence, said : "The word 'jeopardy' is therefore used in the constitution in its defined technical sense at the common law. And in this use it is applied only to strictly criminal prosecutions by indictment, information, or otherwise." Expressing marked disapprobation of the rule, the learned court nevertheless held a constitutional provision similar to that under consideration did not stand in the way of allowing exemplary damages in civil suits, even where the act complained of was punishable as a crime. So, in the case of Elliott *v.* Van Buren, 33 Mich. 49, speaking upon this subject, Campbell, J., said : "The argument that a person is thereby punished twice, within the constitutional and common-law rule, is entirely fallacious. The maxim at common law that no one should be twice vexed for the same cause, when it applied at all, prevented a second prosecution as well as a second punishment, and if it applied to cover civil damages would cover the whole, and not merely what is assumed to be part, of them. But there is no analogy between the civil and criminal remedies. The punishment by criminal prosecution is to redress the grievance of the public, while the civil remedy is for private redress."

With great respect for the learned judges from whose opinions we have quoted, we are neverthless not persuaded to adopt either the reasoning so cogently set forth or the conclusions reached. Whatever may be said in respect of the technical application of the constitutional provision which prohibits double punishment for the same offence to civil remedies, it is difficult to see how the practical result is in any degree mitigated, if, in fact, after all other proper elements of damage are considered and allowed in a civil case for a tort for which the defendant is liable to be punished criminally, the jury may assess an unlimited sum as punishment by way of exemplary damages. It is no answer to the constitutional guaranty against double punishment to say that the penalty limited and prescribed by the Penal Code is to redress the grievance of the public, while the other unlimited and undefined punishment awarded by way of exemplary or punitive damages is for private redress. To the extent that damages are awarded in any case for private redress they cannot be exemplary. The private injury is fully redressed when all its elements are considered and compensated for. Exemplary damages only commence at the point where full private or compensatory damages end ; and so long as there remains any private injury to be redressed, no exemplary damages are or can be awarded.

The result of it is that to the extent that exemplary damages are allowed in any case which is punishable criminally, the defendant is, or is liable to be, twice punished for the same offence : once by the State for the public grievance, and again by the injured party for example's sake, for the supposed benefit of the public, to deter others from the like offending. Austin *v.* Wilson, 4 Cush. 273. The fact that the damages allowed under the name of the punitive or exemplary go to the benefit of the injured party renders the punishment no less real ; and, as is said by a learned author, "after there has been one trial in which the moral culpability of the defendant has been tried with a view to punishment in the interest of the public, any other trial for the same purpose, whatever may be the form of the proceeding, is, in substance and effect, putting the accused again in jeopardy of punishment for the same offence, and vexing him again for the same cause." 1 Suth. Dam. 740, 741. In Fay *v.* Parker, 53 N. H. 342, this question was fully considered in an opinion conspicuous for its research and learning. The conclusion was there reached that the fundamental maxims of the common law, as well as the provision in the bill of rights, were an effectual barrier against the infliction of punitory damages in a civil case where the defendant was subject to be criminally punished for the same offence. PARKER, J., delivering the judgment of the court, said: "These maxims apply both to criminal and civil proceedings. . . . If, then, this constitutional prohibition of a double penalty is indeed nothing more than an affirmation of the general principle of the common law, applicable alike to civil and criminal cases making a judgment in one action a bar to another action founded on the same cause, it follows logically that punitive damages are a violation of the general principle of the common law as well as of the constitution." In further illustration, the learned judge said: "Just as firmly is the right secured to him that in all cases wherein he is charged with conduct such as calls for punishment for the sake of public vengeance or public example—and to him it can make no difference, so long as the blow must fall, whether it comes from the arm of the civil or criminal law—that he shall be permitted to confront his accusers and their witnesses face to face, and not be tried upon depositions; and that he should go free unless his guilt is proven beyond a reasonable doubt."

This much by way of a re-examination of Koerner *v.* Oberly, *supra*, seemed proper with a view of determining the ground upon which the decision in the case before us should rest; and, upon the assumption that the statute there in question authorized the infliction of unlimited, unrestricted exemplary damages as punishment for an offence which was also made punishable as a crime, we adhere to the ruling in that case with renewed confidence. It cannot be said that where the legislature has prescribed one definite penalty as the punishment for an offence, it may, in addition, authorize the injured party, under the guise of exemplary damages, to subject the offender to another uncertain, indefinite punishment, which is to be measured only by the varying and unrestrained discretion, or it may be passion, of the jury. If the provision that "no one shall be twice put in jeopardy for the same offence" is, as this court has recognized it to be, a sure protection against the power of the courts in that regard, it must be deemed equally potential against the power of the legislature. It cannot be maintained in reason that it shall be interpreted to mean that the courts cannot adjudge a second punishment for the same offence except when expressly authorized by the legislature, for the reason that in so far as the legislature attemps to authorize such second punishment the barrier of the constitution is as effectual against it as it is against the court.

While the foregoing considerations lead us to adhere to the ruling in Koerner *v.* Oberly, they at the same time direct us to the conclusion that the act here in question RECOVERY OF FIVE TIMES ILLEGAL FEES NOT A DOUBLE PUNISHMENT; is not obnoxious to the objection claimed. The distinction between the case relied on and that under consideration is that, in the first, the legislature, after affixing to the offence a prescribed punishment, undertook to authorize the recovery of exemplary damages, which, as we have seen, implies nothing less than a second punishment for the same offence by way of unrestricted damages for the sake of public example. In the statute here involved the legislature has done nothing more than to fix or measure by a definite sum the amount which the injured party shall be entitled to recover on the official bond of the public officer. While the act of taking or making the unlawful charge or demand is made a misdemeanor, punishable by a fine to the State, the legislature, not by way of additional or double punishment, but for the purpose of defining the liability of the officer to the injured party, has provided that he shall be liable on his official bond in five times the amount of the fees illegally charged, demanded, or taken. In such a case it can be truly said that " the punishment by criminal prosecution is to redress the grievance of the public, while the civil remedy is for private redress." The legislative assumption is that the injury done by the public officer who makes the illegal charge will not be adequately compensated by leaving the parties to their common-law rights and liabilities, and accordingly it has provided what in its judgment would be adequate compensation to the one, and the just liability of the other.

There is in this no element of exemplary or punitory damages. It cannot be said that part of the recovery is allowed by way of example, or for the punishment of the offender, when it is apparent that the legislative NOR EXEMPLARY DAMAGES.

purpose is nothing more than to fix the amount of civil liability of the officer as a measure of compensation for the injury. Who shall say that a person from or against whom an inconsiderable sum is illegally demanded or charged by an officer who is armed by law with compulsory process to enforce his demand, such person being obliged to incur the expense of a suit to redress his grievance, is more than compensated by a recovery of five times the amount so charged, demanded, or taken? This is the measure of recovery fixed in all cases, and no circumstances of fraud, malice, or oppression can make it greater.

While it may be conceded that the statute which thus fixes the amount is in a sense penal, the penalty prescribed is nevertheless fixed by way of compensation for the injury sustained, and to fix the liability of the officer on his bond executed to the State for the injurious act. The whole penalty prescribed for the offence, taking the statute altogether, is the fine prescribed to the State, and the liability on the official bond fixed by way of recompense to the injured party ; and, even regarding the whole statute as penal, it cannot be said that the person offending has been put in jeopardy of the penalties prescribed until he has been tried for the misdemeanor, and has also answered for the penalty fixed to the injured party as his compensation. Statutes which fix or limit the amount of recovery which may be had by way of compensation on the bond of a public officer, or by way of redress for an injury sustained by the tortious act of another, are one thing ; while those which provide for unrestricted exemplary damages by way of public example, after the injured party has been allowed full compensation, are quite another. As was said in Blatchley *v.* Moser, 15 Wend. 215 : " The one may be said to be a private remedy ; the other, a public one for the same offence."

All criminal punishment is of necessity punitory, and, in a ALL CRIMINAL degree, exemplary ; and where an offender is made PUNISHMENT IS PUNITORY. the subject of example by being once punished criminally, and is again subjected to exemplary damages in a civil suit for the same offence for a public example, he is put to the hazard of being set up as an example twice for the same offence. Where, however, a statute makes certain conduct a misdemeanor, and annexes to it a prescribed fine to the State, and also provides that the wrong-doer shall be liable to the injured party in a fixed or limited sense, it is certain from the beginning what the consequence of the offence may be, and there is no possibility that the penalties may overlap each other, so as to put him in jeopardy of being tried twice, or suffering double the punishment prescribed for the same offence. Of the power of the legislature to fix the amount of liability on an official bond, recoverable as compensation by the person injured, there can be no question ; and this power is not affected by the consideration that the act out of which the liability grows is also punishable criminally ; nor can it be doubted that it has the power to prescribe fines and penalties against certain acts, and at the same time fix or limit the civil liability for the same acts.

LEGISLATURE MAY FIX LIABILITY ON OFFICIAL BOND.

The next objection urged against the complaint is that the statute imposing the liability sued for not having been enacted until after the bond in suit was executed, it is contended that it was not competent for the legislature to increase the common-law liability after its execution. Section 5528 Rev. Stat. 1881, which was in force at the time the bond was executed, and which by force of law became a part of it, provides that " all official bonds shall be payable to the State of Indiana, and every bond shall be obligatory upon the principal and sureties for the faithful discharge of all duties required of such officer by any law then or subsequently in force, for the use of any person injured by the breach of the condition thereof." Section 5534 makes the sureties on an official bond liable as principals, and prohibits them from making any defence which would not be available to the principal. It has been held, as the statute plainly implies, that by force of section 5528 a permanent, continuing liability is created against the officer and his sureties, as well for the failure to discharge any duty imposed by existing law as for duties required under laws subsequently enacted. Davis *v.* State, 44 Ind. 38 ; State *v.* Davis, 96 Ind. 539.

POWER OF LEGISLATURE TO INCREASE LIABILITY ON OFFICIAL BOND AFTER ITS EXECUTION.

One of the duties which the law subsequently enacted was imposed upon the officer, that he should not charge, demand, or take more than the fees specified, and for violating this duty a certain liability was imposed, recoverable on his bond. This it was competent for the legislature to do.

Another objection insisted on is that it does not appear from AVERMENTS the averments in the complaint that the illegal fees THAT ILLEGAL FEES WERE FOR charged were for "official acts done or performed OFFICIAL ACTS, CONSIDERED. under the provisions of this act." The averments in this regard are that Stevens was clerk of the Decatur circuit court; that upon the dismissal of a certain action pending in that court against the relator "said Stevens made up and stated upon the fee-books of said court his taxation of the costs in said case against the said Scobey, due to himself as such clerk of said court, therein claiming due him for his costs in said case against said Scobey for his services therein as such clerk a large sum" in excess of the amount legally due. We think it sufficiently appears from these averments that the fees illegally charged were for acts done in his official capacity as clerk. There is no force in the objection that the suit on the bond for illegal fees is a collateral attack on the judgment for costs, and that the complaint was for that reason subject to a demurrer. It may be true that, as between the parties to a judgment, that part of it which is for costs cannot be impeached collaterally any more than the other, the remedy being by motion to retax; but a failure to do so cannot relieve an officer from his statutory liability, if he has in fact charged, demanded, or taken illegal fees.

The next and last objection made to the complaint is that LIMITATION. the action is for a forfeiture or penalty; and, not having been commenced within two years from the date at which the cause of action accrued, it is claimed that it is barred by the first clause of section 293, Rev. St. 1881, which requires action for the recovery of a forfeiture or penalty to be commenced within two years. The second clause of the same section provides that "all actions against a sheriff or other public officer, or against such officer and his sureties on a public bond, growing out of a liability incurred by doing an act in an official capacity, or by the omission of an official duty," shall be barred within five years. While it may be said that the amount fixed as compensation to the injured person, and as the measure of the officer's liability, is to a degree in the nature of a penalty, it is nevertheless a liability incurred by doing an act in an official capacity for which the officer is made liable on his bond, and it is therefore within the terms of the second clause of section 293 above set out. The cause of action accrued on the thirty-first day of July, 1879, the date when the illegal fees were charged or taxed, and as the action was commenced within five years from that date it was not barred.

Judgment reversed, with costs.

ELLIOTT, J.—I concur in the conclusion reached, but I do not agree to all of the reasoning of the prevailing opinion, or assent to all of the propositions laid down. My opinion is that the question is purely one of legislative power, and that the legislature may provide for the recovery of punitory damages in cases where an injury is caused by an illegal act, although the same illegal act may subject the defendant to a criminal prosecution. As the legislature has this power, unabridged by constitutional limitation, it has the authority either to limit the amount to be recovered or to leave it to be ascertained upon a trial.

It is not a question for the courts whether the power is wisely or unwisely exercised ; the only question for the courts is, does the power exist and has it been exercised ? Once the power is found to exist, all questions of policy and wisdom in its exercise pass outside of the judicial department of the government.

RECOVERY OF EXEMPLARY DAMAGES FOR TORTIOUS ACTS PUNISHABLE CRIMINALLY.—THE NATURE OF EXEMPLARY DAMAGES.—The question whether " exemplary damages " can be recovered in a civil action for an act which is also punishable criminally is one which, on the authorities, is involved in much difficulty and confusion. It is thought that much of this difficulty and confusion is owing to a lack of precise definition of the phrase "exemplary damages." Fay *v.* Parker, 53 N. H. 342. The phrase is used to indicate those damages recoverable beyond the ordinary measure of damages in certain cases of tort, where the tortious act involved fraud or malice, etc., on the part of the defendant. So far the authorities are agreed ; but as to the theory on which such damages are allowed there is much conflict and confusion in the authorities. It would seem clear from the meaning of the word ``exemplary,'' and from the fact that exemplary damages are only allowed in cases where the act of the defendant is morally culpable, that the idea of punishment—of making an example is involved. But is this the principal idea, or is the fundamental idea still compensation for injury to the plaintiff, resulting from the wrongful act, though allowed for injuries for which no damages are ordinarily recoverable ?

EXEMPLARY DAMAGES ALLOWED AS COMPENSATION.—In the case of Fay *v.* Parker, 53 N. H. 342, Judge Foster goes into a learned discussion of this subject, including therein an exhaustive survey of the authorities, and comes to the conclusion that the better reasoning and authority both sustain the view that exemplary damages are damages allowed for mental and moral injuries to the plaintiff, for which damages are not ordinarily recoverable, and that no damages can be allowed by way of punishment of the defendant, pure and simple. Referring to the origin of the idea that damages could be given solely by way of punishment, the learned judge proceeded as follows : " I venture to say that no case will be found, in ancient, nor, indeed, in modern reports, in which a judge explicitly told a jury that they might, in an action for assault and battery, give the plaintiff four damages, viz.: 1. For loss of property, as for injury to his apparel, loss of labor and time, expenses of surgical assistance, nursing, etc.   2. For bodily pain.   3. For mental suffering ; and 4. for punishment of the defendant's crime.   But a critical examination of the cases will show, as I believe, that this fourth item is, in fact, comprehended in the third, but has grown into and become a separate and additional item by inconsiderate, if not intemperate and angry, instructions given to juries when the court was too much incensed, by the exhibition of wanton malice, revenge, insult, and oppression, to weigh with coolness and deliberation the meaning of the language previously used by other judges : instructions prompted by impulses of righteous indignation, swift to administer justice to a guilty defendant, but expressed with too little caution and without pausing to reflect that the court was thus encouraging the jury to give the plaintiff more than he was entitled to—to give him, in fact, as damages, the avails of a fine imposed for the vindication of the criminal law, and for the sake of public example."

That the primary object of exemplary damages is compensation and not punishment, see also Bixby *v.* Dunlap, 56 N. H. 456 ; Detroit Daily Post Co. *v.* McArthur, 16 Mich. 447 ; Chiles *v.* Drake, 2 Met. (Ky.) 146 ; Hendrickson *v.* Kingsbury, 21 Iowa, 379 [which refers to the controversy between Prof. Greenleaf, 2 Gr. Ev. § 253 note, who was of the opinion that exemplary damages were intended to be compensatory, and Mr. Sedgwick, 2 Sedgw. Dam. p. 323, who thinks that purely punitory damages are recoverable].

EXEMPLARY DAMAGES ALLOWED AS PUNISHMENT.— Many cases, however, hold that exemplary damages may be inflicted by way of punishment, pure and simple.   Tillotson *v.* Cheetham, 3 John R. N. Y. 56 ; Brown *v.* Swineford, 44 Wis. 282 ; Railroad *v.* Williams, 55 Ill. 185 ; 1 Suth. Dams. 721, 722, *et seq.* and notes.

In Meidel *v.* Anthis, 71 Ill. 241, the majority of the court draw a distinction between exemplary damages which are not compensatory inflicted for the sake of example, and those inflicted for the sake of punishment. The court held that under a statute allowing a civil action for selling intoxicating liquors to drunkards punitory damages could not be allowed, since the statute itself provided that the act should be punishable by fine, but that damages for the sake of example could be recovered. The court says: " They" (the jury) " may give exemplary damages. We understand by this they may, in a proper case, give, besides actual damages to the party injured, such damages as may operate as a warning to others—they may make an example of the seller by the quantum of damages they shall award against him. We can not believe it was the design of the legislature to give to the jury in such an action the power to punish the violator of the law in the shape of damages," etc. The minority of the court deemed this distinction " verbal," not " substantial."

PUNITORY DAMAGES FOR AN ACT PUNISHABLE AS A CRIME UNCONSTITUTIONAL.—Exemplary damages allowed by way of punishment would seem on principle to be clearly unconstitutional when the act to be punished is also punishable criminally. To allow punitive damages in such a case would seem clearly to be putting a person in jeopardy twice for the same offence. The reasoning of the court in the principal case seems to be unanswerable. The Wisconsin court takes the position that this constitutional provision relates wholly to criminal prosecutions, and has no application to a civil action. Brown *v.* Swineford, 44 Wis. 282, 287. But there would seem to be no good reason for limiting a broad constitutional principle to a mere question of procedure. Whatever else this constitutional clause was intended to provide for, it seems clear that it intended to provide for this, that where a person charged with a crime has been tried and acquitted he should not be subjected to another trial for the same offence. Yet if punitory damages are recoverable in a civil action for an act that is also a crime, the following case might happen : A man might be tried criminally for an act punishable by a fine of $500 and acquitted ; a civil suit might then be brought, and the jury would then allow the exact sum, $500, as punitive damages over and above all compensatory damages. It is difficult to see why such a case is not within the spirit of the constitutional inhibition. Indeed, the chance of incurring the penalty would be greater in the civil suit than in the criminal, inasmuch as a less degree of proof of having committed the act would be required in the former case than in the latter. In the former the jury could find the defendant guilty on a mere preponderance of evidence ; in the latter they could not convict unless convinced of defendant's guilt beyond all reasonable doubt.

It might even be questioned if the allowance of punitive damages for a tortious action that is also criminal and punishable as a crime does not offend against the constitutional inhibition against cruel and unusual punishment. Even apart from all constitutional questions, it would seem that on simple principles of justice and right the court should refuse to allow punitive damages in such a case. Simple justice would seem to require that a person should not be amerced twice for the same offence.

The following cases hold that punitive damages in cases where the act is punishable criminally are unconstitutional, as providing for a double penalty : Austen *v.* Wilson, 4 Cush. (Mass.) 273 ; Tabor *v.* Hutson, 5 Ind. 322 ; Butler *v.* Mercer, 14 Ind. 479 ; Koerner *v.* Oberly, 56 Ind. 284 ; Fay *v.* Parker, 53 N. H. 342; Bixby *v.* Dunlap, 56 N. H. 456, 1 Sutherland Dams, 739; Cherry *v.* McCall, 23 Ga. 193.

In this connection see Meindel *v.* Anthis, 71 Ill. 241, where it was held that where a statute relating to the sale of liquor to drunkards, provided both a civil and a criminal remedy, it must be assumed that the legislature intended that punitory damages should not be recoverable in the civil suit, the matter of punishment being specially provided for in the statute. See also Freese *v.* Tripp, 70 Ill. 496.

In the following cases the court allowed punitive damages for an act punishable criminally. Brown *v.* Swineford, 44 Wis. 282. In this case the court get around the constitutional difficulty by holding that the constitutional inhibition against putting a person in jeopardy twice for the same offence relates only to criminal prosecutions. Pike *v.* Dilling, 48 Me. 539. In this case the judge below charged the jury that they might, if they thought proper, " in addition to the actual damages the plaintiff has sustained, give him a further sum, as exemplary or vindictive damages, both as a protection to the plaintiff and as a salutary example to others to deter them from offending in like cases." The act was punishable criminally. It was held that the charge was unobjectionable. The point of double punishment was taken in the argument and insisted on in the dissenting opinion. It seems to have been wholly ignored in the principal opinion. In Jefferson *v.* Adams, 4 Harr. (Del.) 321, it was said that punitory damages might be recovered, though it does not appear that the exemplary damages allowed in that case were not compensatory wholly. The point of double punishment was not raised.

In Wolff *v.* Cohen, 8 Rich. (S. C.) 144, the court, in discussing the question of whether evidence of a fine inflicted in a criminal prosecution was admissible in mitigation of damage in a civil suit for the same act, decided that such evidence was not admissible. As to the matter of exemplary damages they say : " And where circumstances of aggravation call for vindictive and punitory damages, the range of the jury's discretion should not be narrowed by the sentence of the court."

In Roberts *v.* Mason, 10 Ohio St. 277, an instruction allowing punitive damages in addition to all compensatory damages was held to be correct. See Jockers *v.* Borgman, 29 Kan. 109. In Cook *v.* Ellis, 6 Hill (N. Y.) 466, the court said : " We concede that smart-money allowed by a jury and a fine imposed at the suit of the people depend on the same principle. Both are penal, and intended to deter others from the commission of the like crime. The former, however, becomes incidentally compensatory for damages, and at the same time answers the purposes of punishment. The recovery of such damages ought not to be made dependent on what has been done by way of criminal prosecution any more than on what may be done."

COMPENSATORY EXEMPLARY DAMAGES DO NOT COME WITHIN THE OBJECTION OF BEING A DOUBLE PUNISHMENT.—Where exemplary damages are compensatory, allowing them in the civil action clearly does not amount to providing a double punishment for the same offence, and come within constitutional and other objections involved therein. See principal case.

Bixby *v.* Dunlap, 56 N. H. 456; Fay *v.* Parker, 53 N. H. 342; Wheatley *v.* Thorn, 23 Miss. 62; Hendrickson *v.* Kingsbury, 21 Iowa, 379; Chiles *v.* Drake, 2 Metc. (Ky.) 146.   See also Fry *v.* Bennett, 4 Duer (N. Y.), 247.

PROOF OF A FINE IMPOSED IN A CRIMINAL ACTION OFFERED IN MITIGATION OF DAMAGES IN A CIVIL SUIT.—In many cases it has been held that evidence of a conviction and punishment in a criminal action is not admissible in mitigation of damages in a civil suit for the act punished in the criminal prosecution.   In some of these cases the question of exemplary damages was not raised at all, but merely whether—it being the law that the criminal court will consider a recovery in a civil action in mitigation of damages, regardless of whether those damages are exemplary or not (State *v.* Autery, 1 Stewart (Ala.), 399)—the converse of that rule would hold and permit the imposition of a fine to be considered in mitigation of civil damages.   Phillips *v.* Kelley, 29 Ala. 628.

In other cases the question of exemplary damages was involved, but it did not appear whether the exemplary damages were punitive or compensatory.   Corwin *v.* Walton, 18 Mo. 71; Jefferson *v.* Adams, 4 Harr. (Del.) 321; Wolff *v.* Cohen, 8 Rich. (S. C.) 144; Hoadley *v.* Watson, 45 Vt. 289; Cook *v.* Ellis, 6 Hill (N. Y.) 466.   In Cherry *v.* McCall, 23 Ga. 193, it was held that such evidence was admissible in rebuttal of punitive damages.

NOTE ON THE PRINCIPAL CASE.—If the civil remedy provided by the statute is penal, it would seem perhaps that even if each part of the statute provides only a part of the punishment, the part of the statute relating to the recovery in the civil action was unconstitutional, as putting persons in jeopardy twice for the same offence.   It is conceived that a statute providing a punishment which could only be inflicted by two separate proceedings would fall within that constitutional inhibition.   It is probable that in reality the statute contemplates but one trial for the crime, and that the conviction in the criminal court would dispense with all proof of the commission of the crime in the civil suit, leaving nothing to be proved but the execution of the bond and similar formal matters.

SIMONS *et al.*
v.
COUNTY OF JACKSON.

(63 *Texas*, 428.)

The statutory bond required of a county treasurer (Rev. Stat., art. 989) renders the sureties thereon liable for any misappropriation of the school fund, of any description, without reference to the source from which it might be derived.   It includes all available school funds obtained from the State treasurer, as well as interest arising from bonds procured through the sale of the four leagues of land set aside to each county, and interest on notes given on their sale.

If the county court should, through error, appropriate permanent instead of available school funds, for school expenses, and make the county treasurer their custodian, the sureties on his official bond would be liable for their safe keeping.

The sureties on the official bond of a treasurer will be held liable for the safe-keeping of school money received by him as such, though at the time of the execution of the bond its receipt by the treasurer may not have been contemplated by the parties.

Judgment against a defaulting treasurer, for school funds intrusted to his custody as such, should bear interest from the first of the year succeeding his default.

APPEAL from Jackson. Tried below before the Hon. Wm. H. Burkhart.

Suit by Jackson county against George F. Simons and Frank B. Owens, sureties of Wm. Wood, late treasurer of that county, who, it was alleged, had absconded and was insolvent, and therefore was not sued.

The cause was tried by the court without a jury, and a judgment rendered in favor of the plaintiff for the sum of $1385.19, being for $1233.11 principal, and interest thereon from January 1, 1883.

The sum claimed was interest paid by purchasers of Jackson county school land.

It would seem that none of the interest on the school land notes was in the hands of the treasurer when the bond sued on was executed, and it was alleged in the defendants' answer, to which exceptions were sustained, that the receipt of any school land notes interest was not in contemplation of the parties to treasurer's bond when it was executed.

Glass & Callender and Stockdale & Proctor for appellants.

A. B. Peticolas for appellee.

WILLIE.—The bond upon which this suit was founded was
FACTS.   conditioned that Wood, the county treasurer, would safely keep and faithfully disburse the school fund according to law, and pay such warrants as might be drawn on said fund by competent authority.

These are the conditions prescribed by law for the bond to be given by the county treasurer to secure the school fund belonging to the county. R. S., art. 989.

The language of the statute would make the sureties upon such bond liable for any misappropriation of the school fund of any description without reference to the source from whence it might be derived.

The available school fund, as defined in arts. 3703 and 3704 of the Revised Statutes, embraces only such moneys as are partitioned among the various counties from the treasury of the State. The bond includes that fund within its protection (id., art 4036); but this is not the only fund which in contemplation of law may be made available for the annual expenses of the free school system. Each county has four leagues of lands allotted to it for school purposes. These lands belong to the counties and may be sold in manner as prescribed by commissioners' courts, the proceeds to be invested in bonds, and the interest accruing upon these bonds is to be made available for the current expenses of the free schools of the respective counties to which it belongs. This interest when received by a county must go into the hands of its treasurer, and is secured by the letter and clear intent of the conditions we have recited. It is the duty of the county treasurer to receive all moneys belonging to the county, from whatever source they may be derived (id., art. 9), and the theory of the law is that the bonds prescribed for his execution cover all the moneys thus coming into his custody. Had it been the intention of the law to protect by the bond in question only a portion of the school fund, it would have so stated By using terms comprehensive enough to embrace the entire fund, it was clearly intended to include at least all such amounts as were subject to disbursement by the county commissioners' court. Were the amounts alleged in this case to have been embezzled embraced by words of this description? They consisted of interest upon notes received for the purchase money of the four leagues of land granted to Jackson County for school purposes. If instead of taking notes the county had received money and exchanged it for bonds, the interest upon these bonds would, as we have seen, have been available for the current expenses of the county's free school. The interest upon the proceeds of these bonds are not, therefore, in contemplation of law, a part of the permanent school fund, but of that which is to be used in payment of annual expenses. In this case it was so treated by the commissioners' court, and was by them duly transferred to the available fund, and

[margin note: SCHOOL FUNDS—WHETHER COVERED BY BOND OF COUNTY TREASURER.]

as such committed to the care and custody of the county treasurer. It then became his duty safely to keep it and faithfully to disburse it, and for his default in these respects we think the sureties upon the bond in question were responsible.

If the appropriation of this fund to school expenses made by the commissioners was unauthorized, we do not see that this would excuse the bondsmen, for it is well settled that the sureties of an officer intrusted with public funds are liable for his defalcations, though the moneys in his charge were collected and placed there without warrant of law. For instance, the sureties of a tax collector are responsible for the taxes collected by him, though they were obtained under an illegal or void assessment. County of Mahaska *v.* Ingalls, 14 Iowa, 170; Ford *v.* Clough, 8 Me. 334; Boehmer *v.* Schuylkill, 46 Pa. St. 452; Wylie *v.* Gallagher, Id. 205.

This, in effect, disposes also of the point made that the sureties cannot be held liable for the money recovered in this suit, for the reason that it did not come into the treasurer's hands till after the bond was executed. The money was received during the term of office for which the bond was given, and it was money which, as we have seen, the law contemplated should be taken into keeping by the county treasurer. The condition of the bond including this character of funds, it was not imposing a greater burden upon the sureties than they had agreed to bear, to make them responsible for it.

Numerous cases may be found in the reports of our own and other States where the sureties upon official bonds have been held liable for funds received by their principal after the execution of the bond, which funds it was not at the time contemplated should come under his charge. Borden *v.* Houston, 2 Tex. 594; Houston *v.* Dwyer, 59 Tex. 113; State *v.* Kelly, 43 Tex. 667; Broome *v.* United States, 15 How. 143; United States *v.* McCartney, 10 Cent. L. J. 113; Walker *v.* Chapman, 22 Ala. 116.

But we think the court erred in not adjudging interest upon that amount from January 1, 1881, instead of January 1, 1883.

The defalcation seems to have occurred in 1880, during

[marginal note: SURETIES: LIABILITY FOR DEFALCATIONS OF TREASURER OF MONEY COLLECTED WITHOUT WARRANT OF LAW.]

the existence of the bond upon which this suit is founded. It is only on this supposition that the suit can be maintained upon the present bond. If it occurred after the term for which the defendants were sureties, they were not liable; but the sureties for his next term were alone responsible. Interest should have been computed from the first of the year succeeding the default, which was 1881. The judgment will therefore be reversed and rendered for the appellee for the principal sum recovered below, with interest from January 1, 1881, and the costs of this court and the court below.

Reversed and rendered.

WOOD

v.

CUTTER and others.

(138 *Massachusetts*, 149.)

The school committee of a town, having been required by a vote of the town to appoint a superintendent of schools, may, after having elected such superintendent by ballot, reconsider the vote at the same meeting, and before it has been communicated to the person appointed, and, at an adjourned meeting, elect another person by a yea and nay vote.

S. Hoar for petitioner.

R. D. Smith & F. C. Nash for respondents.

HOLMES, J.—This is a petition for a writ of *mandamus* to the school committee of the town of Acton, com- FACTS. manding them to permit the petitioner to perform the duties and receive the emoluments of the office of superintendent of schools. The only facts material to our decision are that on April 7, 1884, the town by vote required the school committee to appoint a superintendent (Pub. Sts. c. 44, § 43); that, at a meeting of the school committee held the same day, it was voted to proceed to a formal vote for superintendent; that a majority of the votes cast were for the petitioner, the voting being by ballot; that it was then voted "to reconsider the last vote for superintendent if they could do it legally;" and that, at an adjourned meeting, all the members of the board being present, Frederic C. Nash had three votes, the other three members of the board not voting. The votes at this meeting were yea and nay. Nash was duly notified, and has since performed the duties of his office.

We are all of opinion that the petitioner shows no right to the office, and that the writ ought not to issue. This is not the case of a fluctuating body, like a town meeting, nor is it one where the law prescribes a particular mode of voting in the performance of some public duty, as, for instance, the ballot, where it would be open to question whether the power to reconsider, if it were held to exist, would not practically destroy the secrecy intended to be secured. Both these elements concurred in Putnam v. Langley, 133 Mass. 204, and when it was suggested in that case that perhaps, after a ballot had been taken and the result in favor of a candidate announced and accepted, further action by the same meeting would be ineffectual, the suggestion plainly had reference only to the facts of the case before the court.

Here the mode of voting was determined by the pleasure ELECTION: RE- of the voting body. At the meeting of April 7 CONSIDERATION OF VOTE. it was by ballot; at the adjournment, by yeas and nays. Under these circumstances, no reason has been suggested to us why this vote should not stand on the same footing as any other vote of a deliberative body, and remain subject to reconsideration at the same meeting and before it has been communicated. It begs the question to say that the board had once definitively voted in pursuance of the instructions of the town meeting, and therefore was *functus officio*, and could not reconsider its vote. The vote was not definitive if it contained the usual implied condition, that it was not reconsidered in accordance with ordinary parliamentary practice, and it must be taken to have been passed subject to the usual incidents of votes, unless some ground is shown for treating it as an exception to common rules. Whether the board could have cut down their powers of deliberation by communicating their vote before the meeting was closed, or otherwise, is not a question before us. It is enough to say that an implied condition is as effectual as an express one; and that in this case the condition which has been stated must be implied.

Petition dismissed.

KIEFER

v

TROY SCHOOL TOWNSHIP OF PERRY COUNTY.

(Advance Case, Indiana. June 12, 1885.)

A school trustee who advances funds to pay the teacher accrued wages may recover the same from the township.

APPEAL from Perry circuit court.
Simeon Jaseph and *Heber J. May* for appellant.
Wm. Henning for appellee.

MITCHELL, C. J.—From the complaint in this case it appears that Lawrence Kiefer was the trustee of Troy School Township, in Perry County, in the year 1883; that he had made estimates of the funds likely to come into his   FACTS. hands for tuition purposes, and, relying on such estimates, he employed competent and licensed teachers for the several school districts in his township, and entered into written contracts with them at the usual stipulative wages, and that the number employed was necessary to supply the requirements of the school children of the township; that the several teachers employed carried out their contracts in good faith, and taught the township schools in all respects according to their agreements; that at the end of the term for which they were employed the tuition fund, less having been received through some miscalculation than was expected, having been exhausted in making proper disbursements therefrom, and there remaining due the several teachers the sum of $708.96, the appellant advanced and paid the same out of his own funds, and that this sum was received by them for their services; that he made report of his doings in that regard to the board of commissioners, who approved the same, and, at the direction of the board, the county auditor gave him a certificate of the amount found due him from the township, from which action of the board no appeal has been taken; that he has demanded payment from his successor for the money thus advanced and allowed, who refuses to pay; that it was the intention of the several teachers and the trustee, at the time he paid them, not to extinguish their claims against the township, but to transfer to him their rights against it. To this complaint a demurrer was sustained, and the sole question is, did it state a cause of action upon which the plaintiff was entitled to recover?

Of a case in some respects involving the same principles an eminent judge said: "This is an attempt to impale an honest debt on the sharp points of the law which ought not to succeed." Heidelberg School District *v.* Horst, 62 Pa. St. 301.

Two grounds are urged as obstacles in the way of the appellant's right to receive payment of the money advanced by him for the benefit of the township. It is said (1) that because he was trustee of the township the payment of its debts was a voluntary payment, and that a stranger cannot by voluntarily paying the debt of another maintain against the other assumpsit for such payments; (2) that if the payment was not voluntary, the trustee could create no obligation against the township by dealing with himself. The propositions above stated enunciate sound and salutary principles of law, which are of binding obligation in all cases in which they apply; but they have no application to the case before us.

It is conceded by the demurrer to the complaint that the TRUSTEES' AD- teachers were hired in good faith, under the belief VANCES TO TEACHER ARE that the tutition funds provided would be sufficient RECOVERABLE FROM TOWNSHIP. for their payment; that the township had the benefit of their services and became liable for their wages, and, having no funds to discharge its just obligation, the appellant advanced the money out of his own pocket and paid a debt, the benefit of which the school corporation received. Under the rulings of this court in Harmony School Tp. *v.* Moore, 80 Ind. 276, the township was liable for the services of its school-teachers, whether it had the funds to pay or not. It was there held that it was no excuse for the dismissal of a teacher before the expiration of the term for which he was employed that the fund out of which he was to be paid was exhausted. This ruling was followed in Harrison School Tp. *v.* McGregor, 96 Ind. 185, where it was again held that the liability of a township to pay its teachers does not depend upon whether it had the funds for their payment or not. Quoting from an approved authority, this court said in Bicknell v. Widner School Tp., 73 Ind. 501 : " Persons who had in any way advanced money to a corporation, which money has been devoted to the necessities of the corporation, are considered in chancery as creditors of the corporation to the extent to which the loan has been expended." When a necessity exists for so doing, and the trustee in good faith advances money to liquidate a just debt owing by the township for which it is unquestionably bound, and in the creation of which it was benefited, no reason is perceived why he should not be reimbursed as well as a stranger from whom he might have borrowed the money. Bristol Milling & Manuf'g Co. v. Probasco, 64 Ind. 406. It can no more be said in such case that the officer has contracted with himself than in the case of an agent, whose duty it is to attend to the interests of his principal, who in an emergency advances money for the principal's benefit. He has not contracted with himself. He has done nothing except in the interest of the school township whose servant and agent he was, and whose advantage it was his duty to subserve, to advance his money for the liquidation of its debts on contracts which had been made and executed. An equitable obligation is thus raised against the school corporation to pay him the moneys advanced.

In the case of Porter v. Dunlap, 17 Ohio St. 591, one Clark, engaged in teaching school, was advanced on his wages by Porter, the treasurer of the school corporation, under an agreement that he should retain out of his wages, when earned, the amount advanced. It was held that this was a valid assignment in equity, and that a subsequent assignee of Clark could recover nothing until Porter was reimbursed. The principle of this case fully sustains the right of the appellant to recover ; but whether he became the equitable assignee of the claims of the school-teachers or not, he was entitled to recover for money paid to he use of the corporation. That a public officer may not contract with himself is not to be doubted ; but, like any other agent or trustee, he may, within the scope of his agency, when a necessity arises, advance money to save his principal or *cestui que trust* from inevitable loss or damage, or to pay just liabilities growing out of his agency ; and for such advances, upon the same principle that any other agent may be reimbursed, he may be. Story, Ag. § 335. Of course, a public officer, as such, cannot borrow money from himself, nor can he be reimbursed for money paid on contracts which he had no authority to make, nor to pay debts for which the corporation received no benefit, nor for advances made without a necessity therefor; but this record presents no case of the character supposed.

The judgment is reversed, with costs, with instructions to the court to overrule the demurrer to the complaint, and to proceed in accordance with this opinion.

BARKER *et al.*

v.

BARROWS.

(138 *Massachusetts*, 578.)

At the trial of a writ of entry, dated in 1883, it appeared that the demanded premises were conveyed by A, in 1829, to the ancestor of the demandant; that in 1837 A conveyed the same premises to the inhabitants of a school district, "their successors and assigns forever," by a deed which contained, after a description of the premises, the words "said lot of land to be used, occupied, and improved by said inhabitants as a schoolhouse lot, and for no other purpose;" that from 1837 to 1882 the school district had the exclusive use of the premises for school purposes, and had taken exclusive care of it; and that in 1882 the school district conveyed the premises to the tenant, the school-house was removed, and the premises ceased to be used for school purposes. *Held*, that the demandant's ancestor was disseized in 1837; that the deed to the school district was in form a deed in fee; and that the statute of limitations, Pub. Stats. c. 196, was a bar to the action.

WRIT of entry, dated February 15, 1883, to recover a parcel of land in Attleborough. Plea, *nul disseisin.* Trial in the Superior Court, without a jury, before Gardner, J., who reported the case for the determination of this court, in sub-stance as follows:

The demandants offered in evidence a warranty deed from Samual Richards to Elihu Daggett, dated and recorded on August 15, 1829, of certain land, including the demanded premises; also a quit-claim deed from Elihu Daggett to Jesse F. Richards, the father of the demandants, dated December 29, 1829, and recorded January 2, 1830, which the judge found included the demanded premises. The demandants are the children and only heirs-at-law of Jesse F. Richards, who lived in North Attleborough, and died intestate in 1882.

The tenant offered in evidence a deed of the demanded premises, dated July 3, 1837, and recorded March 1, 1843, by which Elihu Daggett conveyed unto the "inhabitants of School District No. Four, their successors and assigns for-ever," the demanded premises. The deed contained, after the description of the premises, the words "said lot of land to be used, occupied, and improved by said inhabitants as a school-house lot, and for no other purpose." The *habendum* of the deed was "to the said inhabitants, their successors and assigns, to them and their use and behoof forever." The deed also contained full covenants of seisin, of freedom from incum-brances, and of warranty.

The tenant also offered in evidence a warranty deed of the demanded premises, from said school district to the tenant, dated and recorded on September 20, 1882, which contained no restrictions as to the use of the lot; also a deed from Lyman W. Daggett, heir-at-law of said Elihu, to Handel N. Daggett, dated September 16, 1882, and recorded September 20, 1882, conveying all the right, title, and interest of said Lyman in the demanded premises; also a deed from said Handel N. to the tenant, dated September 16, 1882, recorded September 20, 1882, conveying the same right, title, and interest set out in the deed of Lyman to Handel.

It was admitted at the trial "that a school-house has been on this lot and a school has been kept there; that, since 1837, School District No. 4 has had exclusive use of the locus for school purposes; and that the district has taken exclusive care of it." It was in evidence that, since said school district was conveyed to the tenant in September, 1882, the premises have not been used for school purposes: and that the school-house thereon was removed before the demandants brought this action.

There was no evidence that Jesse F. Richards, since 1837, ever possessed, occupied, had seisin of, or controlled the de-manded premises, or that its possession by the district (ad-mitted by the parties as above stated) was ever disputed by any one, or was by the license or permission of any one, except

9 Cor. Cas.—14

so far as appears from the evidence herein stated, or may properly be inferred therefrom.

Each party contended that, as matter of law, upon the evi. dence, he was entitled to judgment. The judge found for the demandants.

Final judgment was to be entered for either party, as the court might determine.

T. M Stetson (J. E. Pond, Jr., with him) for the tenant.

C. W. Clifford & F. C. S. Bartlett for the demandants.

W. ALLEN, J.—One inference of law from the facts stated in
FACTS.   the report is that Jesse F. Richards, the ancestor of the demandants, was seized of the premises under the deed of Elihu Daggett to him delivered and recorded in 1829. Another inference of law is, that the same Jesse F. Richards was disseised of the premises by School District No. 4 in Attleborough in 1837; and he never afterwards entered upon the premises or recovered seisin thereof. The statute of limitations is therefore a bar to the action. Pub. Sts. c. 196; Gen. Sts. c. 154; Rev. Sts. c. 119.

The argument for the demandants, as we understand it, is that the school district entered under a deed to it from a stranger, which, while it gave the grantee no right or title, showed that it entered claiming an estate less than a fee simple; and that the purpose of the entry and possession was such that the act could not constitute a disseisin.

Without considering the answer that an actual ouster, the
DEED HELD NOT beginning of a possession exclusive, notorious, ad-
TO REQUIRE USE
OF   PROPERTY verse, and uninterrupted for forty years, cannot
FOR SCHOOL PUR-
POSES   EXCLU- be qualified into something less than a disseisin, by
SIVELY.
showing that it was under the deed of a stranger having neither title nor possession, purporting to convey less than an estate in fee simple, it is a sufficient answer to the argument that the deed in question did purport to convey an estate in fee simple. It is in the common form, and contains the usual covenants of a deed of warranty. The only question made is upon the effect of the words immediately following the description of the land, " Said lot of land to be used, occupied, and improved by said inhabitants as a school-house lot, and for no other purpose." If these words constituted a condition, the deed would still purport to convey an estate in

fee simple, absolute against the true owner and all the world except the grantor and his heirs or devisees. But they do not import a condition, or in any way limit the legal estate granted by the terms of the deed.   Rawson *v.* Uxbridge School District, 7 Allen, 125 ; Sohier *v.* Trinity Church, 109 Mass. 1, 19; Packard *v.* Ames, 16 Gray, 327 ; Episcopal City Mission *v.* Appleton, 117 Mass. 326.   So far as the deed affects the character of the entry, it tends to show that it was under a claim of title in fee simple.

Judgment for the tenant.

BOARD OF EDUCATION
v.
BOARD OF EDUCATION.

(42 *Ohio St.* 680)

The board of education of a township established a central or high school under the provisions of the act of March 14, 1853, S. & C. 1346, as amended May 14, 1868, S. & S. 712, and erected a building in a sub-district of the township for the use of the school, and the building was used, by agreement between the board of education and the local directors of the sub-district, for the central or high school and the school of the sub-district. The territory comprised in the sub-district after the establishment of the central or high school, and before the act of May 1 1873 (70 Ohio Laws, 195), was formed into an incorporated village. *Held*, that the property of the central or high school and the management of the school did not, by virtue of said last-mentioned act, pass to the board, of education of the incorporated village.

ERROR to the District Court of Trumbull County.

The board of education of Hubbard township, Trumbull County, in June, 1868, commenced proceedings under section 21 of the act of March 14, 1853, to provide for the reorganization, supervision, and maintenance of common schools, S. & C. 1346, as amended May 14, 1868, S. & S. 712, to establish in that township a central or high school. Their proceedings resulted in the establishment of such school and the location of a building for that purpose in sub-district number 5 in the township. In 1870, the building being completed, by agreement between the board of education of the

township and the local directors of sub-district number 5, the
rooms in the second story of the building were used for the
central or high school, and the rooms in the first story were
used for the school in sub-district number 5. After the
schools had been in operation for some time in this way, the
territory comprised in sub-district number 5 was formed
into an incorporated village. This occurred some time prior
to the passage of the act of May 1, 1873. The action in the
common pleas was by the board of education of the village
against the board of education of the township, and the
object of it was to enjoin the defendants from exercising any
control or direction over the school-house or over the school
held therein, and to prevent them by injunction from interfering with the sole use, direction, and control of the school
by the board of education of the village. The district court,
upon a trial on appeal, found and decreed for the plaintiffs.
It is now sought to reverse this decree.

Dio Rogers, Volney Rogers, and *C. A. Harrington* for plaintiffs
in error.

McCAULEY, J.—The board of education of the township
FACTS.   legally established a central or high school, and
located the building for it in sub-district number 5 of the
township. The building must have been located in some one
of the sub-districts of the township. It is claimed by the
board of education of the village that because the territory
within sub-district number 5 was formed into an incorporated
village after this central or high school was established, and
prior to the passage of the act of May 1, 1873, 70 Ohio Laws,
195, the 39th section of that act vested the board of education
of the village with jurisdiction and control of all school property within the district. Section 4 of that act, now section
3888 Rev. Stats., provides: " That each village, including the
territory attached to it for school purposes, and excluding
the territory within its corporate limits detached for school
purposes, shall constitute a school district, to be styled a village district." Section 39 of the same act, now section 3972
Rev. Stats., provides: " That all property, real or personal,
which has heretofore vested, and is now held by any board of
education or the council of any municipal corporation, for
the use of public or common schools in any district, is hereby

vested in the board of education provided for in this title, having under this title jurisdiction and control of the schools in such district." The act of May 1, 1873, repealed all provisions relating to central or high schools existing at the time of its passage ; but it provided for the establishment of such schools, and provided, also, that obligations or liabilities incurred and rights acquired under the provisions of any of the acts repealed by it should be in no wise altered or affected, but be enforced as if the act had not been passed. 70 Ohio Laws, 240. The township board of education had established a central or high school according to the statutes in force at the time the school was established. The act of May 1, 1873, gave the board of education of the CONTROL OF SCHOOL PROPERTY. village control of all school property within the village district, and at the same time saved all rights which had accrued under former statutes. The right of the township board to the school property, and to the control and management of the central or high school, had accrued before the act of May 1, 1873 ; and the rights of this board were, therefore, not affected by this act.

Judgment reversed.

STATE *ex rel.* FANGER

v.

BOARD OF PUBLIC WORKS.

(42 *Ohio State*, 607.)

Under the provisions of the act of March 23, 1840 (3 Rev. Stats. 417, §§ 20 to 23 inclusive), relating to the canals of the State, it is the duty, as well as the right, of the board of public works to resume the privilege or right to the use of surplus water, leased or sold for hydraulic purposes, or any portion thereof, whenever, at any time, it may be deemed necessary for the purposes of navigation, or whenever its use for hydraulic purposes shall be found in any manner to interfere with and injuriously affect the navigation of the canal, feeder or stream from which such water is taken.

The board of public works is not authorized by said statute to in any manner surrender, abridge, restrict or limit its power to resume, at any time, the surplus water leased or sold for hydraulic purposes, whenever it may be deemed necessary for the purposes of navigation ; nor to create or impose any burden or obligation upon the State, by reason of the exercise of such right of resumption, other than is authorized by the 23d section of said act.

Hence, a clause providing that on such resumption of surplus water and termination of the lease, the board of public works shall pay to the lessee the value of the lasting improvements erected for the use of such water, is a restriction on the performance of a public duty, and is unauthorized and void.

MANDAMUS.

The relator's intestate was the assignee of a lease, dated June 27, 1853, made by the board of public works, to Riley and Le Blond, whereby certain water-power, out of the Mercer county reservoir, together with about one and three-quarter acres of land adjoining the same, was leased to them for the term of thirty years, from November 1, 1853, with the privilege of a renewal, on the terms as hereinafter stated. The use of said water-power was to be subject to the restrictions, conditions, and limitations stated in said lease.

Among these were the following :

" It is expressly understood and agreed by and between the parties that the party of the second part (the lessees) shall not be entitled to any deduction from the rent hereby made payable, unless said parties shall be deprived of the use of the water for more than one month in any one year, and the party of the first part reserves the right to resume, at any time, the use of the water hereby leased ; and whenever, in the opinion of the acting commissioner in charge of this canal, the interests of the party of the first part require it, the water hereby leased may be resumed, and then, and in that case, all the rights and privileges derivable to said party of the second part from this agreement shall cease and determine, provided the party of the first part shall first pay or tender the party of the second part the value of all lasting improvements now made, or hereafter to be made, by said second party. Said value to be determined by three disinterested persons chosen for that purpose. Each party choosing one, and the two thus chosen to choose the third." Said lease also contains the following stipulations, touching the renewal of said lease for an additional term of thirty years : " And it is further understood and agreed that at the expiration of this agreement, the party of the second part shall be entitled to a renewal of this lease for the like term of years, for such annual rent as may be offered by the highest bidder, who shall also agree to purchase of said party of the second part all permanent and valuable buildings necessarily erected by said party, for the convenient use of the water-power hereby leased, at such price as such buildings shall be adjudged to be worth by three judicious, disinterested freeholders, to be chosen as hereinbefore specified, provided such buildings shall be erected on land belonging to the State, or land which can be purchased by said bidder at a reasonable price, to be determined by said appraisers. And if no such bids shall be made on the terms aforesaid, at a higher rent than is herein specified, said party shall be entitled to such renewal on the terms of this lease."

The first term of thirty years expired on the first day of November, 1883. Prior to that date the board of public works notified the assignee of said lease that said board would not renew said lease for an additional term after the expiration of the first term, for the reason that said leased water was necessary for the purposes of navigation, and its use for hydraulic purposes interfered with the navigation of the canal, and said board proposed to resume the same. On the sixth day of May following, the board passed an order formally resuming the use of the said water.

The petition avers that the said relator and those under whom he claims have performed all the conditions of said lease on their part to be performed; that lasting and valuable improvements have been placed upon the lands of the State, described in said lease; and that the board of public works has resumed the water-power so let, but has neglected and refused to renew said lease or to appoint an appraiser of said improvements, though often requested so to do. The prayer of said petition is for writ of *mandamus* commanding the defendant to select an appraiser so as to ascertain the value of said improvements, and for general relief.

The parcel of land included in said lease, as is expressly stated therein, was leased for the purpose of enabling the party of the second part to use and enjoy the use of the water-power thereby leased. The land was a mere incident to the use of the water, and, independently of that, is of comparatively small value. The lease provided that upon resumption of the use of the water the entire lease should cease and determine.

The main question in this case is the proper construction of the statute authorizing the lease of water-power by the board of public works—being sections 20 to 23, inclusive, of the act of March 23, 1840, found in volume 3 (Supplement), Revised Statutes, page 417. These sections are as follows:

"Sec. 20. Whenever, in the opinion of the board of public works, there shall be surplus water in either of the canals, or in the feeders, or at the dams erected for the purpose of supplying either of said canals with water, or for the purpose of improving the navigation of any river, and constructed at the expense of the State, over and above the quantity of water which may be required for the purpose of navigation, the said commissieners may order such surplus water, and any lands granted to, or purchased by the State, for the purpose of using the same, or such part thereof as they may deem expedient, to be sold for hydraulic purposes, subject to such conditions and reservations as they may consider necessary and proper, either in perpetuity or for a limited number of years, for a certain annual rent, or otherwise, as they may deem most beneficial for the interests of the State.

"Sec. 21. The provisions of the foregoing section shall extend to and include the water passing round locks, from one level to another, on either of the canals of the State.

"Sec. 22. No hydraulic power, nor right to the use of any water, shall be sold, leased or conveyed, except such as shall accrue from the surplus water of the canal, feeders or dams, or from the water passing round any lock, after supplying the full quantity necessary for the purposes of navigation.

"Sec. 23. Every lease, grant, or conveyance of water-power shall contain a reservation and condition that the State, or its authorized agents, may at any time resume the privilege or right to the use of water, or any portion thereof, whenever it may be deemed necessary for the purposes of navigation, or whenever its use for hydraulic purposes shall be found in any manner to interfere with and injuriously affect the navigation of either of the canals, feeders, or streams from which the water shall be taken for such hydraulic purposes; and, whenever such privilege shall be resumed, in whole or in part, the sum paid therefor, or the rent reserved, or such reasonable portion thereof as shall be determined upon, agreeably to the conditions and stipulations of the lease or deed of conveyance aforesaid, shall be refunded or remitted to the purchaser or lessee, his heirs, or assigns."

T. J. Godfrey and *Marsh & Loree* for plaintiff.

James Lawrence, attorney-general, for defendant.

JOHNSON, C. J.—The twentieth section of the above-recited statute authorizes the board of public works to sell, for hydraulic purposes, the surplus water in the canals of the State, their feeders, dams, and locks, " subject to such conditions as they may consider necessary and proper, either in perpetuity or for a limited number of years, for a certain annual rent, or otherwise, as they may deem most beneficial for the interest of the State." *FACTS.*

By section 22, the board is expressly limited to a sale of such surplus water as may remain " after supplying the full quantity necessary for the purposes of navigation."

And to make this limitation effective, section 23 requires that " every lease, grant, or conveyance of water-power shall contain a reservation and condition that the State or its authorized agents may at any time resume the privilege or right to the use of water, or any portion thereof, whenever it may be deemed necessary for the purposes of navigation, or when its use for hydraulic purposes shall be found in any manner to interfere with and injuriously affect the navigation of either of the canals, feeders, or streams from which the water shall be taken for such hydraulic purposes."

The admitted facts of this case show that the lease before us contains such reservation and condition, and that the authorities of the State have properly resumed the right to the use of the water granted by this lease. The sole question involved is as to the validity of a proviso annexed to said reservation and condition, which reads as follows:

" Provided the party of the first part shall first pay or tender to the party of the second part the value of all lasting improvement now made or hereafter to be made by said second party, said value to be determined by three disinterested persons chosen for that purpose, each party choosing one and the two thus chosen to choose the third."

If the clause thus quoted is valid, the relator is entitled to the relief sought, otherwise not. Had the board of public works the power to bind the State to purchase the improvements, should it be deemed neces- *POWER OF BOARD OF PUBLIC WORKS TO PURCHASE WATER IMPROVEMENTS.*

sary to resume the use of the surplus water for the purposes
of navigation or when its use by the lessees will be found
injuriously to affect navigation? We think not. The latter
clause of section 23 provides what shall be the right of the
lessees in case of such resumption. Whenever such privilege
shall be resumed in whole or in part, the sum paid therefor,
or the rent reserved, or such portion thereof as shall be determined upon agreeably to the conditions and stipulations of
the lease or deed of conveyance aforesaid, shall be refunded
or remitted to the purchaser or lessee, his heirs or assigns."

This clause, which section 23 requires shall be inserted in
RESERVING CON-
TROL OF WATER
POWER. the lease, and which seems to embrace the only
right reserved to the lessee in case of the resumption of the surplus water, is, strange to say, omitted from this
lease, and in lieu thereof is the proviso above quoted, which
requires of the State, as the condition precedent to the resumption of such water-power, that the State shall first pay
or tender to the lessee the value of all lasting improvements,
and which further requires that the State shall pay such
amount as shall be fixed by arbitrators mutually chosen by
the parties. Whether we regard the obligation to purchase
as a condition precedent or subsequent, the result is the same,
as in neither case is the power conferred to make such purchase.

It may well be doubted whether the board of public works,
BOARD OF PUB-
LIC WORKS.
CONTRACT DIS-
POSING OF SUR-
PLUS WATER. as the agent of the State, has power to enter into
arbitration that will bind the State in any matter
committed to their charge, in the absence of express
legislative authority. However this may be, it is quite
clear that no authority is delegated to them to contract away
or restrict the right to resume this surplus water whenever
its use for navigation is required. The power to grant or
lease water privileges is incidental and subordinate to the
public use. The duty of those having charge of the canals to
employ all the water, if needed for public use, is imperative.
The public right is paramount; so important was this principle deemed by the legislature that this right to resume the
surplus water was required to be inserted in every lease,
grant, or conveyance. The board possesses no power to
surrender this right or hamper themselves in its exercise. By
this so-called proviso they cannot resume this surplus water,

however much it may be needed for the public use, or however injuriously its use by the lessee may affect the navigation of the canals, without purchasing the improvements. Such a restriction upon the performance by them of an important public trust is clearly unauthorized, and is contrary to that public policy under which the canals have been constructed and operated. They were constructed at great expense for the public convenience and welfare. They are public navigable highways. The statutes in force from time to time show how careful the State has been to preserve these great highways free from all encroachments that might interfere with their usefulness.

The board of public works have power to perfect, render useful, maintain, keep in repair, and protect the same. Revised Statutes, 7691. This is a power of superintendence for the protection and maintenance of the canals, including everything that pertains to them. They posses no powers except such as are expressly conferred by law or that are necessarily implied, the purpose of which is the maintenance of the canals as public highways.

BUT MAY MAINTAIN AND SUPERVISE THE SAME.

It is said, however, in argument, that the 20th section in the act of 1840 authorizes the board to grant this surplus water, "subject to such conditions and reservations as they may consider necessary and proper;" and that this proviso, which makes it a condition precedent that the State shall first pay or tender the value of the permanent improvements upon the resumption of the surplus water, is a condition within the meaning of that clause, which the board could agree to if they deemed it necessary and proper. It is further said that at that day it was to the interest of the State to encourage the development of manufacturing interests along the line of the canals by offering favorable terms to lessees or grantees so that their products would be transported over the canals, and thus increase the revenue of the State. In reply to this it may be said : 1st. As already shown, the board possessed no power to surrender the duty of performing the public trust committed to their charge, and the limitation, self-imposed, to pay for these improvements before resuming the water, though it may be necessary for the purpose of navigation,

POWER OF BOARD OF PUBLIC WORKS TO GRANT SURPLUS WATER ON CONDITIONS.

was against the public policy of the State, which made it the duty of the board to resume this water at any time when needed for the public use, untrammeled by any condition or any right of the lessee to prevent it.

2d. The phrase "subject to such conditions and reservations" has the same meaning as it has in section 23, where it is provided that every lease, grant, or conveyance of water-power shall contain "a reservation and condition that the State or its authorized agents may at any time resume the use of water, or any portion thereof."

What we mean to say is that these terms, "conditions, and reservations" are such as are imposed upon the lessees or grantees of water-power, and not upon the State.

3d. But if we are in error in this construction of the statute, and these words embrace conditions and reservations imposed upon the State, they must be such as relate to the use of the water for hydraulic purposes, which are in the nature of the quantity used, the manner of its use, etc. It is quite clear they are not broad enough to embrace conditions to be imposed upon the State after the right to use the water has expired, or after the State has abandoned the canal as a public highway. By such resumption or abandonment, which are identical in their results so far as lessees are concerned (Hubbard *v.* Toledo, 21 Ohio St. 379), the State is not liable to respond in damages to the lessee. If it were otherwise the State would be compelled to maintain her canals at any sacrifice for the exclusive benefit of the lessees of surplus water, or become the purchaser of the property of the lessee, thus making the incidental purpose paramount to the public use.

If this obligation to purchase is valid in this instance, it is within the power of the board of public works to bind the State to become the purchaser of all the permanent improvements in the State, erected for the use of surplus water leased or granted. They cannot do this, although they might deem it necessary and proper as a means of developing manufacturing interests along the line of the canals, and thereby increasing transportation over them and thus enhancing the revenues from the canals.

4th. This obligation to purchase, when the surplus water is

resumed, is in legal effect a covenant to purchase, and not a condition annexed to the use of the water. OBLIGATION TO PURCHASE WHEN SURPLUS WATER IS RESUMED NOT A CONDITION.

A condition in its legal signification is something annexed to the grant, while this is in the nature of a stipulation binding the State to purchase when the lease is terminated. The State covenants that upon the resumption of the surplus water it will purchase the improvements at a price to be fixed by arbitrators. If it be called a condition instead of a covenant, it can only apply to the right of the State to resume water.

In this sense, it is a condition precedent to such resumption. As such it would be clearly illegal, for, as we have shown, there can be no restriction on the right and duty to resume the use of this surplus water whenever it becomes necessary for the public use.

5th. The statute provides what shall be the relief to which the purchaser or lessee is entitled on such resumption. The last clause of section 23 reads thus: " Whenever such privilege shall be resumed in whole or in part, the sum paid therefor, or the rent reserved, or such reasonable portion as shall be determined upon agreeable to the conditions and stipulations of the lease or deed of conveyance aforesaid, shall be refunded or remitted to the purchaser or lessee, his heirs or assigns."

As was said in Hubbard *v.* Toledo, *supra*, this clause of the statute expressly negatives the liability of the State for the destruction of the privilege, by resuming the grant, beyond what is therein provided; namely, in case of resumption of such surplus water the sum paid therefor, or the rent reserved, or a reasonable portion thereof, shall be refunded or remitted. Hubbard *v.* Toledo, 21 Ohio St. 379; Elevator Co. *v.* Cincinnati, 30 Ohio St. 629; Fox *v.* Cincinnati, 33 Ohio St. 492; Same case, 104 U. S.; State *v.* Railway, 37 Ohio St. 157.

Writ refused.

FULKERTH

v.

COUNTY OF STANISLAUS.

(Advance Case, California. August 22, 1885.)

A sheriff having furnished necessary food to prisoners in jail is entitled to be paid a reasonable compensation therefor, to be determined by the county board, subject to review by the courts in an action for such reasonable compensation, if the sheriff be dissatisfied with what is allowed.

APPEAL from a judgment of the superior court of Stanislaus county, entered in favor of the defendant. The opinion states the facts.

C. C. Wright for the appellant.

Wm. O. Minor for the respondent.

BELCHER, C. C.—The plaintiff was sheriff of the defendant county during the year 1881, and as such furnished meals to the prisoners confined in the county jail. For the meals so furnished he made out an account in proper form and duly verified, and presented it to the board of supervisors for allowance. In this account he charged twenty-five cents for each meal furnished. The board acted upon the account and found it to be a proper county charge, but, considering it greater in amount than was justly due, allowed twenty cents only for each meal. The plaintiff, being dissatisfied with the amount allowed him, within six months after the final action of the board commenced this action to recover the amount claimed by him to be due. The defendant demurred to the complaint on the ground that it did not state facts sufficient to constitute a cause of action, and its demurrer was sustained. The plaintiff declined to amend his complaint, and thereupon judgment was entered in favor of the defendant. The appeal is from this judgment.

For the respondent it is insisted—and this is the only point made—that the board of supervisors, in allowing or disallowing claims against the county, acts in a quasi-judicial capacity, and that its action in this case was made final and conclusive by the provisions of section 1611 of the Penal Code. That section reads as follows: " The sheriff must receive all per sons committed to the jail by competent authority, and provide them with necessary food, clothing, and bedding, for which he shall be allowed a reasonable compensation, to be determined by the board of supervisors."

We do not think the words "to be determined by the board of supervisors" had the meaning and effect claimed for them.   SUPERVISORS TO AUDIT CLAIMS.

All claims against the county must be presented to the board of supervisors for allowance, and where the amount of the claim has not been fixed by statute or the judgment of some competent court, the board is required, if it be a proper county charge, to find and allow the amount which is justly due.   Political Code, sec. 4074.

If the board allows less than is claimed, and claimant is dissatisfied with the amount allowed him on his account, he "may sue the county therefor at any time within six months after the final action of the board, but not afterwards; and if in such action judgment is recovered for more than the board allowed, on presentation of the judgment the board must allow and pay the same, together with the costs adjudged; but if no more is recovered than the board allowed, the board must pay the claimant no more than was originally allowed." Political Code, sec. 4075.

This provision is general, and applies to all accounts presented against the county.

By subdivision 4 of section 4344 of the same code, the "expenses necessarily incurred in the support of persons charged with or convicted of crimes, and committed therefor to the county jail," are made county charges.

The plaintiff, having furnished "necessary food" to the prisoners in jail, was entitled to a "reasonable compensation" therefor.   What was a reasonable compensation was to be determined by the board of supervisors in the first instance, but that determination was no more final than would have been the finding by the board of the amount which was justly due if the account had been presented for any other proper county charge.

"To determine what is a reasonable compensation," and "to find what is justly due," are expressions, we think, of equivalent import.   The plaintiff, being   BUT SUBJECT TO JUDICIAL REVIEW.
dissatisfied with the amount allowed him on his account, had

the right, therefore, to sue the county for the amount which he claimed to be reasonable.

The cases cited by counsel for respondent from the reports of this State do not touch the question involved here, and those cited from New York are not in point, for the reason that no law existed in that State providing for suit upon a claim disallowed, in whole or in part, by the board. Chase *v.* The County of Saratoga, 33 Barb. 603; Martin *v.* Board of Supervisors, 29 N. Y. 645; Price *v.* The County of Sacramento, 6 Cal. 254.

Judgment should be reversed and the cause remanded, with direction to the court below to overrule the demurrer.

SEARLS, C., and FOOTE, C., concurred.

BY THE COURT.—For the reasons given in the foregoing opinion, the judgment is reversed and the cause remanded, with direction to the court below to overrule the demurrer.

THE BOARD OF COMMISSIONERS OF CARROLL COUNTY

v.

GRESHAM.

(101 *Indiana*, 53.)

Where official duties to which no compensation is attached are imposed upon a public officer, they must be performed gratuitously.

The act regulating the fees of sheriffs was intended by the legislature to be a complete fee bill, prescribing, so far as could be, the services for which they should receive compensation, and the fees designated therein are to be deemed a full remuneration for all services incident to the office, and such officer is entitled to no extra compensation for keeping the county jail and caring for prisoners.

There being no statute authorizing the circuit court to commit insane persons, as such, to the county jail, the presumption is that they were duly committed for some offence, and that they were received and held as other prisoners, and for their care the sheriff can claim no extra compensation.

FROM Tippecanoe Circuit Court.

J. C. Nelson, J. C. Odell, R. P. Davidson, and *J. C. Davidson* for appellant.

J. Applegate, C. R. Pollard, J. R. Coffroth, and *T. A. Stuart* for appellee.

MITCHELL, J—The appellee's claim, as finally amended and passed upon in the circuit court, was stated in his bill of particulars as follows: FACTS.

" *The Board of Commissioners of the County of Carroll, in the State of Indiana.*

"TO EDWARD H. GRESHAM, Dr.

" For services rendered personally by plaintiff in keeping the jail of the county of Carroll, in the State of Indiana, for 4 years from Nov. 8, 1876, to Nov. 8, 1880 . . . . $4380

" To cash paid Will H. Haughey, for like services, from Jan. 1, 1877, to Nov. 1, 1879, at $75 per month.   1600

" To cash paid William Scott, for like services, from Sept. 1, 1879, to November 8, 1880, at $75 per month.   712

" To cash paid Frank Gresham, for like services, from November 8, 1876, to November 10, 1880, at $75 per month   . .   2190."

It was specially found by the court that whatever was done by Gresham in "keeping the jail" was done while he was the sheriff of Carroll County, and it was also found that during the whole period of his service as sheriff he had claimed and was allowed by the commissioners compensation for all services for which the statute makes specific provision.

After enumerating various specific services which the court found the appellee and his assistants performed in and about the jail, such as carrying fuel into the jail, cleaning the closets, locking the prisoners in their cells at night and letting them out in the morning, and washing and cleansing some insane persons who were committed to jail by order of the Carroll Circuit Court, etc., the court further found as follows:

" That the duties and services so enumerated, and including the care of said insane persons, and for which no specific pay is allowed, are and were of the value of $1000 per year, and for the whole four years are and were of the value of $4000."

Upon the facts found the court stated as a conclusion of law that the appellee was entitled to recover $4000, and accordingly judgment was rendered against the board of commissioners for that sum. It is apparent from the special findings of the court that for all services rendered by the appellee for which there is a specific compensation fixed by law he has been allowed and paid ; but the argument is pressed that because the services enumerated were rendered, and were necessary, and because the law provides no specific compensation for such services, therefore the county is liable to pay for them as upon a *quantum meruit.*

That an individual is elected to the office of sheriff in a particular county, and because he thereby becomes *ex officio* the jailer of that county, and responsible for the

STATUTE FIXES COMPENSATION OF OFFICERS.

care and custody of the prisoners confined in the jail which is provided and maintained by law in that county, does not imply that the municipality shall come under any other obligation to him except that provided by the very terms of the statute. The statute prescribes, specifically, the duties of the sheriff with respect to receiving and caring for prisoners confined in the county jail, and fixes the compensation which shall be paid him for receiving, discharging, and boarding them ; and when the county, through its board of commissioners, has provided a suitable jail, and maintains in it suitable furniture and appliances for its proper keeping, and pays the jailer the compensation specifically provided by statute, it has discharged its municipal obligation and exhausted its corporate power over the subject.

There can be no such thing in legal contemplation as an

NO IMPLIED ASSUMPSIT AS TO FEES OF COUNTY OFFICERS.

implied *assumpsit* on the part of a county with respect to the services of county officers. In performing services for the county, the officer and the county stand related to each other precisely as an individual and the officer, the statute regulating fees being the measure of compensation for the one and the extent of the liability of the other in each case.

For services imposed by law upon the officer, which are

PREREQUISITES OF LIABILITY OF COUNTY FOR OFFICERS' SERVICES

not specially rendered for the municipality, as a prerequisite to the liability of the county for said services the officer must show: 1. A statute fixing the compensation for the service. 2. A law authorizing or making the county liable to pay for such service out of its treasury. It is of the highest concern to the public that this should be so ; otherwise it would be within the power of one body of county officials to compensate the other county officers out of the public treasury, as a matter of grace and favor, without limit or restraint.

This principle has been recognized in this State from the beginning, and accordingly it has invariably been held that official duties imposed upon a public officer to which no compensation is attached must be performed as all official duties anciently were, gratuitously.

The act regulating the fees of sheriffs was plainly intended by the legislature to be a complete fee bill, prescribing, so far as could be, with precision and certainty, the services for which they should receive compensation, and this makes it all the more apparent that the fees designated therein are to be deemed a full remuneration for all services incident to the office. Rawley *v.* Board, etc., 2 Blackf. 355 ; City of Brazil *v.* McBride, 69 Ind. 244 ; Board, etc., *v.* Leslie, 63 Ind. 492 ; Hartwell *v.* Supervisors, etc., 43 Wis. 311 ; Freeholders of Morris Co. *v.* Freeman, 44 N. J. L. 631 ; Atchison Co. *v.* Tomlinson, 9. Kans. 167. *[FEE BILLS OF SHERIFFS.]*

In the argument of counsel, stress is laid on the provision, in the act above mentioned, that " in all cases where the sheriff shall perform any service for the county required by law to be performed by him, and there is no provision for its payment, the board of county commissioners shall allow and pay such sheriff the same compensation as is allowed by law for similar services." R. S. 1882, sec. 5874.

The services enumerated in the special finding, and for which the appellee had judgment below, were in no sense services performed " for the county." The prisoners and other persons committed to his custody, to whom attention was given, were not committed to the jail by nor for the county, nor was the county interested in them in any respect different from a city or town, or other corporation within the county, except to discharge its statutory obligation of providing, furnishing, and maintaining the jail, and paying the sheriff the compensation provided by law for receiving, discharging, and boarding them while in his custody. *[CARING FOR PRISONERS NOT A SERVICE PERFORMED FOR COUNTY.]*

It is contended further that because the court, in its special finding, found that the appellee had the care of some insane persons who were committed to the jail by the order of the Carrol Circuit Court, this case is thereby distinguishable from that of Bynum *v.* Board, etc., 100 Ind. 90.

Our attention has been called to no statute, nor are we

INSANE PERSONS PRESUMED HELD AS PRISONERS FOR MISDEMEANOR. aware of any, which authorized the Carroll Circuit Court to commit insane persons, as such, to the county jail. We are to presume, therefore, that the insane persons who were committed to the jail by the circuit court were so committed in pursuance of a conviction duly had for some misdemeanor of which they were found guilty, and that they were received and held under the law as other prisoners. Adhering to the ruling in the case of Bynum *v.* Board, etc., *supra*, and the authorities therein cited, it results that on the facts found by the court the conclusion of law should have been that the appellee was not entitled to recover for any of the services mentioned in the complaint.

The judgment is reversed, with costs, with instructions to the court below to state its conclusions of law and render judgment for the appellant in accordance with this opinion.

THE COUNTY OF BRISTOL

v.

FRANKLIN GRAY.

(Advance Case, Massachusetts.   Dec. 6, 1885.)

The statutes of this State provide that the county commissioners shall receive annual salaries which shall be in full for their compensation for services as such commissioners, including their travelling expenses.

A sheriff is responsible for the safe-keeping of prisoners under his charge, and it is the duty of the county commissioners to provide necessary supplies, materials, and implements, establish rules for employing and governing the prisoners, make contracts for their employment, and settle accounts for the productions of their labor with the masters who employ them.

It is the duty of the master to dispose of articles manufactured through the labor of the prisoners, and the necessary and reasonable expenses of making sales thereof should be allowed the master.

PROCEEDING on agreed statement of facts to test the right of a county commissioner to charge for the sale of articles manufactured in the House of Correction.

Mr. Edgar J. Sherman, Attorney-General, for plaintiff.

Messrs. Morton & Jennings for defendant.

FIELD, J.—Public Statutes, ch. 22, sec. 14, provide that "the commissioners and special commissioners of the several counties shall receive from the respective county treasuries, in full payment for all their services and travel, the following annual salaries, to be divided among the county commissioners in proportion to the services rendered, the travel performed, and the expenses incurred by each; and no other or additional compensation shall be paid to them for any service performed by them for their respective counties." By the Revised Statutes, ch. 84, § 4, they were to be paid $1 for every ten miles travelled and $3 a day "for the time employed in discharging the duties of their office." By statute 1859, ch. 163, § 1, they were to be paid, "out of the treasury of each county, a fixed annual salary which shall be in full payment for all services rendered and travel performed by them in discharge of their duties in their respective counties." See, also, Gen. Stat., ch. 17, § 29, and stat. 1863, ch. 185, § 1. Stat. 1864, ch. 280, sec. 1, provides that "the salaries provided for the county commissioners of the several counties by chapter one hundred and eighty-five of the acts of the year eighteen hundred and sixty shall hereafter be taken to be in full payment for all services rendered, travel performed, and expenses incurred," etc., "and no other additional compensation shall be paid them for any service performed by them for their respective counties." Stat. 1867, ch. 340, provided that "the commissioners and special commissioners of the several counties of the commonwealth shall receive," etc., "in full payment for all their services and travel, payable as now provided by law, the following annual salaries," etc. See stat. 1871, ch. 236; stat. 1872, ch. 151, and stat. 1879, ch. 295.

We think these statutes and the Public Statutes mean that the annual salaries shall be in full payment for all their services and travel as county commissioners, and that no other compensation for such services and travel shall be paid to them. *STATUTES AS TO SALARY CONSTRUED.*

The county commissioners provide a house or houses of correction for the counties, Pub. Stat. ch. 220, § 7, and suitable materials and implements, and establish needful rules, etc., Ibid. § 11, and examine all accounts of the master "relating to the earnings of the prisoners, and all expenses of the institution," etc., Ibid. § 12. They may make contracts for work

to be done or for letting out to hire the prisoners, Ibid. secs.
13, 14. The sheriff, except in the County of Suffolk, has "the custody, rule, and charge" of the
house of correction and of all prisoners therein,
"and shall keep the same by himself or by his deputy as jailer, master, or keeper, for whom he shall be responsible," Ibid. §§ 23 and 33. The county commissioners, "without extra charge or commission to themselves or to any other
person," procure the necessary supplies for the house of correction, Ibid. § 53. The charges and expenses, etc., "shall be
paid from the county treasury, the accounts of the keeper or
master being first settled and allowed by the commissioners,"
etc., Ibid. § 54. By § 356 it is provided that each master or
keeper shall cause the articles manufactured by the prisoners
in his custody, or the products of their labor, to be disposed
of to the best advantage, and under the direction of said commissioners "shall cause accounts to be kept of such accounts
to them for settlement semiannually," etc. "He shall pay
into the treasury the amount of sales and the proceeds of the
labor and earnings of the prisoners in his county, or the balance thereof." These provisions are derived from Stat. 1834,
ch. 137, § 18.

The general scheme is that the sheriff, by his deputy as
master, shall be responsible for the safe-keeping of the prisoners, and that the county commissioners shall furnish the neccessary supplies, material, and implements, establish rules for
employing, reforming, governing, and punishing the prisoners, make contracts for the work of the prisoners,
and settle the accounts of the master. But it is
the duty of the master to dispose of the articles
manufactured to the best advantage, and in this the statutes
do not make the master the agent or servant of the commissioners. The commissioners do not appoint him and they
cannot remove him, although they may ask the Superior
Court to remove him, Ibid. § 24; and we cannot see that it is
any part of the duty of the commissioners to make sales of the
articles produced by the labor of the prisoners. The necessary and reasonable expenses of making such sales should of
course be allowed the master. The defendant, therefore, in
making the sales, was not acting as county commissioner, and
whatever may be the propriety of forbidding by law any

such employment of a commissioner by the master, a majority of the court think it is not forbidden by existing statutes. Judgment affirmed.

WALLER

v.

WOOD.

(101 *Indiana*, 138.)

Under the statute, R. S. 1881, section 4993, the county commissioners constitute the board of health of the county, and a physician who is selected by the county board of health as its secretary is entitled to such compensation from the county treasury as such board may determine.

When the secretary's compensation is determined by the board of health, it is the duty of the county commissioners as such to cause it to be paid out of the county treasury by the auditor's warrant for the amount on the treasurer.

Where the county commissioners made an allowance to the secretary of a board of health, the supreme court will presume, in favor of the ruling of the circuit court dismissing an appeal therefrom, that the board of health had determined the amount of his compensation, and that the allowance was made by the county commissioners in payment of the same.

Whether the allowance by the county commissioners to the secretary of the county board of health is not of itself a determination of the amount of such compensation within the meaning of the statute.

No appeal lies from an order of a county board of health fixing the compensation of its secretary, the statute creating boards of health investing them with discretionary power in that regard, and making no provision for appeal.

FROM the Steuben Circuit Court.

S. A. Powers and *G. B. Adams* for appellant.

J. A. Woodhull and —— *Brown* for appellee.

BEST, C.—The appellee filed the following verified claim against the county :

" STEUBEN COUNTY, INDIANA,
            " To H. D. Wood, Dr. :
    " As health officer Steuben county, for the year. 1883, $250."

This claim was allowed by the board of commissioners, and from such order the appellant, who was a tax-   FACTS.

payer of the county, and who felt aggrieved by tne decision, appealed to the circuit court. The appeal, upon motion, was there dismissed, and here such ruling is assigned as error.

It is obvious that this claim was for services rendered as "health officer" of said county, under and by virtue of section 4993, R. S. 1881. This section is in these words:

"The trustees of each town, the mayor and common council of each incorporated city (except where a regularly constituted board of health, by ordinance of such city, now exists or may hereafter be created), and the board of county commissioners of each county shall constitute a board of health, *ex officio,* for each of the several towns, cities, and counties respectively of the State, who shall perform such duties respectively required of them by this act without compensation. They shall annually, in the month of January, complete their organization by the election of a secretary, who shall be a physician. The secretary of such local boards of health, and the secretary of any regularly constituted board of health of any incorporated city, shall be the health officer of every town, city, or county, respectively, for the purposes provided in this act, and shall be allowed such compensation from.the town, city, or county treasury, respectively, as the board electing them may determine: provided that the secretary of each county board of health shall render such medical and surgical services as may be required by persons confined in the county jail of such county, and such other medical services as may be required of him by the board of county commissioners."

By virtue of this section, a physician who is selected by SECRETARY OF the county board of health as its secretary is entitled to such compensation from the county treasury as such board may determine. This the appellant concedes, but insists that the authority to make such officer an allowance for such compensation is conferred upon the board of health, and not upon the board of commissioners ; and as the allowance in this case was, therefore, unauthorized, any person interested and aggrieved might appeal therefrom under the general statute authorizing appeals from the board of commissioners. This position cannot be maintained. The statute above recited does not confer any authority upon the board of health to make such allowance. It simply authorizes such board to determine the amount of compensation, and when determined the duty rests upon the board of commissioners to cause it to be paid out of the county treasury. This is done by an allowance upon which the auditor draws his warrant upon the treasurer. This is the usual mode, and the statute does not change it. If, then, the amount of the appellee's compensation as such officer was determined by the board of health, and the allowance was made for the sum thus fixed, the board of commissioners did have authority to make the allowance. The contrary does not appear; and as this court will indulge every reasonable presumption in favor of the ruling of the circuit court, it will indulge the presumption that the board of health had determined the amount of such compensation, and that the allowance was made by the board of commissioners in payment of the same. Kissell *v.* Anderson, 73 Ind. 485; Coulter *v.* Coulter, 81 Ind. 542; Peck *v.* Board, etc., 87 Ind. 221. *(ALLOWANCE BY COMMISSIONERS.)*

This much has been said upon the assumption that the county commissioners must determine the amount of such compensation while acting strictly as the board of health. This, however, is probably not required. The commissioners constitute the county board of health, and it would seem that an allowance by them to the secretary of such board was of itself a determination of the amount of such compensation within the meaning of the statute, and that such determination need not precede the allowance nor be made by them while formally acting as the county board of health. A substantial compliance is all that is required.

The statute creating boards of health makes no provision for an appeal, and we think, by implication, denies an appeal from an order awarding the "health officer" compensation for his services. The amount *(NO APPEAL FROM BOARD OF HEALTH DECISION.)* of compensation is a mere matter of discretion with the board of health, and from a decision made in matters of discretion no appeal lies. Sims *v.* Board, etc., 39 Ind. 40; Moffitt *v.* State, *ex rel.*, 40 Ind. 217; Grusenmeyer *v.* City of Logansport, 76 Ind. 549.

An appeal cannot be taken without depriving the board of health of the right to determine the amount of compensation to which its secretary is entitled, and, therefore, the statute, by investing the board with such right, impliedly denies an appeal. The appeal in this case was, therefore, properly dismissed. This conclusion is in entire harmony with the doctrine that an appeal lies in all cases where it is not expressly or impliedly withheld, as was decided in Grusenmeyer *v.* City of Logansport, *supra,* and the cases following it.

This conclusion renders it unnecessary to notice the assignment that the claim filed does not state facts sufficient to constitute a cause of action.

The order of the court in dismissing the appeal should, therefore, be affirmed.

PER CURIAM.—It is therefore ordered, upon the foregoing opinion, that the judgment be and it is hereby in all things affirmed, at the appellant's costs.

SMITH

v.

STROTHER, Auditor, etc.

(Advance Case, California. August 27, 1885.)

The act of March 21, 1885, California Legislature, providing that the compensation of official shorthand reporters shall be fixed by the judge in whose court they act, is not unconstitutional. It is neither a delegation of legislative authority to the judiciary, nor a violation of the constitutional provision requiring a uniform system of county governments, although it fixes a different rate of compensation according to differences in the population of the counties served by such reporters; nor is it unconstitutional as imposing a new set of officials on the people.

APPEAL from a judgment of the superior court of the city and county of San Francisco, entered in favor of the defendant, in a proceeding to compel him to audit plaintiff's demand as official reporter.

W. M. Pierson and *A. L. Hart, amicus curiæ,* for appellant. *John L. Love* for respondent.

Ross, J.—The last legislature passed an act, approved

FACTS.   March 21, 1885, entitled "An act to amend section 274 of an act entitled 'An act to establish a civil code of procedure relative to the compensation of court reporters," by which it is provided that the official reporter shall receive as compensation for his services a monthly salary, to be fixed by the judge, by an order duly entered on the minutes of the court, which salary shall be paid out the treasury of the county, in the same manner and at the same time as the salaries of county officers, with a *proviso* to the effect that such salary shall not exceed three hundred dollars per month in counties having a population of one hundred thousand and over, and shall not exceed two hundred and seventy-five dollars per month in counties having a population less than one hundred thousand and exceeding fifty thousand, and so on to and including counties having a population less than five thousand, in which the maximum is fixed at seventy-five dollars per month. The act contains other provisions not important to mention, and further provides that "in civil cases in which the testimony is taken down by the official reporter, each party shall pay a *per diem* of two dollars and fifty cents before judgment or verdict therein is entered; and where the testimony is transcribed, the party or parties ordering it shall pay ten cents per folio for such transcription on delivery thereof ; said *per diem* and transcription fees to be paid to the clerk of the court, and by him paid into the treasury of the county, and such portion as shall be paid by the prevailing party may be taxed as costs in the case."

The act is claimed to be violative of the constitution in three respects : First, as "a delegation of legislative power to the judiciary ;" second, "in violation of the constitutional provision requiring a uniform system of county governments," and, third, because it imposes a new set of officials upon the people, in contravention of section 6, article xi., of the constitution."

Of course, we have nothing to do with the policy of the law, and it is our duty to sustain it unless we can see clearly that it is in conflict with the paramount law of the State. And this we cannot do. In so far as the right to confer upon the judges the power and duty of fixing the compensation of reporters is concerned, the provisions of the act in question are similar to those of all of the former statutes upon the subject, commencing with the act of May 17, 1861, Statutes 1861, page 497. Immediately prior to the adoption of the codes, the law with respect to phonographic reporters of the courts in San Francisco was contained in the act of March 13, 1866, Stats. 1865-6, p. 232; and in the act of March 28, 1868, Stats. 1867-8, p. 425. Each of those statutes, as well as the provisions of the code of civil procedure, authorized the judge to fix the compensation of the reporter in certain cases. And in *Ex parte* Reis, 64 Cal. 234, it was said that whether the acts of 1866 and 1868 or the provisions of the Code were to control the determination of that case was immaterial, as "in either case, just before the adoption of the present constitution, the district court and county court could legally employ the power of appointing a shorthand reporter, fix his compensation in criminal cases, and order such compensation to be paid, and it was the duty of the treasurer to pay the same upon the order of the court." It is true that the point now made was not made in *Ex parte* Reis, nor does the constitutionality of the various statutory provisions conferring upon the courts the power of fixing the compensation of reporters seem ever before to have been raised in this State.

In our opinion, the point is not well taken. Phonographic reporters are officers of the court in the same sense that sheriffs and clerks are. They constitute part of the judicial system of the State. The court may fix the fees of referees, commissioners, keepers, etc., in proper cases—why not of reporters? We see in the act of doing so none of the characteristics of legislation. Nor does it in any manner contravene that provision of the constutition requiring the legislature to establish "a uniform system of county governments." Phonographic reporters are not county officers, and have nothing to do with county governments. They are, as already said, officers of the courts, and constitute a part of the judicial system of the State. Nor does the act in question "impose a new set of officials upon the people, in contravention of section 6 of article xi. of the State constitution." The "officials" referred to in the act of March 21, 1885, were already provided for by law. See *Ex parte* Reis, 64 Cal. 233, and the statutes there and herein before referred to.

Section 6 of article xi. of the constitution, cited in support of this point of respondent, reads:

COURT SHORT-HAND REPORT-ERS NOT A NEW SET OF OFFICERS

" Corporations for municipal purposes thall not be created by special laws; but the legislature, by general laws, shall provide for the incorporation, organization, and classification, in proportion to population, of cities and towns; which laws may be altered, amended, or repealed. Cities and towns heretofore organized or incorporated may become organized under such general laws whenever a majority of the electors voting at a general election shall so determine, and shall organize in conformity therewith; and cities or towns heretofore or hereafter organized, and all charters thereof framed or adopted by authority of this constitution, shall be subject to and controlled by general laws."

The framers of the constitution, as we had occasion to say in Staude *v.* Election Commissioners, 61 Cal. 320, meant something when they inserted the provision that "cities or towns heretofore or hereafter organized, and all charters thereof framed or adopted by authority of this constitution, shall be subject to and controlled by general laws," and we are not at liberty to hold that they did not mean what they said. Giving, as they did, to all cities and towns, and cities and counties, the right to organize under a general act of incorporation, which the legislature was directed to pass, or to continue their existence under their existing charters, as they might elect, they nevertheless said that, whichever course should be pursued, such cities and towns, and cities and counties, should be subject to and controlled by general laws as should be passed by the legislature other than those for the "incorporation, organization, and classification" of cities and towns. The constitution has provided, in effect, that the city and county of San Francisco shall not be compelled to surrender its present charter for one it does not want; and, further, that its charter shall not be changed by special legislation, directly nor indirectly, under the guise of laws relating to cities, or cities and counties, containing a population of more than one hundred thousand inhabitants. At the same time, recognizing the fact that the city and county of San Francisco remains a subdivision of the State, the constitution has said, in effect, that it, as well as all other cities and towns heretofore or hereafter organized, shall be subject to and controlled by such general laws as the legislature shall enact other than those for the incorporation, organization, and classification, in proportion to population, of cities and towns.

Judgment reversed and cause remanded, with directions to the court below to overrule the demurrer.

THORNTON, J., and MORRISON, C. J., concurred.

McKINSTRY, J., CONCURRING.—I concur in the judgment, and in the conclusion that the act of March 21, 1885, is valid and operative.

MYRICK, J., dissented.

THE STATE *ex rel.* SIMMONS

v.

JOHN.

(81 *Missouri*, 13.)

The right to an office cannot be determined in a proceeding by *mandamus* to compel the payment of salary to a person claiming such office, or in a proceeding to compel the performance of official duty alleged to be obligatory by reason of the official character of the claimant. In such cases he who has the better *prima facie* right must be recognized until, by contesting the election, or by proceedings in *quo warranto*, the rights of the parties are finally determined.

The authority which city councils may have possessed to hear and determine a contested election for city officers was abrogated by section 9, article 8, of the constitution, which provides that "the trial and determination of contested elections of all public officers, whether State, judicial, municipal, or local, except governor and lieutenant-governor, shall be by the courts of law, or one or more of the judges thereof."

APPEAL from Lafayette Circuit Court. Hon. WM. T. WOOD, Judge.

Walker & Field and *Alexander Graves* for appellant.

J. D. Shewalter for respondent.

HOUGH, C. J.—This is a proceeding by *mandamus* to compel the respondent, who is mayor of the city of Lexington, to sign a warrant in favor of the relator, Simmons, drawn by Thomas B. Claggett, who is alleged to be register and treasurer of said city of Lexington. The respondent refused to sign said warrant, and alleged as a reason therefor that said Claggett is not register and treasurer of said city, but that Henry Turner is; that said Turner received a certificate of his election from the city council, was duly commissioned by the mayor, qualified and gave bond as such in June, 1880. The relator admits that said Turner was commissioned and qualified as alleged, but avers that thereafter, and within the time provided by law, said Claggett instituted proceedings before the city council to contest the election of said Turner, and that said counsel declared the vote for said parties, who were the only candidates, to be a tie, and ordered a new election, at which said Claggett was duly elected, and, having received a certificate thereof, was duly commissioned and qualified as register and treasurer as aforesaid. The respondent denies the jurisdiction of the city council to determine a contest for the office of register and treasurer, and its authority to order the special election at which Claggett claims to have been elected.

We have stated the issues, not in the order in which they are stated in the pleadings, but in the order in which they should have been stated. It appears from the record that Turner and Claggett each claimed, at the time these proceedings were instituted, to be the rightful incumbent of the office in question, and each assumed to act as register and treasurer, and that no proceedings by *quo warranto* had been instituted by Claggett against Turner, and that Turner had possession of the records, seal, money, books, and papers of said city, and was performing some of the duties of his office, but that Claggett was recognized by a majority of the council as the rightful register, and kept their minutes. It seems to be conceded that the respondent, as mayor, cannot lawfully sign the warrant in question, unless it has been drawn by the register. The mayor refuses to recognize Claggett as register, and the purpose of this proceeding is to compel him to do so. It is contended for the relator that no inquiry can be had in this proceeding into the right of Claggett to the office of register, and that, being a *de facto* officer, the mayor is bound to recognize his official acts. With the ultimate right of either Turner or Claggett to the office of register we can have nothing to do in this proceeding. The right to an office cannot be determined in a proceeding by *manda-* *mus* to compel the payment of salary to a person

OFFICE — TRIAL OF — RIGHT TO MANDAMUS— QUO WARRANTO.

claiming such office, or, in a proceeding like the present, to compel the performance of official duty alleged to be obligatory by reason of the official character of such claimant. In such cases he who has the better *prima facie* right must be recognized until, by contesting the election or by proceedings in *quo warranto*, the rights of the parties are finally determined. Under this view of the law, which is supported by the decision of this court in the case of the State *ex rel.* Vail *v.* Draper, 48 Mo. 213, it is quite plain on the facts in this record that if Turner had instituted a proceeding by *mandamus* to compel the payment of his salary as register, he would have been entitled to a peremptory writ. The votes for Turner and Claggett were duly canvassed. Turner received the certificate, was duly commissioned and qualified. Thereafter, the city council, without authority of law, heard a contest for the office, declared a tie vote, and ordered another election. We say without authority of law, because it is provided by section 9, article 8, of the constitution that "the trial and determination of contested elections of all public officers, whether State, judicial, municipal, or local, except governor and lieutenant-governor, shall be by the courts of law, or one or more of the judges thereof." This provision, under the first section of the schedule, went into effect on the first day of July, 1877, and completely abrogated all authority which the city council may have previously possessed to hear and determine a contested election for city officers. In granting a certificate of election to Turner, the city council exhausted its jurisdiction in the premises, and all further proceedings had by it, which resulted in the election of Claggett, were wholly and utterly void. State *v.* Draper, *supra.* The election held was at most a mere voluntary election, and Claggett acquired no rights thereunder. The city council could not give Claggett any rights superior to those of Turner, by recognizing him as register in its meetings or otherwise. Turner, being regularly commissioned and qualified, and being ready and willing to discharge the duties of the office, and, in so far as he was able, being engaged in discharging his duties, and being possessed of the books, papers, seal, and records of the city, was properly recognized by the mayor as the rightful register, and the writ of *mandamus* should have been by the cir-

CONTESTED ELECTION—TRIAL OF—CONSTITUTION.

cuit court. Its judgment must, therefore, be reversed. All concur.

Reversed.

NOBLE

v.

BOARD OF COMMISSIONERS OF WAYNE COUNTY.

(101 *Indiana*, 127.)

Before a county clerk is entitled to demand compensation from the county treasury for services performed by him in his official capacity, he must show, first, a statute authorizing him to receive compensation for such services and fixing the amount thereof, and, second, a statute authorizing the county commissioners to pay for such services out of the county treasury.

FROM the Wayne Circuit Court.

H. C. Fox for appellant.

MITCHELL, J.—On the 6th day of June, 1882, William T. Noble, clerk of the circuit court for the county of Wayne, filed with the auditor the following account or claim: _{FACTS.}

"Wayne County, Indiana:

TO WM. T. NOBLE, DR.

Statistical reports of marriage: March 50c., April 50c., May 50c.	$1.50
Three certificates for same, with seal, 50c.	1.50
Order to draw jury 10c, index 10c, certificate 50c.	.70
44 certificates to auditor for jurymen, 50c.	22.00
Venire for jury (under seal)	.75
Four appointments judge *pro tem.*, and certificate, 75c.	3.00
Record of marriages for board of health for y'r	12.50
85 civil order-book entries and orders 10c.	8.50
74 probate order-book entries and orders 10c.	7.40
28 criminal order-book entries and orders 10c.	2.80
Filing 54 miscellaneous papers, 5c.	2.70
2 certificates of election of justices of peace to Secretary of State 50c.	1.00
4 certificates of board of equalization, record and copy to each	6.00
Filing 250 election papers, consisting of tally-sheets, poll-books, and certificates, 5c.	13.25
	$83.60"

Of this account the board of commissioners allowed items amounting to about $30, and disallowed others amounting to $53.65. From the order of the board the clerk appealed to the circuit court, where the case was submitted for trial on an agreed statement of facts, in which statement it was admitted that the services charged for were rendered. The court refused to allow any part of the claim, and the case is before us on appeal.

Before the appellant is entitled to demand compensation from the county treasury for services performed by him in his official capacity, it is necessary for him to show—1. A statute authorizing him to receive compensation for such services, and fixing the amount thereof. 2. A statute authorizing the county commissioners to pay for such services out of the county treasury.

It was decided as early as Rawley *v.* Board, etc., 2 Blackf. 355, and it has been the law ever since, that a county cannot be liable for the fees and charges of officers without an express statute on the subject. Board, etc., *v.* Blake, 21 Ind. 32; Board, etc., *v.* Templer, 34 Ind. 322; Taylor *v.* Board, etc., 67 Ind. 383; State *ex rel. v.* Wallace, 41 Ind. 445; Wright *v.* Board, etc., 98 Ind. 88.

In the absence of a statute, a county is liable to pay fees and charges to the clerk precisely in the same manner that an individual is, and not otherwise, and except where a statute expressly authorizes the boards of commissioners to make allowances to him for services which he performs in the course of his official duties, they have no more authority, and are under no greater liability, to pay him for such services than to pay for any other services not performed for the county. We have been unable to find any statutes which fix any compensation for the clerk for performing any of the services above specified, or which authorize the county boards to pay for such services out of the public treasury; and as neither the appellant nor his counsel have pointed out any law for either, we have some confidence that none exists.

The judgment is affirmed.

ALDRICH, Clerk,

v.

PICARD, Comptroller.

(14 *Lea, Tenn.* 456.)

The compensation of clerks and other officers for making sales of the land of delinquent taxpayers does not, as between them and the State, depend upon the validity of the sales made.

The clerk is entitled to fifty cents for each tract of land sold since the passage of the act approved March 20, 1883, for the taxes assessed under the act of 1881, chapter 171.

APPEAL in error from Circuit Court of Davidson county. FRANK T. REID, J.

Pilcher & Weaver for Aldrich.

Attorney-General Lea for Pickard.

FREEMAN, J.—This is an agreed case, showing that the real estate of Davidson county was duly assessed   FACTS. for taxes for the year 1882, as provided by the act of Legislature passed April, 1881. Page 198 *et seq.* of Acts.

The list of delinquents, amounting to 3,123 tracts of land, was sold for taxes of that year, on the first Monday of July, 1883, and within thirty days a certified report of said sale was made to the circuit court, and on the first day of August, 1883, said court entered judgment on said report, condemning said list of lands and town lots. The above lands were all purchased by the State—this being the only sale of lands for taxes of 1882 made in said county.

The clerk claims, and so reported to the comptroller, that he had performed all the duties required by the act of 1883, chapter 105, and insists he is entitled to the sum of fifty cents for each separate tract of the said lands, which the comptroller denies, and this is the question to be decided.

The defence is rested on the ground, as we understand it, that the act of 1881, chapter 171 (passed April 6), providing for the assessment of taxable property, entitled " An act to provide more just and equitable laws for the assessment and collection of revenue for State and county purposes, and to repeal all laws now in force whereby revenue is collected from the assessment of real estate, personal property, and privileges," has been declared unconstitutional and void. This act proposed to regulate sales of real estate for taxes, and by section 86 fixed the fees of the "trustee, clerk, and printer" on all sales of land to the treasurer of the State, and directed the comptroller to issue his warrant for the same. By this section the clerk's fee was fixed at fifty cents for each separate tract, lot, or parcel of land.

The act of 1881, approved April 7, fixed the rate of taxation of property, and defined what privileges should be subject to privilege tax, and was an amendment to the act of 1879 in some of its features.

By the revenue act of 1883, approved March 30th of that year, a complete system for assessment and collection of revenues of the State, counties, ánd municipalities was enacted by the Legislature, which, among other things, provided for sale of real estate by the tax-collectors, and a report to the circuit court in section 73, as follows : "That when sales have been completed, and within thirty days after the first Monday in July of said year, the tax-collector of each county shall certify all of said sales to the circuit court of his county." The form of such certificate is given, and then it is provided, "said court, if in session, or if not in session, then at next term of said court, shall enter said sales of record as valid judgments, vesting title to the property so sold in the purchaser thereof, and writs of possession shall be granted to the purchasers during said term, or at any time on demand, whether said purchaser shall be any person, company, firm or corporation, or the treasurer of the State." By section 85 of this act it is provided "that the comptroller of the treasury shall issue his warrant for the fees of the trustee, clerk, and printer on all sales of land to the treasurer of the State, said fees to be as follows: Printer's fee of five dollars for notice in section 68; clerk's fee and trustee's fee each fifty cents for each separate tract, or lot, or parcel of land." The 87th section then repeals chapter 81 of act of 1875, chapter 73 of act of 1877, chapter 245 of act of 1879, chapter 171 of act of 1881, and all other acts in conflict with this law.

The duties required of the clerks under the act of 1883 are precisely the same as those required by the act of 1881. The fees for the service by the clerk are the same in both acts. The Legislature, in repeal- ing all these acts, certainly knew there were taxes in process of collection for 1882, which had been enforced by sales of land, and that clerks had rendered service in such cases, and the treasurer of the State had become the purchaser. Con- cede the sales were invalid because the law under which the taxes had been assessed or the property valued for taxation was void, and the sales, therefore, gave no title; still, it can- not be presumed it was intended that these clerks should receive no compensation for work honestly done.

The compensation of the clerk or other officer in such cases does not depend on the validity of the sales made, as held by this court in Akers and Union & American Publish- ing Company *v*. Burch, 12 Heis. 611, 612. Judge McFar- land says, in that case: "We conclude, therefore, that the fact of an actual sale and purchase in the name of the treasurer is sufficient, and we hold this the more readily as these claims do not depend upon the validity of the sale."

It is conceded, however, that no public officer can receive as fees anything but by a provision of law fixing such fees. But when this service was done the act of 1883 was in force, which provided a fee for such service, and it may well be held to include all such service done after its passage in favor of a meritorious claim; especially as by that act all the previous laws on the subject were repealed, and the rule prescribed in this act left alone to regulate such compensation. This may not be a strict construction, but it is a fair one, and reaches the right of the case.

The judgment of the court below will be affirmed, with costs.

BARNES

v.

TOWN OF BAKERSFIELD.

(Advance Case, Vermont.   January, 1885.)

A lister can recover only such compensation for his services as the town votes him, in a case where long usage is not an element.

GENERAL *assumpsit.* Plea, general issue and notice. Trial by court, September term, 1884; Royce, Ch. J., presiding. Judgment for the defendant.

The action was brought to recover pay for the plaintiff's services performed as lister. He was elected one of the listers of the defendant town at the annual March meeting in 1882, accepted the office, and rendered the services charged in his specification. The court found that the amount charged was reasonable, and that the plaintiff should recover it, if he was entitled to recover anything. The plaintiff's specification was: " Twenty days' services as lister, and expenses of self and team, $40; making list for said town, $10; two days' expenses, self and team, at St. Albans before equalizing the board, $10," making $60 in all. At the March meeting in 1883, the town accepted by vote the following amendment to the auditors' report:

" Resolved, by the legal voters of the town of Bakersfield, in town meeting assembled, that the auditors' report just read and submitted to the town be and is hereby amended by allowing Junius Barnes and William B. Shattuck for services as listers of said town, in 1882, fifteen days' work as services each, and the sum of $1.50 per day each, in lieu of the sum the auditors allowed them, making $22.50 for Mr. Barnes, and also $20 for making the list and attending the equalizing board at St. Albans, and $22.50 for Mr. Shattuck.

The town tendered the plaintiff $42.50. It did not appear that the town ever promised to pay the plaintiff for his services as lister; or that it took any action in regard to his compensation when he was elected; or what the town had paid its listers per day, except in 1881, when $2 per day was paid. The town records showed what amount had been paid the listers for a long series of years—sometimes showing what was paid the whole board, as in 1875, viz., $100, and then what was paid each lister, as in 1876, viz., $13.30. It appeared by these records that the plaintiff was paid for his services as lister in 1879 $32.

G. W. Burleson for plaintiff.

Cross & Start for defendant.

POWERS, J.—The right of town officers to recover pay for official services is regulated by statute. Section 2673 reads: "Towns, at the annual meeting, may fix the compensation of town officers." Section 2727 requires the auditors to examine and adjust the accounts of town officers, and report the items of such accounts to the town at its annual meeting. Section 2728 forbids the allowance by the auditors of any claim for personal services except when compensation is fixed by law or by vote of the town, but requires the auditors to report the nature and extent of such services to such meeting.

LISTER'S COMPENSATION IS STATUTORY.

By these sections it is clear that the plaintiff is not entitled to recover for his services beyond the sum tendered. When he accepted office he was bound to know that the "nature and extent of his services" would be reported to such meeting by the auditors, and that at such meeting the town, being informed by the auditors of the character of his services, would "fix the compensation."

He took office impliedly agreeing to accept pay as the law contemplates. It is not a case where long usage has made the law, but a case of explicit statutory regulation.

Judgment affirmed.

HARRRISON, etc.,

v.

COMMONWEALTH

(Advance Case, Kentucky. June 18, 1885.)

A statute fixing an assessor's compensation provided that "the amount allowed shall not exceed fifteen cents for each person's list of taxable property, and the same shall be paid by the treasurer upon the warrant of the auditor."

Held, that the assessor was entitled to pay for each list taken by him, whether it embraced property or not. Such construction of the statute, having been followed by the executive department for years, will be adopted by the courts.

APPEAL from Louisville Chancery Court.

T. L. Burnett, Isaac T. Woodson, Hargis & Easton, and *Good loe & Roberts* for appellants.

Helm & Bruce and *P. W. Harden* for appellee.

HOLT, J.—The assessor of Jefferson county returned upon his books for 1883 a report in accordance with the statutory FACTS.   form as to 76,205 persons, of whom only 21,232 owned any taxable property.

The number returned by him in 1884 was 78,343, of whom but 21,871 had any estate; but the entire number returned for both years were either tithables or property owners; and the question is now for the first time presented to this court whether an assessor is entitled under the statute to pay for each and every list taken by him whether it embraces property or not. Its decision involves the construction of the statute, which provides that "the amount allowed shall not exceed fifteen cents for each person's list of taxable property, and the same shall be paid by the Treasurer upon the warrant of the auditor. (Gen. Stats. ch. 92, art. 5, sec. 8.) The form prescribed by it, and the blanks in accordance therewith which are furnished to the assessor, contain forty-five items as to which the person being listed must make answer under oath to be administered by the assessor; and he can not return anyone as delinquent without first applying at his residence for his list; nor is he entitled to any compensation until he makes oath that the person "rendering the list" made oath to its truth. It is urged upon the part of the State that a blank space, where the items of property are to be enumerated in case the person being listed owns them, is not a "list of taxable property;" that these words in the statute divest it of all doubtful import, and that they must be disregarded in order to allow the assessor pay for taking the list of one who has no estate. Upon the other hand it is asserted that when the officer has taken the sworn statement of the person liable to pay tax in accordance with the statutory form, that it is in legal contemplation his "list of taxable property," although in point of fact it embraces no property. For instance, his name is first entered ; and even if he has no property, yet the assessor must enter his statement upon oath as to the number of his children, if any, between six and twenty years of age, and the other items or information as required by the form ; and it is insisted that when this has been done it is his "list of taxable property" within the meaning of the law.

A brief review of the former legislation upon the subject, and the light in which it has been regarded by those charged with its execution, will aid in arriving at a correct conclusion. REVIEW OF LEGISLATION.

The form for the list prescribed by the act of January 13, 1814, enumerated twenty-two items ; and by the act of February 2, 1819, entitled "An act to alter the mode of taking in lists of taxable property," and in the body of which is found the expression, "list of taxable property," the commissioner of tax, as the assessor was then called, was allowed such compensation as the county court might see proper to certify to the Auditor.

This was changed by the act of January 29, 1829, which like the present law, provided "that it shall be the duty of such commissioners to apply at the residence of every individual in his county or district liable to taxation for his list of taxable property," and allowed not exceeding five cents for each list taken by "the commissioners of taxable property."

By the act of January 4, 1840, entitled "An act to change the form of the commissioners' books of taxable property, and to equal all the duties of the commissioners of tax, and other officers in the relation to the same," a new form, containing twenty-nine items, was provided ; and it by way of illustration gives the names of supposed persons and their lists ; and the last one named is "Peter Mosby," whose list is an entire blank save the statement that he is a white male over twenty-one years of age, and has six children between seven and seventeen years of age. By an act approved March 3, 1842, it was provided that the county courts should make allowances to "commissioners of taxable property" of not more than eight cents for each list ; and by the revised statutes adopted in 1852 the same pay was allowed for "each list of taxable estate."

They also prescribed a new form of assessments of thirty-five items, and interchangeably speak of it as a list of "taxable property" or "taxable estate;" and sec. 14, art. 6, ch. 83, required the person giving the list to enumerate as a part of it the estate owned by him, and taxed in any other State. The General Statutes adopted in 1873 provide still another form, and which is the one now in force; and which furnishes to the State when returned by the assessor much valuable information, aside from taxation. By it the number of voters; the number of children between six and twenty years of age, and many other facts necessary to the existence of the State and the proper conduct of its affairs are ascertained; and this list is repeatedly spoken of in the statute now in force, as it was in the previous ones, as the "list of taxable property."

The expression read in the light of all the previous legisla-
TAXING LIST DE- tion leads to the conclusion that the allowance to
TERMINES COM-
PENSATION. the assessor does not depend upon the property returned, but upon the taking of the list; and that the entry of the name of Peter Mosby and his six children, as prescribed in the act and from *supra* in which he is mentioned, and which related to "taxable property," constituted his "list of taxable property" within the meaning of law. Again, if this be not so, and the pay is to depend upon property being returned, which will add to the State's revenue, then in case an assessor, under the provision of the Revised Statutes providing that a person should list his property situated in and taxed by another State, had taken the list of one who had no other property, yet he would not have been entitled to any pay for it because it was not subject to taxation in this State, and no benefit by way of taxes would have been obtained save the poll tax on the tithable. It would seem from this that it is not the items embraced in the list, but the taking of it which gives the right to compensation; and that it is based upon the lists, and not the items in them. Technically speaking it requires more than one item to make a list; and yet it will hardly be claimed that an assessor is not entitled to pay for taking one which contains no property save one tract of land worth thousands of dollars; and yet in a strict sense this would not be "a list of taxable property."

In construing a statute the object to be accomplished must be considered. In this instance it is to obtain the sworn statement of the person liable to taxation as to his property, and the other information required by the law. He may not own any taxable estate; but he must state on oath whether his statement is true. It cannot be said that if one has no property that the oath should not be administered to him; or that if he refuses to take it, or disclose his condition as to property, that he is not liable to a penalty.

When his sworn statement has been obtained, its truth or falsity may under the law be otherwise ascertained; and it should not be presumed that the Legislature in enacting the law relied for a faithful performance on the part of the assessor upon the character or amount of his compensation, which at most is hardly supportable, instead of his oath of office and the bond he is required to execute. If so, and his compensation is to depend entirely upon the property returned, then with equal force it can be contended that he would neglect his duty in obtaining the other information required by law and which is highly important to the State, and yet does not relate to property. But let us turn to the meaning of the expression, "list of taxable property," as used in the statute, and suppose that one of the citizens of Louisville should contract with its mayor to ascertain the taxable property of each citizen living on Jefferson Street at the price of ten cents for each list. Now would it be any answer to the claim for compensation that the mayor was not bound to pay for the list of those who, upon investigation, appeared to own no property? Certainly not, because this would not accord with the meaning of the contract or the intention of the parties. Here the State has said to the assessor, If you ascertain each man's taxable property in your county you shall have not exceeding fifteen cents for each person's list. But it is claimed that when he applies for his compensation he must be told that although he applied to A for his list, and he was subject to taxation, yet as he rendered a return of *nulla bona*, and you made the same return to the State, you have no claim for taking the list.

But although the question is *res integra* in this court, yet it is not required by its opinion to establish a practical construction of the statute. The very fact that persons and even courts are differing as to its meaning tends strongly to show that it is at least of doubtful import. Contemporaneous construction adopted.

It is alleged in the answer, and admitted by the demurrer to it, that the State, through its county courts and its executive department, has for many years allowed and paid for each list whether it embraced property or not. The executive branch of a government must necessarily give a construction to the laws which it must execute ; and if its construction has been followed for years, and in view of and without interference by the law-making power, then such contemporaneous and long-continued construction should not be departed from without the most cogent reasons. A long-continued practice under a statute under such circumstances ripens into an authoritative construction of it. The law, in its regard for the public good, goes so far in some cases as to hold that *communis error facit jus ;* but courts should be slow to set up a misconception of the law as the law ; and there is no need of it in this instance ; but it is proper to regard a. long-continued *communis opinis* in construing it.

The object of construction is to give effect to the legislative intent. Its will and not its words are the law. In the language of the Supreme Court of the United States in the case of the United States *v.* Moore, 95 U. S. 763, "a thing may be within the letter of a statute and not within its meaning ; and it may be within the meaning though not within the letter ;" and the meaning and not the letter must control.

A case within even the reason but not the letter of a remedial statute is embraced by it. Admitting for argument sake that the letter of the statute under consideration does not allow the assessor any pay for the list which does not embrace property, yet the legislative meaning has been placed beyond question by the action of the State. It was said by Chief Justice Marshall in the case of Cohens *v.* Virginia, 6 Wheaton, 418, that "great weight has always been attached, and very rightly attached, to contemporaneous exposition ;" and this rule is so well settled that citation of authority is needless. Not only those claiming rights under the law now in question, as well as the county courts of the State, and those who have had charge of its execution have for over half a century interpreted it otherwise, but while this was being done the various legislatures and the people behind and over them have known of it and recognize it by failing to interfere. They have in fact not only ratified it by their silence, but by their action.

Knowing the practical construction which was being put upon the provision of the statute as contained in the Revised Statutes of 1852, the legislature re-enacted it in equivalent and nearly the same language in the one now in force; thus virtually re-enacting that construction; giving it the force of a positive law and placing beyond question that it was the one intended by the law-making power. Judicial precedent or exposition could not give greater sanctity to it; and as the language of the statute and the legislation upon the same subject in force prior to its enactment render it at least of doubtful import, we cannot doubt, in view of the long continued legislation, executive and judicial action as to it, that the interpretation placed upon it by the lower court is incorrect. It is urged that if the pay of the assessor be insufficient, yet that this is a matter for legislative consideration. This is conceded; but yet every statute should be construed according to its equality; and it must be assumed that the legislature intended to give a fair compensation for the services to be rendered; and if the view now taken by the State of the statute were to prevail, then the assessors would by no means receive a compensation adequate to the labor required of them; and this is an argument against the soundness of the position, and leaves little room to doubt the wisdom of the construction which has been followed for so many years, undisturbed by legislative or judicial action. It takes the assessor of Jefferson County and his nine assistants, each furnishing a horse, six months to assess the county; and if only allowed for the lists which embrace property they would each receive but about three hundred dollars.

The pay of the assessors of other counties would be still more inadequate, and especially so in the sparsely settled ones. Moreover, the proportion between those who own taxable property and those who have none would vary greatly in different counties, and there would be little uniformity in the compensation for the labor.

In this instance the assessor, in accordance with the long continued practice, has received his pay for each list whether it embraced property or not; and has disbursed the most of it to his assistants; and the legislative intention shown by a long continued practical construction under the act ought not to be defeated by a decision of this court, even admitting

that it would accord with the letter of the law. The demurrer to the answer of the appellants reached back to the petition, and it should have been dismissed ; and the judgment is
reversed, with directions to do so.

VANDERCOOK

v.

WILLIAMS, Treasurer, etc.

(*Advance Case, Indiana.   June* 16, 1885.)

A statute making it the official duty of the county auditor " to diligently
search for and discover, in a lawful manner, omitted, concealed and unassessed taxable property," and to add such property when discovered to
the tax duplicate, with the proper valuation and charge tax thereupon to
the owner, and investing the auditor in discharge of this duty with the
powers of an assessor, does not authorize a contract by which a county
board agreed to pay such auditor 30 per cent of the money and taxes recovered by the treasurer of the county by reason of such discoveries by
the auditor.

A statute allowed a county auditor a specified sum annually "and no
more for his services." *Held*, that a county board could not lawfully
allow him additional compensation for duties already his.

The invalidity of a contract allowing a county auditor thirty per cent
of all taxes paid by reason of his discovering property secreted from taxation will not invalidate a tax assessed upon property so discovered.

APPEAL from Steuben Circuit Court.
Morris, Aldrich & Barret for appellant.
A. A. Chapin for appellee.

HOWK, J.—In this case the circuit court sustained the demurrer of the appellee, Williams, to the complaint
of the appellant, Vandercook. This ruling is the only error
assigned here by the appellant, and it presents for our decision
the question of the sufficiency of the facts stated in his complaint to constitute a cause of action.

In his complaint Vandercook alleged that on the twelfth
day of June, 1883, one Robert H. Johnson, then and since the
auditor of Steuben County, entered into a contract with the
board of commissioners of Steuben County, in the words and
figures following, to-wit:

" Whereas, it appearing that large sums of taxable property escape taxation, by reason of evasions and concealments on the part of the owners thereof; and, whereas, the board of commissioners find an indispensable public necessity that a competent person should be employed to collect the necessary facts and evidence for the recovery of such taxes and all other moneys due the county and State aforesaid, order the following: That Robert H. Johnson, auditor of Steuben County, be, and he is hereby, employed and directed to make search for all such omitted and concealed taxables, and also for the evidence of all other moneys due said county, and proceed with reference thereto in the manner provided by law, and in accordance with the written contract executed this day; which contract is in these words, to-wit: This agreement, made and entered into this twelfth day of June, 1883, by and between the board of commissiòners of Steuben County, of the first part, and the auditor of said county, of the second part, witnesseth: That, by the contract, the party of the second part is hereby employed by the party of the first part to diligently search for and discover, in a lawful manner, omitted, concealed and unassessed taxable property, as provided for by section 6416 of the Revised Statutes, the taxes upon which property being lawfully due said county and State. The party of the second part shall also make diligent search and examination for evidence of other moneys due said county which, by reason of negligence, have been lost to the county. Said second party, after the said discoveries, shall be governed by the laws in relation thereto, and act accordingly.

"For and in consideration of the services above named being done and performed by the party of the second part, and the necessary expert assistance, the party of the first part covenants and agrees to pay the party of the second part, a sum equal to thirty per centum of the money and taxes recovered by the treasurer of said county, by reason of the aforesaid discoveries: provided that said percentage, or any part thereof, shall not be paid or deemed due and owing until such money and taxes have actually been paid into the county treasury, and that, immediately upon such money and taxes having been paid into the treasury, then, and in that case, the aforesaid commissions shall become due and payable by the board of commissioners of Steuben County, whenever they may be in session. This contract shall continue in force for one year from this date; the work to be proceeded with as soon as possible. In witness whereof," etc.

(We omit the signatures to this contract.)

And the appellant averred that afterwards, on the ——— day of ———, 1883, the said Johnson, as such auditor, under and pursuant to the foregoing contract, and as the employee of' such board of county commissioners, notified the appellant to appear before him at his office in Steuben County, and show cause why certain pretendedly omitted personal property, alleged to belong to the appellant, should not be entered upon the tax duplicate of such county by such auditor, acting under and pursuant to the aforesaid contract with such board of commissioners; that the appellant having failed to appear before such auditor as required by such notice, the aforesaid' auditor, acting as the employee of such board of commissioners under the foregoing contract, on the day and year last named, without authority of law, placed upon the tax duplicate of the county personal property of the appellant of the nominal amount of $1,000, and then and there, under such contract, valued the same at $1,000 for taxation for the years 1876 to 1883, inclusive, and then and there, under such contract, assessed taxes thereupon for State and county purposes for such years; that the taxes for the years 1876 to 1883, ranging from $51.75 to $195.30, inclusive, so made by special assessment, were not returned to the county treasurer until the date hereinbefore given for any of such years, amounting in all to the sum of $2,489.94, and the auditor afterwards delivered such duplicate, with such property valuation and assessment thereon, entered by such auditor, to the appellee, as treasurer, for collection, which duplicate was then in the hands of appellee, as treasurer of such county, who would, if not restrained by an order of the court, proceed to collect the taxes so assessed of and from the appellant; that such taxes, as entered upon the tax duplicate, constituted a cloud upon the appellant's title to ——— acres of land, owned by him in Steuben County. And the appellant averred that the taxes so assessed by Robert H. Johnson, as such auditor, under the foregoing contract, were and are absolutely void, for the reason, among others, that he, Johnson, was, at the time he made such valuation and assessment, interested therein to the amount of thirty per cent of the taxes so assessed, under the aforesaid contract, against the appellant, and was by reason of such interest disqualified and incompetent to make such assessment; and the appellant averred that he had paid all taxes legally assessed against him for State and county purposes, and then due, and was the owner of real estate in such county. Wherefore, the appellant prayed that the appellee, as treasurer of such county, might be forever enjoined from collecting the aforesaid taxes, etc.

Several objections are urged by the appellant's counsel to the decision of the circuit court in sustaining the appellee's demurrer to the foregoing complaint. In their brief of this cause, the appellant's counsel contend that "the following propositions are indisputably the law: (1) That the auditor, in determining what property of appellant was taxable, and what was its value, acted judicially; (2) that an interest in the questions thus to be determined would render his decision void; (3) that if, by a contract with the board of commissioners, he secured thirty per cent of the amount of taxes to be by him assessed against the appellant, his decision of the question was void, though the contract was illegal and not enforceable against the board."

In their brief, the appellant's counsel, in speaking of the circuit court's decision, say: "In passing upon the demurrer, the court below held the contract between the board and the auditor void. The judge also held that because the contract was void, though believed to be valid by the auditor, its legal invalidity had the effect to render him an impartial and disinterested judge, and his judgment as to the taxability of the property alleged by him to belong to the appellant, and his estimate of its value, fair and valid; that for this reason the judgment of the auditor upon the question raised by the demurrer must be legally regarded as free from bias and the corrupting taint of selfish partiality. And this is the question, and the only question, presented to this court for decision. Though the auditor contends, and will in this case contend, and though he seems to believe, that the contract which gave him one-third of the taxes which he might adjudge and assess against the appellant is valid, will this court hold, as did the court below, that, because the contract is void in law, the auditor was, though acting under it in the belief that it was valid, for that reason a disinterested and impartial judge in the sense of the law? Was he a man in whose impartiality and fairness the appellant should, by the law of Indiana, be compelled to confide, without appeal and without complaint, though he believed that the auditor was adjudging his own case, and, by his judgment, putting money in his own pocket? This is the question. Its statement seems to shock every man's sense of right and justice."

We have quoted thus liberally from the able brief of the appellant's learned counsel, not alone to show the grounds upon which they ask for the reversal of the judgment below, but also to disclose the line of argument they have pursued in endeavoring to support their positions. The first question for decision in this case, as it seems to us, may be thus stated: Is the contract by and between the board of commissioners and the auditor of Steuben County, a copy of which is set out in the appellant's complaint, authorized by law, and therefore a valid, legal, and binding contract? Upon the face of such contract, it is manifest that it was executed by the parties thereto upon the supposition, at least, that its execution was fully authorized by the provisions of section 6416 Rev. St. 1881, in force since March 29, 1881. This section of the statute is mentioned in such contract, and provides as follows: "Whenever any county auditor shall discover or receive credible information, or if he shall have reason to believe, that any real or personal property has, from any cause, been omitted in whole or in part in the assessment of any year or number of years, from the assessment book or from the tax duplicate, he shall proceed to correct the tax duplicate and add such property thereto, with the proper valuation, and charge such property and the owner thereof with the proper amount of taxes thereon: to enable him to do which he is invested with all the powers of assessors under this act. But before making such correction or addition, if the person claiming to own such property, or occupying it, or in possession thereof, reside in the county and be not present, he shall give such person notice in writing of his intention to add such property to the tax duplicate, describing it in general terms, and requiring such person to appear before him at his office, at a specified time, within ten days after giving such notice to show cause, if any, why such property should not be added to the tax duplicate; and if the party so notified do not appear, or if he appear and fail to show any good and sufficient cause why such such assessment shall not be made, the same shall be made. The county auditor shall, in all cases, file in his office a statement of the facts or evidence on which he made such correction; but he shall in no case reduce the amount returned by the assessor without the written assent of the auditor of State given on the statement of facts submitted by the county auditor. No person other than the officials provided for in this law shall be employed by the county commissioners to discover omitted property."

Assuming to act under these statutory provisions, the board of commissioners of Steuben County and the audi- CONTRACT ALLOWING AUDITOR 30 PER CENT OF TAXES COLLECTED IS INVALID. tor of such county entered into the contract or agreement set out in the appellant's complaint. It will be seen from such contract or agreement, a copy of which we have heretofore given in setting out the substance of appellant's complaint, that the county board thereby attempted to employ the county auditor, *inter alia*, " to diligently search for and discover, in a lawful manner, omitted, concealed, and unassessed taxable property, as provided for by section 6416 of the Revised Statutes, the taxes upon which property being lawfully due such county and State." It will be further seen that in such contract or agreement, for and in consideration of the services above named being done and performed by the county auditor and necessary expert assistants, the county board covenanted and agreed to pay such county auditor a sum equal to 30 per centum of the money and taxes recovered by the treasurer of such county, by reason of such discoveries of the county auditor. Applying the ordinary rules of statutory construction to the provisions of section 6416, above quoted, we are of opinion that the execution of such a contract as the one set out in appellant's complaint is wholly unauthorized by that section of the statute. It was the official duty of the county auditor, without regard to any contract, under that section of the statute, as we construe its provisions, " to diligently search for and discover, in a lawful manner, omitted, concealed, and unassessed taxable property," and to add such property when discovered to the tax duplicate, with the proper valuation, and charge such property and its owner with the proper amount of taxes thereon; and, to enable such auditor to discharge this statutory duty, he was invested with all the powers of an assessor under the law.

In section 5907 Rev. St. 1881, in force since May 31, 1879, it is provided that the county auditor shall be

allowed an annual specified sum, "and no more, for his services," except a certain addition thereto dependent upon the population of his county, as shown by the last preceding United States census, and except, also, an annual allowance of $100 for making reports to the auditor of State. It was not competent, therefore, for the county board to covenant and agree to pay the county auditor any additional compensation for his services in the discharge of any of his official or statutory duties; nor was it competent for such county auditor to contract for, or to accept and receive, any such additional compensation for his services. City of Fort Wayne *v.* Lehr, 88 Ind. 62; Miller *v.* Embree, Id. 133.

It is probable, we think, that the contract or agreement set out in appellant's complaint was executed by the parties thereto upon the supposition that its execution was authorized by the language used in the last sentence of section 6416, above quoted, namely: "No person, other than the officials provided for in this law, shall be employed by the county commissioners to discover omitted property." We are of opinion, however, that this provision of the statute is not fairly open to the construction that the legislature intended thereby to authorize the county commissioners to employ any of the officials named in that law to discover omitted property, at an additional compensation to the compensation elsewhere given them by law for their services in the discharge of their official duties. On the contrary, it was the manifest intention of the legislature, in the enactment of the statutory provision last quoted, as it seems to us, to prevent and forbid the employment by the county commissioners of outside parties, who, at the time, for a consideration, made it their special occupation to diligently search for and discover omitted, concealed, and unassessed taxable property in the several counties of this State. The provision quoted "hath this extent and no more."

We conclude, therefore, that the contract or agreement set

out in the appellant's complaint is wholly unauthorized by the statute, and therefore is void. Such
contract or agreement is also void as against public
policy. The law will not tolerate the employment of
a public officer to discharge his plain official duty at a compensation other or different from, or in addition to, the compensation given him by law for his official services ; especially so
where, as in this case, the amount of such additional compensation is, by contract, made to depend upon the exercise of
his individual judgment, in the discharge of his official duty.
Public policy as well as law forbids the execution or enforcement of such a contract or agreement. The question remains
for decision, what effect does the fact that the assessment
of appellant's omitted property, of which he complains in this
action, was made by the county auditor under and pursuant
to the provisions of such invalid, unauthorized, and void contract, have upon the sufficiency or insufficiency of the appellant's complaint? It is true, perhaps, that the execution and
existence of such illegal and void contract prompted and
induced the county auditor to make the assessment of appellant's omitted property, of which he complains, and that if
there had been no such contract in existence the county
auditor would not have made such assessment. But does it
follow from these facts, conceding them to be such, that the
assessment of appellant's omitted property and the valuation
thereof, and the taxes charged against such property and appellant on the tax duplicate by such county auditor, were and
are of necessity, under the allegations of the complaint,
wrongful, unjust, and void? We think not. It will be observed that the appellant has nowhere averred in his complaint that he did not own the omitted property wherewith
he was assessed by the county auditor, nor that such property
was, for any cause, exempt from taxation, nor even that the
county auditor had placed an unjust or excessive valuation
on such property. In the absence of such averments as these,
we are bound to conclude that the appellant did own such
omitted property; that it was lawfully subject to taxation,
that the valuation of such property by such county auditor
was neither unjust nor excessive ; and that the taxes thereon
were properly charged by such auditor against appellant
and his property on the tax duplicate. If the appellant

owned the omitted property which had not been assessed for taxation, if it was lawfully subject to taxation, and if no unjust or excessive valuation was placed thereon, then the taxes assessed on such property are a proper and legal charge against appellant and his property, whatever motive may have prompted and induced the county auditor to assess such omitted property and to enter it and the taxes thereon on the tax duplicate.

We conclude, therefore, that the facts stated in the appellant's complaint herein are not sufficient to constitute a cause of action in his favor, nor to entitle him to any relief. The demurrer to such complaint was correctly sustained.

The judgment is affirmed, with costs.

DISCOVERY OF PROPERTY OWNED BY CITY—PAYMENT FOR.—The Common Council of the city of New Orleans passed a resolution in the year 1856, whereby the city bound itself to pay to any person who should discover and make report and give due information of the location and description of any real estate in the city belonging to it, of which there was no record on the books of the city, and to which it shall appear that the city has a valid title, a commission of five per cent on the value of the same. In pursuance of this resolution, Louis H. Pilie, then holding the office of city surveyor, made examination, and discovered certain real estate previously unknown to the city, of which it took possession, and sold for the benefit of the corporation. *Held*, that in the absence of proof showing that the discoveries and report formed a part of his official duties as city surveyor, he was entitled to recover the percentage allowed by the resolution. Pillie *v.* New Orleans, 19 La. An. 274.

SUPERVISORS OF SENECA CO.

v.

ALLEN.

(*Advance Case, New York. October* 6, 1885.)

The compensation of the county treasurers of Monroe and Seneca counties is limited to the salaries as fixed by the supervisors of those counties.

Where it is diminished by an act of the legislature, which does not in terms apply to treasurers in office at the time of its passage, it will be presumed that it was intended to operate only as to future treasurers.

A county treasurer having received funds by virtue of an act of the legislature, which directed that they should be allowed to him for the benefit of his county, cannot set up the invalidity of the act under which he received the money, and on that ground claim to retain it for himself as against the party for whose benefit he received it.

APPEAL from a judgment of the general term affirming a judgment of nonsuit at the circuit.

The action was instituted to recover money which came into the hands of the defendant Allen, as county treasurer of the county of Seneca, during his term of office, and which he refused to pay over, claiming that the compensation of the county treasurer, as fixed by the board of supervisors, was not the whole compensation to which he was entitled, and that in addition thereto he might receive one per cent for receiving and paying over the State tax. He also claimed that the act chapter 605, Laws of 1875, authorizing the supervisors of Seneca and Monroe counties to fix the compensation of the county treasurers of those counties, was unconstitutional, on the ground that it conflicted with section 18 of article 3, which provides " that the legislature shall not pass a private or local bill, creating, increasing, or decreasing fees, percentages or allowances of public officers during the term for which said officers are elected or appointed." And, further, that it was in conflict with section 16, article 3 of the Constitution, as containing more than one subject.

W. F. Cogswell for appellant.

Chas. A. Hawley for respondents.

RAPALLO, J.—The act of 1875 (chap. 605) and that of 1879 (chap. 213), construed together, clearly indicate STATUTES CON- an intention to limit the compensation of the STRUED TO- GETHER. county treasurers of Monroe and Seneca counties to the salaries authorized by the sixth section of the act of 1875, and to take from them the percentage to which they were formerly entitled on State as well as on other funds.

The sixth section of the act of 1875 provides that such treasurers, whether elected or appointed, shall receive for their services, as such treasurers, an annual salary to be fixed by the board of supervisors, and that they shall not receive to their own use any interest, fees, or other compensation for their services, as such treasurers except in proceedings for the sale of land, etc.

Although the money received by them for State taxes is

COUNTY TREAS-
URERS ARE
COUNTY OF-
FICERS. collected for the benefit of the State, the county treasurers receive it by virtue of their office of county treasurer. They are county and not State officers, and, receiving and depositing the State money they discharge in behalf of the county an obligation resting upon it.

Under the Revised Statutes, county treasurers were COMPENSATION
OF COUNTY
TREASURERS. entitled to retain to their own use, as compensation for their services, a commission of one per cent on all moneys received and paid out by them. 1 R. S. 370, § 26.

By chapter 189 of the Laws of 1846, the several county treasurers of this State were to receive for their services, instead of the fees then allowed by law, such compensation as should be fixed by the boards of supervisors of their respective counties, not exceeding one-half per cent for receiving and one-half per cent for disbursing the moneys received and disbursed, and in no case to exceed the sum of $500 per annum. This act was not applicable to the counties of New York and Kings. There can be no doubt that by this act the boards of supervisors were empowered to fix the compensation of county treasurers for receiving and paying out State as well as county moneys.

The act of 1846 was amended by chapter 110 of the Laws of 1871, by providing that, in addition to the compensation fixed by the boards of supervisors, county treasurers should be entitled to retain a commission of one per cent on every dollar belonging to the State which they should receive and pay over, but in no case to exceed the sum of $500; and that the act should not apply to the counties of New York, Kings, Albany, Otsego, Onondaga, Erie, and Westchester.

The act of 1875 applied to the county treasurers of the counties of Seneca and Monroe only. It provided for their compensation by an annual salary, and that they should not receive to their own use any other compensation for their services as such treasurers. It did not in terms refer to the one-per-cent commission allowed under the Revised Statutes and the acts of 1846 and 1871, upon moneys collected for the State, but simply provided that no compensation, in addition to their salary, should be received by county treasurers for their own use for their services as such, and repealed all acts, parts of acts, and special laws inconsistent therewith. If any doubt could be entertained as to the applicability of this act to commissions on State moneys, such doubt is dispelled by reference to the act of 1879, chap. 213, which amends the act of 1875, applicable to Seneca and Monroe counties, by adding section 12, declaring that "nothing in this act contained shall be construed as preventing the treasurers of the said counties from retaining for the benefit of their counties, respectively, the same compensation for receiving and paying the money belonging to the State every year, as that allowed by chapter 110 of the Laws of 1871 ; but the comptroller is hereby authorized to allow to the said treasurers, for the benefit of their respective counties, on the State taxes heretofore and hereafter received and paid over by them, where not already allowed, the compensation provided by said chapter 110."

These enactments, relating to the same subject, should be construed as if contained in the same act ; and, in fact, the provision last cited is incorporated by amendment in the act of 1875. Thus construed, they are very plain and show that their intention was not to relieve the State of the burden of the commission of one per cent which, under the Revised Statutes and the acts of 1846 and 1871, was chargeable on the quota of State taxes collected in each county, but simply to preclude the treasurers of the counties of Monroe and Seneca from retaining such commission to their own use, and to confine them to the salaries paid by the boards of supervisors, at the same time authorizing them to retain or receive such commission for the benefit of their respective counties.

In this manner the counties are indemnified in part for the salaries paid to their county treasurers. The practice of the principal officers of the State in leaving undrawn or paying over to the county treasurers so much of the funds collected for the State as would cover their commissions is entirely in accord with this construction. It simply recognizes the liability of the State to bear the commissions, but does not affect the question whether they are to go to the counties or to the treasurers for their own use.

Our conclusion in this respect brings us to the questions raised by the respondents as to the constitutionality of the acts of 1875 and 1879.

The first objection is, that the act of 1875 is a local bill and violates section 18 of article 3, which prohibits the passage of any private or local bill increasing or decreasing fees, percentages, or allowances of public officers during the term for which such officers are elected or appointed.

Passing the question whether the act in question is a private or local bill, it is a sufficient answer to this

INCREASING OR DECREASING SALARY APPLICATION TO COUNTY TREASURERS.

objection that it did not, in terms, apply to county treasurers in office at the time of its passage; and as it might lawfully operate to affect the compensation of future treasurers, we must presume that such was the intention. Kerrigan *v.* Force, 68 N. Y. 381. Although it did not affect treasurers in office in 1875, it is not, for that reason, invalid as to the defendant, whose term did not begin until January 1, 1879.

Section 23 of article 3 is next referred to. This section directs the legislature by general laws to confer upon boards of supervisors such further powers of local legislation and administration as the legislature may from time to time deem expedient, but it contains nothing prohibitory. The act does not contravene section 16 of article 3. All its provisions relate to the treasurers of the counties of Seneca and Monroe, and the subject is sufficiently embraced in the title. The provisions authorizing the supervisors to designate the banks

WHETHER ACT AFFECTING TREASURERS IS LOCAL.

in which such treasurers shall deposit the State moneys, and directing such banks to give bonds, pay interest and keep accounts with the State treasurer, are all parts of the system established by the act for the custody and disposition of the State funds collected by the treasurers designated in the title of the act, and are connected with the same subject. The title of the act of 1879 is, in our judgment, sufficient. It not only refers to the act of 1875, but it recites the title of that act which expresses the subject of the act amended, and the amendment is simply declaratory of the meaning of that act.

It is further claimed that the act of 1879 appropriates public money for local purposes, and consequently

WHETHER ACT IS AN APPROPRIATION ACT.

under section 9 of article 1 of the constitution required a two-thirds vote. The act does not appropriate any money of the State. It simply directs that the commissions which under former laws were payable to the county treasurers as their own compensation be retained by or allowed to them for the benefit of their respective counties, instead of being retained by them for their own benefit. This money belonging to the counties, having come under the control of the State treasurer by being deposited to his credit, he was authorized to allow the same to the treasurers for the benefit of their respective counties. The money in question in this action was not collected until after the passage of the act. But beyond these answers to the objections raised is the fundamental one that the defendant having received these funds by virtue of the act which directed that they should be allowed to him for the benefit of his county, he cannot set up the invalidity of the act under which he received the money, and on that ground claim to retain it for himself as against the party for whose benefit he received it. Ross *v.* Curtiss, 31 N. Y. 606; People *v.* Mead, 36 Id. 224; First Nat. Bank *v.* Wheeler, 72 Id. 201. The judgment should be reversed and a new trial ordered, costs to abide the event.

All concur.

COMPENSATION OF MUNICIPAL OFFICERS. GENERALLY NONE AT COMMON LAW.—The fundamental principles of the common law were formulated at a time when municipalities were comparatively few in number, small, and inconsequential.

There were usually found in all towns citizens competent to fill town offices properly, and willing to discharge their duties gratuitously, influenced by motives of public spirit, or by the honor or incidental advantages of the position. Sikes *v.* Inhabitants of Hatfield, 13 Gray (Mass.), 352. It therefore has become a firmly established rule of common law, that all services rendered by municipal officers are presumed to have been rendered gratuitously, unless compensation is provided by statute. Boyden *v.* Brookline, 8 Vt. 284; Barton *v.* New Orleans, 16 La. Ann. 317. Besides the fact that sufficient service might readily be obtained gratuitously, there is perhaps another reason: Municipalities, being corporations, are limited to their charter powers in disbursing money, and in the absence of charter authority to pay salaries it might be held that they lacked authority so to do. And services rendered a town have been held gratuitous, even though payments for such service had been previously made. Jones *v.* Mayor of Carmathen, 8 M. & W. 605. Therefore, no assumpsit is implied on the part of a municipal corporation in respect to services performed by one of its officers for which the ordinances allow no compensation. Lock *v.* The City of Central, 4 Colo. 65; see also Baker *v.* City of Utica, 19 N. Y. 326.

These considerations suggest the first prerequisite to the recovery of compensation by a municipal officer, which is a

CONSTITUTIONAL OFFICE.—It is essential that the office of which the claimant for compensation is the incumbent shall be a constitutional office,—that is, an office authorized by the Constitution. Meagher *v.* Storey County, 5 Nev. 245.

STATUTE OR ORDINANCE MUST FIX AND AUTHORIZE PAYMENT OF COMPENSATION.—Not only must the office be constitutional, but it must also be created, its compensation fixed, and payment thereof be authorized by some statute of the State or ordinance of the municipality. This has been decided, for example, in Bosworth *v.* City of New Orleans, 26 La. Ann. 494, wherein plaintiffs sued on an open account to recover salaries as Commissioners of Waterworks, and commissions on two millions of dollars for adjusting and settling the accounts between the Commercial Bank and the city of New Orleans. On July 31, 1868, the resolution which authorized the appointment of plaintiffs was adopted, but neither it nor any other resolution, law, ordinance, or contract fixed any salary or compensation for the services of said commissioners. It was held that none, therefore, could be claimed, and that, as a general principle, an ordinance by city councils to pay a municipal officer his salary should be founded upon another ordinance fixing the salary of the office; for public officers ought to have a fixed compensation, so as not to be dependent upon councils, who are but trustees of public functions, and ought not to vote money as matter of grace or favor. Smith *v.* Commonwealth, *ex rel.* 41 Pa. St. 335.

Consistently with this rule it is held that such ordinances, since ordinances are not judicially noticed; must be pleaded or otherwise shown. Thus where the relator presented a petition, averring that the city council had passed an ordinance to pay him $50 to apply to his services as high constable, and that the mayor, in violation of his duty, refused to sign a warrant on the treasurer therefor, but did not set forth the law or ordinance imposing that duty on the mayor, or show it on the trial of the issues of fact raised, or on writ of error, it was held that he had shown no ground for the mandamus asked for in his petition, and that it was error in the court below to award a peremptory mandamus thereon. Smith *v.* Commonwealth, *ex rel.* Dillon, 41 Pa. St. 335.

And where the statute provided that no debt shall be binding on a city unless authorized by law or ordinance, and a sufficient appropriation made therefor by the council, it was decided that where only $1400 was appropriated only that sum could be recovered, although the Board of Health had fixed the officer's compensation at $2000. Bladen *v.* Phila. 60 Pa. St. 464. That a statute is essential to recovery of fees, see Askin *v.* London District Council, 1 U. C. Q. B. 292.

NO CONTRACT BETWEEN OFFICER AND MUNICIPALITY EVEN WHERE STATUTES OR ORDINANCES FIX COMPENSATION.—Even where a statute or ordinance creates the office, fixes the compensation, and provides for its payment, there is no contract between the officer and the city. Love *v.* Mayor, etc., Jersey City, 40 N. J. L. 456; Augusta *v.* Sweeney, 44 Ga. 463; Smith *v.* Mayor, 37 N. Y. 518; Hoboken *v.* Gear, 3 Dutch. (N. J.) 266; Commonwealth *v.* Mann, 5 W. & S. Pa. 403; Iowa City *v.* Foster, 10 Iowa, 189; Commonwealth *v.* Bacon, 6 Serg. & Rawle (Pa.), 322; Barker *v.*

Pittsburgh, 4 Pa. St. 51; Marder *v.* Portsmouth, 59 N. H. 18; Ridge *v.* Lamb, 58 N. H. 278; City of Brazil *v.* McBride, 69 Ind. 244.

There may, of course, be a strong moral obligation to pay a compensation, but this does nor create a legal contract. Barker *v.* Pittsburgh, 4 Pa. St. 51. In fact, the relation between a municipality and its officers is very different from the relation between employer and employee. In that relation, if either party violates his agreement with the other, he may sue for breach of contract. If the employer discharge the employee before the expiration of his term of service, he can be made to respond in damages. But if an officer neglects to perform his duties, the municipality has no remedy against him for breach of contract. At his pleasure he may relinquish his office. His remuneration for services to be rendered may, in the absence of any charter restriction, be changed from time to time at the will of the city council. Locke *v.* City of Central, 4 Colo. 65, and in City of Hoboken *v.* Gear, 3 Dutch. (N. J.) 278, the court says: "An appointment to a public office, therefore, either by the government or by a municipal corporation, under a law fixing the compensation and the term of its continuance, is neither a contract between the public and the officer that the service shall continue during the designated term, nor that the salary shall not be changed during the term of office. It is, at most, a contract that while the party continues to perform the duties of the office he shall receive the compensation which may from time to time be provided by law." See also Baker *v.* The City of Utica, 19 N. Y. 326; Smith *v.* The Mayor of New York, 37 Id. 518; The Commonwealth *v.* Bacon, 6 Serg. & Rawle, 322.

Accordingly, it is held that votes of a town to raise a certain sum of money for the repairs of highways, and that the same be a labor tax, and "to pay the surveyors one shilling per hour, teams one shilling per hour, and hands fifteen cents per hour," are no evidence of a contract by the town to pay a surveyor for work voluntarily performed by himself upon the highways, beyond the appropriation, even if the town has paid for such services in past years. Sikes *v.* Inhabitants of Hatfield, 13 Gray (Mass.), 347.

One case at least presents a different view. Thus the Massachusetts court said: "Whatever may be the authority of the legislature to shorten the term of offices, when that term is not fixed by the Constitution (Taft *v.* Adams, 3 Gray (Mass.), 126), we are of opinion that cities and towns have no such authority as to city or town offices (unless it be expressly conferred by statute), except in cases where the officer misbehaves in his office or otherwise becomes unfit to perform its duties," and accordingly held, that the appointment by a city council, for a definite time, of a city officer entitled to a compensation for his services, if accepted by him, constitutes a contract between him and the city which cannot be changed by a subsequent ordinance of the city and vote of the city council without his consent. Chase *v.* Lowell, 7 Gray (Mass.), 33.

Upon the point whether a contract exists or not between a municipal officer and the municipality, a distinction exists between those cases where the officer may resign at will before his term expires, and those where the service is obligatory during the whole term.   In Commonwealth *v.* Bacon, 6 Serg. & R. (Pa.) 322, the existence of a contract was denied, the court pointing out that "this cannot be considered in the nature of a hiring, *because it was not obligatory on the mayor to serve out the year.*"   But in Trustees *v.* Walden, 15 Ala. 655, the tutors of the University of Alabama were required by law to hold their offices two years, unless permitted to resign by the executive committee.   The salary was by ordinance $1000 per annum, and it was decided that under such a law the election of a tutor and his acceptance of the office while such law and ordinance existed made a contract between him and the university, and that his salary could not be reduced.

OFFICER MUST BE QUALIFIED.   BOND—OATH.—In order to be able to collect compensation for his services the officer must fully qualify.   If a bond is required he must give it in the prescribed form and with sufficient sureties.   Smith *v.* Dillon, 41 Pa. St. 335; Philadelphia *v.* Given, 60 Pa. St. 136.   In the last case Given was returned elected city commissioner, and submitted the names of sureties which were, by resolution of council, approved, and the solicitor directed to draw the official bond; the mayor vetoed the resolution.   Given was not duly elected, but he performed the duties of the office to the time of the decree.   *Held,* that not having given bond he was not entitled to the emoluments of the office.   Phila *v.* Given, 60 Pa. St. 136.   The officer must take the necessary oath in order to entitle him to recover.   Riddle *v.* County of Bedford, 7 Serg. & R. (Pa.) 386. And a bill of particulars must be furnished if demanded.   Idem.

TITLE.   DE FACTO AND DE JURE OFFICERS.—Salary being an incident of the office, People *v.* Oulton, 28 Cal. 44, it follows that the right to the emoluments of the office depends upon the title to the office.   Philadelphia *v.* Given, 60 Pa. St. 136.   One having the legal right to an office, but not in possession of it, is entitled to the salary for the term for which he was elected; and the payment of the salary to one in possession of the office without title will not prevent the one having the title from recovering the salary.   People *v.* Smyth, 28 Cal. 21.   See also Carroll *v.* Siebenthaler, 37 Cal. 193.   And where an officer, duly elected, is kept out of office by one to whom the returning board has given a certificate of election, he is not at fault for not qualifying before he has obtained judgment of ouster, as such an attempt might be nugatory in the absence of the documentary title. He is therefore entitled to recover damages for the whole official term, from the beginning until he obtains possession of the office.   He is entitled to recover for that period the entire official salary, without any deduction for the services of the incumbent, or for what he may have earned himself while ousted.   An official salary is not made dependent on the amount of work done, and belongs to the office itself without regard to the personal services of the officer.   People *v.* Miller, 24 Mich. 458.   In fact, the occupation of an office by an intruder does not have even the effect of deferring the time of payment of the salary until the intruder is ousted.   Carroll *v.* Siebenthaler, 37 Cal. 193.

Again, W. was elected physician to the Memphis City Hospital, and the Mayor of the city was about to induct him into office, when L., the prior incumbent, obtained an injunction restraining the Mayor and W. from interfering with his enjoyment of the office; and, under this injunction, made perpetual at the hearing, L. succeeded in retaining the office himself until its discontinuance, some six months afterward, for which period he drew the salary. The injunction bill was dismissed by the Supreme Court, which declared that W. was validly elected, and entitled to all the privileges and emoluments of the office; whereupon W. sued the city for the salary of the office during the period of his merely de jure incumbency,— he having always been willing and ready to perform the duties, and to receive the salary. *Held,* that he was entitled to recover; that the payment of the salary for this period to L., a mere officer *de facto*, was wrongful, the injunction only preventing L.'s extrusion from the office, and not requiring the payment to him of the salary. Mayor *v.* Woodward, 12 Heisk. (Tenn.) 499; Lynch *v.* Lafland, 4 Col. 103; Dodd *v.* Weaver, 2 Sneed (Tenn.), 670; Payne *v.* State, 3 Hum. (N. Y.) 480; Pearce *v,* Hawkins, 2 Swan (Tenn.), 87. And it is to be believed to be the general rule that officers *de facto* cannot recover compensation for their services. Meagher *v.* Storey, 5 Nev. 245; Auditors *v.* Benoit, 20 Mich. 176.

But some cases hold that a mere offer to perform the duties of the office is not enough to entitle a de jure officer to recover, and that a person is not entitled to the salary of a public office unless he both obtains and exercises the office. Farrell *v.* Bridgeport, 45 Conn. 191. See also Samis *v.* King, 40 Conn. 298; Smith *v.* Mayor, 37 N. Y. 518; City of Central *v.* Sears, 2 Colo. 588.

It has also been held that disbursing officers charged with the duty of paying official salaries have, in discharge of that duty, a right to rely upon the apparent title of an officer *de facto*, and to treat him as an officer *de jure* without inquiring whether another has the better right. On December 31, 1872, plaintiff, who was assistant clerk of the Sixth District Court of the city of New York, was unlawfully excluded from that office by K., who, claiming under an appointment of a justice of that court, entered upon and continued to occupy the office until March 1, 1874, when by virtue of a judgment of ouster, in an action of *quo warranto,* plaintiff again came into possession. The salary of the office was by statute required to be paid by the comptroller of the city in monthly installments. It was paid to K. from the time of his intrusion to December 1, 1873. Plaintiff, during the time he was excluded, was ready to perform the duties of the office and proffered his services to the clerk, which were refused. In an action to recover the salary, *held,* that plaintiff was not entitled to recover the salary for the period during which it was paid to K.; that defendant was in no way a party to the usurpation or responsible for the unlawful exercise of the power of appointment by the justice; that such appointment, although unauthorized, when joined with the possession of the office, constituted K. an officer *de facto;* that, while as an officer *de facto* only, he was not entitled to the salary and could not maintain an action to recover it, yet payment to him while in possession was a good defence, the comptrollor being justified in acting upon the apparent title; and that plaintiff's remedy was by action against the usurper. But, *held,* that plaintiff was entitled to recover the unpaid salary, he having the right to the services of K. as having been rendered for him.   Dolan *v.* Mayor, 68 N. Y. 274.

And in Kansas where a person is in the possession of the office of county clerk, under color of title, and is county clerk *de facto*, and claims to be county clerk *de jure*, and the board of county commissioners pays to him the quarterly salary due to the rightful incumbent of such office, it was *held*, that the county clerk *de jure* has no action against the county board for such salary; and this, notwithstanding the fact that the county board may have known, at the time they paid such salary, that the question as to the title to said office was in litigation ; and notwithstanding the fact that the county clerk *de facto* may be insolvent.   Commissioners *v.* Anderson, 20 Kansas, 298; Benoit *v.* Auditors of Wayne County, 20 Mich. 176; Smith *v.* Mayor of N. Y. 37 N. Y. 518; Conner *v.* Mayor of N. Y. 5 N. Y. 285; Parker *v.* Supervisors, 4 Minn. 59; McAffee *v.* Russell, 29 Miss. 84, 97; Wheatly *v.* City of Covington, 11 Bush (Ky.), 18, 22 ; The Queen *v.* Mayor of Cambridge, 12 Adolphus & Ellis, 702; People *ex rel.* Dorsey *v.* Smith, 28 Cal. 21 ; Carroll *v.* Siebenthaler, 37 Cal. 193.

CHANGING SALARY.—As a general rule, the duties and emoluments, in fact the office itself and all that appertains thereto, may be abolished or changed at will by the legislature, or if it be a purely municipal office, by the common council, commissioners, or other such municipal legislature; Butcher *v.* Camden, 29 N. J. Eq. 478; Chicago *v.* Edwards, 58 Ill. 252; Love *v.* Mayor, 40 N. J. L. 456; Barker *v.* Pittsburgh, 4 Pa. St. 49; Commonwealth *v.* Bacon, 6 Serg. & R. (Pa.) 322; Warner *v.* People, 2 Den. (N. Y.) 272; People *v.* Detroit, 38 Mich. 636; City of Madison *v.* Kelso, 32 Ind. 79; Augusta *v.* Sweeney, 44 Ga. 463; Waldraven *v.* Mayor, etc., of Memphis, 4 Cold. (Tenn.) 431 ; and the officer need not be notified of the reduction; Doolan *v.* Manitowoc, 48 Wis. 312; and in Louisiana it is decided that a resolution of the council empowering an individual to collect the taxes due the city, at a given rate per cent on the amount collected for his compensation, may be repealed or modified at any time by the corporation, on the sole condition that it shall be liable for any compensation earned under the resolution previous to its repeal or modification ; Hiestand *v.* New Orleans, 14 La. Ann. 330 ; and if after his salary is reduced an officer continues to serve, and receives warrants for monthly payments of his salary during the term, he waives thereby all objections to the reduction thereof.   Love *v.* Mayor, etc., Jersey City, 40 N. J. L. 456.   But an officer's submission to a reduction by a superior officer who has no power to make it, will not stop him from claiming his full pay.   Kelm *v.* State, 65 How. Pr. (N. Y.) 488.

There are, of course, exceptions to the rule that the legislature or council may abrogate or alter an office and its fees at will.   Thus a board of auditors, after fixing a salary, cannot change it by parol or without some further action spread upon their records.   People *v.* Auditors, 41 Mich. 4. Generally, too, the salary of judges is exempt from legislative reduction. Commonwealth *v.* Mann. 5 W. & S. (Pa.), 403.   Nor is it to be understood that city councils have any power to withhold payment from a State officer whose salary or perquisites are fixed by law, such as the officers of the courts, jurors, or indeed any of the necessary expenses of the administration of justice. The municipality has no more control over such matters in the city than commissioners have in their several counties. They can no more be reduced or denied than can the amounts ascertained in the fee bill when the city has occasion either to claim or defend in the courts, or transact other business in the offices. These claims stand on an entirely different ground. Bladen *v.* Phila. 60 Pa. St. 464.

Where the charter of the city of St. Louis established the office of Recorder, and fixed his fees, it was held that the corporation could pass no by-laws reducing his fees, or depriving him of them in any case in which, by the charter, he would be entitled to receive them. Carr *v.* City of St. Louis, 9 Mo. 190. And where a city, organized under a special charter, abandoned its organization and reorganized under the general law, its marshal under the old charter was elected under the new, and continued without interruption to discharge the duties of the office, it was held, that it was not competent for the city council, after re-incorporation, to diminish the salary of the officer for the term for which he was first elected. Cox *v.* The City of Burlington, 43 Iowa, 612.

And a provision in the charter, by which the corporation is empowered to fix the compensation of its officers, does not necessarily carry with it the power to take away fees allowed by the charter. Carr *v.* City of St. Louis, 9 Mo. 190.

The office of patrolman is not within the constitutional clause prohibiting an increase or decrease of compensation. Shanley *v.* Brooklyn, 30 Hun, 396. But salaries cannot be reduced by limiting the amount of appropriations for them. Cashin *v.* Dunn, 58 Cal. 581. And where the salary is to be fixed by the board of public works and approved by the council, the council cannot alone reduce it. Fountain *v.* Mayor of Jackson, 50 Mich. 15.

EXTRA COMPENSATION FOR EXTRA SERVICES.—The New Jersey court discuss this matter in the following explicit language:

" It is a well settled rule that a person accepting a public office with a fixed salary is bound to perform the duties of the office for the salary. He cannot legally claim additional compensation for the discharge of these duties, even though the salary may be a very inadequate remuneration for the services. Nor does it alter the case that by subsequent statutes or ordinances his duties are increased and not his salary. His undertaking is to perform the duties of his office whatever they may be from time to time during his continuance in office for the compensation stipulated,—whether these duties are diminished or increased. Whenever he considers the compensation inadequate, he is at liberty to resign. Andrews *v.* United States, 2 Story's C. C. R. 202; People *v.* Supervisors, 1 Hill (N. Y.), 362; Bussier *v.* Pray, 7 Sergt. & Rawle (Pa.), 447; Angell & Ames on Corporation, sec. 317.

" This rule is of importance to the public. The successful effort to obtain office is not unfrequently speedily followed by efforts to increase its emoluments; while the incessant changes which the progressive spirit of the times is introducing effects almost every year changes in the

9 Cor. Cas.—18

character and additions to the amount of duty in almost every official station; and to allow these changes and additions to lay the foundation of claims for extra services would soon introduce intolerable mischief. The rule, too, should be very rigidly enforced.   The statutes of the legislature and the ordinances of our municipal corporations seldom prescribe with much detail and particularly the duties annexed to public offices; and it requires but little ingenuity to run nice distinctions between what may and what may not be considered strictly official; and if these distinctions are much favored by courts of justice it may lead to great abuse. . . .

"But the rule, nevertheless, has its limit.   It does not follow, from the principles laid down, that a public officer is bound to perform *all manner of public service* without compensation because his office has a salary annexed to it.   Nor is he in consequence of holding an office rendered legally incompetent to the discharge of duties which are clearly extra official, outside of the scope of his official duty." Evans *v.* Trenton, 24 N. J. L. 767.   And in this case the rule of distinction above suggested was applied.   The fact were these: An ordinance authorized a twenty-thousand-dollar loan, and it was made the duty of the treasurer of the city to sign, issue, and redeem the certificates and disburse the money raised. He prepared these tickets for circulation; separated, trimmed, and numbered them; issued them; loaned out the money thus obtained; redeemed the tickets when called upon; re-issued them; kept them in circulation for more than two years; and finally paid them off.   These, he alleged, were extra services, for which he was entitled to the five hundred dollars which he claimed.   "But clearly," said the court, "*a large part of these services* were within the scope of his official duty.   The issuing, re-issuing, and redeeming these certificates and the loaning of the money were acts performed as treasurer of the city—acts that nobody but the treasurer was authorized to perform; and however totally inadequate the compensation he received by way of salary may have been, and undoubtedly was, we have nothing to do with it—" and the jury had nothing to do with it.

But to carry this ordinance into effect, a large number of these certificates or tickets were to be prepared for the action of the treasurer. Paper was to be purchased, the certificates were to be printed, separated, trimmed and numbered.   The ordinance required the treasurer to sign, issue, and redeem the certificates, and this pre-supposed that the council was to procure the certificates and have them prepared for the treasurer's action.   "These," said the court, "were in no sense official duties—they were not within the scope of his general duties as treasurer, nor within the duties prescribed by the special ordinance.   They might as well be performed by one person as another—by a private citizen as by a public officer—and if he could show that he had incurred this expense or performed this duty by request of the proper authority of the city, he should have been permitted to do so.   The claim he thus established would have been a claim, not for extra services as treasurer of the city or services as treasurer of a finance committee, but simply for services rendered in his private, individual capacity." (Evans *v.* City of Trenton, 24 N. J. L. 767.)

The question whether services are extra so as to entitle the officer to extra compensation must obviously depend largely upon the facts of each particular case. And no better way can probably be taken to illustrate the distinction than to state briefly the facts of the cases (1) in which no extra compensation was allowed, the duty performed being held within the scope of the official's employment, and (2) those in which an allowance of extra compensation was sustained.

1. EXTRA COMPENSATION REFUSED.—A watchman of the city of Boston, who, while in discharge of his duty as such, discovers a person setting fire to a building, and prosecutes him to conviction, is not entitled to claim a reward offered by the city government for the detection and conviction of an incendiary. Pool *v.* Boston, 5 Cush. 219. See also Gilmore *v.* Lewis, 12 Ohio, 281,

A special justice of the city of New York, receiving an annual salary for his services in that capacity, cannot recover extra compensation for services performed on Sunday. Palmer *v.* Mayor, etc., N. Y. 2 Sandf. (N. Y.) 318.

The chief clerk of the post office department of the United States Government is not entitled to charge a commission for negotiating loans to the use of the government. Brown *v.* U. S. 9 How. U. S. 487.

Officer not entitled to a commission on a debt collected by levying execution placed in his hands. Preston *v.* Bacon, 4 Conn. 472.

No extra pay to supervisor for selling stock owned by county. Andrews *v.* Pratt, 44 Cal. 309.

City marshal cannot recover from county for fees earned in administering criminal law, although ordinarily such expenses are charged to the county. Christ *v.* Polk County, 48 Iowa, 302.

The sheriff will not be allowed extra expenses of summoning special jurors on account of their residing at a distance from each other; and court will make a rule absolute for the sheriff to refund money received on this account, although he has actually expended all the money. Lane *v.* Sewell, 1 Chitty, 175. *Vide* Pearson *v.* Maynard, 1 Taunt. 416; where the court refused to allow the expenses of sheriff of Yorkshire in summoning knights to appear at Westminster in a real action. The sheriff cannot maintain an action for expenses in keeping possession of goods, under fi. fa. at request of plaintiff. Bilke *v.* Havelock, 3 Campb. 374, 2 M. & S. 294. And see Imp. K. B. 8th ed. 378, as to fees on special jury.

The office of township treasurer having been abolished in Cincinnati, and the county treasurer of Hamilton county being required to hold all moneys in his hands belonging to the township of Cincinnati subject to the orders of the trustees of the township, the county treasurer cannot charge the fees allowed by law to the township treasurer for the receipt and disbursement of township funds, in the absence of any law allowing him to do so. Debolt *v.* Trustees, 7 Ohio St. 237.

The treasurer of the city of Covington, Kentucky, is not entitled to recover from the city any compensation in addition to his salary by reason of his being required to receive from the taxpayers the amounts assessed against them, without any express contract for additional compensation.

Receiving taxes is a duty pertaining to the office of treasurer. The increase of such duties by extending the time the taxpayers were required to pay to him, from June 15 to July 1, to avoid an additional penalty for not paying to him, did not imply that the city thereby placed itself under any legal obligation to increase the treasurer's salary as then fixed by ordinance, and the fact that the treasurer continued to receive taxes between June 15 and July 1 was a recognition of the right of the council to require this service at his hands. Covington *v.* Mayberry, 9 Bush (Ky.), 304.

Especially cannot a public officer receiving a fixed salary for his services rightfully claim a compensation beyond his salary for performing a new duty, or one imposed upon him since the salary was fixed, if he accepts the office with full knowledge of the resolution requiring the extra duties to be performed. Palmer *v.* Mayor, etc., N. Y. 2 Sandf. (N. Y.) 318. Or where he has, at the end of every quarter during his term of office, rendered an account against the corporation for the amount of his salary, and has received his pay, without making any claim for extra compensation. Palmer *v.* Mayor, etc., N. Y. 2 Sandf. (N. Y.) 318. A tillerman of a hook and ladder company is within the constitutional provision prohibiting extra compensation to be given to officers. Wright *v.* Hartford, 50 Conn. 546.

And in some instances it is an indictable offence, in public officers, to exact and receive anything more for the performance of their legal duty than the fees allowed by statute. Gilmore *v.* Lewis, 12 Ohio, 281.

And generally promises to pay extra compensation are void for want of consideration. Gilmore *v.* Lewis, 12 Ohio, 82 ; Evans *v.* Trenton, 24 N. J. L. 764 ; Blanchard *v.* La Salle, 99 Ill. 278 ; Wendell *v.* Brooklyn, 29 Barb. (N. Y.) 204.

"Not only," says Judge Dillon, "has an officer under such circumstances no legal claim for extra compensation, but a promise to pay him an extra fee or sum beyond that fixed by law is not binding, though he renders services and exercises a degree of diligence greater than could legally have been required of him." 1 Dill. Mun. Corp. § 234. Citing Heslep *v.* Sacramento, 2 Cal. 580 ($10,000 voted to Mayor for meritorious services held void). Hatch *v.* Mann, 15 Wend. (N. Y.) 45, reversing s.c., 9 Wend. 262 ; approved, Palmer *v.* Mayor, etc., of New York, 2 Sandf. (N. Y.) 218; Bartho *v.* Salter, Latch. 54 ; W. Jones, 65 ; s. c. Lane *v.* Sewell, 1 Chitty, 175, 295; Morris *v.* Burdett, 1 Camp. 218 ; 3 Camp. 374 ; Callaghan *v.* Hallett, 1 Caines (N. Y.), 104 ; Preston *v.* Bacon, 4 Conn. 471 ; Shattuck *v.* Woods, 1 Pick. (Mass.) 175; Bussier *v.* Pray, 7 Serg. & R. (Pa.) 447; Carroll *v.* Tyler, 2 Har. & Gill. (Md.) 54; Smith *v.* Smith, 1 Bailey (S. C.), 70; DeBolt *v.* Cincinnati, 7 Ohio St. 237; Pilie *v.* New Orleans, 19 La. Ann. 274.

2. EXTRA COMPENSATION ALLOWED.—A judge of the county courts who attends at the clerk's office to witness the drawing of juries is entitled to compensation for such attendance. People *v.* Supervisors, 12 Wend. (N. Y.) 257.

Where a county attorney goes beyond the limits of his county to do business for his county, he may recover reasonable compensation for such services, in addition to his salary. Huffman *v.* Board of Comrs. Greenwood Co. 23 Kan. 281. See also Commissioners *v.* Brewer, 9 Kan. 307.

When a town agent employs an attorney in a suit in favor of or against the town, the town is legally holden to pay for the attorney's services without an express vote to that effect; and the rule is the same if the town agent, being himself an attorney, renders professional services for the town. Langdon *v.* Town of Castleton, 30 Vermont, 285.

And if such a town agent, after his term of office has expired, continues in the management of the suits in which the town is interested, without any objection from or any express employment by the town or his successor, he is entitled to recover of the town for the professional services rendered after his term of office as town agent has expired. Langdon *v.* Town of Castleton, 30 Vermont, 285.

Under ordinances of Lowell, prescribing the duties of city solicitor, he is entitled to recover against the city for services rendered by virtue of his office, without special employment, as assistant counsel, in the preparation and trial of a case of flowing land in which the city was one of numerous complainants, and for services in drafting exceptions and reports of cases; but not for examining records and making a report of the business of his office to the city council. Caverly *v.* Lowell, 1 Allen (Mass.), 289.

The town of C. held a public meeting in regard to the proposed alteration, by a railroad company, of the channel of a stream, and passed resolutions directing legal proceedings to be commenced against the company to prevent such alteration. The plaintiff spoke at the meeting in favor of the resolutions, and said he would indemnify the town against all expenses arising from such legal proceedings for six cents. It was the general expectation among the inhabitants of the town that the expenses of such legal proceedings would be borne by another railroad company, of which plaintiff was a director, but there was no evidence that this expectation was based on anything said or done by the plaintiff or any one in behalf of that company. The officers of the town, in consequence of these resolutions, caused a bill for an injunction against the proposed alteration of the stream to be brought in the name of the town, in which plaintiff, having subsequently been appointed town agent, rendered professional services for the town as a solicitor, *Held*, that plaintiff was entitled to recover of the town for such services. Langdon *v.* Town of Castleton, 30 Vermont, 285.

When the fees of a particular officer are mentioned in the statutory fee bill of 1814, he can charge no other fees for any service whatever than those specified in the act. But where the officer is not mentioned in the act, he may receive fees under other acts of Assembly. Bussier *v.* Pray, 7 Serg. & R. (Pa.) 447.

A Municipal Council, in 1850, passed a vote assigning to the clerk of the peace a fixed salary for that year, "in lieu of all fees." *Held* (the Jury Act, 13 & 14 Vic. ch. 55, having been subsequently passed), that this could not debar him from claiming the fees allowed by the statutes for preparing the jury books for the following year.   Pringle *v.* McDonald, 10 U. C. Q. B. 254.

A clerk of the peace cannot charge fees for any service for the remuneration of which no provision is made by statute or otherwise, and the payment of such fees by a district council in accounts rendered for services in former years will not prevent their afterwards disputing the charges in the accounts of subsequent years.   If a clerk of the peace accept a salary in lieu of all fees, he is not afterwards entitled to any remuneration except such salary, and an action will not lie against the district council for fees charged for services performed by a clerk of the peace.   Askin *v.* London District Council, 1 U. C. Q. B. 292.

Where the collector of Ipswich claimed a commission on drafts drawn by him on the collector at Boston, in payment of bounties due to fishermen, under the act of 1813, ch. 34, it was held that there being no provision by which a commission is allowed thereon, the collector could not charge a commission, Andrews *v.* United States, 2 Storey, C. C. 202.

Where the sheriff sells lands under an order of court, he is entitled to the same commissions as are allowed to the Master and Commissioner in Equity for similar services ; but he is confined to the rate fixed by the fee bill : and no usage of the Court of Equity will warrant his making a higher charge for his services.   Smith *et al. v.* Smith, 1 Bailey (So. Car.), 70.

The register of wills of a county where letters testamentary were granted, acting as the agent of an executor or administrator in the settlement of an estate, is entitled to compensation for his services as agent. Carroll *v.* Tyler, 2 Harris & Gill (Md.), 55.

A city controller having been appointed agent of the city to receive certain bounty bonds, and apply them in the manner prescribed by the special act authorizing their issue, is entitled to the same compensation as any other man designated by the council would have.   The services being performed at the request of the city, the law implies a promise to pay what they are reasonably worth.   Detroit *v.* Redfied, 19 Mich. 376.

All expenditures made by a collector for office rent, clerk hire, fuel, and stationery, are incidents to his office, and should be allowed as proper charges against the United States : and if he do not keep and transmit yearly accounts thereof he does not forfeit his right to be reimbursed for such expenditures, but only subjects himself to the payment of a penalty. Andrews *v.* United States, 2 Storey C. C. 202.

And where the county treasurer occupied for his office a room belonging to plaintiff, and defendant made no other provision for such office than by suffering him to occupy said room, and plaintiff gave notice pending the occupation to at least two of the members of the county board that he should expect and demand compensation for its use, and said occupation was with the kuowledge and consent of the defendant, it was *held* that the defendant was liable for the value of the use of the room, although there was no express contract between the plaintiff and defendant that he should receive compensation therefor.   Butler *v.* Board of Neosho County, 15 Kan. 178.

Mandamus lies to supervisors of a county to compel them to allow the account of the clerk of the county for advances made by him in purchasing books for recording deeds and mortgages, etc., and for sending notices to judges and justices of the peace, of the pedlars who are licensees, with interest on such advances. Such services being required by law of the clerks, and no specific compensation provided for them, are properly chargeable to the county, and ought therefore, to be allowed by the supervisors and paid according to the act (Sess. 36, ch. 49, s. 1, 2 N. R. L. 137, 1 Rev. Statutes, 386) for defraying the public and necessary charges in the respective counties, etc. Bright *v.* Supervisors, 18 Johnson (N. Y.), 242. *Vide* Hull *v.* Supervisors of Oneida, 19 Johns. Rep. 259. *Ex-parte* Nelson, 1 Cowen's Rep. 417. Supervisor, etc., of Sandlake *v.* Supervisor, etc., of Bulin, 2 Cowen's Rep. 485.

The collector of any port being authorized by the Act of 1817, ch. 282. sec. 7, to appoint a deputy, with the approbation of the secretary of the treasury, a deputy so appointed should receive a reasonable compensation for his services, although no compensation therefor be fixed. Andrews *v.* United States, 2 Storey, C. C. 202.

See also, generally, McBride *v.* Grand Rapids, 47 Mich. 236. *In re* Building Inspectors' Accounts, 12 Phila. 226. Powers *v.* Oshkosh, 56 Wis. 660.

WHO LIABLE FOR COMPENSATION.—Obviously that municipality and no other is liable for the compensation claimed whose officer the claimant is. It may sometimes be difficult to determine what municipality the officer serves, and the courts have been called upon to decide the question. Thus:

Commissioners created by the legislature to sign warrants to be issued by the city of St. Louis, are State officers whom the city is under no obligation to pay for such service. Garnier *v.* St. Louis, 37 Mo. 554.

Since, by the charter of the city of New York (L. 1873, chs. 335 and 755), the police department is made a distinct and separate branch of the municipal government, and has complete control over the funds annually appropriated for its support and maintenance, the plaintiff, who had been employed by such department, could not—at least in the absence of proof that the appropriations were insufficient to meet its necessary expenses— recover from the corporation of the city of New York for services rendered upon such employment. Waterman *v.* Mayor, etc., of New York, 7 Daly (N. Y.), 489.

The services of the clerk of the police court of the city of Detroit are not "services rendered for Wayne county" within the meaning of section 10, article 10 of the constitution, and, therefore, the provision of the statute (Laws of 1863, p. 332), empowering the common council to prescribe the salary of such clerk, is not in conflict with said section of the constitution, and is valid. People *v.* Auditor of Wayne Co. 13 Mich. 233.

FIXING COMPENSATION. BY WHOM, HOW, WHEN DUE, METHOD OF PAYMENT, AUDITING.—The board of supervisors of the city and county of New York have power to fix or increase the salary of the clerk of a police court; more especially if such increase is made in pursuance of an act of the legislature, or is subsequently ratified by them. Devoy *v.* Mayor, etc., of New York, 39 Barb. (N. Y.) 169.

See Canniff *v.* The Mayor, etc., of New York, 4 E. D. Smith (N. Y.), 430.

The provision of the constitution of Michigan (Art. 10, Sec. 10), that "the board of supervisors, or, in the county of Wayne, the board of county auditors, shall have the exclusive power to prescribe and fix the compensation for all services rendered for and to adjust all claims against their respective counties, and the sum so fixed or defined shall be subject to no appeal," does not embrace those cases where charges have been laid on counties simply as a fair way of apportioning the public debt, and where no benefit accrues to them in their corporate capacity. Where the law has, in such cases, pointed out any other mode of adjustment or regulation of salaries or compensation than that by the county boards, the latter have no right to review, but must allow and pay them as thus adjusted. People *v.* Auditor of Wayne Co. 13 Mich. 233.

The legislative powers of council under, as in fixing the compensation of city officers, must be exercised by ordinance, when such fixing is intended to be permanent. Compensation of a city officer, fixed only by such a resolution of the council a year previous to the appointment of the officer, was not paid. He brought suit therefor, and it was held that the officer could not recover. City of Central *v.* Sears, 2 Colo. 588.

A salary of an office which is fixed at a monthly rate becomes due and payable monthly. Carroll *v.* Siebenthaler, 37 Cal. 193.

And any peculiar method provided for compensating employee controls. Baker *v.* Utica, 19 N. Y. 326; Cumming *v.* Mayor, 11 Paige Ch. (N. Y.) 597.

FORFEITURE OF SALARY. An officer may forfeit his salary, as by being removed or suspended from office for misconduct. Steubenville *v.* Culp, 38 Ohio St. 18. See Mayor *v.* Fahm, 60 Ga. 109; and Reilly *v.* Mayor, 48 N. Y. Superior Ct. 274. But the acceptance by an officer of less fees than he was entitled to, does not waive or forfeit his right to the balance. People *v.* Auditors, 41 Mich. 4.

A board of commissioners, however, cannot punish a subordinate by withholding a month's pay from him, although they had power to make regulations for his conduct and annex $50 penalty for their breach. Tyng *v.* Boston, 133 Mass. 372. See also Murphy *v.* Webster, 131 Mass. 482.

The discharge of a policeman for seduction forfeits his salary for the balance of his term. Queen *v.* Atlanta, 59 Ga. 319. But the compulsory suspension of an officer by his superior, without cause and without his consent, is no defence to an action by him for his salary during the suspension. Alker *v.* New York, 27 Hun. (N. Y.) 413.

ACTION FOR COMPENSATION.—An ordinary action at law lies to recover payment of compensation earned by municipal officer, although *mandamus* is also a proper remedy to compel payment thereof. Page *v.* Harden, 8 B. Mon. (Ky.) 650; Mc Bride *v.* Grand Rapids, 47 Mich. 236

Suit for fees wrongfully obtained lies even after the expiration of the term. Hunter *v.* Chandler, 45 Mo. 452.

Equity will also restrain the payment of an officer's salary pending a contest for the office. Colton *v.* Price, 50 Ala. 425. The officer is of course a necessary party to such a suit. Butchef *v.* Camden, 29 N. J· Eq. 478. But see People *v.* Smyth, 28 Cal. 21.

JOHNSON *et al.*

v.

WHITESIDE COUNTY.

(110 *Illinois*, 221.)

An attorney at law appointed by the court to defend one on a trial of an indictment, who does defend, is not entitled to recover of the county in which the trial was had any compensation for his services. An attorney takes his license with its burdens, among which is, to defend persons charged with crime when required by the court.

Section 422 of the Criminal Code, making it the duty of the court to assign counsel to a person charged with crime when he is unable to employ one, conferred no new power, nor did it impose any additional duty. It but formulated the common law already in force.

WRIT OF ERROR to the Appellate Court for the Second District;—heard in that court on writ of error to the Circuit Court of Whiteside county;—the Hon. John V. Eustace, Judge, presiding.

C. C. Johnson for the plaintiffs in error.

Walter Stager for the defendant in error.

WALKER, J.—At the August term, 1882, of the Whiteside circuit court, seven indictments were returned against four persons for forgery. The accused were unable to FACTS. employ counsel, and plaintiffs in error were, without their consent, appointed by the court to make their defence. The case against two of the accused was tried, plaintiffs in error appearing for them, and they were convicted, and the others pleaded guilty, and all were sentenced to the penitentiary. The judge who appointed plaintiffs in error to defend, gave them a writing requesting the board of supervisors to allow and pay them $100, as compensation for such service. The board refused to make the allowance, and plaintiffs sued the county. On the trial of the case in the circuit court, judgment was rendered in favor of the county. The case was removed to the Appellate Court for the Second District. The judgment of the circuit court was affirmed, and the case is brought to this court, and a reversal is urged.

The only question presented by this record is, whether the
LIABILITY OF COUNTIES TO COMPENSATE ATTORNEYS FOR DEFENDING CRIMINALS. county is liable for compensation to attorneys appointed by the court to defend persons indicted for crime, and who are unable to employ counsel for their defence. Under the ancient common law, persons accused of treason or felony were not permitted to defend, under the plea of not guilty, by counsel. The practice was, not to permit counsel to be heard on questions of fact, but the court would assign counsel to discuss questions of law arising on or after the trial. In such cases the prisoner proposed the point, and if the court supposed it would bear discussion, it assigned him counsel to argue it. (2 Hawkins' Pleas of the Crown, chap. 39, sec. 4, p. 555 ; 1 Chitty on Crim. Law, 407.) Thus it appears that at the common law the court exercised the power of assigning counsel to argue legal questions, and it seems counsel could only appear for that purpose after being assigned by the court. The Bill of Rights (or article 8, section 9,) of the constitution of 1818, provided, " that in all criminal prosecutions the accused hath a right to be heard by himself and counsel," and the constitution of the United States contains a similar provision regulating the practice in the Federal courts. This constitutional provision is retained in the present organic law, and modified the rigor of the common law by extending the privilege of the accused to be heard by counsel on both the facts and the law ; but it still left the common law in force as to the power of the court to assign counsel, and is the present chapter 28 of the Revised Statutes of 1874, which has been in force since September 17, 1807. This State was then a part of Indiana Territory, the legislature of which adopted the provisions of chapter 28, adopting the common law in substantially the same language of the present law. In 1809 the Governor and judges of the Illinois Territory adopted the laws of Indiana, so far as they were not local to that territory. That law appears in Pope's

Revision of 1815. The State legislature, in 1819, re-enacted the law as it now stands, and it has so remained ever since.

Thus it is seen, under the common law, and the 9th section of article 8 of the constitution of 1818, the courts DUTY OF COURTS TO ASSIGN had the power, and it was their duty, to assign COUNSEL TO DEFEND CRIMINALS. counsel to defend persons charged with crime who were unable to employ counsel, and such has ever been the practice in this State. Nor has the power ever been questioned. Our criminal codes, from the earliest period of legislative history, have provided that trials for criminal offences shall be according to the course of the common law, except as otherwise provided. It then follows, that it was by express enactment that the common law should be in force as to this power, and was as binding as is the 422d section of the act of 1874, Rev. Stat. page 410. That section conferred no new power, nor did it impose any additional duty. It but formulated the common law then in force. It left the law in all respects as it was previously under the common law.

Under the common law, this court, in the case of Vise *v.* Hamilton County, 19 Ill. 78, *held* that when an attorney was thus assigned to defend a pauper prisoner, there was no law which rendered the county liable to compensate the attorney for his services. It was there said the county was not a party to the prosecution, and had no power to control the matter, nor did the county employ the attorney to perform the services; that the prosecution was carried on "in the name and by the authority of the People of the State of Illinois," and with it the county had no concern or power of interference, and was under no obligation to furnish counsel for the accused. It was further said: "The law confers on licensed attorneys rights and privileges, and with them imposes duties and obligations which must be reciprocally enjoyed and performed. The plaintiffs but performed an official duty, for which no compensation is provided. Edgar County *v.* Mayo, 3 Gilm. 82." That case is conclusive of this.

It, however, seems to be supposed that because the legislature has declared, in terms, the duty previously COUNTY NOT LIABLE TO SUCH imposed by the common law, there is a change of ATTORNEYS. legislative intention, and that we must infer it was intended to render the county liable. We are wholly unable to see such a purpose. Substantially there was no change in the

law. Counties are only liable for the expense of apprehend-
ing, keeping and prosecuting persons accused of crime, by
force of statute, or the common law as adopted by the
statute. There is no statute or rule of the common law that
imposes the duty of paying attorney's fees for defending
paupers from criminal accusations, and the courts have no
power to enact laws authorizing counties to levy taxes for
such purposes. The taxing power is a legislative, and not a
judicial, function, and it would be a palpable violation of the
constitution for the courts to usurp the power. The courts,
no doubt, have the power, in proper cases, to compel counties
to exercise the taxing power, where it has been conferred on
them by the legislature ; but they are destitute of power to
compel them to levy and collect a tax not authorized by the
statute. Plaintiffs in error are presumed to have known,
when they applied for a license, that the office was burthened
with this duty, and they must be held to have accepted the
place subject to the burthen. The legislature had the power,
in conferring such privileges. to impose duties and obligations such as it might choose. Plaintiffs in error voluntarily
accepted the privileges with this obligation, and they must be
held to its performance. This being so, there is no pretense
that the law deprives them of their property or labor without compensation. They received a compensation in the
privileges conferred by their licenses.

This doctrine is announced in the cases of Wayne County
v. Waller, 90 Pa. St. 99, and Rowe *v.* Yuba County, 17 Cal.
61. We are aware that in Iowa, Indiana, and Wisconsin the
courts have reached a different conclusion; but we are not
disposed to overrule our former decision. To do so would
not produce harmony in the decisions. Moreover, we are
satisfied that we have announced the true rule in Vise *v.*
Hamilton County, *supra.* If a correction is required it is at
the hands of the legislature, and when that body sees proper
it will afford the remedy.

Perceiving no error in the record, the judgment of the Appellate Court is affirmed.

Judgment affirmed.

COMPENSATION OF COUNSEL ASSIGNED TO THE DEFENCE OF PAU-
PERS CHARGED WITH CRIME.—There is a conflict of authority as to the

right of counsel appointed by the court to defend paupers charged with crime, to recover compensation for their services from the county. It was held in Vise *v.* County of Hamilton, 19 Ill. 78 ; Wayne County *v.* Waller, 90 Pa. St. 99 ; and Rowe *v.* Yuba County, 17 Cal. 61, that they could not. In Carpenter *v.* County of Dane, 9 Wis. 274 ; Webb *v.* Baird, 6 Ind. 13 ; Hall *v.* Washington, 2 Greene (Iowa), 473, it was held that they could.

That the court has the right to compel counsel to appear in defence of persons charged with crime who are unable to retain counsel on their own behalf, seems to be generally conceded. Carpenter *v.* Dane County, 9 Wis. 274; County of Dane *v.* Smith, 13 Wis. 585 ; Wayne County *v.* Waller, 90 Pa. St. 99 ; White *v.* Polk County, 17 Iowa, 413 ; Hall *v.* Washington, 2 Greene (Iowa), 473 ; Rowe *v.* Yuba County, 17 Cal. 61 ; Vise *v.* County of Hamilton, 19 Ill. 78 ; Regina *v.* Fogarty, 5 Cox Cr. Cas. 161. Indeed, this right would seem to be a natural consequence of the position of counsel as officers of the court ; Bacon Abr. " Attorney," prefatory remarks ; 3 Blk. Comm. 26 ; and Vise *v.* Hamilton County ; Wayne County *v.* Waller ; Rowe *v.* Yuber County, all *supra.* It has even been intimated that a constitutional provision, that the accused shall have the right to be heard by counsel, imposes upon the court the duty of appointing counsel where the accused is too poor to employ them. Carpenter *v.* Dane County, 9 Wis. 274; Wayne County *v.* Waller, 90 Pa. St. 99.

The court of Indiana appear to deny the right of the court to compel counsel to defend. They say that the State statutes have rendered counsel no longer officers of, or part of, the court. They hold, however, that the court has authority to employ counsel to defend pauper criminals, acting in so doing as agents of the county. Webb *v.* Baird, *supra.*

Admitting the right of the court to compel counsel to appear in defence of persons charged with crime, it is difficult to see how any liability on the part of the county to pay for the services of counsel so defending in obedience to the order of the court, can arise. It may be urged that, although the court has this right, it can only exercise it on reasonable provision for compensation of counsel thus appointed being made. Conceding this to be true where the accused has the means for making such provision, it is obvious that where he has not, the court cannot itself make it. The court has no funds with which to pay lawyers ; the only way it can provide for their being paid, is by contract binding on the county. In the absence of special statutory authority, it cannot bind the county by contract. Wayne County *v.* Waller, 90 Pa. St. 99; Dane *v.* Smith, 13 Wis. 585; see also principal case.

To maintain, then, that the court has in no case authority to compel counsel to defend unless a reasonable compensation for their services is, provided for, is to deny that the court has authority to compel them to defend paupers charged with crime—practically the only case where the right to compel counsel to defend is ever exercised.

Admitting that the court has the right to compel counsel to appear in defence of paupers charged with crime, and that the court has no authority to bind the county by contract, it seems illogical to hold that the performance of services in defending the accused in obedience to the order of the court can give rise to any implied obligation on the part of the county. Yet this fallacy appears to have been fallen into by the Wisconsin court in the case of Dane *v.* Smith, 13 Wis. 585. At p. 587 the court say : " Having established that the courts had the power to make the appointment and order the services, it follows as a necessary legal consequence that the person appointed and who rendered them was entitled to a just compensation. This was of course to come from the county, that being the municipality to which, under our system, all such expenses are chargeable. The liability of the county, therefore, results from the existence and exercise of the power : not perhaps because the court is authorized to contract for the county or its officers ; for, strictly speaking, it has no such power ; but because the law, which gave the power to order, implied the promise to pay. This is agreeable to the general doctrine that whoever knowingly receives or assents to the services of another, which are of value and contribute to his benefit, impliedly undertake to pay such sum as the services are reasonably worth."

The Indiana court deny the right of the court to compel counsel to appear in defence of paupers ; they base their decision in part on a clause in the State constitution providing " that no man's particular services shall be demanded without just compensation." Webb *v.* Baird, 6 Ind. 13.

In conflict with the views expressed in the above note, is the following opinion of an eminent American text-writer : " Can counsel thus assigned sustain an action against the county for their fees ? The first impression is in the negative. Counsel are officers of the court, and are obliged as such to render to the court any services that may be necessary to the maintenance of public justice. Counsel, with the emoluments must take the burdens of their profession. Among the burdens is the gratuitous defence of the poor ; and the remuneration for this, in those cases in which no remuneration can be had from the State, must be found, it is urged, in the general income of a profession of which such service is one of the incidents, as well as in the consciousness of duty performed. For these and other reasons, it has been held that counsel cannot recover from the county commissioners compensation for such services. Yet a more careful examination teaches us that this view is not consistent either with English precedent or sound public policy. Counsel for the defence are as essential to the due examination of the case as are counsel for the prosecution ; and to have the services of the one unremunerated is as impolitic as it would be to have the services of the other unremunerated. If the State pays to convict its guilty subjects, it should pay also to acquit such as are innocent." 3 Wharton Crim. Law (7th ed., 1874), § 3006.

JONES

v.

MORGAN.

(Advance Case, California. August 18, 1885.)

The statute requiring that the board of supervisors shall audit claims against the county and order them paid before a valid warrant can issue, *held*, in a petition for a writ of *mandamus*, that an averment that the board of supervisors audited and allowed said claim of plaintiff, and ordered the auditor of said county to draw a warrant on defendant, as county treasurer, for the same, was sufficient without an express averment that said claim was ordered paid by said board of supervisors.

The official position of a district attorney of a county would render any contract made between him and the county supervisors providing for compensation for work falling within the scope of his official duties, in addition to his regular salary, absolutely void. But a contract on the part of the county to retain a district attorney to attend to county litigation in another county, after his term of office has expired, is valid and binding on the county where such contract was entered into in good faith on both sides.

COMMISSIONERS' decision.

Department 1. Appeal from superior court, county of Butte.

John H. Gray for appellant.

T. B. Reardon & Son for respondent.

FOOTE, C.—The plaintiff brought a petition for a writ of mandate in the superior court of Butte county,   FACTS. against the defendant, as treasurer of that county, the object being to compel the treasurer to pay a warrant issued to the plaintiff previously by the auditor of the said county. In referring to the action of the board of supervisors of said county, in his petition the plaintiff, among other things, avers:

"That at the said December session of said board of supervisors the said board audited and allowed said claim of plaintiff in the sum of $500, and ordered the auditor of Butte county to draw a warrant in favor of plaintiff on the defendant, as treasurer of said county, for said sum of $500."

This petition was demurred to and answered at the same time. The grounds of demurrer were "that the petition did not state facts sufficient to authorize the court to grant the writ of mandate, or to give any relief." The demurrer was overruled. A trial on the merits was then had of the case by the court, a jury being waived. The judgment of the court was to order a peremptory writ of mandate as prayed for, and for costs against the defendant. A new trial was moved for and denied. On this motion a statement was agreed upon in open court, and by a stipulation it was afterwards agreed that it should be the statement upon appeal. From the judgment of the court, and its order denying the motion for a new trial, an appeal was taken.

The only ground relied on in argument by the appellant to reverse the court below in its ruling on the demurrer is that the complaint did not set out, in reference to the claim of plaintiff, " it was ordered paid," in the very language of the statute. The complaint recited that the board of supervisors of Butte county "audited and allowed said claim of plaintiff in the sum of $500, and ordered the auditor of Butte county to draw a warrant in favor of plaintiff on the defendant, as treasurer of said county, for said sum of $500."

It further alleged " that on the twelfth day of December, 1884, the auditor of said county of Butte, in pursuance to said order of the said board of supervisors of said county, issued, drew, and delivered to plaintiff a warrant for said sum of $500."

The allegations in the complaint thus demurred to were, we think, entirely full and sufficient. A similar complaint to the one under discussion was held to be good by this court in the case of Connor *v.* Morris, 23 Cal. 451.

Upon the trial of the case at bar it was stipulated by counsel in open court that the only questions and issues to be submitted to the court were: (1) Is the petitioner the party beneficially interested, and owner of the warrant set forth in the petition? (2) Has the warrant set forth in the petition been duly presented to the defendant for payment, and payment demanded thereof, and payment refused? (3) Has plaintiff (petitioner) suffered any damage by reason of the refusal of defendant to pay the warrant set out in the petition? (4) Is the warrant set forth in the petition founded on a legal claim against the county of Butte?

The court found that the warrant was the property of the

petitioner; that it was duly presented to and refused payment by the defendant; and, by reason of such refusal to pay it, no damage had resulted to the plaintiff.

Upon the first three propositions there can be no doubt of the correctness of the findings, and this is so plain that discussion of them is needless. It is strenuously argued by the appellant that the board of supervisors of Butte county never ordered the claim of the petitioner to be paid; but in his answer to the petition he did not deny the allegations of the complaint upon that point; hence those allegations are, by the pleadings, admitted to be true. It being thus virtually admitted by the pleadings that the question raised by the appellant, above alluded to, is without the issues to be tried, and that, too, by the act of the defendant, he cannot be heard to complain here. The appellant further contends that the trial court erred in overruling his objection to the introduction of warrant "No. 773" in evidence; but as the objector did not see proper to include in the stipulation of issues to be passed on by the court any question as to the validity of the warrant on its face, but expressly agreed to exclude it, by agreeing that the issues thus submitted by the stipulation were the only issues, he could not, under those issues thus limited, be heard legally to object to the introduction of the warrant in evidence, nor can we entertain such objection here.

WHETHER CLAIM WAS ORDERED PAID—ISSUES.

As to the point made, that the contract was void, and the warrant likewise, because the petitioner sought to have his salary increased, and that in allowing his claim, and ordering the warrant to be drawn for it, the board of supervisors of Butte county increased his salary, it is plain, from the evidence, that no such thing was in contemplation or was done.

WHETHER SALARY WAS INCREASED OR NOT.

The evidence shows that the petitioner was district attorney of Butte county up to January 5, 1885; that the board of supervisors of that county employed him to attend to a case which was not to be tried until his term of office should expire; that the case had been transferred before his employment to Sutter county; and that the petitioner was retained to go into that county and look after the case and protect the interests of Butte county. The board of Supervisors in their discretion certainly had the power, in this sort of a case, to

9 Cor. Cas.—19

employ counsel to attend to Butte county's interests in Sutter county, and the fact that they retained their then district attorney to go out of his own county and attend to the case like any other attorney, and agreed to pay him for it, was not an increase of his salary for anything he had done, or ought to have done, or was to do, while holding his office in Butte county.

But the last and most important objection raised by the defendant is that the contract on which the claim

POWER OF COUN-
TY   ATTORNEY
TO   CONTRACT
WITH COUNTY.

is based is void, for the reason, as he contends, that neither the petitioner could make such a contract with the board of supervisors nor the board of supervisors with him. · In this connection it is urged that a district attorney, being by law the legal adviser of the board of supervisors of his county, cannot make any contract with them as to any employment which entails any payment of money to him other than his compensation fixed by law. It is urged that this cannot be done, because as a county officer the district attorney cannot contract with the board of supervisors of a county, he being like a director in a corporation, or a member of a town council, or a member of such board of supervisors.

The district attorney is the legal adviser of the board of supervisors of his county, and as to all cases of the county pending in the courts which it is his duty as district attorney to appear in and conduct, he can make no contract with that board to receive any compensation outside of that allowed him by law; but when it is sought by that board to secure his services as an attorney-at-law, and the services are to be rendered outside of the county of which he is district attorney, and the contract for their rendition is made in good faith, and they are of a character for which such a board, in its discretion, has the lawful right to employ counsel, we are not prepared to say it cannot be done.

The case of Mayor, etc., *v.* Muzzy, 33 Mich. 62, is a case in point. Muzzy was an attorney-at-law, and also mayor and councilman of the town of Niles. While occupying the municipal office, that corporation employed him as an attorney-at-law, through its council, to attend to a suit in which it was interested in a neighboring court. He attended to the case in that tribunal, demanded his fee, it was refused payment, and he brought suit for it. On the part of the town the point was urged that by reason of Mr. Muzzy being a municipal officer he could not claim pay for his services as an attorney-at-law; but the Supreme Court of Michigan declared that he was entitled to pay for such services, as there had not been shown in the case any fraudulent or collusive conduct on his part, or that of any other of the municipal officials.

In Kansas a county attorney recovered for services performed upon an implied contract, in prosecuting a criminal action, in a county of which he was not an officer, the action being one in which his county was interested. Huffman *v.* Board Com'rs Greenwood Co., 23 Kan. 281.

We hold to the doctrine held heretofore by this court in the cases of Andrews *v.* Pratt, 44 Cal. 317, and San Diego *v.* San Diego and La. R. R. Co., 44 Cal. 106; but they were dissimilar to the case under consideration. The petitioner here is neither a member of the board of supervisors of a county, nor a stockholder or director of a railroad corporation, seeking to contract with himself on the part of the corporation or board of which he is a member.

There does not appear in the record before us any evidence that the petitioner has been guilty of the least bad faith in making his contract with the board of supervisors of Butte county, or that he, or any one for him, has exercised any undue influence over that board in the matter; neither is it evidenced in any way that such board of supervisors was beneficially interested in the claim, or were actuated throughout the transaction by any motive save that proceeding from an honest desire as guardians, so to speak, of protecting, to the best of their skill and judgment, the interests of said county and in the utmost good faith towards all concerned.

We are of the opinion that the judgment and the order of the court denying a new trial ought to be affirmed.

We concur—SEARLES, C.; BELCHER, C. C.

By the court. For the reasons given in the foregoing opinion the judgment and order are affirmed.

MANGAM, as Administratrix, etc.,

v.

CITY OF BROOKLYN.

(98 *New York Reports,* 585.)

The provision of the State Constitution (Art. 3, § 18), prohibiting the legislature from passing a private or local bill "creating, increasing or decreasing fees, percentage or allowances of public officers, during the term for which said officers are elected or appointed," does not apply to officers receiving fixed salaries ; it includes only those irregular and uncertain modes of compensating public servants indicated by words of like meaning with fees, percentage, etc.

The provision of the act of 1877 (§ 6, chap. 459, Laws of 1877), in relation to the salaries, etc., of officers of the city of Brooklyn, which declares that the act "shall not apply to any officer who, under the provisions of the Constitution, cannot have their fees, percentage or allowances increased during their present terms of office," and the similar provision of the act of 1879 (§ 7, chap. 467, Laws of 1879), amending said act of 1877, have reference to the constitutional provision above referred to. It was not the intent of the legislature, however, to limit the operation of said acts to subsequently elected or appointed officers, but simply to save them from possible condemnation as being in conflict with the Constitution.

Where, therefore, under the act of 1877, the common council of the city reduced the salaries of patrolmen from $1100 to $1000, the same deduction being also made by the act of 1879, *held,* that the salary of a policeman then in office was thereby lawfully reduced.

APPEAL from judgment of the General Term of the Supreme Court, in the second judicial department, entered upon an order made September 9, 1884, which affirmed a judgment in favor of defendant, entered upon a verdict directed by the court.

The nature of the action and the material facts are stated in the opinion.

Erastus Cooke for appellant.

John A. Taylor for respondent.

RUGER, Ch. J.—The plaintiff brought this action to recover FACTS. the sum of $100, for each of the years 1879, 1880, 1881 and 1882, as the balance of her intestate's salary as policeman in the city of Brooklyn, alleged to be remaining unpaid by the defendant. Said intestate was appointed policeman prior to

1877. The claim is made by virtue of the charter of that city, appearing in chapter 863, Laws of 1873, which fixed the compensation of patrolman at the sum of $1100 per annum. It is answered to this claim that the common council of Brooklyn, by virtue of authority conferred upon them in chapter 459, Laws of 1877, have reduced the annual compensation payable to patrolmen in that city from $1100 to $1000. It is also claimed that the same reduction was effected by chapter 467 of the Laws of 1879. If the validity of the reduction made under either authority is established, it constitutes a defence to the plaintiff's cause of action. The appellant asserts, however, that these acts do not affect the questions in dispute, for the reasons:

First. That both of them were, by their terms, restricted to officers to be thereafter elected or appointed; and

Second. In case the first proposition fails, that such acts are obnoxious to the provisions of section 18, article 3 of the Constitution, as being local bills, and "creating, increasing or decreasing fees, percentage or allowances of public officers during the term for which said officers are elected or appointed."

The first proposition depends upon the meaning and effect to be ascribed to the following sections of the acts in question: Section 6 of chapter 459, Laws of 1877, and section 7 of chapter 467 of the Laws of 1879, is similar, reads as follows: "The provisions of this act shall not apply to any officers who, under the provisions of the Constitution, cannot have their fees, percentages or allowances increased or diminished during their present terms of office; but said provisions shall apply to all of those hereafter elected or appointed to perform any service within the city of Brooklyn." The language of this section is upon its face ambiguous and equivocal, and requires an inquiry into its meaning before the provisions of the act can be understandingly enforced.

In a proper sense there are no public officers in the State, whose compensation may not be increased or diminished by the legislature during their terms of office, except those of governor, lieutenant-governor and other State officers named in the Constitution, judges of the Court of Appeals and justices of the Supreme Court, county judges and surrogates. These are, by the terms of the Constitution, expressly exempted from the power of the legislature to diminish, and in some cases to increase, during their existing terms. None of these persons, however, are officers of the city of Brooklyn or paid from its treasury, and they are not, therefore, the officers referred to by the acts in question. All other public officers are subject to the power of the legislature to increase or diminish their compensation at any time, provided it be done by general law. In a strict sense, therefore, the language of this exception does not apply to the officers in question, for the inhibition is against such legislation by local or private bills only, and not to enactments accomplishing these objects by general law.

In accordance with settled canons for the construction of statutes, however, some effect must be given to all of the lan-guage employed in framing them, provided the intent of the legislature is discoverable from the words employed, or other sources of information open to the consideration of the court, and such constrnction is reasonable and does not lead to absurd or unjust results.

It is quite obvious, from the language of the act, that the legislature had in mind section 18 of article 3 of the Constitu-tion in framing it, because they use the precise language em-ployed in that section in describing the class of officers who are not to be affected by its provisions. Thus, they say it is those officers " who, under the provisions of the Constitution, cannot have their fees, percentage or allowances increased or dimin-ished during their present terms in office." This language is used in section 18, article 3, and in no other place in the Con-stitution, and unless held to apply to that section, it must be denied any application whatever. It does not follow, from this circumstance, however, that we must give it the effect claimed for it by the appellant. It is quite clear, if the legis-lature intended the provisions of the act to apply only to fu-ture elected officers, that any reference to the constitutional provision was utterly unnecessary, as their power of legislation over that subject was undeniable. It is also quite obvious, from the inclusion of the official names of the officers in ques-tion in the provisions of the act, and the clauses specially pro-viding that the amount of their compensation should be left to the power of the common council to regulate, that the leg-islature did not suppose they were transcending their consti-tutional power in legislating as they did. If the legislature had intended that the act should affect subsequently elected or appointed officers only, they would have said so directly, and omitted all reference to the constitutional provisions.

It would seem, therefore, that the first clause of section 6 was inserted merely as a tentative provision to save the act from possible condemnation as being in conflict with the Constitution.

It is evident, from the consideration suggested, that no conclusive inference can be drawn from the insertion of the clause in question, that the legislature intended thereby to exempt officers from the operations of the act who would otherwise be included in its provisions, but it would seem that they intended to leave the act open in that respect, to be determined by the solution of the question as to their coustitutional power to pass it.   The act is clearly hypothetical, and its true reading, if paraphrased according to its apparent object and meaning, would be as follows : This act shall not affect any officers named therein whose compensation cannot constitutionally be increased or diminished during their existing terms : and if so read, there is afforded no room for the contention that the legislature intended thereby to exempt the existing police force from its operation.

We thus arrive at the question whether the statutes referred to violate section 18 of article 3 of the Constitution.

It is quite certain that the act of 1877 does not infringe upon its letter, and it is only by a resort to principles of construction that the appellant can hope to nullify its provisions.

The Constitution prohibits the legislature, by local or private bills, from increasing or diminishing the "fees, percentage or allowances" of certain officers during existing terms of office. The act of 1877 refers only to salaries, and does not purport, in itself, either to increase or diminish those, but attempts only to confer power upon the common council to fix and regulate such salaries as are payable from the municipal treasury.

The appellant claims, however, that the act is within the spirit and meaning of the constitutional provisions, RULES OF CONSTRUCTION CONSTITUTIONAL PROVISIONS. and that, therefore, the attempt, by the common council, to reduce the patrolmen's salaries was ineffectual. The rules applicable to the construction of constitutional provisions are the same generally as those applying to statutes, and the object in both cases is to arrive at the intention of the law-makers.

If the meaning of a given provision be clear and unambiguous, and leads to no absurd or unjust result, it leaves no room for the application of rules of interpretation, and must, therefore, be enforced according to its letter and spirit. Potter's Dwarris on Stat. and Const. 9; Jackson *v.* Lewis, 17 Johns. 475. It was said in Newell *v.* People, 3 Seld. 97, " Whether we are considering an agreement between parties, a statute or a constitution, with a view to its interpretation, the thing we are to seek is the thought which it expresses. To ascertain this the first resort in all cases is to the natural signification of the words employed in. the order and grammatical arrangement in which the framers of the instrument have placed them. If thus regarded, the words embody a definite meaning which involves no absurdity and no contradiction]between different parts of the same writing, then that meaning upon the face of the instrument is the one which alone we are at liberty to say was intended to be conveyed." See, also, McCluskey *v.* Cromwell, 11 N. Y. 602; Johnson *v.* H. R. R. R. Co., 49 Id. 455. If the words used in a statute are susceptible of different meanings, that one must be ascribed to them which accords with the natural and obvious signification and import of the language used. For the purpose of arriving at an understanding of its signification, it is the duty of the courts to examine the whole act, and by a comparison of, and a consideration of its various clauses and provisions, determine the meaning of any doubtful or ambiguous phraseology used therein. Beebee *v.* Griffing, 14 N. Y. 244. But where the same words are used in different parts of the same act, in connection with the same subject-matter, it is contrary to settled rules of construction to give them different meaning, in the several places where they occur. It was said by Lord Denman in Reg. *v.* The Com. of the Poor Laws, cited in Potter's Dwarris, 195 · " We disclaim altogether the assumption of any right to assign different meanings to the same words in an act of Parliament on the ground of a supposed general intention in the act, we think it necessary to give a fair and reasonable construction to the language used by the legislature; but we are not to assume the unwarrantable liberty of varying that construction for the purpose of making the act consistent with any views of our own." Fol

lowing the rule referred to in examining the question presented for our consideration, we can see no reasonable ground for
holding that salaries of public officers are included in the provision in question.

The omission of the word "salaries," and the use of the
rather uncommon word "allowances" in section "SALARIES" AND
18, considered by itself, would be quite signifi- ALLOWANCES
cant, and suggestive of great doubt as to the FICERS.
real signification of the provision, but when considered
in connection with other occasions where the framers of
the Constitution and the law-makers have been called
upon to express themselves on the subject of payments
to public servants, we shall find a uniform and invariable use
of language, showing that the respective phrases of " compensation," " salary," and " allowances" have been used discrimi-
natingly by them, and with a perfect understanding of their
true meaning. Thus we find that the Constitution provides
that "each member of the legislature shall receive for his
services an annual salary of $1500;" but senators, when serv-
ing as members of the court for the trial of impeachments, and
such members of the assembly as shall be appointed managers
of an impeachment, "shall receive an additional allowance of
$10 a day." § 6, art. 3. The governor "shall receive for his
services an annual salary." § 4, art. 4. The lieutenant-governor shall receive for his services an annual salary, " and shall
not receive or be entitled to any other compensation, fee, or
perquisite for any duty or service he may be required to perform by the Constitution or the law." § 8, art. 4. The secretary of State, treasurer, and attorney-general shall each
"receive for his services a compensation which shall not be increased or diminished during the term for which he shall have
been elected." § 1, art. 5. A superintendent of public works
"shall receive a compensation to be fixed by law." § 3, art.
5. Three deputy superintendents "shall receive for their
services a compensation to be fixed by law. Id. Judges of
the Court of Appeals and justices of the Supreme Court
"shall receive for their services a compensation to be established by law, which shall not be diminished during their
official terms." § 14, art. 6. It is provided for the county
judge that "his salary and the salary of the surrogate, when
elected as a separate officer, shall be established by law," and

' shall not be diminished during his term of office." § 15, art. 6. The compensation of the clerk of the Court of Appeals "shall be fixed by law ' § 20 art. 6.

"No officer whose salary is fixed by the Constitution shall receive any additional compensation. Each of the other State officers named in the Constitution shall, during his continuance in office, receive a compensation to be fixed by law, which shall not be increased or diminished during the term for which he shall have been elected or appointed, nor shall he receive to his use any fees or perquisites of office, or other compensation." (§ 9, art. 10.)

" Judicial officers in office when this Constitution shall take effect may continue to receive such fees and perquisites of office as are now authorized by law, until the first day of July, 1847." § 11, art. 14. "Any person holding office under the laws of this State, who, except in payment of his legal salary, fees or perquisites," shall receive, or consent to receive, "directly or indirectly, anything of value," etc., shall be deemed guilty of a felony. § 1, art. 15.

It is seen by this review that the word "allowances" is used in the Constitution in a sense entirely different and distinct from that of salary. The only instance in which it is employed, aside from the section in question, being to denote something to be given or yielded by the State in addition to a stated compensation, termed a salary. The generic term used by them to cover all forms of payments made to public officers for services is invariably that of compensation, and the specific term used to denote payments to officers having a fixed, definite and stated compensation, is that of salary.

A brief reference to the action of the several conventions which preceded the adoption of the present Constitution will show that the words of the existing section were deliberately selected after the rejection, by the people, of a provision couched in more comprehensive language. Among the sections submitted to the people by the constitutional convention of 1867, was the following : § 17. "The Legislature shall not grant any extra compensation to any public officer, servant or contractor, nor increase or diminish any compensation, except that of judicial officers, during their term of office." Proceedings and Debates, p. 3961, Atlas Ed. This provision, together with the Constitution of which it was a part, was rejected by the people. Subsequent to this rejection, a convention assembled under the authority of chapter 884, Laws of 1872, and framed provisions which, after being revised by the action of the subsequent legislature, resulted in the submission to the people of the Constitution as it now stands, and as thus submitted it was approved and adopted by them.

It will thus be seen that the framers of the Constitution, when they attempted to draw provisions specifically limiting the power of the legislature over the compensation of public officers, used the most appropriate, natural and comprehensive language adaptable to the purpose which they had in view, and with a discriminating sense of the meaning of the words used by them. It is impossible to resist the conviction that by the use of the words "salary and "compensation" in all of the provisions attempting the inhibition of the legislature from interfering therewith, and their exclusion from the clause in question, they intended to exempt persons whose services were payable by a fixed and stated compensation from the operation of the section. It will also be observed that in the structure of the clause referred to, the words first used, and presumably those to which the most importance was attached are those of "fees and percentages," and then follows the word "allowances," which seems to have been employed by way of repetition, and as a possible cover for some form of compensation of a similar character not included in its previous language. The rule embraced in the maxim of *noscitur a sociis* seems to be peculiarly applicable to the question presented, and requires a definition of the word "allowance" similar to that of the language to which it is so closely allied.

The natural interpretation of these provisions is that they were intended to include only those irregular, indefinite and uncertain modes of compensat- FEES, PERCENT-AGES, ETC., OF OFFICERS. ing public servants which were indicated by words of like character and meaning, as those of "fees," "percentages," etc. The case of McGaffin *v*. City of Cohoes, 74 N. Y. 389, is illustrative of the rule referred to. There the words "contract, obligation or liability" were held, by force of the maxim in question, to exclude liability for torts; the late Chief Judge Church saying that "words are often used redundantly or repetitiously, without strict regard to the meaning of each, but for greater caution to express the full meaning of the principal subject. In such cases, the maxim *noscitur a sociis* is applied." In the case of Corning *v.* McCullough, 1 N. Y. 47, it was held that a clause in a statute prescribing three years limitation " for any forfeiture, or cause, the benefit and suit whereof is limited to the party aggrieved," should be construed as meaning actions for a forfeiture, or cause of action of like nature only, and not to apply to cases of contract liability. See, also, Aikin *v.* Wasson, 24 N. Y. 484 ; Coffin *v.* Reynolds, 37 Id. 644.

It seems to us that we cannot, without doing violence to the meaning and intent of the authors of the Constitution, ascribe to them, by the use of such a word, in such a relation, an intention to reach and affect so important a subject as that embraced in regulating the compensation of those numerous ALLOWANCES, public servants whose services are compensated by ETC. fixed salaries. Whether we consider the ordinary and popular signification of the word, or the more accurate and technical meaning attached to it by lexicographers, it is entirely inappropriate to express the idea of a fixed compensation adopted for the payment of services rendered by one person to another. The word " allowance" imports the voluntary act of one party in doing something which is in his discretion to perform or withhold at pleasure. To allow implies the right to determine, and is the act of a superior toward a dependant granting a privilege which he has authority to confer or deny. It does not express the relations existing between co-contractors, vendor and vendee, or employer and employee where there is a right secured by contract on one side, and no power of voluntary action on the other.

Allowances are made by husband to wife, parents to children, the head of a family to its members, superannuated dependants and servants, from the benevolent to the poor, and in cases where the act is discretionary with the donor, as a reward for benefits conferred, or services voluntarily rendered by one to another.

Referring to some of the uses of the words in question adopted by the legislature in statutes, we find by section 3, chapter 521, Laws of 1880: " No officer or person who is paid a salary from the city treasury shall receive to or for his own use any fees, costs, allowances, perquisites of office, commissions," etc., and the comptroller is empowered to examine any such officer under oath touching "the amount of any fees, costs, allowances, perquisites," etc. Allowances have been authorized to be made by the court to parties in actions in certain cases, and extra allowances in actions to foreclose mortgages, for partition of real property, and to obtain construction of wills, etc. (Code of Pro. §§ 303–309; and Code of Civ. Pro. §§ 3252, 3253); also for expenses of poor witnesses (§ 1, chap. 155, Laws of 1869), and so, too, in cases of divorce, infancy, lunacy and wards of court, salvage, and all discretionary awards. They are also made to sheriffs on attachment proceedings when no fixed charges are provided. Code of Civ. Pro. § 656. They were formerly authorized in some special cases to be made to canal contractors for work and labor (§ 2, chap. 273, Laws of 1841; 1 R.·S. 632, § 37; 653, §§ 76, 77; 655, § 2), and to compensate appraisers appointed by loan commissioners. 3 Stat. at Large, 87, § 35. *Per diem* allowances were made to the justices of the Supreme Court in addition to their salaries, and it was provided that the compensation of those residing in New York City should not thereby be deemed to be reduced. (Chap. 308, § 9, Laws of 1870.) The health officer receives an allowance by way of commission on collections from coasters. Chap. 302, Laws of 1829. The clerks of the senate and assembly received an allowance for stationery (§ 1, chap. 1, Laws of 1859), but were to receive a salary and no extra allowance by section 3, chapter 379, Laws of 1879. Commissioner of public accounts receives a *per diem* compensation and additional allowance for mileage. Chap. 223, Laws of 1862. Pilots have an allowance for extra service (§ 8, chap. 69, Laws of 1847), as do also receivers of insolvent financial and life-insurance companies. §1, chap. 141, Laws of 1821 ; §2, chap. 3, Laws of 1841 ; chap. 442, Laws of 1871 ; chap. 902, Laws of 1869.

To the uses of the words shown by these citations, others of the same character could be made indefinitely, and we have yet to discover any employment of the word "allowance" by law-makers or others which is the exact equivalent of either of the words "salary" or "compensation." Reference to the works of the lexicographers shows Webster's definition to be, "The act of allowing, granting or admitting." "Permission or license." "That which is allowed ; a portion appointed ; a limited quantity of meat and drink when provisions fall short."

" A customary deduction from the gross weight of goods."
The substance of the definitions in Crabbe's English Synonyms is that an allowance is gratuitous; it ceases at the
pleasure of the donor.   Stipends and salaries are the requital
of some supposed service, and are paid yearly or at even
portions of a year, and are the subject of contract between
the parties.

Worcester gives a definition similar to that of Crabbe, but
refers to the word " salary" as one of the synonyms of " allowance," distinguishing them, however, by stating that the latter
is gratuitous and the former a stated compensation, payable
under a contract.   Richardson's English Dictionary gives,
" to permit, to concede, to suffer, to assent, to yield." Other
lexicographers give definitions similar to those of Worcester
and Crabbe, and seem to exclude the idea that the terms are
analogous, except, perhaps, in a very loose and imperfect
sense.

It would seem from the foregoing illustrations that the
word "allowance" has a plain, definite and precise meaning
attached to it by authors and law-makers, and the duty of
the court to enforce it as it reads, is clear and unmistakable.
We have no power, and it is not our office, to stretch the
meaning of words used, for the purpose of covering an object which we have no other means of determining to have
been within the contemplation of the authors of the Constitution, than that of the language employed by them.   It therefore seems to us not only a reasonable but a neccessary
inference from the invariable use by the authors of the Constitution of the words "salary" and "compensation" when
referring to that kind of payment made to public officers by
way of salary, and their deliberate exclusion from the clause
in question, that they did not intend to include salaried officers within its meaning.

This view is greatly strengthened by the express provisions
made in that instrument with reference to the immutability
of the compensation of a large number of such officers, and
the inference which may be drawn therefrom that they did
not intend to enact general provisions to accomplish a similar
object.

In opposition to our views it is urged that such a construction would leave no subject of importance for the provisions

in question to operate upon, but we do not think this is so. While it is obvious that it does, to a certain extent, narrow its application, yet a large body of public officers whose compensation consists solely of fees,' percentages and allowances, such as sheriffs, county clerks, registers of deeds, coroners, port-wardens, harbor-masters, pilots, commissioners, health-officers, justices, constables, and others who might be named, are still left to be affected by those provisions of the Constitution.

We are quite aware of the great importance of the question presented, and of the divers views existing with reference to it by judges and members of the legal profession; but no sufficient. reason has been suggested, as we think, which authorizes the importations into the Constitution of a meaning which does not flow naturally and obviously from the language employed in it.

Other minor questions raised by the learned counsel for the appellant have been examined by us, but we find none of sufficient plausibilty to raise serious doubt as to the correctness of the judgment appealed from. The judgment should therefore be affirmed.

All concur.

MAYOR, ALDERMEN AND COMMONALTY OF THE CITY OF NEW YORK

v.

KELLY, Administratrix, etc., Impleaded, etc.

(98 *New York Reports*, 467.)

The sureties to a bond, given by one appointed to a position in a public office, for the faithful discharge of his duties, are not discharged by the imposition of new duties, which are distinct and separable from those protected by the bond, unless they render impossible, or materially hinder or impede, the proper and just performance of the duties so guaranteed; and this, although the new duties so imposed expose the principal to temptation, and give broader opportunity for dishonesty.

Upon the appointment of B. as book-keeper in the department of docks, in the city of New York, he gave a bond with two sureties in the penal sum of $5000, conditioned that he would "truly and faithfully perform the duties that may be legally required of him . . . during his continuance in the office." B. was required to assist the treasurer in receiving and depositing, to the credit of the treasurer, the funds of the department. He embezzled, at various times, moneys of the department, amounting in all to over $40,000, and to conceal this, made false entries of deposits in the books, or omitted to make any entries of receipts. In an action upon the bond it was not claimed that the additional duties in any manner impeded or hindered the faithful performance of the duties of book-keeper. The complaint was dismissed on trial. *Held*, error; that conceding B. could not be held liable, as book-keeper, for the whole amount embezzled (as to which *quære*), as there was a clear breach of the condition of the bond, the amount of damages resulting therefrom was a question of fact for the jury, and might reasonably have been found to have at least equalled the penalty.

APPEAL from judgment of the General Term of the Court of Common Pleas, in and for the city and county of New York, entered upon an order made November 5, 1884, which affirmed a judgment in favor of defendant Kelly, entered upon an order dismissing the complaint on trial.

This action was a bond given by William W. Burnham upon his appointment as book-keeper in the department of docks in the city of New York.

The facts, so far as material, are stated in the opinion.

D. J. Dean for appellant.

Wallace Macfarlane for respondent.

FINCH, J.—The sureties who defend, resist the action brought upon their bond, with proof which they claim establishes that their principal, in addition to the duties of book-keeper, was required to perform, and did continuously perform, the duties of treasurer of the department of docks; so that, besides keeping the accounts, which was his specific duty, he was intrusted with the public money, and exposed to risks and temptations not contemplated by his bondsmen. The defence founded upon this fact assumed two forms, expressed in the separate grounds upon which a motion for the dismissal of the complaint was based. It was claimed, first, that the added employment was an extension of the risk and liability of the sureties which discharged them at once and entirely; and, second, that if not so discharged, and remaining liable for Burnham's false book-keeping, the breach created by his fraudulent entries was merely technical, and

. the injury flowed from an embezzlement not protected by the bond.

The sureties are never discharged by the imposition of new duties which are distinct and separable from those protected by the guaranty, unless such new employment renders impossible, or materially hinders or impedes, the proper and just performance of the duties guaranteed. Where the new employment is separate and distinct, and in no respect essentially interferes with the duty covered by the bond, the imposition of such added duty is wholly a matter between the employer and servant with which the sureties have no concern. For misconduct as to the new employment, the bondsmen are in no manner responsible, and have no right to complain so long as the added and separable duties do not prevent or tend to prevent the proper and just performance of those which are guaranteed. In such a case, if misconduct occurs, the sole question is whether it was a violation of the duties guaranteed, or of those outside of the bond and its protection. Ordinarily, that proves to be the only inquiry ; and in all the cases cited by the respondent was the substantial point of investigation. Thus in Nat. Mech. B'k'g Ass'n *v.* Conkling, 90 N. Y. 116, to which our attention is especially called, the book-keeper had been promoted to the office of teller. When we held that the guaranty related wholly to the duties of book-keeper, and such others as might be temporarily added while he remained such, it followed that his promotion to a new office terminated his duties as book-keeper, and so ended his responsibilities in that character, and of course the liability of his sureties, while as to his new and separate duties, the sureties had made no contract. If in that case he had remained book-keeper, the liability of the sureties as to that office would have continued, although the duties of a teller had been added to it (Rochester City Bank *v.* Elwood, 21 N. Y. 88), unless it further appeared that his failure to keep correct accounts was naturally and necessarily occasioned by the pressure or interference of his new duties. That the latter exposed him to temptation, or gave broader opportunity for dishonesty, is immaterial. For it is the very substance of the contract of the sureties, that as book-keeper he will be honest and faith-

[margin note:] IMPOSITION OF NEW DUTIES DOES NOT DISCHARGE BONDS-MEN, EXCEPT WHEN.

9 Cor. Cas.—20

ful whatever temptation may approach. By their bond they vouch for his integrity, and invite the employer to repose trust and confidence. They know that the book-keeper is to be introduced into the office and the business; that the whole range of the employer's transactions must come under the servant's observation, and be intrusted to his silent fidelity; and that out of the situation will necessarily arise unforeseen opportunities and temptations. It is of no consequence how ' many or what, so long as they in no respect become part of, or hinder or prevent, his guaranteed duty, or the preservation of his guaranteed integrity in rendering the services covered by the contract. If that were not so, proof that the money-drawer in the book-keeper's room was left unlocked and often unwatched, or the combination of the safe was disclosed to him, might serve as a defence against dishonestly kept accounts. In People *v.* Pennock, 60 N. Y. 426, the sole question considered was whether the sureties upon a supervisor's bond were liable for his default as to moneys which he was not authorized to receive in his official capacity. The board of supervisors had directed certain moneys to be paid to him, and which were so paid without legal authority, and this court held that as to such sums, his default was not within the condition of the bond. The decision went wholly upon that ground, without even a hint that the imposition of the new duty discharged the real and existing liability of his sureties for his official acts. In Ward *v.* Stahl, 81 N. Y. 406, the question again was upon the construction of the bond, and whether it covered anything more than the collection of village taxes. In People *v.* Vilas, 36 N. Y. 460, the rule as to private parties and the ground upon which it rests is thus stated: " Any alteration in the obligation or contract in respect of which a person has become surety without· consent of the latter, extinguishes his obligation. The reason upon which the rule is founded is, that the surety has never made the contract upon which it is sought to charge him." In all these cases, the question hinged upon the construction of the bond. If the employer has not materially altered the employment guaranteed ; if that remains as contemplated by the contract; it is no defence of faithlessness in that, to say that employer and servant have contracted in addition for new services with which the sureties had no concern, and which did not in their nature interfere with or injuriously affect the services guaranteed.

It is not here pretended that the additional duties imposed upon Burnham of receiving and depositing the funds of the department were of a nature to prevent or in any manner impede or hinder his faithful performance of the duties of bookkeeper. It may correctly be said that it furnished him greater opportunity for embezzlement and so put temptation in his way. But precisely that suggestion was overruled in Rochester City Bank *v.* Elwood, *supra.* There the bond was given for the faithful discharge by the principal of the trust reposed in him as assistant book-keeper of the bank. In consequence of the absence of the cashier and the duties of the teller having become more onerous, the assistant book-keeper was required to assist the teller in keeping the credit journal. Availing himself of that opportunity, Gold credited a deposit of $1625 as $625, and embezzled $1000 of it. The court conceded that by this added duty imposed upon the book-keeper the latter was "better able" to cover up an embezzlement and conceal it from detection. There was thus opportunity and temptation resulting from the new duty; but it was held that the true interpretation of the bond extended to Gold's honesty in his position, the court saying that " the contract did not define the trust reposed, but indicated the department of duty to be assigned and guaranteed that the appointee was a trustworthy person to be introduced into the bank to discharge that duty."

The sureties were held liable. The new opportunity for wrong-doing furnished by the new action of the employer was not permitted to operate as a defence. If the rule were otherwise it would compel the employer to put no confidence in the honesty of the book-keeper, and sedulously guard his money and valuables against any opportunity for embezzlement. The true question thus is, was the loss inflicted upon the employer within the condition of the bond, and the contract of the sureties, or in other words, was the contract essentially altered or modified? The bond recited that Burnham had been appointed to the office of book-keeper of the department of docks, and was conditioned that he should "in all things well, truly and faithfully perform the duties that may be legally required of him to perform and do during his

continuance in the said office of book-keeper of the department of docks." If this condition, which is very broad in its
terms, is narrowed by the recital, and limited to the duties of
book-keeper simply, the facts show that those duties were
not faithfully performed. Burnham not only emblezzled the
money of the department, but made false entries of deposits in
the books, and omitted to make entries of receipts which
should have been made, and all this purposely and with a
view to conceal his wrong.

There was thus a breach of his bond. His duties as book-
keeper were never terminated by promotion or change to a
new or different office, nor were they in any respect altered
or modified by the imposition of the entirely distinct and
separate duties as to which the sureties were not bound.
The respondent argues that while Burnham was not promoted
to the office of treasurer he was in fact made treasurer by
the act of the department. Even so much cannot justly be
said. It was the duty and authority of the treasurer to receive and disburse the funds. No authority was given to
Burnham to disburse a dollar. The money paid went to the
credit of the treasurer and remained within his control.
None of it could go to the credit of Burnham except as he
stole and concealed it. His duties were merely clerical in
the receipt and deposit of moneys and as an assistant to the
treasurer, and his services were temporary in the sense that
they could be dispensed with at any moment and were wholly
within the control of the treasurer. So that his duty as
book-keeper remained and was not terminated, nor was it at
any time essentially or necessarily altered or modified.

That duty, it is conceded, was wilfully and fraudulently
violated; but it is said, as the second ground of defence, that
ALLEGED TECH- the breach was purely technical; that the loss
NICAL BREACH resulted wholly from the embezzlement against
OF BOND EX-
AMINED. which the sureties had not contrᵃcted; and so
that only nominal damages could be recovered. Precisely
the same contention was urged in the Elwood Case,
supra, and overruled. The court there said that, " where
a person is introduced into and employed by a bank to assist
in keeping its books, and avails himself of his situation to
defraud his employers, the surety who has vouched for his
honesty should answer for any loss accruing from his fraud-

ulent or criminal conduct. Irrespective, therefore, of false entries, the abstraction of the money by Gold would render the surety liable for the loss. But more especially would he be liable if the false entries were concurrent and simultaneous, and each a part of the *res gestæ* of guilt." That doctrine thus declared would make Burnham liable as book-keeper for the embezzlement. But the present case does not require that we should go so far, or follow the doctrine stated to its full extent, for here the amount of damages resulting from the conceded breach was a question for the jury, and might reasonably have been found by them upon the facts to have at least equalled the penalty of the bond. That penalty was $5000. The total defalcation of Burnham exceeded $40,000. The embezzlements were between 1875 and 1878, or through a period of about three years. During the last eleven months of the time the books were not written up at all, and in that period Burnham's thefts reached $11,000. The largest single item which the evidence shows to have been stolen is less than $2400. So that it is quite apparent that a jury might justly trace to the system of false or omitted accounts, a loss of more than the penalty of the bond. If Burnham had simply stolen the funds from time to time, but had not falsified the accounts, a jury might well conclude that the robbery would have been promptly discovered, and much more than $5000 of it have been prevented. The court, therefore, should have held the defendants liable for a breach of the bond in the failure of their principal to faithfully perform his duty as book-keeper, and submitted to the jury the question of damages resulting from that breach.

The judgment should be reversed, and a new trial granted, costs to abide the event.

All concur.

Judgment reversed.

LIABILITY OF SURETIES WHEN OFFICERS' DUTIES ARE ENLARGED.—There are several cases very much to the point upon the question involved in the principal case. In People *v.* Vilas, 36 N. Y. 459, it was held that the sureties upon the bond of a public officer, are not discharged by the imposition upon their principal of new duties of a similar nature and character by an act of the legislature. In this case J· was in 1850 appointed a commissioner for the county of St. Lawrence, to loan the moneys of the United States deposited with the State under an act of 1839, and the defendants became sureties for the faithful performance of his duties as such commissioner, and during the continuance of his office the legislature transferred to such commissioner, for the same purpose, moneys formerly held by another commissioner under acts of 1792 and 1808, and J· became a defaulter, to the amount of $500, in the funds last transferred to him, and to a larger amount of the original fund. *Held*, that his sureties were liable for the whole amount of his default. In Board of Supervisors *v.* Clark, 92 N. Y. 391, it was held that the imposition by the board of supervisors of a county upon the county treasurer, during his term of office, of the duty of raising, keeping, and disbursing large sums of money in addition to the usual and ordinary duties of his office, for instance the raising and disbursing money during a war for bounty purposes, does not discharge the sureties upon his bond from all liability.

To the same general effect are the following authorities : Commonwealth *v.* Holmes, 25 Gratt. (Va.) 771 ; Hatch *v.* Inhabitants of Attleborough, 97 Mass. 533; United States *v.* Kilpatrick, 9 Wheat. 720; White *v.* Fox, 9 Shepley (Me.), 341 ; Colter *v.* Morgan, 12 B. Monroe (Ky.), 278 ; German American Bank *v.* Auth, 87 Pa. St. 416; Kindle *v.* State, 7 Black (Ind.), 586; Rochester City Bank *v.* Elwood, 21 N. Y. 88.

In Gaussen *v.* United States, 97 U. S. 584, the court remarks: " If it be conceded, as it may be, that the addition of duties different in their nature from those which belonged to the office when the officer's bond was given will not impose upon the obligor in the bond, as such, additional responsibilities, it is undoubtedly true that such addition of new duties does not render void the bond of the officer as a security for the performance of the duties at first assumed. It will still remain a security for what it was originally given to secure."

There are some English authorities which maintain a contrary doctrine, but they have been repudiated in the United States. Pybus *v.* Gibbs, 6 Ell. & B. (88 Eng. C. L.) 902. See, also, Bonar *v.* McDonald, 3 N. L. Cas. 226; Bartlett *v.* Att'y-Gen'l, Parker, 277 ; Napier *v.* Bruce, 8 C. & F. 470.

CHANGE OF STATUTORY DUTIES.—The sureties of an official are generally liable for the faithful performance by him of all the duties imposed by statute, whether before or after the execution of the bond, provided, of course, that they belong to and come properly within the scope of the office. Governor *v.* Ridgway, 12 Ill. 14; Compher *v.* People, 12 Ill. 290; People *v.* Leet, 13 Ill. 261 ; Smith *v.* Peoria Co., 59 Ill. 412 ; People *v.* Tompkins, 74 Ill. 482 ; People *v.* Vilas, 36 N. Y. 459; Mayor of New York *v.* Silberns, 3 Abb. Pr. New Cas. (N.Y.) 236 ; Commonwealth *v.* Holmes, 25 Gratt. (Va.) 771 ; Commonwealth *v.* Galbert's Adm'r, 5 Bush (Ky.), 438, United States *v.* Gaussen, 2 Woods, C. C. 92; Postmaster-General *v.* Munger, 2 Paine U. S. C. C. 189; King *v.* Nichols, 16 Ohio St. 80 ; State *v.* Bradshaw, 10 Ired. (N. Car.) L. 229; Dawson *v.* State, 38 Ohio St. 1 ; Board of Supervisors *v.* Clark, 2 Am. & Eng. Corp. Cas. 333.

A total change in the functions of the office may discharge the sureties, as they will be considered to have assumed the obligation on the faith of the law existing at the time of the execution of the bond, Van Epps *v.*

Walsh, 1 Woods C. C. 598; Fillden *v.* Lahens, 6 Blatch. C. C. 524; Romans *v.* Peters, 2 Rob. (La.) 479; Denis *v.* State, 60 Miss. 949.

CAVANAGH

v.

CITY OF BOSTON.

(Advance Case, Massachusetts. June 19, 1885.)

The city has no power to appropriate private property, without the owner's consent, for the purpose of abating a nuisance existing on adjacent lands. Such power can only be conferred by statute providing due compensation for the property taken.

Such acts being beyond the power and authority of the common council, the city cannot be held responsible in damages.

It seems that the liability, if any, rests upon the individuals who per-. formed the acts.

ACTION of tort to recover damages by reason of the construction of a dam across South bay in the city of Boston. At a trial in the superior court, the plaintiffs offered evidence tending to show that they were at the time of doing the acts complained of, and had ever since been, the owners in fee of Wales Island and the flats adjacent thereto, situated in South bay ; that at a meeting of the common council of the city of Boston, held June 3, 1880, the following order was passed : " Ordered, that the board of health be requested to cause to be abated the nuisance at present existing in the South bay east of the New York & New England R. R., and the expense attending the same to be charged to the appropriation for health." At a meeting of the board of aldermen, held June 10, 1880, the said order was referred to the committee on health, in concurrence with the vote of the council, passed June 3. At a meeting of the common council, held July 12, 1880, the committee on health recommended the passage of the following order:

" Whereas, The board of health has declared a nuisance exists, consisting of effusive flats on the territory between the track of the New York & New England R. R. Co. and Dorchester avenue, which can be abated by the construction of a dam, at an estimated cost of $4600, and as the annual appropriation, granted to said board, does not contemplate such an expenditure, it is hereby

"Ordered, That the committee on finance be directed to furnish the means for the abatement of the aforesaid nuisance."

This report was accepted and the order passed by both branches of the city government. At a meeting of the board of aldermen, held July 26, 1880, the committee of finance reported the following order granting the request:

"Ordered, That the auditor of accounts be, and is hereby authorized to transfer from the reserve fund, the sum of $4600, and that said sum constitute a special appropriation for the purpose of constructing a temporary dam across South bay between the New York & New England R. R. track and Dorchester avenue, for the abatement of the nuisance on the flats therein located; and that the board of health is hereby authorized to have said temporary dam constructed at an expense not exceeding the sum herein provided."

At a meeting of the common council, held July 29, 1880, the report and order of transfer of $4600 from the reserved fund for the abatement of the nuisance was passed in concurrence.

Upon the petition of the city engineer, the State board of harbor commissioners also granted a license to construct the dam. The defendants offered as evidence, subject to the plaintiff's objection, the record of the board of health of the city of Boston, from which it appeared that, at a meeting of the board, held September 6, 1880, it was ordered that the city engineer be requested to abate the nuisance, by erecting a dam, according to the plan proposed, at a cost not exceeding $4600.

Upon all the evidence in the case, the court ruled that the action could not be maintained, and directed a verdict for the defendant, and the plaintiffs alleged exceptions.

W. E. L. Dillaway for plaintiffs.

T. M. Babson for defendant.

C. ALLEN, J.—The difficulty with the plaintiffs' case is that neither the board of health nor the city government had

any authority to abate the nuisance in the manner which was adopted. That manner was by the erection of a dam, the easterly portion of which was built across the flats and upon the upland of the plaintiffs, for the purpose of raising the water so as to flow AUTHORITY OF CITY OR BOARD OF HEALTH TO ABATE NUISANCE over other flats away from the flats of the plaintiffs, the plaintiffs' evidence tending to show that no nuisance existed on their own flats. This was an occupation of the plaintiffs' land, which the city had no power to make without the plaintiffs' consent. No statute conferred the power of appropriating the plaintiffs' property for public uses, nor provided compensation to them for damages sustained by such appropriation. When the preservation of the public health has been thought to require such acts as the filling of land or raising the grade over a considerable extent, of territory, or the covering of land with water, or the removal of dams from streams in order to allow better drainage, or to prevent the accumulation of offensive materials, it has been usual to pass statutes giving the requisite authority and mak ing due provisions for the protection of the property of individuals. Instances of such legislation may be found in Stat. 1867, chap. 308, which was before the court for consideration in Dingley *v.* Boston, 100 Mass. 544 ; and Cobb *v.* Boston, 109 Id. 438 ; s. c., 112 Id. 181. In Stat. 1869, chap. 378, which was under consideration in Phillips *v.* Co. Comm'rs, 122 Mass. 258 ; s. c., 127 Id. 262. In Stat. 1872, chap. 299, which was before the court in Cambridge *v.* Munroe, 126 Mass. 496 ; Bancroft *v.* Cambridge, Id. 438 ; and Read *v.* Cambridge, Id. 427. In Stat. 1873, chap. 340, which was considered in Farnsworth *v.* Boston, 121 Mass. 173. The general power vested in boards of health and the city governments is not adequate to dealing with such cases if it is impossible to come to an agreement with the owners of property to be affected. There is no general statute vesting in these bodies the right of eminent domain or making provision for the compensation of persons whose property may be taken. The general phrases contained in the city ordinances which have been referred to, authorizing the city council to exercise the powers vested in them for the preservation of the public health in any manner which they may prescribe, cannot be held to give them authority to take private property for public uses. No such power existed in the body which enacted the city ordinances. In the present case, the acts of which the plaintiffs complain amount to an occupation of their land for the purpose of building a dam thereon in such a manner that clearly it was an appropriation of the land to a public use. It was not a mere transient entry and occupation, though the dam was styled temporary, but there was a substantial and practically exclusive occupation of a portion of the plaintiff's land. Such an act was clearly illegal. It does not fall within the principle upon which a brief or momentary occupation of private lands is sometimes justified through necessity, as, for example, for the purpose of making an arrest, or for the perambulation of the boundaries of towns by the selectmen, or of ascertaining boundaries for public purposes. Winslow *v.* Gifford, 6 Cush. 327. The present case is a much stronger one than Brigham *v.* Edmunds, 7 Gray, 359. See, also, Baker *v.* Boston, 12 Pick. 194. No doubt the plaintiff might have obtained an injunction to restrain the prosecution of the work if he had sought his remedy in that form. Boston Water Power Co. *v.* Boston & Worcester R. R., 16 Pick. 525. The acts done having been beyond the authority and power of the city to do, the city cannot be held responsible in damages for what was done under the supposed authority of illegal and void votes. Spring *v.* Hyde Park, 137 Mass. 554; Lemon *v.* Newton, 134 Id. 476; Cushing *v.* Bedford, 125 Id. 526. But the liability, if any, rests upon the individuals who performed the acts, as in Brigham *v.* Edmunds, 7 Gray, 359.

Exception overruled.

ABATEMENT OF NUISANCES BY EXERCISE OF EMINENT DOMAIN.— Practically the same conclusion as that reached in the principal case was arrived at in New York. A statute was passed in 1871, authorizing the draining of private lots in the city of New York by the department of public works, on the certificate of the board of health that the same was necessary, etc., and providing for collecting the expense by an assessment on the property benefited. It was, however, held unconstitutional in making no provision for compensation to the landowners. *In re* Chessbrough, 17 Hun (N. Y.), 561.

POWER OF MUNICIPALITIES TO ABATE NUISANCES.—It is well settled that municipal authorities cannot arbitrarily declare a thing a nuisance or destroy valuable property which was lawfully erected or created, where such thing or property is not a nuisance *per se*, until this fact has been lawfully ascertained. Further, that where the necessary power has been expressly conferred by the legislature, it is inoperative and void unless the thing is in fact a nuisance, or was created or erected after the passage of the ordinance and in defiance of it; and, except in cases of emergency, or where the use is clearly a nuisance, that fact should first be established by judicial adjudication. Yates *v.* City of Milwaukee, 10 Wall. 497; Everett *v.* Council Bluffs, 46 Iowa, 66; Chicago, R. I. & P. R, R. *v.* Joliet, 79 Ill. 25; Rye *v.* Patterson, 45 Tex. 312; Chicago *v.* Laflin, 49 Ill. 172; Darst *v.* People, 51 Ill. 286; Underwood *v.* Green, 42 N. Y. 140; Pieri *v.* Shieldsboro, 42 Miss. 493.

See North Chicago, etc., Ry. *v.* Town of Lake View, 2 Am. & Eng. Corp. Cas. 6; Rolfs *v.* Shallcross, 2 Am. & Eng. Corp. Cas. 191; City of Denver *v.* Mullen, 4 Am. & Eng. Corp. Cas. 304; River Rendering Co. *v.* Behr, 4 Am. & Eng. Corp. Cas. 320; Vogt *v.* Mayor, etc., of Baltimore, 4 Am. & Eng. Corp. Cas. 329; State of Maryland *v.* Mott, *Ibid.* 334.

It is also said, however, that these two propositions of law are not irre-concilable; that where a municipal corporation is authorized by its charter to remove and prevent nuisances, generally speaking, the only restriction upon that right is that what is done shall clearly be for the public health, safety and convenience. Roberts *v.* Ogle, 30 Ill. 459; Lake View *v.* Letz, 44 Ill. 81; Comm. *v.* Worcester, 3 Pick. (Mass.) 462; Dubuque *v.* Maloney, 9 Iowa 450; Commissioners *v.* Gas Co., 12 Pa. St. 318; Comm. *v.* Goodrich, 13 Allen, 546; Salem *v.* Railroad, 98 Mass. 431; Dingley *v.* Boston, 100 Mass. 544; Whyte *v.* Mayor, 2 Swan (Tenn.), 364; Williams *v.* Augusta, 4 Ga. 509; Mobile *v.* Yuille, 3 Ala. 137; New Orleans *v.* Philippi, 9 La. Ann. 44; People *v.* Albany, 11 Wend. (N. Y.) 539; St. Paul *v.* Colter, 12 Minn. 41; Collins *v.* Hatch, 18 Ohio, 523; St. Louis *v.* Bents, 11 Mo. 61; Taylor *v.* Griswold, 2 Green (N. J.), 222; Peck *v.* Lockwood, 5 Day (Conn.), 22; Phillips *v.* Allen, 41 Pa. St. 481; Baltimore *v.* Radecke, 49 Md. 217; King *v.* Davenport, 98 Ill. 305; s. c., 38 Am. Rep. 89; Green *v.* Lake, 60 Miss. 451.

But see Lake *v.* Aberdeen, 57 Miss. 260.

HOUGHTON COMMON COUNCIL
v.
HURON COPPER MINING COMPANY.

(Advance Case, Michigan.   September 29, 1885.)

Where a municipal corporation seeks to condemn certain land for its use, and there are separate pieces of land that are necessary to the full en-joyment of either piece of land, they must all be condemned in the same action.

Where it appears that the jury called are biassed in the matter to be passed upon, a challenge to the array should be sustained.

Under the statute (act 124, Super. Laws 1883, p. 115), village corporations not empowered by their charters to purchase and hold lands outside
of corporation limits cannot condemn lands beyond corporation for use of
the village.

APPEAL from Houghton.

T. M. Brady for petitioner.

Chandler, Grant & Gray for appellant.

SHERWOOD, J.—The common council of the village of
Houghton, on the twelfth day of April, 1884, filed a petition
FACTS. in the circuit court for the county of Houghton to
condemn for the use of the village, and to supply the village
and its inhabitants with water, a piece of land having upon it
a spring, and certain rights of way over it, and other parties'
lands, for a pipe-line between the spring and village limits. The appellant, the Huron Copper Mining Company, was
made a party to the petition, with one other land-owner who
did not appeal, and two others who were not served with any
notice or process, or otherwise proceeded against than by the
filing of the petition. The petition was filed and the jurisdiction of the court invoked under the provisions of law contained in an act of the legislature entitled " An act to authorize cities and villages to take private property for the use and
benefit of the public, and to repeal act numbered 26 of the
public acts of 1882" (see Pub. Acts 1883, p. 115); and the
petitioner also showed to the court that it desired and should,
in addition thereto, "avail itself of the provisions of law contained in How. St. §§ 3090, 3109, and of any and all the laws
of the State of Michigan applicable to the premises." The
petition further described the land desired to be taken, the nature and extent of its proposed use, and claimed that the fee
was necessary for the proposed improvement; states that
the common council of the village had declared the proposed
public use and improvement necessary; "also had declared
that they deemed it necessary to take the private property
described for such improvement for the use and benefit of the
public;" and further asked that a jury be summoned and im-
panelled to ascertain and determine the necessity to take
the property described for the use and benefit of the public
aforesaid, and to determine the just compensation to be made
therefor.

Summons was issued in accordance with the prayer of the petition, and served on the twelfth day of May following, upon the defendants, the Huron Copper Mining Company and the Dacotah Mining Company. The Huron Company appeared and moved to quash the proceedings, for the following reasons:

"(1) Because act No. 124 of the Session Laws of 1883, under which the petition in this case is filed, is unconstitutional in these respects, viz.: (*a*) The title of the act only allows condemnation inside the city or village, and does not allow the condemnation of lands outside the city or village limits. (*b*) The act provides for the summoning of a jury to condemn property within the city or village limits, only from the city or village. (*c*) As to property outside the village limits, the act provides for the summoning of a jury from the vicinity of the property to be taken. (2) Because neither the charter of the village of Houghton nor any statute of this State authorizes the common council of said village to take or hold property outside of their corporate limits for obtaining and securing a supply of water."

The motion of defendants' counsel was denied, and in the entry of the order denying the motion the following order was made by the court for obtaining a jury : " It is further ordered, pursuant to the prayer of said petitioner, no sufficient cause to the contrary being shown, that the sheriff of this county make a list of twenty-four freeholders, residing in the vicinity of the property in the petition described, from which to strike a jury for the hearing of said petition as against said respondents, and that the attorneys of said petitioners and said respondents, respectively, attend at the office of the clerk of this court on the first day of July, 1884, at 10 o'clock in the forenoon of that day, for the purpose of striking such jury, and that the sheriff, under-sheriff, or deputy-sheriff have then and there such list of freeholders, and that when such jury shall have been struck, the clerk of this court issue, under the seal of this court, a *venire* summoning such jury to attend this court on the fifth day of July, A.D. 1884, at 9 o'clock in the forenoon of that day, which *venire* shall be served by said sheriff."

Thereupon the respondent's agent made and filed in the case an answer, setting forth that the spring is situated but a short distance from the respondent's stump-mill, which is but a mile from the village; that it obtains its supply of water for the mill from a pond, which is insufficient in quantity and quality for its business; and that it had already commenced preparations for the purpose of utilizing the water of the spring for its boilers at its mill, and it cannot obtain water elsewhere for the purpose except at great expense, and the spring will soon become a necessity in its business; that the spring will not afford a sufficient supply for the use of the village; that a supply can be obtained elsewhere for the village, at very little, if any, greater expense to the village; that the taking is not necessary for public use; that the reasonable compensation therefor would be an amount sufficient to enable the respondent to obtain an equal supply of good water from other sources, and reasserting the reasons given why the proceeding should not be further prosecuted, stated on the motion to quash.

The sheriff thereupon, after having taken an oath for the purpose, made a list of the names of 24 persons from which to select a jury in the case, and the respondent, the Huron Copper Mining Company, by its agent, refusing to strike six names from the list, the court did so for it. The petitioner then struck off six, and the remaining twelve constituted the jury by whom the case was tried.

Counsel for respondents, before the same were sworn, challenged the array of jurors for the reason they were not summoned from the vicinity of the property or body of the county. The facts were made to appear that they were all taken from a single township, and all but one taken from the village of Hancock, in that township, where the subject of water supply for that village and others had been freely discussed with a strong feeling in favor thereof, and in which discussion several of the jurors had taken an interest. The court overruled the motion, and exception was taken, and the case was ordered to trial.

None of the rest of the property necessary to be obtained had been secured, or proceedings taken for its condemnation. The deeds offered for that purpose came too late, and should have been ruled out. Testimony was taken upon the trial by both parties, upon the conclusion of which, under the charge given by the court, the jury returned a verdict that it was necessary to take said premises for the use and purposes described in said petition, and assessed the damages of the said respondent, the Huron Copper Mining Company, at the sum of $750. This finding of the jury was confirmed by the circuit judge on the fifth day of August thereafter.

The four pieces of property mentioned in the petition all lay outside the corporate limits of the village of Houghton, and the appellant's parcel was the most remote therefrom. It will be noticed, by a careful reading of the statute, that all the proceedings were had or intended to be had under act 124, Super. Laws 1883, p. 115. The whole proceeding must stand or fall, find its support or condemnation, under the provisions of that act. The sections of our laws found in Howell's Statutes, to which counsel for the petitioner has referred us, cannot be relied upon to aid the jurisdiction of the court in the case or to give warrant for the proceedings taken. Section 3090 does no more than to authorize the raising of money to pay for property taken and improvements made in cases when the same has been legally done. How. St. § 3109 says the act therein referred to "shall apply to all cities and villages," but it can have no application to any proceedings not taken under the act. We must, therefore, lay aside all the statutes except that of 1883 in the consideration of the case in hand.

Counsel for the respondents, at the close of the trial, asked the court to charge the jury: "(1) The lands of the respondents, the Huron Copper Mining Company and the Dacotah Mining Company, which the petitioners in this case seek to condemn for the benefit of the village of Houghton, are situated outside the limits of the village. Neither the charter of the village of Houghton, nor any statute of this State, gives to the petitioners the right to take and condemn lands outside of the corporate limits of the village. You are therefore instructed to find a verdict for the respondent. (2) These lands, which the petitioner seeks to condemn, are not the only lands necessary and requisite for the use' of the village in obtaining water from the spring described in the petition. In order to utilize said spring, the petitioners must obtain the use of other lands in order to reach the village of Houghton. They have not obtained such lands by agreement, and have not proceeded against the owners of such lands, although they made them parties in their petition. This proceeding is

an indivisible one, and all the owners of the lands, the use of which, or the title to which, it is necessary to obtain in order to make the water available, must be made parties to the suit; and all must be before the court at the same time, in order that the same jury may pass upon the necessity of taking and condemning their lands. You are therefore instructed to find a verdict for these respondents. (3) The petitioners have not shown any proceedings taken by them to obtain, by agreement or condemnation, land within the village limits for water purposes, nor that they have or own any such land for such purposes. In order to enable the jury to pass upon the necessity of taking lands outside the village limits, the petitioners must show that they have the necessary lands and facilities within the village in order to utilize the water taken from outside. The petitioners not having shown this, you are instructed to find a verdict for these respondents. (4) The petitioners have made no such case against these respondents as entitled them to a condemnation of their lands described in the petition. You are therefore instructed to find a verdict for the respondents." (8) " The title of act No. 124 of the public acts of the State of Michigan for the year 1883, under which the petitioners in this case have proceeded, only allows condemnation of lands within the city or village limits, and that portion of said act purporting to authorize cities and villages to take and hold lands or property outside of their corporate limits is unconstitutional and void. You will therefore find a verdict for the respondents. (9) The petitioners have not shown any authority conferred upon them by a vote of the inhabitants of the village of Houghton to take these proceedings, and therefore your verdict must be for the respondents."
To the refusal of which to give each and every of said requests, this respondent then and there duly excepted.

These exceptions and the reasons stated in the respondent's motion raise all the questions in the case requiring our consideration. The proceeding was one to condemn land containing a spring of water and a strip of land 20 feet wide for a right of way over which to conduct the waters. The land and spring were of no use for the purposes sought without the right of way over the other respondent's lands. The entire right of way was rightly, therefore, included in the petition and asked to be condemned in the proceeding. The object was entire, as much so as in the condemnation of land for a highway, and the proceeding should have been had against all the owners at the same time; all should have had the notice required by the statute and the opportunity to be heard before the same jury, and the privilege of participating in selecting and impanelling the same. This was not done. The petitioner proceeded upon the theory that it could have as many juries as there were different pieces of property belonging to different owners in the case to be condemned. I do not think the legislature ever intended such a construction, or such expense and confusion as such a practice would be likely to entail upon the parties. The consequences which might follow forbid such construction, some of which are suggested by respondent's counsel in their brief and argument, wherein he says if the petitioner's theory upon the subject is correct, then one jury might hold that there was no necessity for introducing water into the village, while another jury might hold that there was; one jury might find that one piece of land was necessary, while the next might find that the intervening piece, without which the first piece would be of no use, was not necessary; one jury might be in favor of taking water from one place, another jury from another place. The bare statement of the proposition demonstrates its absurdity. Public policy will not permit such a multiplicity of suits, especially where such evil results might follow. The jury must pass upon the necessity of obtaining a supply of water and then upon the necessity of taking each parcel of land sought to be condemned for that purpose. I think such a proceeding is indivisible, and the same jury in the same case should decide as to all. Brush *v.* Detroit, 32 Mich. 43. I think the court should have given the respondent's second, third, and fourth requests.

In selecting the jury the sheriff took them all from a single township, and all from a village where the subject-matter of the petition had been discussed freely with some apparent bias. As the testimony tended to show there was good reason for believing some might be biassed, the challenge to the array should have been sustained; the jury should have been summoned from the body of the county. Large property interests are frequently at their dis-

JURY—BIAS—
CHALLENGE TO
ARRAY.

posal in this class of cases, and great care and circumspection should be observed in their selection. The requirements of the statute must be strictly complied with. *In re* Convers, 18 Mich. 467; Swart *v.* Kimball, 43 Mich. 448; Powers' Appeal, 29 Mich. 504.

There is nothing in the charter of the village of Houghton authorizing these proceedings to be taken. The act of 1883 does not authorize them. The provisions of that VILLAGE CAN- act are confined to condemning land within the NOT CONDEMN LANDS OUTSIDE municipality. Section 20 of the act reads as fol- ITS LIMITS. lows: " The cities and villages of the State authorized to take or hold land or property outside of their corporate limits for obtaining and securing a supply of water to the municipality, or for any other public purpose, may take private property therefor, provided it is for the use or benefit of the public. . . ." By this provision the act itself limits its application to cities and villages authorized to take and hold lands outside of their corporate limits under their charters. It is entirely unnecessary to consider the constitutionality of the act, so long as its provisions do not apply to the case under investigation. I know of no statute, general or special, in force at the time this petition was filed authorizing by its expressed terms the prosecution of the proceedings under the theory of the petitioner's counsel; and certainly the powers of the village of Houghton so to do cannot be implied, because by the proceedings it is proposed to take land against the will of the respondent. Dill. Mun. Corp. § 469; Cooley, Const. Lim. 528–541; Kroop *v.* Forman, 31 Mich. 144; Detroit Sharpshooters' Ass'n *v.* Highway Com'rs, 34 Mich. 36; Powers' Appeal, 29 Mich. 504; Specht *v.* Detroit, 20 Mich. 168.

I think the proceedings in this case are without the authority of law, and the order entered, affirming the finding of the jury, should be vacated and the petition dismissed, with costs.

CAMPBELL, J., concurred.

COOLEY, C. J.—I concur in the result.

AUSTERBERRY

v.

CORPORATION OF OLDHAM.

(*L. R.* 29 *Ch. D.* 750.)

The doctrine in Tulk *v.* Moxhay, 2 Ph. 774, is limited to restrictive stipulations, and will not be extended so as to bind in equity a purchaser taking with notice of a covenant to expend money on repairs or otherwise which does not run with the land at law.

Semble, that the burden of a covenant (not involving a grant) never runs with the land at law except as between landlord and tenant.

Cooke *v.* Chilcott, 3 Ch. D. 694, overruled on this point.

Morland *v.* Cook, Law Rep. 6 Eq. 252, explained.

Holmes *v.* Buckley, 1 Eq. C. Ab. 27, discussed.

Consideration of the circumstances under which a covenant will be held to touch or concern the land of the covenantee so that the benefit may run with the land.

A, by deed, conveyed for value to trustees in fee a piece of land as part of the site of a road intended to be made and maintained by the trustees under the provisions of a contemporaneous trust-deed (being a deed of settlement for the benefit of a joint-stock company established to raise the necessary capital for making the road) ; and in the conveyance the trustees covenanted with A, his heirs and assigns, that they, the trustees, their heirs and assigns, would make the road, and at all times keep it in repair, and allow the use of it by the public, subject to tolls. The piece of land so conveyed was bounded on both sides by other lands belonging to A. The trustees duly made the road, which afforded the necessary access to A's adjoining lands. A afterwards sold his adjoining lands to the plaintiff, and the trustees sold the road to the defendants, both parties taking with notice of the covenant to repair.

Held, that the plaintiff could not enforce covenant against the defendants.

The promoters of an intended road by deed declared that the road should not only be enjoyed by them for their individual purposes, but "should be open to the use of the public at large for all manner of purposes, in all respects, as a common turnpike road," but subject to the payment of tolls by the persons using it.

Held, that this was not a dedication of the road to the public, and that the road was not a highway repairable by the inhabitants at large under section 150 of the Public Health Act, 1875.

Semble, an individual cannot, without legislative authority, dedicate a road to the public if he reserves the right to charge tolls for the user; and the mere fact that a number of persons form themselves into a company for making and maintaining a road, and erect gates and bars and charge tolls, does not make the road a "turnpike road" in the sense of a turnpike road made such by act of Parliament, and so dedicatèd to the public.

IN the year 1837, the owners of property adjacent to an old circuitous highway leading from Higgenshaw to Lower Moor, in the borough of Oldham, being desirous of constructing a shorter and more direct road between those places, it was proposed that the owners of the lands through which the new road was to pass should sell the necessary slips of land for agreed sums of money amounting in the aggregate to £173 19s. 10d., the sum agreed to be paid to one of these landowners, John Elliott, through whom the plaintiff in this action claimed, being £14 11s. 8d. It was also proposed that the construction and maintenance of the road should be undertaken by an association or company of proprietors who were to be represented by trustees.

To carry out this arrangement a deed of settlement was executed on the 3d of March, 1837. The parties to this deed were Joshua Milne, John Milne, and Samuel Lees, of the first part; James Milne and John Travis, of the second part; the said James Milne and various other persons whose names and seals were comprised in the 2d schedule thereto, and the several other persons who should from time to time execute the deed and whose names and seals should be comprised in the 3d schedule thereto, of the third part. The deed then recited as follows: That the making of the proposed new road would be of great public advantage; that the several parties thereto, being willing at their own expense to carry out the undertaking, had agreed to form amongst themselves a joint-stock company, under the style of the Higgenshaw and Lower Moor Road Company, and to raise capital for the purchase of land for the formation of the road and making and maintaining the same; that it had been agreed that the said Joshua Milne, John Milne, and Samuel Lees should be the trustees in whose name the lands necessary for the road should be purchased, and that the road when completed should not only be appropriated, used, and enjoyed by the parties thereto "for their individual purposes, but (subject as thereafter mentioned) should be open to the use of the public at large for all manner of purposes in all respects as a common turnpike road"; that contracts had been entered into by or on behalf of the said company for the purchase of the necessary lands for a total sum of £173 19s. 10d., and proper conveyances had been prepared and were awaiting execution for vesting such lands in the said Joshua Milne, John Milne, and Samuel Lees, who were to stand possessed thereof upon the trusts thereinafter declared; and that the business of the said company should be carried on subject to the provisions thereinafter contained; it was then witnessed and agreed that the said Joshua Milne, John Milne, and Samuel Lees, and the survivors and survivor of them, and the heirs of such survivor, should forever thereafter stand possessed of the lands intended to be granted to them, upon the trusts thereinafter declared. And it was further witnessed and agreed that the said parties thereto, and all other persons who should thereafter become proprietors as thereinafter mentioned, should, whilst holding shares in the capital of the said company, be and they were thereby united into a company for making and maintaining the said road, and should be and continue the proprietors thereof under the name of " The Higgenshaw and Lower Moor Road Company"; that for the purpose of making and maintaining the road and other general purposes attending the same a capital of £1600 should be raised in thirty-two shares of £50 each ; that the number of shares held by each person should be written opposite his or her name at the time of his or her executing the deed; that the said £173 19s. 10d. should be paid out of the capital of the company for the purchase of the land necessary for the road as aforesaid, and that the remainder of the money to be received by the said company, whether by way of capital or profits, or otherwise, should be applied by the trustees in paying the costs of the present deed, of the conveyances, and of the establishment of the said company, and that the remainder of the capital should be applied in making and afterwards maintaining in repair the said road pursuant to the specification, ground-plan, and cross-section contained in a schedule of even date, and in setting up necessary toll-gates.   Then followed provisions describing the line of road; for the erection of tables of tolls to be fixed from time to time by a majority in value of the company at a meeting for the purpose,—" that no person or persons (except such persons and for the purposes only as are mentioned in the said several conveyances of the said land so purchased by the company as aforesaid) shall be allowed to travel upon, use, or enjoy any part of the said road, or pass through any such toll-gate, side-bar, or chain, to be erected or set up as aforesaid, without having previously paid such toll as may from time to time be demanded of him, her, or them, pursuant to the table of tolls for the time being authorized by the said company to be demanded and taken as aforesaid" for payment of tolls by the parties to the present deed; that the trustees should apply the tolls in payment of the current expenses of the company, "and in repairing and keeping in repair the said road," and in discharge of the principal and interest of any moneys borrowed on the security of the tolls, and then in payment of the dividends declared to the proprietors of the company. Then followed various provisions as to meetings, rights of voting, keeping of the company's books, calls on and forfeiture of shares, declaration of dividends, appointment of new trustees by the shareholders, variation or modification of any clauses in the present deed, and enrolment of the present or any future deed of settlement by the trustees if deemed expedient.

The schedule of even date referred to in this deed was signed by the parties to the deed, and the owners of the slips of land which were to be conveyed as the site of the road, and contained a specification describing the construction of the road, with a plan attached showing its course, and the lands, with the owners' names, through which it was to run. Amongst the owners' names appearing on the plan was that of John Elliott, the plaintiff's predecessor in title, who owned the land on each side of the slip agreed to be conveyed by him.

John Elliott conveyed his slip of land to the trustees by an indenture dated the 8th of April, 1837, being one of the intended conveyances referred to in the deed of settlement. This deed was made between the said John Elliott, of the one part, and the said Joshua Milne, John Milne, and Samuel Lees, of the other part; and thereby the said John Elliot, in consideration of the sum of £14 11s. 8d., paid to him by the said Joshua Milne, John Milne, and Samuel Lees, granted and released unto the said Joshua Milne, John Milne, and Samuel Lees, their heirs and assigns, the plot of land therein described —being part of certain lands belonging to him, Elliott, called Higher Moor Fold, and which said plot of land was therein

expressed to be intended to form part of the said intended
line of road from Higginshaw to Lower Moor—together with
liberty to enter upon the adjoining lands of the said John
Elliott for making and completing the said road, and to erect
on the said plot of land toll-gates with toll-houses, and to demand and take the tolls mentioned in any table of tolls put up
at any such toll-gate before any horse, beast, cattle, cart,
wagon, or carriage (except as thereinafter mentioned) should
be permitted to pass through such toll-gate, except mines and
minerals, "and also except such rights and privileges of passing toll-free over the said line of road for certain purposes as
hereinafter is mentioned and expressed." To hold the said
plot of land, liberties, powers, and privileges, unto and to the
use of the said Joshua Milne, John Milne, and Samuel Lees,
their heirs and assigns, forever, for the ends, intents, and purposes therein in that behalf expressed and declared of and
concerning the same (that was to say): "Provided always,
and it is hereby agreed and declared by the said parties to
these presents, and each of them, the said Joshua Milne, John
Milne, and Samuel Lees, for himself severally and respectively,
and to and for his several and respective heirs and assigns,
doth covenant and agree with the said John Elliott, his heirs
and assigns, by these presents in manner following (that is to
say), that they the said Joshua Milne, John Milne, and Samuel
Lees, their heirs or assigns, or some or one of them, shall and
will within the space of three years now next ensuing, at
their or his own costs and charges, convert, make, and form,
and fence off, in a good, workmanlike, and proper manner,
the whole of the said plot of land, hereditaments, and premises
hereby granted and released, into a road or way to form part
of the said line of road from Higginshaw to Lower Moor
aforesaid, and in like manner make and form the remainder
of the said line of road, which when so finished shall be of the
length, width, dimensions, and construction, and made of such
stone and other materials and in such manner as is set forth
and expressed and as drawn and laid down or delineated in
the specification, ground-plan, and cross-section contained in
a certain schedule or writing bearing date the 3d day of
March last past, and since the date and execution hereof
signed by the said several persons parties to these presents,
and by several other persons owners of other lands over

which the said intended line extends; and also that the said
line shall from and immediately after the expiration of the
said term of three years (subject nevertheless to such tolls
for horses, cattle, beasts, carts and carriages passing thereon
as may by the said Joshua Milne, John Milne and Samuel
Lees, their heirs and assigns, from time to time be fixed and
determined upon) be used by the public; and shall and
will forever hereafter be kept open and used as and for a
road for the use of the public (subject as aforesaid); and
also that they the said Joshua Milne, John Milne and Samuel
Lees, their heirs and assigns, shall and will from time to time
and at all times hereafter keep and maintain the said road
and every part thereof in good repair, order and condition,
except such part thereof as hereinafter is mentioned." Then
followed a proviso that no toll should be taken or demanded
from Elliott, his heirs or assigns, lessees, tenants or occupiers, for any horse, cattle, beast, or carriage laden with
materials for repairing the fences or drains thereinafter
covenanted to be kept in repair and maintained by Elliott,
his heirs or assigns, or his or their tenants, etc., of the lands
adjoining the said plot of land thereby granted, nor for any
horses, etc., or carriages passing over the said line of road
for any purpose connected with the occupation of the said
lands called Higher Moor Fold for farming or agricultural
purposes only or relating to the cultivation thereof. And
Elliott covenanted that he, his heirs or assigns, or the
tenants, etc., of the lands adjoining the said plot of land
thereby granted, would at all times keep in repair and maintain the fences and ditches on each side of so much of the
said road as passed over the lands of him, Elliott, and also
keep the drains thereof in repair.

Elliott, though a vendor, was not a member of the company of proprietors of the new road, and he never executed
the trust deed. In or about the month of May, 1837, four
conveyances in similar terms of sites for the new road were
executed to the trustees by other landowners. At the time
the trust deed and conveyances were executed the lands
through which the new road was to pass were and had been
used for agricultural purposes.

The trustees having taken possession under their several
conveyances, the new road, afterwards called Shaw Road, was

duly made and, until the purchase thereof by the Corporation of Oldham hereinafter mentioned, was maintained by the trustees or their successors in title under the trust deed out of the tolls levied upon the traffic. A footpath was made down one side of the road, and this was left free for foot-passengers, tolls being charged only upon the traffic over the roadway.

After the completion of Shaw Road, Elliott and other owners of land adjoining the road from time to time erected houses on their land at irregular intervals along the line of and abutting on the road, the property in its vicinity thus gradually losing its agricultural character and becoming absorbed into the town of Oldham. The plaintiff, who had subsequently purchased Elliott's land, alleged that the expenditure in the erection of these houses was made upon the faith of the covenants in the above-mentioned conveyances and the provisions of the trust deed, and with the full knowledge and acquiescence of the persons for the time being entitled to Shaw Road, such persons being in fact the predecessors in title of the defendants, the corporation of Oldham ; also that the access afforded by Shaw Road was essential to the proper use and enjoyment of the houses.

In the year 1865 the Oldham Borough Improvement Act, 1865, was passed. Sect. 27 of that Act contained the following provisions as to the "road or street called Shaw Road ": (1) The corporation were empowered to purchase all rights in or over the said road or street and all rights of levying tolls on the traffic thereon, and the interests of all persons in any tolls so levied; (2) for the purposes of such purchase the said rights and interests were to be deemed lands within the meaning of the Act and any Act incorporated therewith: (3) On the completion of such purchase all the rights and interests aforesaid were to be absolutely extinguished, the corporation were to remove all gates, etc., and thenceforth the said road or street was to be a street open to the public and subject to all provisions relative to the sewering, draining and paving of streets not being highways repairable by the inhabitants at large: (4) The corporation's powers of compulsory purchase under this section were not to be exercised after the expiration of five years from the commencement of the Act, and (5) were not to extend to the soil of the said road or street.

By an indenture dated the 21st of April, 1868 (the 27th section of the above Act being then still in force, though from the evidence it appeared that the plaintiff was not aware of it at the time), in consideration of the sum of £580 paid to the said John Elliott by the plaintiff, Elliott conveyed to the plaintiff in fee simple the said lands called Higher Moor Fold and all other the lands of him, Elliott, adjoining Shaw Road, together with the houses and buildings thereon and the appurtenances. At the time of his purchase the plaintiff had notice of the conveyances relating to Shaw Road as part of his title, and he stated in evidence that the fact that the trustees had to repair the road materially influenced him in making the purchase. After the completion of his purchase the plaintiff expended a considerable sum in building other houses on the property, and he paid the usual tolls when using the road. Down to the year 1880 Shaw Road was kept in repair by the trustees. In that year the Oldham Improvement Act, 1880, was passed, which—after referring to the 27th section of the Act of 1865 and reciting that the corporation had not exercised their powers within the period limited by the latter Act, and that a transfer of Shaw Road to them without compulsion had been agreed on for the sum of £6000—enacted as follows : Sect. 62, "nothing contained in the Act of 1865 or in this Act shall exclude, limit, or affect the right of the corporation to exercise the powers conferred upon them by sect. 150 of the Public Health Act, 1875, as regards the road or street within the borough called Shaw Road." Sect. 63, so far as is material, was as follows: " With respect to Shaw Road the following provisions shall take effect; namely,

" (1) On the corporation paying to the said Joshua Milne Cheetham, William Taylor, and Charles Edward Lees"—the then trustees of the deed of settlement and defendants in the present action—" or two of them, or to the survivor of them, or to the executors or administrators of the survivor of them, out of the borough fund or borough rate, or out of moneys which the corporation are by this act authorized to borrow for the purpose, the consideration money aforesaid, and on a copy of this Act being produced to the Commissioners of Inland Revenue, stamped with such an *ad valorem* stamp as would be required by law to be impressed on a deed of conveyance of Shaw Road by them or him to the corporation, then and in that case, but not sooner or otherwise, all the rights, interests, property and things comprised in sect. 27 of the Act of 1865, as subsisting at the time of the vesting thereof under this section, and the soil of Shaw Road, shall by virtue of this section vest absolutely in the corporation and their successors for all the estate and interest therein of Joshua Milne Cheetham, William Taylor, and Charles Edward Lees, each of them, their and each of their heirs, executors, and administrators, and of all persons and bodies claiming through or under them:" (2) The receipt of the said trustees for the consideration money paid to be a good discharge; "(3) The persons to whom payment is so made shall hold the money received by them, subject to payment and discharge of all debts and liabilities (if any) properly payable thereout or chargeable thereon, in trust for such persons as are at the time of payment beneficially interested in Shaw Road, and according to the proportions or respective amounts of the interests of those persons : (4) On the vesting aforesaid taking effect all rights of levying tolls in respect of traffic on Shaw Road, and the interests of all persons in any tolls so levied, shall be by virtue of this section absolutely extinguished."

In November, 1880, and in pursuance of the last-mentioned Act, the corporation paid to the defendants, the trustees of the deed of settlement, the said sum of £6000 for the purchase of Shaw Road, which thereupon became absolutely vested in the corporation as owners thereof. The toll-gates were then removed and tolls ceased to be collected.

On the 2d of March, 1881, the corporation, acting under the powers conferred upon them by sect. 150* of the Public ·

---

* The material parts of sect. 150 of the Public Health Act, 1875, are as follows :—

"Where any street within any urban district (not being a highway repairable by the inhabitants at large) or the carriageway footway or any other part of such street is not sewered levelled paved metalled flagged chanelled and made good or is not lighted to the satisfaction of the urban authority, such authority may, by notice addressed to the respective owners or occupiers of the premises fronting adjoining or abutting on

Health Act, 1875, and reserved to them by sect. 62 of the Oldham Improvement Act, 1880, resolved that Shaw Road, as not being a highway repairable by the inhabitants at large, should be sewered, drained, paved and otherwise completed to their satisfaction; and accordingly, on the 3rd of June, 1881, notices were served upon the plaintiff and other owners and occupiers of premises fronting on Shaw Road, requiring them to do the work within a specified time. The plaintiff and the other owners, however, failed to comply with the notices, whereupon the corporation executed the work themselves, and subsequently served notices and took out summonses before the justices against the plaintiff and the other owners for the recovery of the expenses which had been apportioned on the several frontages. Upon these summonses orders were made for payment, but, pending an appeal, no further steps had been at present taken to enforce such orders.

On the 4th of July, 1883, the corporation duly declared Shaw Road a public highway, pursuant to sec. 152 of the Public Health Act, 1875, which enacts that, upon such a declaration being made of any "street," "the same shall become a highway repairable by the inhabitants at large."

The plaintiff's grounds for resisting the claim of the corporation were, that he and the other persons served with the notices had no such interest in Shaw Road as to render them liable under the Public Health Act, 1875, or otherwise, for works executed thereon of the nature alleged by the corporation; that Shaw Road was not a "street" within the meaning of the Public Health Act, 1875, but that, on the contrary,

---

such parts thereof as may require to be sewered levelled paved metalled flagged or channelled, or to be lighted, require them to sewer level pave metal flag channel or make good or to provide proper means for lighting the same within a time to be specified in such notice," Plans and estimates of the works to be made and referred to in such notice. "If such notice is not complied with, the urban authority may, if they think fit, execute the works mentioned or referred to therein; and may recover in a summary manner the expenses incurred by them in so doing from the owners in default, according to the frontage of their respective premises, and in such proportion as is settled by the surveyor of the urban authority, or (in case of dispute) by arbitration in manner provided by this act; or the urban authority may by order declare the expenses so incurred to be private improvement expenses . . . ."

it was and always had been a road repairable by the owners
thereof, and that the corporation, on behalf of the ratepayers
or inhabitants at large, having become the owners, the road
thereupon became "a highway repairable by the inhabitants·
at large"; and that, as to any portion of the expenses alleged
by the corporation to have been incurred in relation to the
road and necessary for the maintenance thereof, the corporation, having purchased the road with notice of and subject to
the provisions of the trust-deed and the conveyances to the
trustees, were estopped from making any claim against the
plaintiff and other adjoining owners on account of such expenses, and thus evading liability as assigns of the grantees
under the conveyances and trust-deed or in respect of covenants running with the land purchased by them the corporation.   The plaintiff further contended, in the alternative,
that if the corporation were entitled to be repaid their said
expenditure, or any part thereof, as being necessary for the
maintenance of Shaw Road in good repair, such right constituted a "liability" within the meaning of the provisions of
sec. 63, sub-sec. 3, of the Oldham Improvement Act, 1880,
and that such expenditure was properly payable out of the
purchase-moneys in the hands of the trustees, and that the
plaintiff and the other adjoining owners were entitled to have
such purchase-moneys or a sufficient part thereof applied in
·satisfaction of the claim of the corporation by way of indemnity or otherwise.

In order, then, to ascertain the rights of the owners of property fronting and adjoining Shaw Road, the plaintiff brought
this action on behalf of himself and all other such owners
against the corporation and the trustees, claiming (1) a declaration that the corporation were not entitled to recover
from the plaintiff and other adjoining owners any sums or
charges for the bedding or paving of, or execution of repairs
upon, Shaw Road, or other works necessary for keeping the
road in good repair; (2) an injunction to restrain the corpo·
ration from proceeding further upon the orders made by the
justices, the plaintiff submitting to any order which the
court might make in the present action for the purpose of
finally determining all questions between the parties; (3) in
the alternative a declaration that the defendants, the trustees,
were liable out of the purchase-money paid to them by the

corporation to keep the plaintiff and such other owners indemnified against the said charges; (4) to have the trusts of
the said purchase-moneys executed by the court, and ac-
'counts thereof directed, and to have provision made thereout
to answer such indemnity, or to satisfy the claim of the corporation as a "liability" within the meaning of the Oldham
Improvement Act, 1880, sec. 63; (5) damages; and (6) costs.

The corporation, in their statement of defence, insisted
that at the date of the conveyances and trust-deed the land
forming the site of Shaw Road and the other adjoining lands
were agricultural lands of small value, and that the work to
be done to the road under the covenants and provisions in
such deeds was only applicable to the road and neighborhood as existing at that time, and that owing to the subsequent entire change in the character of the neighborhood
consequent upon the growth of population, the erection of
buildings and improvements within the township and borough
of Oldham, and otherwise, such covenants and provisions at
the time of the purchase of the road by the corporation
ceased to be applicable or to have any binding effect, and
had in fact wholly lapsed; that the plaintiff purchased with
full knowledge (which, however, the plaintiff denied) that
under the Oldham Borough Improvement Act, 1865, s. 27,
the corporation were empowered to purchase all rights over
Shaw Road within the period of five years; also that the·
plaintiff purchased with notice of the liability to the payment
of tolls in respect of Shaw Road, and of the fact that the said
covenants and provisions relating to the maintenance and
repair of the road and the liability of the trustees thereunder
had wholly lapsed and ceased to be binding. They also asserted that the work executed by them in making Shaw
Road under their statutory powers was entirely different
from that provided for by the said covenants and provisions,
which had become wholly inapplicable and inoperative; that
at the time they purchased Shaw Road it was not a highway
repairable by the inhabitants at large, but was liable to be
paved, sewered, and put into thorough repair, under the
provisions of sec. 150 of the Public Health Act, 1875, at the
expense of the adjoining owners; that, even if the covenants
in the said conveyances were binding, the plaintiff and the
other owners had forfeited all right to relief thereunder by

laches and delay in standing by and permitting the Oldham Acts of 1865 and 1880 to pass into law without objection, in making no objection to the notices served on them by the corporation, and in permitting the corporation to execute the work without contesting their right to do so; and they submitted that if the said covenants and provisions were binding on the trustees, and if the moneys due from the plaintiff and the other adjoining owners to the corporation constituted "debts and liabilities" within the meaning of sub-sec. 3 of sec. 63 of the Oldham Act of 1880, then that the same were payable to the plaintiff and the other owners out of the purchase-money in the hands of the defendants, the trustees, and not by the corporation.

Issue having been joined, the action came on for trial on the 30th of April, 1884, before the Vice-Chancellor of the County Palatine of Lancaster, who held that the plaintiff's case failed against all the defendants, and dismissed the action with costs.

The plaintiff appealed. The notice of appeal was served upon the defendants the corporation only.

Henn Collins, Q.C., and *Maberly* for appellant.

Cookson, Q. C., and *Pankhurst*, for respondents the corpo ration :

COTTON, L. J.—This is an appeal by the plaintiff against the decision of the Vice-Chancellor of the County Palatine, who did not grant the relief which he ^FACTS. sought. The nature of the case is this: The plaintiff is the owner of land lying on two sides of what is now a street in Oldham; he had got a notice from the corporation, under the 150th section of the Public Health Act, 1875, to do certain work, which, if the road or street is within that section, they are entitled to require to be done, in the nature of paving and sewering the street. He did not do it; then they executed the work, and sought to recover from him, in the way pointed out by the act, his proportion of the expense which they had incurred in paving and sewering the road or street, part of which divided his property. He contended before the Vice-Chancellor unsuccessfully, and has contended on appeal, that for various reasons the corporation had no power to put in force against him section 150 of the Public Health Act, 1875,

and the consequential powers given by that act in respect o
work done under that section. That was, of course, saying
"you have no right at all as against me to claim any part of
this money;" but there was also a subsidiary point. He contended that, if he was wrong on the first point, yet they were
only entitled to claim from him the expense of part of the
work which they had done, on the ground that under the
deed which I shall have to refer to, the corporation were
bound to bear the remainder of the expense under a covenant
entered into by their predecessors in title.

Now, the point first argued was as to the general power
under sec. 150 of the Public Health Act, 1875. [His Lordship read the section and continued:] Of course, if Shaw
Road is not a street within this section, the corporation have
no power at all to give the notice under it or to do the work
with the consequential result of being able to claim from the
plaintiff any proportion of the expense. Now, the plaintiff's
contention was this: It was admitted that it was a street, but
it was said that the 150th section only applies to streets not
being highways repairable by the inhabitants at large, and
that this street was "a highway repairable by the inhabitants
at large;" that before it became vested in the corporation it
had been a turnpike road—a highway—and, therefore, being
a highway, was repairable by the inhabitants at large. Well,
is that so? It appears that this street was originally made as
a matter of private adventure by persons who had formed
themselves into a joint stock company. There was a line of
road agreed upon, which would cut off a great angle, and
make a very much shorter line of access than had existed previously; and apparently the landowners on the line of that
contemplated new road joined together and formed a joint
stock company in order to make this road, and put upon it
bars, which they did not allow people to pass unless they paid
money. It was said that that alone made it a turnpike road.
I will not enter into the question as to whether that made it a
turnpike road, because certainly that is not the question we
have to deal with. It did not make it a turnpike road in the
sense of a turnpike road made such by Act of Parliament,
which by Act of Parliament is dedicated to the public; or
rather, a road which by Act of Parliament—although there is
no expressed dedication—is constituted a public highway,

subject only to the obligation imposed by the act of payment to the trustees of the road of certain tolls. But the question we have to consider is this: Was the road at the time when the corporation acquired it under the act which has been referred to, a road, whether turnpike or not, repairable by the inhabitants at large? That, in my opinion, depends upon this further question—was it really dedicated to the public so as to make it a public highway? The Vice-Chancellor considered that on the true interpretation of the 150th section, the road was not repairable by the inhabitants at large, and that if it was repairable under the trust deed out of the tolls, it was not within the exception in the section. I do not give any decision upon that question, because in my opinion this road was never dedicated to the public in such a way as to become a public highway, repairable as such by the inhabitants at large.

I have mentioned how it was that this road came to be formed, and we have before us the deed of settlement of the company of proprietors. It mentions the object of making this road, that the parties had DEDICATION OF TURNPIKE TO PUBLIC BY DEED. agreed to raise the necessary capital, and that the road, when made, should not only be enjoyed by them "for their individual purposes, but (subject as hereinafter is mentioned) shall be open to the use of the public at large for all manner of purposes in all respects as a common turnpike road." It was contended that those words dedicated it to the public; that it then became a public highway, and that consequently it would be repairable by the inhabitants at large. But though there are the words, "shall be open to the use of the public at large," there are also the words "subject as hereinafter is mentioned," and we must look to see what is "hereinafter mentioned." We then find this—"that no person or persons (except such persons and for the purposes only as are mentioned in the said several conveyances of the said land so purchased by the company as aforesaid) shall be allowed to travel upon, use, or enjoy any part of the said road, or pass through any such tollgate, side-bar, or chain, to be erected and set up as aforesaid, without having previously paid such toll as may from time to time be demanded of him, her, or them, pursuant to the table of tolls for the time being authorized by the said company to be demanded and taken as aforesaid." Now the exception there is this, that the persons who conveyed their land to the trustees for the site of this road reserved for themselves, by covenant on the part of the trustees, a right to use the road as a road for agricultural purposes free of toll; that is, for carts to pass for any purpose of agriculture connected with their land; but subject to that, they and everybody else can only use it if they are willing to pay a toll, and it is not a fixed toll, but the " tolls for the time being authorized by the said company to be demanded and taken as aforesaid." Now I here give no opinion as to whether there can be a dedication by an individual of a road as a highway subject to a toll without the aid of an Act of Parliament. Authorities were cited containing some passages apparently to the effect that this might be done. I do not think it necessary in this case to give any opinion upon that point, though I certainly hesitate to say, and I do not in any way encourage the idea, that an individual without any authority from the Crown, and without the authority of an Act of Parliament, can be said to dedicate a road to the public when it can only be used on payment of a toll; but if this is a highway, it would be an infringement of the prerogative to stop the Queen's subjects on it and demand toll from them, either in consequence of any repairs which might be done or any improvements which might be made. If it is once a highway there can be no question of toll after that. Whether originally a road could be dedicated to the public so as to become a highway subject to a toll to be paid to the man who dedicates it, I give no opinion, because it has not been really fully discussed. But here the case is very different ; it is not that all the public are to use the road, but only such persons are to use it as are willing to pay this toll—" that no person or persons. . . shall be allowed to travel upon, use, or enjoy any part of the said road, or pass through any such tollgate, side-bar, or chain to be erected and set up as aforesaid without having previously paid such toll," and it is not a fixed toll, but it is " such toll as may from time to time be demanded from him, her, or them, pursuant to the table of tolls for the time being authorized by the said company, to be demanded and taken as aforesaid." So that this company, formed for the profit of the individual shareholders—because the deed of settlement shows that they contemplated realizing a profit and making a dividend—are from time to time to charge such tolls as they may think fit, not merely for the purpose of keeping up the road, but for the purpose of keeping the road open, as a source of profit to them, as well as a matter of convenience to those members of the public who may be willing to pay such tolls as they may from time to time fix.   They might increase the tolls from time to time, and there is no limit, except their own interest, placed on the tolls; and though it is true that, as. far as it was a footpath, there never has been any toll, yet under the deed of settlement they were at liberty, if they thought fit, to charge a toll on that footpath as well as any other part of the road.   However, down to the time when the corporation got this road, they did not charge anything on the footpath ; but there was nothing, as I say, to prevent them from so doing.   In my opinion there was no such dedication to the public as to make this a public highway, and consequently it does not come within the exception of section 150 of "a highway repairable by the inhabitants at large."

Then comes this other point.   Assuming that this corporation had the power to act under sec. 150, it was COVENANT TO MAINTAIN ROAD, WHETHER BINDING UPON ASSIGNS said that when the land, forming the portion of the road about which this question arises, was originally purchased from Mr. Elliot—he being one of those over whose land the new road went—there was a covenant by the trustees who bought on behalf of the joint stock company to preserve and maintain it as a road.   The covenant was by those trustees with John Elliott, his heirs and assigns, that they should, within the space of three years, at their own cost, make and form and fence off in a good and workmanlike manner the road; and then it goes on to prescribe the mode of making the road, and "that the said line shall from and immediately after the expiration of the said term of three years (subject, nevertheless, to such toll for horses, cattle, beasts, carts, and carriages passing thereon as may by the said Joshua Milne, John Milne, and Samuel Lees—who are the trustees—their heirs and assigns, from time to time be fixed and determined upon) be used by the public, and shall and will forever hereafter be kept open and used as and for a road for the use of the public (subject as aforesaid), and also that they, the said Joshua Milne, John Milne, and Samuel

Lees, their heirs and assigns, shall and will from time to time, and at all times hereafter, keep and maintain the said road and every part thereof in good repair, order, and condition." It is said that this covenant having been entered into by the trustees, the corporation, as purchasers from them, are now subject to that covenant. The corporation bought this road under an Act of Parliament which was passed in the year 1880. I do not think it necessary, in the view I take of this case, to go in detail into that Act of Parliament, but sec. 63 gives the power of purchase. There had been a previous act which had given them the right to enter into a contract with the trustees for the purchase of this road; they had not done that, and then sec. 63, with respect to this road, which is called Shaw Road, gave them this power, that on their paying to the trustees out of the borough funds, or the moneys borrowed, the consideration money which they were to pay, and, on a copy of the act being produced to the Commissioners of Inland Revenue (duly stamped), "then, and in that case, but not sooner or otherwise, all the rights, interests, property, and things comprised in sec. 27 of the act of 1865" (that was the previous act), "as subsisting at the time of the vesting thereof under this section, and the soil of Shaw Road shall by virtue of this section vest absolutely in the corporation and their successors for all the estate and interest therein" of the trustees.

It seems by the immediately preceding section that this act contemplated that probably the corporation might have power to exercise the rights given by sec. 150, but in the view which I take of this case I shall not enter minutely into that question, or as to the general effect of this Act of Parliament with regard to the question in dispute. But it is said, on behalf of the appellant, here is this covenant by the trustees; the corporation are their successors under that Act of Parliament, taking all the estate and interest of the trustees in Shaw Road, and, that being so, they must be bound by the covenant: it is a covenant the burden and benefit of which run at law, or at least in equity, they having taken with notice, which undoubtedly they did; and, if not enforceable at law, it is a covenant which can be enforced in equity, and the consequence must be that they cannot claim under the Public Health Act, 1875, the expense of repairing this road, or, at any rate, they cannot claim from the plaintiff the full amount, but only such proportion as would meet the amount that would have been required to put the road in the state of repair required by the covenant with Mr. Elliott, through whom the plaintiff claims.   Now, as to enforcing this covenant in equity, I will deal with that point first.   In my opinion, if this is not a covenant running at law, there can be no relief in respect of it in equity; it is not a restrictive covenant; it is not a covenant restraining the corporation or the trustees from using the land in any particular way, at least so far as this case is concerned.   If either the trustees or the corporation were intending to divert this land from the purpose for which it was conveyed, that is, from its being used as a road or street, that would be a very different question; then one would have to consider this—how far, having regard to the act of 1880, the equitable right would travel; because, undoubtedly, where there is a restrictive covenant, the burden and benefit of which do not run at law, Courts of Equity restrain any one who takes the property with notice of that covenant from using it in a way inconsistent with the covenant.   But here the covenant which is attempted to be insisted upon on this appeal is a covenant to lay out money in doing certain work upon this land; and, that being so, in my opinion—and the Court of Appeal has already expressed a similar opinion in a case which was before it—that is not a covenant which a Court of Equity will enforce; it will not enforce a covenant not running at law when it is sought to enforce that covenant in such a way as to require the successors in title of the covenantor, to spend money, and in that way to undertake a burden upon themselves.   The covenantor must not use the property for a purpose inconsistent with the use for which it was originally granted; but in my opinion a Court of Equity does not and ought not to enforce a covenant binding only in equity in such a way as to require the successors of the covenantor himself, they having entered into no covenant, to expend sums of money in accordance with what the original covenantor bound himself to do.   The case principally relied upon by the appellant was one before Vice-Chancellor Malins. That was the case of Cooke *v.* Chilcott, 3 Ch. D. 694.   Now undoubtedly the vice-chancellor did decide that case on the

equitable doctrine, and said that he would enforce the covenant; but that is an authority which in my opinion was not
right on that point.   In the subsequent case of Haywood *v.*
Brunswick Permanent Benefit Building Society, 8 Q. B. D.
403—both Lord Justice Lindley and myself were members
of the court which decided that case—we expressed our opinion against Cooke *v.* Chilcott being a correct development of
the doctrine established by Tulk *v.* Moxhay, 2 Ph. 774, or for
which Tulk *v.* Moxhay was an authority.

Then there was another case, before the late Lord Romilly,
of Moreland *v.* Cook, Law Rep. 6 Eq. 252, which was relied
upon; but that was really a case not turning upon that doctrine, because it was this: There was a deed of partition of
land all of which was below the sea level and was protected
by a river or sea wall, and a covenant was entered into by
the different parties to pay their proportion of the expense of
repairing the sea wall, whoever should do it; and that covenant was enforced for and against the successors of those who
were parties to the deed.   But in that case it appeared that
there was, according to the view of the Master of the Rolls,
a common law liability, independently of that covenant, to
repair the sea wall, so that it would be very different from
the case of creating a new liability: the covenant there was
framed in such a way as to create a grant by the different
persons who took, on partition, portions of the property, of a
rent-charge out of their lands in order to provide for the ex
pense.   The covenant was in this form.   The parties covenanted for themselves, etc., "severally and respectively, in
manner following, that is to say, that the charges, damages,
and expenses of or attending the keeping and maintaining the
walls and gutts of or belonging to the said lands, fresh marsh
lands, hereditaments and premises hereby granted and released, or intended so to be, in good order and repair, shall be
borne and paid by them (naming them), their respective heirs
and assigns, out of the said lands and hereditaments hereby
divided in proportion, and by an acre-scot to be from time to
time for that purpose made thereon and payable thereout in
the same proportions in ready money."   So, although in terms
it was a covenant, it was a covenant by these parties that the
expense should be paid out of their proportions of the land
by an acre-scot payable thereout in the same proportions in

ready money. That is, therefore, really a grant by each of the parties of a rent-charge of so much money as would be equivalent to his proportion of the total expense of repairing the sea wall.

Those, I think, were the principal cases which were relied upon. As to the case of Holmes *v.* Buckley, 1 Eq. C. Ab. 27, although that was a case which came from equity, yet I apprehend it was not decided on the ground taken in Tulk *v.* Moxhay, 2 Ph. 774; therefore I do not think it necessary on this part of the case to refer to that decision. In my opinion, therefore, if the plaintiff here cannot say he is entitled at law to sue on the covenant, he cannot have any relief on the equitable doctrine of Tulk *v.* Moxhay.

Then, is there here a covenant enforceable at law? For this there are two things to be considered—the burden of the covenant, and the benefit of the covenant; and unless the plaintiff can show, he being an assign of the original covenantee, that he is entitled to the benefit of the covenant, and unless he can also show that the corporation, being assigns of the original covenantor, are subject to the burden of the covenant, he cannot establish in this court any covenant which can be enforced at law. If the plaintiff fails in either of these two points, he fails on this part of the case. As I think my learned brethren will consider more particularly the question whether this burden runs with the land, I do not propose to enter into this part of the case. If I had to do so, I ought to give my opinion upon the debated point whether the burden of a covenant can properly run with the land; and for that purpose I should like, before giving any opinion on the subject, to consider the authorities which are supposed to lay down the proposition that it can; but I in no way say that the burden of a covenant can be so annexed to the land as to run properly with the land. But does the benefit of the covenant in the present case run with the land? In order that the benefit may run with the land, the covenant must be one which relates to or touches and concerns the land of the covenantee. Here, undoubtedly, what was to be done was not to be done on the land of the covenantee at all, but simply on the land of the purchasers from him—these trustees; and when we look at the particular form of covenant entered into with him it is clear that it was not pointedly with reference to his land that this covenant was entered into—it was a covenant that this strip of land should be kept as a road for the use of the public. Of course that was insufficient to dedicate it as a public highway so as to make it repairable by the parish, for it was only a matter of covenant as between him and the purchasers from him. Looking at the terms of the covenant, it is rather a covenant for the benefit of such of the public as might be willing to use this road, not a covenant having a direct reference to the land, or the enjoyment or the benefit of the land, of the covenantee, the predecessor in title of the plaintiff. There was undoubtedly a reservation to the covenantee which was for the benefit of his land and the occupiers of it in relation to his right to cross this road in respect of and for agricultural purposes without paying tolls; but it is conceded that this right or easement, or whatever it was, is gone, and here we are dealing with a covenant in which the public is constantly referred to, not the owners and assigns of the land. The words are, "shall and will forever hereafter" (that is, the road) "be kept open and used as and for a road for the use of the public." That shows this, that although the covenantee thought it would benefit himself and the other owners of the adjoining lands to have a road which they as members of the public might use, this covenant is not a covenant which was made and entered into in such a way as that it relates to or touches and concerns the land reserved by the covenantee. In my opinion, therefore, the plaintiff fails to make out that the benefit of this covenant can be said so to run with the land as to enable him, as the assign of the covenantee, to maintain this action. This being so, I think I need scarcely go through many of the cases; but some of them, perhaps, one ought to mention. Holmes *v.* Buckley, 1 Eq. C. Ab. 27, is one. . It is doubtful whether that case was decided on the ground that the covenant ran with the land, because there the land of the plaintiff was nothing but the easement of a watercourse: and it is suggested that that decision really must not be looked upon as an authority that the benefit of the covenant would run with such an easement; but I should think myself that the watercourse must have been used to convey water to adjoining land of the plaintiff, and probably it was in respect of that land that the covenant was said to run with the land. However, I will not enter further into that case, because one of my learned brethren will do so more fully; but even if that is an authority as to the burden or the benefit of a covenant running with or against the land, one can see it has no application to the point on which I decide this case, because there the watercourse must undoubtedly have been for the benefit of the adjoining land of the grantee.

· Then as to the other case of Morland *v.* Cook, Law Rep. 6 Eq. 252, I have explained what the case really is, and although Lord Romilly did decide that the covenant would run with the land, I do not think, having regard to the explanation which I have given, one need consider that an authority which ought to trouble one either as regards the benefit to or burden of the covenant; but, as regards benefit, a covenant for the keeping up of a sea wall which would prevent the land in question owned by the plaintiff from being flooded was undoubtedly a covenant with reference to the benefit to be enjoyed by the land by the keeping of the sea out.

Then Western *v.* Macdermott, Law Rep. 1 Eq. 499, 2 Ch. 72, was another decision of Lord Romilly, and he did express his opinion that there the covenant ran with the land; but there the covenant was one which was much more pointedly and directly for the benefit of the land of the plaintiff, or the predecessor in title of the plaintiff, because it was a covenant not to build on adjoining land, the evidence being that it was not for the benefit of mere members of the public other than the owner of the adjoining land, but to prevent the adjoining land being made less commodious by the erection of buildings on the land of the covenantor.

Then there is the case of Cooke *v.* Chilcott, 3 Ch. D. 694, which was before Malins, V.C., where he likewise expressed an opinion that the covenant ran with the land. He did not base his opinion on the cases I have mentioned, but the case was one in which there was very little, if any, difficulty as regards the benefit of the covenant touching and relating to land of the plaintiff, because it was to erect a pump and pump water from the land of the defendant's predecessor in title to the land of the plaintiff's predecessor in title, and there was reference to the benefit of the land, which showed that that was the object of the covenant. As to whether it was right to express any opinion as to the burden running with the land I say nothing; but there is no authority which can in any way interfere, when fairly regarded, with the opinion which I express, that the covenant in the present case was neither in terms nor in its obvious sense such as to be a covenant relating to, or touching and concerning, the land of the plaintiff's predecessor in title. So, in my opinion, this point that there is a covenant on which the plaintiff can sue the corporation at law is one which cannot be maintained, and, so far as this case depends on that, in my opinion the appeal fails. If one had been of opinion that either at equity or at law the plaintiff could have relied on this covenant as against the corporation, it would have been necessary to consider what would have been the effect of the 268th section of the Public Health Act, 1875, which points out what is to be done if a person charged considers that he has been charged too much; but as I decide this case on the other point, that neither in equity nor law can the plaintiff successfully rely on this covenant, I think it is not necessary to enter into the question as to how far that section would prevent him from arguing the contention before us that what he has been called upon to pay should be reduced by striking off such proportion of this expense as is attributable to repairs which ought to be done by the trustees under the deed of covenant.

LINDLEY, L. J.—The controversy in this case has arisen in
FACTS.   this way: There is a road called Shaw Road, in Oldham, and the defendants, who are the corporation of Oldham have recently paved, flagged, sewered, and repaired it. The plaintiff has some land adjoining the road, and the corporation have sought to charge him with what would be, under ordinary circumstances, his share of so making the road, paving and draining it. He says that the corporation have no right to charge him with any of that expense; and he says, if they have, they have no right to charge him with the whole of it. Now, the first point, whether they have a right to charge him with any of it, depends upon the question whether this Shaw Road is or is not "a highway repairable by the inhabitants at large" within the meaning of sec. 150 of the Public Health

Act. Mr. Austerberry maintains that it is a highway repairable by the inhabitants at large. The Vice Chancellor has
expressed a doubt whether that expression in sec. 150—
"highway repairable by the inhabitants at large"—is synonymous with all highways; whether it does not mean highways repairable by the inhabitants at large primarily, and
whether the turnpike roads, and so on, which are primarily
repairable by the public, though they may be repairable at
common law by the inhabitants at large, are within that expression. I think there is some doubt about that, but it is
unnecessary to decide the question for the reasons that have
been mentioned at length by Lord Justice Cotton, and to
which I will very shortly refer.

I think it is very doubtful, but it is unnecessary to decide,
whether it is possible to dedicate to the public a DEDICATION OF
highway subject to a toll. I do not say it is not, ROAD TO THE
PUBLIC TOLL.
but I am very far from saying that it is. But whatever
doubt there may be upon that point, which if we had to decide it, I should like to investigate further, it appears to me
impossible to hold that a highway is dedicated to the public
subject to a toll which may fluctuate from day to day. This
highway was constituted under a trust deed giving the trustees
power to levy tolls if they liked, and to change them whenever they liked; and it appears to me quite impossible not to
see that that is not a dedication to the public—it is liberty to
such of the public as choose to pay the toll to use the road—
that is all. I cannot come to the conclusion that the road
ever was dedicated to the public. That appears to me to be
the short answer (I need not go further into it) to the first
point; and in my opinion this road is within sec. 150 of the
Public Health Act, and upon the first point the corporation is
right.

But then arises another and a totally different point. The
plaintiff says: "You, the corporation, have bought or acquired this road under an act of Parliament which places you
in the position of, and in no better position than, those from
whom you got it; you acquired it from certain trustees, and
those trustees covenanted with my predecessors in title to
keep this road open for the public, and to repair it: you are
bound by that covenant to repair, and I am in a position to
enforce against you that covenant." First, it seems to have

been thought that that covenant was so worded as to cover everything which the corporation had done—I mean by "everything" the metalling, and paving, and sewering; but when the covenant is looked at it is seen that it is not extensive enough to cover that; and, therefore, whatever may be the merits of the case, the corporation must be right as to a great portion of the charges made against the plaintiff. But then there is the covenant which extends (to use a short word) to repairing, and the plaintiff says that at all events to the extent to which you, the corporation, have incurred expense in repairing the road, to that extent you are bound to exonerate me by virtue of that covenant. That gives rise to one or two questions of law.

The first question which I will consider is whether that covenant runs with the land, as it is called—whether the benefit of it runs with the land held by the plaintiff, and whether the burden of it runs with the land held by the defendants; because, if the covenant does run at law, then the plaintiff, so far as I can see, would be right as to this portion of his claim. Now, as regards the benefit running with the plaintiff's land, the covenant is, so far as the road goes, a covenant to repair the road; what I mean by that is, there is nothing in the deed which points particularly to that portion of the road which abuts upon or fronts the plaintiff's land—it is a covenant to repair the whole of the road, no distinction being made between the portion of that road which joins or abuts upon his land and the rest of the road; in other words, it is a covenant simply to make and maintain this road as a public highway; there is no covenant to do anything whatever on the plaintiff's land, and there is nothing pointing to the plaintiff's land in particular. Now it appears to me to be going a long way to say that the benefit of that covenant runs with the plaintiff's land. I do not overlook the fact that the plaintiff as a frontager has certain rights of getting on to the road; and if this covenant had been so worded as to show that there had been an intention to grant him some particular benefit in respect of that particular part of his land, possibly we might have said that the benefit of the covenant did run with this land; but when you look at the covenant it is a mere covenant with him, as with all adjoining owners, to make this road, a small portion of which only

COVENANT. WHETHER RUNNING WITH THE LAND.

abuts on his land, and there is nothing specially relating to his land at all. I cannot see myself how any benefit of this covenant runs with his land.

But it strikes me, I confess, that there is a still more formidable objection as regards the burden. Does the burden of this covenant run with the land so as to bind the defendants? The defendants have acquired the road under the trustees, and they are bound by such covenant as runs with the land. Now we come to face the difficulty: does a covenant to repair all this road run with the land—that is, does the burden of it descend upon those to whom this road may be assigned in future? We are not dealing here with a case of landlord and tenant. The authorities which refer to that class of cases have little, if any, bearing upon the case which we have to consider, and I am not prepared to say that any covenant which imposes a burden upon land does run with the land, unless the covenant does, upon the true construction of the deed containing the covenant, amount to either a grant of an easement, or a rent charge, or some estate or interest in the land. A mere covenant to repair, or to do something of that kind, does not seem to me, I confess, to run with the land in such a way as to bind those who may acquire it.

It is remarkable that the authorities upon this point, when they are examined, are very few, and it is also remarkable that in no case that I know of, except one which I shall refer to presently, is there anything like authority to say that a burden of this kind will run with the land. That point has often been discussed, and I rather think the conclusion at which the editors of the last edition of Smith's Leading Cases have come to is right, that no case has been decided which does establish that such a burden can run with the land in the sense in which I am now using that expression. The case of Holmes *v.* Buckley, 1 Eq. C. Ab. 27, looks a little like it at first; but the observation to be made on that case I think is this: In the first place it is quite plain that there the plaintiff had a cause of action; he was entitled to an injunction of some sort to restrain the defendants from interrupting his watercourse. The right of the plaintiff to enforce specifically the covenant to repair, or rather to cleanse the watercourse, is obscure, and we have not got the decree which was pronounced; and I confess that having only that short note of it which is to be found in "Equity Cases Abridged," I fail to understand the exact grounds of that decision, specifically enforcing that covenant to cleanse. I doubt whether it was a decision to that effect; but the case is too loosely reported to be a guide on the point.

Morland *v.* Cook, Law Rep. 6 Eq. 252, another case in which it was said that the covenant ran with the land, is intelligible on this ground—that there was there that which amounted to a creation of a rent charge for the repair of the sea wall which was in question. That was intelligible enough, and if the covenant in the present case amounted to anything of the kind, of course the observations I am now making would not be applicable.

The case before Vice-Chancellor Malins of Cooke *v.* Chilcott, 3 Ch. D. 694, has been so shaken that I cannot rely upon it as an authority at all. I think the Vice-Chancellor did intimate an opinion that the covenant there would run with the land. I confess I doubt the correctness of that opinion. He decided the case upon another point, and upon that other point only has it been followed. There is no other authority that I am aware of that such a covenant as this runs with the land, unless it is Western *v.* Macdermott, Law Rep. 1 Eq. 499, 2 Ch. 72, where the Court of Appeal did not sanction the notion that the covenant in that case ran with the land, although the covenant was a purely restrictive covenant. I am not aware of any other case which either shows, or appears to show, that a burden such as this can be annexed to land by a mere covenant, such as we have got here ; and in the absence of authority it appears to me that we shall be perfectly warranted in saying that the burden of this covenant does not run with the land. After all it is a mere personal covenant. If the parties had intended to charge this ʃand for ever, into whosesoever hands it came, with the burden of repairing the road, there are ways and means known to conveyancers by which it could be done with comparative ease ; all that would have been necessary would have been to create a rent-charge and charge it on the tolls, and the thing would have been done. They have not done anything of the sort, and, therefore, it seems to me to show that they did not intend to have a covenant which should run with the land.

That disposes of the part of the case which is perhaps the most difficult.

The last point was this—that even if it did not run with the land at law, still, upon the authority of Tulk *v.* Moxhay, 2 Ph. 774, the defendants, having bought the land with notice, of this covenant, take the land subject to it. Mr. Collins very properly did not press that upon us, because after the two recent decisions in the Court of Appeal in Haywood *v.* Brunswick Permanent Benefit Building Society, 8 Q. B. D. 403, and London & South Western Ry. Co. *v.* Gomm, 20 Ch. D. 562, that argument is untenable. Tulk *v.* Moxhay cannot be extended to covenants of this description. It appears to me, therefore, that upon all points the plaintiff has failed, and that the appeal ought to be dismissed with costs.

FRY, L. J.—I have very little to do in this case except to express my assent and concurrence with the conclusion of my learned brothers.

Upon the question of dedication, I think it plain that there has been no dedication to the public of the road in DEDICATION. question. I doubt whether there can be a dedication of a road to the public with a levy of a toll, unless under a grant from the Crown; but that point is one which it is not needful now to decide. In the present case what is relied upon as a dedication is the language used in the deed of settlement; but I regard that as a mere convention between the parties who associated themselves together for a private enterprise and covenanted that they would open the road to the public subject to a toll to be varied from time to time, with an eye, no doubt, to the dividends which they were to declare amongst the shareholders. I consider that they no more dedicated the road to the public than a company formed for the purpose of carrying on a theatre or a pleasure garden dedicated the theatre or the pleasure garden to the public because they agree among themselves that they will admit the public, subject to the payment of a toll.

Upon the second point I have not much to add. It appears to me that the questions are three. In the first COVENANT. place, did the benefit of this covenant run with the land—the land of Mr. Elliott? Upon that point my opinion is perhaps not quite as confident as that of my learned brothers. I am rather more inclined to think that the road connecting the

land with the public highway was so far an incident to the
use and occupation of the remainder of Mr. Elliott's land that
it might be conceivable that it came within the principles of
covenants relating to things incident to the land; but, at the
same time, I do not desire to express any difference of opinion
upon that. But upon the point whether the burden of the
covenant ran with the land of the covenantors, I am clearly of
opinion that it did not so run; and I share the doubt which
has been expressed by my learned brothers whether in any
case, except that of landlord and tenant, the burden of covenants of this description does ever run with the land.

There is one authority which appears to me very closely
parallel to the present case. I think the most favorable way
of stating the case for the appellant is to hold that there was
the grant by the covenantors to Mr. Elliott of a right of way
over the land of the covenantors, with a covenant by the covenantors that they would maintain the land subject to the
right of way in repair as a road. Now, putting the case in
that manner, it is extremely like the circumstances which
occurred in the case of Brewster *v.* Kidgill, which is best
reported in 12 Modern Reports, 12 Mod. 166. That was a
case which came before Lord Holt and the King's Bench,
and was evidently very elaborately argued. There one
Brewster, who was seised in fee of a manor, in consideration
of £800 granted a rent-charge in fee of £40 per annum, and
on the back of the deed was indorsed a memorandum declaring it to be the true intent and meaning of that deed, "that
the grantee and her heirs shall forever hereafter be paid the
said rent-charge without any deduction or abatement of
taxes, charge or payment out of, for or concerning the said
rent, or the said manor or lands charged herewith." The
question then arose whether the memorandum was really
part of the grant of the rent-charge, or a covenant collateral
to the grant. Lord Holt conceived it to be a collateral covenant; the other Judges of the King's Bench thought that it
was part of the grant. They all agreed in the view that if it
was a part of the grant it ran with the land; but that if it was
a covenant to pay it did not run with the land. Now what
Lord Holt said upon that point is this, 12 Mod. 170: "I make
no doubt, but that the assignee of the rent shall have covenant against the grantor, because it is a covenant annexed to

the thing granted; but that covenant should run with the rent against the assignee of the land, I see no reason. If this rent was granted so to be paid, it would be another matter; but here is only a covenant, and no words amounting to a grant; and therefore there can be no relief in this case against the terre-tenant, but," his Lordship added, "in equity;"— I will consider that point presently—"and, therefore, for this point I do not see how the plaintiff can have his judgment." The learned judges differed on the question of construction, but they do not appear to have differed on the point of law which Lord Holt discussed.

There remains, therefore, only the question whether there is any relief in equity in a case of this description where there is none at law. The point was not pressed upon us by the appellant. I do not think it is arguable after the recent decisions. A covenant of this description requiring the outlay of money upon the land is not a covenant which, if it does not run at law, runs at equity by reason of any doctrine such as that in Tulk *v.* Moxhay, 2 Ph. 774. I agree, therefore, that this appeal must be dismissed with costs.

DEDICATION OF PRIVATE PROPERTY FOR PUBLIC USE.—See note to case of Landis *v.* Hamilton, 4 Am. & Eng. Corp. Cas. 501.

HURLEY

v.

MISSISSIPPI AND RUM RIVER BOOM CO.

(Advance Case, Minnesota. September 30, 1885.)

Dedication of streets and public places, properly designated upon the plat of a survey of a tract of land into lots and blocks, is to be deemed complete upon conveyances being made of lots with reference to such plat, though it be not properly certified for record.

But where an open, unplatted space appearing on such plat is not so marked or designated, it is ordinarily a question of fact to be determined by the trial court from evidence of acts *in pais*, user, etc., in connection with the plat, whether the same has been dedicated for a particular public use or purpose. So held in respect to an alleged common-law dedication of a parcel of land for a public wharf or landing.

Grantees of lots fronting on unplatted land of the grantor are entitled to a way or street; and where such lots are situated on a line with the boundary of a street which, if continued, would, as indicated by the plat within which they are included, extend along the front thereof, it may in such case be implied from the plat, and the situation of adjacent blocks and streets as indicated thereon, that such street was intended to be so extended and opened in front of such lots, though no external line of division is marked on the plat.

And where there is an intervening street between lots so conveyed and other lands of the grantor, whether subject to a public easement or not, the grantees take the fee to the centre of such street only.

As against the owner of the soil, a trespasser cannot interpose as a defense the existence of an easement which the public or a third person may have in the premises.

APPEAL from an order of the District Court, Hennepin County.

Rea, Woolley & Kitchel and *Worrall & Jordan* for respondent, Henry P. Hurley.

J. B. Gilfillan for Mississippi and Rum River Boom Co.

VANDERBURGH, J.—In the year 1850 a survey and plat of FACTS. what is known as Bottineau's addition to St. Anthony was made, but the plat, not being properly acknowledged and certified, constituted no statutory dedication to the public of any streets or public grounds. A plat purporting to represent such survey was, however, filed in the office of the register of deeds of Ramsey County, in which the land was then situated, and there still remains among the files and records of that county a map or plat of that description. The land in controversy is indicated by a blank space on the plat, as shown by the diagram opposite, between block 26 (or Water street, if deemed extended in front of the block) and the river, and one material question of fact litigated is whether this open space on the river front was marked and designated " Public Wharf " on the original plat.

The plaintiff claims title under the original proprietor, Pierre Bottineau. The defendants lay no claim to the land themselves, but deny plaintiff's title and right of possession. The controversy embraces substantially two issues—First, whether the *locus in quo* was dedicated to public use for a public street and wharf; and, second, whether the fee had, prior to the deed to plaintiff, passed to other parties by deed of the abutting lots. Of course, a common-law dedication is meant, to establish which the defendant relies upon evidence of acts *in pais* of the original proprietor, including the survey and representations upon the plat, public user, and conveyances made with reference to the plat. It is, however, found by the trial court upon this issue " that there has been no dedication to or acceptance by the public of this land as or for a

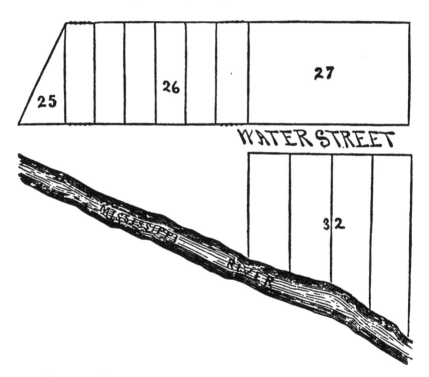

public wharf or steamboat landing, and that no part of said land has been used for such purpose for more than twenty years prior to the commencement of this action."

This includes a finding that there were no acts *in pais* by Bottineau, either separately or in connection with and explanatory of the survey, sufficient to constitute a dedication. It would have been more satisfactory if the court had specifically found whether the *locus in quo* was designated on the plat by the words " public wharf" written thereon,—a

very material question in the case,—but we think it must be
assumed to be involved in the general finding and determined
in the negative. If more specific findings are deemed important or material, the defendant should have made an application to the court for such purposes. Smith *v.* Pender-
gast, 26 Minn. 318; Rep. 978; Bradbury *v.* Bedbury, 31
Minn. 163.

The evidence that the original plat was so marked is cir-
cumstantial. The words in question do not appear on the
plat now remaining of record in Ramsey County. No witness swears that they were originally placed thereon, or that
he remembers seeing them there. But they appear upon
copies, some of which were made for record in Hennepin
County, though not certified by the register of deeds of
Ramsey County, but which the witnesses believe were
accurate from the circumstances under which they were
made and compared. On the other hand, they do not appear upon other maps which were also made from the
records at an earlier day, and which the compilers intended
should be accurate copies, and which were copied from the
original records. Though the evidence in defendant's favor,
taken in connection with the circumstances of the survey and
situation of the premises and the navigation on the river as
then contemplated, is strong and persuasive, yet we are not
prepared to say that the finding of the court embracing this
issue is without support.

Dedication of streets and public places, properly marked
DEDICATION COM- and designated upon the plat of a survey of urban
PLETED BY SALE
OF LOTS WITH REF- property, is complete upon conveyances being
ERENCE THERETO. made of lots included in such survey with refer
ence to such plat, though not properly certified for record.
Such conveyances work an estoppel in favor of the grantees,
and no subsequent revocation can be made without their
consent, and the rights so granted may be adopted and enforced by the public authorities. State *v.* Trask, 27 Amer.
Dec. 568, notes and cases; 2 Dill. Mun. Corp. (3d ed.) § 640;
White *v.* Cowen, 4 Paige, 510; Bartlett *v.* Bangor, 67 Me.
460; Mankato *v.* Willard, 13 Minn. 27. It is clear, therefore,
that the question of fact whether or not the land in question
was represented on the plat to be a " public wharf" was im-

portant and material on the question of the alleged dedication. Assuming that it was not so marked, as we think we
must, and it does not appear to be established by the plat
itself, standing alone, that the blank space in question was
intended to be set apart and dedicated for a public wharf or
any special purpose. Downer *v.* Railway Co. 23 Minn. 273;
Cowles *v.* Gray, 14 Iowa, 4; Warden *v.* Blakley, 32 Wis. 693;
2 Dill. Mun. Corp. (3d. ed.) § 64. Whether it was intended
to be dedicated for some public purpose would properly be
determined as a question of fact upon all the circumstances
by the trial court. Eastland *v.* Fogo, 58 Wis. 275; and cases
last above cited.

The claim is made that the space at least between Water
street and the river is dedicated for a public wharf or landing, and purposes impliedly accessory thereto. This is a
specific purpose distinct from that of a street merely, or a
public square, and the public right is determined by the
character of the grant. The public take *secundum forman
doni.* What the nature of the dedication is must, therefore,
in some way be made to appear by proper evidence. And
in this case we are unable to say that the court erred in its
reference that if the land in question was not so marked or
designated, the fact that it was left a blank open space was
insufficient to show such dedication.

2. The grantees of lots in block 26 are entitled to a street,
and it would be implied from the plat and the situation of
Water Street that the same was intended to be ex- RIGHT OF GRAN-
tended and opened in front of the block, though TEE TO STREETS.
no external line of division is marked on the plat; and so the
evidence tends to show it has been used. Warden *v.* Blakley,
32 Wis. 693. But this does not follow, in respect to the
wharf, in the absence of proof of a dedication therefor. Accordingly it was properly adjudged by the trial court that
such grantees took the fee in front of their lots to the centre
of Water Street so extended. In the case of a common-law
dedication, which operates not as a grant, but as an estoppel
in pais, the fee remains in the donor, subject only to the
public use for which the dedication is made, and he is entitled
to the beneficial enjoyment of the land for any purpose not
inconsistent with such public use. The fee of the land in

question between Water Street and the river remained in the original proprietor, and passed by grant to plaintiff, though it was dedicated for a public landing, unless it had passed by his conveyances previously made. It certainly remained in the original proprietor as long as he retained the ownership of the abutting lots, and as lots adjoin this open space on three sides, and, in case of a public square, front on all sides, it would be hardly consistent to attempt to apportion the fee among the several lots; but it is presumed the grant in such case would stop with the intervening streets, where they can be ascertained, and with the right to enjoy the public easement in common. In the situation of the abutting lots with reference to Water Street, in this case the construction that the grant of these lots stopped with the centre of that street, which it is apparent was in any event to be open for use for the benefit of such lots, is the most reasonable.

In any view of the case, then, the defendants' use and appropriation of the premises was unauthorized, and was an unlawful interference with plaintiff's riparian right as owner of the soil. As against the owner of the soil, a trespasser cannot interpose as a defence the existence of an easement which the public or a third person may have in the premises. Jackson *v.* Hathaway, 15 Johns. 447; Gardiner *v.* Tisdale, 2 Wis. 115.

Order affirmed.

PELLS

v.

BOSWELL *et al.*

(8 *Ontario Reports,* 680.)

P. owned a small piece of land at the south end of a lane or street called Johnson Street, 26 feet wide, in the City of Toronto, leading from Adelaide Street to King Street, extending nearly to the line between these streets, and continued to King Street by an irregular private footway. M. and T. owned the adjoining lots on King Street, extending back to the centre line, and P. had refused to sell his piece of land to them. They then, with other owners purporting to be owners of adjacent land, petitioned the city council under the local improvement clause of the Municipal Act, reciting that they "were desirous of securing communication between King and Adelaide Streets for vehicles by means of the above street, and certain lanes to the south thereof," and asking that said street might be opened up of the full width of 26 feet from Adelaide Street to the centre line of the block between King and Adelaide Streets at the expense of the property benefited. The sub-committee of the council, to whom this petition was referred, and before whom the plaintiff had appeared to oppose it, said that nothing further should be done without notifying him, but about eight months afterwards, without any further notice to him, they passed a by-law opening up the lane to the centre of the block as prayed, but making no provision for extending it to King Street. It was shown that M. and T., through whose land such extension would pass, had refused to give a right of way for vehicles, as expressed in the petition, and had agreed to pay all costs of opening the lane.

Held, that the by-law had been passed improperly, not in the public interest, but in that of M. and T. · and the corporation on the application of P. was enjoined from proceeding under it.

That a by-law purports to be for local improvement, and not for the general benefit of the municipality, does not affect the principle which prevents corporate powers from being exercised for the benefit of one individual at the cost of another.

THIS was an action brought by Thomas Pells against Arthur R. Boswell as Mayor, John Blevins as City Clerk, and the Corporation of the City of Toronto, for an injunction to set aside a by-law and restrain the defendants from taking any proceedings thereunder.

The plaintiff's statement of claim set out that he was, at the time of the passing of the by-law, and still is, the owner of certain property on the west side of Johnson's Lane in Toronto, and also of a parcel of land situate at the south end of said lane, between the said south end and the centre line of the block between King and Adelaide Streets in Toronto; that about May, 1884, the plaintiff became aware that a by-law had, at the instance of Alex. Manning and M. A. Thomas, been introduced into the Council of Toronto entitled, "A by-law to extend, open up, and establish Johnson Street in the Ward of St. Andrew;" that said by-law had been introduced on the. petition of the said Alex. Manning and others, which petition was in the words following:

" To the Council of the Corporation of the City of Toronto:

" The petition of the undersigned, being owners of the real property situate adjacent to and fronting or abutting on Johnson Street, otherwise known as Johnson's Lane, in the Ward of St. Andrew, and owners of lands interested in the improvement of said street, humbly showeth:

" That your petitioners are desirous of securing communication between King Street and Adelaide Street for vehicles, by means of the above street and certain lanes to the south thereof, and for this purpose it is necessary and they desire to have Johnson Street aforesaid extended, opened up, and established as a public street, of the full width of twenty-six feet from Adelaide Street southward to the centre line of the block between King Street and Adelaide Street, being the southern limit of lot number three on the south side of Adelaide Street, west of Yonge Street; and they also desire to have a cedar block pavement constructed thereon within the limits aforesaid, and to have the same done and the said pavement constructed as a local improvement by special assessment according to the conditions and regulations adopted by the committee on works and prefixed hereto, and under the provisions of the Consolidated Municipal Act of 1883, and amendments thereto.

" Your petitioners therefore pray that the said street may be extended, opened up, and established as a public street or highway as aforesaid, and that a cedar block pavement may be constructed thereon and therein, and that all necessary steps may be taken, by-laws passed, and assessments made for the purpose. And your petitioners will ever pray.

(Sgd.) Alexander Manning.	(Sgd.) Neil C. Love,
(Sgd.) M. A. Thomas.	Executor to Drummond
(Sgd.) H. A. Drummond.	estate.
(Sgd.) Jethro Warden.	(Sgd.) W. V. Carlysle.
(Sgd.) John Kay.	(Sgd.) Mason & Risch,
Toronto, May 9th, 1884."	*per* Robert S. Gourlay.

That the plaintiff immediately took steps to oppose said by-law, and petitioned the council against the same; that the sub-committee to whom it was referred, and before whom the

plaintiff and his solicitor appeared to oppose the by-law, disapproved of said by-law, and agreed that nothing further
should be done without notifying the plaintiff; but that afterwards, on the 12th January, 1885, the council of the defendants
assumed to read a third time and pass a document purporting
to be a by-law in the words and figures following:

No. 1529. A BY-LAW

*To extend, open up, and establish Johnson Street, in the Ward of
St. Andrew.*

[Passed January 12th, 1885.]

WHEREAS, Alexander Manning and others have, by their
petition presented to this Council pursuant to the Statute in
that behalf, represented that it is desirable and necessary to
extend, open up, establish and improve Johnson Street, otherwise known as Johnson's Lane, in the Ward of St. Andrew,
as a public highway, from Adelaide Street southerly to the
centre of the block between Adelaide Street and King Street,
at the expense of the property benefited ;

And, whereas, it is expedient to grant the prayer of the said
petition ;

Therefore the Council of the Corporation of the City of
Toronto enacts as follows :

I.

That Johnson Street, in the Ward of St. Andrew, in the
City of Toronto, be opened up southerly to the centre of the
block between Adelaide Street and King Street, and that the
line of road or street surveyed and laid out by Messieurs
Unwin, Browne & Sankey, Provincial Land Surveyors, as
appears by their description and plan of survey of the same
dated the third day of May, one thousand eight hundred and
eighty-four, and which is particularly described as follows,
that is to say : All and singular that certain parcel or tract of
land and premises, being composed of part of Town Lot number three on the south side of Adelaide Street, west of Yonge

Street, in the City of Toronto, and which may be more particularly known and described as follows, that is to say :
Commencing at a point on the south side of Adelaide Street
aforesaid, distant two hundred and fifty feet westerly from the
intersection of the west limit of Yonge Street with the south
limit of Adelaide Street, said point being the intersection of
the west face of the west wall of the Grand Opera House ;
thence southerly along said face of said wall two hundred and
five feet and ten inches to the centre line of the block between
Adelaide Street and King Street ; thence westerly along said
centre line twenty-six feet ; thence northerly parallel with the
west face of said wall two hundred and five feet and ten
inches to the south limit of Adelaide Street ; thence easterly
along the south limit of Adelaide street twenty-six feet to the
place of beginning ; be and the same is hereby established and
confirmed as a public highway, to be known and designated
as Johnson street, in the Ward of St. Andrew, in the City of
Toronto, and that that portion (if any) of the said above described lands not heretofore dedicated for street purposes be
and the same is hereby taken and expropriated for and established and confirmed as part of the said street, and that the
said Johnson Street, as above described, be forthwith opened
up throughout its whole length to the use of the public under
the direction of the city engineer, who, with servants, workmen, agents, and contractors is hereby authorized to enter
into and upon the same and every part thereof for the purposes aforesaid.

I certify that I have examined this bill, and that it is correct.

JOHN BLEVINS,
City Clerk.

COUNCIL CHAMBERS,

    Toronto, January 12th, 1885,

[L. S.]   ARTHUR R. BOSWELL,

Mayor.

That neither the sub-committee nor the council notified the
plaintiff of their intention to proceed with said by-law, and it
was passed without an opportunity being given to him to ob-

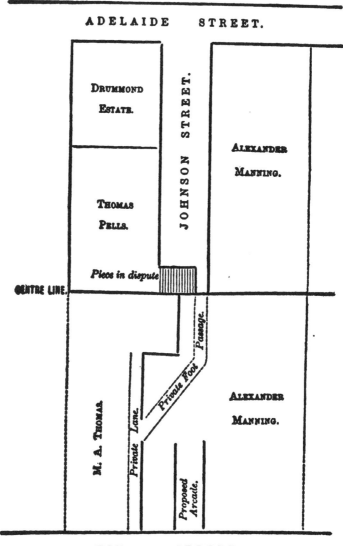

ject to same; that the only land that can be taken or expropriated under said by-law is a piece belonging to the
plaintiff, which separates the south end of said lane from the
properties of said Manning and Thomas, which they have
tried to obtain from the plaintiff and the former owner, one
Clarke, and having failed to do so sought to obtain it by
means of the said by-law; that the said Council pretended to
pass said by-law in the public interest, but the facts were that
it was passed in the private interests of Manning and Thomas,
and was therefore illegal; that the signatures to the petition
were obtained by misrepresentation; that the petition is
framed to mislead, in first setting out that it was desirable to
secure communication between King and Adelaide Streets,
and in the prayer only asking to have Johnson's Lane
opened up to the centre line of the block, and so gave no
communication for vehicles between Adelaide and King
Streets.

The defendants' statement of defence denied any irregular
or improper conduct, and claimed that the by-law was regularly passed, and that they had full power and authority to
pass it, and proceeded in the exercise of their discretion in
doing so.

An interim injunction was granted on 21st January, 1885,
by Boyd, C., and continued on 17th March by Ferguson, J.,
to the trial, both parties agreeing thereto; and the action
came on for trial at the sittings at Toronto on May 19th and
20th, 1885, before Boyd, C.

The position of the lane and property in question is shown
by the sketch on page 363.

H. D. Gamble for plaintiff.

W. A. Foster and *W. G. McWilliams* for defendants.

BOYD, C.—That a by-law purports to be for local improvement and not for the general benefit of the municipality, does

CORPORATE AC-
TION WILL BE
RESTRAINED BY
COURTS.   not affect the cardinal principle which governs the
exercise of corporate powers, as well expressed by
Osler, J., *In re* Morton and St. Thomas, 6 A. R.
325, to this effect: "Corporations are trustees of their powers
for the general public, and when they prostitute them for
the benefit of one individual at the cost of another, the general

public not being interested, their action will be restrained by the courts."

It is impossible to come to any other conclusion, after hearing the testimony and perusing the documents in evidence in this case, than that the impeached by-law was passed in the sole interest of Messrs. Manning and Thomas, and to the detriment of the plaintiff.

By-law held passed in interest of private persons.

The true "inwardness" of the by-law would be properly illustrated if it were entitled " A' by-law to coerce the expropriation of Pell's land at the foot of Johnson's Lane or street which he refuses to sell at a reasonable price to the adjoining proprietors." The only property owners upon Johnson's Lane or abutting thereon are Manning, Pells, and the representatives of the Drummond estate.

If the lane is opened up as prayed by the petition and by-law, it would extend to the rear of the property of Mr. Thomas. Manning and Thomas have been for some years very anxious to purchase the strip of land now owned by the plaintiff, and have offered $1500 therefor at different times, but a larger sum was demanded. The expedient of a petition was then resorted to in May, 1884, by which the city council was prayed to open up this lane to the centre line of the block between King Street and Adelaide Street. This would bring the lane down to the rear of Thomas' lot on King Street, and also give a wider open space at the rear of Manning's lot.

There is an opening for foot passengers of a private character now used, and which has been for many years in existence between this lane and King Street. But to give a color of general benefit to the application for a by-law, the petitioners set forth that " they are desirous of securing communication between King and Adelaide Streets ·for vehicles by means of the above street and certain lanes to the south thereof." These lanes for vehicles would be of necessity through the property of either Manning or Thomas, but it is well established that neither of them contemplates giving a right of way for vehicles as expressed in the petition. It was certainly refused when the matter was before the sub-committee of the council, to whom it was referred. The by-law as passed simply provides for opening up and extending

Johnson Street to the centre of the block, and for expropriating such land (if any) as may be needed therefor.

It is evident, and was indeed proved by the alderman who had the by-law in charge, that taking it *per se* it would as a matter of public benefit amount to nothing. It was justified only as the first step or instalment of a scheme which should afterwards be carried out by Messrs. Manning and Thomas. But their manner of carrying out the subsequent instalments would be an arbitrary matter resting in their own hands and to be used for their own convenience.

Contemporaneously with the petition Messrs. Manning and Thomas signed an agreement setting forth "that they were individually interested in the opening of this lane in the rear of their premises, for the purpose of acquiring access by said lane from their premises," and that the petitioning of the city was being done for their immediate benefit and convenience; and they agreed to contribute equally to the payment of all costs incurred and to be incurred in opening the lane, making special mention in that connection of "the purchase of the right of way over property claimed by a person named Pells, which claim will be decided by arbitration by direction of the corporation."

The only persons who had, strictly speaking, a right to petition were the property owners on the lane or street, whom I have mentioned. The signature on behalf of the Drummond estate was given upon a belief that the purport of the petition was to open up Johnson Street to King Street; but any objections on this score were silenced by a bond being given to the representatives of that estate by Mr. Manning, dated 6th June, 1884, by which he agrees "to indemnify that estate from and against all costs and charges, loss, damages, and expenses which may arise out of, or be incurred or assessed in respect of, the said proposed opening up and establishing of Johnson Street pursuant to the prayer of the said petition."

The sub-committee to whom the matter was referred by the council heard the parties interested for and against and took no action, because it was considered to be a matter more of private than public interest, and the parties were advised to settle it themselves. A promise was given by that sub-committee, and relied on by the plaintiff, that no further action would be taken without his being notified. This was not done, and after the matter had remained in abeyance for seven or eight months, the by-law was passed by the expiring council, in order, as was said, to leave a clean sheet behind them.

All the direct evidence and all the circumstances of the case made against the efficacy of this by-law as a bona fide piece of municipal legislation. When the facts are examined there is not even a color of public interest attaching to its enactment or its provisions. The whole thing is palpably passed in the interests of two individuals, who object to pay what the plaintiff seeks to get for this coveted strip of land.

Having regard to the pleadings and evidence it is my duty to continue the injunction as prayed, so far as the plaintiff's land is affected thereby, and to give the plaintiff his costs.

CONSTITUTIONALITY OF STATUTES PROVIDING FOR THE OPENING OF "PRIVATE" OR "TOWN" ROADS BY CONDEMNATION.—This is a subject on which there is much conflict of authority. Statutes providing for the opening of private roads or ways from highways to the premises of individuals over the property of others by process of condemnation have been held unconstitutional, as authorizing the condemnation of private property for the private use or accommodation of an individual. Taylor *v.* Porter, 4 Hill (N. Y.), 140; Sadler *v.* Langham, 34 Ala. 311; Bankhead *v.* Brown, 25 Iowa, 540; Nesbitt *v.* Trumbo, 39 Ill. 110; Crear *v.* Crossly, 40 Ill. 175; Wild *v.* Deig, 43 Ind. 455; Witham *v.* Osburn, 4 Oreg. 318; Osborn *v.* Hart, 24 Wis. 89; Clark *v.* White, 2 Swan (Tenn.), 540.

On the other hand it is held that such a road, though primarily for the benefit of an individual, is a public road in the sense that the public have the right to travel on it, and that, therefore, the right of eminent domain may properly be exercised in opening such a road, without infringing on constitutional rights. See Shaver *v.* Starrett, 4 Ohio St. 494; Ferris *v.* Bramble, 5 Ohio St. 109; Sherman *v.* Buick, 32 Cal. 241; Brewer *v.* Bowman, 9 Ga. 37; Hickmann's Case, 4 Harr. (Del.) 580; Robinson *v.* Swope, 12 Bush (Ky.), 21; Snyder *v.* Warford, 11 Mo. 513.

NATURE OF A "PRIVATE" OR "TOWN" ROAD AS BEARING ON THE QUESTION OF CONSTITUTIONALITY.—The conflict of authority above adverted to grows out of the opposite views which courts take of the nature of "private" or "town" roads. Of course the nature of such roads depends wholly on the statute providing for them; but it is thought there is little difference in the provisions of the statutes in the different States relating to such roads. The object of these roads is to afford means of access to private individuals living off the high-road, and who have no other means of access to the high-road. In general, the statutory provisions

in regard to laying out such roads conform as closely as possible to those
in regard to laying out highways. The power to open such roads is, as
in the case of highways, vested in some municipal body or in certain
public officers. The chief difference is that in the case of a private road,
the petition of the individual to be benefited by the road is sufficient to
authorize the body empowered to open the road to act; and that the
expenses of opening the road and of keeping it in repair are to be borne
by that individual, or by him and the town in such proportions as shall
be deemed proper. See Public Statutes of Mass. Ch. 49, § 65; and cases
cited above as to constitutionality or unconstitutionality of the statute;
see also R. S. Del. 1874, p. 332; R. S. Ill. 1871. Ch. 93, § 60; Gen. Stats.
Ky. 1883, p. 770; R. S. Mo. 1879, p. 1373, *et seq.*

It would seem, on principle, that ways or roads opened under statutes
of the general character above described were both public and private,—
private in the sense that they are primarily for the benefit of an individual, and public in the sense that they are open to the public and intended
to give a means of communication or access between the individual and
the public, and that this means of communication is for the use and benefit of the public as well as of the individual. Of course, the interest
which the public have in the opening of " private" roads depends on the
special circumstances of the case. Where the public will have no means
of access to the individual unless the road is laid out, it would seem clear
that the laying out of the road was of sufficient interest to the public to
warrant an exercise of the right of eminent domain. The principle is
clearly stated in Brewer *v.* Bowman, 9 Ga. 36, 40 : " But the complainant's
land is surrounded by the lands of other proprietors so that he is excluded from any public road ; he cannot get out to vote at elections, to
perform jury or road duty, to perform either militia or patrol duty, to
give evidence in courts of justice, or to carry the productions of his
farm to market. . . . It would seem, therefore, that to have a private
road, as contemplated by the act of 1834, would not necessarily, in the
view in which we have been considering the question, be *exclusively* for
the benefit of the party applying for it, but that the public interest would
also be promoted, by enabling every citizen to perform all the duties
which are required of him by law, for the benefit of the whole community." See also Robinson *v.* Swope, 12 Bush (Ky.), 21. Indeed, means
of access to the individual has been deemed of sufficient public importance to warrant the laying out a public highway against the will of the
individual to whom the road was to give access. Johnson *v.* Supervisors
of Clayton County, 61 Iowa, 89.

In Sherman *v.* Buick, 32 Cal. 241, 255, the court says : " Roads, leading from the main road, which run through the country to the resi-
dences or farms of individuals, are of public concern and under control
of the Government. Taking private property for the purpose of such
roads is not a taking for private use. They are open to every one who
may have occasion to use them, and are, therefore, public. Their character as public roads is unaffected by the circumstance that, in view of their
situation, they are but little used and are mainly convenient for the use

of a few individuals, and such as may have occasion to visit them socially or on matters of business ; nor by the circumstance that in view of such conditions the Legislature may deem it just to open and maintain them at the cost of those most immediately concerned instead of the public at large. The object for which they are established is none the less of a public character, and, therefore, within the supervision of the Government. To call them "private roads" is simply a legislative misnomer, which does not affect or change their real character. By-roads is a better name for them, and one which is less calculated to mislead the uninitiated."

See also Metcalf *v.* Bingham, 3 N. H. 459 ; Allen *v.* Stevens, 29 N. J. L. 509. Hickman's Case, 4 Harr. (Del.) 580.

Nearly all the cases holding that statutes for the opening of "private roads" by condemnation are unconstitutional, do so on the ground that such roads are not intended to be open to the use of the public. Bankhead *v.* Brown, 25 Iowa, 542–548 ; Sadler *v,* Langham, 34 Ala. 311–332 ; Taylor *v.* Porter, 4 Hill (N. Y.), 140, 142 ; Clark *v.* White, 2 Swan (Tenn.), 540, 548 ; Wild *v.* Deig, 43 Ind. 455, 460 ; Witham *v.* Osburn, 4 Oreg. 318, 323, 324 ; Osborn *v.* Hart, 24 Wis. 89.

It would seem that the courts have been misled by the use of the word "private." Indeed, this is pointed out in the dissenting opinion in the case of Bankhead *v.* Brown, 25 Iowa, 540. The court had held that the description of the roads as "private," and the fact that they were to be opened and kept up at the expense of the applicants, showed that the public had no interest in them or right to use them. Judge Beck, in his dissenting opinion, p. 551, says : "The fact that, in the title of the act the word "private" is used, to my mind gives no strength to the argument in support of the conclusion that the road is private, or for the benefit of the petitioner, and subject to his control. This word is simply to indicate the manner of its establishment. It by no means indicates that it is to be owned or controlled by a private citizen." Again he says : "It cannot be argued that the mere use of the term "private" in the title of the act, without one word of limitation in the body thereof, or any provision that the road established thereunder is a private way, will, of itself, determine that the road is under the control of, owned by, and established for the sole use of the party who petitions for its establishment." See Wild *v.* Deig, 43 Ind. 455, 460 ; Witham *v.* Osburn, 4 Oreg. 318, 323, 324.

BY SPECIAL PROVISION OF STATUTE "PRIVATE" ROAD MAY BE ONLY FOR PRIVATE USES.—It is thought that under the ordinary provisions of statutes relating to the opening of "private" roads, such roads when opened are for the use of the public. But, of course, special provisions may change this, and make it clear that such road is strictly private and not intended for the public use. Thus in Dickey *v.* Tennison, 27 Mo. 373, a special act of legislature was passed authorizing an individual to open and keep open a "neighborhood" road. The individual was to mark out and report the road to the county court, who were then to appoint commissioners to assess the damages. The individual was required to pay all damages and costs assessed before he could open the road. The court held that the statute left the matter of opening the road or not entirely to the will of the individual, and that it was apparent that the road contemplated was private in the strict sense of the word. [The Missouri court held in Snyder *v.* Warford, 11 Mo. 513, that a statute providing for the opening of "private roads" by condemnation was not unconstitutional.]

Where the statute provided that "every such private road, when so laid out, shall be for the use of such applicant, his heirs and assigns, and also that the occupant or owner of the land through which such road should be laid out, should not be permitted to use the same as a road unless he shall signify his intention so to do to the jury or commissioners to assess the damages," it was held that these provisions showed that roads contemplated by the statute were to be for private use, and that the public were to be excluded. Taylor *v.* Porter, 4 Hill (N. Y.), 140; Osborn *v.* Hart, 24 Wis. 89.

STATUTES AUTHORIZING THE OPENING BY CONDEMNATION OF "PRIVATE" OR "TOWNSHIP" ROADS FOR THE MERE CONVENIENCE OF INDIVIDUALS UNCONSTITUTIONAL.—Although it is thought that the exercise of the right of eminent domain in the opening of a road to give the public access to an individual, is a proper and constitutional exercise of that right, yet this right should not be exercised to open a road purely for the convenience of an individual or individuals, where the public would have no use for the road. The fact that the public would have the right to use such road would, in this case, be immaterial. In order to warrant the exercise of the right of condemnation, it is necessary that the public should have more than a mere barren right of user. The road must be such a road as the public will in fact use or in the use of which the public is directly interested. A Kentucky statute authorized the opening of private roads or pass ways in several cases. One of the cases was where an individual had no access to any public road; another was where he owned two pieces of land entirely separated from each other, It was held that the statute was constitutional as to the first case, but unconstitutional as to the second. Robinson *v.* Swope, 12 Bush (Ky.), 21.

CONCLUDING REMARKS.—It is deemed that the following propositions of law are established by the cases reviewed in this note. I. That the ordinary so-called "private" or "town" roads, opened by public authority are public in the sense that the public have a right of user in them. II. That being public roads in the sense just described, they may be opened by condemnation in cases where the public welfare demands their being opened. III. That the public welfare does demand their being opened where the public otherwise have no means of access to individuals.

It may be here remarked that the opening of "private" or "town" roads by condemnation is especially provided for and allowed in the State constitutions of Georgia, New York, and Michigan. Cooley Const. Lim. (4th ed.) 662 *n.*

WHAT PUBLIC NECESSITY WILL AUTHORIZE THE OPENING OF PUBLIC ROADS BY CONDEMNATION UNDER STATUTES AUTHORIZING A PUBLIC

BODY TO OPEN SUCH ROAD WHEN IN THEIR JUDGMENT IT IS OF COM-
MON CONVENIENCE OR NECESSITY.—Under a statute of the character above
indicated it was held that where proceedings are had to open a highway,
and it appears from the record of the proceedings that it is to be opened
rather in the interest of individuals than in that of the public, such proceedings will be quashed on certiorari. Commonwealth *v.* Cambridge, 7
Mass. 158; Commonwealth *v.* Sawin, 2 Pick. (Mass.) 547.

In the latter case the record of the judgment was as follows: "It appears to the court here, that the common convenience or necessity for the
highway prayed for is not sufficient to warrant the laying out the same
wholly at the expense of the town of Natick, but considering the quantity
of travel that will be accommodated by the road, and that M. S., a
petitioner who will be peculiarly benefited by the establishment of it, has
filed in court a bond obliging himself to the inhabitants of said town for
their use, if they will accept the same, to make a certain portion of said
road, by which the expense of said town will be considerably lessened, the
court do adjudge and determine that it is of common convenience or
necessity to have the highway prayed for in said petition laid out." On
certiorari it was held that, unless the public need or convenience was
pressing enough to warrant the laying out of the road at the expense of
the town, there was no authority to lay it out at all.

But where the body, vested with authority to lay out or alter streets
whenever in their opinion the safety or convenience of the inhabitants
shall require it, shall adjudge that the laying out or altering of a
street is required by public safety and convenience, their having taken a
bond from an individual to contribute towards the expense will not vitiate
their proceedings, provided the bond was not made the basis of their
proceedings, and the adjudication was not colorably for the use of the
city and really for the benefit of the individual. Parks *v.* Boston, 8
Pick. (Mass.) 217. See also Jones *v.* Andover, 9 Pick. (Mass.) 146; Cope-
land *v.* Packard, 16 Pick. 217; Crockett *v.* Boston, 5 Cush. (Mass.) 182.

·

CORNELL

v.

MAYOR AND ALDERMEN OF NEW BEDFORD.

(138 *Massachusetts*, 588.)

A petition that a way be laid out fifty feet wide in a city was presented
to the board of mayor and aldermen; and the usual order of notice was
issued and served. An order introduced in the board to lay out the way
fifty feet wide was lost by a vote of three to three, and then "was laid on
the table until the next meeting of the board." Three months later, the
city surveyor was instructed to survey a way forty feet wide, and, on his

return being made, the board adjudicated that public necessity and convenience required that the way be laid out forty feet wide, and gave due notice of an intention so to lay out the way. Subsequently a new order, laying out the way fifty feet wide, and giving the same metes and bounds as in the order first mentioned, was adopted by the board, concurred in by the common council, and approved by the mayor. *Held,* that the proceedings under the first order were not terminated by its being laid on the table, nor waived by the proceedings relating to the forty-foot way; and that a person whose land was taken by the location of fifty feet, but not by the location of forty feet, could not maintain a writ of certiorari to quash the proceedings laying out the way.

Petition for a writ of certiorari to quash proceedings of the respondent, in laying out an extension of Pleasant Street in New Bedford. Hearing before Colburn, J., who reserved the case for the consideration of the full court. The facts appear in the opinion.

F. A. Milliken for petitioner.

T. M. Stetson & L. L. Holmes for respondents.

FIELD, J.—The questions submitted to us by the report are QUESTIONS. whether the common council of New Bedford should not also have been made a respondent; and whether "the power of the city authorities in respect of laying out the fifty-foot way was terminated when the vote of three to three was had, on January 31, 1884, in respect of the passage of the order of that date, and by the subsequent notice and proceedings for a forty-foot way in May."

Assuming that the common council should have been made a respondent (St. 1847, c. 60, § 12,), it may nevertheless be useful to consider the second question, because, if no error appears in the record, further proceedings in the case become unnecessary.

It appears from the report of the mayor and aldermen on FACTS. the petition of Francis Hatheway and others, recommending that the way be laid out fifty feet wide, was received in the board of aldermen on January 3, 1884, and referred to the next city government. We infer that the next city government came in on the first Monday of January, 1884 (St. 1857, c. 2,), which was January 7. On January 17, 1884, the usual notice of an intention to lay out the way was given and served upon the petitioner. The notice recited that, in the opinion of the board, the safety and convenience of the inhabitants required that the way be laid out fifty feet wide.

On January 31, 1884, an order was introduced in the board of mayor and aldermen laying out the way fifty feet wide, and taking certain parcels of land therefor, and was lost by a vote of three to three, and thereupon, after a motion to amend the order so that the way should be forty feet wide instead of fifty, which was withdrawn, "the order was laid on the table until the next meeting of the board."

On May 8, 1884, the city land surveyor was instructed to survey a way forty feet wide, and his return of this survey was received at a special meeting of the board of mayor and aldermen, on May 15, 1884; and at that meeting the board of aldermen adjudicated that the public necessity and convenience of the inhabitants required that the way be laid out forty feet wide, and gave due notice to all persons interested that the board intended to lay out such a street. The way as surveyed, if forty feet wide, did not touch the land of the petitioner; if fifty feet wide, it included a part of his land. No order laying out the way forty feet wide, however, appears ever to have been introduced in the board of aldermen, or voted upon by that board; but, on June 4, 1884, a new order laying out the way fifty feet wide was introduced and adopted, was concurred in by the common council, and approved by the mayor. This order did not differ from the order which, on January 31, 1884, "was laid on the table until the next meeting of the board," in the description of the metes and bounds of the way, or of the parcels of land taken.

The contention is, that, as the first order was defeated in the board of aldermen, and the vote was never reconsidered, the original proceedings were thereby terminated,—certainly when the next meeting of the board of aldermen adjourned without having taken the order from the table; that the subsequent proceedings in regard to a forty-foot way also show that the laying out of a fifty-foot way had been abandoned; and that, in order afterward to lay out a way fifty feet wide, it was necessary to begin *de novo*, because the jurisdiction over the original petition of Hatheway and others was exhausted.

Whether the board of aldermen had adopted by vote any rules of procedure, we do not know, as no rules appear, neither is there any evidence of the cus-

tomary rules of the board. The function of the common
council was to concur or non-concur in the orders of the
board of aldermen. It is obvious that there might be differences of opinion between the two bodies; and that, until
the subject was finally disposed of, the orders must be subject
to amendment in the board of aldermen. The consideration
of any order in the board of aldermen might be postponed
from time to time until the final action of that board upon it,
and whether that board has or has not taken final action upon
an order must be determined by the intention of the board as
shown by its record. New Marlborough *v.* County Commissioners, 9 Met. 423.

In the absence of any evidence that the board had adopted,
TAKING UP A either by custom or by vote, any special rules, it
MATTER FROM
THE TABLE. might perhaps be considered that it proceeded under what may be called the common parliamentary law. By
that law, a motion to lay on the table, if carried, disposes of
the motion to which it is applied for the time being; but this
motion can be brought up for consideration of the subject, or
by a motion to reconsider. The order "was laid on the table
until the next meeting of the board;" but, if not taken from
the table at the next meeting, it was still on the table of the
board, and could be taken up for consideration, provided the
order was not disposed of so that nothing remained to be
considered, and then it could be taken up for the purpose of
being reconsidered, if special rules did not forbid it. "When
there is no special rule on the subject, a motion to reconsider
may be made at any time, or by any member, precisely like
any other motion, and subject to no other rules." Cushing's
Law and Practice of Legislative Assemblies, §§ 1266, 1449,
1451. But, without applying too strictly to such a body as a
board of aldermen the common parliamentary law of legislative assemblies, and interpreting its record by the construction which would be given to it by persons unskilled in parliamentary proceedings, we think it is clear that the order
was laid upon the table until the next meeting of the board
that the board might thereafter take some action upon it.
The order had failed to pass, but, if it had been the intention
to regard this as a final disposition of the order, no motion
would have been carried to lay it upon the table, unless such
a motion was by the special rules of the board a method of

disposing of a subject so that it could not thereafter be re-considered. As the order, when laid upon the table, had been voted upon and declared lost, the technical method of procedure would have been to move to take it from the table, and then to move to reconsider it. The resolve and order introduced and put upon their passage on June 4, 1884, were in effect a motion to take the original order from the table, to reconsider it, to amend it in certain particulars not material to this case, and, as thus amended, to pass it. As the subject was still open to consideration by the board, and the substance of what was done was within its power to do, its action cannot be declared void, because the manner of do-ing what it did was not in accordance with approved prece-dents. The petitioner has not been injured by the method of procedure.

Petition dismissed.

THE WASHINGTON ICE COMPANY OF CHICAGO *et al.*, Appts.

v.

LAY *et al.*

(Advance Case, Indiana. September 17, 1885.)

A motion to dismiss an appeal, taken from an inferior court to the Circuit Court, not made a part of the record by order of the latter court, and not contained in any bill of exceptions, cannot be considered on appeal to this court, notwithstanding the clerk below has inserted in the transcript what purports to be a copy of the motion; and no ruling had thereon can be reviewed in this court.

Where the motion to dismiss is not before the court, the objection that notice of the original proceedings before the Commissioners was not given, cannot be raised in this court for the first time; the fact of their appearance without objecting to the want of notice, is deemed a waiver of the objection.

The general highway law provides that the petition shall be signed by freeholders, but it does not require that this shall appear on the face of the petition. Whether or not it is so signed is a question for the county board, to whom all objections to the qnalification of the petitioners should be made, and if not so made at the time, they are deemed waived.

Where it appears that the appellants were owners of all the land over which the highway passes, and without any objections in the Commissioners' Court they made a voluntary appearance in the proceeding, so far as concerns notice to landowners, such defect will not justify a reversal.

Where the petition and the evidence agree that there was a highway commencing at the north end of a certain road, running through a certain section of land, and they disagree only as to the distance of the said north end from the corner of the section, it is not such a variance as to overthrow the proceedings.

When a highway has been established and opened by the county board, there is no longer involved any question of public utility, and where a way has become a pnblic highway by use, it is such, regardless of the question of public utility, and remains so till vacated, or by non-use, whether entered of record or not, and refusing to order a highway located upon the lines of an existing highway, will not vacate the existing highway, not will it bar the proceeding to have a highway entered of record, the two proeeedings being dissimilar.

APPEAL from the Laporte Circuit Court.
Mortimer Nye and *David Turpie* for appellants.
L. A. Cole for appellees.

ZOLLARS, J.—Appellee instituted this proceeding before the
FACTS.   board of county commissioners under section 5035, R. S., 1881, to have an alleged highway ascertained, described and entered of record, on the ground that it had been used as such for twenty years. From a decision of the board against them, they appealed to the Circuit Court. In that court the appellants here moved to dismiss the appeal. The overruling of the motion is assigned as error. The clerk below has inserted in the transcript what purports to be a copy of the motion, but it was not made a part of the record by order of the court, nor is it contained in any bill of exceptions.

We cannot disregard the contention of appellees, that the
MOTION HELD   motion is not a part of the record, and hence, is
NOT PART OF   not before us for any purpose. Crumley *v.* Hick-
RECORD.
man, 92 Ind. 388, and cases there cited.

Without the motion, we have no way of knowing upon what it was based, and, hence, have nothing upon which to base a decision that the ruling upon it was right or wrong. The assignment predicated upon that ruling, therefore, presents no question for decision here.

The second assigned error is, that the court below erred

in overruling appellant's motion to dismiss the Notice held waived. petition, and the proceedings under it.   Under this assignment, the argument is, that the petition and all the proceedings under it should be dismissed because of defects in the petition, and because there was no notice given of the pendency of the petition and proceeding.

Upon the question of notice, it is sufficient to say that the record before us requires no decision as to its necessity. We, therefore leave that question where it is left by former decisions.   Appellants, who seem to own all of the land over which the alleged highway passes, appeared in the Commissioners' court and without making any question as to notice, made a full appearance by filing what is denominated an answer.

At the first Term of the Circuit Court after the appeal, the parties all appeared by counsel, and the cause was continued without any question as to notice.   At a subsequent term appellants moved to dismiss the appeal, and also to dismiss the proceedings.   The clerk below has inserted in the transcript copies of these motions.   As they were not made a part of the record by order of the court, and are not contained in any bill of exeeptions, they are not properly in the record, so far, at least as they relate to or are based upon the want of notice.   There are, therefore, two conclusive reasons why this court cannot, upon the question of notice, overthrow or interfere with the final judgment below.

In the first place, the motions to dismiss, not being properly before us, there is nothing upon which to predicate a decision, that notice was not given, or that appellants, at any time, made any question as to notice.

In the second place, appellants should have made the question as to the notice, at their first opportunity, before the board of commissioners.   Having appeared and having made no objections there, as to notice, they waived whatever objections they might have.

Having thus waived the objections, they were not in a condition to make them upon appeal.   This is the rule in other highway and analogous cases, and the reasonable rule to be applied here.   We cite some of the cases : Milhollin *v.* Thomas, 7 Ind. 165 ; Smith *v.* Alexander, 24 Ind. 454 ; Fisher *v.* Hobbs, 42 Ind. 276 ; Green *v.* Elliott, 86 Ind. 53, and cases there cited; Vandever *v.* Garshwiler, 63 Ind. 185; Peed *v.* Brenneman, 89 Ind. 252; Lowe *v.* Ryan, 94 Ind. 450; Bradley *v.* Frankfort, 99 Ind. 417.

Under the assignment, based upon the motion to dismiss the proceedings, and the fourth assigned error, that the PETITION FOR HIGHWAY NEED NOT PURPORT TO BE SIGNED BY FREEHOLDERS. petition does not contain a sufficient statement of facts to constitute a cause of action against appellants, it is argued that the petition is defective because it does not contain the names of the persons over whose land the alleged highway passes, and because it does not purport to be signed by any freeholder or citizen of LaPorte County.

Assuming that the petition should be signed by freeholders, as in an ordinary highway case, appellant's counsel argue that it is insufficient, because it does not purport to be so signed.

But if the correctness of the assumption should be granted, about which we decide nothing in this case, counsel's conclusion would not follow. The general highway law provides that the petition shall be signed by freeholders, but it does not require that this shall appear upon the face of the petition. The petition needs not, in any case, " purport to be signed by freeholders." Brown *v.* McCord, 20 Ind. 270.

Whether or not the petition is so signed, is a question for the decision of the County Board, before taking further action upon it. Objections to the qualifications of the petitioners should be made at the first opportunity before the County Board. If not made then and there, they will be deemed as waived. Little *v.* Thompson, 24 Ind. 146; Fisher *v.* Hobbs, 42 Ind. 276; Wilson *v.* Whitsell, 24 Ind. 306; Sowle *v.* Cosner, 56 Ind. 276; Turley *v.* Oldham, 68 Ind. 114.

It is further contended under these assignments of error, PETITION. NAMES OF PERSONS OVER WHOSE LAND HIGHWAY PASSES NOT NECESSARY. that the petition is fatally defective because it does not give the names of the persons over whose land the highway passes. This contention is based, in the main, upon the case of Vandever *v.* Garshwiler, 63–185, *supra.*

It was said in this case, that when the moving parties are other than the county board, the petition should give the names of the owners of the land over which the road is claimed to run, so that the court can cause proper notice to be given to them of the pendency of the petition.

In the case before us, however, the reason has no application. Here it appears, by appellant's motion to dismiss and otherwise, that they were the owners of all the land over which the highway passes, and that without any objections in the commissioner's court, they made a voluntary appearance to the petition and proceeding. So far, therefore, as concerns notice to land owners, no beneficial end could have been accomplished by inserting their names in the petition.

Nor would the ends of justice be subserved by reversing the judgment on account of this alleged defect in the petition. Without deciding more, as to the requisites of the petition in this regard, it is sufficient to say that, upon the record before us, the judgment should not be reversed on account of the alleged defect in the petition.

It is contended that the motion for a new trial should have been sustained first, because the petition was not introduced in evidence; second, because there was no proof that the petitioners were freeholders; and third, because the proof as to the line and location of the highway did not agree with the description as given in the petition.

The petition was a paper in the case, as the complaint in an ordinary case, and there was no necessity of introducing it in evidence. Daggy *v.* Coats, 19 Ind. 259. PETITION NEED NOT BE PUT IN EVIDENCE.

Not having made the question before the county board, there was no question before the court on appeal as to the qualification of the petitioners. In ordering the highway entered of record, the County Board and the Circuit Court were confined, of course, to the highway as described in the petition. The verdict and final order have reference to this highway. Unless the proof showed that this had become a public highway by twenty years' use, the case failed, and a new trial should have been granted. HIGHWAY DESCRIBED IN PETITION. VARIANCE

The petition describes the beginning of the highway as commencing at the north end of the road running through Wilson's second addition of out lots to the City of LaPorte, being 275, 75-100 feet east of the southwest corner, of west fractional part of section thirty-four, etc. The evidence shows that the highway does begin at the north end of the

road running through Wilson's said addition, but that this
road at that point is 285 1–10 feet east of the said corner, as
measured by the witness. The north end of the road
through Wilson's addition seems to be well known, and is
the visible monument by which the beginning of the alleged
highway should be determined, rather than the measurement from the corner of the section of land.

It is easy to mistake, in the measurement, but it is not likely
that there would be any mistake about the Wilson road.
The petition and the evidence agree that there was a highway commencing at the north end of the Wilson road. They
only disagree as to the distance of the north end of that
road from the named corner of land. This is not such a
variance as ought to overthrow the proceeding. Gray *v.*
Stiver, 24 Ind. 174; Simonton *v.* Thompson, 55 Ind. 87;
Hedge *v.* Sims, 29 Ind. 574.

In the Circuit Court appellants filed what purports to be,
OPENING HIGH- and what they style, an answer in bar of the pro-
WAY. SUFFICI-
ENCY OF ANSWER ceeding, in substance, that at a previous term of
the county board, appellees had petitioned for the location
and opening of a highway, upon the line of the highway that
they here seek to have entered of record, and that upon that
petition and a report of viewers the board adjudged that the
proposed highway would not be of public utility, and should
not be opened, and that the judgment remained in full force.

If this answer is sufficient to bar this proceeding, it was
error to sustain the demurrer to it. If it does not constitute such a bar, it was not error to sustain the demurrer to
it, whatever weight the facts set up might be entitled to for
any purpose, other than as a bar to the proceeding.

That the county board may have refused to open a new
highway upon the line of that here sought to have entered of
record as an existing highway, surely cannot bar this proceeding. The proceedings are entirely dissimilar. One
goes upon the theory that there is no highway, and that
one should be opened; the other goes upon the theory
that there is an existing highway, and that no action by the
county board nor any other authority is necessary to establish it. In the latter proceeding, the county board is not
asked to locate and open a new highway, but simply to
ascertain, describe, and enter of record one already existing

and open for travel. The board might well refuse to order a highway to be established and opened upon the line. of an existing highway without debarring itself or others of the right to have the existing highway entered of record. Refusing to order a highway located upon the line of an existing highway will not vacate the existing highway.

It is contended in argument that appellees might have joined, in their petition for the location and opening of the highway, an application such as that made in this case, and that as they did not do so they are estopped to institute and maintain this proceeding. It would seem to be an inconsistent proceeding to join in the same petition an application to have a highway entered of record as an existing highway, and also an application to have a new highway opened upon the same line. The. contention cannot be maintained.

One question remains. It is contended that the question of public utility is a material question here, and that that question was adjudicated in the former proceeding. When a highway has been established and opened by the county board there is no longer involved. any question of public utility. So when a way has become a public highway by use it is such regardless of any question of public utility, and it will remain such until it shall be vacated in a proper proceeding or by non-user, and that, too, whether entered of record or not. The order for entering of record is not the establisment of a highway, but an adjudication of the fact that there is already such a highway. If indeed there is no such highway, the order will have the effect of establishing one, but this is not the purpose or theory of the order or proceeding.

PUBLIC UTILITY OF HIGHWAY NOT CONSIDERED, WHEN.

It must follow that the question of public utility in a proceeding like this cannot in any way constitute a bar to the proceeding.

There was no error, therefore, in sustaining the demurrer to the answer. As we find no available error in the record, the judgment is affirmed with costs.

ZIMMERMAN *v.* CANFIELD *et al.*
ZIMMERMAN *v.* PRICKETT *et al.*

(42 *Ohio State*, 463.)

Section 4452 (Rev. Stats.), which authorizes the county commissioners to view the line of a proposed ditch, and determine, by actual view of the premises along and adjacent thereto, whether the ditch is necessary, or will be conducive to the public health, convenience or welfare, invests the commissioners with political and not judicial powers, and notice of such proceedings to the owners of lands crossed by the ditch is not essential to the validity of such enactment or of such proceedings thereunder.

Sections 4461, 4471 and 894 (Rev. Stats.) authorize the payment of money out of the county treasury as compensation for lands taken for a county ditch, within the meaning of section 10 of the bill of rights, which ordains that : "When private property shall be taken for public use, a compensation therefor shall first be made in money, or first secured by deposit of money."

The statutes relating to county ditches, in force in the year 1881, were valid and constitutional enactments.

In an action by a resident owner of land crossed by the line of a proposed ditch, who has neither notice nor knowledge of such proceeding prior to the hearing upon the engineer's report, to enjoin the construction of the proposed ditch, it is error in the court to send the proceedings before the commissioners for hearing upon the plaintiff's claim for compensation and damages, and leave the commissioners at liberty to proceed with the construction of the ditch without regard to whether his compensation for lands taken be first made in money or first secured by deposit of money, as required by section 19 of the bill of rights,

ERROR to the District Court of Fulton county.

These cases are considered together. The first was one to enjoin the construction of a proposed ditch about eight miles in length, seventeen rods of which crossed the plaintiff's lands seven miles below the initial point and about one mile above the outlet.

The object of the second was to enjoin all proceedings upon a petition to locate and construct a ditch across the plaintiff's land along the route of the proposed ditch involved in the first case.

In the first case the proceedings were regular, except that the plaintiff (who was a resident of the county) had no notice or knowledge of the ditch proceedings prior to the hearing of the engineer's report. The proceedings were under the statutes in force in 1880 as amended in 1881 (78 O. L. 204–210).

A preliminary injunction was allowed by the probate judge against all work on the ditch. A judge of the court of common pleas dissolved the injunction as to all of the ditch except that crossing the plaintiff's lands.

Two judges of the district court modified this last order by restraining the construction of the ditch above and across the plaintiff's land ; leaving the part below to be completed.

Thereupon the second petition was filed with the commissioners, to establish a ditch across plaintiff's land of the same dimensions as the first proposed ditch.

Before the time for hearing this second petition plaintiff filed another petition for an injunetion, which is the second of the above mentioned cases, upon which a preliminary injunction was allowed.

Upon trial in the common pleas both injunctions were dissolved, except so much of the first as related to the seventeen rods across plaintiff's land, which was held in force until his damages, if any, were legally ascertained and paid.

Upon appeal, the district court found the foregoing facts and that the ditch was necessary and would be conducive to the public health, convenience and welfare, and proceeded to make the following order:

" And the court upon the conclusions of fact and law aforesaid, do order, adjudge and decree: That said county commissioners shall and they are hereby ordered, to give said plaintiff an opportunity to be heard before them and to present any claim for compensation or damages that he may have or sustain by reason of the construction of said ditch, and said commissioners shall give him such notice of the time and place, when and where such hearing is to be had, and claim to be presented, as is prescribed by statutes in case of proceedings to establish ditches by county commissioners ; and plaintiff shall have the right of appeal and all other remedies, as is provided by said statute, upon said question of compensation and damages, and no other question shall be heard by said commissioners or upon such appeal. It is further considered, that the injunction heretofore granted in this case be and the same hereby is dissolved, and said plaintiff shall have and recover his costs in this case, taxed at $—, which shall be paid by said County of Fulton, upon the warrant or order of the auditor thereof. It is ordered that the further construction of this ditch and all proceedings to establish the same or to ascertain said damages or compensation shall be delayed for sixty days. To all and each of which action, rulings and judgment of said court said plaintiff then in due form excepted."

Pratt & Bentley and *W. C. Kelly* for plaintiff in error.

Henry Newbegin representing parties having like interests as plaintiff in error.

OWEN, J.—1. It is maintained by the plaintiff (1) that the statutes in force in 1881, under which the commissioners were proceeding, were unconstitutional and void, and (2) that the order of the district court directing proceedings before the commissioners was unauthorized.

One of the grounds relied upon to support the first proposition is that these statutes were in contravention of section 19 of the bill of rights of the constitution of Ohio, which ordains that : " Where private property shall be taken for public use, a compensation therefor shall first be made in money, or first secured by a deposit in money, and such compensation shall be assessed by a jury."

(side note: COMPENSATION BEFORE LANDS ARE TAKEN DISCUSSED.)

It is contended that the legislation in question failed to provide for payment or deposit of compensation in money before the lands are "taken" by the construction of the ditch. The Revised Statutes, § 4461, provides that : " The commissioners shall, upon actual view of the premises, fix and allow such compensation for lands appropriated, . . . to each person or corporation making application as provided in the preceding section." . . .

By this provision the commissioners are called upon to do two things : First to " fix " the amount of compensation, and second to " allow " it.

Let us inquire what it is to allow a sum of money which has been " fixed," that is, determined upon by the commissioners.

(side note: "ALLOWING" A SUM OF MONEY AS COMPENSATION.)

Section 894 (Rev. Stat.) provides that : " No claims against the county shall be paid otherwise than upon the allowance of the county commissioners, upon the warrant of the county auditor, except in those cases in which the amount due is fixed by law, or is authorized to be fixed by some other person or tribunal, in which case the same shall be paid upon the warrant of the county auditor, upon the proper certificate of the person or tribunal allowing the same; but no public money shall be disbursed by the county commissioners, or any of them, but the same shall be disbursed by the county treasurer, upon the warrant of the county auditor specifying the name of the party entitled to the same, on what account and upon whose allowance, if not fixed by law."

When the commissioners have caused to be entered upon their journal an order fixing and allowing the amount of compensation to a land owner who has made application therefor, they have exhausted their powers, and it only remains for the county auditor to draw his warrant on the county treasurer for the sum so allowed.

If an appeal is taken from the allowance of the commissioners to the probate court, and " the verdict of the jury be in favor of the appellant, the commissioners shall cause to be made on their journal an entry carrying out the findings of the jury," etc., § 4471.

How may the commissioners "carry out the findings of the jury" except by the allowance of the amount of the compensation found by the jury? Whether the amount of compensation for lands taken be " fixed " by the commissioners or " found " by the jury, the provision for first paying or depositing the compensation in money is ample; and it is no answer to this to say that the particular fund to be drawn upon is not designated.

The case of Ohio *ex rel.* McConahey *v.* Seaman, 23 Ohio St. 389, where it was held that orders drawn on the county treasurer for the cost of constructing a ditch were not payable out of the general county fund, has no application to the present case.

It is to be supposed that when the commissioners enter upon the location and construction of a ditch which must involve the " taking" of lands, they do so in contemplation of the fact that compensation for lands so taken must, if applied for, be first paid or deposited, and it seems clear that if no other fund is provided, nor payment or deposit otherwise made by those to be benefited by the ditch, the general county fund is to be resorted to. Ample provision is made to reimburse this fund.   Section 4479 provides for assessments on benefited lands to raise the amount of compensation and damages, and section 2834 provides for the transfer of these special funds so raised to the general fund.

The position contended for, that the allowance by the com-missioners or even the drawing of his warrant by the auditor is neither the payment nor deposit of money in the sense in which these terms are employed in the bill of rights, is not well taken.   There is no complaint that the county was in-solvent, nor that for any other cause the warrant of the audi-tor would not be honored.

The solvency of the State and of her municipal subdivis-ions is presumed in the absence of a showing to the contrary. Talbot *v.* Hudson, 16 Gray, 431 ; Hill *v.* United States, 9 How. 386 ; Long *v.* Fuller, 68 Pa. 170 ; Yost's Report, 17 Pa. 524 ; Mills on Eminent Domain, § 126.

This question was considered by the supreme court of Indiana in Rudisill *v.* State, 40 Ind. 490, where it is said: " The author is authorized to draw his warrant upon the treas-urer for a sum allowed or certified to be due . . . by the board of county commissioners.   We are of the opinion that, when the amount of damages is ordered to be paid out of the county treasury, as in this case, the commissioners may treat the case as one where the amount it deposited in the treasury for the use of the parties entitled to the same." It is not easy to conceive how a more efficient scheme can be devised for either the payment or deposit of money for compensation for lands taken, then the statutes in question have provided.

2. It is further maintained that the statutes under considera-tion are in contravention of the constitution, for

NOTICE OF PETI-TION FOR DITCH. HEARING. the reason that no notice is provided of the hear-ing of the petition for the ditch.   That it is the fil-ing of this petition which confers upon the commissioners jurisdiction to act, and that the failure of the statutes to pro-vide for notice of the hearing of such petition, and permitting the commissioners to proceed to " find for the improvement" without giving parties to be affected by the improvement their day in court is fatal to the validity of the statutes.

It is not denied that opportunity is afforded to all parties affected by the ditch to be heard upon appeal in the probate court; and this leads to the inquiry whether they are entitled to such hearing in the first instance.

The proposition contended for contemplates that the commissioners, in determining upon the necessity of the ditch or whether it will conduce to the public health, convenience or welfare, are acting judicially.

Section 4452 provides that the commissioners, upon receiving a copy of the petition, shall proceed at once to view the line of the proposed ditch and determine by actual view whether it is necessary, or will be conducive to the public health, convenience or welfare, and whether the line described is the best route.

Section 4453 provides that if the commissioners shall find against the improvement, they shall dismiss the petition and proceedings at the cost of the petitioners.

By section 4454, if the commissioners find for the improvement, they shall direct a survey, etc., of the line described in the petition. Up to this point in the proceedings, none of the interested parties except the petitioners for the ditch have notice. So far the proceedings are preliminary. The State has delegated to the commissioners so much of her power of eminent domain as is necessary to determine whether the construction of the ditch is so far a public necessity as that it is demanded by consideration of public health, convenience, or welfare. There is nothing in the constitution of our State which guarantees to the owners of lands traversed by a ditch a trial by jury, or other judicial investigation, to determine upon its necessity or whether it will conduce to the public good.

While the statutes in question do provide for such a hearing upon appeal, it is so rather as a matter of favor than of right.

The commissioners, in determining this preliminary question of the necessity of appropriating lands for the purposes of a ditch, are called to the exercise of political and not judical powers. It is a question rather of public policy than of private right. McMiken *v.* City of Cincinnati, 4 Ohio St. 394; Giesy *v.* Railroad Co., 4 Ohio St. 325; People *v.* Smith, 21 N. Y. 597; Bowersox *v.* Watson, 20 Ohio St. 507; Mills's Eminent Domain, § 11;

Cooley's Constitutional Limitations, 528; Kramer *v.* C. & P. Railroad Co., 5 Ohio St. 146.

It is not upon the question of the appropriation of lands for public use, but upon that of compensation for lands so appropriated, that the owner is entitled, of right, to a hearing in court and the verdict of a jury.

What remedies the courts afford for the perversion or abuse of this power of appropriation we are not now called upon to inquire.

3. The remaining constitutional objections to these statutes are predicated upon the assumption that all proceedings looking to the appropriation of lands for ditch purposes are judical in their nature, and that the owner is entitled to a jury trial or other judical investigation, and are sufficiently answered by the conclusions already declared.

4. It is also assigned for error that, even if the statutes in question are valid, the district court erred in ordering the proceedings before the commissioners for hearing upon any DISSOLVING IN- claim of the plaintiff for compensation and dam- JUNCTION BE- FORE HEARING ages; and in dissolving the injunction theretofore HELD ERROR. granted in the case, and staying the proceedings to establish the ditch for only sixty days.

It is maintained by the defendants that this order was warranted by section 4491, which provides that: "The court in which any proceeding is brought . . . to declare void the proceedings to locate or establish any ditch . . . . shall, if there is manifest error in the proceedings, allow the plaintiff in the action to show that he has been injured thereby. · · The courts in which any such proceedings are begun shall allow parol proof that said improvement is necessary and will be conducive to the public health, convenience, or welfare, . . . and without finding error, the court may correct any gross injustice in the apportionment made by the commissioners; the court shall, on final hearing, make such order in the premises as shall be just and equitable," etc.

How far this provision may authorize the court to cure jurisdictional defects in the proceedings of the commissioners by ordering proceedings, in their nature *de novo*, in which the plaintiff would be permitted to make every claim and assert every right allowed to him in case of notice of the original proceedings, or whether it was the duty of the district court to proceed in the case before it, to administer such relief, we need not now inquire.

No opportunity had been afforded the plaintiff to claim or prove compensation and damages.

The court dissolved the injunction theretofore granted, and thus left the commissioners entirely at liberty to proceed (after the expiration of the sixty days for which proceedings were stayed) with the construction of the ditch across the plaintiff's land regardless of whether his compensation should "first be made in money, or first secured by a deposit of money" (as required by section 19 of the bill of rights). In this there was error for which the judgment of the district court is reversed.

Judgment will be entered enjoining all further proceedings until the ditch is legally established.

5. In the second case, the commissioners, when their proceedings were enjoined, were proceeding to act upon a petition for a ditch across the plaintiff's lands along the identical route, and of the same dimensions, of the ditch involved in the first case. It represented that a large extent of country above was in need of drainage and would be drained by the proposed ditch. It was alleged by the plaintiff that this second ditch proceeding was the result of a conspiracy between the commissioners and the petitioners to ignore and defeat the injunction against the first ditch proceedings.

So far as the proceedings for the last ditch had progressed, they were regular.

The district court found the facts which embraced the proceedings in the first case up to that time, and then stated their conclusions of law, and ordered as follows:

" And the court upon the facts aforesaid, and those admitted in the pleadings herein, find as matters of law, that it is not a question material for the introduction of testimony, whether or not there was any conspiracy between the county commissioners and said petitioners for said shorter ditch, or what the motives of said parties might have been or were; that the plaintiff began this action for an injunction prematurely, and that for the matters complained of in his petition, he has an adequate remedy at law by hearing before said county commissioners, and an appeal thence to the probate court of said county. That the statutes of the State of Ohio relating to the establishment of county ditches under which the proceedings complained of in this action were had, are not in conflict with the constitution of the State of Ohio."

And the court upon the conclusion of fact and law aforesaid, do order, adjudge, and decree as follows, to wit:

" That said petition of the plaintiff in this case be dismissed at the costs of the plaintiff, and that the temporary injunction heretofore allowed in this case, be, and the same is hereby dissolved. That the defendants recover of the plaintiff therein, their costs herein, taxed at $—. But that the farther construction of the said ditch and proceedings to establish the same, or to ascertain damages and compensation therefor, shall be delayed for sixty days.

" To all and each of which actions, rulings, and judgment of said court, the said plaintiff then in due time excepted."

The objection chiefly urged against the second ditch proceeding (aside from the constitutional question relied upon), is that the proposed ditch was a short one. It is not the length of a proposed ditch, but the extent of the drainage to be effected by it, which determines the power to establish it. Kent *v.* Perkins, 36 Ohio St. 641. The question was properly addressed to the commissioners.

There was no error in the action of the court.

Judgment in Zimmerman *v.* Canfield reversed.

Judgment in Zimmerman *v.* Prickett affirmed.

Town of Leominster
v.
Conant.

(*Advance Case, Massachusetts. June* 25, 1885.)

While no particular form of words is made necessary by the statute to be used by the authorities in laying out a sewer, yet there must be such a laying out before any assessment therefor can be made; and this must be done with sufficient precision to show what the sewer is, or is to be, for which parties are liable to be assessed, or for the construction of which their estates may receive damage.

The authority of the selectmen of a town to keep a record of their proceedings carries with it the right to amend such record at a subsequent date.

While, ordinarily, the laying out of a sewer by the town authorities should be made before any work is done, yet if a sewer be actually constructed and completed without a formal previous order, there is no reason why. it may not then be formally laid out and appropriate proceedings be had thereafter in regard to assessments.

No previous notice to parties in interest is required in order to lay out a sewer.

The town laid out and built a sewer in the street on which defendant's property was situated, and subsequently, but before any assessment was laid, adopted a general system of sewerage. The expense of the sewer first constructed was included in the cost of the general system, which increased defendant's assessment beyond his proportional share of the cost of the first sewer.

Held, that the action of the town was lawful, no assessment having been laid for the particular sewer, at the time of adopting the general system.

A warrant, by virtue of which real estate is sold for an assessment, is not invalid because it fails to direct the collector how to dispose of the money when received.

Writ of entry to recover possession of premises in Leominster, sold by the collector of taxes for Leominster for the non-payment of an assessment made for the construction of a sewer.

The case was heard upon an agreed statement of facts. Judgment was entered for the defendant in the Superior Court, and the demandant appealed.

H. Mayo for demandant.

G. A. Torrey and *C. W. Carter* for defendant.

DEVENS, J.—The plaintiffs seek to recover certain demanded premises which were sold by the collec- FAOTS. tor of taxes for Leominster, for the non-payment of an assessment, laid thereon by the selectmen of Leominster, for the construction of a sewer. Their title depends upon the validity of this assessment and of the proceedings had to enforce the same. While no particular form of words is made necessary by the statute to be used by the authorities in laying out a sewer, yet there must be such a laying out MODE OF LAYING before any assessment therefor can be made, and OUT SEWER. this must be done with sufficient precision to show what the sewer is, or is to be, for which parties are liable to be

assessed, or from the construction of which their estates
may, to some extent, receive damage. Bennett *v*. New Bedford, 110 Mass. 433; Sheehan *v*. Fitchburg, 131 Id. 525.
There can be no doubt but the record accurately states the
action of the selectmen at their meeting on July 29, 1880, and
had it been actually made on the date which it bears it would
have constituted a sufficient laying out of the sewer in question. It was, in fact, recorded at a subsequent date, by the
authority of the selectmen who had passed it, who still continued in office and had the custody of the records, although
some seven months had elapsed. An accident, such as occurred by the failure to record the vote at the time, should
not deprive the town of its rights, when the means existed
AMENDMENT OF of correcting it and were within the reach of the
TOWN RECORD. tribunal whose proceedings were defectively recorded. The authority to keep a record carries with it the
right to amend it, otherwise the rule which excludes evidence to control a record would often work great injustice.
It has, therefore, been often exercised after a great lapse of
time. Batty *v*. Fitch, 11 Gray, 184; Winchester *v*. Thayer,
129 Mass. 129; Halleck *v*. Boylston, 117 Id. 469. Nor could
the rights of the land-owner have been in any way prejudiced
so far as the assessment made upon him was concerned. All
his right to contest the assessment were preserved, if he was
dissatisfied therewith. He was entitled to appeal to a jury
for a revision of the assessment within three months after
receiving notice of it, and such notice was not given until a
long time after the actual laying out. Pub. Stat., chap. 50,
§ 6.

But, if the vote of July 29, 1880, be held defective, either
from failure to then record the same, or for any other reason,
the laying out of February 21, 1881, actually established it.
ESTABLISHMENT On that day, which was the day when the record
OF SEWER HELD
SUFFICIENT. was actually made, and undoubtedly with the
view, should their former proceedings prove defective, of
remedying the defect, the selectmen passed a vote, which
was recorded, laying it out as then actually constructed.
While ordinarily a laying out should be made before any
work is done, and sometimes necessarily so, where incidental
injury is liable to be done to abutting estates, for the protection of the selectmen or their servants, yet, if a sewer be

actually constructed and completed without a formal previous order, there is no reason why it may not then be formally
laid out and appropriate proceedings be had thereafter in
regard to assessments upon those who receive benefit therefrom, or damages to those whose estates are injured thereby.
These may often be ascertained at that time most conven-
iently and accurately, and no previous notice to parties in
interest is required in order to lay out a sewer. Allen *v.*
Charleston, 111 Mass. 123.

Assuming that there was a valid laying out of the sewer,
we must consider whether there was a valid assessment upon
the defendant, as the owner of an estate abutting VALIDITY OF
SEWER ASSESS-
on the street through which it passed. The town MENT.
had not, when the sewer was laid out, whether by the earlier
or later order, or when it was built, adopted any system of
sewerage, although it was then authorized to do so. Stat.
1878, chap. 232, § 3; Stat. 1879, chap. 55; Pub. Stat., chap.
50, § 7. Before any assessment was laid, it did adopt such a
system under the existing statute, which provided, that assessments might be made upon the owners of estates within
the territory for which the system was adopted, by a fixed
uniform rate, based upon the estimated average cost of all
the sewers therein, according to the frontage of such estates
on any street or way where a sewer is constructed. The
sum assessed to those whose estates abutted on this sewer
was more than the cost of this particular sewer, and the
assessment was made under the system thus adopted. It
was not for a proportional part of the sewer, which had been
constructed, but according to the uniform rate which had
been determined upon for the sewerage territory. It is the
contention of the defendant that this could not properly have
been done; that the liability to which his estate was subjected when the laying out took place was an incumbrance
thereon for its proportional share of the expense of constructing that particular sewer, under Pub. Stat., chap. 50,
§ 4; Gen. Stat., chap. 48, § 4: Stat. 1878, chap. 231, § 2, which
could not thereafter be increased or differently assessed, by
including it in a sewerage territory by a system subsequently
adopted. The liability to assessment is certainly an incum
brance upon the abutting estate, where the sewer is laid out,
although its amount cannot be ascertained. Carr *v.* Dooley,

119 Mass. 294. As the law existed, the town might lawfully provide for a system of sewerage and prescribe the territory to which it should be applicable.   It could incorporate therein this sewer and make the expense of constructing it a part of the expense to be provided for under that system. If, before any assessment was made, it determined to adopt a general system, it might properly do so.   Whatever system it might lawfully adopt the defendant's estate was subjected to it.   It is suggested that Pub. Stat., chap. 50, § 7, which accurately restates Stat. 1878, chap. 232, § 3, and Stat. 1879, chap. 55, applies' only to those persons described in Pub. Stat., chap. 50, § 4, who enter their drains into the sewer, or by more remote means receive benefit thereby.   But its meaning is, that assessments such as are made under section 4 shall be made upon the owners of estates within the sewerage territory, according to fixed uniform rates, as are therein provided for.   The last clause of section 7, which provides that no assessment shall be made where " by reason of its grade, level or for any other cause," it is impossible to drain an estate into the sewer, sufficiently shows that in all other cases the assessment is to be laid.

It is further contended by the defendant that, even if the system of the sewerage might have been adopted by the town subsequently to the laying out of this sewer, and an COLLECTOR'S   assessment made thereunder for its cost, this as- WARRANT NEED NOT SHOW DIS- sessment does not appear to have been laid in POSITION OF MONEY.   accordance with this system.   In form the order states that the assessment is laid upon the abutters, " as their proportional part of the charges of making and repairing the main drain and common sewer, constructed by said town in Main Street."   These assessments, when added together, exceed the whole cost of the particular sewer.   The order sufficiently shows that the assessment is based on the estimated average cost of all the sewers in the territory, according to the number of feet of frontage of their estates thereon, and that it was for the defendants' proportional part, as thus ascertained, that the assessment was made upon his estate. The defendant further contends that the warrant of the collector, by virtue of which he sold this estate, was informal, illegal, and did not authorize him to sell the estate.   Chapter 50, section 5, prescribes that the sale of an estate " shall be

conducted in like manner as sales for the payment of taxes."
The warrant should properly state what the collector is to
do, and the preliminary steps to be taken by him in the collection of the assessment. Pub. Stat., chap. 11, § 63. The
assessment was made by the selectmen on July 19, 1881, and
the warrant issued and signed by the selectmen, referring to
a copy of it, simply directs the collector to collect it, according to law. But while the warrant is thus brief, every preliminary step, as well as the sale itself, was made in conformity with that which was the legal power and duty of the
collector. The defendant does not suggest a failure in any
respect. Its defects were those of omission, King *v.* Whit-
comb, 1 Metc. 328 ; Barnard *v.* Graves. 13 Id. 85. Nor is the
warrant, in the case at bar, invalid, because it failed to direct
the collector how to dispose of the money when he received
it. He executed the warrant as a valid process, received
the money under it, by virtue of his office, and he cannot
deny his liability to the town for it.

Judgment for demandant.

GENET, Appellant,

v.

THE CITY OF BROOKLYN, Respondent.

(99 *New York Reports,* 296.)

The provisions of the statutes in reference to street-openings in the city
of Brooklyn (chap. 384, Laws of 1854 ; chap. 63, Laws of 1862; chap. 631,
Laws of 1868) contemplate and authorize the application of assessments
for benefits upon residues of lots, parts of which are taken for a street improvement in reduction of awards for the parts taken, and that the liability
of the city shall be limited to the excess of award over assessment; but in
ascertaining such liability, each lot or parcel is to be separately considered,
so that an assessment on one lot may not be applied to reduce an award
in respect to another, where they are separately valued and assessed,
although both are owned by the same person.

The authority thus given to reduce an award, by an assessment for benefit on the residue of the same lot, is not in conflict with the constitutional
prohibition against taking private property for public use without just
compensation. State Const., art. 1, § 6.

It does not render the act obnoxious to the constitutional provision that

by it the fixing of the district of assessment and the assessment for benefits are distinct proceedings, conducted by different bodies, or because it
requires the commissioners of estimate and assessment to assess the whole
expense of the improvement upon the district of assessment fixed by the
park commissioners.

The fact that the act of 1868 for the widening of Sackett and other
streets in the city of Brooklyn (chap. 631, Laws of 1868) requires the commissioners therein named, before an assessment is made, to fix a district of
assessment to which the assessment shall be limited, and that the whole
expense, including the damage to landowners, shall be assessed upon the
lands embraced in the district, making the assessment relatively equal as
between the different parcels of land, and may not limit the assessment to
the actual benefit to each parcel, and then authorizes an assessment to be
applied in satisfaction of an award for a portion of the lot taken for the
improvement, does not render the act obnoxious to said constitutional
provision. The assessment authorized is an exercise of the legislative
right of taxation, all the incidents of which are within the control of the
legislature, and in respect to which its determination is final, and the
application of the sum assessed in satisfaction of an award for land taken
is just compensation within the meaning of the Constitution.

APPEAL from decision of the General Term of the Supreme
Court, in the second judicial department, entered upon an
order made December 8, 1884.

This action was brought by plaintiff as grantee and assignee
of one Davis to have certain assessments for the widening of
Sackett street, in the city of Brooklyn, upon lands conveyed
by said Davis, set aside as illegal and void ; or, in case the
validity of the assessment should be sustained, to recover the
amount of certain awards made to said Davis for lands taken
for said improvement.

The material facts are stated in the opinion.

George C. Genet, appellant, in person.

John A. Taylor for respondent.

Joshua M. Van Cott for intervenors.

ANDREWS, J.—The act (chapter 631 of the Laws of 1868) for
the widening of portions of Sackett and other streets in the
FACTS.　　city of Brooklyn defined the land to be taken for
the improvement, and appropriated it for public use. It made
provision for the appointment of commissioners to estimate
and ascertain the expense of the improvement and the damages sustained by the landowners for the lands taken, and
also for the apportionment and assessment of such damages

and expenses upon a limited assessment area to be fixed by the commissioners of Prospect Park. (§§ 4 and 5.) It provided that the proceedings subsequent to the appointment of commissioners of estimate should be governed by the laws then in force relating to street-openings in the city of Brooklyn, so far as they were not inconsistent with the act. (§ 7.) There was no express provision embodied in the act itself for paying the landowners for the lands taken. But the duty of payment was cast upon the city by force of section 16 of the fourth title of the charter of 1854, which was incorporated into the act of 1868 by force of the seventh section. This was expressly adjudged in the case of Sage *v.* Brooklyn, 89 N. Y. 189.

There are two questions upon the determination of which this case depends, not involved, or at least not decided, in Sage *v.* Brooklyn. The plaintiff sues to recover from the city of Brooklyn the sum of $9576, being the aggregate damages sustained by his predecessor in title and interest by the taking for the improvement of a part of several city lots owned by him, embraced in a single tract, as estimated by the commissioners of estimate appointed under the act, whose report was confirmed November 24, 1869. Each lot was separately described and numbered in the report, and the value of the part taken from each was separately stated. The same commissioners who estimated the damages, after their report thereon was confirmed, proceeded, in pursuance of the further authority conferred by the act, to assess the expense of the improvement upon the property benefited within the district of assessment. They separately assessed the residue of each of the lots above referred to—that is, the part of each lot not taken for the improvement—for benefits. The assessment for benefit on such residues in some cases exceeded and in other cases was less than the damages previously awarded for the parts taken. The commissioners' report of assessments was tabulated as required by section 15 of the charter of 1854 as amended by chapter 63 of the Laws of 1862, and in their report the commissioners stated in respect to each lot of which a part had been taken, the amount awarded for damages for the part so taken, the assessment for benefit on the residue, and the balance of award over assessment, or of assessment over award, as the case might be. In respect to five lots, the

awards exceeded the assessments thereon in the sum of about
$1035; and in respect to five other lots the assessments exceeded
the awards by about the sum of $1020.   The final report of
the commissioners was confirmed February 28, 1870.

The two questions to be determined are, first, whether, by
the true construction of the statute of 1868, a landowner,
part of whose land was taken for the improvement, is entitled to recover the whole sum estimated by the commissioners in their first report as his damages for the land taken,
or only the balance of award over assessment stated in their
final report; and whether, in the case of several lots owned
by the same person, but treated in the proceedings as distinct and separate parcels in respect to some of which the
assessment exceeds the award, and in others the award exceeds the assessment, the city is entitled to have the balances each way aggregated and set off the one against the
other.   The other question is, whether the scheme of the
statute for ascertaining and providing compensation to the
landowners satisfies the constitutional provision and guaranty that private property shall not be taken for public use
without just compensation.   (Const., art. 1, § 6.)

The general scheme of street-openings in the city of Brooklyn seems to contemplate that assessments for benefits upon
residues of lots, part of which are taken for the improvement,
shall be applied to reduce and limit the awards for the parts
taken, and that the liability of the city to pay awards to the
landowner in such cases shall be limited to the excess of
award over assessment; but that in ascertaining such liability
each lot or parcel is to be separately considered, so that an
assessment on one lot will not reduce an award in respect to
another lot, although both lots may be owned by the same
person.   By the charter of 1854 (Laws of 1854, chap. 384),
power was conferred on the common council to cause streets
and avenues to be opened under certain limitations, and to
fix a district of assessment.   The act provided for the appointment of commissioners of estimate and assessment, and
it was made their duty to ascertain the damages for land
taken, and to assess the expenses of the improvement upon
the land embraced in the district of assessment according to
benefit.   (Tit. 4, §§ 3 and 6.)   The commissioners were required to designate in their report the pieces of land to be

taken by the map number, and any residues; the pieces assessed for benefits; the names of the persons interested in the property taken or assessed; the awards made; the amount assessed on each piece of land, and the balance of award over assessment, or of assessment over award in each case. (§ 7.) In case part only of the land of any person should be taken, the residue was subject to assessment for benefit (§ 9), and it was provided that when only a part was required, the excess of damages for the part taken over the assessment for benefit on the residue " shall be assessed and be a lien on other lands and premises according to the estimated benefit to be derived by them from the improvements." Upon the final confirmation of the report of the commissioners, the common council was authorized to cause the improvement to be made (§ 15), and by section 16 it was made the duty of the comptroller to pay to the persons to whom damages were awarded in the report of the commissioners the amount of such SET-OFF OF damages, without deduction by way of " fee or BENEFITS AGAINST AWARD. commissions." These provisions in the act of 1854 plainly indicate that it was the intention that the assessment on the residue of a lot, for benefit, should be applied by the commissioners in reduction of the estimated value of the part taken, and that the award to be paid by the city, under section 16, was the balance remaining after such application. It was to accomplish this purpose that the statute required that the balances to be received and to be paid, respectively, should be stated by the commissioners in their report. Any other construction would leave the act incomplete, since by the tenth section it is only the excess of damages which is to be assessed and which is made a lien upon other lands and premises. The amendment of 1862 (Laws of 1862, chap. 63) separated the functions of the commissioners of estimate and assessment, which, under the charter of 1854, as has been seen, were united in the same persons. By the amendment the damages for land taken were to be ascertained by commissioners, and the assessment was to be made by the board of assessors. (§§ 14, 17.) But the provision for ascertaining and stating balances was preserved, that duty being devolved upon the assessors, and it was only upon confirmation of their report that the rights of landowners to awards became fixed. There was no departure in the act of 1868,

under which the proceedings in question were taken, from
the policy of the Charter Acts, that awards should be reduced
and limited by assessments on residues. Under the act of
1868, both awards and assessments were to be made by the
same commissioners as under the charter of 1854, but the
awards were to precede the assessment. The expense of the
improvement was to be determined before the assessment
should be made. After the report of the commissioners estimating the expense of the improvement and the damages of
the landowners had been made and confirmed, the same
commissioners were then to proceed to make the assessment,
and in making their assessment and report, the provisions of
the Charter Acts are to govern when not inconsistent with
the act of 1868. The form of the report, including the stating
of balances, is governed by the Charter Acts, and the same
policy of reducing awards by assessments is by force of the
seventh section applied to proceedings under the act of 1868.
It is insisted by the counsel for the plaintiff, and it is conceded
by the counsel for the city of Brooklyn, that under the
Improvement Acts an assessment is not a personal charge
against the owner of the land, and is enforceable only by a
proceeding *in rem* against the land assessed. The exemption
of the owner of land from personal liability for an assessment
does not, however, conflict with the policy of charging
against an award an assessment against a residue. An
assessment for benefit proceeds on the assumption that the
land assessed is increased in value by the improvement, and
the extinguishment of the award in whole or in part by the
assessment relieves the land assessed from the burden of the
assessment. In theory the cancelled assessment is the exact
equivalent of the amount by which the award is reduced.
But we think the court below erred in aggregating the balances of awards and the balances of assessments, and offset-
ting the one aggregate against the other. The lots were separately valued and separately assessed. In cases where the
assessment exceeds the award, the owner may prefer that the
land should be sold for the assessment rather than pay the
lien. This, we think, he has the right to do. The statute only
contemplates the reduction of an award by an assessment
when both relate to the same lot, and the balance is to be
ascertained and struck by the commissioners and embodied

in their report. The plaintiff was not personally bound to pay the assessments, and no general right of set-off is given by the act, and in the absence of a statutory provision we perceive no equity upon which such right can rest. See Hatch *v.* Mayor, etc., 82 N. Y. 436.

The constitutional objection is based upon the claim that the authority given to the commissioners of as- SAME   HELD "JUST"   COM- sessment by the act of 1868, to reduce the award PENSATION. for the land taken, by the assessment for benefit on the residue of the same lot or parcel, is not just compensation within the constitutional requirement. It is not claimed that actual benefit to a residue of land owned by a person whose land has been taken in part for a local improvement may not, if the legislature so direct, be set off against the value of the land taken, and the money payment limited to the balance of the award remaining after such application. This course has been sanctioned by a uniform course of legislative and judicial precedent, commencing at an early period. By the Street Opening Act relating to the city of New York, re-enacted in the Revised Laws of 1813 (2 R. L. 408) it was provided (§ 178) that the commissioners of estimate and assessment shall proceed to make a just and equitable assessment of the loss or damage to any person by reason of the taking of land, over and above the benefit or advantage, or of the benefit and advantage over and above the loss and damage, and that the commissioners "should estimate and report the excess and surplus only of the said loss and damage over and above the value of said benefit and advantage, as and for the compensation and recompense to such owner or owners for his loss or damage, etc., and for relinquishing the said lands," etc. The validity of the mode of compensation provided by this act was considered in the case of Livingston *v.* Mayor, etc., 8 Wend. 85, and the decision in that case has been frequently approved. People *v.* Mayor, etc., 4 N. Y. 435; Betts *v.* Williamsburg, 15 Barb. 255; L. I. R. R. Co. *v.* Bennett, 10 Hun, 91. The principle of the New York act has been incorporated into very many of the acts subsequently passed authorizing the laying out and opening of streets in cities and villages. But the particular point of objection now made is that the statute of 1868 does not limit the reduction of the award by the actual estimated benefit resulting from the improvement to the lands of the owner other than those taken, but that under the scheme of the statute the assessment for benefit may exceed the actual, intrinsic benefit to the land assessed, and it is claimed that a law permitting an award to be reduced by the deduction of such arbritrary sum, not measured by actual benefit, does not provide just compensation within the purview of the Constitution. The facts upon which the argument proceeds may be briefly stated. The act requires the commissioners of Prospect park, before any assessment is made, to fix a district of assessment, beyond which the act declares the assessment shall not extend. (§ 5.) The whole expense of the improvement is to be estimated by the commissioners of estimate and assessment, including the damage to the landowners. (§ 16.) When this estimate is made and confirmed, the commissioners of estimate and assessment are then required to assess the amount so ascertained upon the lands embraced in the district of assessment which they deem benefited by the improvement, and as they shall deem just and equitable. (Id.) The argument is that under this plan the whole expense must be assessed upon the lands embraced in the assessment district fixed by the park commissioners, although the aggregate benefit to such lands from the improvement may not, in fact, or in the judgment of the commissioners of assessment, equal the aggregate expense; the only duty resting upon the commissioners being to make the assessment relatively equal and just as between the different parcels in the assessment district. So, as is claimed, it may result that the assessment on each parcel may exceed the actual benefit thereto. It is insisted that the reduction of an award by applying thereon an assessment not measured by actual benefit is not just compensation.

We think the argument fails in omitting to separate the two powers exercised by the legislature in framing the act of 1868, viz., the power of taxation, and the right of eminent domain. The constitutional requirement that just compensation shall be made for lands taken for public use must be absolutely performed, and a mere colorable compliance will not satisfy the constitutional guaranty. The right to compensation is the right of the citizen whose land is taken, which the legislature can neither ignore nor deny. The power of taxation on the other hand is vested in the legislature and is practically absolute, except as restrained by constitutional limitations. The power of taxation being legislative, all the incidents are within the control of the legislature. The purposes for which a tax shall be levied; the extent of taxation; the apportionment of the tax; upon what property or class of persons the tax shall operate; whether the tax shall be general or limited to a particular locality, and in the latter case the fixing of a district of assessment; the method of collection, and whether the tax shall be a charge upon both person and property, or only on the land, are matters within the discretion of the legislature and in respect to which its determination is final. Livingston *v.* Mayor, etc., *supra;* People *v.* Mayor, etc., 4 N. Y. 419; Thomas *v.* Leland, 24 Wend. 65; Town of Guilford *v.* Sup'rs of Chenango, 13 N. Y. 143; *In re* Church, 92 Id. 1.

There is no constitutional guaranty that taxation shall be just and equal, although a law plainly departing from the principle of equality in the distribution of public burdens would be justly obnoxious, as contrary to natural equity and as practical confiscation; but the remedy must ordinarily be found in an appeal to the justness of the legislature. The principle of local assessments for public municipal improvements has been recognized and applied during the whole history of the State, although its absolute justice has been sometimes questioned. The legislature may itself fix a district of assessment, or the power may be delegated by the supreme legislative body to the authorities of subordinate political and municipal divisions, or other official agencies, as may also the incidents of the power, such as the apportionment and distribution of the tax, as between the persons and property upon which it is laid. The learned counsel for the intervenors is compelled to admit that the legislature may distribute the burden of public improvements on its own notions of policy, its own sense of justice, and its own assumptions of benefit.

The imposition of local assessments for benefits is an exercise of the taxing power (People *v.* Brooklyn, *supra;* Matter of Van Antwerp, 56 N. Y. 261; Litchfield *v.* Vernon, 41 Id. 123), and it is clear that the legislature may, in its discretion, make assessments a personal charge against the owners of the land assessed, and impose upon them the duty of payment. The assessment district, under the act of 1868, was fixed by

the park commissioners, under its authority ; and although the
act does not in terms require them to include therein all the
property which, in their judgment, would be specially benefited by the improvement, this is the fair intendment.   In executing this authority the commissioners may have erred in
judgment, as the legislature might have done if it had itself
defined the district of assessment.   But the judgment of the
commissioners was final, unless it was subject to revision in a
direct proceeding in review, as to which it is not necessary to
inquire.   The assessments imposed upon the lands of the
plaintiff's grantor, was, as has been said, a tax, and represented the proportion of the aggregate sum which, in the
judgment of the commissioners exercising by delegation the
power to distribute the tax, should be charged upon the several parcels as their respective contributions to the aggregate
expense.   Assuming that the charge exceeded the benefit, it
was nevertheless made under the authority and direction of
the legislature in the exercise of an undoubted legislative
power, and it cannot be invalidated by proof that the charge
was unjust or unequal, or even arbitrary.   Bringing together,
then, the two proceedings under the act of 1868, we are of
opinion that there is no constitutional objection to a legislative direction setting off against an award made to an individual for lands taken for public use an assessment for benefit
against his other lands made in the same proceeding.   The
act provides in the first instance, for the ascertainment,
through constitutional commissioners, of the full value of the
land taken.   It next provides for the assessment by the same
commissioners, acting as representatives of the taxing power,
of the whole expense of the improvement upon a limited district, defined by the commissioners of Prospect Park.   There
can be no doubt that the assessment, when made, became a
valid charge on the lands assessed.   It was competent for the
legislature to have made the owners personally liable for the
assessment.   It did not adopt this general policy.   But in respect to the owners of lands taken, and also of lands assessed,
it declared, in substance, that the claim for compensation, ascertained in the mode defined by the Constitution, should be
satisfied in whole or *pro tanto* by the satisfaction, in the manner pointed out by the statute, of a valid and legal charge for
benefit imposed upon his other lands.   This, we think, was

just compensation within the principle of Livingston *v.* Mayor, etc., *supra*, and the cases following it. If there is any departure from sound principle in the method of adjusting compensation provided in the act of 1868, it is sanctioned by a long line of legislative and judicial precedents which the court is not at liberty to disregard.

There are no other questions which require particular notice. The result is that the judgment should be reversed for the error of the court below in aggregating the balances and setting off the one aggregate against the other. The subtractions in the copy of the tabulated report, as printed, seem to be inaccurate. Upon a new trial the parties will have an opportunity to correct any amendable error in the computation.

All concur, except MILLER and DANFORTH, JJ., not voting.

Judgment reversed.

COHEN

v.

CITY OF CLEVELAND.

(Advance Case, Ohio. April 28, 1885.)

Under the Acts of 1872 and 1876, 69 Ohio L. 138; 73 Ohio L. 107; 3 R. S. 616, 617, a viaduct 64 feet wide, with a level roadway, was constructed in Cleveland across the Cuyahoga River. On the south side of Superior Street, between Water Street and the river, a distance of 768 feet, the city condemned a strip of ground and the viaduct was constructed over that strip and over a part of Superior Street, about 37 feet being over the strip opposite Cohen's premises, and the balance over the street; so that, in effect, Superior Street, which was 93 feet wide, is reduced in width between Water Street and the river, and opposite Cohen's premises its present width is 66 feet. The elevation of the roadway of the viaduct above Superior Street gradually increases from Water Street to the river, and opposite the premises of Cohen, which are on the north side of Superior Street, midway between Water Street and the river, the elevation is 45 feet; and it is alleged that the viaduct diverts travel from that part of Superior Street, impairs the light and air to Cohen's premises, causes noise and the jarring of his house day and night, and has impaired the value of his property and reduced its rental value.

Held: 1. The viaduct is a lawful structure.

2. On proof of the alleged injury, Cohen is entitled to damages.

3. Cohen is not owner of a lot "bounding or abutting upon the proposed improvement," within the meaning of the Municipal Code, sec. 564;
R. S. sec. 2315, and hence it was not necessary for him to file a claim for
damages under that section.

ERROR to the District Court of Cuyahoga County.

G. E. & J. J. Herrick and W. S. Collins for plaintiff in error.
John F. Weh for defendant in error.

OKEY, J.—Elias Cohen, on August 30, 1879, brought suit
FACTS.   in the Court of Common Pleas of Cuyahoga
County against the city of Cleveland for injuries to his
real estate, which it is alleged he sustained by reason of
the construction of a bridge, commonly called the viaduct,
across the Cuyahoga River.   An answer and a reply were
filed, and on the trial testimony was offered to show that the
plaintiff was entitled to a verdict; but it appearing that the
plaintiff had filed no claim for damages in accordance with
the Municipal Code, sec. 564, 66 Ohio L. 245 ; 75 Ohio L.
324; R. S. sec. 2315, the court, in effect, directed a verdict
against him, which was returned accordingly. Judgment
was rendered on the verdict, and the District Court having
affirmed the judgment, this petition in error was filed to reverse as well the judgment of the Court of Common Pleas
as that of the District Court.

The city of Cleveland, situated upon Lake Erie, is divided
by the Cuyahoga River, which runs north to the lake.
Superior Street, for more than sixty years one of the principal thoroughfares of the place, extends westerly to the
river, crossing Water Street, which is parallel with the river,
and distant about 768 feet therefrom.   Midway between
Water Street and the river the premises of Cohen are situated.   His lot, fronting twenty-two and one half feet on the
street, has a depth of ninety feet, and his house is a three-
story brick with stone basement.   The street at this point is
ninety-three feet wide.   At the time the alleged grievance
was committed, Cohen was, and he continued to be, sole
owner of the premises, and in possession.

The viaduct is a magnificent structure, extending from
Water Street, above mentioned, to Pearl Street near its
junction with Dayton Street, on the other side of the river,
and its roadway is nearly level.   Its width is sixty-four feet,

and it is so constructed as to accommodate travel of every sort. In order to construct this work, the city condemned a strip of ground on the south side of Superior Street, extending from Water Street to the river, and the viaduct covers that strip, to the width of thirty-seven feet opposite Cohen's premises, and also covers part of Superior Street, such part opposite Cohen's premises being twenty-seven feet in width on the south side of the street. The elevation from the roadway of the viaduct to the surface of Superior Street gradually increases from Water Street to the river, and in front of Cohen's property the elevation is forty-five feet.

The viaduct was constructed in 1877 and 1878, and the authority for building it is found in the Act of 1872, 69 Ohio L. 138; 3 R. S. 616, and the Act of 1876, 73 Ohio L. 107; 3 R. S. 617.

These acts are supplementary to the Municipal Code; no objection which has been urged against their validity in this case is tenable; and, in our judgment, those acts in connection with the Municipal Code contain ample power for the erection of such structure. Hence, the viaduct cannot be, in contemplation of law, a nuisance, but is a lawful structure; and there is no complaint that there was negligence, malice, or bad faith which caused injury to the plaintiff.

But the right of Cohen to damages is not determined adversely to him by these facts. He is not entitled to compensation under the letter of the Constitution, article 1, section 19, but may be entitled to such compensation in COMPENSATION analogy to that provision. Injuries resulting from TO ABUTTER ON VIADUCT. the change of established grades in streets, though made in accordance with the statute and without negligence or malice, and other injuries of a kindred character, have been held to afford ground for the recovery of damages against municipal corporations. Rhodes *v.* Cleveland, 10 Ohio, 159; McComb *v.* Akron, 15 Ohio, 479; s. c., *sub nom.* Akron *v.* McComb, 18 Ohio, 229; s. c., 51 Am. Dec. 453; Crawford *v.* Del., 7 Ohio St. 459; Youngstown *v.* Moore, 30 Ohio St. 133; Keating *v.* Cincinnati, 38 Ohio St. 141; and see Little Miami R. R. Co. *v.* Naylor, 2 Ohio St. 235; Street R. R. Co. *v.* Cumminsville, 14 Ohio St. 523; Richard *v.* Cincinnati, 31 Ohio St. 506; Story *v.* N. Y. Elevated R. R. Co., 90 N. Y. 122.

This court has, however, constantly acknowledged that

McComb *v.* Akron, and cases following it, is a departure from the current of authority elsewhere ; and although these cases have not found favor with the Judges delivering the opinions in Radcliff *v.* Brooklyn, 4 N. Y. 95 ; s. c., 53 Am. Dec. 357, 366 *n.*; Hill *v.* Boston, 122 Mass. 344, 378 ; Alexander *v.* Milwaukee, 16 Wis. 247, 256 ; Transportation Co. *v.* Chicago, 99 U. S. 635 (XXV. Law. ed. 336), we are entirely content with the doctrine, and would not change it if we could.

But the justice of the Ohio rule, the firmness with which it has been adhered to for nearly half a century, and the manner in which it is recognized and enforced in our statutes, have established the doctrine as a rule of property, and it is now too late to inquire whether McComb *v.* Akron was properly decided. In other States, the same rule is, in part or wholly, adopted by constitutional or statutory provision.

If we look alone to the allegations in the plaintiff's petition, and the facts which the evidence tended to establish in his favor, a far stronger ground of recovery was shown than in either of the Ohio cases cited. We have seen that the roadway of the viaduct, in front of Cohen's premises, is forty-five feet above the surface of Superior Street ; and it is averred, and there was evidence given tending to show, that the viaduct, to some extent, shuts out light and air from his premises ; that, by reason of the viaduct, dust and other obnoxious substances are constantly thrown on the premises of plaintiff, and on persons passing along the street ; that there is constant noise and jarring his premises, day and night, by reason of travel on the viaduct ; that the viaduct has diverted travel from that part of Superior Street between Water Street and the river ; and that, by reason of the premises, the value of the plaintiff's property and his rents have been reduced one half. True, evidence was offered by the city, tending to show there was no ground of recovery and, therefore, it was for the jury to determine in whose favor the evidence preponderated. But while the title to the street is in the city, it must be remembered that the abutting owner has a special interest in the street, which the law will not only recognize, but protect. The court below seemed to recognize this view as correct, but the learned judge who presided at the trial virtually directed a verdict for the defendant, as already stated, upon the ground that plaintiff had failed to comply with the Municipal Code, sec. 564, R. Stats. sec. 2315, and the question before us is whether, in so directing the jury, there was error.

Section 564 was as follows: "Any owner or owners of lots or lands bounding or abutting upon the proposed improvement, claiming damages therefor, shall file a claim, in writing, with the clerk of the corporation, setting forth the amount of damages claimed, together with a description of the property owned for which the claim is made, within two weeks after the expiration of the time required for the publication of said notice; and all such owners as shall fail or neglect to file their claim for damages aforesaid, within the time aforesaid, shall be deemed to have waived the same, and be forever barred from filing any claim or receiving any damages therefor." Section 575 of the same code, R. S. sec. 2326, provided: "No claimant for damages shall commence any suit until he shall have filed a claim therefor with the clerk of the corporation, and sixty days shall have elapsed thereafter to enable such corporation to appoint assessors to assess such damages, return the same to the proper officers, and sufficient further time shall have elapsed, not exceeding twenty days after the return of such appraisal, to enable the corporation to pay the assessment." In the Act of 1872, 69 Ohio L. 138; 3 R. S. 616, providing for the construction of the viaduct, it is provided, section 2, that "Owners of land or property of any kind, and lessees of said canal, claiming damages therefor, shall file a claim therefor in writing with the clerk of the corporation, as required by section 544 of said Act; and said claims for damages shall be determined, and said work shall be done, in accordance with the provisions of the Act to which this is supplementary, in so far as the same may be applicable."

Manifestly, there is a mistake in the figures "544," as that section of the Municipal Code has no relation to filing claims, while section 564, as we have seen, does provide for filing such claims. Perhaps if that section alone made provision on the subject, we would have no difficulty in agreeing with the defendant that it was intended; People *v.* King, 28 Cal. 265; Tappan *v.* Tappan, 6 Ohio St. 64; Jenks *v.* Langdon, 21 Ohio St. 362; Com. *v.* Marshall, 69 Pa St. 328; Sedg. Con.

L. 2d ed. 354; Hard. Stats. 241, 247; but the difficulty is, that section 575, with which plaintiff complied, provides for filing claims as well as section 564, and the plaintiff, conceding the mistake, insists that section 575 was intended, and not section 564. The difference between the sections, it will be seen, is marked. The former section, 575, is much broader than the latter, 564, and embraces not only the cases provided for by section 564, but apparently all claims arising from improvements; possibly others. But failure to comply with section 564, where that section is applicable, is a bar to any action; while failure to comply with section 575, though it would defeat the pending action, would not be a bar to another suit based on a claim properly filed under that section subsequently to the first suit.

If we were required to determine whether section 564 or section 575 was intended by the figures 544 in the Act of 1872, the case would not be free from difficulty. Much may be said in favor of either construction. We are of the opinion we need not determine the question. Let it be conceded that section 564 was intended. Then we are of opinion that the case would not have been different so far as lot owners are concerned, if section 564 had been in terms incorporated into the Act of 1872, instead of such reference to section 564, if that be the section, and hence only the owners of lots bounding or abutting upon the proposed improvement, were required to give such notice. No doubt many houses are on substantially the same plane as the roadway of the viaduct, and the real estate on which they are built are lots "bounding or abutting upon the proposed improvement;" but is that WHETHER LOT true of the premises of Cohen? We are clear WAS "BOUNDED OR ABUTTING ON that it is not. The street, as we have seen, is in PROPOSED IM- PROVEMENT," front of his house, forty-five feet below the road-CONSIDERED. way of the viaduct. That structure has furnished a new route for travel, and has largely diverted travel from that part of Superior Street, and if Cohen desires to cross the viaduct, he must travel nearly one hundred and thirty yards to get upon it. In no just sense is his property a lot "bounding or abutting upon the proposed improvement." In reality, this was no more an improvement of Superior Street than an elevated railway is an improvement of a street, but the viaduct furnishes an additional and substantially ·

an exclusive route of travel to persons going across the river.

Doubtless, it is true, that the words bounding and abutting have no such in flexiblemeaning as to require the lots assessed or injured to touch the improvement, though the usual meaning of the words is that the things spoken of do actually adjoin. Without entering very much into the origin of the word abutting, it is sufficient to say that, according to Latham, it does not imply that the things spoken of are "necessarily in contact;" and to the same effect see Webster, Worcester and Murray. In ascertaining the meaning of such word, of course regard must be had to the intent of the law-maker, though it will be seen that the usual meaning conveyed is that the things spoken of touch or come together. Holt v. Somerville, 127 Mass. 408; Wakefield, etc., v. Mauder, 5 C. P. Div. 248.

So with the word bound. True, it was held in Richards v. Cincinnati, 31 Ohio St. 507, that "Where a strip of land ninety-one feet in width was dedicated for a street and the municipal authorities improved a street thereon, of the width of ninety feet, leaving one foot on one side thereof unused; except in sloping the embankments and excavations, the owners of property abutting on such foot of land are liable to be assessed as owners of property abutting on the improvement." In that case McIlvaine, J., said: "It seems to us that in order to exempt these proprietors from assessment as abuttors on the improvement, it must appear that this intervening foot of land deprives them of full, free and lawful access to the street improved; but such deprivation could result only when the right and exclusive use thereto have reverted to the original dedicators and their heirs. If the public right to its use still continues, or if the right to the strip has vested absolutely in the owners of lands abutting upon it; after abandonment by the public, then, in either case, their liability to assessment is certain. That this foot of land, before the improvement of the avenue, was subject to the use of the public, as part of a highway, is not disputed; and we are unable to find any ground upon which it can be held that such right in the public has terminated. The greater part, if not the whole of this strip, is utilized by the public in making slopes to embankments and excavations of the street; a use as important and germane to public travel and convenience as if located in the centre of the street." And see Fass *v.* Seehawer, 60 Wisc. 525.

It seems to us, a just consideration of this reasoning leads to the conclusion that property situated as the plaintiff's is, with respect to the viaduct, is not lands "bounding and abutting upon the proposed improvement," and that the court below erred in this respect. He is deprived, and in no merely technical sense, of the full, free and lawful use of Superior Street as it existed before the viaduct was constructed.

Judgment of the District Court and Court of Common Pleas reversed, and cause remanded to the Court of Common Pleas for a new trial.

PROPERTY AND "TAKING" THEREOF FOR PUBLIC USE.—Property is a right of ownership of any object. Sir G. C. Lewis, Use and Abuse of Political Terms, 170. It is the right to possess, use and enjoy it, Weynehamer *v.* People, 13 N. Y. 433, 1 Bl. Com. 138; to the exclusion of all others, Mills Em. Dom. 31; indefinite in point of user, 2 Austin Jur. 965; unrestricted in point of disposition and unlimited in point of duration, 2 Austin Jur. 817. The term property in the constitution includes a right of action for injuries to land proposed to be taken for public use. Morris *v.* Townsend, 24 Barb. 658. It also includes the following, none of which may be taken for public use without compensation :

A right of reversion, Heard *v.* Brooklyn, 60 N. Y. 242 ; a right to use water-power, Bank *v.* Roberts, 44 N. Y. 192; an easement over the land of another, People *v.* Haines, 49 N. Y. 587; Arnold *v.* Railroad Co., 55 N. Y. 661; the lien of a mortgage, Astor *v.* Hoyt, 5 Wend. 605; a riparian right to use running water, Gardner *v.* Newburgh, 2 Johns. Ch. 161 ; Yates *v.* Milwaukee, 10 Wall. 497; an easement of way over the road of a turnpike company, Troy, etc., Railroad Co. *v.* Turnpike Co., 16 Barb. 100; a corporate franchise, West Railroad Co. *v.* Dix, 6 How. 507; Richmond *v.* Railroad Co., 13 How. 71 ; a right in land subject to the easement of a public highway, Williams *v.* Railroad Co., 16 N. Y. 97 ; a contested claim to unliquidated damages, Erwin *v.* U. S., 97 U. S. 392.

In all the foregoing things their owners have property rights and interests which cannot be taken for public use without compensation being made therefor. And it goes almost without saying that lot-owners have rights of property in the streets adjacent to their lots, and any new burden, servitude, or use to which a street is subjected outside of its use as a public thoroughfare, which impairs or destroys such rights, is a taking of private property for which compensation must be made to such lot-owners. Instances of takings of private property for public use and for which compensation has been adjudged are, among others, the following :

Where an exclusive right to the franchise of taking toll is granted, the grant of a similar privilege to another is a taking, State *v.* Noyes, 47 Me. 189; a partial destruction or a diminution of value is a taking, Glover *v.* Powell, 10 N. J. Eq. 211; acquiring an easement to run on another's road, Jersey, etc., R. R. Co., 20 N. J. Eq. 61; the destruction by the State of a waterfall in a private stream, People *v.* Appraisers, 13 Wend. 355; changing a private into a public stream, Morgan *v.* Keeig, 35 N. Y. 454; digging a ditch by authority of the legislature on the land of a private person, People *v.* Nearing, 27 N. Y. 306; appropriating land by the public, allowing nothing for widow's dower. In matter, etc., 19 Wend. 678; laying gas pipes in country highway, 62 N. Y. 386; building sewer in city street, Kelsey *v.* King, 33 How. Pr. 39; interfering with use of shade trees on street, Village *v.* Richardson, 4 Lansing (N. Y.), 136; building railroad across a turnpike, Seneca *v.* Railroad Co., 5 Hill, 170; flooding land by excavating for a railway, so that the waters of a river ran through the cut upon adjoining farms, Robinson *v.* Railroad Co., 27 Barb. 512. See, also, Eaton *v.* Railroad Co., 51 N. H. 504; Story *v.* Elevated R. R. Co., 90 N. Y. 170.

Still other instances of the taking of private property for public use are these: By laying a rail for a street railway track within two or three feet of the sidewalk, Street Railroad Co. *v.* Cumminsville, 14 Ohio St. 543; changing easement for a canal into an easement for a railway, Hatch *v.* Railroad Co. 18 Ohio St. 92; building railroad on road owned by Turnpike Co., Railroad Co. *v.* Zinn, 18 Ohio St. 417; building railroad in public street, Railroad Co. *v.* Williams, 35 Ohio St. 169; Shurmeier *v.* Railroad Co., 10 Minn. 79; placing earth upon land to support an embankment, Dodson *v.* Cincinnati, 34 Ohio St. 276; cutting ditches in such a manner as to cause water to overflow and wash away land, Rhodes *v.* Cleveland, 10 Ohio, 159; People *v.* Haines, 49 N. Y. 587; building a house in a street, Corning *v.* Lawerse, 6 Johns. Ch. (N. Y.) 439; flowing or backing of water upon land, Hooker *v.* Canal Co., 14 Conn. 146; Pumpelly *v.* Green Bay Can. Co., 13 Wall. 166; Nevins *v.* Peoria, 41 Ill. 502; damaging mill privilege, Emporia *v.* Soden, 25 Kan. 588; an order permitting a plaintiff in proceedings to condemn land for a public use to enter into possession of the same during the pendency of the proceedings and until their conclusion, San Mateo Water Works Co. *v.* Sharpstein, 50 Cal. 284.

ENGLE

v.

SOHN & CO.

(41 *Ohio State,* 691.)

A person who purchases and slaughters hogs, for the purpose of adding to the value thereof by certain processes and combination with other materials,—whereby they are converted into bacon, lard and cured meats,—with a view of making a gain or profit thereby, is a manufacturer, and taxable as such, under Section 2742 of the Revised Statutes.

ERROR to the District Court of Butler County.
John F. Neilan and *Thomas Millikin* for plaintiff in error.
Slayback & Shaffer for defendants in error.

DICKMAN, J.—During the years 1870 and 1880, John W. Sohn & Co. were a firm engaged in the business of purchasing
FACTS. and slaughtering hogs, and packing pork, in the city of Hamilton, Butler county. They bought and slaughtered hogs, and subjected the same to certain processes and combination with other materials, requiring the application of skill, labor, and capital, and converted them into lard and cured meats, for the purpose of adding to the value thereof, with the view of making gain or profit. It required about forty men to carry on the business, which was conducted under several departments, each requiring the supervision of a foreman possessed of skill and experience. In rendering lard, curing sides and shoulders, curing, smoking and canvasing hams, and packing pork, it became necessary to use other raw material of various kinds, such as salt, saltpetre, saleratus, sugar, molasses, flour, chrome yellow, linseed oil, canvas, wood, paper, barrels, tierces and kegs, and also to use various tools, implements, and mechanical devices. The process of curing hams required about three months. They were then ready for smoking, which occupied from six to eight days, when they were wrapped, canvased, and dipped in a mixture, to render them air-tight and proof against atmospheric influences and insects. The different branches of the business were carried on together in one building. Sohn & Co. cured all their own meats, and did not deal in meats cured by others. In former years, those that slaughtered were not in the packing business, and packers did not slaughter; but for several years the two branches of business had been, as now, combined.

In listing their property for taxation for the year ending on the day preceding the second Monday of April, 1880, Sohn & Co. took the greatest value of raw material which they had on hand on any day in each month of the next preceding year, and adding those sums together and dividing the aggregate by twelve, listed the quotient, $5130, as their average stock of manufactures for that year—such raw material being articles purchased, received or otherwise held, for the purpose of being used in their packing business. At the time of listing they did not have on hand any articles which had been by them manufactured or changed in any way, either by combination or adding thereto, one year or more previous to such listing. Subsequently to making their return to the assessor, the special board of equalization of the city of Hamilton added to the return the sum of $16,067.90, as an addition " to the monthly average value of pork on hand from time to time during the year,"—thus treating the article as personal property, purchased in its then existing shape, with a view of being sold at an advanced price or profit, and thereby compelling Sohn & Co. to list as merchants. Sohn & Co. filed their petition in the court of common pleas of Butler county, against the county treasurer, to enjoin the collection of taxes upon such addition to their return, on the ground that they should be taxed as manufacturers, and not as merchants; and a perpetual injunction was thereupon granted. On appeal by the county treasurer the district court rendered a like decree as in the court below, and this proceeding is prosecuted to reverse the judgment of the district court.

The question for our consideration is, whether upon the facts in the case at bar the defendants in error were taxable as merchants or manufacturers. If taxable as manufacturers only, they were required to return for taxation—as they did— the monthly average value of the raw material which they had on hand during the preceding year, in the same condition in which it was purchased, received or otherwise held for the purpose of being used by them in their manufacturing business. But they were not required to list for taxation such material in a manufactured or partly manufactured state— unless manufactured one year or more previous thereto—as it was not the intention of the legislature to tax the labor, skill and capital which, when in combination with the raw material, produced the manufactured article. Sebastian *v.* Ohio Candle Co., 27 Ohio St. 459.

The question therefore recurs, were Sohn & Co., for purposes of taxation, merchants under section 2740, or manufacturers under section 2742 of the Revised Statutes? By " Sec. 2740. Every person who shall own or have in his possession, or subject to his control, any personal property within this State, with authority to sell the same, which shall have

been purchased either in or out of this State, with a view to
being sold at an advanced price or profit, or which shall have
been consigned to him, from any place out of this State, for
the purpose of being sold at any place within this State, shall
be held to be a merchant."

And under " Sec. 2742. Every person who shall purchase,
receive, or hold personal property of any description, for the
purpose of adding to the value thereof by any process of
manufacturing. refining, rectifying, or by the combination of
different materials, with a view of making a gain or profit by
so doing, shall be held to be a manufacturer."

In both definitions there is the common element of purchas-
 "MANUFACT ing personal property, with a view of making a
UER " AND
"MERCHANT " gain or profit. But the definition of a manufac-
C NSIDERED.
turer contemplates the attainment of such object by adding
to the value of the property after purchase, by some process
or combination with other materials, while the merchant is
supposed to get his advanced price or profit by selling the
article as it is, without subjecting it to any change by hand,
by machinery, or by art.   The material entering into the manufactured article may be modified, more or less, in its identity,
as it passes through the several stages of a manufacturing
process ; but the merchant deals in the manufactured article
itself, or its constituents, by buying and selling them in the
same condition in which he purchases them.   His business is
that of exchanges, and not of making or fabricating from raw
materials.

The occupation of the defendants in error was, we think,
PORK PACKER essentially that of manufacturers.   By the use of
HELD A MANU-
FACTURER. tools, implements, and mechanical devices; by subjecting the slaughtered animals to divers processes, running—
some of them—through several months; by a combination
with various materials and ingredients requiring skill, care
and attention, products were obtained in the form of pork,
lard and cured meats, to which may appropriately be applied
the term "manufactured articles."   The original substance,
though not destroyed, was so transformed through art and
labor that without previous knowledge it could not have
been recognized in the new shape it assumed, or in the new
uses to which it was applied.   One who produces such results
may as correctly be designated a manufacturer as he who

buys lumber, and planes, tongues, grooves, or otherwise dresses the same ; or as he who by a simple process makes sheets of batting from cotton; or as he who buys fruit and preserves the same by canning—all of whom have been held to be manufacturers, and taxed as such, under the internal revenue laws of the United States. 9 Internal Revenue Record, 193 ; 5 Id. 180; Internal Revenue Decisions, 117, No. 171. And as to the article of ice, to which reference has been made in argument, he is not inappropriately termed a manufacturer who produces artificial ice by the method of vàporization and expansion. The dressed lumber, cotton batting, canned fruits, and artificial ice, though but slightly changed from the original material, could not, we think, be properly classified as unmanufactured goods. Indeed, the term manufacture has been extended to include every object upon which art or skill can be exercised, so as to afford products fabricated by the hand of man, or by the labor which he directs. Curtis on Pat. § 74.

During the past forty years the business of slaughtering and meat packing, from a small beginning, has grown to such magnitude that it is now ranked as one of the great industries of the country. It is placed in our Federal Census among the mechanical and manufacturing industries of our large cities. In its different departments the aid of science, and art, and inventive talent has been invoked, and new and improved methods have been devised for facilitating and perfecting its various processes. "The perfection of manufacturing," it has been said, "consists in the being able to effect the wished-for changes in the raw material, with the least expenditure of labor or at the least cost." With such a test alone there would be no hesitation in ranking this indnstry, in its present advanced state, among our most effective branches of manufacture.

These views, it may be urged, are in conflict with the decision of the court in Jackson *v.* The State, 15 Ohio, 652. The facts in that case appear to be meagrely reported. The appellant, who was a citizen of the State of Pennsylvania, "engaged in the business of purchasing, slaughtering and packing pork for transportation and sale," at Columbus, Ohio. Hitchcock, J.·, was "not prepared to say," that a person so engaged was a manufacturer within the meaning of the statute.

We are, however, satisfied, that if the facts had been the same as in the case at bar, if there had been in the year 1846 the same perfection in the art of packing and curing meats which has since been reached and now exists, Jackson would have been held to be a manufacturer and not a merchant.

The conclusion to which we have arrived is, that Sohn & Co. were manufacturers; that, as such, they made proper return to the assessor of the personal property of the firm subject to taxation; that the addition to their return by the board of equalization was illegal; and that the district court did not err in rendering judgment, that the county treasurer be perpetually enjoined from collecting any tax upon the addition so made by that board.

Judgment affirmed.

KNICKERBOCKER ICE COMPANY
v.
. PEOPLE.

(99 *New York Reports*, 181.)

A corporation organized under the act of 1855 (chap. 301, Laws of 1855), extending the operation of the General Manufacturing Act (chap. 40, Laws of 1848), by authorizing the formation of corporations "for the purpose of collecting, storing, and preserving ice, of preparing it for market, of transporting it, . . . and of vending the same," and whose business is confined to the purposes expressed in the act, is not a manufacturing corporation, and so is not within the provision of the act providing for the taxation of certain corporations (§ 3, chap. 542, Laws of 1880, as amended by chap. 361, Laws of 1881), which exempts manufacturing corporations from the operation of the act, and such corporations are taxable under said act.

The provision of the said act of 1855 (§ 2), giving to the corporations organized under it the privileges conferred by the act of 1848, was not intended to put them, in all respects, upon the same footing as manufacturing corporations, and does not exempt them from taxation. The exemption is limited to corporations which are in fact manufacturing corporations, and carry on manufacture.

APPEAL from judgment of the General Term of the Supreme Court, in the third judical department, entered upon an order made the first Tuesday of May, 1884, which affirmed a judgment in favor of plaintiff, entered upon the report of a referee. (Reported below, 32 Hun. 475.)

The nature of the action and the material facts are stated in the opinion.

Matthew Hale for appellant.

D. O'Brien, attorney-general, for respondent.

DANFORTH, J.—This action was brought to recover State taxes for the year ending November 1, 1881, under the provisions of chapter 542, Laws of 1880, section 3, as amended (Laws of 1881, chap. 361), and also for the penalty prescribed (Laws of 1881, *supra*, § 2), for their non-payment. FACTS. The answer, in substance, avers that the defendant " is a manufacturing corporation, carrying on manufacture within this State," and therefore, exempt from such imposition by the very terms of the statute (*supra*). Upon trial of the issue before a referee, it appeared that the defendant was a corporation organized under the Manufacturing Act of this State (Laws of 1848, chap. 40); and in pursuance of an act passed April 12, 1855 (Laws of 1855, chap 301), to extend the operation of said act of 1848; that its business was " collecting ice from the Hudson River and Rockland Lake, storing, preserving and preparing it for sale ; transporting it to the city of New York or elsewhere and vending the same," and the referee found that the defendant was not a manufacturing corporation carrying on manufacture. If this finding is correct, judgment properly followed the prayer of the complaint.

The business of the defendant is described in language found in its articles of association, and for the ICE COMPANY doing of which it was organized. The perform- NOT A MANUFAC-TURER. ance, therefore, corresponds with its license, and while the phrase by which the incorporation was effected might not be important, we cannot fail to see that neither it nor its operations are in any way concerned with the manufacture or sale of an artificial product. Its dealing is with "ice," as an existing article, not the manufacture or production of ice by combination of materials, or the application of forces, or otherwise. It collects, stores, and preserves that which natural causes created and which other natural causes would destroy and waste. It seeks only to hold these last in check. Similar applications would equally apply to water, fruit, sand, gravel, coal, and other natural productions.   Water might be improved by filtration, fruit by judicious pruning of the tree or vine, or protection by glass, sand and gravel by screening, cobble-stones by selection, and coal by breaking, and each, by various processes, stored until the season of demand, when, having been " collected, stored, preserved and prepared for sale," the natural articles and no other would be put upon the market.

No doubt ice may be manufactured and frigoric effects produced by artificial means.   Corporations exist for that purpose and come literally within our manufacturing laws. Their methods in no respect resemble those of the defendant. Its tools and implements are for convenience in handling and marketing a product, and not at all for making it.   Many cases are cited by the learned counsel for the appellant, but we find none so comprehensive as to include this case.   They all, so far as they have any application, require the production of some article, thing, or object, by skill or labor, out of raw material, or from matter which has already been subjected to artificial forces, or to which something has been added to change its natural condition.   Whether, therefore, the words of exemption in the act of 1881 (*supra*) are taken in their usual and ordinary sense, or according to their legal interpretation (Gas-light Co. *v.* Brooklyn, 89 N. Y. 409), they do not include the defendant.   The statute (Laws of 1855, *supra*), under which the existence of the defendant was made possible, seems to require the same conclusion.   By it the Manufacturing Act of 1848 (*supra*) was extended so as to permit the formation of such a company.   It became a law on the 12th of April, 1855, and on the 19th day of the same month the defendant was organized, and its object, as above described, follows literally the language of the act.   We have, therefore, both a practical and a legislative interpretation of the earlier act—that of 1848.   The defendant did not rely upon it in describing the purpose for which the company was to be formed, and it cannot be assumed that the later act would have been passed if, in the opinion of the legislature, it did not provide for a new subject.   No doubt it is the province of the court to declare what the law is, but where there are two statutes relating to the same general purpose, they are both to be considered and each construed in the light of the other. Here the act of 1855 may be regarded as a legislative declaration that the object to which it was directed was not included in the act of 1848. It is, however, provided, that a corporation organized under the act of 1855 (*supra*, § 2), shall be entitled to the privileges conferred by the act of 1848 (*supra*), and hence the learned counsel for the appellant argues that a legislative intent may be implied to put it on the same footing in all respects as a manufacturing corporation. This does not follow. Equality under that act is provided for, but nothing more. Exemption from taxation is not given by it. That subject is regulated by the statute under which this action was brought (Laws of 1881, *supra*), and it is limited to corporations which are in fact manufacturing corporations, and do carry on manufacture. We think the defendant is of a different character.

The judgment appealed from should therefore be affirmed. All concur.

WHO ARE NOT MANUFACTURERS.—One who carries on the business of buying timber and converting it into lumber is a manufacturer, and not a trader. State *v.* Chadbourn, 80 N. C. 479. A gas company is a manufacturing company. Commonwealth *v.* Lowell G. L. Co., 12 Allen, Mass. 75; Williams *v.* Rees, 2 Fed. Repr. 882. An aqueduct company is not a manufacturer, although it uses filters and screens in preparing its water for circulation through mains into a city. Dudley *v.* Jamaica Pond A. Co., 100 Mass. 183. "But an aqueduct company manufacturers nothing," said the court. "Nothing is put into the article which it supplies to change its natural condition, and the whole operation of the water-works is designed merely to keep foreign substances from mingling with it." An ice cream confectioner is not a manufacturer. New Orleans *v.* Mannassier, 32 La. Ann. 1075. "We cannot assent to the proposition," said the court "that a person making and selling ice-cream is a manufacturer in the sense of the law, or in any other sense of the word. The attempt to magnify a confectionery, which is defendant's business, into a manufacture must fail. We are told that any one seeing the steam engine, complicated apparatus, and large force needed to produce defendant's goods, would at once conclude that he is a manufacturer. With as much force it might be said that any one visiting the mammoth kitchen of the Grand Union Hotel at Saratoga, together with their myriads of employees and their colossal apparatus, would at once magnify the cooks and pastrymen into manufacturers." In People *v.* N. Y. Floating Dry Dock Co., 63 How. Pr. 451, it is decided that the builder and repairer of vessels is a ship-carpenter, or builder, and not a manufacturer.

Undoubtedly in a certain broad sense any builder may be called a manufacturer—that is, he takes raw material, and, either by hand or machinery, fashions it into shape for use.   But this is not what is ordinarily and generally understood as meant by "manufacturing,"—and it is in the general ordinary sense that "manufacturing" is to be taken in a tax law, or other statute.

THE GALVESTON WHARF CO.

v.

THE CITY OF GALVESTON.

(63 *Texas Reports*, 14.)

The decree of the District Court of Brazoria County, rendered April 1, 1869, in the case of The City of Galveston *v.* The Galveston Wharf Company, consolidating the interests of the respective parties thereto, vested the undivided one third of the property of the consolidated wharf company in the city of Galveston, with the exception of certain property specified in the decree.   Said one third interest was represented by one third of the stock of the consolidated company.

The effect of said decree was to vest in the city of Galveston, not only the right to receive one third of the dividends accruing to the wharf company, but the further right to one third of the entire property of the company as consolidated; it being, however, subject to the control of the Galveston Wharf Company for the uses and purposes for which the consolidation was made.

The power to alienate one third of the wharf company property, which was reserved to the city in said decree, is inconsistent with any other relation to the one third interest than that of ownership by the city.

Said decree clothes the wharf company with a power to be exercised in the management of said one third interest, through a directory to be selected, in which the city of Galveston is to be represented as provided by said decree.

The fact that compensation is received for the use of a wharf across which the commerce of a country passes does not divest it of its public character.

Sec. 1, art. 8, of the State constitution, which enumerates certain property which is exempt from taxation, cannot be construed to subject all property not specified to taxation; that section simply indicates the character of things and the uses to which they must be appropriated in order to entitle them to the exemption.

In the absence of any statute controlling the subject, such property as a municipal corporation owns and uses for a public purpose is not affected by general laws regulating taxation.

The city of Galveston owns such a beneficial interest in the property of the Galveston Wharf Company, and of the dividends to arise from its use, as renders it improper for the city to impose taxes which would ordinarily deprive the city of a part of the dividends of the company which it is entitled to receive.

The two thirds interest owned by the wharf company is subject to State and municipal taxation.

The rights of the city of Galveston and of the wharf company, in respect to dividends, resulting from the fact that the interest of one is taxable, and that of the other is not, must be adjusted as would the rights of persons holding shares of stock in other corporations, except that the city cannot diminish the dividends by the imposition of a tax in its own favor not authorized by law.

An injunction properly issued to restrain the city of Galveston from, collecting taxes on its interest in the property of the Galveston Wharf Company.

APPEAL from Galveston.   Tried below before Hon. Wm. H. Stewart.

The opinion states the case.

Ballinger, Mott & Terry, and *Trezevant & Franklin* for appellant.

James B. Stubbs for appellee.

STAYTON, A. J.—The nature and result of this action is correctly stated in the brief of counsel for appellant as follows:
FACTS.

"Suit was brought by the Galveston Wharf Company, a corporation chartered in 1854, against the city of Galveston, to enjoin the sale of certain property advertised for sale for the payment of taxes to the city of Galveston from the wharf company, so far as the taxes were assessed on the one third interest in certain wharf property in possession of the company, under compromise between the city and the company, confirmed by the legislature, on the ground that the said interest is the property of the city, in trust for its present and future inhabitants, and is used only for public purposes, and not taxable by the constitution and laws of the State. An injunction was granted against the enforcement of the tax by the district judge of Harris County, in the absence of the district judge of Galveston County.   But on the trial of the case before the latter judge the injunction was dissolved and the suit dismissed.   There were various other injunctions to the tax as levied by the city, all of which were overruled by the judgment below, and some of which cannot be considered, owing to a failure to obtain the signature of the judge to the statement of facts. So far as the case is presented for review by this court, the pleadings and special agreement of the parties concurred in the facts."

The petition sets out very fully the history of the grant to M. B. Menard, on which is situated the city of Galveston, through which and subsequent legislation conflicting claims to the flats and wharf privileges arose between the city of Galveston and others, who were claiming through the grant to Menard, out of which grew the suit which was decided in this court in 1859. A full history of that case and the questions involved and decided will be found in City of Galveston *v.* Menard, 23 Tex. 349.

The ownership of the soil in the flats in front of the lots out of the channel was held, in that case, to be in Menard and his vendees, who were declared to have the right to devote it to wharf or other like purposes, free from the control of the public, under the qualification incident to all property; that it was not to be so used as to be a common nuisance, and at the same time, in view of the purposes for which the grant to Menard was made, it was held that the city had a like right to build and control wharves in front of the streets of the city, which might be extended to or over the flats to the channel.

Within a year after the decision was made in the case of The City of Galveston *v.* Menard, a suit was brought by the city of Galveston against the Galveston Wharf Company, which has been organized pending the prior litigation, and was composed of the owners of wharves sued in the former case, and other owners of wharves and wharf property. That action was transferred to Brazoria County, where it was pending until April 1, 1869, when, by agreement of parties, a consent decree was entered by the district court of that county, which was intended by the parties to be a full settlement and compromise of all matters in controversy between the city of Galveston and the Galveston Wharf Company. The decree thus rendered was confirmed by an act of the legislature of June 23, 1870. There therefore arises no question as to the binding force and effect of that decree, which might arise but for the confirmatory act.

The assignment of errors are as follows:

1. "The court erred in its judgment in holding that the

interest or share of the city of Galveston in the property assessed and taxed by the city of Galveston is subject to taxation by the city of Galveston."

2. " The court erred in its judgment in holding that the sale against which the writ of injunction was sued out could lawfully be made to satisfy taxes assessed by the city of Galveston on its own interest, held in trust for the public, in the property assessed by it for taxes."

3. " Because the interest of the city of Galveston in the wharf property, the subject of controversy, is held by the city of Galveston in trust for its present and future inhabitants, and solely for public purposes, as authorized by the legislature of the State, and is not lawfully subject to taxation by the city of Galveston, the court erred in its judgment in holding the same liable to such taxation."

The question which arises is : Has the city such interest in the one third interest in the property sought to be taxed as exempts it from taxation by the city?

The character of interest held by the city in the Galveston Wharf Company's property depends on the true construction to be given to the decree of the District Court for Brazoria County before referred to.

So much of that decree as is necessary to an examination and determination of that question is as follows:

" It is considered, ordered, adjudged, and decreed by the court that the present capital stock of the Galveston Wharf Company, consisting of twelve thousand four hundred and forty-four shares of stock of $100 per share, amounting in the aggregate to $1,244,400, shall be increased the full one half thereof, viz.: by six thousand two hundred and twenty-two shares of $100 each, amounting to the sum of $622,200, which said stock of said sum of $622,200 shall be the property of the mayor, aldermen, and inhabitants of the city of Galveston and the same shall stand and remain on the books of said company as the property of said mayor, aldermen, and inhabitants of the city of Galveston; and the equal, undivided one third of the property of said company, to be consolidated and vested in it by this decree, shall be owned by said city, and represented by its said stock; and the said stock, and the rights and interests therein, and in said property, of said mayor, aldermen, and inhabitants of the city of Galveston, shall be in trust for the present and future inhabitants of the city of Galveston, and all and every part thereof shall be alienable, and not subject to conveyance, assignment, transfer, pledge, mortgage, or any liability for debt whatever, in any other manner than by the vote of four fifths of all the qualified voters of said city in favor of some clear and specific proposition therefor. The dividends and net earnings of said stock shall be regularly paid to said mayor, aldermen, and inhabitants of the city of Galveston, to be disbursed and expended for the public good and benefit of said present and future inhabitants of said city."

Said decree then proceeds to fix the respective representation and rights of said city and company on the board of directors, giving the city three directors in said board of nine—one to be the mayor, and one of the committee on finance, another an alderman, and the third an alderman or citizen, but to be elected by the council. And said decree further provides:

"In consideration of all which, it is further agreed between the parties, and is now considered, ordered, adjudged, and decreed by the court, that all the property, rights, and claims of every kind and description (except certain lots and property hereinafter specified) of the said Galveston Wharf Company, and also all the right, title, interest, and claim of every kind and description whatsoever of the said mayor, aldermen, and inhabitants of the city of Galveston, in and to all the land and ground extending from the shore or ordinary high-water mark of the island of Galveston to the channel of the bay or harbor, from and including the street known on the map and plan of said city of Galveston as Ninth Street, on the east, to and including the street known as Thirty-first Street, on the west, including all the ground known as the Flats within said limits, and also all rights, capacity, powers, and claims of said plaintiffs to build and erect wharves and take and receive wharfage therefor, at the end of streets now or hereafter running or extending to said channel, be and the same are hereby vested in the said Galveston Consolidated Wharf Company, and to be henceforth the corporate property, right, and title of the said Galveston Wharf Company, and owned, held, possessed, controlled, used, and administered by said company—all the said united and consolidated property, rights, and claims being represented by said aggregate of $1,866,600—the original two thirds thereof held by the present stockholders, and one third by the said plaintiff in trust as aforesaid."

Said decree further provided that the result of certain suits then pending should inure to carry out said decree and compromise, and also excepted from its operation certain lots and blocks south of Avenue A, in said city, and others named, the benefit of which was to belong to the stockholders of said company, prior to the compromise; and said decree further provided as follows:

" It is further the agreement and intention of the parties that this settlement shall, if practicable, result in and secure the final settlement of all controversy, and prevent future controversy in regard to all the wharf privileges in front of the city of Galveston, and that the whole of said wharf privileges shall be united and consolidated in the present parties hereto."

The true construction of this decree is to be arrived at by considering the whole decree, which had for its object the settlement of the conflicting claims of the respective parties to the action.

The city was controverting the ownership of the wharf company, claiming through Menard, to the property in the flats, and the resultant right to maintain wharves; and the wharf company was controverting the right of the city, not only to the property in the flats, but also the right of the city even to use, for wharf purposes, the termini of its streets on the bay.

The title of the one to property in the soil embraced in the flats, with the right to use it for wharf and other purposes, had been practically determined by the former suit; as had been the right of the city to use for wharf purposes, notwithstanding the ownership of the soil had passed by the grant to Menard, that part of the flats at the termini of its streets.

The last part of the decree, above set out, evidences the fact that it was intended to consolidate and to put into the hands of the Galveston Wharf Company all the wharf privileges possessed by both or either of the contesting parties; and that this was done, both parties agree; but it is claimed by the one that all the property vested by the decree absolutely in the wharf company; and by the other, that one third of the entire consolidated property not excepted from the operation of the decree vested in the city of Galveston, subject only to the use and control by the wharf company for the purposes for which the consolidation was made.

The latter part of the decree, in terms, vests in the "Galveston Consolidated Wharf Company" all the property, rights, and claims of every kind and description (except certain property specified) of the Galveston Wharf Company; as did it all the right, title, interest, and claim of every kind and description of the city of Galveston in and to all land and ground embracing the flats between and inclusive of Ninth and Thirty-first streets, and also all rights, capacities, powers, and claims of the city to erect wharves and receive wharfage at the ends of streets then extending, or to be extended, to the channel; and it declared those things and rights "to be henceforth the corporate property, right, and title of the said Galveston Wharf Company, and owned, held, possessed, controlled, used, and administered by said company."

The purpose of this part of the decree was, evidently, to vest in the consolidated company, which, in all instances but one, is called "The Galveston Wharf Company," the rights, even of property, as well as of use, which had formerly been owned or claimed by the wharf company and the city, or either of them, except as limited on the face of the decree.

The language used seems, in many respects, sufficient to vest the absolute title in all property and rights to which it applies in the consolidated company; but when considered in connection with the language which immediately follows, it is not inconsistent with an intention to give to the stockholders of the wharf company existing before consolidation title to two thirds of the property, and to the city one third; all to be under such qualified ownership and dominion of the consolidated company as was necessary to enable it to carry out the purposes for which the consolidation of the respective interests was made.

The beneficial interests to accrue from profits, as well as the proprietary interests which would inure to the respective parties in interest in case of dissolution of the Galveston Wharf Company, are evidenced by the shares of stock of which the parties were respectively declared the owners and holders.

It is not clear from this part of the decree whether the

declaration in reference to the holding of "one third by the said plaintiff (the city) in trust as aforesaid" refers to the shares of stock or to the property as well, but the preceding part of the decree, to which reference is made, which relates to the property as well as the shares of stock, renders it highly probable that it was in this connection used in relation to the property as well as the shares of stock; it is, however, immaterial in reference to the matter under consideration, whether it refers to one or both, for in either event the beneficial interest to arise from the use of the property would inure to the benefit of the "present and future inhabitants of the city of Galveston."

Prior to this decree, it will be remembered that there was a contest about the ownership of the property, as well as the right to use all or parts of it, and the latter part of the decree was evidently intended to settle that question by vesting, it may be, the absolute as well as the qualified rights held by the respective parties in or to the property in the consolidated company, as a starting-point for the clear investiture of unquestioned title in each to shares in the property, as well as the profits to be derived from its use, to which, by the agreement made the basis of the decree, each party would be entitled.

The former part of the decree evidences that it was thought such a course was necessary before the rights of the parties, as they desired them to exist in the future, could by the decree be determined.

The more natural order would have been to vest the property in the consolidated company in the first part of the decree, and in the subsequent part to have vested in the respective parties the property or rights which it was agreed they should severally own, if separate ownership was desired or thought necessary.

However this may be, the order in which things were done by the decree cannot control its construction; for the true inquiry is, What does the entire decree show was the declaration of law made on the agreement of the parties as to the rights of the respective parties?

The first part of the decree, after directing the issue of additional shares of stock and determining the number of shares which each of the parties should have, declares that "the

equal undivided one third of the property of said company
(the consolidated company) to be consolidated and vested in it
by this decree shall be owned by said city, and represented by
the said stock, and the rights and interests therein, and in said
property of said mayor, aldermen, and inhabitants of the city
of Galveston, shall be in trust for the present and future inhabitants of the city of Galveston; and all and every part thereof
shall be inalienable, and not subject to conveyance, assignment, transfer, pledge, mortgage, or any liability for debt
whatever, in any other manner than by the vote of four fifths
of all the qualified voters of said city in favor of some clear
and specific proposition therefor."

This part of the decree declares what shall be the rights of
the parties then before the court, after the rights and property of both were consolidated and vested by the decree in
the consolidated company.

It would seem that the declaration as to how the ownership
should stand after the property and rights of both parties
should by the decree be vested in the one in whose name the
business was to be transacted in the future, should control
that part of the decree by which the contemplated consolidation was made.

Taken all together, the apparent intent of the decree is to
vest in the city of Galveston not only a right to receive one
third of the dividends, but also the further right to one third
of the entire property of the company, as consolidated; it
being, however, subject to the control of the Galveston Wharf
Company for the uses and purposes for which the consolidation was made.

This view is much strengthened by the fact that a power is
recognized, and a method is provided, in the decree, by which
not only the right and interests of the city in the stock which
it holds, but also in the property, *i.e.*, an undivided one third
of the whole property consolidated and vested in the Galveston Wharf Company, by the decree, may be alienated by the
city.

Such a power of alienation is inconsistent with any other
relationship to the property than that of ownership, it not
appearing that a naked power was intended to be conferred.

The trust spoken of in the decree is evidently one imposed
not only on the Galveston Wharf Company, but also on the

municipal government of the city of Galveston for the benefit of the inhabitants of that city.

We are of the opinion that the decree vests in the city of Galveston title to an undivided one third of the property consolidated by the decree, and that it clothes the wharf company with a power to be exercised in its management through the directory to be selected in which the city is to be represented as provided by the decree. TITLE OF GALVESTON TO WHARF PROPERTY.

Section 1, article 8, of the constitution, in providing for taxation, seems to exempt all property belonging to municipal corporations from taxation; but section 9, article 11, provides: "The property of counties, cities, and towns owned and held only for public purposes, such as public buildings and sites therefor, fire-engines and the furniture thereof, and all property used or intended for extinguishing fires, public grounds, and all other property devoted exclusively to the use and benefit of the public, shall be exempt from forced sale and from taxation."

It is contended that under this provision of the constitution, even if the one third of the property belongs to the city, it is subject to taxation, because not such property and so used as to be entitled to the exemption.

It is property held only for purposes essentially public, and may be said to be devoted exclusively to the use and benefit of the public; indeed it would be hard to imagine a use more essentially public than is that of a wharf which extends along the front of a city, and upon which is received a large part of the articles which go to make up the inward and outward commerce of the State. It is a property which all persons and vessels have a right to use, under proper regulations, and without the use of which the business of the city could not be conducted. That compensation is received for its use does not withdraw from it its public character. Dillon on Municipal Corporations, 103–113. CITY WHARF PROPERTY IS PUT TO A PUBLIC USE AND IS EXEMPT FROM TAXATION.

There may be property owned by municipal corporations which would be subject to taxation, but the enumeration of certain things in the section of the constitution quoted, as exempt from taxation, was not intended to operate as a declaration that things not enumerated were subject; but simply to indicate the character of things, and the uses to which they must be appropriated, in order to be entitled to the exemption.

The decree provides that dividends received by the city " shall be disbursed and expended for the public good and benefit of said present and future inhabitants of said city."

In the absence of any law expressly providing otherwise, such property as a municipal corporation owns and uses for a public purpose is held not to be affected by general laws regulating taxation. Cooley on Taxation, 130, 131; Dillon on Municipal Corporations, 773, 774, and cases cited in the notes.

Many cases exist in which examples are given of the character of property and uses to which it must be put, when owned by municipal corporations, to make it, within the meaning of the law, property " held only for public purposes, or devoted exclusively to the use and benefit of the public," which, in this case, it is not deemed necessary to review, among which are the following: Klein *v.* New Orleans, 99 U. S. 150; Water Commissioners *v.* Gaffney, 34 N. J. 131; Gibson *v.* Howe, 37 Iowa, 170; Fall *v.* Mayor of Marysville, 19 Cal. 392; Piper *v.* Singer, 4 S. & R. 354; Directors of the Poor *v.* School Directors, 42 Pa. St. 24; Louisville *v.* Commonwealth, 1 Duval, 295; Trustees *v.* Champaign Co., 76 Ill. 185.

The words "held only" and "devoted exclusively," used in the section of the constitution quoted, would seem to convey the idea that a municipal corporation may own property which will not be exempt from taxation; if so, the property involved in this case is not of that character; and it will be time enough to consider what kinds of property, if any, belonging to a municipal corporation, is subject to taxation when a case requiring its decision is presented.

If, however, the decree did not vest in the city the title to one undivided one-third of the property of which it purports to dispose, there can be no doubt that the decree vests in the city such a beneficial interest in the property, and in the dividends to arise from its use, as would, on principle, render it improper for the city to impose taxes which would indirectly deprive it of a part of the dividends, which, under the decree, it was evidently intended the city should receive.

In other words, can the city tax the property to the extent

of its beneficial interest therein, when to do so will diminish its dividends, and in addition to this incur the increased ex pense of collecting the tax.

In our opinion, it might just as well tax any other property it owns, and pay the tax out of its own treasury, with a loss to itself of the cost of collecting.

If the only beneficial interest of the city be to dividends, these cannot be declared and paid until the expenses of oper- ating and keeping up the entire property is first deducted for dividends are not paid on gross receipts; hence, it the city can tax the entire property, the tax so levied and col- lected must be deducted before a dividend is paid, and thus the dividend be diminished.

A power to tax, under such circumstances, involves the power of a municipal corporation to tax itself or its own property, which it certainly cannot do, for obvious reasons.

There are no equities arising in favor of the city from the fact that the dividends which the city will receive are dimin- ished by the taxes paid to the city on the interest of the wharf company in the property, for the city receives the en- tire tax, and only accounts for one-third of it in receiving a diminished dividend, caused by this tax, as do the other stockholders.

If the dividends of the city will be diminished by the pay- ment of State and county taxes on the interest owned by the wharf company, this furnishes no reason to sustain the impo- sition of an unauthorized tax. It is true that the taxation of two-thirds of the property, which, under the decree, is the interest of the wharf company, by the State and county, will diminish the dividends which the city will receive; but this results from the fact that under the law that property is sub- ject to taxation, as is the property of other persons, and its association in ownership with other interests not subject to taxation does not create an exemption in its favor. No pro- vision is made, in the decree for adjusting what may seem to be the equities of the parties in reference to dividends, result- ing from the fact that the part of the property owned by the wharf company is subject to taxation, while the part owned by the city is not; but in the absence of some such provision, the rights of the parties would have to be adjusted in refer- ence to dividends, as would the right of persons holding

9 Cor. Cas.—28

shares of stock in other corporations, except that the city cannot diminish the dividends by the imposition of a tax in its favor not authorized by law.

The rights of the parties, in respect to such matters, rest as fixed by the decree, which, having been confirmed by the legislature, must be held to indicate the will of the law-making power, as fully as though embodied in a statute. The legislature might have withdrawn from the city the right to receive any dividends at all.

The court below erred in dissolving the injunction sued out to restrain the city from collecting the tax on an undivided one-third of the wharf property, and its judgment will be here rendered perpetuating the injunction heretofore granted, and adjudging costs of the court below and of this in favor of the appellant against the appellee.

And it is accordingly so ordered.

Reversed and rendered.

MUNICIPAL PROPERTY IS NOT TAXABLE.—That a municipal corporation should for its own purposes assess and collect from itself a tax on its own property is an absurdity so great that it may be dismissed without consideration. Whether the State or the United States may tax municipal property, or whether one municipality may tax the property of another, are questions of greater difficulty. There is a case in 1 Duval (Ky.), 298, where the following rule is laid down: "Where property, such as court-house, prison, and the like, which became necessary or useful to the administration of the municipal government, and is devoted to that use, is exempt from State taxation; but whatever is not so used, but is owned and used by Louisville in its social or commercial capacity as a private corporation, and for its own profit, such as vacant lots, market-houses, fire-engines, and the like, is subject to taxation," and the county judge was directed to correct an assessment in accordance with this principle. Judge Dillon, with reference to this decision, "ventures to observe that in his judgment the exemption should have been extended to all the property. Municipal corporations are not usually allowed to hold or deal in property directly for profit; and this is not the purpose for which authority is given to erect market-houses or wharves, or to purchase and own fire-engines." 2 Dill. Mun. Corp. § 775. To this it may be added, that the putting out of fires and prevention of conflagrations would seem to make fire-engines as much the instruments of a public purpose as a court-house or jail. And it may also be questioned whether the taxation of any part of the property of a municipality does not fall within the reason stated by Judge Cooley, thus: "A State may, if the legislature see fit, tax all the property owned by its municipal divisions; but to do so would render necessary new taxes to meet the demand of this tax, and thus the public would be taxing itself in order to raise money to pay over to itself, and no one would be benefited but the officers employed." Cooley, Taxation, 131.

These reasons, however, hardly apply with as much force to a case where one municipality owns property not used for its corporate purposes in another. Such was the fact in West Hartford *v.* Board of Water Commissioners, 44 Conn. 361. To supply the City of Hartford with water, the Board bought a large tract of land in the neighboring town of West Hartford. It was held that the portion used for storing and supplying the water was not taxable, but that the unused portion was not exempt. And in so far as the exemption of a part was concerned, it was held not to affect the matter that the Board sold the water to consumers and paid interest on the investment and incidental expenses by the water rents so derived. ·

In an Alabama case, Stein *v.* Mayor, etc., of Mobile, 24 Ala. 591, the interest of the lessee of a city water-works system was held not exempt from taxation.

But the general rule is that municipal property is not taxable. People *v.* Solomon, 51 Ill. 37; Directors *v.* School Directors, 42 Pa. St. 21, 25; State *v.* Gaffney, 34 N. J· 133; People *v.* Doe, 36 Cal. 220; People *v.* Austin, 47 Cal. 353; Gibson *v.* House, 37 Iowa, 168; Trustees *v.* Champaign Co., 7 Leg. News, 160; Piper *v.* Singer, 4 S. & R. 354; Hall *v.* Marysville, 19 Cal. 391; Low *v.* Lewis, 46 Cal. 549; Ft. Dodge *v.* More, 37 Iowa, 388.

The lands of a county used for a court house and other county purposes cannot be taxed by the city in which they are situated, nor are they liable for a street assessment. Worcester Co. *v.* Worcester, 116 Mass. 193.

A municipal corporation cannot levy a tax on bonds issued by the State even though they be properly within the corporation limits. It is not to be presumed that the State intended, without an express grant to that effect, to confer upon a municipal corporation a power thus to depreciate the State securities, and do what the State itself ought not to be presumed to have done, in the absence of clear language so declaring. City Council *v.* Dunbar, 50 Ga. 387.

SPECIAL EXEMPTION OF CEMETERIES FROM TAXATION. REPEAL BY SUBSEQUENT GENERAL STATUTE.—Some of the States, either by statute or constitutional provision, exempt cemeteries from taxation. For example, Missouri, by section 6, article 10, constitution of 1875, provides that "the property, real and personal, of the State, counties, and other municipal corporations, and cemeteries shall be exempt from taxation." The questions which arise in this kind of litigation are usually questions of interpretation and construction. In State *v.* Wesleyan Cemetery Association, 11 Mo. App. 561, it was held that if the property was used as a cemetery at the time the taxes sued for were assessed, there could be no recovery. In another case, between the same parties, 11 Mo. App. 570, the same point was affirmed. It appeared that the cemetery company was exempt from taxation by a special charter granted it in 1851. It was contended that the exemption was repealed by certain general enactments subsequently, but this was denied by the court which applied the

rule *generalia specialibus non derogant.*   Earl Derby *v.* Commissioner,
L. R., 4 Exch. 222 ; Fitzgerald *v.* Champenys, 2 Johns. & Hun. 31, 53, 54,
Jenk. Cent. 120.   The reason why a general enactment will not repeal a
prior particular enactment unless it specially refers to it, is well stated by
Sir W. Page Wood: "The reason in all these cases is clear.   In passing
the special act, the legislature had their attention directed to the special
case which the act was meant to meet, and considered and provided for
all the circumstances of that special case; and having done so they will
not be considered by a general enactment passed subsequently, and making no mention of such intention, to have intended to derogate from that
which, by their own special act, they had thus carefully supervised and
regulated.   Fitzgerald *v.* Champenys, *supra.*   See also upon this point
Sedg. Stat. and Const. Law (2 ed.), 98 note.   St. Louis *v.* Alexander, 23
Mo. 483 ; State *v.* McDonald, 38 Mo. 529; Deters *v.* Renick, 37 Mo.
597 ; State *v.* Macon, 41 Mo. 453 ; Williams *v.* Pritchard, 4 Term R. 2;
State *v.* Minton, 23 N. J. L. 529; Blain *v.* Bailey, 25 Ind. 155.

In Appeal Tax, etc., *v.* Baltimore Cem. Co., 50 Md. 432, the charter of
the company provided that "the land of the company dedicated to the purposes of a cemetery shall not be subject to taxation of any kind."   The
assessors assessed it, including gate-houses and all permanent improvements of the cemetery.   The court, however, held that the special exemption in the charter constituted a contract not subject to impairment.

WHAT PROPERTY OF CEMETERY IS TAXABLE.—It is obvious that the
property of a cemetery company may be put to various uses.   Some of it
may lie idle, another portion may be used for burial purposes, and upon part
of it buildings may be erected.   It became a question, in Appeal Tax, etc., *v.*
Baltimore Cem. Co., 50 Md. 433.   The exemption was of "*the land* of the
company dedicated to the purposes of a cemetery," and it was argued that
this exemption does not extend to, or include, the *improvements* on the
land, because by the tax-law the assessors were required, in valuing real
estate, to estimate the value of the land per acre and "separately to value
the improvements thereon."   But the court held the point not well taken.
"But this requirement," said Bartol, C. J., "was not designed to convert
the improvements into personalty, or to separate them from the realty,
nor can it be construed to have that effect ; it was intended only to point
out the mode in which the assessment should be made, and the whole
aggregate value of the land, with the improvements, ascertained.   The whole
context shows that the permanent improvements are treated as realty, as
the law regards them ; and in our judgment the exemption of the lands
from taxation necessarily embraces also an exemption of the permanent
improvements thereon *used for the purposes of a public cemetery, and which
are essential to the use and enjoyment of the land for the purpose contemplated in the charter.*   Such was the character of the improvements in this
case."   Appeal Tax, etc., *v.* Balto. Cem. Co., *supra.*

In Hoboken *v.* North Bergen, 43 N. J. L. 148, there was about five acres
of land in the cemetery property that was not used for burial purposes,
but was cultivated by the superintendent of the cemetery, who resided in
a house on the five acres.   This house and five acres was assessed, but the

court held it exempt, under a law providing that the cemetery and all burial lots sold therein should be free from taxation. Replying to the contention that the exemption extended only to land actually used for burial purposes, the court said: " Such construction of the general act is too narrow. The space required for burial purposes constantly increases, and a reasonable quantity of land for future occupancy should be provided. Land acquired for such purpose is not taxable. Seventeen acres is not an unreasonable quantity of land for a cemetery in the vicinity of the city of Hoboken."

A somewhat different view was taken in Woodlawn Cemetery *v.* Inhabitants of Everett, 118 Mass. 354, wherein it was held that under the statutes of the Commonwealth land is not "dedicated for" a cemetery or for the burial of the dead, so as to be exempt from taxation, or " used or appropriated" to the purpose of a burial ground, so as to entitle the owner to use it for that purpose for the future without municipal permission, until it has been devoted or set apart and some active measures taken toward preparing the ground for that purpose.

In 1850 a parcel of land was conveyed to a cemetery corporation organized under the St. of 1881, c. 114, and the corporation voted to appropriate it to the purposes of a cemetery or burial place of the dead. In 1858 the vendor foreclosed a mortgage given by the corporation and took possession of the land. In 1868 another cemetery corporation voted to purchase the land for the purposes of a cemetery, and applied to the town in which the land lay for permission to use the land for burial purposes; the town refused to grant permission. The corporation then bought the land, and gave notice to the town that it was dedicated to the uses and purposes of a cemetery, and passed a vote that it was so dedicated. A house on the land was used by the gardener of the corporation, a hot-house for propagating, for the cemetery was built thereon, and the land was used to pile manure, grave markers, stone posts, wood and lumber for the cemetery, and for cutting sods for lots therein; but no part of the land was ever used for burials, or laid out into lots or permanent avenues, and no attempt was made to sell any part of it for burial purposes. *Held*, in an action to recover back a public tax levied on the land in 1870, that the land had not become so " dedicated to the burial of the dead" within the General Sts. c. 11, § 5, cl. 8, as to be exempt from taxation.

In People *v.* Cemetery Co., 86 Ill. 337, the exemption was of property held by the company "subservient to burial uses." The company had 153 acres of land in two tracts near Chicago, besides the land which they had in actual use for burial purposes, and upon this 153 acres were built certain stables, etc., occupied by men and teams employed in the cemetery. The court held the property not within the exemption. " Here are two large tracts of land," said the court, " not used, or likely for years to come to be used, for cemetery purposes. While we may concede the right of the company to purchase and hold the land to be appropriated some time in the distant future for burial purposes, yet we cannot hold, under a fair or reasonable construction of its charter, that the land can be held free from taxation."

In Mulroy *v.* Churchman, 52 Iowa, 238, where out of 40 acres of land alleged to be held by a church as a burying ground, only one acre was actually used for burial purposes, the 39 acres remaining were held taxable. WHETHER EXEMPTION FROM TAXATION APPLIES TO SPECIAL ASSESSMENTS.—In Barry *v.* Wesleyan Cemetery Co., 10 Mo. App. 587, it was held that where, by the charter of a corporation, its realty is exempted from taxes *and assessments,* so long as the same is used for a cemetery, such property, while so used, is exempt from liability for special taxes for improvements of the street in front thereof. `

In Olive Cemetery Co. *v.* Philadelphia, 93 Pa. St. 129, the charter of a cemetery company contained the following clause : That no street, lane, or road shall hereafter be opened through the said tract occupied as a cemetery without the consent of a majority of the lot-holders; and the same, when used as a place of sepulchre, shall be exempt from taxation except for State purposes." A sewer was constructed on a street along the line of which were a number of these burial lots, and an assessment was charged against such lots to defray, in part, the cost of the sewer. In a suit to recover this assessment, *held,* that the assessment was a species of local taxation, and within the exemption clause of the charter, and that the lot-holders were not liable.

As to taxation of cemeteries, see Lima *v.* Cemetery Association, 5 Am. & Eng. Corp. Cas. 547, and note.   .

CAMERON

v.

CAPPELLER, Auditor, *et al.*

(41 *Ohio State Reports,* 533.)

A statement for the taxation of personal property, moneys, credits, investments in bonds, stocks, joint stock companies, or otherwise, which omits a judgment, in reference to which proceedings in error are pending in the Supreme Court, may be corrected by the county auditor under the power conferred by sections 2781 and 2782, Revised Statutes.

In putting such judgment on the tax duplicate the auditor should place it there at its true value at the time the owner should have listed it, and not at its nominal value.

ERROR to the District Court of Hamilton County.
Alfred Yaple for plaintiff.
Goss & Cohen for defendant.

NASH, J.—The most important question involved in this case is this : A judgment has been obtained in a court of com-
QUESTION.   mon pleas, and it is involved by proceedings in error

in the Supreme Court. Does section 2734, Rev. Stats., require the listing of such a judgment for taxation? This section requires the listing of all credits due or owing from any person or persons, body corporate or politic. By section 2730, Rev. Stats., the word "credits" is held "to mean the excess of the sum of all legal claims and demands, whether for money or other valuable thing, or for labor or service due or to become due to the person liable to pay taxes thereon . . . (estimating every such claim or demand at its true value in money), over and above the sum of legal *bona-fide* debts owing to such person."

Surely when a legal claim is reduced to judgment, although there is alleged error in so doing, it does not so lose its taxable character as to excuse its owner from return- JUDGMENT IS TAXABLE. ing it for taxation at its true value. When he does not do so the county auditor, acting under the authority conferred by sections 2781 and 2782, Rev. Stats., may place it upon the tax duplicate. In the case of Bank *v.* Hines, 3 Ohio St. 1, it was held that choses in action must be listed for taxation. Every reason requiring this to be done applies with equal force to such a judgment as the one we are now considering.

But such judgment should be listed at its true value at the time of listing. In the opinion in the case just BUT LISTABLE AT ITS TRUE VALUE. referred to, 3 Ohio St. 25, it was correctly said:
" In estimating the taxable valuation of credits, they are not to be taken at their nominal amount, but, like the valuation of other property, every circumstance affecting, in any manner, their value should be taken into consideration. If the debtor be wholly insolvent, the credit is of no value, and therefore has no basis for taxation. If the debtor be in doubtful or failing circumstances, if the claim be disputed, contested, or involved in litigation, or if any defence by way of payment, or otherwise, either in whole or in part against the claim be known to exist, it should be considered and all proper allowances made in estimating its taxable valuation.

The district court in the case now before us proceeded to render the judgment, which the Court of Common Pleas, in its opinion, should have given, and in doing this valued the interest of Cameron in the judgment at its nominal value in 1876, 1877, and .1878, only deducting therefrom the amount of his attorney's fees. In these years there was a proceeding in error, pending and undecided, in the Supreme Court, to reverse the judgment. By it important, novel, and difficult questions of law were raised, and it was uncertain whether the judgment would be affirmed. This situation certainly lessened the value of the judgment during its pendency. In fact the petition averred that these things wholly destroyed the value of Cameron's interest in the judgment, and when the District Court acted the averments of the petition had not been denied.

Therefore we think that there was error in the judgment of that court for which a judgment of reversal is entered herin.

Judgment reversed.

BENTLEY
v.
BARTON.

(41 *Ohio State Reports,* 410.)

Where the United States appropriated section number sixteen in every township . . . for the use of schools in such township, and vested the same in the legislature of the State " in trust for the use aforesaid, and for no other use, intent, or purpose whatever," in an action by a county treasurer against a lessee of such lands, who held a lease for ninety-nine years, renewable forever, whose lands were taxed under section 2733, Rev. Stats., as the property of the lessee, to enforce the payment of the taxes so assessed, *held*—

That, in the absence of a provision in the terms of acceptance of such lands by the State that they should be forever free from taxation, they are taxable after sale or lease by the State, as other lands in the State.

That section 2733, Revised Statutes, provided for the taxation of such lands held under such lease as the property of the lessee.

ERROR to the District Court of Columbiana county.

The plaintiff in error, William G. Bentley, treasurer of Columbiana county, brought his action against Henry Bar. ton, defendant in error, alleging that there stood charged on the duplicate of taxes for that county for the year 1880, the sum of $9.23 against eighty-three acres of land in section sixteen of Elkrun township, in the name of Henry Barton, and prayed that in case said taxes were not paid by a day to be fixed by the court, the lands should be sold to satisfy such taxes.

The defendant answered: that the tract of land described in the petition in this case, is a part of section sixteen, in Elkrun township, Columbiana county, Ohio; that said section sixteen was, by act of the Congress of the United States, set aside for the use of schools in said township; that said section, so set aside, was accepted by the people of Ohio for the use and support of schools in said township, the title thereof being vested in the legislature of said State, in trust for said purpose; that, in pursuance of the several acts of the legislature of said State, ordering and authorizing the leasing of said section sixteen, the township trustees of said original surveyed township of Elkrun, on the 28th day of April, 1821, by a written lease, duly executed, acknowledged and delivered, leased to Alexander Rodgers, the northeast quarter of said section sixteen, of which the tract described in petition is a part, at the rate of six per cent on the appraised value thereof, said appraised value being six dollars ($6.00) per acre, to be paid into the treasury of the school funds of the money arising from said section sixteen, for the use of the inhabitants of said township for school purposes, for the full term and period of ninety-nine years from said date of said lease, renewable forever, subject to a re-valuation of said real estate at the end of thirty-three years from said date of said lease, and at the end of each thirty-three years during said term of said lease, according to the true intent and meaning of the act of the legislature ordering and authorizing said lease; that said Alexander Rodgers accepted said lease of said real estate, and under it entered into possession of the same; that said Alexander Rodgers and his grantees and assigns have ever since continued in possession of said real estate, and have fully paid said rental and performed their part under said lease; that the defendant is a grantee and assignee of said Alexander Rodgers, holding possession of said tract, in the petition described, under and by virtue of said lease; that the rental of six per cent on the valuation, and re-valuation, has been and still is paid into the school funds of said township, and has been and still is wholly and exclusively applied for the use and support of the schools of said township for the free

education of the school youth therein without charge; that
said real estate described in the peittion in this case, is
exempt from taxation, and has been, and is wrongfully placed
on the tax duplicate of said county, and has been and is
wrongfully taxed thereon; that said taxes sued for in the
petition in this case are general taxes for State, county, township, and other purposes, and that there is nothing lawfully
due from the defendant to the treasurer of said county, or to
said county, for taxes on said tract of land.

To this answer the plaintiff demurred generally. The
court sustained the demurrer, and thereupon gave judgment
for the plaintiff. This judgment was reversed by the District Court. A petition in error is brought here to reverse
the judgment of the district court.

R. W. Tayler for plaintiff in error.

J. W. & H. Morrison for defendant in error.

McCAULEY, J.—By section 7 of an act of Congress approved April 30, 1802, entitled " An act to provide for the
government of the territory northwest of the river Ohio,"
1 Chase Statutes, 70, it was provided: " That the following
propositions be, and the same are hereby offered to the convention of the eastern State of the said territory when
formed, for their free acceptance or rejection; which, if
accepted by the convention, shall be obligatory upon the
United States. First. That the section number sixteen in
every township . . . shall be granted to the inhabitants of
such township for the use of schools." This proposition was
accepted by the convention assembled to form a constitution
for the State of Ohio, with the modification thereof to be
assented to by Congress, that all lands appropriated for the
use of schools shall be vested in the legislature of this State,
in trust for said purpose. This modification was afterwards
assented to by Congress. Act of March 3, 1803, Chase
Statutes, 72.

The answer in the court below sets forth the nature of the
defendant's title and the mode provided by law for taxing the
property. Section 2733, Rev. Stat., which is a re-enactment
of a former statute, provides that:

" Lands held under a lease for a term exceeding fourteen
years, belonging to the State or to any religious, scientific

or benevolent society, or institution, whether incorporated or unincorporated, and school and ministerial lands, shall be considered, for all purposes of taxation, as the property of the persons so holding the same, and shall be assessed in their names."

The defendant in error insists first, that under the statutes the taxation of his lands is not provided for; and second, that if the statutes do provide for the taxation of LEASED SCHOOL the land, they are unconstitutional and invalid. LANDS TAXABLE. The lands of the defendant are school lands and held under a valid lease for ninety-nine years, renewable forever. This clearly brings the property within the provisions of section 2733 above. This section applies only to lands held under a lease, and describes two kinds of property, that belonging to the State or to any religious, scientific or benevolent society, and school and ministerial lands. It could not apply to school and ministerial lands belonging to the State, before the same had been leased or sold. It must therefore apply to lands the legal title to which is in the State, but which have been leased for a term greater than fourteen years. The lands were properly assessed for taxes under this section, if they are taxable at all.

Are the lands taxable? They were appropriated by the United States to the inhabitants of each township for the use of schools, and the title thereto was vested in the legislature of the State "for the use aforesaid, and for no other use, intent or purpose," and were accepted by the State "upon the trust aforesaid." The State, in accepting the lands upon this trust, impliedly agreed that they or the rents and profits or proceeds of the sale thereof, should be applied to the use of schools in the several townships; and in the absence of a provision in the terms of acceptance that they should be forever free from taxation, after the lands were leased or sold, and the proceeds applied to the use upon which they were held by the State, the trust by which they were effected was fully executed; and when the land became private property it was subject to taxation as any other private property in the State.

It is insisted that the taxation of these lands would appropriate them to a purpose other than the support TAXATION IS NOT of schools, and the State being under the obliga- AN APPROPRI-
ATION OF PROP-
tion not to appropriate them to any other pur- ERTY.

pose, the lands are not taxable.   This argument is at fault in assuming that the taxation of the lands would appropriate them to a purpose other than the support of schools.   The taxation of property is in no proper sense an appropriation of it to any purpose.   In a general sense it is nothing more than the exercise of that attribute of sovereignty by which the State provides the means of self-preservation.   The trust upon which the lands were accepted did not affect them after they were leased or sold by the State, but was thereby transferred to the fund arising from the lease or sale—directng and defining the only use or purpose to which such fund should be applied.

Judgment reversed.

CITY OF CLEVELAND

v.

HEISLEY.

(41 *Ohio State Reports*, 670.)

A village was annexed to a city in A.D. 1872, pursuant to chapter 57, Municipal Code (66 Ohio Laws, 267).   The "terms and conditions of such annexation" authorized the city (in order to pay certain bonds theretofore issued by the village, under ordinances that contemplated their payment by taxes upon its general duplicate), to collect the money "in the manner and from the property specified or contemplated in" the said village ordinances.   The village territory formed two wards of the city.   The city council levied a tax upon the general duplicate of those wards alone, to pay said bonds.   This, when added to the other taxes on said duplicates, exceeded the authorized limit of eleven (11) mills.   *Held:*

The levy of said tax upon the village territory alone, pursuant to the "terms and conditions of such annexation," is not forbidden by Article XII, Constitution of 1851.

The tax as actually levied was illegal because the statutory limit was exceeded.

In A.D. 1872, the village of East Cleveland was annexed to the city of Cleveland.   The "terms and conditions of such annexation" included (with others) the following stipulations:

" 1. That the territory comprised within the limits of East Cleveland shall, until otherwise ordained by the city council, constitute two wards of the city of Cleveland; so much of said territory as lies south of Euclid Street shall be designated and known as the 'Sixteenth ward,' and so much as lies north of said street shall be designated and known as the 'Seventeenth ward.'

" 3. All rights and property of every description whatever, belonging to either of said corporations, shall become the rights and property of the city of Cleveland, and all existing legal liabilities of each of said corporations shall be assumed by the city of Cleveland; Provided, however, that all assessments made or bonds issued for street or other improvements, under the authority of existing ordinances, shall be collected at the times and in the manner and from the property specified or contemplated in such ordinances respectively, except the sum of ten thousand dollars of the indebtedness of East Cleveland, the estimated cost of paving street intersections, which is to be assumed and paid for by the city of Cleveland.

"6. As soon as practicable after such annexation is consummated, the city council shall pass all such ordinances as may be necessary and proper to carry into effect all the terms and conditions in this agreement of annexation mentioned and set forth."

In A.D. 1870, the council of the village duly ordered an improvement of a part of Euclid avenue, and resolved " That the cost and expense of making said improvement, except at street crossings and one half in front of school house in District No. 2, be defrayed by assessing the whole cost of said grading and one third of said paving on the lands abutting on said improvement by the foot front, and the balance be defrayed by a tax to be levied on the general duplicate of property, both real and personal, in this village."

Similar action had been taken as to other street improvements. In anticipation of levies, and assessments, the village had issued its bonds. All the bonds based upon assessments were paid by assessments. Of the other bonds the city paid $10,000 (the estimated cost of the street intersections), with moneys raised by a general tax on the city duplicate. In A.D. 1873, the city levied a tax, upon the general duplicate of the two wards, to pay said remaining village bonds, and $45,000 was collected. No tax-payer of said wards made any objection.

In A.D. 1879, the city made a similar levy. John W. Heisley and others, acting for themselves and other tax-payers of said wards, sued out an injunction against this tax. At a final hearing, the common pleas court dissolved the injunction and gave judgment for the city. On appeal the district court made a decree perpetually enjoining the collection of said tax. The city and the county treasurer (the defendants below) ask a reversal of this decree.

Kain, Sherwood & Bunts for plaintiff in error.

C. C. Baldwin and *E. J. Estep* for defendants in error.

GRANGER, C. J.—We are satisfied that the third stipulation, CITY—TAXATION OF ADDITION TO PAY A DEBT CONTRACTED BY SUCH ADDITION. in "the terms and conditions of such annexation," authorized the city to collect, by a tax levied upon the general duplicate of the two wards, enough money to pay the bonds theretofore issued by the village, for so much of the cost of said street improvements, as exceeded the aggregate formed by the sums assessable under the original ordinances upon the abutting lots, and the $10,000, estimated cost of street intersections.

Sec. 590, Municipal Code (66 Ohio Laws, 249), was then in force. The entire cost of the improvement of street intersections was a debt of the village, payable out of the proceeds of a tax "upon the general duplicate of all the real and personal property subject to taxation within the limits of the" village.

The express exception of this cost, out of the bonds that the city was authorized to pay by collections from villagers' property, necessarily implies that the power granted to the city, by the stipulation itself, included the power to levy and collect a tax, upon the general duplicate of the two wards alone, to pay bonds of the same character as those theretofore issued by the village for the cost of the improvement of street intersections. If the intent was to give power to assess abutting lots only, the exception has no meaning whatever. Neither city, nor village, had, or by agreement could confer, power to assess upon the abutting lots any part of the estimated cost of the street intersection improvements. The record shows no attempt by the village to make any such assessment. It is true that the ordinance to grade and improve Madison avenue, from Euclid avenue to the north line of the village, provided that the entire cost and expense of that improvement should be levied and assessed upon the abutting lots and lands. But it does not appear that any street intersection was included in said improvement. None of the bonds, about which the parties here contend, were issued for Madison avenue. The $10,000, estimated cost of street intersections, was made up of $6476.45 for Euclid avenue; $2378.47 for Cedar street, and $1145.08 for Fair-mount street. The ordinances, as to those streets, imposed only two thirds of the entire expenses of the respective improvements upon the abutting lots, and charged the general duplicate with much more than the entire cost of said street intersections.

It seems plain that the ordinances, as to those streets, "contemplated" the payment of at least one third of the bonds issued for said improvements, by the proceeds of taxes to be levied upon the general duplicate of the village. If no annexation had been made, such bonds could be paid in no other way. When the council had before it the question of making the improvement, and providing for a distribution of its cost, and, by ordinance or resolution, decided to charge only two thirds of the cost upon the abutting lots, and made the improvement under such ordinance, it had no power to, afterwards, re-distribute the burden, and increase the share to be assessed upon the lots.

The conduct of the parties to the stipulation, soon after the annexation, indicates that they both understood the intent to be precisely what we hold it was. The annexation was completed in 1872. The terms were agreed upon on August 3, 1872. In 1873, the city, by a tax limited to the two wards, collected $45,000, to pay bonds of the same class as those for which the tax before us was levied. Some of the men, who acted for the village in making the stipulation, were tax-payers then, as now. No tax-payer, in any manner, objected to the tax of 1873. The fair presumption is, that it was quietly paid, because it was understood that the terms of annexation granted to the city the power to levy and collect it. ·

But it is urged that the stipulation, so construed, was ineffective, because section 2, of Article XII, of the State Constitution, requires that all taxes shall, by a uniform rule, rest upon all taxable property within the municipality.

So long as East Cleveland continued its separate existence, its council could levy taxes on its duplicate to pay these bonds.

The two municipalities were by statute given power to fix any terms, not conflicting with existing laws. Sec. 705, Municipal Code (66 Ohio Laws, 268), provided that, " such annexation shall not affect, or in anywise impair, any rights, or liabilities, existing at the time of the annexation, either in favor of, or against, said corporations ; and suits, founded upon such rights and liabilities, may be commenced, . . . and carried to final judgment and execution, the same as though such annexation had not taken place."

If such annexation had not taken place, the holder of one of these bonds, after default, could obtain judgment against the village ; and, through a proper court, compel the levy of a tax upon the village duplicate to pay it.

The annexation having taken place, the rights of such a bondholder remain the same, but the order for the levy of the tax, to pay his judgment, can only be enforced through the city council.

The effect of the statute was, to continue so much of the existence of the village, as is necessary to secure the payment of its debts. The effect of the stipulation before us was, to continue the existence of these bonds, as debts of the village as between the city and village. As between bondholder and village, they of course remained obligations of the village.

In levying the tax, the city does no more than the bondholder could enforce through a court. If this were the only objection to the tax as levied, we feel sure that a court should not, at the instance of a taxpayer, enjoin the voluntary doing of the very act that, at the suit of a judgment creditor of the village, it would order to be done.

As already said, the effect of the statute and the stipulation, taken together, is to continue the existence of the village, so far as is necessary to legalize a tax, upon its duplicate, to pay a village debt, which, as between city and village, still remains a village debt. We think that the levy of the tax in question is not forbidden by Article XII. of the

Constitution. It is simply a levy upon all taxable property within East Cleveland, to pay East Cleveland's debt; to pay a debt that that property is legally bound to pay in that way.

But it is urged that the city was, by the statute in force, forbidden to levy a greater aggregate tax than eleven mills, in addition to the tax for school and school-house purposes, and such further rate as LEVY EXCEEDING LIMIT OF TAX ALLOWED BY LAW. was necessary to pay the interest on its public debt, and for cemetery purposes; and that the levy actually made, exclusive of the tax complained of, aggregated $10\frac{8}{10}$ mills. The tax complained of was $3\frac{6}{10}$ mills, making the aggregate in the two wards $13\frac{4}{10}$ mills.

A village aggregate might be eight mills.

It is plain that the village could not confer upon the city power to exceed the village aggregate. The city had and retained full power to tax, up to its own aggregate. Its power to tax was given by the statute. Hence it could not legally pass the statutory limit. If the village limit had been greater for the year of the levy than that of the city, under the doctrines hereinbefore stated, the city could, within the two wards, for the purpose before us, tax up to said village limit.

In making the levy complained of, the city exceeded both limits. An ordinance levying a tax on the two wards, which, when added to the other taxes, computable in fixing the aggregate that could lawfully be imposed, did not exceed eleven mills, would have been valid. The levy actually made was wholly void, because it made an aggregate greater than eleven mills. No part of it is sustained by valid action of the council. Ohio *v.* Humphries, 25 Ohio St. 520; Cummings *v.* Fitch, 40 Id. 56.

The city claims that the levy complained of is not a tax computable as part of the eleven mills, but is a WHETHER LEVY IS A TAX OR A SPECIAL ASSESSMENT. special assessment upon specified property.

Sec. 581, Municipal Code (66 Ohio Laws, 248), reads thus:

"If, in the opinion of the council, it would be equitable, the whole, or a proportion of the cost of the improvement, as may be fixed by the council, . . . may be raised by the levy and assessment, by the council, of a tax upon the general

9 Cor. Cas.—29

duplicate of all the real and personal property subject to tax-ation within the limits of the corporation." If the village had continued to exist, the levy to pay these bonds would have been a tax under this section. As already stated, the village, having once exhausted its power to determine the distribution of the cost of the improvement, could not, afterwards, increase the burden upon the abutting lots. That distribu-tion finally determined how the respective shares of the cost should be paid. In levying such tax, the city council acts instead of the village council, and can make no change in the nature of the levy. In the words of Judge White (The State *v.* Strader, 25 Ohio St. 536), " we see no just ground on which taxes raised by general levy, for the improvement of streets, can be excluded from the aggregate amount of taxes, to the levying of which corporations are restricted."

As already said, this is a tax levied upon the general dupli-cate of East Cleveland. It must be counted as part of the aggregate levy for the two wards.

This conclusion may make it difficult for the city to enjoy the full benefit of Stipulation 3, but no court can help it. The legislature of course has power to raise the limit of taxation for municipalities. Whatever that limit may be at the time of making a levy, the city can go to it, but not beyond it.

Therefore the district court did not err in enjoining the collection of the tax, and its action in so doing is

Affirmed.

TAX LEVY CANNOT EXCEED LIMITS FIXED BY STATUTE OR CON-STITUTION.—It is well settled that the levy of a greater amount than is authorized by law is void. Greedup *v.* Franklin Co., 30 Ark. 101. It has been held that a tax cannot be levied to pay a judgment against a fund when the tax already levied for that fund equals the maximum—10 mills —fixed by law. Sterling School Furniture Co. *v.* Harvey, 45 Iowa 468; Iowa R. L. Co. *v.* Sac. Co., 39 Iowa, 124. Where county commissioners levied a tax of one per cent for current expenses, which came up to the limit fixed, and they then levied an eight-mill tax to make up a deficit in the preceding year's revenue, the second levy was held void. Atchison, T. & S. F. R. R. Co. *v.* Woodcock, 18 Kans. 20. County commissioners have no power to assess an additional tax for previous years on land, on a subse-quently increased valuation, after taxes for the previous years have been paid. Sudderth *v.* Britain, 76 N. C. 458. They have no power to increase the levy beyond the constitutional limit without legislative authority given in advance. Cromartie *v.* Commmr's, 87 N. C. 135. French *v.* New Hanover Co., 74 N. C. 692; Trull *v.* Madison Co., 72 N. C. 388;

Clifton *v.* Wynne, 80 N. C. 145; Mauney *v.* Montgomery Co., 71 N. C. 486. In Texas the limitation of the constitution on the power of counties to levy taxes applies only to the erection of public buildings. Texas & P. R. R. Co. *v.* Harrison Co., 54 Tex. 119. But while the constitutional restraint imposed on the taxing power applies to taxes levied to meet the ordinary expenses of county government, it does not extend to such as may be necessary for the payment of obligations incurred before the adoption of the constitution. In such cases the limit may be exceeded. Clifton *v.* Wynne, 80 N. C. 147; Haughton *v.* Comm'rs, 70 N. C. 466; Street *v.* Commr's, 70 N. C., 644; Brothers *v.* Currituck Comm'rs, 70 N. C. 726; Trull *v.* Madison, 72 N. C. 388; French *v.* New Hanover Co., 74 N. C. 692.

JUSTICE
v.
THE CITY OF LOGANSPORT.

(101 *Indiana,* 326.)

Municipal corporations in levying taxes are instrumentalities of government, and taxes levied by them are, in legal effect, levied by the State, so that the lien for such taxes is of equal rank and priority to taxes levied for State or county purposes.

A purchaser at a tax sale made by the county officers takes the land subject to the lien for city taxes existing thereon, if the land is of sufficient value to pay all taxes; but, if the land is not of sufficient value to pay all taxes, then the sale first rightfully made will divest the lien for the other taxes.

FROM Cass Circuit Court.
D. C. Justice for appellant.
J. C. Nelson and *Q. A. Myers* for appellee.

ELLIOTT, J.—The appellant foreclosed a mortgage executed to him by Jacob J. Puterbaugh, and acquired title   FACTS. under the sale made on the decree. In 1877 the city of Logansport assessed taxes against the real estate embraced in the mortgage amounting to $600. At the time the taxes for 1877 accrued Puterbaugh was the owner of the property, and was also the owner of $10,000 worth of personal property subject to seizure for the taxes assessed against him. State and county taxes were assessed against the property for the years 1877, 1878, and 1879, and in the latter year the property was sold to pay the delinquent and current State and county taxes. The appellant was the purchaser at the sale, and received a deed in due course of law. He seeks by the present suit to restrain the city from enforcing the taxes assessed by it against the real estate bought by him at the sale for State and county taxes.

The theory of the appellant is that the title acquired through the sale made for State and county taxes swept away all liens of the city, and vested in him the property discharged from all liens for municipal taxes.

This theory is constructed on an unsubstantial foundation.

Taxes levied by a municipal corporation are levied for a public purpose and by public officers. A municipal corporation is part of the government; it is a governmental organization, invested with the powers of government over a designated locality. One of the oldest as well as one of the best definitions of a municipal corporation is, " an investing the people of the place with the local government thereof." Cuddon *v.* Eastwick, 1 Salk. 193. Cities are much older governmental institutions than counties, and they were influential agencies in securing stable and liberal government centuries before counties were organized. Robertson says : " The institution of cities into communities, corporations, or bodies politic, and granting them the privilege of municipal jurisdiction, contributed more, perhaps, than any other cause to introduce regular government, police, and arts, and to diffuse them over Europe." Chancellor Kent and Judge Dillon accept as correct De Tocqueville's theory, that municipal corporations are important governmental institutions, and essential to the preservation of free government. 2 Kent Com. (12th ed.) 275 ; 1 Dillon Munic. Corp. (3d ed.), section 9, n. 2. The chancellor says : " Public corporations are such as are created by the government for political purposes, as counties, cities, towns, and villages ; they are invested with subordinate legislative powers, to be exercised for local purposes connected with the public good." Counties do not, therefore, rank higher than cities ; they are not as ancient; they are not more important instrumentalities of government, nor have they more comprehensive powers. It is not possible, therefore, to successfully maintain that taxes for county purposes take precedence of taxes levied by a city pursuant to legislative authority.   It might with quite as much reason be affirmed that taxes levied by a city have precedence of taxes levied by a county as to assert the contrary. The position which best comports with reason and authority is this: There is no difference in priority, PRECEDENCE OF LIENS FOR MUNICIPAL TAXES. and a purchaser at a tax sale made by the county authorities takes the property subject to the city taxes, except, perhaps, in cases where it is made to clearly appear that the property is not of sufficient value to pay both city and county taxes. Where the property is not of sufficient value to pay both city and county taxes, then the sale first rightfully made divests the lien of the other governmental corporation.

The power to levy taxes is an attribute of sovereignty. ·Sovereign powers reside in the State, but the power to exercise the sovereign power of taxation may be delegated to a municipal corporation.   In exercising this sovereign power the corporation invested with it is exercising a power of the State, and the taxes levied by it as an instrument of the government are, in legal effect, levied by the State.   The State acts through one of its governmental subdivisions, and is the source of power.   Whether the taxes are levied by a county or a city, they are taxes laid upon the people by the State, acting through its chosen representatives.   This view is supported by the well-reasoned case of Denike *v.* Rourke, 3 Bissell, 39, where it was said: "Municipal taxes are levied by virtue of the same general authority which levies and enforces a payment of State and county taxes—the municipal authorities acting by virtue of the power delegated to them by the State government, and a sale by municipal authority is, therefore, essentially in all respects a sale by State authority." The question was presented in Dennison *v.* City of Keokuk, 45 Iowa, 266, as it is here, and it was held, as we hold, that the sale by the county officers did not divest the lien for city taxes.

Counsel for appellant makes some criticism upon the provision of the statute that city taxes are to be a lien " to the same extent as a judgment of a court of record of general jurisdiction;" but, in making this criticism, ALL OF A STATUTE TO BE READ TOGETHER. counsel pursues the illogical course of wresting the phrase from its connection and completely isolating it. Statutes are not to be thus treated.   The context is to be read as an entirety, not subjected to a process of dissection.   Treating the statute logically, there can be no doubt that it creates an enduring lien; it does, indeed, do this in very plain words, for it declares that " such lien shall be perpetual for all taxes due from the owner." It would be difficult, if not impossible, to have employed stronger words. It is obvious that a perpetual lien cannot be destroyed by a sale made upon a lien of equal rank. The purchaser may, perhaps, secure a right to redeem from the city taxes, but he does not secure a title divested of the lien.

Judgment affirmed.

CARLTON
v.
NEWMAN.

(*Advance Case, Maine. August* 8, 1885.)

When an entire school-district tax is illegal, equity will, at the suit of all or a part of the taxpayers, enjoin its collection in order to prevent a multiplicity of suits.

Municipal officers erecting a school-house can lawfully expend therefor no more money than is voted for the purpose.

Nor, if more than this sum is expended, can the legislature authorize the excess to be taxed upon the polls and estates of the district.

Joseph C. Holman and *Drummond & Drummond* for plaintiffs.
E. O. Greenleaf for defendants.

VIRGIN, J.—While the defendant admits the facts, he denies that equity can enjoin the collection of the pretended tax, even on the assumption that it was assessed without the authority of law and, therefore void, and he contends that the only remedies open to the plaintiffs, and all the other taxpayers on whose polls and estates the tax has been assessed are simply such as the law affords, viz.: Each to defend the action of debt against himself, provided the collector shall proceed to enforce the collection by such action, under the provisions of Rev. Stat., chap. 6, § 141; or, in case the collector shall resort to the more usual mode of seizing their individual property under the other statutory provisions for the collection of taxes, then for each taxpayer whose property shall be taken to bring an action for damages, or recover back the money when collected, and these remedies are said to be "plain, adequate, and complete."

If a tax against an individual be illegal, simply by reason of some irregularity in its assessment, as for instance, on account of over-valuation, or if laid on property which the tax-payer did not own at the time, he would then have ample remedy therefor by a seasonable application for an abatement. Rev. Stat., chap. 6, §§ 68, 69; Gilpatrick *v.* Saco, 57 Me. 277. Moreover, it is generally held that a bill to restrain the collection of a tax cannot be maintained on the sole ground of its illegality. Greene *v.* Mumford, 5 R. I. 472; Sherman *v.* Leonard, 10 Id. 469; Guest *v.* Brooklyn, 69 N. Y. 506; Loud *v.* Charlestown, 99 Mass. 208; Whiting *v.* Boston, 106 Id. 89, 93; Hunnewell *v.* Charlestown, Id. 350. There must be some allegation presenting a case of equity jurisdiction. Dows *v.* Chicago, 11 Wall. 108; Hannewinkle *v.* Georgetown, 15 Id. 547; State Railroad Tax Cases, 92 U. S. 575, 614; cases cited 2 Dest. Tax, 676, 677. In Hunnewell *v.* Charlestown, *supra*, brought b a single plaintiff, the court adds: "The question is not affected by the fact that there are others, whether few or many, who are subjected to a like assessment by the same proceedings of the city council and who propose to contest their liability."

But we are of opinion that when it appears that an entire school-district tax is illegal, because assessed without authority of law, a bill to enjoin its collection, brought ILLEGAL TAX WILL BE ENJOINED. by all of the taxpayers of the district jointly on whose polls and estates the tax has been assessed, or by any number thereof on behalf of themselves and all the others similarly situated, may be sustained upon the ground of inherent jurisdiction of equity to interpose for the purpose of preventing a multiplicity of suits; that, although each taxpayer has some legal remedy, it is grossly inadequate when compared with the comprehensive and complete relief afforded by a single decree.

The general doctrine, coeval with equity proceedings, asserted in a multitude of decisions, that, in certain cases, where parties have some remedy, equity may interpose and take cognizance for the purpose of preventing a multiplicity of suits, was declared by Chancellor Kent to be "a favorite object with a court of equity." Brinkerhoff *v.* Brown, 6 Johns. Ch. 151, and the number of parties and the multiplicity of actual or threatened suits, as stated by Comstock, J., sometimes justify a resort to equity when the subject is not at all of an equitable character and there is no other element of equity jurisdiction. N. Y. & N. H. R. R. *v.* Schuyler, 17 N. Y. 608. And yet the precise extent and limitations of the doctrine are still unsettled, the decisions being quite inharmonious even as to its fundamental grounds. It is said that "bills of peace" were founded upon this ground—to quiet unnecessary litigation as to titles, and where one person claimed or defended a right against many or many against one. Sto. Eq., § 864. In these bills originally, whether brought by or in behalf of many against one, or by one against or on behalf of many, "chancery confined its jurisdiction to cases wherein there was common interest in the subject-matter of the controversy, or a common title from which all their separate claims and all the questions at issue arose, it not being enough that the claims of each individual being separate and distinct, there was a community of interest merely in the question of law or fact involved, or in the kind and form of remedy demanded and obtained by or against each individual." Pom. Eq., § 268. But, at an early day, the limitations began to yield and the jurisdiction to extend. Thus, in York *v.* Pilkington, 1 Atk. 282, Lord Chancellor Hardwicke at first intimated that the bill could not be maintained for want of any general right or privity among the parties, and because the nature of the defendants' claims was different, and that, therefore, injunction would not quiet the possession, as other persons not parties might likewise claim a right. But after argument, he changed his opinion, saying bills might be maintained, although there were no privity between the plaintiffs and defendants, nor any general right on the part of the defendants, and when many more might be concerned than those before the court.

This jurisdiction has continued to extend until it comprises a great variety of cases, which do not come strictly within bills of peace, but which courts have declared to be analogous thereto and within the principles thereof, and in which there was no common title or community of interest in anything, save the question at issue and the remedy sought. Thus, in a recent case, where the owner of lands on a river sought, by a bill against them jointly, to restrain several owners of mines from depositing the débris thereof in the river and its tributaries, where it floated down and was deposited on the plaintiff's lands, on demurrer, Sawyer, J., sustained the bill, saying: "The rights of all involve and depend upon identically the same question, both of law and fact. It is one of the class of cases, like bills of peace and bills founded on analogous principles, where a single individual may bring a suit against numerous defendants, where there is no joint interest or title, but where the questions at issue and the evidence to establish the rights of the parties and the relief demanded are identical." Woodruff *v.* North B. G. M. Co., 8 Sawy. 628. This case has been cited and approved by this court in the very recent case of like nature. Lockwood *v.* Lawrence, *ante*, 403, to appear in 77 Me.

So in a late English case, the bursting of the plaintiff's reservoir occasioned an inundation which damaged the property of many persons. The statute commissioners issued certificates to such as satisfactorily proved their damages and entitled them to costs and could be enforced by action at law. Fifteen hundred of these certificates were alleged to be invalid; and to avoid a multiplicity of suits against itself, the bill was brought by the plaintiff against five holders of the certificates "on behalf of themselves and all other the persons named in any of certain pretended certificates." On demurrer, the bill was sustained first by Vice-Chancellor Kindersley, and on appeal by Lord Chancellor Chelmsford, who said: "Perhaps, strictly speaking, this is not a bill of peace, as the rights of the claimants under the alleged certificates are not identical; but it appears to me to be within the principle of bills of this description. The rights of the numerous claimants all depend upon the same question." And after remarking that if the certificates had no validity, the executions could not be set aside until considerable expense had been incurred by many, he concluded: "It seems to me to be a very fit case by analogy, at least to a bill of peace, for a court of equity to interpose and prevent the unnecessary expense and litigation, which would be thus occasioned, and to decide once for all the validity or invalidity of the certificates upon which the claims of all the parties depend." Sheffield Water-

works *v.* Yeomans, L. R., 2 Ch. App. 8, 12.   See, also, N. Y.
& N. H. R. R. *v.* Schuyler, *supra ;* Board Sup. *v.* Deyoe, 77
N. Y. 219.

In Brinkerhoff *v.* Brown, *supra*, a bill by various distinct
judgment creditors to render effectual their executions
against their debtor was sustained in order to prevent a
multiplicity of suits, although their only community of interest was in the relief demanded.   See, also, Cadigan *v.*
Brown, 120 Mass. 493, and Ballou *v.* Hopkinton, 4 Gray, 324,
wherein one of the reasons assigned for holding jurisdiction
in equity was, that at law each owner must bring a separate
action to obtain a remedy for his particular injury, and
equity prevents a multiplicity of suits.

After an exhaustive examination of the subject both upon
principle and authority, an eminent legal author sums up his
conclusions as follows : " Under the greatest diversity of
circumstances and the greatest variety of claims arising from
unauthorized public acts, private tortious acts, invasion of
private property rights, violation of contract obligations, and
notwithstanding the positive denials by some American
courts, the weight of authority is simply overwhelming that
the jurisdiction may and should be exercised either on behalf of a numerous body of separate claimants against a
single party or on behalf of a single party against a numerous
body, although there is no ' common title ' nor ' community
of right,' . . . or of ' interest in the subject-matter,' among
these individuals ; but where there is and because there is
merely a community of interest among them in the questions
of law and fact involved in the general controversy, or in the
kind and form of relief demanded and obtained by or against
each individual member of the numerous body.   The same
overwhelming weight of authority effectually disposes of
the rule laid down by some judges as a test, that equity will
never exercise its jurisdiction to prevent a multiplicity of
suits, unless the plaintiff, or each of the plaintiffs, is himself
the person who would necessarily and contrary to his own
will be exposed to numerous actions or vexatious litigation.
This position is opposed to the whole course of decisions in
suits of the third and fourth classes from the earliest period
down to the present time."   Pom. Eq., § 269.

These principles apply to the case at bar.   They have

been applied to a large number like this. Each of the plaintiffs has, of course, some remedy at law or else equity could not interpose on the ground mentioned. But at law he must wait and suffer the wrong before he can begin his action for redress, and when his legal remedy is exhausted it is not much else than nominal when viewed in the contrast with the full relief in equity which decides in advance of actual litigation once for all, the validity or invalidity of the tax.

The court in Rhode Island, although they in Greene *v.* Mumford, 5 R. I. 472, and in Sherman *v.* Leonard 10 Id. 469, referred the complainants therein to their remedies at law (the validity of the assessment in each case on the complainants only being involved), nevertheless declared the court would enjoin the collection of a tax where the question involves the validity of the whole tax. Sherman *v.* Benford, 10 R. I. 559.

So the United States Supreme Court, although they had denied jurisdiction in suits brought by a single plaintiff in the case already cited, they also disavow in the State Railroad Tax cases, *supra,* any purpose of fixing any absolute limitation in restraining the collection of illegal taxes; and in Cummings *v.* Nat'l Bank, 101 U. S. 157, say: " We are of opinion that when a rule or system of valuation is adopted by those whose duty it is to make the assessment, which is designed to operate unequally and violate a fundamental principle of the Constitution, and when this rule is applied not solely to one individual but to a large class, that equity may interpose to restrain the operation of this unconstitutional exercise of power."

That our opinion is sustained by the weight of judicial authority to-day, see Dill. Mun. Corp. §§ 731, 736; Bur. Tax., § 143 and cases; Pom. Eq., §§ 258–260, 1343, and cases in notes.

Was the tax assessed by authority of law? If any part is illegal the whole is; therefore the provisions of Rev. Stat., chap. 11, § 78, and chap. 6, § 142, do not apply.

Under the general statutory provisions, it is common knowledge that political subdivisions, such as EXPENDITURE FOR SCHOOL towns, created for the more efficient administra- LIMITED TO SUM VOTED. tion of the affairs of the State, have only such power of

taxation as is delegated to them by the State. In the provisions of Rev. Stat., chap. 11, defining the duties and obligations of towns and school districts in relation to education,
we find no authority for assessing a tax on a school district
for the purpose of building a school-house, unless: (1) The
district, at a legal meeting thereof called for the purpose,
vote to raise the money therefor—chap. 11, § 48—or to borrow
it—§§ 81, 83—or (2), the town, on application of five voters
of the district, under a proper article, deeming the sum
voted by the district insufficient, vote a larger sum—§ 51;
Powers v. Sanford, 39 Me. 183—or (3), the town, on the
written opinion of the school committee that the district un-
reasonably neglects or refuses to raise money for a school-
house such as the wants of the district require, shall vote a
sum. § 52. No action was ever taken under sections 51 or
52, but the district, under section 48, voted to raise by
assessment $500. There is no general statutory warrant for
the tax, unless it is found in section 56.

The authority of the municipal officers to build a school-
house for a school district is derived solely from section 56.
When they had "decided where the school-house should be
placed," and seasonably certified " their determination to
the clerk of the district," their authority ceased *pro hac*.
Then it became the duty of the district to " proceed to erect
the house as if determined by a sufficient majority of " its
voters. But when the district had neglected " for sixty days
to carry such determination into effect," then it became the
duty of the municipal officers, " at expense of the district, if
need be, to purchase a lot for said house and cause it to be
erected." § 56.

What house were the municipal officers directed by the
statute to " cause to be erected "?—" said house" for which
they might " purchase a lot ," " the house" which the statute
directed the district to " proceed to erect" on the location
fixed by the municipal officers ; the house which it might
build under its vote, viz., a $500 house. The building com-
mittee of the district could not bind the district by expend-
ing more money than the district voted. Wilson v. School
District, 32 N. H. 118, recognized in Jenkins v. Union School
District, 39 Me. 220. The legislature could not have intended to confer on the municipal officers unlimited power

as to the "expense" to which they might subject the district,
for the decision of that question is rightfully vested in the
discretion of the tax-payers, except in the two instances
coming under sections 51 and 52, when all the voters of the
town take part in the decision. It is very evident, therefore,
that the municipal officers transcended their authority and
could not bind the district by thus virtually undertaking to
hire money on the district's credit; nor could the payment
by the treasurer of the orders drawn by them for the expenditure, in excess of the sum voted by the district, create
any liability or debt of the district to the town. The relation
of creditor and debtor the law does not allow to be created
in that manner. Brunswick *v.* Litchfield, 2 Me. 32; Hampshire *v.* Franklin, 16 Mass. 84. We find no authority for the
tax in the general statutes.

Did the special act of 1883, chap. 348, afford a legal foundation for it? We think not. Assuming that the legislature
might constitutionally confer authority for assessing on the
district the excess mentioned, did the act answer the object?
Giving to it that strict construction which well-established
rules of law require to be put upon statutes affecting the
property of the citizen, and by which it may be EXCESS CANNOT
taken from him, as by taxation—Merritt *v.* Vil- BE TAXED.
lage of Port Chester, 71 N. Y. 309; s. c., 27 Am. Rep. 47, and
cases therein cited; Burr. Tax, § 128; 1 Dest. Tax. 257—the
assessment was without legal authority, it having been made,
not by the "municipal officers," as provided in the act, but
by the "assessors," an entirely different and distinct board
of officers. Rev. Stat., chap. 3, § 12. Moreover the act
authorized the tax to be assessed for the purpose of reim-
bursing the town "for making repairs on the school-house,"
and not for building a school-house, as the fact was. No money
was paid by the town for "making repairs" on the district's
school-house. Districts may raise money for both purposes
—§ 48—and the school agent may appropriate a certain per
cent of the school money to repairs, but not to building.
§ 93. They are considered by statute distinct matters.
Courts can give effect to legislative enactments only to the
extent to which they may be made operative by legal construction of the language in which they are expressed, and
cannot make defective enactments carry out fully the pur-

poses which may have occasioned them. Swift *v.* Luce, 27 Me. 285.

Moreover, the last clause in the act satisfies us that the legislature must have supposed that the object of the act was the very common one of validating a former assessment, which was defective for some irregularity therein; for, as said by Mellen, C. J., "we cannot, without disrespect to the legislature, presume they intended, *ipso facto,* to create a debt from one man or corporation to another." Brunswick *v.* Litchfield, *supra.* And in that of Parker, C. J.: "It certainly must be admitted that, bv the principles of every free government, and of our Constitution in particular, it is not in the power of the legislature to create a debt from one person to another, or from one corporation to another, without the consent, express or implied, of the party to be charged." Hampshire *v.* Franklin, *supra.*

Bill sustained. Collection of the tax perpetually enjoined.

WALTON, DANFORTH, LIBBEY, FOSTER, and HASKELL, JJ., concurred.

SNOW

v.

WEEKS.

(Advance Case, Maine.   August 6, 1885.)

Without a distinct vote determining when taxes are payable, interest on them cannot be collected, even though it be voted by the common council that "on all taxes unpaid after the last day of December, interest must be collected."

But if the assessor's warrant contain such a recital of facts as authorizes a collection of interest, then an arrest thereunder would be justified, although such recitals were not true.

A. P. Gould for plaintiff.

D. N. Mortland for defendant.

WALTON, J.—The plaintiff having been arrested on a warrant issued by the defendant as treasurer and collector of taxes of the city of Rockland, claims that the arrest was illegal, and brings this action to recover the damages which he says he thereby sustained.

The city council of Rockland had voted that the collector be instructed to allow a discount of eight per cent on all taxes paid during the month of August, and four per cent on all taxes paid during the month of September, and WHEN INTEREST that "on all taxes unpaid after the last day of IS PAYABLE ON TAXES. December, interest must be collected." But there was no distinct vote by the city council determining when the taxes should be payable; and the question is whether, without such a vote, the payment of interest could lawfully be enforced. We think it could not. The statutes authorizing the collection of interest are explicit, and make it a condition precedent, that the town or city shall first fix the time when the taxes are payable.

The Revised Statutes of 1871, chap. 6, § 93, declare that "towns at their annual meetings may determine when their taxes shall be payable, and that interest shall be collected after that time," and the act of 1876, chap. 92, extending this power in terms to cities as well as towns, and limiting the amount of interest, declares that "whenever a city or town has fixed a time within which taxes assessed therein shall be paid, such city, by its city council, and such town, at the meeting when money is appropriated or raised, may vote that on all taxes remaining unpaid after a certain time, interest shall be paid at a specified rate, not exceeding one per centum per month; and the interest accruing under such vote or votes shall be added to and be a part of such taxes."

We think it is clear that under a fair interpretation of these statutes, a compulsatory collection of interest cannot be justified, without a definite and distinct vote, fixing the time when the taxes are payable. A vote declaring that interest shall be collected after a time named is not sufficient. Interest may and generally does commence to run before the principal is payable; and a vote declaring when interest shall commence is by no means equivalent to a vote, fixing a time when the principal shall be payable.

Such being the law, we are forced to the conclusion that the warrant issued by the defendant for the arrest of the plaintiff was illegal. It directed the sheriff or his deputy to collect interest as well as the principal remaining due upon the plaintiff's taxes. We think an arrest upon such a warrant would be an actionable wrong. No justification is found in the defendant's warrant from the assessors, for that did not direct him to collect interest. It directed him to collect the taxes actually assessed, but it did not direct him to collect the interest. It made no mention of interest. And no justification is found in the vote of the city council, for that is defective and insufficient upon its face. If the warrant from the RECITALS IN WARRANT JUSTIFYING ARREST assessors had contained such a recital of facts as would justify a collection of interest, and also a direction to the defendant to collect interest, then, being an instrument legal upon its face, and coming from competent authority, the defendant could justify under it, although the recitals were not in fact true. But the warrant from the assessors to the defendant contained no such recitals, and the principle invoked in his defence, and the authorities cited in support of it, do not apply.

When this case was before the law court, on a former occasion, the court held that inasmuch as the warrant which the defendant issued to the sheriff contained an averment of the vote by the city of Rockland, fixing a time when its taxes should be payable; this averment should be deemed to be true unless the contrary should be proved—in other words, that such a recital by a sworn officer is *prima-facie* evidence of the fact. But the contrary is now proved. An inspection of the city records and the testimony of the clerk show that no such vote was passed. Consequently, the averment must be disregarded and the truth allowed to prevail.

The result is, that the defendant must be defaulted and the damages assessed by a jury, as agreed in the report.

Defendant to be defaulted. Damages to be assessed by a jury.

PETERS, C. J., DANFORTH, VIRGIN, LIBBEY, FOSTER, and HASKELL, JJ., concurred.

KLOKKE

v.

STANLEY.

(109 *Illinois*, 192.)

A county clerk who has once executed a tax deed at the instance of the holder of the certificate of purchase, upon evidence furnished by such holder, cannot subsequently be compelled, by *mandamus*, to execute to the same party another tax deed under the same certificate of purchase, the holder thereof having filed with the clerk additional and more perfect evidence of his having complied with the law in respect to giving notice of his purchase, etc.

If, however, the county clerk himself makes a mistake in executing a tax deed, whereby it is rendered inoperative for the purpose for which it was intended, he may be compelled, by *mandamus*, to correct his mistake, and he may make the correction without being coerced thereto by the court.

A party applying for a *mandamus* must show a clear legal right to have the thing sought by it to be done; and if the granting of the writ will be of no avail to the party applying for it, it will be refused.

It is contrary to the policy of the law that *mandamus* should issue, where its sole purpose and effect is to relieve the party seeking it from the consequences of his own mistakes or omissions.

APPEAL from the Appellate Court for the First District;— heard in that court on appeal from the Superior Court of Cook County; the Hon. Joseph E. Gary, Judge, presiding.

A petition for *mandamus* was filed in the Superior Court of Cook County, on the 22d of September, A.D. 1882, in the words following, omitting the caption:

"The petition of Philiskey E. Stanley, of Cook County, State of Illinois, complains that on the 10th day of October, A.D. 1879, at a tax sale then being held in said Cook County, by Samuel H. McCrea, county treasurer and *ex-officio* collector of revenue of said county, the petitioner bid off and became the purchaser at said sale of lot four (4), in block thirty-five (35), in school-section addition to Chicago, situate in said Cook County; that thereupon petitioner paid to said collector the sum of $377.33, and afterwards, on said 10th day of October, 1879, the county clerk of said county made out and delivered to petitioner, duly executed and countersigned, a tax-sale certificate of purchase of said lot, said cer-

9 Cor. Cas.—30

tificate being numbered No. 15,663; that said petitioner, as
owner of said certificate, duly caused to be served a partly
written and partly printed notice of such purchase, on every
person in actual possession or occupancy of said premises,
and upon all the owners or parties interested in said premises, three months before the expiration of the time of
redemption of said sale, in which notice petitioner stated
when he purchased said lot, in whose name the same was
taxed, the description of the premises so purchased, for what
years the same was taxed, and when the time of redemption
would expire; that petitioner caused diligent inquiry to be
made for the person in whose name said lot was taxed; that
upon such inquiry said person could not be found in said
county, and thereupon petitioner caused said notice to be
published in a newspaper printed in said county, said notice
being inserted three times in said newspaper,—the first time
not more than five months, and the last time not less than
three months, before the time of redemption from said sale
would expire; that said premises were not redeemed by any
one from said sale during the time limited by law for such
redemption; that on the 11th day of November, 1881, petitioner made affidavit (still being owner and holder of said
certificate of sale, supposed by him at that time to be in compliance with the conditions of section 216 of the Revenue
act, chapter 120, of the Revised Statutes of the State of Illinois), stating particularly the facts relied upon as complying
with said act, and thereupon delivering said affidavit and
certificate of sale, and the receipt for the payment of all taxes
upon said premises for the two years following said tax sale,
to the county clerk of said county; that petitioner at that
time requested said county clerk to execute and deliver to
petitioner a tax deed of said premises; that thereupon said
county clerk duly filed said affidavit, certificate of sale, and
the papers accompanying the same, in the office of the county
clerk of said county, and afterwards, to wit, on November
25, 1881, executed and delivered to petitioner a tax deed of
said premises, said tax deed being tax deed No. K 1952; that
the papers upon which petitioner obtained said tax deed
were, the affidavit of petitioner, the said tax-sale certificate,
the said tax receipts, the affidavits of William E. Winholtz,
George M. French and James Mois, the tax-purchaser's

notices, the published tax-sale notice, and the certificate of
publication of said notice, certified copies of which are hereto annexed and made a part of this petition; that Mary
Conners was in possession of said premises at the time when
notices were served as aforesaid, but they do not show that
said notice was at any time served upon said Mary Conners;
that said notice was duly served upon said Mary Conners,
by delivering a copy thereof to her, on the 15th day of
March, 1881; that the same was served upon her by said
George M. French, agent of petitioner, for that purpose, but
at the time of making said affidavit of service of said notice
by said French, the allegation that he had so served said
notice upon said Mary Conners was left out of said affidavit
by mistake, and that neither petitioner, nor said French, nor
said clerk, nor any one else, discovered said mistake until
long after the execution and delivery of said tax deed; that
petitioner believes it to be the law that said tax deed, so far
as it relates to the premises aforesaid, 'was prematurely
issued, unauthorized, and void, for the reason that said
papers, so filed as aforesaid, show that said Mary Conners
was in possession of said premises at the time of service of
said notices, but show no service of said notice upon said
Mary Conners, and that said papers so filed are not in compliance with section 216 of said act, and are not *prima-facie*
evidence that your petitioner had complied with the conditions of said section 216 at the time when said tax deed was
issued;' that petitioner has made no conveyance of said
premises at any time after discovery of said mistake in the
affidavit of said French; that petitioner made a new affidavit,
accompanied with a copy of said notice and a second affidavit of said French, stating that he served said notice on said
Mary Conners on the 15th day of March, 1881; that petitioner
presented said last-mentioned papers to said county clerk,
Ernst F. C. Klokke, and requested him to file the same, and
to deliver to petitioner a new deed for said premises, offering to pay any additional fee to said clerk which it might be
necessary to pay, but said clerk refused, and still refuses, to
deliver to petitioner such new deed; that the time limited
for taking out a valid deed upon said premises will expire on
the 10th day of October next; that petitioner believes it is
the duty of said clerk to deliver to him a new deed of said

premises in time for filing the same for record, before the 10th day of October, 1882; wherefore petitioner prays this court to grant a writ of *mandamus* to compel said Ernst F. C. Klokke to receive and file in his office said papers last presented to him, and to execute and deliver to petitioner a new deed of said premises, and to do such acts and things as the law requires, for petitioner's relief."

Copies of the affidavits, notices of purchase, etc., are referred to in the petition as exhibits.

The defendant demurred to the petition, and for cause of demurrer assigned, " that as the county clerk of said county has regularly issued a tax deed in compliance with section 216 of the Revenue law, and that such deed having been in all respects issued regularly and according to law, as appears from said petition, the respondent, as such county clerk, has no power or authority in law to issue a second deed." The demurrer concludes: " Wherefore, and for other good causes of demurrer appearing in said petition, defendant prays judgment whether he shall be compelled to make further answer." The court overruled the demurrer, and the defendant making no further answer, the court adjudged that the petition be taken for confessed, and that a peremptory *mandamus* issue, etc. An appeal was prosecuted from that judgment to the Appellate Court. That court affirmed the judgment of the Superior Court, and the case comes here by appeal from the last-named judgment, on certificate as to the importance of the question involved, by two of the judges of that court.

E. R. Bliss and *H. W. Magee* for the appellant.

Abbott, Oliver & Showalter, for the appellee.

SCHOLFIELD, J.—The question presented by this record is, whether a county clerk who has once executed a MANDAMUS DOES NOT LIE TO COM-PEL CLERK TO RE-EXECUTE TAX DEED, WHEN. tax deed at the instance of the holder of the certificate of purchase at a tax sale, upon evidence then furnished by such holder, can be subsequently compelled, by *mandamus*, to execute to the same party another tax deed under the same certificate of purchase, the holder thereof having filed with the clerk additional and more perfect evidence of his having complied with the law in respect to giving notice, etc., since the execution of the first deed. Our answer must be in the negative. It is true, where a clerk has himself made a mistake in executing a tax deed, whereby it is rendered inoperative for the purpose for which it was intended, he may subsequently be compelled, by *mandamus*, to correct his mistake, and, of course, may make the correction without being coerced thereto by judgment of court. Maxcy *v.* Clabaugh, 1 Gilm. 26. And to the same effect is McCready *v.* Sexton, 29 Iowa, 356. But here the clerk has made no mistake. The mistake made is that of the party applying for the deed, and relates to proof which it was his duty to furnish to the clerk, and which he assumed to furnish to the clerk, before applying for his deed. If he may have *mandamus* to compel the clerk to make a new deed upon his alleged correction of one mistake, may he not also have it to compel the clerk to make a new deed upon his alleged correction of another mistake? Where is it to end? The owner of the land to be affected is not before us, and has no opportunity to be heard upon this question. If this *mandamus* will lie, will it not afford a precedent whereby purchasers at tax sales may, by adroit manipulation, obtain the opinion of the court upon the validity of a given title before the landowner has any opportunity to be heard? The rule is, a party applying for a *mandamus* must show a clear, legal right to have the thing sought by it to be done, and if the granting of the writ will do the party applying for it no good, it will be refused. People *v.* Chicago & Alton R. R. Co., 55 Ill. 95 ; Commissioners of Highways *v.* Bonker, 66 Id. 339; People *v.* City of Elgin, Id. 507; People *v.* Klokke, 92 Id. 134; People *ex rel. v.* Dulaney, 96 Id. 503; People *ex rel. v.* Johnson, 100 Id. 537. And so the question of the sufficiency of the deed to convey the title, when made as asked, would always be a pertinent question in such cases.

We think it is contrary to the policy of the law that *mandamus* should issue where its sole purpose and effect is, as it is here, to relieve from the consequences of the mistakes or omissions of the party applying for it.

The judgment is reversed and the cause remanded.

Judgment reversed.

BERRY

v.

BICKFORD.

(*Advance Case, New Hampshire.   July* 31, 1885.)

A town which becomes the purchaser of land sold for taxes, under G. L., c. 59, § 6, is not estopped to set up the title so acquired by the fact that for two years after the sale and before a deed had been given by the collector the premises were taxed to the owner and the taxes paid by him.

WRIT of entry.   Trial by the court.   The land in question was conveyed in mortgage to the Gonec Five Cents Savings Bank by one Nutter, February 4, 1869.   February 28, 1874, Nutter's assignee in bankrupcy quitclaimed it to the bank, and October 10, 1882, the assignee of the bank quitclaimed it to the plaintiff.

The defendant's title was a quitclaim deed of the premises from the town of New Durham, dated March 14, 1882; and the title of the town was through a deed of quitclaim, dated January 14, 1882, from its collector of taxes for 1878.   May 31, 1879, the land was duly sold for the taxes of 1878, and was bid off by the town.   In 1880, and also in 1881, the land was taxed to the bank, and the bank paid the taxes.

The court ordered judgment for the defendant, and the plaintiff excepted.

Sanborn & Cochrane for plaintiff.

R. G. Pike for defendant.

ALLEN, J.—The only point raised by the plaintiff in the case is, that the town, by assessing a tax upon the land to the bank, the plaintiff's grantor, and receiving the tax in 1880 and 1881, after it had purchased the land and had a right to a deed, was estopped from denying the title of the bank, and as against that title took nothing from the collector's deed and conveyed nothing to the defendant.

Although the town had a right to demand and receive a deed at the end of a year from the time of sale, the land was open to redemption by the bank, which had an interest to protect at any time prior to the reception of a deed from the town. G. L., c. 59, §§ 8, 14. The bank had a title to the land as early as 1874, and there is nothing to show it was not the duty of the bank to pay the tax of 1878. The proceedings of the collector, in selling the land in 1879 for the unpaid tax of 1878, were matters of public record in the town and were constructively known to the bank, and the bank had the right and privilege of paying the delinquent taxes and protecting its title at any time up to January, 1882, when the town took its deed. The fact that, during all the time, between the tax sale in May, 1879, and January, 1882, or any part of it, when the land was open to redemption, it was taxed to the bank whose duty it was to pay the tax, cannot estop the defendant nor the town under whom the defendant claims from asserting a title, which the bank might have defeated, but did not take the necessary steps to do. So long as the land was open to redemption, neither the town nor its selectmen could know that the bank would not pay the tax and make its title sure. Having a right to redeem the land, the bank had such an interest in it that the town, during the existence of such right, might well assess the tax against the bank, and in doing so there would be no estoppel nor waiver of a right on its part to assert a title not before defeated or destroyed by a redemption of the land from a tax sale. The position of the bank, the plaintiff's grantor, was not changed to its injury or disadvantage by anything which the town did. Even if neither the plaintiff, at the time of his purchase, nor the bank at the time of the proceedings, in the sale of the land to and by the town, had actual notice of the same, there could be no estoppel against a purchaser at a tax sale, notice of the proceedings, as provided by law, having been given, and actual notice not having been intentionally or fraudulently withheld. No question is raised by the case upon the effect of want of notice to the bank, beyond the bearing of the fact upon the question of estoppel, and that question cannot be affected by want of notice, if the want did not arise or was not promoted by the fraud of the defendant or the town. It was no fault of the town that the bank was ignorant of the assessment of the tax of 1878, or of the sale of the land for that tax in 1879; nor was it the fault of the town that the bank did not redeem the land and protect its title by paying the tax sometime in the two and one half years after the sale and before the deed was taken, and neither the plaintiff nor his grantor, the bank, can now complain, if the defendant and his grantor, the town, insist upon asserting a title, which they, the plaintiff and the bank, might by reasonable diligence have easily defeated.

ESTOPPEL OF
TOWN.

The selectmen of the town are public officers, whose duties are defined by law, and the town could not be estopped from claiming title to its land by any wrongful or unauthorized act of its selectmen in assessing a tax upon the land against one not the owner, nor in collecting and receiving the tax. Rossin *v.* Boston, 4 Allen, 57, 58; St. Louis *v.* Gorman, 29 Mo. 593; Ellsworth *v.* Grand Rapids, 27 Mich. 280; McFarlane *v.* Kerr, 10 Bosworth (N. Y.), 249.

Exceptions overruled.

BLODGETT, J., did not sit; the others concurred.

SNELL

v.

CAMPBELL, Co. Treasurer, and others.

(Advance Case, Circuit Court, N. D. Iowa. June, 1885.)

Action to set aside tax sale and enjoin execution of tax deed in so far as the validity of the tax in controversy is concerned, *held*, barred by a former suit brought by complainant and others against the county treasurer to test the validity of said tax, and decided against them in the State court.

The repeal of a statute under which a penalty is assessed against a taxpayer who fails to pay his taxes within a specified time is a remission of the penalty. It cannot be collected after such repeal, and, when the penalty has not been collected of the delinquent tax-payer, he may redeem from tax sale without making a tender of the penalty in addition to the tax properly assessed, with legal interest thereon.

IN Equity.

Cole, McVey & Clark and *Barcroft & Bowen* for complainant.
J. F. Duncombe for defendants.

SHIRAS, J.—The complainant, who is a citizen of the State of Illinois, avers in his bill of complaint that he is now, and

FACTS.

was in 1877, the owner of certain realty, situated in Wahkonsa township, Webster county, Iowa; that in 1877 a tax of 5 per cent was levied on said realty in aid of the Fort

Dodge & Fort Ridgely R. R. Co., in pursuance of a vote of the electors in said township under the provisions of an act of the general assembly of the State of Iowa, approved March 15, 1877; that on or about the eighteenth of June, 1883, the treasurer of said Webster county, at a sale of lands for delinquent taxes, sold the realty owned by complainant for said railroad tax, the same remaining unpaid; that Wm. M. Grant, one of the defendants, bought said realty at such tax sale ; that the treasurer, in making said sale, added to the amount of the tax at five per cent a penalty for the non-payment thereof at the rate of 1 per cent a month for the first three months, 2 per cent per month for the second three months, and 3 per cent a month for the remaining months thereafter up to the day of the sale; that, unless restrained from so doing, the county treasurer will execute a treasurer's deed to the purchaser or his assignee, thereby casting a cloud upon complainant's title to said realty ; that the act of the general assembly of March 15, 1877, is contrary to the provisions of the constitution of the State of Iowa; that the vote taken was not in pursuance of the act in question, and the tax levied is void and of no effect; that taxes in aid of railroads had already been voted in Wahkonsa township in excess of 5 per cent, and that the power to vote a tax under the statute was exhausted ; that if valid no penalty attached to the failure to pay the tax assessed, and that the sale by the treasurer is void, because these penalties had been added.

To this bill the proper county officers, together with the purchaser at the tax sale and the owner of the certificate of sale, were made parties, and have fully answered thereto.

The first question made by defendants upon the pleadings and the evidence is that the matters relied upon by complainant have already been adjudicated against him, and that he is now estopped from relitigating them in the present action. TAX IN AID OF RAILROAD—RES ADJUDICATA.

It appears that the complainant, Snell, uniting with a number of other tax-payers owning property in Wahkonsa township, filed a bill in equity in the district court of Webster county, Iowa, at the February term, 1879, against A. Leonard, the then county treasurer of Webster county, to enjoin and restrain the collection of the tax voted and levied in aid of the Fort Dodge & Fort Ridgely R. R. Co. In substance, the grounds of complaint were that the petition asking for a submission of the question of aiding the railroad was not signed by the requisite number of freeholders; that the trustees had no power to order an election; that the company had not complied with the provisions of the proposition submitted to the voters; and that the road was not properly constructed, and had been changed from a narrow to a standard gauge road.

A temporary injunction, restraining the treasurer from collecting the tax, was granted by the judge of the district court. The defendants answered the bill thus filed, and upon a hearing the temporary injunction was dissolved, and the bill ordered to be dismissed. The order dissolving the injunction is in writing, signed by the judge, and was made in vacation, and it is not shown that a formal judgment or decree based thereon was entered upon the records of the court. The plaintiffs, however, appealed the case to the supreme court of the State, and in that court attacked the constitutionality of the act of the general assembly under which the tax was voted. The supreme court held the act constitutional, and affirmed the order or decree of the district court. See Snell *v.* Leonard, 55 Iowa, 553; s. c., 8 N. W. Rep. 425.

The defendants in the present suit plead and rely upon the action had in Snell *v.* Leonard as an adjudication estopping the complainant from again questioning the validity of the tax assessed upon complainant's property in aid of the Fort Dodge & Fort Ridgely R. R. Co.

Upon part of complainant, it is insisted that it has not been proven that there was any legal or binding adjudication had in that cause, in that it does not appear that the order of the judge dissolving the injunction and dismissing the bill ever ripened into a full and final decree entered of record during a term of the court. It clearly appears that the answer filed in that cause took issue upon the merits of the bill of complaint, and that the judge upon the hearing dissolved the injunction previously granted and ordered the dismissal of the bill. The complainants evidently treated this as the end of the case in the district court, and appealed the cause to the supreme court, stating in the notice of appeal that "the plaintiffs in said action have appealed from the judgment of the district court·rendered in favor of the defendant at the March term thereof," etc.

In the supreme court the case was fully heard upon its merits, and the judgment of the district court was affirmed. •Under these circumstances it is not open to the complainant to say that there was not an adjudication against him upon the merits of the controversy involved in the bill of complaint filed against the treasurer of Webster county.

Treating the record as sufficient evidence of an adjudication upon the merits of that controversy, the question then arises whether that adjudication bars the complainant from the relief sought in the present proceedings.

In Cromwell *v.* Sac Co., 94 U. S. 351, the general rule applicable to this plea of *res judicata* is very fully and clearly stated. It therein appeared that one Smith had brought an action against Sac county upon certain coupons attached to bonds issued by the county. It was therein adjudged that the bonds were fraudulent, and, it not appearing that Smith was an innocent holder for value, it was further adjudged that he could not recover. Subsequently an action upon other coupons attached to the same bonds was brought in the name of Cromwell against Sac county, and by way of defence the adjudication in the case of Smith *v.* Sac Co. was pleaded, with the averment that Cromwell had been at all times the owner of the coupons sued on, and that the suit in name of Smith was really for his benefit. The supreme court held that,—

" There is a difference between the effect of a judgment as a bar or estoppel against the prosecution of a second action upon the same claim or demand, and its effect as an estoppel in another action between the same parties upon a different claim or cause of action. In the former case, the judgment, if rendered upon the merits, constitutes an absolute bar to a subsequent action. It is a finality as to the claim or demand in controversy, concluding parties and those in privity with them, not only as to every matter which was offered and received to sustain or defeat the claim or demand, but as to any other admissible matter which might have been offered for that purpose. Thus, for example, a judgment rendered upon a promissory note is conclusive as to the validity of the instrument and the amount due upon it, although it be subsequently alleged that perfect defence actually existed, of which no proof was offered, such as forgery, want of consideration, or payment. If such defences were not presented in the action, and established by competent evidence, the subsequent allegation of their existence is of no legal consequence. The judgment is as conclusive, so far as future proceedings at law are concerned, as though the defences never existed. . . . . Such demand or claim, having passed into judgment, cannot again be brought into litigation between the parties in proceedings at law upon any ground whatever. But when the second action between the same parties is upon a different claim or demand, the judgment in the prior action operates as an estoppel only as to those matters in issue or points controverted upon the determination of which the finding or verdict was rendered ; . . . only upon such matters is the judgment conclusive in another action."

Applying these principles to the facts of the case, the court held that the second suit, being upon different coupons than those involved in the first suit, was for a different cause of action ; that the judgment in the former suit, holding the bonds invalid against the county, estopped the plaintiff from averring the contrary in the second suit, but that plaintiff was not estopped from showing that he was an innocent holder of the coupons declared on in the second suit, because that question was not involved in nor passed upon in the first suit.

In Block *v.* Commissioners, 99 U. S. 686, it appeared that one Lewis was the owner of 100 coupons attached to bonds issued by Bourbon county, Kansas. In 1873 he applied to the supreme court for a *mandamus*, for the purpose of compelling the county commissioners to levy a tax and provide for the payment of the coupons held by him. An alternative writ was issued, and the commissioners answered it, setting up, among other things, that the bonds and coupons held by Lewis were unauthorized by law, because a majority of the electors of the county had not sanctioned the issuing of the bonds. The supreme court gave judgment for the defendants, refusing the *mandamus*. Thereupon Lewis delivered the coupons to Block, who brought suit thereon, in reality in the interest of Lewis. To this suit, brought in the United States circuit court, the judgment in the *mandamus* case was pleaded as a defence, and the supreme court held it was a conclusive bar to the action.

In Stout *v.* Lye, 103 U. S. 66, the record presented the following facts : On the tenth of November, 1873, one Lye executed to the First National Bank of Delphos a mortgage on certain real estate in Allen county, Ohio, to secure a debt due the bank. On the twenty-ninth of December, 1875, John W. and Jacob O. Stout brought suit in the United States circuit court for Northern district of Ohio against Lye and others to recover judgment on a debt due thereon. On the fifteenth of January, 1876, the bank commenced suit in the State court of Allen county against Lye for the foreclosure of its mortgage. To this suit the Stouts were not made parties. On the thirty-first of January, 1876, the Stouts obtained judgment against Lye in the United States circuit court. This judgment was a lien upon the mortgaged realty. On the twenty-third of February, 1876, the Stouts commenced a suit in the United States circuit court, making the bank a defendant, in which they sought to set aside the mortgage as illegal for want of authority to take it, and also seeking to have certain payments of usurious interest credited on the principal debt. On the seventh of March a judgment was rendered in the State court in the suit of the bank againt Lye for the full amount of the note, and ordering a sale of the mortgaged property. Thereupon the bank answered in the suit pending in the United States court, setting up the judgment of foreclosure as a bar to the action on part of the Stouts. The supreme court held that the suit to foreclose the mortgage in favor of the bank was pending when the Stouts obtained a lien upon the realty by virtue of the judgment in their favor against Lye; that, consequently, they were in privity with Lye, and although they were not parties to the record in the foreclosure suit, they were nevertheless bound by the decree therein; that although Lye, in the foreclosure suit, did not in fact set up the defence of want of authority in the bank to take the mortgage, yet he was at liberty to do so, and that he could not, nor could the Stouts, afterwards be heard to say in the suit in the United States court that the mortgage was for any reason invalid or void.

In the cases of Corcoran *v.* Chesapeake, etc., Canal Co., 94 U. S. 741, and Louis *v.* Brown Tp., 109 U. S. 162; s. c., 3 Sup.

Ct. Rep. 92, it is ruled that in chancery cases adverse interests between defendants will be deemed settled, as between
such defendants, by a decree in the cause, if the parties had
an opportunity of asserting their rights.

Applying the rules thus enunciated to the facts of the
present case, what is the result? In the case brought in the
State court, the present complainant was one of the complain
ants therein, and so far as he was concerned the record shows
that that proceeding, like the present one, was brought to
restrain and enjoin the collection of the 5 per cent tax voted
in aid of the Fort Dodge & Fort Ridgely R. R. Co.
and levied upon complainant's property. The object and
purpose of both suits is identical, and the ultimate question
presented for decision is the same, to wit, whether the tax
voted is legal and binding. The former suit was against the
then treasurer of the county in his official capacity ; the present
suit is against the present treasurer, the auditor, and the purchaser at the tax sale. It is apparent that these latter parties
are in privity with and represent exactly the same interests as
did the defendant in the former suit. In the former suit the
decision was that the act of the general assembly under which
the tax was voted was constitutional, and the tax was legal
and binding, and the complainant's property liable therefor.
The judgment in that case concluded the complainant upon
these questions, no matter whether the same objections were
then made to the validity of the tax or not.

It is not now open to the complainant in this case to litigate
the validity of the tax in question. In the former suit, he had
the opportunity to present for decision every question touching
the constitutionality and validity of the tax voted ; and as the
two suits are for the same relief and based upon the same facts,
the former adjudication concludes him, not only upon the
objections he then made, but upon all he might have made.
None of the points made, therefore, against the constitutionality of the act of the general assembly, or against the validity
of the tax as voted and levied, are open for investigation
before this court in the present cause.

The bill filed, however, presents another question, and that
TENDER NECES- is as to the amount necessary to be paid in order to
SARY TO REDEEM
FROM TAX SALE. redeem the property from the tax sale. This sale
did not take place until after the final decision of the case of

Snell *v.* Leonard, and the question of the right of redemption and the amount to be paid was not involved therein. The rights of the parties growing out of the sale of the realty for the tax in question have not been adjudicated, and are open to contest in the present proceeding.

The stipulation of facts filed in the present cause shows that after the decision of the supreme court in the case of Snell *v.* Leonard was rendered, the complainant herein tendered to the treasurer of Webster county the amount of the tax assessed upon his property in favor the Fort Dodge & Fort Ridgely R. R. Co., together with interest thereon at the rate of 10 per cent up to the date of the tender, which was made on May 10, 1881, The treasurer refused to accept the amount thus tendered, and in June, 1883, sold the lands as already stated.

The reason assigned by the treasurer for refusing to accept the tender was that, under the act of the general assembly authorizing the voting and levy of the tax, the complainant must pay a penalty at the rate fixed in the general tax law of the State, and the question is now presented whether, under the act of the general assembly, this penalty can be exacted.

Counsel for complainant criticise the language of the act providing for the penalty, claiming that the provision that "said taxes shall be collected at the time or times specified in said order, in the same manner, and be subject to the same penalties for non-payment after they are collectible, as other taxes, or as may be stated in the petition asking said election." is meaningless, because it declares that the tax shall be subject to the penalty, instead of declaring that the property, or the owner thereof, is subjected to the penalty.

While the language used may be open to exception, still it is sufficiently clear that the legislature intended to thereby provide that if not paid when due, the tax was liable to be increased by the amount of the penalty. By section 3 of the act it is provided that the aggregate amount of the tax to be voted or levied under the act in any township shall not exceed 5 per centum of the assessed value of the property in the township. Section 4 provides that the moneys collected under the provisions of the act shall be paid by the county treasurer to the treasurer of the railroad company. All sums, therefore, collected as penalties belong to the railroad com-

pany.   In Barnes v. County of Marshall,5 6 Iowa, 20; s. c., 8
N. W. Rep. 677, it was decided that the county acquires no
beneficial interest in the taxes voted in aid of the railroad
company and paid to the county treasurer, and is not liable
for the repayment thereof if the company forfeits the same.
All sums, therefore, collected from the tax-payers under the
provisions of the act in question, whether called a tax or a
penalty, are sums contributed by the property owner to the
railroad company for the purpose named in the statute, to wit,
to aid in the construction of a designated line of railroad.

As already stated, the limitation on the amount of tax that
can be levied under the act is 5 per cent.   If, therefore, as in
the case now under consideration, the full amount of 5 per
cent is levied as a tax, it is very questionable whether any
further sum can be collected and paid to the railroad company, even under the guise of a penalty.   This additional
amount is not to cover expenses.   It goes into the treasury
of the company, just as the amounts realized from the 5 per
cent. tax do, and for the same purpose.   Under the decision
of the supreme court of Iowa, that the beneficial interest in
the tax voted in aid of a railway belongs, not to the county,
but to the railway company, it is difficult to distinguish the
amount due from a given tax-payer to the company for the
tax voted from any other debt he might owe to the company.
The tax-payer is under legal obligation to pay, and the railroad company has a legal right to demand and enforce payment of the tax.   The statute, however, expressly limits the
amount that the tax-payer can be compelled to pay to 5 per
cent.   If, therefore, a tax for the full amount of 5 per cent is
levied, is it within the power of the county treasurer or the
railroad company to insist upon payment of a sum equal to 10
per cent if the tax-payer does not promptly pay the tax when
due ?

The claim is not made that the additional sum is to be con-
PENALTY — TEN- sidered as interest upon an overdue debt.   In that
DER.
case the rate would be fixed by other provisions of the law.
The additional sum is claimed to be due as a penalty; but it
is a penalty, not for a failure to pay a tax due to and belonging to the State or county, but for a failure to pay a sum due
to the railroad company.   The penalty, when paid to the
county treasurer, belongs to the railway company, and in

effect is a sum paid by the tax-payer to aid in the construction of a line of railway. In no respect, therefore, does it seem to differ from the sum paid as a tax, and there is reason in the proposition that calling the sum a penalty does not change the fact that it is a sum paid by the tax-payer to aid in the construction of a railway, and that under the act in question the sums thus collected from the tax-payer for that purpose shall not exceed in the aggregate the amount of 5 per cent.

But, without deciding this proposition, it is clear that under the provisions of the act in question the tax-payer cannot be subjected to a tax greater in amount than 5 per cent. If any further sum can be collected, it must be as a penalty; that is, an amount assessed against the tax-payer over and above the full legal amount of his tax as a punishment for his failure to pay the sum due as a tax at a given date. The sum in excess of 5 per cent, if collectible at all, can only be collected as a penalty, and not as part of the tax. If, therefore, it is a penalty pronounced against the delinquent tax-payer for the failure on his part to perform the duty and obligation of payment cast upon him by the act of the general assembly, then as a penalty its enforcement may be waived, and a repeal of the act providing for the penalty, before the penalty is enforced, will terminate the right to enforce the penalty. "The repeal of the law imposing the penalty is of itself a remission." State *v*. Baltimore & O. R. R. Co., 3 How. 534; Confiscation Cases, 7 Wall. 454.

The act of March 15, 1877, was expressly repealed by chapter 159 of the acts of the twentieth general assembly. Being thus repealed, its penal provisions cannot be enforced; that is to say, the repeal of the act terminated the right to collect any penalty that remained uncollected at that date. If the realty had not been sold at a tax sale by the treasurer before the repeal of the act, it could not now be sold in order to collect the penalty claimed.

The record shows that in 1881 the complainant tendered to the treasurer the full amount of the 5 per cent tax assessed upon his property, with 10 per cent interest added, but the treasurer refused to accept the tender, and in June, 1883, sold the realty for the taxes and penalty added. The complainant, denying his liability to the penalty, brought the present action in order to determine whether such penalto could be collected from him. He has, as yet, paid nothing, and one object of the present suit is to determine the amount which he is under legal obligation to pay in order to discharge the tax assessed against him, and redeem his property from the sale made thereof. It cannot, therefore, be fairly said that the penalty in this case has been collected and distributed, so far as the question lies between the complainant and the railway company. The right to collect the penalty is in dispute, and if the complainant can show that he has been relieved from the payment thereof, he has the right so to do, as against the company. So far as the tax is concerned, the company may obtain or perfect a vested right therein before it is collected; but to the penalty no vested right attached until it is collected, and thus placed beyond the power of the tax-payer to contest its validity. So long, therefore, as the right to the penalty has not vested in the company by its collection, the same may be remitted by the legislature, and, in the language of the Supreme Court of the United States in State *v.* Baltimore & O. R. R. Co., *supra,* " the repeal of the law imposing the penalty is of itself a remission."

What the rule would be as against some third party not interested in the tax, who should, at a tax sale, bid in the property for the tax and penalty, and actually pay such amount into the treasury, is not considered or determined. The certificate of sale in this case was issued to W. M. Grant, who was a stockholder in the company. It does not appear that he has as yet paid any money on such purchase, or that he bought the property in his own right. The testimony of the county treasurer, who conducted the sale, shows that no money was paid him on the bid made, but that he accepted the receipt of the treasurer of the company instead of the money, and delivered the certificate of sale to the treasurer.

Under these circumstances the question of the right to exact the penalty as a condition to the right to redeem the land from the sale is one solely between complainant and the company, and, as between them, the right to exact the penalty, if it ever existed, was terminated by the repeal of the act under which the tax was voted. The complainant, having pleaded the tender made May 10, 1881, and relied thereon, which was for the full amount of the tax levied, and interest thereon at 10 per cent to that date, has thereby admitted that, equi-

tably, that amount was then due to the railroad company
The payment of that amount, with interest thereon at 6 per
cent from May 10, 1881, will fully discharge the indebtedness
due from complainant, and relieve his property from any lien
or claim by reason of the tax levied in aid of the Fort Dodge
& Fort Ridgely R. R. Co.

The order and decree will therefore be that, upon the payment of the amount above indicated to the treasurer of
Webster county within 90 days from the date of this decree,
the sale of said realty for taxes as aforesaid shall be cancelled
and set aside, and the defendants, and parties claiming under
them, be restrained and enjoined from executing or receiving
a treasurer's deed of said realty, or from asserting any title
to said realty under the sale for taxes made June 18, 1883.
The complainant, having sought by his bill to set aside the
sale as wholly void, and escape the payment of any sum, and
having failed to make good his bill in these particulars, is adjudged to pay the costs of this proceeding.

INHABITANTS OF WEST BRIDGEWATER

v.

INHABITANTS OF WAREHAM.

(138 *Massachusetts*, 305.)

A town may, by its vote, admit that a person had a settlement therein.

The records of a town showed votes "to hire out F. and take his wages
for to support his family," and "to vendue the poor," followed by the
record of the bidding off of F.'s children, and to pay various bills for the
support of him and them ; a vote, at a meeting held under a warrant "to see
what the town will do with the town poor," that "the children of F. be sold
to the lowest bidder," and that whatever it should cost to get them kept
until they were twenty-one should be paid in one year ; and also that "the
rest of the town's poor that are not provided for be left to the care of the
selectmen." *Held,* that these votes contained admissions that F. had his
settlement in the town, and warranted a finding of such settlement.

CONTRACT for expenses incurred in the support of George
M. Fryes, a pauper, whose settlement was alleged to be in the
defendant town. The case was submitted to the Superior
Court, and, after judgment for the plaintiff, to this court, on

appeal, upon agreed facts, the material parts of which appear
in the opinion.

H. J. Fuller for the plaintiff.

E. B. Powers (*S. L. Powers* with him) for the defendant.

HOLMES, J.—The question whether the pauper George M.
QUESTION. Fryes was settled in the defendant town depends
on whether his grandfather, James Fryes, senior, was settled
there. The plaintiff says that certain ancient votes of the
defendant amount to admissions which warranted a finding
in its favor. The defendant denies that it either did or could
make admissions that would have that effect.

Taking the latter contention first, the defendant says that,
as the statute provides that settlements shall be gained in certain ways and not otherwise, and also in view of the limited
power of towns, proof of admissions of the conclusion of law
that a pauper had a settlement cannot take the place of
proof of the facts that warrant that conclusion.

We are unable to assent to this argument. In the first
place, such admissions are not mere statements of law. They
might be, if they set forth the constituent facts relied on as
establishing the conclusion. But when the conclusion alone
is stated, the statement affirms or admits by necessary implication that facts exist which warrant that conclusion. Again,
to establish a settlement against a defendant in this way is no
more introducing a new mode of gaining a settlement than
to establish a marriage by admissions in a suit against a husband for necessaries furnished his wife is introducing a new
mode of marriage. The admission is not conclusive, and, if
it does not induce the inference of the facts prescribed by
statute as necessary to constitute a settlement or a marriage,
it goes for nothing. Finally, we see no more reason to doubt
the power of towns to make admissions in town meeting
prejudicial to their own interests, in a case where they have
power to act on the general subject-matter, than to doubt
their power of doing the same thing through their counsel in
court; especially on a question which they have statutory
power to settle, as the defendant could have done in this case,
by town vote admitting the pauper as an inhabitant. The case
of New Bedford *v.* Taunton, 9 Allen, 207, cited by the defendant, only denies the power of overseers of the town to bind

the town; it does not suggest that an admission of the town itself would not be evidence against it, and pretty strongly implies the contrary. See East Greenwich *v.* Warwick, 4 R. I. 138; Hopkinton *v.* Springfield, 12 N. H. 328, 330.

The votes put in warranted the inference that was drawn from them. In 1824, at a town meeting held under VOTES HELD TO a warrant "to see what the town will do with the ESTABLISH SETTLEMENT. town poor," it was "voted the children of James Fryes be sold to the lowest bidder," etc., and that whatever it should cost to get them kept until they were twenty-one should be paid in one year. The record then continues, "Voted the rest of the town's poor that are not provided for be left to the care of the selectmen to dispose of." The foregoing language clearly means that the children of James Fryes are a part of the town poor. "The town's poor," in its natural sense and unexplained, means poor whom the town is permanently bound to support. St. 1793, c. 59, § 1. It does not include persons receiving temporary relief under the St. of 1793, c. 59, §§ 9, 13. Coupling this with votes of previous years, "to hire out James Fryes and take his wages for to support his family," "to vendue the poor," followed by the record of the bidding-off of James Fryes's children, and to pay various bills for the support of him and them, we find ample admissions that James Fryes had his settlement in the defendant town. The force of these admissions is not affected by the question whether the town was usurping the functions of the overseers of the poor by passing the votes, upon which we express no opinion. For, as the town had power to act on the general subject-matter, an admission with regard to it is evidence against the town, even if the particular act directed to be done was *ultra vires.*

Judgment for the plaintiff.

THEILAN

v.

PORTER *et al.*

(14 *Lea* (*Tennessee*), 622.)

The act of the Legislature which empowers Taxing Districts to condemn and abate as nuisances all houses which shall be found unhealthy, is not in violation of the provision of the constitution which provides "that no man's particular services shall be demanded or property taken or applied to public use, without the consent of his representatives, or without just compensation being made therefor." This inhibition has no application as a limitation of the exercise of those police powers which are necessary to the safety and tranquillity of every well-ordered community.

APPEAL in error from the Circuit Court of Shelby county. J. O. Pierce, J.

T. W. Brown for Theilan.

C. W. Heiskell for Taxing District.

DEADERICK, C. J.—The plaintiff brought an action of tres-
FAOTS.   pass on April 27, 1880, against the Taxing District
of Shelby county and its legislative council and officers for damages for destroying his dwelling-house in Memphis.

About thirty pages of demurrers, pleas and demurrers, and replications thereto, resulted in issues upon the material questions arising in the cause, upon the record.

The defendants justified the pulling down of the house under the acts of 1879, conferring the power to remove all buildings, etc., found to be unhealthy.

Allowing the objection by demurrer to defendants' pleas to have been improperly overruled, the objection was cured by pleas subsequently filed by leave, in which the justification is placed solely on the ground that the house was a nuisance because unhealthy, and not because of its dilapidation and danger on this account. So, as before stated, it is not neces-sary to follow and dispose of the various questions raised by demurrers, as the issue rests upon the right of defendants to do the act complained of, and this they rely upon by their plea of justification, which their amended or additional pleas fully and formally set up. The circuit judge, who tried the case without a jury, does not recite the facts upon which h rendered his judgment, but recites, in his judgment, that " having heard the evidence the court finds for the defendants," etc., and renders judgment against plaintiff for costs, etc.

The plaintiff appealed, and the referees have recommended an affirmance of the judgment, and plaintiff has excepted to their report, and his exceptions go to the error in overruling his demurrer to the first batch of pleas, and in failing to sustain it, to the additional pleas, and to the right of the Legislature to authorize the acts complained of to be done, and to the failure of the referees to report the facts.

No action was taken to the demurrer to the additional pleas, and in such a case the demurrer is regarded as waived. 3 Head, 602; 4 Heis. 236. And issue thereon was taken. WAIVER OF DEMURRER.

The most material exception is that which denies the power of the Legislature to authorize the taxing district to do the act complained of. The authority claimed is found in two acts of the Legislature, one passed January 29, 1879, entitled, " A bill to establish Taxing Districts in this State, and to provide the means of local government for the same:" Acts of 1879, p. 15 ; and an amendment thereto passed March 12, 1879: Ibid. p. 98. Both acts have this provision: The city government "shall have power, and it shall be their duty to condemn as nuisances all buildings, cisterns, wells, privies and other erections in the Taxing District, which, on inspection, shall be found to be unhealthy, and cause the same to be abated, unless the owners thereof, at their own expense, upon notice, shall reconstruct the same in such manner as shall be prescribed by the laws of the Taxing District." They are also required to have buildings, etc., so constructed in future as not to interfere with the health of the citizens; and other powers are given and duties imposed in respect to the cleanly and healthy condition of the houses, etc., of the city. POWER OF LEGISLATURE TAXING DISTRICT TO ABATE NUISANCE.

In the bill of exceptions, it is recited that on the trial there was evidence on behalf of plaintiff tending to prove that the destruction and removal of the house was attended with great oppression to him personally, and with unnecessary loss of his property, and that the house had been the home of the plaintiff for many years before the Taxing District was created;

and on behalf of the defendants, evidence was introduced
tending to prove that said house was unsafe by reason of its
rotten and tumble-down condition, and unsanitary by reason
of its filthiness and its rotten condition ; and was for both o
these reasons a nuisance, and that no unnecessary force or
oppression was used to accomplish its destruction, etc., and
that defendants pursued the District law in its condemnation
and destruction, and that defendants were the officers of the
Taxing District, intrusted with the duties imposed by said
statutes.

It is also recited in said bill of exceptions, that the court
found that defendants did destroy said house, or cause it to
be destroyed and removed, with no more force than was
necessary, and that it was not oppressively, but carefully, done
without loss or unnecessary injury to its contents; that said
house was unsanitary and unsafe to a degree that made it a
nuisance; and that defendants were protected under the acts
of 1879, above referred to, and acted in discharge of their
duties as public officers.

It is argued that the acts in question are in violation of that
DESTRUCTION OF clause in our State constitution, which declares
UNHEALTHY
HOUSE WITHOUT that no man's property shall be taken or applied to
COMPENSATION
IS LAWFUL.   public use without the consent of his representa-
tives, or without just compensation being made therefor.

But this inhibition has no application as a limitation of the
exercise of those police powers which are necessary to the
safety and tranquillity of every well-ordered community, nor
of that general power over private property which is necessary for the orderly existence of all governments : Sedg. Const.
Law, 434-5 ; and in a note on page 435-6 it is said: " In very
many instances, summary proceedings, without the usual
POLICE POWER forms of a regular judicial trial, have been held
DISCUSSED.   valid as falling within the police powers of the
State," because the necessities of society and good government demand a certain amount of summary and repressive
measures which would be ineffectual if delayed by ordinary
machinery of more regular judicial trial; and numerous
examples and cases are given in which such summary proceedings were held valid ; and it is added, abating a nuisance
does not take away property without due process of law, for

the common law recognized the power to abate a nuisance in a summary manner.

Chief-Justice Shaw said: "Every holder of property, however absolute his title, holds it under the implied liability that his use of it shall not be injurious to others, nor to the rights of the community. If it be hurtful he is restrained, not because the public makes any use of it, or takes any benefit or profit from it, but because his own use would be a noxious use, contrary to the maxim, *sic utere tuo ut alienum non lædas.* It is not an appropriation of the property to a public use, but the restraint of an injurious private use by the owner." Sedg. on Stat. & Const. Law, 438-9, citing 7 Cush. 53. So that the summary abatement of a nuisance is not in violation of the constitution, as taking private property for public use without compensation, or depriving one of his property without giving him his day in court. ONLY ONE TAXING DISTRICT AFFECTED—PARTIALITY OF LAW DISCUSSED.

The further objection is made that the law is partial, because it applies only to the Taxing District of Shelby county; even if the Legislature had not the authority to confer on different municipal corporations different powers according to their several circumstances and necessities, by its first section the act applies to "the several communities embraced in the territorial limits of all such municipal corporations in this State as have had or may have their charters abolished," etc., thus showing the law not to apply to one specified locality only, but to all who have brought or may bring themselves within the class described. Acts of 1879, p. 15.

If the law is otherwise unobjectionable, all that can be required is that it be general in its application to the class or locality to which it may apply; it is then public or general in its character; of its policy or propriety the Legislature must judge. Cooley Const. Lim. 390.

Where the Legislature in terms confers on a municipal corporation power to pass ordinances of a specified or defined character, if the power thus delegated be not in conflict with the Constitution, an ordinance passed in pursuance thereof cannot be impeached as unconstitutional, because it would have been regarded as unreasonable if it had been passed under the incidental power of the corporation, or under a grant of power general in its nature. 1 Dillon on Mun. Cor., sec. 262.   And where the power is given the ordinance must conform to it.

The statutes cited conferred the power, upon inspection, if unhealthy, to condemn, and upon notice given, if the nuisance was not abated by the owner, the municipal government were directed to cause the same to be abated.   Under ordinances in conformity to the acts of the Legislature the nuisance was abated.

The case in 10 Wallace, 506, is not in conflict with the cases cited.   It is there said, the mere declaration of the city council that a certain structure was a nuisance, did not make it so, unless it in fact had that character.   It, says the court, is a doctrine not to be tolerated, that a municipal corporation without any general laws by the city or State within which the structure can be shown to be a nuisance can, by its mere declaration that it is one, proceed to abate it.   That is the point of that decision, and the court held that the structure in fact was not a nuisance.

The responsibility of the officers is certainly of a very grave character, and to be assumed only when the paramount obligation of protecting the public health and safety impera- tively requires it, and justified only when the exercise of the powers conferred upon them is strictly within the line of their duty.   But when so exercised they cannot be held liable for damages to compensate a party for the removal of a nuisance dangerous to the public health, which such party himself ought to have removed.

The objection is also made that the referees, although they report that it was error to dismiss the suit as against the Tax- ing District, refused to recommend a reversal on this ground. The referees say that the plaintiff would not derive any advantage from such course, as it is manifest he cannot recover, even if the cause were remanded for a new trial.

From the view we have taken of this case, we think the referees are correct in this conclusion, as a reversal on this ground would be of no practical benefit to complainant.

We concur with them therefore in this particular, as well as in their recommendation of affirmance of the judgment, and confirm their report.

AUTHORITY OF THE SOVEREIGNTY TO ABATE NUISANCES.—The authority of the sovereignty to abate public nuisances is obvious, and must necessarily inhere in every sovereignty. It may take whatever means are necessary to abate the nuisance, although this may involve the destruction of the property. Hart *v.* Mayor, etc., of Albany, 9 Wend. 571. See also Meeker *v.* Van Rensselaer, 15 Wend. 397. It must not, however, do unnecessary damage to private property, or unnecessarily destroy private property. Brown *v.* Perkins, 12 Gray (Mass.), 89; Gray *v.* Ayres, 7 Dana (Ky.), 376; Moody *v.* Supervisors, 46 Barb. (N. Y.) 659; Welch *v.* Stowell, 2 Dougl. (Mich.) 332; Barclay *v.* Commonwealth, 25 Pa. St. 503.

MARX

v.

PEOPLE.

(99 *New York,* 377.)

The right to liberty secured to the citizen by constitutional prohibitions (State Const., art. 1, §§ 1, 6, U. S. Const., 14th Amend.) includes not only the right to freedom of the person from restraint, but also the right to adopt and follow such lawful industrial pursuits not injurious to the community, as he may see fit.

A legislative enactment, therefore, which absolutely prohibits an important branch of industry, not injurious to the community, and not fraudulently conducted, solely for the reason that it competes with another, and may reduce the price of an article of food, is unconstitutional.

Accordingly *held,* that the provision of the act of 1884 (§ 4, chap. 202, Laws of 1884), prohibiting the manufacture or sale as an article of food of any substitute for butter or cheese produced from pure, unadulterated milk or cream, is unconstitutional, inasmuch as the prohibition is not limited to unwholesome or simulated substitutes, but absolutely prohibits the manufacture or sale of any compound designed to be used as a substitute for butter or cheese, however wholesome, valuable, or cheap it may be, and however openly and fairly the character of the substitute may be avowed and published; and that a conviction under said provison for a sale of oleomargarine, where it appeared that the true character of the article was avowed, and that the substitute was wholesome as an article of food, was error.

People *v.* Marx (35 Hun, 528), reversed.

APPEAL from judgment of the General Term of the Supreme Court, in the fourth judicial department, entered upon an order made March 4, 1885, which affirmed a judgment of the court of General Sessions of the Peace, in and for the city and county of New York, entered upon a verdict convicting the defendant of a violation of section 6, of chapter 202, Laws of 1884. (Reported below, 35 Hun, 528.)

The material facts are stated in the opinion.

F. R. Coudert and *Wheeler H. Peckham* for appellant.

Samuel Hand for respondent.

RAPALLO, J.—The defendant was convicted in the Court of General Sessions of the city and county of New York, of a FACTS. violation of the sixth section of an act entitled " An act to prevent deceptions in sales of dairy products." Chap. 202 of the Laws of 1884. On appeal to the General Term of the Supreme Court in the first department, the conviction was affirmed, and the defendant now appeals to this court from the judgment of affirmance.

The main ground of the appeal is that the section in question is unconstitutional and void.

The section provides as follows:

" § 6. No person shall manufacture out of any oleaginous substances, or any compound of the same, other than that produced from unadulterated milk or of cream from the same, any article designed to take the place of butter or cheese produced from pure unadulterated milk or cream of the same, or shall sell or offer to sell the same as an article of food. This provision shall not apply to pure skim-milk cheese produced from pure skim milk." The rest of the section subjects to heavy punishments by fine and imprisonment "whoever violates the provisions of this section."

The indictment charged the defendant with having on the 31st of October, 1884, at the city of New York, sold one pound of a certain article manufactured out of divers oleaginous substances and compounds thereof, other than those produced from unadulterated milk, to one J· M., as an article of food, the article so sold being designed to take the place of butter produced from pure unadulterated milk or cream. It is not charged that the article so sold was represented to be butter, or was sold as such, or that there was any intent to deceive or defraud, or that the article was in any respect unwholesome or deleterious, but simply that it was an article designed to take the place of butter made from pure milk or cream.

On the trial the prosecution proved the sale by the defendant of the article known as oleomargarine or oleomargarine butter.   That it was sold at about half the price of ordinary dairy butter.   The purchaser testified that the sale was made at a kind of factory, having on the outside a large sign " Oleo. margarine."   That he knew he could not get butter there, but knew that oleomargarine was sold there.   And the district attorney stated that it would not be claimed that there was any fraudulent intent on the part of the defendant, but that the whole, claim on the part of the prosecution was that the sale of oleomargarine as a substitute for dairy butter was pro. hibited by the statute.

On the part of the defendant it was proved by distinguished chemists that oleomargarine was composed of the same elements as dairy butter.   That the only difference between them was that it contained a smaller proportion of a fatty substance known as butterine.   That this butterine exists in dairy butter only in a small proportion—from three to six per cent. That it exists in no other substance than butter made from milk, and it is introduced into oleomargarine butter by adding to the oleomargarine stock some milk, cream, or butter, and churning, and when this is done it has all the elements of natural butter, but there must always be a smaller percentage of butterine in the manufactured product than in butter made from milk.   The only effect of the butterine is to give flavor to the butter, having nothing to do with its wholesomeness. That the oleaginous substances in the oleomargarine are substantially identical with those produced from milk or cream. Professor Chandler testified that the only difference between the two articles was that dairy butter had more butterine. That oleomargarine contained not over one per cent of that substance, while dairy butter might contain four or five per cent, and that if four or five per cent of butterine were added to the oleomargarine, there would be no difference ; it would be butter; irrespective of the sources, they would be the same substances.   According to the testimony of Professor Morton, whose statement was not controverted or questioned, oleomargarine, so far from being an article devised for purposes of deception in trade, was devised in 1872 or 1873 by an eminent French scientist who had been employed by the French Government to devise a substitute for butter.

Further testimony as to the character of the article being

offered, the district attorney announced that he did not propose to controvert that already given. Testimony having been given to the effect that oleomargarine butter was precisely as wholesome as dairy butter, it was, on motion of the district attorney, stricken out, and the defendant's counsel excepted. The broad ground was taken at the trial, and boldly maintained on the argument of this appeal, that the manufacture or sale of any oleaginous compound, however pure and wholesome, as an article of food, if it is designed to take the place of dairy butter, is by this act made a crime. The result of the argument is that if, in the progress of science, a process is discovered of preparing beef tallow, lard, or any other oleaginous substance, and communicating to it a palatable flavor so as to render it serviceable as a substitute for dairy butter, and equally nutritious and valuable, and the article can be produced at a comparatively small cost, which will place it within the reach of those who cannot afford to buy dairy butter, the ban of this statute is upon it. Whoever engages in the business of manufacturing or selling the prohibited product is guilty of a crime ; the industry must be suppressed ; those who could make a livelihood by it are deprived of that privilege, the capital invested in the business must be sacrificed, and such of the people of the State as cannot afford to buy dairy butter must eat their bread unbuttered.

The references which have been here made to the testimony on the trial are not with the view of instituting any comparison between the relative merits of oleomargarine and dairy butter, but rather as illustrative of the character and effect of the statute whose validity is in question. The indictment upon which the defendant was convicted does not mention oleomargarine, neither does the section (§ 6) of the statute, although the article is mentioned in other statutes, which will be referred to. All the witnesses who have testified as to the qualities of oleomargarine may be in error, still that would not change a particle the nature of the question, or the principles by which the validity of the act is to be tested. Section 6 is broad enough in its terms to embrace not only oleomargarine, but any other compound, however wholesome, valuable, or cheap, which has been or may be discovered or devised for the purpose of being used as a substitute for butter. Every such product is rigidly excluded from manufacture or sale in this State.

One of the learned judges who delivered opinions at the General Term endeavored to sustain the act on the ground that it was intended to prohibit the sale of any artificial compound, as genuine butter or cheese made from unadulterated milk or cream. That it was that design to deceive, which the law rendered criminal. If that were a correct interpretation of the act, we should concur with the learned judge in his conclusion as to its validity, but we could not concur in his further view that such an offence was charged in the indictment, or proved upon the trial. The express concessions of the prosecuting officer are to the contrary. We do not think that section 6 is capable of the construction claimed. The prohibition is not of the manufacture or sale of an article designed as an imitation of dairy butter or cheese, or intended to be passed off as such, but of an article designed to take the place of dairy butter or cheese. The artificial product might be green, red, or white instead of yellow, and totally dissimilar in appearance to ordinary dairy butter, yet it might be designed as a substitute for butter, and if so, would fall within the prohibition of the statute. Simulation of butter is not the act prohibited. There are other statutory provisions fully covering that subject. Chapter 215 of the Laws of 1882, entitled "An act to regulate the manufacture and sale of oleomargarine, or any form of imitation butter and lard, or any form of imitation cheese, for the prevention of fraud, and the better protection of the public health," by its first section prohibits the introduction of any substance into imitation butter or cheese for the purpose of imparting thereto a color resembling that of yellow butter or cheese. The second section prohibits the sale of oleomargarine or imitation butter thus colored, and the third section prohibits the sale of any article in semblance of natural cheese, not the legitimate product of the dairy, unless plainly marked "imitation cheese." Chapter 238 of the Laws of 1882 is entitled "An act for the protection of dairymen, and to prevent deception in the sales of butter and cheese," and provides (§ 1) that every person who shall manufacture for sale, or offer for sale, or export any article in semblance of butter or cheese, not the legitimate product of the dairy, must distinctly and durably stamp on the side of every cheese, and on the top and side of every tub, firkin, or package, the words "oleomargarine butter," or if containing cheese, "imitation cheese,' and chapter 246 of the Laws of 1882, entitled "An act to prevent fraud in the sale of oleomargarine, butterine, suine, or other substance not butter," makes it a misdemeanor to sell at wholesale or retail any of the above articles representing them to be butter. These enactments seem to cover the entire subject of fraudulent imitations of butter, and of sales of other compounds as dairy products, and they are not repealed by the act of 1884, although that act contains an express repeal of nine other statutes, eight of which are directed against impure or adulterated dairy products, and one against the use of certain coloring matter in oleomargarine. The provisions of this last act are covered by one of the acts of 1882 above cited, and the provisions of the repealed acts in relation to dairy products are covered by substituted provisions in the act of 1884, but the statutes directed against fraudulent simulations of butter, and the sale of any such simulations as dairy butter, are left to stand. Further statutes to the same effect were enacted in 1885. Consequently, if the provisions of section 6 should be held invalid, there would still be ample protection in the statutes against fraudulent imitations of dairy butter, or sales of such imitations as genuine.

It appears to us quite clear that the object and effect of the enactment under consideration were not to supplement the existing provisions against fraud and deception by means of imitations of dairy butter, but to take a further and bolder step, and by absolutely prohibiting the manufacture or sale of any article which could be used as a substitute for it, however openly and fairly the character of the substitute might be avowed and published, to drive the substituted article from the market, and protect those engaged in the manufacture of dairy products, against the competition of cheaper substances, capable of being applied to the same uses, as articles of food.

The learned counsel for the respondent frankly meets this view, and claims in his points, as he did orally upon the argument, that even if it were certain that the sole object of the enactment was to protect the dairy industry in this State against the substitution of a cheaper article made from cheaper materials, this would not be beyond the power of the legislature. This we think is the real question presented in the case. Conceding that the only limits upon the legislative power of the State are those imposed by the State constitution and that of the United States, we are called upon to determine whether or not those limits are transgressed by an enactment of this description. These limitations upon legislative power are necessarily very general in their terms, but are at the same time very comprehensive. The constitution of the State provides (Art. 1, § 1), that no member of this State shall be disfranchised, or deprived of any of the rights and privileges secured to any citizen thereof, unless by the law of the land, or the judgment of his peers. Section 6 of article 1 provides that no person shall be deprived of life, liberty, or property, without due process of law. And the fourteenth amendment to the Constitution of the United States provides that "no State shall make or enforce any law which shall abridge the privileges or immunities of citizens of the United States, nor shall any State deprive any person of life, liberty, or property, without due process of law, nor deny to any person within its jurisdiction the equal protection of the laws." These constitutional safeguards LAWFUL INDUSTRIES MAY BE FOLLOWED WITHOUT RESTRAINT. have been so thoroughly discussed in recent cases that it would be superfluous to do more than refer to the conclusions which have been reached, bearing upon the question now under consideration. Among these no proposition is now more firmly settled than that it is one of the fundamental rights and privileges of every American citizen to adopt and follow such lawful industrial pursuit, not injurious to the community, as he may see fit. Live-stock Ass'n *v.* The Crescent City, etc., 1 Abb. (U. S.) 398; Slaughter-house Cases, 16 Wall. 106; Corfield *v.* Coryell, 4 Wash. C. C. 380; Matter of Jacobs, 98 N. Y. 98. The term "liberty," as protected by the Constitution, is not cramped into a mere freedom from physical restraint of the person of the citizen, as by incarceration, but is deemed to embrace the right of man to be free in the enjoyment of the faculties with which he has been endowed by his Creator, subject only to such restraints as are necessary for the common welfare. In the language of Andrews, J., in Bertholf *v.* O'Reilly (74 N. Y. 515), the right to liberty embraces the right of man " to exercise his faculties and to follow a lawful avocation for the support of life," and as expressed by Earl, J., *In re* Jacobs, " one may be deprived of his liberty, and his constitutional right thereto violated, without the actual restraint of his person. Liberty in its broad sense, as understood in this country, means the right

LIBERTY DE- not only of freedom from actual servitude, impris-
FINED. onment, or restraint, but the right of one to use his faculties in all lawful ways, to live and work where he will, to earn his livelihood in any lawful calling, and to pursue any lawful trade or avocation." Who will have the temerity to say that these constitutional principles are not violated by an enactment which absolutely prohibits an important branch of industry for the sole reason that it competes with another, and may reduce the price of an article of food for the human race? Measures of this kind are dangerous, even to their promoters. If the argument of the respondents in support of the absolute power of the legislature to prohibit one branch of industry for the purpose of protecting another with which it competes can be sustained, why could not the oleomargarine manufacturers, should they obtain sufficient power to influence

OLEOMARGARINE or control the legislative councils, prohibit the man-
MAKING IS A LAW- ufacture or sale of dairy products? Would argu-
FUL INDUSTRY. ments then be found wanting to demonstrate the invalidity under the constitution of such an act? The principle is the same in both cases. The numbers engaged upon each side of the controversy cannot influence the question here. Equal rights to all are what are intended to be secured by the establishment of constitutional limits to legislative power, and impartial tribunals to enforce them.

Illustrations might be indefinitely multiplied of the evils which would result from legislation which should exclude one class of citizens from industries, lawful in other respects, in order to protect another class against competition. We cannot doubt that such legislation is violative of the letter as well as of the spirit of the constitutional provisions before referred to, nor that such is the character of the enactment under which the appellant was convicted.

The judgment of the general term and of the court of sessions should be reversed.

All concur.

PROHIBITION OF THE MANUFACTURE AND SALE OF OLEOMARGARINE.
—In Missouri the legislature passed an act as follows: "An act to prevent the manufacture and sale of oleaginous substances, or compounds of
the same, in imitation of the pure dairy products.

"Section 1. Whoever manufactures, out of any oleaginous substances,
or any compound of the same other than that produced from unadulterated milk, or cream from same, any article designed to take the place of
butter or cheese produced from pure unadulterated milk, or cream of the
same; or whoever shall sell or offer for sale the same as an article of food,
shall, on conviction thereof, be confined in the county jail not exceeding
one year, or fined not exceeding one thousand dollars, or both." Approved March 24, 1881. The validity of this statute came before the St.
Louis court of appeals and was affirmed by Judge Seymour D. Thompson of
that court in a carefully written opinion, in which the main point discussed
was whether the statute was an uureasonable exercise of the police power of
the State. After affirming that the police power was extensive and undefined, and conceding that it could not be exercised to prohibit a legitimate industry—although, under the police power, such industries might be
regulated—Judge Thompson says: "The substance of the objections urged
against it (the law) is that it is a sweeping prohibition of the manufacture
and sale of an article of food which is not only harmless but wholesome,
the manufacture of which is beneficial to the people—an industry which
should be encouraged and not repressed. We are disposed to concede
that it is beyond the power of the legislature to prohibit the manufacture,
the cultivation, the mining, or the importation of any known article of commerce, innocuous in itself, the production of which is known to be useful
to the people. We do not think it would be competent for the legislature to prohibit the commerce in any of the ordinary productions of
agriculture, of mines, or of manufacture, because the production of these
things is universaily recognized as beneficial to the people. Such a prohibition could not be justified on any pretence of public safety or utility;
and the common-sense of mankind would agree that an interference by
the legislature of the usual and ordinary industries by which life is supported would be an unjustifiable interference with private right. It would
be oppression under the pretence of police regulation.

"But we do not concede that the mere fact that scientific men may pronounce a manufactured article intended for human food to be wholesome
or harmless renders it incompetent for the legislature to prohibit the
manufacture and sale of the article. Laws, in order to be wholesome,
must not only conform to the needs of the people, but must also respect
their tastes, their prejudices, and even their superstitions. Hence it is conceded by jurists and publicists that laws which in one age or nation are
beneficial, in another age or nation may be unwholesome, injurious, or
oppressive. The test of the reasonableness of a police regulation prohibiting the making and vending of a particular article of food is not alone
whether it is in fact unwholesome or injurious. If an article of food is of
such a character that few persons will eat it, knowing its real character; if,
at the same time, it is of such a character that it can be imposed upon the

public as an article of food which is in common use, and against which there is no prejudice ; and if, in addition to this, there is probable ground for believing that the only way in which to prevent the public from being defrauded into purchasing the counterfeit article for the genuine is to prohibit altogether the manufacture and sale of the former,—then we think such a prohibition may stand as a reasonable police regulation, although the article prohibited is, in fact, innocuous, and although its production might be found beneficial to the public, if, in buying it, they could distinguish it from the production of which it is the imitation.   Upon this ground rests, in part, those laws which prohibit the counterfeiting of trade-marks.   A trade-mark may be a guaranty of the genuineness of an article which, through the excellence of its manufacture or the care and skill of its manufacturer, has acquired a high reputation. A statute which punishes the counterfeiting of such a mark is founded in the double policy of protecting the owner in his proprietary interest and of protecting the public against imposition.   The State *v.* Gibbs, 56 Mo. 135.   It would be idle to declaim against the reasonableness of such a law, on the ground that the imitator of the article in question has produced an article exactly the same as, or equally good with, the one the mark to which he has imitated.   Every person has the right to buy the article which he seeks ; and if he pays his money thinking he is buying this article when he is not, is he not cheated, although he may, in fact, get an article which, but for his prejudice, would be just as good for him ?   The question is not what some one else may think is for his good.   He has a right to his free-dom of choice ; and when, through fraud, that freedom of choice has been violated, is he not wronged and injured ?   Here is an article made from the fat of dead animals, in so close an imitation of pure butter that a non-expert person cannot distinguish between them.   Noticing, judicially, things which are matters of common knowledge, we know that the people will not knowingly eat this counterfeited article, and that it cannot be sold, and is not sold, to those who buy butter for their personal consumption except under the belief that it is real butter.   Even though we may not know this judicially, we may, at least, indulge in so reasonable a supposi-tion in support of the action of the legislature.   The manufacturer may brand it with his real name.   It may carry this brand into the hands of the broker or commission merchant, such as this defendant is ; this brand may follow it into the hands of the retail grocer ; but there it will be taken off, and it will be sold to the customer as real butter, or it will not be sold at all.   The fact that, in the present state of the public taste, the public judg-ment, or the public prejudice with respect to it, it cannot be sold except by cheating the ultimate purchasers into the belief that it is real butter, and defrauding their judgments and their freedom of choosing what they will eat and what they will not eat, stamps with fraud the entire business of making and vending it, and furnishes justification to a police regulation prohibiting the making and vending of it altogether.

  " Let us see where the argument of the learned counsel for the defendant would lead.   Abundance of scientific evidence could, no doubt, be pro-duced to show that the flesh of horses, dogs, cats, and rats is not unwholesome. But a universal popular prejudice—in some cases even a religious feeling—prohibits the eating of the flesh of such animals. If the flesh of such animals could be prepared so as not to be distinguished from the flesh of animals whose flesh is deemed wholesome,—if butchers were known in some instances to be engaged in the business of so preparing and selling it in fraud of the choice and judgment of their customers,—would any one say that a statute prohibiting, in general terms, the selling of the flesh of horses, dogs, cats, and rats would transcend the police power of the legislature? Upon what principle could a judicial tribunal undertake to say that a statute less sweeping in its terms would be effective to protect the public from such an imposition?

" It seems to us, then, that this whole question comes to this : A practice has sprung up which operates to defraud the people of their right of choice as to what they will eat, with reference to an article of food of constant and universal consumption. The legislature has passed an act which, if properly administered, will nip the practice in the bud. The courts must uphold and administer this act as a valid exercise of the police power of the State." The State *v.* Addington, 12 Mo. App. 214.

This judgment of the Court of Appeals was affirmed by the Supreme Court of Missouri. State *v.* Addington, 12 Mo. App. 223 ; s.c., 77 Mo. 117. But the Supreme Court did not add anything either to Judge Thompson's reasons or improve upon the manner of their expression.

With great respect for these decisions, we are constrained to believe them wholly unsound, and that the correct conclusion is that reached by the New York court.

In the first place, Judge Thompson's opinion is based largely upon assumptions of fact not well founded. " Noticing, judicially," says he, " things which are matters of common knowledge, we know that the people will not knowingly eat this counterfeited article, and that it cannot be sold, and is not sold, to those who buy butter for their personal consumption except under the belief that it is real butter. Even though we may not know this judicially, we may, at least, indulge so reasonable a supposition in support of the action of the legislature." Again he says, " It will be sold to the consumer as real butter, or it will not be sold at all." This is neither true nor reasonable. A large and growing class of people buy oleomargarine or some form of compound butter daily. Nor is it unreasonable that they do so. They know it to be oleomargarine. They know also that it is a clean, wholesome product, from twenty-five to fifty per cent cheaper than the best butter and infinitely better in quality than butter which, though a genuine " product of the dairy," is yet strong, rancid, and dirty. They are not deceived in buying it, nor defrauded of their "right of choice." Neither do they require an expert to distinguish oleomargarine from butter. And, in the writer's opinion, the attempt to deprive the people of a wholesome, economical article of food by suppressing the manufacture of it deserves signal failure.

Nor can the substitution of oleomargarine for butter be regarded in the light of the imitation of a trade-mark. A trade-mark is private property, and its imitation is prohibited because it infringes a right of private property. It is true that one of the effects of prohibiting the imitation of trade-marks may be, and often, if not generally, is, the prevention of imposition of an inferior article on the public. But this is not the object of the prohibition. It is not the reason of it. That is the protection of private property. Now, butter-making belongs exclusively to no man or woman. It is an industry open alike to all the public. No individual's rights are infringed by others going into a similar business. The analogy between making a substitute for butter and imitating a trade-mark therefore fails in the very particular essential to make the analogy of any logical value.

Nor is the sale of oleomargarine comparable to the sale of the flesh of dogs, horses, cats, and rats. In the first place, there is no " universal prejudice" against the flesh of these animals. The French eat horseflesh, and the Chinese are said to eat rats, whatever may be the fact with reference to cats and dogs. However it may be as to the flesh of any of these animals, there is no such prejudice, nor indeed any prejudice at all, against oleomargarine. Compound butter, in the form of oleomargarine, butterine, suine, etc., etc., is readily bought and sold in the markets of France, England, and the United States without deception or fraud. It is advertised in the leading newspapers, and exhibited in fairs and industrial expositions side by side with all the "products of the dairy"—with which it does not suffer by comparison either as to cleanliness of manufacture, wholesomeness of ingredients, or cheapness of price.

It is true there is a prejudice against being imposed upon. No man is willing to pay for butter and get oleomargarine. Nor is this prejudice unreasonable. But fraud of this kind is becoming exceptional, owing to several reasons. In the first place, oleomargarine is sold by many dealers, among whom the most sell it for what it is. Secondly, the name butterine, or oleomargarine, is stamped either upon the package or the commodity itself. Inspection by municipal authorities also compels honesty in many other instances, and this is the true remedy for frauds of this nature. But the fact that there is fraud in the sale of a useful commodity should not lead courts to sanction the prohibition of its honest manufacture and sale. And it is believed that the decisions in Missouri will not be sanctioned either by public opinion, by legislative enactment, or by other courts.

LAWFUL INDUSTRIES CANNOT BE SUPPRESSED.—The true view to take is that so well expressed in Live-stock, etc., *v.* Crescent City, 1 Abb. (U. S.) 398 : " But so far as relates to the question in hand, we may safely say it is one of the privileges of every American citizen to adopt and follow such lawful industrial pursuit—not injurious to the community—as he may see fit, without unreasonable regulation or molestation and without being restricted by any of those unjust and odious monopolies or exclusive privileges which have been condemned by all free governments. It is also his privilege to be protected in the possession and enjoyment of his property so long as such possession and enjoyment are not injurious to the community, and he cannot be deprived thereof without due process of law. It is also his privilege to have, with all other citizens, the equal protection of the laws. These privileges cannot be invaded without sapping the very foundation of republican government. A republican government is not merely a government of the people, but it is a free government. Without being free it is republican only in name, and not republican in truth ; and any government which deprives its citizens of the right to engage in any lawful pursuit, subject only to reasonable restriction, or at least subject only to such restrictions as are reasonably within the power of the government to impose, is tyrannical and unrepublican. And if, to enforce arbitrary restrictions made for the benefit of a favored few, it takes away and destroys the citizen's property without trial or condemnation, it is guilty of violating all the fundamental privileges to which I have referred, and one of the fundamental principles of free government. There is no more sacred right of citizenship than the right to pursue unmolested a lawful employment in a lawful manner. It is nothing more nor less than the sacred right of labor."

—BUT MAY BE REGULATED.—It is not denied, however, that the legislature may regulate the adulteration of food, the sale of dangerous articles, and noxious, unwholesome trades and business which endanger the health or welfare of the people. Illustrative of this rule may be cited the following cases :

THE SALE OF GUNPOWDER, INFLAMMABLE OILS, AND FIRE-ARMS MAY BE REGULATED.—A city may regulate the keeping and sale of gunpowder within its limits. Williams *v.* Augusta, 4 Ga. 509. The prohibition may extend to the mere act of receiving the powder into a store, though for the purpose of being immediately packed and shipped to another State. Foote *v.* Fire Department, 5 Hill (N. Y.), 99. The sale of naphtha may be regulated. Commonwealth *v.* Wentworth, 118 Mass. 441, and if in a prosecution for violating a regulation of the sale of naphtha the jury are instructed to decide whether the article sold was " substantially naphtha or not," no exception will be sustained to the use of the word " substantially." Commonwealth *v.* Wentworth, 118 Mass. 441. And if a person is injured by an explosion of oil sold by a dealer when it was not of the standard fixed by the statute, the dealer in an action for damages for the injury cannot defend on the ground that he was ignorant that it was not of the required standard. Hourigan *v.* Nowell, 110 Mass. 470 ; see also Wellington *v.* Downer Kerosene Oil Co., 104 Mass. 64 ; Wright *v.* C. & N. W. R. R. Co., 7 Brad. (Ill.) 446, is a close case. When on the night of October 9, 1871, the city of Chicago was on fire, Wright, the plaintiff, had a large amount of property—horses, carriages, etc., etc., being such property as a liveryman would have—in his stables. He could have saved this property from the advancing conflagration but for the fact, as he alleged, that the Northwestern R. R. Co. had a large quantity of inflammable oils in a neighboring freight-house, contrary to a municipal ordinance regulating the keeping of the same. These oils caught fire long before the buildings in the neighborhood, and the fire from them spread to Wright's place, preventing him from saving his property, as he might otherwise have done. A demurrer to the plaintiff's declaration was sustained in the circuit court, but overruled by the appellate court. The case presents a question of proximate cause rather than one of the power of a municipality to regulate the sale of oils.

In Dabbs *v.* State, 39 Ark. 353, it is decided that an act making it a misdemeanor to sell "any pistol except such as are used in the army or navy of the United States, and known as the navy pistol," is constitutional. The court said the act was "levelled at the pernicious habit of wearing such dangerous or deadly weapons as are easily concealed about the person."

In State *v.* Burgoyne, 7 Lea (Tenn.), 173, it is held competent for the legislature to pass a law that may in the future interfere with rights that once existed under a license that has expired before the law goes into effect. This rule was applied to the case of a merchant who, under his license, bought a stock of pistols for sale, which was not exhausted at the expiration of his license. He was tried and convicted for selling such stock as remained after his license expired and after the prohibitory law had been passed.

In Binford *v.* Johnston, 82 Ind. 426, the principle was affirmed that one who sells dangerous explosives to a child, knowing that they are to be used in such a manner as to put in jeopardy the lives of others, must be taken to contemplate the probable consequences of his wrongful act, including injury to the child. The merchant was sued for selling a toy pistol and cartridges to a child who shot it off and killed his brother. The court held that the sale of the cartridges was in violation of the criminal law, and was *per se* negligence.

Nunn *v.* State of Georgia, 1 Kelly (Ga.), 243, tends to sustain the decision of the New York court in the principal case. It decides that a law which merely inhibits the wearing of weapons in a concealed manner is valid. But that so far as it cuts off the right of a citizen altogether to bear arms, or, under color of prescribing the mode, renders the right of itself useless, it is void. See also State *v.* Buzzard, 4 Ark. 19; State *v.* Mitchell, 3 Blackf. (Ind.) 229.

DANGEROUS MACHINERY is also subject to regulation. For example, elevator shafts may be required to be inclosed by a railing, and also to be closed by a trapdoor after the close of business during the day. Mayor, etc., *v.* Williams, 15 N. Y. 502.

DANGEROUS DRUGS.—A law prohibiting the sale of opium is constitutional. State *v.* Ah Chew, 40 Am. Rep. 488, 16 Nev. 50.

DANGEROUS ANIMALS—DOGS.—An act "to discourage the keeping of useless and sheep-killing dogs" by assessing a penalty or license fee upon their owners is constitutional. Mitchell *v.* Williams, 27 Ind. 62; State *v.* Cornnall, 27 Ind. 120. Generally, license fees may be imposed as a means of restraining the carrying-on of a business or the keeping of property when to carry on such business or to keep such property to an unlimited extent would injuriously affect the health, safety, or welfare of society. Those who have not the means to pay the license fee will of course be debarred from the business. Tenney *v.* Lenz, 16 Wis. 566; Carter *v.* Dow, 16 Wis. 299.

The government may even go further and require dogs to be muzzled on penalty of their being killed. Haller v. Sheridan, 27 Ind. 494.´ The legislature may authorize the killing of dogs found without a collar bearing the owner's name, and the putting of the initials (J. P. M.) of the owner's name on the collar is not such an affixation of the owner's name to the collar as will protect the dog, or render the person who kills him liable for so doing. Morey v. Brown, 42 N. H. 373.

In Mayor v. Meigs, 1 McArth. D. C. 59, Judge Humphreys waxed sentimental about dog history and poetry. "Not only," said he, "has the dog been the subject of discussion in the courts, as involving the question of property, but his virtues have been celebrated in song. The wrongs done him have been touchingly described by poets, and hours have been occupied at the camp-fires of huntsmen in narrating the achievements of favorite hounds." The learned judge then proceeded to indulge in a dog story, that of the rescue of William of Orange "from the grasp of the enemies of toleration on the morning of the 12th September, 1572, by the action of a little dog." Admitting, however, that "the historian and moral philosopher" more appropriately than the court could discuss "the influence which the watchfulness of the little spaniel had upon the destinies of the world," the court proceeded to hold that the law recognizes property in dogs ; that a city ordinance requiring the owner of dogs to obtain a license for keeping them is illegal, and that the dog-owner who failed to take out and pay for a license could not be arrested and fined for so doing.

ADULTERATION OF MILK AND FOOD-PRODUCTS.—The legislature may make it a criminal offence to sell milk and water, and in a prosecution for so doing a certificate of analysis by a sworn municipal milk-inspector is admissible as evidence. Commonwealth v. Waite, 11 Allen, 264. It is not necessary to convict for selling adulterated milk to show knowledge of the adulteration by the seller, nor to aver that the milk was cow's milk. Nor is it a defence to show that the woman who sold it was acting as her husband's agent. Com. v. Farren, 9 Allen, 489 ; but see Dilley v. People, 4 Brad. (Ill.) 52. The result of a test by a lactometer is admissible in evidence. Com. v. Nichols, 10 Allen, 199 ; see also Com. v. Flannelly, 15 Gray, 195 ; Thompson v. Howe. 46 Barb. 287. But tests of milk made more than a year after the violation complained of are inadmissible. Stearns v. Ingraham, 46 T. & C. (N. Y.) 218. Further, as to evidence in a prosecution for selling adulterated milk, see State v. Smith, 10 R. I. 258.

The adulteration of confections may also be prohibited ; but an indictment charging defendant with fraudulently adulterating "a certain substance intended for food—to wit, one pound of confectionery"—does not sufficiently describe the substance adulterated, and if reasonably objected to, will be quashed. Commonwealth v. Chase, 125 Mass. 202. But an act prohibiting the sale of adulterated milk does not embrace the offence of bringing such milk into the city. Polinsky v. State, 73 N. Y. 65.

In State v. Newton, 45 N. J. L. 469, an act conferring authority upon a State milk-inspector to condemn milk, and either pour it upon the ground or return it to the consignor, was held constitutional, and it was also held that the legislature might fix a standard and authorize the condemnation of milk falling below it. Same point in Com. v. Evans, 132 Mass. 11, holding an act constitutional declaring adulterated milk containing more than 87 per cent water and less than 13 per cent milk solids.

LICENSE FEES.—In Allerton *v.* Chicago, 20 Am. Law Reg., N. S. 473, a license fee of $50 per car imposed on street-car companies was held valid. See also Johnston *v.* Phila., 60 Pa. St. 445; Frankford & P. R. R. Co. *v.* Phila., 58 Pa. St. 119. But the Court of Appeals in New York, in Mayor *v.* Second Ave. R. R. Co., 32 N. Y. 261, held a street-car-license ordinance void on the ground that although in form a license, it was in fact a tax in disguise, and as such beyond the power of the municipality.

In Cincinnati *v.* Bryson, 15 Ohio, 625, a fee of $3 was held authorized to be charged for a license to run a dray. In Cincinnati *v.* Buckingham, 10 Ohio, 257, an ordinance that no person should be licensed or permitted to occupy any place in the market but upon making payment of 25 cents for every market-day and occupation was held valid. The Supreme Court of Michigan, Campbell, J., dissenting, held that a fee of $5 required for a license to keep a stall to sell fresh meats outside the public markets was not a tax, but a reasonable compensation which the city of Detroit could demand from those who would not sell in the public markets. In Boston *v.* Schaeffer, 9 Pick. 415, it is decided that the city could require the proprietor of a theatre to take out a license and to pay therefor a fee of $1000. In Baker *v.* Cincinnati, 11 Ohio St. 534, the city charged $63.50 for a license to give theatrical performances, and it was held not to have been illegally exacted. See also Mays *v.* Cincinnati, 1 Ohio St. 268; Cincinnati G. L. & C. Co. *v.* State, 18 Ohio St. 242. In Van Baalen *v.* People, 40 Mich. 258, pawnbrokers were required to take out a license. It was held that the business of pawnbroking gave rise to heavy city expense, especially through the increase of police duty and supervision which it needed, and that the sum charged ($200) did not greatly exceed the incidental and consequential expense of issuing the license, and that therefore the ordinance was valid.

Chicago Packing Co. *v.* Chicago, 88 Ill. 221, decides that packing-house proprietors doing business within one mile of the city limits may be required to take out a license at a cost of $100. The packing company had taken out a license required to be procured by the *town* within whose limits it actually did business. " Nor does the fact," said the court, "that appellant is liable to pay a fee to each municipality for the privilege of pursuing a vocation the General Assembly regards of such a character as to require regulation and control militate against the grant or exercise of the power" to regulate and control such establishments by requiring them to take out and pay for a license.

In Mayor *v.* Yuille, 3 Ala. 137, a city ordinance required bakers to take out a license at a cost of $20. The court said it was "inclined to doubt the propriety of that portion of the by-law . . . which requires $20 to be paid as a license, unless the latter can be supported under the taxing power of the corporation." This suggests the objection most commonly made to these license fees. The power to require a license is conceded to the municipality, but it is urged that the fees are taxes in disguise, and as such beyond the power of the municipality to levy. They are not taxes, however.   The objects for which license fees are charged and taxes levied are widely different.   Taxes are assessed to procure revenue, license fees are imposed to regulate traffic, and although the license fee may ultimately go into the treasury, it is nevertheless not a tax.   Frankford, etc., R. R. Co. *v.* Phila., 58 Pa. St. 119; Johnson *v.* Phila., 60 Pa. St. 445 ; State *v.* Herod, 29 Iowa, 123; Louisville, etc., R. R. Co. *v.* Louisville, 4 Bush (Ky.), 478 ; People *v.* Thurber, 13 Ill. 554; East St. Louis *v.* Wehrung, 46 Ill. 392; St. Paul *v.* Colter, 12 Minn. 51 ; Rochester *v.* Upman, 19 Minn. 108.

So long as the fee charged is one reasonably calculated to effect the object sought, the licensure is valid as an exercise of police power.   If, however, the fee is unreasonable, and is more than enough to effect the legislative purpose, it is a tax, and as such is unauthorized and uncollectable, unless the corporation has power to impose it for revenue purposes. Mays *v.* Cincinnati, 1 Ohio St. 268; Cincinnati *v.* Bryson, 15 Ohio, 625 ; Freeholders *v.* Barber, 7 N. J. L. 64; Kip *v.* Paterson, 26 N. J. L. 298; Bennett *v.* Birmingham, 31 Pa. St. 15; Commonwealth *v.* Stodder, 2 Cush. 562 ; Chilvers *v.* People, 11 Mich. 43; Mayor *v.* Yuille, 3 Ala. 137; Johnson *v.* Phila., 60 Pa. St. 451 ; State *v.* Herod, 29 Iowa, 123; Mayor *v.* Second Ave. R. R. Co., 32 N. Y. 261 ; Home *v.* Ins. Co. *v.* Augusta, 50 Ga. 530.

But courts will not closely scrutinize a license fee with the purpose of adjudging it a tax.   Courts will not review municipal discretion in this matter, unless it be manifestly unjust. "The subject" (i.e., what sum shall be charged ?) says Graves, J., "will not admit of nice calculation, and it would be futile to require anything of the kind."   Van Baalen *v.* People, 40 Mich. 258; Ash *v.* People, 11 Mich. 347 ; Burlington *v.* Putnam Ins. Co. 31 Iowa, 102.

MISCELLANEOUS BUSINESS REGULATIONS.—In Wisconsin à banker or broker who receives deposits, knowing himself to be insolvent or unsafe, is punishable.   Baker *v.* State, 54 Wis. 369.

Jacob's case, 98 N. Y. 98, decides that an act prohibiting the manufacture of cigars or preparation of tobacco in any form on any floor, or in any part of any floor, in any tenement house, if such floor or any part of it was by any person occupied as a home or residence for the purpose of living, sleeping, cooking, or doing any household work therein, was unconstitutional, on the ground that it interfered with the profitable and free use of the cigarmaker's or tobacconist's own property, or of the property of the lessee of a tenement-house who is a cigarmaker or tobacconist, and trammelled them in their industry and the disposition of their labor, and thus, in a strictly legitimate sense, arbitrarily deprived them of their property and of some portion of their personal liberty.   See also *In re* Paul, 18 N. Y. Week. Dig. 487.

In District of Columbia *v.* Saville, 1 McArth. 583, an act provided in substance that no proprietor of a theatre shall, after the door of such theatre is open for the reception of spectators, sell tickets so as to reserve particular seats, or to mark or describe as reserved or taken any seats which have not been reserved by the sale of tickets therefor previous to the opening of such exhibition.   The act was held void.   "In short," said the court, by Olin, J., "the provision is that when the doors of the theatre are opened for the reception of spectators, whoever purchases a ticket to enter the same may plant himself in any unoccupied seat he can discover, unless the proprietor can convince him that the seat he had selected had been sold prior to the time of opening the doors of the theatre for the reception of spectators, or at least before the commencement of the exercises, and this without reference to the fact whether the spectator purchased a ticket for twenty-five cents which would entitle him to a seat in the upper gallery, or whether he paid the price of the most desirable seat in the house.

"Indeed if this law can be enforced it is made a penal offence for the manager or proprietor to reserve for the use of his friends a few desirable seats, who, he thinks, by their presence and approbation, might give success to his entertainment.

"He cannot, however, reserve these seats if not sold before the commencement of the exhibition. Nay, under this section the proprietor or manager of a theatre could not reserve a private box for himself and family without incurring the penalty imposed in the third section of the act."

The court, therefore, held the act not a police regulation, but an "unwise, vexatious, and unlawful interference with the rights of private property."

In Illinois an act requiring the owner or agent of a coal-mine or colliery employing ten men or more to make, or cause to be made, an accurate map or plan of the workings of such coal-mine or colliery was held constitutional. Daniels *v.* Hilgard, 77 Ill. 640.

In Robinson *v.* Hamilton, 60 Iowa, 134, a statute requiring physicians and midwives to report births and deaths to the clerks of courts was held not unreasonable nor unconstitutional; while in Washington Territory a statute prescribing the qualifications of medical practitioners has been held constitutional. Fox *v.* Territory, 5 W. C. Repr. 339.

The police power of governments is all-pervading. It has never been defined within narrow limits, and the foregoing are but a few of the multitude of instances of its exercise. In the language of Judge Redfield in Thorpe *v.* Rutland, etc., R. R. Co., 27 Vt. 140, under it "persons and property are subjected to all kinds of restraints and burdens in order to secure the general comfort, health, and prosperity of the State; of the perfect right to do which no question ever was, or, upon acknowledged general principles, ever can be, made, so far as natural persons are concerned." It need only be added that artificial persons are, as well as natural persons, subject to its legitimate exercise.

BARTHET

v.

CITY OF NEW ORLEANS.

(Advance Case, Louisiana, U. S. Circuit Court. July, 1885.)

An ordinance of the city of New Orleans prescribed the place where slaughter-houses must be located. Relying upon this designation of such place, complainant secured land within its limits and proceeded thereon to erect houses and make other improvements for slaughtering purposes, when the city amended the ordinance by making it unlawful to maintain slaughter-houses in the prescribed place " except permission be granted by the council of the city of New Orleans," and proceeded to prevent complainant who had no such permission from carrying on his slaughtering business.

Held, that the amendment is unconstitutional because it would in effect deny complainant the equal protection of the laws guaranteed. by the XIVth Amendment of the United States Constitution.

The prevention by the city of complainant's exercise of his business is enjoinable in equity, as being likely to do him irreparable injury for which damages at law would be no adequate compensation.

RULE to show cause why an injunction *pendente lite* should not issue.

A. H. Leonard and *E. Sabourvin* for complainant.

W. H. Rodgers for the city.

BOARMAN, J.—Article 258 of the constitution of Louisiana prohibits any monopoly. Article 248 invests the defendant city with power to regulate the slaughtering of cattle, etc., within its limits, provided no monopoly or exclusive privilege exist within the State. Nor shall such business be FACTS. restricted to the land or houses of any individual or corporation ; and provided, further, the place designated for slaughtering is approved by the board of health. By several ordinances, approved by said board, the city designated the place at which the slaughtering of cattle may be carried on, and prescribed in detail the regulations under which such business should be conducted.

The complainant, a citizen of France, whose trade and business is the slaughtering of cattle for food, desiring and intending to engage in such business in New Orleans, leased, with the privilege of buying, two squares of ground situated within the limits defined by said ordinances, and proceeded to repair such buildings, and construct on said ground other buildings and improvements suitable for the trade in which he is engaged, investing in said improvements a considerable sum of money.   Subsequently, on May 19th, an ordinance was • passed by the council which is styled " An ordinance amending ordinance 7336, as passed September 13, 1881, designating the places for slaughtering animals intended for food under article 248 of the constitution."   The original ordinance provided that "it shall be lawful for any person or corporation to keep and maintain slaughter-houses, etc., within certain limits, under certain regulations."   The amendment mentioned makes it unlawful to keep and maintain slaughter-houses within said limits prescribed in original ordinance, and under said regulations, "except permission be granted by the council of the city of New Orleans."

It appears that defendant corporation intends actively to enforce, or attempt to enforce, as against Barthet, the amended ordinance; that it is about to obstruct, hinder, and prevent him from carrying on his legal business in the limits already laid out in pursuance of article 248.

The complainant, alleging that, acting on the good faith of said articles and ordinances, he has acquired vested rights, and that the ordinance of May 19th is unconstitutional, brings a bill for injunction to enjoin and restrain the defendant from interfering in any manner with him in carrying on his business.   Complainant prays, on final hearing, for an injunction absolute, and in the meanwhile has taken this rule to show cause why an injunction *pendente lite* should not issue. Defendant has filed no answer or made any denials, even in argument, of complainant's allegations.

The amendment of May 19th is, we think, unconstitutional, in the fact that if it is carried out, as the city attorney admits it will be, it will make Barthet's right to engage in a lawful PROHIBITION OF BUSINESS. business dependent on the arbitrary will of an individual or body of individuals acting for the city.   The city has no governmental or special power to prevent any one who complies with the law regulating such business from engaging in any lawful business he prefers.

The fourteenth amendment to the United States constitution forbids any State to make or enforce any law which shall abridge the privileges or immunities of citizens of the United States, and prohibits a State from denying to any person " within its jurisdiction the equal protection of the law." That amendment does not enlarge the rights of persons; it clearly recognizes and emphasizes principles imbedded in the common law, and which underlie the structure of all free governments.

The right to grant permission to A to carry on his lawful business carries with it necessarily the power to deny permission to B to exercise the same privilege. The complainant is entitled, in common with all persons, to equal protection. Applying this principle to this case, as it is made up by the bill and admissions of the city's council, Barthet is entitled to carry on his trade within the limits already laid out by the city in pursuance of the articles herein cited. If the city council, as the matter now stands, can prevent him from so doing simply because he has not their permission, then he has not that equal protection of the law guaranteed in the constitution. The ordinance of May 19th transcends not only the limitations or legislative authority presented in the constitutions of the Federal and State governments, but in our opinion it transcends those limitations, also, which spring from the very nature of free government.

The city council have the right, generally, in the exercise of governmental powers, such as belong to municipal corporations, to regulate the business of slaughtering animals for food; but under the articles 248, 258, State constitution, —responsive as those articles are to a public sentiment long offended in this city by oppressive monopolies in the slaughtering of cattle for food,—it must be apparent that the city cannot, directly nor indirectly, prohibit the business of this complainant under the pretence of exercising an ordinary governmental police power. It is clear that those articles were intended to prohibit all monopolies, and to limit rather than to enlarge the police powers of the city in relation to slaughtering cattle, etc., and if the city can refuse to permit Barthet to carry on his business, it can adopt the same course with others. By giving its permission to an individual or to a corporation, and refusing it to all others, a monopoly could be established by the favored suitor. An ordinance which permits one person to carry on an occupation within municipal limits, and prohibits another who had an equal right from pursuing the same business, is void. So, also, is an ordinance which alleges the rights and privileges conferred by the general law of a State. Cooley, Const. Law, 243, 245–247, 155, 202, 491.

If the amendment of May 19th becomes operative as a law, the investment made by Barthet, on the faith of the law existing when he erected his buildings, will be lost or greatly diminished in value, and his privilege, which is of more value, may be wholly destroyed by the refusal of the city. It is urged in argument that the corporation is a legislative body, endowed with police powers, to be exercised with absolute discretion; that this court has no power to control or limit its action in directing when, and upon what particular lot in the territory laid out and defined by the city, Barthet, or any other person following the same business, may locate and carry on his business of slaughtering animals for food. The proposition of the city attorney, in view of the many cases that have been decided by the State and Federal courts, in which just such assumptions of power have been contended for and denied to municipal authorities, need not now be considered, further than to say that the court does not think the proposition maintainable under the law and facts found on the hearing of this bill.

The city does not deny the equity of the bill, nor does she deny that she intends to hinder and prevent Barthet from INJUNCTION. REMEDY AT LAW. carrying on his business in the territory laid out; but it is contended that in these proceedings an injunction will not be allowed because the complainant has an adequate remedy at law; that if he is damaged he can recover fully at law. It is true that the sixteenth section of the judiciary act prohibits suits in equity when there is a plain, adequate, and complete remedy at law; but in Boyce's Ex'rs *v.* Grundy, 3 Pet. 210, the court said, referring to that section, that "it is merely declaratory on the subject of legal remedy. It is not enough that there is a remedy at law; it must be plain and adequate; or, in other words, as practical and efficient to the ends of justice and its prompt administration as the remedy in equity." It does not appear that the adoption of the statute mentioned has impaired the jurisdictional powers of the equity courts of the United States for the protection of the property of individuals, or the privileges that belong, as a common right, to all persons to whom the courts are open for the administration of justice. The jurisdictional power of these courts is certainly not less now than it was in England at the time of the adoption of the constitution. The English authorities show that the granting or continuance of an injunction cannot be controlled by any inexorable rule, but that such orders must rest largely in the sound discretion of the court, to be governed in each case by the equitable rights of all parties, as well as by the nature and effect of the relief sought in the particular case. To grant such writs to prevent an irreparable injury is quite common.

The defence of the city is not based upon any denial that she is going to do the thing complained of; but she seems to rely wholly upon some several petitions, signed by several citizens living in the neighborhood of the place where Barthet has begun his business, protesting against allowing him to proceed with his business. These petitions, if they had been seasonably presented to the council, might have caused the particular place occupied by Barthet's buildings to be not included in the limits; but the counsel for the city would hardly be considered serious should he rest the city's defence on the merits of the bill upon such petitions or papers. An injunction, however, is not, in the Federal courts, issued as a matter of course; and it may be well to consider more definitely the matter as to the jurisdictional power of the court to issue the injunction prayed for. The buildings and improvements were erected in the view of the city for the well-known purposes of Barthet's trade. Would it not be inequitable and violative of a proper, efficient, and practical administration of justice to allow the city now to stop him in the exercise of his lawful business, in the gratification of his legal rights, and to turn him over to an action at law, against whoever should become instrumental in executing the city's unconstitutional ordinance, for the recovery of damages. If such is the effect of the sixteenth section of the judiciary act, the courts of the United States will find themselves often without power to afford to suitors a practical and efficient administration of justice.

We do not think the act complained of is an attempt at a mere
9 Cor. Cas.—33

trespass. The mischief and injury it would work in this case cannot be repaired as efficiently or as adequately by an action at Damage irre- parable. law for damages as in the case of a mere trespass upon property. This is not a case where the city may or will have an ultimate right to do the thing complained of, as sometimes happens when a city is attempting to do a thing lawful to be done, but prematurely; like, for instance, the taking of property for streets before making the compensation required by law; but the city can never do the act complained of without violating Barthet's constitutional rights. In a government like ours it may be said that any act which would deprive a citizen of the power to exercise his lawful trade or privileges must be considered as working an irreparable injury, particularly when the wrong-doer is attempting to do an act clearly forbidden by the State and Federal constitutions.

Our opinion will be better understood when we say that the city authorities have no power, legislative, judicial, or administrative, to pass the ordinance complained of; because the power, by whatever name it may be called, delegated to the city in articles 248, 258, as far as Barthet is now concerned, was exhausted when the city officials laid out the limits in which it was declared lawful to slaughter animals for food. The bill shows that an unlawful act is threatened against the privileges of complainant. In our opinion, such an act, if carried out, would not only work an irreparable injury to Barthet, but would be a decided step, whatever may be the motive, causing the council to move in the matter, in the direction of allowing a monopoly in the slaughtering of animals for food in this city.

The injunction will be operative *pendente lite.*

A City Ordinance Prohibiting the Maintaining of Slaughter-houses within Certain Specified Limits, except on Permission Granted by the City Council, is not an Infringement of the XIVth Amendment of the Federal Constitution.—It is hard to see how the decision in the principal case can be supported. The court bases its decision that the ordinance in question was an infringement of the XIVth Amendment of the Federal Constitution on the clause of the ordinance requiring permission of the city council to be obtained before the business of maintaining a slaughter-house could be lawfully carried on. The court held that this clause vests in the city council the absolute right to grant or refuse permission as it shall see fit; that the council might grant permission to A and refuse it to B, although there was no reason why the permission should be refused or granted in one case more than in the other; and that this power to discriminate deprived citizens of the equal protection of the laws within the meaning of the XIVth Amendment. This reasoning is unsatisfactory. It would seem clear on reason and authority that an ordinance prohibiting the maintaining of slaughter-houses within the city limits, or within other prescribed limits, was a valid exercise of the police powers of the sovereignty. Metropolitan Board of Health *v.* Heister, 37 N. Y. 661; Inhabitants of Watertown *v.* Mayo, 109 Mass. 315. If so, how can a provision that the sovereignty may, in cases where it sees fit so to do, make exceptions to this law by giving permission to certain persons or corporations to carry on the prohibited business within the prescribed limits deprive any one of the equal protection of the laws? The law being that no one may carry on the prohibited business, the exceptions made in case of persons permitted by the council is a matter of favor, not of right. The fact that the law may give scope for injustice and discrimination does not in the least affect the constitutional question involved.

For a case similar to the principal case, except that the statute excepted those slaughter-houses in existence at its passage, see Inhabitants of Watertown *v.* Mayo, 109 Mass. 315. In that case, however, the question of the constitutionality of the statute under the XIVth Amendment of the Federal Constitution was not raised. The statute was held a valid exercise of the police power to restrain and regulate the carrying-on of a business likely to cause danger or annoyance to the public unless properly regulated.

MAKER

v.

SLATER MILL AND POWER CO.

(Advance Case. Rhode Island, July 18, 1885.)

A statute requiring fire-escapes to be put upon certain buildings, but not specifying who, whether the owner or a tenant, is to put them there, nor when or how they are to be erected, and giving to an inspector a certain discretion as to exempting buildings from being equipped with fire-escapes, but not definitely indicating the limits of such discretion, is too vague and indefinite to sustain a criminal prosecution for its violation.

TRESPASS on the case. On demurrer to the declaration.

This is one of several cases brought against the defendant for neglecting to provide fire-escapes in alleged violation of Pub. Laws R. I., chap. 688, of April 12, 1878, in consequence

of which the plaintiff was injured by a conflagration in the
building in which he was employed.   See Grant *v.* Slater
Mill and Power Co., 14 R. J. 380; s. c., 30 Alb. L. J. 310;
Baker *v.* Same, 14 R. I. 531.

Spooner, Miller & Brown for plaintiff.

Charles Hart, Benjamin T. Eames and *Stephen A. Cooke, Jr.,*
for defendant.

STINESS, J.—Plaintiff sues under Pub. Stat. R. I., chap. 204,
§ 21, claiming that he has suffered an injury to his person by
the commission of a " crime or offence" on the part of the de-
.FAcm.   fendant.   The crime or offence consists in an
alleged violation of the Building Act, so called.   Pub. Laws
R. I., chap. 688, of April 12, 1878.   Since the decision of the
court sustaining a demurrer to the declaration in Baker *v.*
Slater Mill and Power Co., 14 R. I. 531, complaint has been
made against the defendant, pursuant to Pub. Stat. R. I., chap.
204, § 22, and process has issued thereon, which is duly
averred in this declaration, but there is no averment of service
of such process or of any proceedings thereon.   A demurrer
is filed to this declaration.   Several grounds have been urged
in support of the demurrer, which need not now be considered ; *e.g.,* that the statute gave a right of action for injury
sustained " by the commission of any crime or offence" does
not include a mere neglect of duty or omission to comply
with the requirements of law ; that such a statute does not apply to a plaintiff to whom the defendant owed no duty outside of statutory requirements; that the terms "crime and
offence" do not apply to a violation of the act in question,
upon the ground that it is not a public statute, but a local
police regulation ; that the injury for which an action can be
sustained must be the immediate and not the consequential
result of the omission charged.   Assuming all these points in
favor of the plaintiff, the fundamental question remains,
whether the defendant's omission to provide its building with
fire-escapes or stairways, as required by chapter 688, is a
" crime or offence."   If, under the act, an owner of a building
is not criminally liable for neglect to comply with its requirements, the foundation of the plaintiff's action fails.   The
penal provision in the act is in the general terms of section
37, "any person violating any provision of this act" shall be

fined, etc.   Our inquiry, then, is whether an owner complained of for neglecting to provide fire-escapes or stairways
could be found guilty under the provisions of the act.   The
requirements of the act are minute and manifold.   Some
clearly pertain to the owner, some to the contractor or
builder, some to tenants, and some to other persons ; while in
many cases it is by no means clear to whom the duty imposed
by the act belongs.   The duty to provide fire-escapes or
stairways is explicit.   The section reads as follows: "§ 23.
Every building already built or hereafter to be erected, in
which twenty-five or more operatives are employed in any of
the stories above the second story, shall be provided with .
proper and sufficient strong and durable metallic fire-escapes
or stairways, constructed as required in this act, unless
exempted therefrom by the inspector of buildings, which
shall be kept in good repair by the owner of such building,
and no person shall at any time place any incumbrance upon
any of such fire-escapes."

But upon whom does the duty rest, when is it to be performed, and what facts are neccessary to constitute a violation of the duty?

The plaintiff claims that the reasonable construction of the
act puts the duty upon the owner.   He argues that, as there   .
is an alternative between fire-escapes or stairways, Statute examined.
the duty must be upon one and the same person, and that person the owner, because only he could provide stairways.   We
do not see that this is necessarily so.   Of course, permanent or
structural improvements are ordinarily made by an owner;
but if a lessee takes a building as it stands and then lets into
it twenty-five or more operatives, it is difficult to see why by
his act a burden should be cast upon the owner which may
not have been expected or provided for when the contract
was made.   It is said that no one but the owner would have
the right to put fire-escapes on a building; but, on the other
hand, if a building was under lease, what right would the
owner have to enter and interfere with the lessee's occupation
by erecting stairways such as are required by the act?   Moreover, if the duty is solely upon the owner, why should the act
particularly specify that he should keep the stairways or es-
capes in repair?   The plaintiff further urges that the defendant in this case is liable because it is both the owner and

the party in control of the building. Without control over
the number of persons which tenants may employ, the same
unexpected burden might suddenly be cast upon the person
in control of a building by the act of a tenant. Under the
construction claimed, such person would be made criminally
liable by the act of another person, which he had no power to
prevent. But if an owner is to be held responsible by reason
of his control, then it follows that a lessee must be held
responsible when he is in control; and so the question recurs,
Whose is the duty? In most cases it would not be an unreasonable construction to say that the duty of complying
with a statute is upon the one who creates, and has the power
to prevent, the necessity of complying with it. Under the present act, this might be the owner or tenant, and the very alternative which is given is possibly significant. It may have been
thought that owners could make the permanent, structural
provision of stairways, and that lessees or tenants, if they create
the necessity, could provide the light, temporary, and less
expensive fire-escapes. A more troublesome question arises
in the case of a building let out to tenants, when no one of
them employs twenty-five persons, but when, all together,
they exceed that number, thus bringing the building within
the law in this respect. Undoubtedly it would be most
natural to look to the owner for the provision, but the statute
does not say whose the duty is, nor whose the responsibility
for neglect. It is one of the omissions that frequently occur
in legislation, but an omission that we do not think we can
cure by construction. Suppose, however, we assume that the
duty is upon the owner, having control of a building, the
problem is by no means solved. The act does not say when
or under what circumstances the duty is to be performed.
The act went into effect in ten days after its passage, and it
does not seem probable that it was intended to make all
owners of buildings, already built, immediately responsible
for its multitudinous provisions and liable to its penalties.
Immediate compliance with the law in all respects would
probably have necessitated changes in many, perhaps nearly
all, of the buildings then built. But if the liability of an owner
did not attach at once, when did it attach? If there were
nothing in the act to indicate the contrary, all its provisions
would take effect at the same time. But we think there are

indications that the act did not contemplate an immediate compliance with reference to existing buildings. The inspector of buildings is charged with the enforcement of the act, but in the very section in question is given authority to exempt buildings from its requirements. Section 33 provides that, upon complaint, he shall examine buildings already erected, including any workshop having the employees on any story above second story, and require such building to be provided with proper and sufficient fire-escapes, stairways, and exits, constructed as described in the act. This section must relate to buildings where there are more than twenty-five employees, for no others are required to have fire-escapes, and, taken in connection with the authority to exempt, indicates that the requirement is to be discretionary with the inspector, dependent, perhaps, upon his judgment of danger in a particular case or of other equivalent provisions for safety. It also indicates that the time for requiring the fire-escapes is when the inspector requires them. In regard to " buildings for public assembly already built, and also boiler-houses and rooms and their heating apparatus, now built," an express discretion is given to the inspector, namely: " If in his judgment the safety of the public requires it, he shall require that the same be made to conform to the provisions of this act." It is hardly probable that in respect to fire-escapes the act was intended to be more restrictive. If this is so, an owner would not be in default until after examination and notice by the inspector. To construe the provision otherwise, the inspector would be obliged to require only what the law itself had already required, and that, too, without pointing out how or from whom he should require it. In Willy *v.* Mulledy, 78 N. Y. 310 ; s. c., 34 Am. Rep. 536, the court said the defendant " was not permitted to wait until he should be directed to provide" a fire-escape by the commissioners. " He was bound to do it in such way as they should direct and approve, and it was for him to procure their direction and approval." But under the law in that case there was no discretion in the commissioners whether to require a fire-escape or not. There was no power of exemption. The owner was bound to provide one in any event ; the commissioners were simply to direct and approve the kind to be used. But under that act no penalty was to be imposed until after notice by the commissioners. The case was not based upon the "commission of a crime or offence," but upon a negligence of duty to the plaintiff as tenant of the defendant. With reference to our statute, it has already been decided, in Grant *v.* Slater Mill & Power Co., 14 R. I. 380; s. c., 30 Alb. L. J. 310, that the act does not create a duty between an owner and the employees of his tenant such as tó give them a right of action for neglect. In Parker *v.* Barnard, 135 Mass. 116; s. c., 46 Am. Rep. 450, it was held that the plaintiff, having a license to enter a building, could maintain an action for neglect to protect the elevator well, as required by statute. The court conclude their opinion, however, by saying: "We have not considered the respective duties of the owners and of the occupants of the building as te the protection of the elevator well. Upon this inquiry the case is not before us, and the facts are not reported."

There are many peculiarities and difficulties in the act as it stands, some of which have already been noticed by the court in previous cases; but upon this fundamental point we think it sufficiently appears that the provisions in regard to fire-escapes and stairways are too indefinite and uncertain to impose a criminal liability upon an owner of a building for not providing one or the other before the inspector required it. Penal statutes must be strictly construed and a duty must be clearly imposed upon a particular person before we can say that he has violated the law by neglecting it.

We do not think the plaintiff states a case against the defendant under the law, and therefore the demurrer to the declaration must be sustained.

Demurrer sustained.

INWOOD

v.

THE STATE.

(42 *Ohio State*, 186.)

A statute which authorizes a penalty by fine only, upon a summary conviction under a police regulation or of an immoral practice prohibited by law, although imprisonment, as a means of enforcing the payment of the fine is authorized, is not in conflict with either section 5 or 10 of article 1 of the constitution, on the ground that no provision is made for a trial by jury in such cases.

ERROR to the District Court of Van Wert county.

The case is sufficiently stated in the opinion of the court.

The cases of Ohio *v.* Frysinger, error to the district court of Van Wert county, and Curtis *v.* State of Ohio, error to district court of Erie county, were argued and decided with the principal case.

Ban & Alexander for Inwood.

J. L. Price and *J. R. Shissler* for the State.

J. L. Bigelow for Curtis in Curtis *v.* State.

E. B. Saddler for the State.

MCILVAINE, J.—Are those statutes which define and punish by fine certain immoral practices and offences, QUESTIONS. *mala prohibita*, in a summary manner and without trial by jury, in conflict with the constitution of the State? There are scores of such offences upon the statute-book, and many of them have remained there unchallenged since the organization of the State government. The validity of all such statutes is within our present decision.

The plaintiff in error, Herbert Inwood, was arrested and fined, under section 3 of the act of February 17, 1831, "for the prevention of certain immoral practices" (Swan and Critchfield, 447), which provides " that if any person or persons shall, at any time, interrupt or molest any religious society, etc., the person or persons so offending shall be fined in any sum not exceeding twenty dollars. And any judge of the court of common pleas, or justice of the peace within the proper county, is hereby empowered, authorized, and required to proceed against and punish every person offending against the provisions of this act ; and upon view and hearing may, or on information given under oath or affirmation shall, if need be, issue his warrant to bring the body of the accused before him, and shall inquire into the truth of the accusation ; and if guilty shall enforce the penalty of this act annexed to the offense ; and said offender (if the judge or justice should think necessary) may be detained in custody and committed until sentence be performed." The arrest was made under a warrant issued by a judge of the court of common pleas, and upon the hearing the accused

demanded a trial by jury, which was refused on the ground
that the offence was not, under the statute, triable by a jury,
whereupon the accused was found guilty by the judge, and
fined in the sum of fifteen dollars, and ordered to stand committed until the fine be paid.   This judgment is now sought
to be reversed, on the ground that the statute under which
the fine was imposed is unconstitutional, for the reason that
it did not provide for a jury trial.

The provisions of the constitution relied on as nullifying
PERPETUITY OF the statute are sections 5 and 10 of article 1.   The
TRIAL BY JURY
GUARANTEED. former provides, " The right of trial by jury shall
be inviolate."   It is settled beyond further discussion that
this clause in the constitution was not intended to enlarge or
modify the right of trial by jury.   Its sole purpose was to
guaranty the perpetuity of the institution as it then existed
and as it had long existed at common law.   Work *v.* State, 2
Ohio St. 296.

The question therefore arises : At the time of the adoption
DID RIGHT OF of the constitution in 1851, did the right of trial by
TRIAL BY JURY
EXIST IN OHIO IN jury exist in cases like the present in the State of
1851?
Ohio, either under its own system of jurisprudence or by the
rules of the common law?   The constitution of 1802 contained
the identical provision now under consideration, and yet, in
Markle *v.* Akron, 14 Ohio, 14, this court held an ordinance to
prohibit, under a money penalty, persons not tavern-keepers,
from selling intoxicating liquors within the corporate limits
to be constitutional, notwithstanding the mayor, without the
intervention of a jury, was authorized to try the case and impose the penalty.   The case was appealed to the common
pleas, where a declaration in debt was filed, and upon recovery, the cause was reviewed, in error, by this court, where
the judgment was affirmed.   In the opinion it is said: " It appears to have been urged against a recovery in the court
below that the ordinance under which the plaintiff in error
was arrested contemplated a criminal prosecution, and that
debt was not the proper remedy.   It is true, for offences
strictly criminal or infamous, punishment can only be inflicted
through the medium of an indictment or presentment of the
grand jury.   There are, however, many offences made so by
statute which are but *quasi* criminal, and in which the legislature may direct the mode of redress untrammelled by the

constitution; such as sabbath-breaking, selling spirituous liquors on Sunday, and the disturbance of religious meetings. Long acquiescence in these enactments goes far to show the construction whicn has been placed by all on the constitution, and that there be many offences which, though decidedly immoral and mischievous in their tendencies, are not crimes, but at most are only *quasi* criminal. Of such, jurisdiction may be given to justices of the peace or the mayor of an-incorporated town." Wightman *v.* State, 10 Ohio, 452, is to the same effect. These cases clearly show that at common law the right to demand a trial by jury in such cases does not exist, and, also, that the common-law rule was not changed by the constitutional provision under consideration. The doctrine of the common law that fines for such minor offences could be imposed and collected without the intervention of a jury, and by magistrates who had no jurisdiction in the trial of jury cases, is abundantly established by many cases and text-writers. Indeed, the doctrine is nowhere denied. 3 Blackst. Comm. 161; Swan's Treatise, Ed. of 1871, p. 678; Sedgwick's, 491, and note; 3 Park. Cr. 544; 1 Curtis C. C. 311; 45 Ill. 218; 31 Conn. 572; 50 N. Y. 274; 6 Lans. 44; 12 Ohio St. 124; 1 Head (Tenn.) 71; 1 Williams (Vt.), 318, 325.

A more difficult question arises on section 10, above referred to. This section reads: "Except in cases of impeachment, and cases arising in the army and navy, or in the militia when in actual service in time of war or public danger, and in cases of petit larceny and other inferior offences, no person shall be held to answer for a capital or other infamous crime, unless on presentment or indictment of a grand jury. In any trial, in any court, the party accused shall be allowed to appear and defend in person and with council; to demand the nature and cause of the accusation against him and to have a copy thereof; to meet the witness face to face and to have compulsory process to procure the attendance of witnesses in his behalf; and to have a speedy public trial by an impartial jury of the county or district in which the offence is alleged to have been committed." The question is: Was the phrase "in any trial, in any court," intended to apply to cases like the present, where the penalty is by fine, NECESSITY OF JURY IN MISDE-merely, inflicted on the violator of a mere police MEANOR CASES. regulation, only *quasi* criminal?—a class of cases for the punishment of immoral and pernicious practices by pecuniary penalties, but in which, by the common law, as above shown, the accused was never entitled to demand a trial by jury. The provision of the constitution is that the person accused shall have a speedy public trial by an impartial jury of the county or district in which the offence is alleged to have been committed. Accused of an offence—to wit, such an offence as would, before the adoption of the constitution, have entitled the accused to a jury trial. This provision, in our opinion, was not intended to extend the right of jury trial, but was intended to define the characteristics of the jury.

In Thomas *v.* Ashland, 12 Ohio St. 124, it was *held*, that an ordinance of a village which imposed imprisonment as a penalty for an offence, where no provision was made for a trial by jury, was in conflict with section 10 of the 1st article of the constitution above quoted; but the court was careful to exclude from the operation of the rule there laid down cases where the punishment was by fine only, although imprisonment was authorized as a means of enforcing the payment of the fine. We think the discrimination between imprisonment as part of the penalty and as a means of enforcing the penalty is well made. Hence, we find no constitutional objection to the statute under which Inwood was arrested.

Judgment affirmed.

MOORE *et al.*
v.
THE PEOPLE OF THE STATE OF ILLINOIS.

(109 *Illinois*, 499.)

Where a village ordinance prohibits the sale or giving-away of intoxicating liquors within the limits of the village, concluding with a proviso that druggists may sell such liquors for purely medicinal, chemical, and sacramental purposes, and fails to provide for the issue of any written permit, this will, within the meaning of the statute, be of itself a permit to all druggists in the village to sell such liquors for the purposes named.

A druggist having a permit to sell intoxicating liquors for medicinal chemical, and sacramental purposes from city or village authorities is not required to give the bond of $3000 required by section 5 of the Dram-shop Act of persons taking out licenses to retail such liquors, and he may sell such liquors for the purposes above stated without giving such bond.

The questions involved in this case did not arise in Wright *v.* The People, 101 Ill. 136, and any general expressions to be found in the reasoning in that case which may seem not to be in entire harmony with the conclusion here reached must be limited in their effect by the case then before the court.

WRIT of Error to the Appellate Court for the Third District, heard in that court on writ of error to the Circuit Court of Vermilion County ; the Hon. J. W. WILKIN, Judge, presiding.

W. R. Lawrence for the plaintiff in error.

C. M. Swallow, State's attorney, for the People.

MULKEY, J.—Charles Lynch and Manzo Moore, the plaintiffs in error, were indicted, in the Vermilion County   FACTS. Circuit Court, at its October term, 1882, for unlawfully selling intoxicating liquors without a license. The cause, by consent of parties, was submitted to the court without a jury, upon an agreed state of facts. The court, on consideration of the case as submitted, found the defendants guilty on fifteen counts of the indictment, and fined them, severally, $20 on each count. This conviction having been affirmed by the Appellate Court for the Third District, the defendants bring the case here for review.

It appears from the stipulation on which the case was tried that the defendants, for eighteen months prior to the finding of the indictment, were doing business together as druggists in the village of Ridge Farm, in said county, during which time the sales of intoxicating liquors complained of were made, in due course of business. There is no controversy as to the fact of the sales, but they are sought to be justified on the alleged ground that in making them they were acting under a druggist's permit, granted to them by the village authorities. To this it is replied by the State, first, that within the meaning of the law no such druggist's permit was ever granted to them by the village authorities ; and, second, conceding such a permit was granted, it was inoperative and void because of the defendants' failure to give bond, as required by the fifth section of the Dram-shop Act.

The first section of the ordinance relied on by the defendants as showing a permit, after prohibiting the sale and giving-away of intoxicating liquors altogether within the limits of the village, and providing a penalty for its violation, concludes with the following proviso, viz. : " Provided druggists may sell such liquors for purely medicinal, chemical, and sacramental purposes." The second section then makes it the duty of druggists to report, under oath, all sales to the village board of trustees, and prescribes a penalty for any violation of the provisions of that section. No written permit was ever issued by the board to the defendants, nor, indeed, does the ordinance contemplate such a permit, though the stipulation shows the defendants made regular reports to the village authorities of all sales made by them, as required by the ordinance.

It must be conceded that the ordinance in question, by its express terms, authorizes all druggists within the corporate limits of the village to sell intoxicating liquors for the purposes above specified, on the conditions named in the ordinance, and this we think was, within the meaning of the statute, a " permit" on the part of the village authorities to the defendants to sell for those purposes. It remains to inquire whether sales of intoxicating liquors under such a permit, when *bona fide* for the purposes specified in the above ordinance, as appears to have been the case here, are subject to the provisions of the fifth section of the Dram-shop Act. That section is as follows: " No person shall be licensed to keep a dram-shop, or to sell intoxicating liquors, by any county board, or the authorities of any city, town, or village, unless he shall first give bond in the penal sum of $3000, payable to the People of the State of Illinois, with at least two good and sufficient sureties, freeholders of the county in which the license is to be granted, to be approved by the officer who may be authorized to issue the license, conditioned that he will pay to all persons all damages that they may sustain, either in person or property or means of support, by reason of the person so obtaining a license selling or giving away intoxicating liquors," etc.   Rev. Stat. 1874, p. 439, sec. 5.

If this was the only provision of the statute bearing on the AUTHORITY OF MUNICIPALITIES TO AUTHORIZE RETAILING OF LIQUOR. question, it might well be concluded that the municipal authorities of counties, cities, towns, and villages have no power to authorize the retailing of intoxicating liquors for any purpose, unless the party acting under their authority has complied with the provisions of this section by entering into bond, with approved security, as therein directed. But this is not the only provision bearing on the question. The 46th sub-section of section 62 of the Revised Statutes of 1874, after declaring incorporated towns, cities, and villages shall have power " to license, regulate, and prohibit the selling or giving-away of any intoxicating, malt, vinous, mixed, or fermented liquor," then adds, by way of proviso, "that the city council in cities, or president and board of trustees in villages, may grant permits to druggists for the sale of liquors for medicinal, mechanical, sacramental, and chemical purposes only, subject to forfeiture, and under such restrictions and regulations as may be provided by ordinance." This language is supplemented with the following additional proviso: "Provided, further, that in granting licenses such corporate authorities shall comply with whatever general law of the State may be in force relative to the granting of licenses." Now, if the legislature had added the words "or permits" after the word "licenses" in the concluding part of this last proviso, there would be no room to doubt it was the intention of the act that the keepers of dram-shops, and druggists, should be placed upon the same footing with respect to the observance of the provisions of the general law relating to the sale of intoxicating liquors, and hence the defendants in this case would have been bound to give bond, as required by the fifth section of the Dram-shop Act. But such is not the case, and the question is, shall we, by mere judicial construction, add these words, in order to sustain the conviction, which the legislature has seen proper to omit. It is not pretended we have power to do this, but the contention is that the word "licenses" in this last proviso is used in its popular or extended sense, and that it therefore includes the word " permits" as used in the preceding proviso. We do not think a fair construction of this sub-section, taking it altogether, sustains the view suggested. If the legislature had intended druggists should be placed upon the same footing with other persons engaged in the retail of intoxicating liquors, there would not have been the slightest occasion, as it seems to us, to have made any special reference to druggists at all. To adopt the construction contended for would give no effect or operation whatever to the first proviso in said sub-section. Again, it will not do to hold that the word "license" as used in the first part of the section is not synonymous with the word "permits" in the first pro-

DRUGGISTS HAV-
ING PERMITS MAY
SELL LIQUOR.

viso, and then, for the purpose of bringing the case within the provisions of the Dram-shop Act, enlarge its meaning so as to include druggists' permits. On the contrary, we are of opinion that the word "license," or "licenses," is used in the same sense wherever it occurs in this section and that it is used in a different sense and for a different purpose from the word "permits," and it therefore follows druggists having "permits" do not fall within the provisions of the fifth section of the Dram-shop Act, and consequently the conviction was improper.

Defendants in error rely upon Wright *v.* The People, 101 Ill. 126, as sustaining the contrary view. It is sufficient to say the question involved in this case did not arise in that, and consequently could not have been decided by it. It may be admitted, general expressions in the reasoning of that case are to be found which are not in entire harmony with the conclusions here reached, but the expressions made in that case *in arguendo*, like all other similar expressions, must be limited by the facts of the case then before the court, and it is hardly necessary to observe it is not within the power of this or any other court to make a binding adjudication upon a question which is not presented by the facts of the case then in hand.

The judgment of the appellate court is reversed, and the cause remanded, with directions to that court to reverse the judgment of the circuit court, and remand the cause for further proceedings in conformity with this opinion.

Judgment reversed.

WALKER, J.—I dissent from the decision in this case.

BRONSON

v.

OBERLIN.

(41 *Ohio State*, 476.)

The act of March 29, 1882 (79 Ohio Laws, 59), authorizing incorporated villages having within their limits a college or university to provide against the evils resulting from the sale of intoxicating liquors therein, is not repugnant to the provisions of the constitution.

A village council acting under the authority conferred by this law exceeds its power when it makes an ordinance which prohibits the sale of intoxicating liquors to all persons and for all purposes except mechanical and medicinal, and the sections of the ordinance so providing are void.

ERROR. Reserved in the District Court of Lorain county. On the 29th of March, 1882, the General Assembly passed the following act (79 Ohio Laws, 59):

"AN ACT

"Authorizing Certain Incorporated Villages to Regulate the Sale of Intoxicating Liquors Therein.

"SECTION 1. Be it enacted by the General Assembly of the State of Ohio. That the following section be enacted as supplementary to chapter 3, division 3, title 12, sec. 1692 of the Revised Statutes of Ohio, with sectional numbering as follows:

"Sec. 1692 *b*. That all incorporated villages within this State having within their limits a college or university shall have the power to provide by ordinance against the evils resulting from the sale of intoxicating liquors within the limits of the corporation.

"Sec. 2. This act shall take effect and be in force from and after its passage."

Attempting to act under the authority conferred by this statute, the council of the village of Oberlin, a village in which a college has been located for many years, on the 6th of September, 1882, passed the ordinance which follows:

9 Cor. Cas.—34

" AN ORDINANCE

"To Provide Against the Evils Resulting from the Sale of Intoxicating Liquors.

" Be it ordained by the incorporated village of Oberlin—

" SECTION 1. It shall be unlawful for any person, by himself or agent, to sell or furnish within the limits of said village any intoxicating liquors whatever to or for any student or students in any of the departments of Oberlin College, or of the Telegraph School, or of the Business and Writing School, located in said village, except on the written order of the President or one of the Professors of said Oberlin College, presented by or in behalf of any student of said Oberlin College, or except upon the written order of the principal Manager of said Telegraph School, or the principal Manager of said Business and Writing School, presented by or in behalf of any students of their respective schools, or except on the written order of the parent or parents of any such students.

" Sec. 2. It shall be unlawful for any person, by himself or agent, to sell or furnish, or keep for sale or furnishing, to any person or persons who are not students in the College or the Schools named in Section One of this Ordinance, within the corporate limits of said village, any intoxicating liquors whatever, except for medicinal or mechanical purposes, under the conditions hereinafter provided.

" Sec. 3. It shall be, and is hereby made, the duty of every person selling or furnishing intoxicating liquors within said village to keep and preserve a record of every sale or furnishing in a book kept for that purpose, wherein he shall enter, at the time said liquor is sold or furnished, the amount and kind of liquor sold or furnished, and to whom sold or furnished, and said record shall be subject at all times to the inspection of such person as the mayor, with the approval of the council, may appoint.

" Sec. 4. It shall be unlawful for any person to sell or furnish to any other person or persons within said village any intoxicating liquors whatever, except upon reasonable and satisfactory evidence that such liquors are needed and will be used for medicinal or mechanical purposes aforesaid.

" Sec. 5. It shall be unlawful for any person to buy or receive from any other person or persons within said village any intoxicating liquors to be·used for other than medicinal or mechanical purposes.

" Sec. 6. Any person who shall violate any of the provisions of this ordinance shall, upon conviction thereof, be fined in any sum not exceeding fifty dollars, or be imprisoned for a period not exceeding thirty days, or both, at the discretion of the mayor.

" Sec. 7. If any person called to testify on behalf of the prosecution before the mayor of said corporation upon any complaint or information for any offence defined in sections one to five, inclusive, of this ordinance disclose any fact tending to criminate himself in any matter made punishable by said sections, he shall thereafter, and by reason thereof, be discharged from all liability to prosecution or punishment for such matter of offence.

" Sec. 8. The ordinance entitled 'An ordinance to provide against the evils resulting from the sale of intoxicating liquors,' passed April 17, 1882, and all ordinances amendatory thereof, and July 5, 1882, are hereby repealed.

" Sec. 9. This ordinance shall take effect upon its passage and legal publication."

On the 25th day of September, 1882, a complaint was filed with the mayor of Oberlin charging that the plaintiff in error, Frank E. Bronson, on or about the 22d day of September, A.D. 1882, at the village of Oberlin, did unlawfully sell intoxicating liquors to one Nathan B. Doane, he not being a student in any of the departments of Oberlin College, or of the Telegraph School located in the village, or of any Business or Writing School located in the village, and the intoxicating liquors were not sold by Bronson to Doane for either medicinal or mechanical purposes. Bronson knew that the intoxicating liquors so sold by him were not intended by Doane to be used for either medicinal or mechanical purposes.

On this complaint Bronson was convicted. The court of common pleas affirmed the judgment of the mayor's court. A petition in error was then filed in the district court of Lorain county, and that court, upon motion of the village of Oberlin, reserved the case for the decision of the supreme court. It was partially presented to this court by oral argument on the 31st day of October, 1884; but the last printed brief of counsel for the village was filed November

29th, and the reply of opposing counsel upon the 29th day of December.

E. G. Johnson and *S. M. Eddy* for plaintiff.

W. W. Boynton, I. A. Webster, and *C. A. Metcalf* for defendant in error.

NASH, J.— 1. Does the act of March 29, 1882 (79 Ohio Laws, 59), authorizing incorporated villages having within their QUESTION. limits a college or university to provide against the evils resulting from the sale of intoxicating liquors therein, contravene the limitations imposed by the constitution upon legislative power?

In considering this question it must be borne in mind that it is well settled that the presumption is always in favor of VALIDITY OF the validity of the law; and it is only when manifest LAW PRESUMED. assumption of authority and a clear incompatibility between the constitution and the law appear that the courts will refuse to execute it. Railroad Co. *v.* Commissioners, 1 Ohio St. 77; Goshorn *v.* Purcell, 11 Id. 641; Lehman *v.* McBride, 15 Id. 573.

It is contended that a classification of incorporated villages such as is sought to be made in this act, and the clothing of CLASSIFICATION the councils of such villages with powers not pos- OF VILLAGES AND CITIES. sessed by the councils of other villages, are prohibited by the constitution.

The Revised Statutes divide cities into grades and make provisions for each grade so established. Municipal corporations are divided into three classes—cities, villages, and hamlets. Cities are divided into two classes—first and second. Cities of the first class are divided into three grades—first, second, and third. Cities of the second class are divided into four grades—first, second, third, and fourth. This classification depends upon the number of inhabitants within a city. In The State *v.* Brewster, 39 Ohio St. 653, it was held that sections 1546–1550 of the Revised Statutes, which make the classification referred to, are authorized by the constitution. . Judge Okey, in the opinion of the court, says: " The validity of that classification has been repeatedly recognized in this court, and the reasons for adhering to that construction of the constitution are cogent and satisfactory."

The principle seems to be that a law which relates to certain municipal corporations as a class, and having a like effect upon all within the class, is general, but one that relates to a particular municipality of a class is special. Judge Okey, in the case of McGill *v.* The State, 34 Ohio St. 228, said: "Under the power to organize cities and villages (Const. article 13, section 6), the general assembly is authorized to classify municipal corporations, and an act relating to any such class may be one of a general nature." Judge McIlvaine, in the case of The State *v.* Powers, 38 Ohio St. 54, said that "judicious classification and discrimination between classes will not destroy the uniformity required by the constitution." In the case of The State *v.* Parsons *et al.*, 40 N. J. Laws, 123, the principle is well stated as follows:

"A law framed in general terms, restricted to no locality, and operating equally upon all of a group of objects, which, having regard to the purposes of the legislation, are distinguished by characteristics sufficiently marked and important to make them a class by themselves, is not a special or local law, but a general law."

The classification must be just and reasonable, and not arbitrary. In the act under consideration the classification is just and reasonable. It groups in a class all incorporated villages in the State having within them a college or university. There are many of these, and they are located in all sections. Large numbers of boys and young men are congregated in them for the purpose of acquiring an education. Many of them are away from home and parental restraints, and at a time when they are acquiring habits which will make them useful men, or will destroy all hopeful prospects for the future. Such villages are small, and do not have the police restraints of the larger cities. They require regulations which are unnecessary in other villages and in larger cities. The value of their property, and their greater value as suitable resorts for the education of youth, depend upon such villages being kept free from the unrestrained traffic in intoxicating liquors. These considerations and many others which could be enumerated, show the just and substantial character of the classification made in this law, and the wisdom of the general assembly in making it.

It is also claimed that the legislature cannot delegate the power to regulate the sale of intoxicating liquors to the

councils of incorporated villages.   This is a settled question
DELEGATION TO in Ohio.   Several years ago the council of the vil-
VILLAGES OF
POWER TO REGU- lage of McConnellsville provided by ordinance that
LATE SALE OF
LIQUOR. it should be unlawful for any person to keep in its
midst a house, shop, room, booth, arbor, or place where ale,
porter, or beer is habitually sold, or furnished, to be drank in,
upon, or about the house, shop, room, booth, arbor, cellar, or
place where so sold or furnished.   This it did under an
authority conferred upon municipalities by statute " to regulate, restrain, and prohibit ale, beer, and porter houses or
shops, and houses and places of notorious or habitual resort
for tippling and intemperance."   This act was a delegation of
power by the general assembly.   In Burckholter *v.* McConnellsville, 20 Ohio St. 309, the supreme court held the
ordinance to be valid, and in so doing of necessity concluded
that the legislature could confer a power possessed by itself
upon municipal corporations.

2. The plaintiff in error was found guilty of violation of
the second and fourth sections of the Oberlin ordinance.
These sections prohibited the sale or furnishing of any intoxicating liquors whatever, or in any quantity, to any person,
except for two purposes—mechanical and medicinal.   In making these sections did the council exceed the power conferred
by the act of March 29, 1882 ?   Whether the legislature could
confer the power to prohibit the sale of intoxicating liquors,
or whether the council by ordinance could prohibit with this
power conferred, are questions not involved in this case.
The question simply is, " What power did this act·confer?"
We are of the opinion that it did not give authority to pro-
VILLAGE HELD hibit.   As expressed in the body of the law, it was
WITHOUT AU-
THORITY a power to provide against the evils resulting from
PROHIBIT.
the sale of intoxicating liquors.   Section 16, article 2 of the
Constitution, provides that the subject of a bill pending before
the general assembly shall be clearly expressed in its title.
In trying to determine what the object of the words of a
statute are, we are authorized to look at its title.   The title
of the law under consideration is " An act authorizing certain
incorporated villages to regulate the sale of intoxicating
liquors therein."   Considering the words of this act, together
with its title, we conclude that the power conferred was to
regulate the sale of intoxicating liquors, and to provide against

evils resulting therefrom, but not to prohibit. We are confirmed in this conclusion from the fact that in previous legislation the word " prohibit" has been used when that was the object sought, and not alone the words "to regulate" and "to provide against evils." It follows that sections 2 and 4 of this ordinance are void.

A part of an ordinance may be void and the remainder valid, but the other sections of this ordinance are not involved in this case, and therefore we express no opinion in regard to them.

Judgment reversed.

BUTZMAN
v.
WHITBECK.

(42 *Ohio State*, 223.)

The written consent of the landlord to his tenant to engage in the traffic of intoxicating liquors on his property, required by the Scott law, is a license; hence the law is in this particular unconstitutional.

Whether a statute is in effect a license law, and therefore in conflict with the eighteenth section of the schedule to the constitution of 1851, must be determined from the operation and effect of the statute, and not from the form it may be made to assume. State *v.* Hipp, 38 Ohio St. 199, followed and approved.

The act of 1883, commonly called the Scott law (80 Ohio Laws, 164), so far as it provides for a lien on real estate occupied by a tenant who is a dealer in liquors, is, in effect, such license law, and therefore unconstitutional, whether the lease be executed before or after the passage of the act, and it will make no difference that the owner, in any case, has consented in writing to such traffic.

Whether the act known as the Scott law is in any other respect unconstitutional is a question not presented by the record in this case, and it is therefore not decided.

ERROR to the district court of Cuyahoga county

Foran & Dawley and *S. Burke* for plaintiff in error.

R. P. Ranney, Carlos M. Stone, and *Alex. Hadden* for defendant in error.

OWEN, J.—On December 29, 1883, H. N. Whitbeck, treasurer of Cuyahoga county, commenced an action against William Butzman and Jacob Mueller to obtain an order for **FACTS.** the sale of premises in Cleveland, owned by Mueller, to satisfy an assessment of $200, with 20 per cent penalty thereon for non-payment, levied pursuant to the act of April 17, 1883, better known as the Scott law (80 O. L. 164), which assessment was upon the business of Butzman, as a dealer in intoxicating liquors on the premises, for one year ending on the second Monday of April, 1884. Butzman has occupied the premises since April 20, 1883, as the tenant of Mueller, and with his consent that the business should be carried on upon the premises. The petition also contains two supposed causes of action and a prayer for personal judgment against Butzman. The demurrers of Butzman and Mueller were overruled and judgment was rendered against Butzman as prayed, and an order was made that in default of payment of the judgment within ten days the premises should be sold to satisfy the same. The district court dismissed a petition in error to reverse the judgment, and Butzman and Mueller prosecute this petition in error to reverse the order of dismissal and also the judgment and order of the court of common pleas.

The act in question provides : " Section 1. That upon the business of trafficking in intoxicating liquors there shall be assessed, yearly, and shall be paid into the county treasury by every person engaged therein, the sum of $200."

If the traffic is exclusively in malt and vinous liquors the assessment is but $100. Section 2 provides : "That said assessment, together with any increase thereof, as penalty thereon, shall attach and operate as a lien upon the real property on and in which such business is conducted , . . . and that whoever shall engage or continue in the business aforesaid of selling intoxicating liquors in or upon land or premises not owned by him, and without the written consent of the owner thereof, shall be held guilty of a misdemeanor," and liable to be fined or imprisoned or both ; and each day's contin uance upon such premises shall be an additional offence.

Section 5 provides : " That the county treasurer shall collect and receipt for all assessments so returned to him. And if any assessment shall not be paid when due, he shall forth with proceed, as provided by section one thousand one hundred and four (1104) of the Revised Statutes, to enforce the lien for the same and penalty; and the provisions of said section and any other provisions of the law of this State relative to the collection of taxes or assessments are hereby made applicable to the enforcement of such liens and the collection of such assessments and penalties. . . ."

Section 1104 of the Revised Statutes above referred to provides that the treasurer, in addition to all other remedies provided by law, may enforce the lien for such taxes and assessments by a civil action in his own name as treasurer, for the sale of the premises, in the court of common pleas in the same way as mortgage liens are enforced. This section provides that judgment shall be rendered for the taxes or assessment, penalty, and costs, and that the premises shall be sold to pay the same, etc. The proceeding below was clearly under this section and for the sale of Mueller's property to pay an alleged debt of Butzman. If Butzman was a proper party, it was merely with reference to the amount due, and possibly his interest as lessee in the premises; and a careful examination of the provisions of section 1104 makes it clear that no personal judgment against Butzman was authorized in such action, whatever remedies the treasurer may have under other provisions of the statute.

The treasurer evidently obeyed the direction of section 5 to " proceed forthwith as provided by section 1104 of the Revised Statutes to enforce the lien for the same and penalty."

While section 1104 provides for a judgment, that a judgment against any other party than the owner of the land is not contemplated is apparent from this language : " And the owner or owners of such property shall not be entitled to any exemption as against such judgment."

The proceeding is plainly stamped as one to effectuate the lien for the assessment.

If, therefore, no lien attached to the property of Mueller, the proceeding must fall.

The act in question assumes to attach a lien for the assessments and penalties upon the premises, whereon the traffic in liquors is prosecuted, without regard to the question whether the person so engaged is owner or tenant; and then the act further provides (section 2) that " whoever shall engage or continue in the business aforesaid of selling intoxicating liquors in or upon land or premises not owned by him, and without the written consent of the owner thereof, shall be held guilty of a misdemeanor, and each day's continuance is made an additional offence.

Does this provision authorize a license and therefore contravene the first clause of the 18th section of the schedule to the constitution which ordains that "no license to traffic in intoxicating liquors shall hereafter be granted in this State; but the general assembly may by law provide against evils resulting therefrom?"

It has been assumed by counsel that this question has been adjudicated by this court in the cases of State *v.* Frame and Benner *v.* Bauder, 39 Ohio St. 398, known as the Scott law cases, and that we are called upon either to approve or overrule those cases. It will be seen that the question involved in these cases was simply whether the Scott law, so far as it authorized assessments upon the business of trafficking in intoxicating liquors, was a valid and constitutional enactment, with perhaps the other incidental question, whether section 2 could be stricken from the act and leave it capable of enforcement according to the legislative intent. The question of lien or license was not necessarily involved in either case. After holding the assessment features valid and that the act could be enforced without the penalty clause of the second section, the opinion proceeds:

"Upon this view, further consideration of this question might be, with propriety, omitted from this opinion, as the cases before us do not depend upon the validity or invalidity of the second section of the statute.

"But inasmuch as the validity of this clause of the statute has been fully and ably discussed by counsel, and a large number of the citizens of the State are personally interested in the question, I have concluded to state the views entertained by a majority of the court, after full consideration."

There is nothing in the present case which calls upon us to reconsider either of the questions actually before the court and adjudicated in those cases. So much of the opinion as follows the above quotation, being that of a majority of the eminent judges who composed this court at that time, comes to us with much force and weight, and is entitled to that high consideration and respect which is freely accorded it by the writer of the present opinion. But being an opinion upon questions not necessary to a determination of the cases then under consideration, its examination by this court is comparatively free from the embarrassment and delicacy which must attend a reconsideration of a question necessarily adjudicated by the court.

Not unmindful of the grave responsibility assumed in considering the validity of a legislative enactment, and fully aware that only a fixed conviction after the fullest consideration, and that, beyond every substantial doubt, will justify this court in declaring such an act unconstitutional, we proceed to inquire: 1. Does the penal clause of section 2, which declares it a misdemeanor to engage in the liquor traffic upon the premises of another without the written consent of the owner, authorize a licence to traffic in intoxicating liquors? Fortunately, the field of inquiry is narrowed by the previous discussions of the license question by the members of this court, and by the court itself. In the State *v.* Hipp, 38 Ohio St. 199 (the Pond law case), license, in a general LICENSE DEsense, was said to be "permission granted by com- FINED. petent authority to do an act which without such permission would be illegal." In the Frame case, McIlvaine, J., says: " A license is essentially the granting of a special privilege to one or more persons not enjoyed by citizens generally, or, at least, not enjoyed by a class of citizens to which the licensee belongs." Cooley, J., in Youngblood *v.* Sexton, 32 Mich. 419, says: "The popular understanding of the word license undoubtedly is a permission to do something which without the license would not be allowable. This, we are to suppose, was the sense in which it was made use of in the constitution. But this is also the legal meaning."

Applying these definitions of a license to the Scott law, the opinion in the Frame case proceeds: "No citizen or class of citizens is required by this statute to perform any condition before the right to traffic shall vest in him."

Let us see. This act found three classes of traffickers in intoxicating liquors. (1) Those who prosecuted the traffic upon their own premises; (2) the class of dealers who carry on the traffic upon the numerous water craft floating upon the waters within the jurisdiction of the courts of the State; and (3) those who carry on the traffic upon lands owned by others.

Just how numerous the latter class may be we may not know. We see, however, that they were sufficiently numer. ous to justify the general assembly, in its wisdom, in making them the subject of special legislation.

We can suppose that when this law took effect very few of them were equipped with what legalized their business—the written consent of the owners of the premises occupied. As to all of this class who were not thus supplied, the act was a prohibitory law. Their business was illegalized, and severe penalties were denounced against it; and each day's continu. CONSENT OF ance of the traffic scored against them a distinct offence. The law prescribed just one condition upon which their traffic could be rendered as lawful as that of those against whom no penalties were denounced and upon whom no conditions were imposed. It said to the dealer upon another's premises : Procure the written consent of the owner of the lands you occupy, or bow to the penalties denounced against you. Without such writing the dealer is a criminal. Armed with it, and his business (if he avoid the special offence defined in the act) is as lawful as the traffic in dry-goods. But eminent counsel contend that the offence here created is that of occupying the premises of another without his written consent. This argument is conclusively answered by the language of the act itself: " Whoever shall engage or continue in the business aforesaid of selling intoxicating liquors in or upon land or premises not owned by him, and without the written consent of the owner thereof, shall be held guilty of a misdemeanor."

Counsel illustrate this argument by asking us to suppose that our statutes had provided that whoever shall carry on the business of bread-making or brick-making upon the lands of another without his written consent shall be held guilty of a misdemeanor, and an imposing array of eminent counsel submit this test as decisive of this question. But to keep the analogy good, we are to supplement the illustration with the further supposition that the constitutional convention had been foolish enough to submit, and the people thoughtless enough to adopt, a provision ordaining that " no license to carry on the business of brick-making or bread-making shall be granted in this State; but the general assembly may, by law, provide against evils resulting therefrom."

With the analogy complete, the argument fails. In the opinion of the majority in State *v.* Frame, this argument is urged:

" We think this statute is no more a license law than was section two of the liquor law of 1854, which provided ' that it shall be unlawful for any person or persons, by agent or otherwise, to sell intoxicating liquors to minors, unless upon the written order of their parents, guardians, or family physician.' Surely, it cannot be contended that that section granted a license to traffic in intoxicating liquors with minors."

With great respect it is submitted . that this argument is conclusively answered in the dissenting opinion in that case, as follows :

" The difference is very marked. The requirement that a sale could only be made to a minor on such order was a mere regulation, which left in the dealer the right to traffic in liquors; but one who is not the owner of real estate is absolutely prohibited from dealing in liquors in any way, without the written consent of the owner of the property in which he proposes to carry on the business. There is no analogy between the cases."

It may be added that upon the slightest reflection, it will be seen that to keep the analogy good the argument must assume that a doctor's or parent's written order for liquor for a minor, addressed to a liquor-dealer, is a written consent to carry on the business of trafficking in intoxicating liquors ; for this is what the " written consent of the owner" contemplates.

But it is maintained that the definition of license contemplates that it shall be issued by authority, whereas the written consent provided for in this act is a mere private permit. Such a construction requires that we utterly ignore the operation and effect of the act and regard only its form _{CONSTITUTION-} and letter. It is settled in State *v.* Hipp that the _{ALITY OF} _{STATUTE DE-} _{PENDS ON ITS} constitutionality of a statute depends upon its oper- _{EFFECT,} _{NOT} _{UPON ITS FORM.} ation and effect, and not upon the form it may be made to assume. Upon this subject, it was said by White, C. J., in the District Court Cases, 34 Ohio St. 431 : " An act violating the true intent and meaning of the constitution, although it may not be within the letter, is as much within the purview and effect of a prohibition as if within the strict letter ; and an act in evasion of the terms of the constitution, as properly interpreted and understood, and frustrating its general and clearly expressed or necessarily implied purpose, is as clearly void as if in terms forbidden." The act provides that whoever engages in the liquor traffic upon premises not owned by him, and without the written consent of the owner thereof, shall be guilty of a misdemeanor, etc.

Stripped of the weak disguise with which a cunning phrase has invested it, this provision plainly confides to the owner the authority to say whether the dealer occupying his premises shall stand as a criminal before the law, or whether his business shall be entirely lawful. Suppose the act had provided that "whoever shall engage in the liquor traffic upon premises not owned by him without the written permission of the probate judge of his county, who is hereby authorized, in his discretion, to grant such permission, shall be guilty of a misdemeanor," etc. Would the judge be in a more emphatic sense clothed with authority to issue such permission than the owner now is? Is the owner any the less authorized to legalize the business of his tenant than if he were a public officer? And is not this authority derived from the State through this act? If the tenant be put upon his trial for a violation of this provision, is not his acquittal as abundantly assured by exhibiting the written consent of the owner as if it bore the seal of a commissioned, sworn, and salaried officer?

The Pond law said to the dealer: Procure a bond signed by two sureties, or stand condemned before the law. The Scott law says to the dealer upon another's premises: Procure the written consent of the owner of your place of business, or suffer the penalties denounced against you. Nor does the analogy fail because the tax is not the price of the license.

"There is no necessary connection between them. A business may be licensed and yet not taxed, or it may be taxed and yet not licensed." *Per* Cooley, J., in Youngblood *v.* Sexton, 32 Mich. 425.

The State has plainly invested the owner with the vast discretion of determining whether the dealer upon his premises shall prosecute his business as a lawful traffic, or whether he shall remain under the condemnation of the law; and to say that this is a mere private permit—that there is no element of public authority in it, is to allow a principle of government which the people have ordained as a feature of their organic law to be subverted by mere subterfuge. If the dealer fails to procure the written license of the only person authorized to issue it, the owner, he continues a daily transgressor against the law. If he procure it, his business is as lawful as that of the dealer who owns his business place, or the dealer upon a water craft against whom neither penalties nor lien are provided; for, "said assessment shall attach and operate as a lien upon the real property on, and in which such business is conducted." Here is discrimination between classes. Here, under the definition of license in State *v.* Hipp, is permission granted by authority to do an act which without such permission would be illegal. Here, by the definition of license in State *v.* Frame, is "the granting of a special privilege to one or more persons . . . not enjoyed by a class of citizens to which the licensee belongs."

Does not this act clearly and negatively answer the proposition that "no citizen or class of citizens is required by this statute to perform any condition before the right to so traffic shall vest in him?"

The "condition" required in the Pond law was to procure a bond. The "condition" required by the Scott law is to procure the written consent from the owner. The failure to comply with either condition alike invoked the penalties of fine or imprisonment, or both.

Whether this provision was intended to cause the lien to attach, or to protect the owner by enabling him to invoke its penalties against the tenant, we need not say. This provision and that concerning the lien upon the owner's premises of the assessment against the business of the tenant so depend upon each other in the general scheme and purpose of section 2 that both are involved in a common infirmity and must fall together.

These provisions, in our opinion, upon the authority of State *v.* Hipp, constituted the act a license law, so far as the act attempts to secure a lien upon real estate occupied by tenants, whether the lease be executed before or after the passage of the act ; and, the provisions being unconstitutional, it is obviously immaterial whether the owner has or has not consented, either verbally or in writing, to the prosecution of the traffic.

We are prompted by considerations which seem urgent to confine our discussions and determination to the questions necessary to a disposition of the case before us. Upon a well-established principle, it is the duty of this court, if there is other clear ground upon which to rest its judgment, to leave the question of the constitutionality of a legislative enactment for consideration until a case arises which cannot be disposed of without considering it, and when a decision upon such question will be unavoidable. Cooley's Const. Lim. 199; Ireland *v.* Turnpike Co., 19 Ohio St. 373. Stability of judicial decision of a court of last resort upon all questions, especially upon questions of great public concern, is one of the safeguards of popular government. It is essential to such stability that the questions determined here are those actually before us and necessary to the determination of the case under consideration.

Whether the Scott law is in any other respect unconstitutional, and how far the rule of *stare decisis* should control, are questions not presented by the record in this case, and therefore they are not decided.

Judgment reversed and action dismissed.

JOHNSON, C. J.—For reasons given in former cases involv-

LANDLORD'S CONSENT IS NOT A LICENSE. ing the same question, I do not assent to the second point of the syllabus, which in substance holds that the written consent of the landlord to his tenant to engage in the traffic in intoxicating liquors on his property, given after the act in question took effect, is a license.

The re-arguments of this question and further reflection have confirmed the views heretofore expressed as to the legal signification of the 18th section of the schedule.

I also dissent from the statement in the 3d point of the

WHAT QUESTIONS PRESENTED BY RECORD. syllabus, to the effect that the validity of the "other provisions" of the Scott law "is a question not presented by the record."

This is a question of fact rather than of law, to be determined by an inspection of the record.

Learned counsel who represented the plaintiffs in error, in oral as well as written argument, made no such claim. They asked us to review the decision of the common pleas and district courts, which, following this court had held, these "other provisions" were valid. For that purpose we allowed a petition in error to be filed, and upon that single question the case was ably argued at great length, but the majority have, *sua sponte*, disposed of the case on the ground that the question is not made in the record.

That this position is untenable will appear from a statement of the issues presented by the pleadings. It will be seen by an inspection of this record that the validity of the first section of the law as well as the landlord clause of the second section was directly involved, and that there was no way of avoiding a decision of it. The petition contains two causes of action; the first, against Butzman, to recover a personal judgment for the tax and penalty under section 1 of the act: the second, against Butzman as tenant and Mueller as landlord, to enforce a specific lien created by statute on the premises owned by Mueller, and to sell the same to pay such judgment. In view of this fact, the statement that this is an action to enforce the lien merely is a clear misapprehension of the pleadings.

In the first cause of action, after stating the facts constituting a personal liability of Butzman under section 1, for the tax and penalty, it concludes as follows:

" Wherefore he (the plaintiff) prays judgment against said William Butzman for the sum of $240."

Standing alone, this would have been a civil action under Revised Statutes, § 2859, to recover a personal judgment on which execution could issue.

The second cause of action is to enforce against the real estate the lien authorized by section 2 of the act. Its allegations are against Mueller as landlord and Butzman as tenant. If this clause is valid, it is conceded these allegations are sufficient to entitle the plaintiff to a decree for the sale of the property.

The prayer to this cause of action is:

" Wherefore this plaintiff prays for a judgment against said defendant, William Butzman, for the sum of $240, that the court may take an account of the amount of assessments, with the penalties thereon, against said real estate, and declare the same a lien thereon, and order such real estate sold for the payment of said assessments and penalties and the costs of this action, and for such other and further relief as he is entitled to by reason of the premises."

The defendants, Butzman and Mueller, filed separate demurrers—that of Butzman alleging that the petition did not state a cause of action against him, and that of Mueller, that as to him there was no cause of action,—that is, no ground to enforce a lien on his property.

These demurrers were separately submitted to the court, and separately decided. Thereupon, on submission and proof, a personal judgment was rendered against Butzman for the assessment and penalty, $240, and a decree for the sale of the real estate to pay the same was entered on the second cause of action.

This judgment and order of sale were affirmed by the district court, that court holding that neither of these demurrers was well taken.

This statement taken from the record clearly shows that two distinct questions of law were before the courts below and are now before us for review,—namely, Was there a good cause of action against Butzman for a personal judgment, and, second, Was there a good cause of action to enforce the lien against the property of Mueller?

Either cause of action might have been brought without joining the other. Mueller's demurrer would be well taken if the opinion of the majority be correct, and a good cause of action would still remain against Butzman. The decision of the majority holding that the lien cannot be enforced disposes of the second cause of action against the property, but leaves the first cause of action undisposed of. That this is so is too apparent to admit of question. The statement, therefore, that there is practically one cause of action, and that to enforce the lien merely, is manifestly at variance with the record.

But it may be claimed that these two causes of action cannot be united in a single petition; and it is claimed, erroneously as we have shown, that this is merely a proceeding to enforce a lien. That neither of these grounds is tenable will appear from a summary statement of the statutes on the subject.

Section 1 of the Scott law assesses upon the business of trafficking in intoxicating liquors a specific sum of money yearly, which "shall be paid by every person engaged therein." This created a statutory liability against Butzman wholly independent of the second section of said act.

Section 2 provides that said assessment, etc., shall attach

and operate as a lien on the real property on which said business is conducted. By the latter clause of said section it is made a misdemeanor for one to engage in such business on land owned by another without his written consent. Section 3 provides for a return by the assessors of the places where such business is carried on.

Section 4 makes it the duty of the county auditors to make out a duplicate of such assessments and to deliver the same to the county treasurers for collection.

Section 5 specifically provides for the collection of these assessments.

If they are not paid by the persons carrying on the business when due, the treasurer shall forthwith proceed, as provided by Rev. Stats. § 1104, "to enforce the lien for the same, and penalty; and the provisions of said section, and any other provisions of the law of this State relative to the collection of taxes or assessments, are hereby made applicable to the enforcement of such liens and the collection of such assessments and penalties."

It is thus made clear by this section that the treasurer is not only clothed with power to enforce the lien, but is further invested with power to resort to "any other provisions of law relative to the collection of taxes and assessments." By section 1104 the treasurer, "in addition to all other remedies provided by law," may enforce by civil action the lien for taxes "in the same way as mortgaged liens are enforced."

Among the "other remedies provided by law" are to be found the general provisions for the collection of taxes. Revised Statutes, §§ 2838 to 2863.

Section 2859 provides, "in addition to other remedies provided by law" for the collection of personal taxes, for a civil action. This action is to be brought in the name of the treasurer against the person whose duty it is to pay.

A personal judgment may be rendered against him, and he shall not be entitled to the benefit of the laws for the stay of execution or exemption of homestead, or any other property from levy or sale or execution in the enforcement of any such judgment. By section 2860 the term personal taxes includes all taxes "except only tax on real estate as such."

This provision of law authorizing a civil action and a per-

sonal judgment has, inadvertently, as we suppose, been overlooked by the majority, or else it has been wholly ignored.

Upon this section, 2859, rests the first cause of action
against Butzman for a personal judgment.

The second cause of action to enforce the lien against the
property is founded upon provisions contained in section
1104. The right to join these separate causes of action is
clearly authorized by section 5021, Revised Statutes.

Section 1104 authorizes the enforcement of the statutory
lien of taxes and assessments on real estate " in the same way
as mortgaged liens are enforced." Section 5021 provides that
" in an action to foreclose a mortgage given to secure the payment of money, or to enforce a specific lien for money, the
plaintiff may also ask in his petition for a judgment for the
money claimed to be due; and such proceedings shall be
had thereon, as in a civil action for the recovery of money
only."

The plaintiff is strictly within the terms of these several
statutes. Under section 2859 he has a civil action for money
only on which he is entitled to a personal judgment. By
section 1104 he has an action in equity to enforce a specific
lien on real estate. By section 5021 plaintiff may ask for a
personal judgment as well as for the enforcement of the
specific lien, "and such proceedings shall be had as if it were
a civil action for money only."

If, therefore, it be assumed that the action to enforce the
specific lien fails by reason of the invalidity of the last clause
of section 2, the first cause of action against Butzman stands
untouched and unaffected.

This presents for the consideration of this court the validity " of the other provisions" of the Scott law.

If it be claimed these two causes of action cannot be joined
"OTHER PRO-
VISIONS" in a single petition, inasmuch as they each do not
SCOTT LAW CON-
SIDERED. affect all the parties to the action, the reply is that
that question is *res adjudicata.* That was, perhaps, the law
prior to the amendment of the code in 1864, which is now
section 5021 R. S.

In McCarthy *v.* Garrahty, 10 Ohio St. 438, the court expressed a doubt of the joinder of two causes of action, one on
a note and the other on a mortgage, but held that as no objection for misjoinder was made in the court below, it could

not be taken advantage of in this court. In consequence of that doubt the act of 1864 (now section 5021) was passed. Malcomb *v.* Marshall, 29 Ohio St. 616. Soon after this act was passed it received an authoritative construction by this court, which has ever since been followed.

In King *v.* Safford, 19 Ohio St. 587, it was held that "the holder of a note secured by mortgage may in a single action demand and have a judgment against all the makers of the note, although the mortgage is executed only by part of the makers of the note."

The fact, therefore, that one cause of action was against Butzman, and the other to enforce the lien against him and Mueller, is no ground for claiming a misjoinder since the act of 1864; nor was it prior to that act where, as in this case, no objection was made to such joinder in the court below.

The validity of the first section of the Scott law was, therefore, directly involved in the first cause of action. The courts below either erred, or they did not, in overruling Butzman's demurrer.

That the majority have doubts as to the correctness of their conclusion is manifest from the final judgment rendered. If there was but a single cause of action, to enforce a lien, then as they held the lien invalid, a judgment against plaintiff should have been rendered that would bar a future action.

Instead of such a judgment the journal entry, after dismissing the action against both defendants, adds: "And it is ordered and adjudged that the action be and the same is hereby dismissed, but without prejudice to the defendant in error to proceed against said Butzman in such manner as the law may warrant."

This leaves the whole question as to the personal liability of Butzman open to future litigation.

We know of no reason why his liability to a personal judgment should not have been decided in this case.

Every consideration of public policy seems to have demanded that this vexed question so fairly made should be settled at the earliest practicable period. Such was the desire of both parties, evidenced by their pleadings and arguments, and such appears to be in the plain path of judicial duty. These views are expressed with all proper respect for the majority.

McILVAINE, J., concurs in the foregoing dissent, and refers to his opinion in the Frame case for his views on the second point of the syllabus.

In re SCHNEIDER.

(Advance Case, Oregon. March, 1884.)

A "barroom or drinking shop" means a place where the business of selling liquor to be drunk on the premises is carried on.

The word "quarter" in an ordinance providing that a license tax shall be payable "five days from the beginning of each quarter," is not ambiguous. From the connection in which it is used it can only mean the quarter of the year for which the applicant desires a license.

A clause in a city charter authorizing it to "license, tax, regulate, and restrain barrooms and drinking shops," empowers the city to require of keepers of barrooms, before granting them license, bonds to observe and obey all city ordinances relating to barrooms, although the bond may be conditioned in a penal sum larger than the fine which the city is authorized to impose for breach of its ordinances.

The city cannot require a bond unreasonable as to its amount or conditions.

Where the bond required was conditioned for the observance of "all other ordinances of said city," *held* that, from the context, this would be construed to refer only to all other ordinances relating to drinking shops.

APPEAL from Multnomah county. Application for writ of *habeas corpus.*

Drake & Stephans and *N. B. Knight* for appellant.

R. Williams contra.

WATSON, C. J.—This is an appeal from an order of the circuit court refusing to discharge the appellant from custody upon a writ of *habeas corpus* directed to the chief of police of the city of Portland. It is impossible to notice all the questions raised in the argument of the case in an opinion of reasonable length, and I shall therefore restrict my examination to such as appear fairly open to controversy. That the legislature has the power, under the State constitution, to invest the subordinate municipal governments with control of the traffic in intoxicating liquors, is not a debatable question. The only questions of real difficulty presented in the record arise upon the construction of the several provisions of the charter conferring power over the subject upon the city council, and the ordinances adopted by the council in attempted pursuance of the power conferred.

1. What is the power "to license, tax, regulate, and restrain barrooms and drinking shops" bestowed upon the council by subdivision 5 of section 37 of the charter? The "BAR-ROOM" OR "DRINKING-SHOP" INCLUDES terms "barrooms" and "drinking shops" are "TAVERN." obviously used here to signify the business of conducting or keeping such places. They are susceptible of no other reasonable interpretation in the connection in which they are found in this provision of the charter. It is such business, therefore, that the council is empowered " to license," etc.

In this view, the legal character of the place would be determined by the nature of the business for which it is occupied. The council, then, in requiring license to be taken out before engaging in the business of disposing of liquors to be drunk on the premises owned or occupied by the dealer, simply exercised its rightful authority; for the business of disposing of liquors to be drunk on the premises where disposed of is identical with the keeping of a " barroom" or " drinking shop," and every place where liquors are disposed of to be drunk on the spot is a " barroom" or " drinking shop" within the meaning of the charter. There can be no essential difference between the original meaning of the word " tavern" and the word " barroom" or " drinking shop," as used in the charter. And a " tavern" has been judicially defined to be " a house licensed to sell liquors in small quantities to be drunk on the spot." State *v.* Chamblyss, 34 Amer. Dec. 593. And such is doubtless the common understanding of the terms " barroom" and " drinking shop," and the sense in which they are employed in the charter.

It is true the language of the ordinance is somewhat broader, covering any sale, barter, or delivery of the liquors specified to be drunk on the premises without license; but a reasonable construction, in view of the particular subject before the council at the time the ordinance was adopted, justifies the restriction I have placed upon it. Albrecht *v.* People, 78 Ill. 510.

The proviso to subdivision 5 of section 37 of the charter also justifies the inference that the legislature intended to confer a large measure of control over the traffic in liquors upon the local government. It is found in the same subdivision of the section by which the power "to license," etc., is given, and declares that "all persons vending liquors within the city of Portland" are exempted from the necessity of taking out license under the general laws of the State. I think, therefore, the ordinance fairly conforms to the power given by the charter in this respect.

2. The objection that the ordinance is ambiguous as to the time when the license fee is to be paid is not maintainable. LICENSE-FEE PAYABLE EACH "QUARTER."—NO AMBIGUITY. It is to be paid each quarter, and the term "quarter" in this connection can only mean the quarter of the year for which the applicant desires a license. And, inasmuch as he may not engage in the proposed business without a license, it is apparent the "five days of the beginning of each quarter" within which he is required to file the receipt of the city treasurer for the amount of the license fee with the city auditor, who is authorized to issue the license, must be the five days immediately preceding the beginning of such quarter.

3. A question is made as to the power of the city council to pass an ordinance requiring a bond from an applicant for a license to keep a " bar-room" or " drinking-shop" within the city limits. I think I may safely assume the existence of the power under the authority to "regulate and restrain bar-BOND MAY BE REQUIRED FROM SALOON-KEEPER. rooms and drinking-shops," unless some limitations can be implied from other parts of the charter. There is no express limitation, and the authority to " regulate and restrain," uncontrolled by other provisions, would clearly give the power to require the bond. In fact, the requirement of a bond from the applicant for license to engage in such business is universally recognized as a proper and legitimate measure of regulation and restraint wherever such power is to be exercised. And as the State exercised the power in the same manner until it withdrew its jurisdiction in favor of the city government, there seems good ground for concluding that the legislature intended the latter should enjoy the power in the same ample and efficacious measure.

The opposite view rests upon deductions from the provisions of subdivision 36 of section 37 of the charter, prescribing the mode and measure of punishment for violations of city ordinances.

These provisions unquestionably limit the power of the council to provide punishment for the offence of violating such ordinances. But the penalty in a bond of this character, which the obligor may become liable to pay on breach of its conditions, is not, either technically or in fact, a punishment for a violation of any city ordinance. If the council passes an ordinance requiring a bond as one of the conditions of granting license, and a person engages in the business for which the license is required without first obtaining it, he might be punished for a violation of the ordinance, and the limitation as to punishment would apply. But if he gives the bond and procures the license, subsequent breaches of the conditions of the bond would not amount to violations of the ordinance. He would simply render himself liable on his contract; and the real question must be, not as to the power to punish, but as to the power to exact the obligation by contract as a legitimate measure of regulation or restraint.

Now, is it to be inferred from the fact that the legislature has limited the amount which the council may impose as a punishment for a violation of a city ordinance, that it intended to withhold the power to require a bond, because a person might thereby incur a liability to pay an amount greater than could be imposed as a punishment? If this reasoning is admissible, no bond can be exacted in any case under the authority given to the city government, for the mode as well as measure of punishment is prescribed, and one operates as a limitation just as much as the other. Certainly, no one will contend that the council has any authority under the provisions relating to punishment for violations of city ordinances to require any bond or other security. A bond to secure in advance the payment of penalties for violations of city ordinances which may happen subsequently, and not warranted as a measure for securing the performance of some special or peculiar duty to the public, would be additional punishment in itself, and plainly not within the authority to punish conferred by the charter. And if a bond for this purpose might be exacted from one, it might from all; and, indeed, no ordinance requiring it of any particular person or class only could, in any event, be deemed valid. How, then, can the city government insure the performance of public duties on

[marginal note: Power to require saloon-keeper to give bond not limited by limiting penalty that may be imposed on him for violating ordinance.]

the part of its officers and citizens in those positions of special trust and power where dereliction would be cheaply purchased at the amount which might be exacted as punishment for the violation of city ordinances, if no security in any greater amount can be required?

The only principle which will sustain the objection to the power of the council to require a bond in such cases proceeds to the extent of denying its authority to create an obligation, or require the execution of a contract, by ordinance which may impose a liability in excess of the amount which may be exacted as a punishment for the violation of such ordinance. But if there is a sufficient consideration for the obligation or contract, as there is in cases of this character, I am unable to perceive any reason why the extent of liability upon it should be affected in any manner by the provisions in relation to punishment for violations of the ordinance creating the obligation or requiring the execution of the contract. Punishment for a violation of a city ordinance under the charter cannot exceed three hundred dollars and ninety days' imprisonment. The amount to be paid for license to keep a "bar-room" or "drinking-shop" must be established by ordinance. If the ordinance requires a greater sum to be paid for license than could be exacted as punishment, if a person should proceed to engage in such business without obtaining license, would it therefore be void? Has the amount of such punishment any relation to the amount which may be required for the license? The bond required as a measure of regulation or restraint stands on the same footing as the license fee in this respect. If the council has the power under the charter to require the bond as a proper measure of regulation or restraint, then the only limitation upon its amount or conditions is that of reasonableness, and the provisions as to the amount of punishment which may be imposed for a violation of the ordinance exacting it can have no bearing. There is no essential connection or correspondence between the legal obligation of an ordinance and the penalty for its violation. If the latter is insufficient, the ordinance may be ineffectual, but is not therefore invalid. In the case at bar, the requirement of the bond is part of the obligation of the ordinance, and quite distinct from the penalty provided for its violation. State *v.* Whitener, 23 Ind. 124; Whalin *v.* City of Macomb, 76 Ill. 49. I think the power of the council to require a bond from the applicant should be sustained.

4. It is claimed that the provision in the form of bond given in section 5 of the ordinance for the observance of "all other ordinances of said city" is illegal, and renders SUBJECT OF OR-
the entire ordinance void. The claim is put upon DINANCE CON-
SIDERED.
a literal construction of the provision. If this were the proper construction, I should not deny the effect contended for. A requirement to observe all other ordinances of the city would be unequal, oppressive, and void; and as the bond required by the ordinance in this instance is an essential part of the consideration for granting the license—as much so as the license fee itself—the manifest intention of its framers would be violated by permitting the license to issue on any other or different terms. An ordinance thus void in part is wholly void. The good part is incapable of separation from the bad. Austin *v.* Murray, 16 Pick. 121; Warren *v.* Mayor, etc., of Charlestown, 2 Gray, 84. But the rule of construction with reference to the subject of the ordinance before considered applies,here with equal force. The subject before the council being the licensing of bar-rooms and drinking-shops, as the title as well as the body of the ordinance abundantly shows, the expression "all other ordinances of said city" must be held to mean all other ordinances on that subject, and therefore not invalidating the ordinance. State *v.* McGarry, 21 Wis. 502.

5. The validity of the ordinance is also assailed on the ground that its requirements as to the qualifications of sureties are unreasonable and oppressive. Under the ORDINANCES
MAY PRESCRIBE
power to restrain, it has been held that a license QUALIFICATIONS
OF SURETIES.
fee may be exacted. Smith *v.* City of Madison, 7
Ind. 86. And if a fee may be required under this power, why not a bond with sureties possessing certain prescribed qualifications? The word "restrain," appearing as it does in immediate association with the word "regulate" in the charter, must be accorded some additional effect. And even if the requirements as to qualifications of sureties could not be considered as justified by the power to regulate, it is by no means so clear that they cannot be sustained under the power to restrain. Judgment affirmed.

WALDO, J., dissenting; LORD, J., concurring.

CITY OF TIFFIN

v.

SHAWHAN.

(Advance Case, Ohio.   April 28, 1885.)

A court of equity will not specifically enforce a contract to purchase land where the title which the purchaser would acquire would be doubtful and unmarketable.

The mode in which at common law corporations execute deeds is by affixing thereto their corporate seal.

By § 1745, Rev. Stat. of Ohio, the Mayor is entrusted with the custody and use of the corporate seal; this being so, and the proper mode of executing a deed of land owned by the corporation being by affixing the seal of the corporation, *quaere*, can the corporation empower the city clerk to make a valid deed of corporate real property?   •

ERROR to district court, Seneca county.

On the third day of July, 1873, Rezin W. Shawhan, defendant in error, duly conveyed to the city of Tiffin, for city park purposes, about six acres of land for the consideration of $2680, which was then paid him.   On the same day, Shawhan agreed in writing with the city that he would, at any time within two years from the first day of July, 1873, upon receiving a reconveyance of the same land, repay to the city the sum of $2680, with interest at 8 per cent per annum from the first day of July, 1873; and that the right to reconvey the lands to Shawhan and receive repayment therefor from him should be at the option of the city during the term of two years.   On the thirty-first of May, 1875, the council of the city of Tiffin adopted a resolution that the lands so conveyed to the city by Shawhan be reconveyed to him by the city. Shawhan was promptly notified of the action of the council. The reconveyance of the land to Shawhan within the period limited by the agreement of July 3, 1873, was mutually waived by the parties.   On the nineteenth day of July, 1875, the city council duly passed an ordinance providing for the reconveyance to the respective grantors of three tracts of land, including that conveyed to the city by Shawhan.   By this ordinance it was ordained: ". . . Sec. 3. That the city of Tiffin does hereby bargain and sell to Rezin W. Shawhan the lands and tenements described as follows: [Description.] Sec. 4. That the city clerk of said city is hereby authorized and directed to make, execute, and deliver to each of the persons named in sections one, two, and three of this ordinance a proper deed of conveyance, under the corporate seal of said city, for the lands so by them severally purchased from said city." On the twenty-second day of April, 1876, Sylvester J. Kintz, city clerk of Tiffin, executed a writing of the tenor following:

" C.

"Know all men by these presents: That, whereas, the city council of the city of Tiffin, in the county of Seneca, and State of Ohio, on the nineteenth day of July, A.D. 1875, duly passed an ordinance of said city, entitled ' An ordinance to authorize the conveyance of certain lands therein described,' whereby said city council bargained and sold the lands and tenements hereinafter described to Rezin W. Shawhan for the sum of two thousand six hundred and eighty dollars to said city, then paid by said Rezin W. Shawhan.

" And whereas, by said ordinance of said city, the city clerk of said city was authorized and directed to make, execute, and deliver to said Rezin W. Shawhan a proper deed of conveyance of said lands:

"Now, therefore, I, Sylvester J. Kintz, city clerk of the city of Tiffin, by virtue of the powers in me vested by said ordinance, and in pursuance thereof, do hereby give, grant, bargain, sell, and convey unto the said Rezin W. Shawhan, his heirs and assigns forever, the lands and tenements described as follows, to wit: [Description.] To have and to hold the same, to him, the said Rezin W. Shawhan, his heirs and assigns, forever.

" In witness whereof, I have hereunto set my hand and seal, and the corporate seal of said city of Tiffin, this twenty-second day of April, 1876.   SYLVESTER J. KINTZ,
          " City Clerk, City of Tiffin. [Seal.]
[City clerk's seal.]
" Executed in the presence of
     "JOHN MCCAULEY,
     " S. DAHM.

" The State of Ohio, Seneca County—ss.:
"Before me, John McCauley, a notary public, within and for said county, personally came Sylvester J. Kintz, and ac-

knowledged the signing and sealing of the above conveyance to be his free act and deed.

"Witness my hand and notarial seal this twenty-second day of April, 1876.   " JOHN MCCAULEY,

[Seal.]   " Notary Public, Seneca Co., O."

This instrument was promptly tendered to Shawhan, of whom the repayment of the money agreed upon was demanded. Acceptance and payment were refused. Thereupon the city commenced her action in the court of common pleas of Seneca county, to enforce specific performance of the agreement of July 3d, for the reconveyance of, and repayment for, the lands in question. The petition, among other averments, alleges "that the plaintiff tendered to the defendant a reconveyance of said lands, and demanded repayment of said sum of money ;" and further avers "that a deed for the said lands and tenements, above mentioned and described, from the said plaintiff to the said defendant, is herewith filed and tendered to him." The tender of the deed, and the filing of it with the petition, are not denied by the answer. The cause was appealed to the district court, which, upon the issues joined, found the equities with the defendant, Shawhan, and decreed accordingly, expressly remanding the parties to their legal remedies. The bill of exceptions taken at the trial shows that the deed, which was tendered to the defendant and filed with the petition (a copy of which is given above), was offered in evidence by the plaintiff, received without objection, and made part of the bill of exceptions. The foregoing statement sufficiently presents the questions which the court deem important to the disposition of the case. The present proceeding is prosecuted to reverse the judgment of the district court.

Perry M. Adams, city solicitor, for plaintiff in error.

James Pillars and *N. L. Brewer* for defendant in error.

OWEN, J.—1. By the conveyance from Shawhan to the city, VALIDITY of the latter was invested with the title to the lands in DEED HELD IN QUESTION. question. The city had ample capacity to reconvey the same lands to Shawhan. If the deed which was tendered to him was such an instrument as could reinvest him with his former title, unclouded by substantial doubt of the validity of the conveyance, the plaintiff was entitled to the relief prayed for, and there was error in refusing it. If it be suggested that the defendant admitted that the deed tendered to him was sufficent to pass the title of the land to him, by failing to deny the averments of the petition that the plaintiff "tendered a reconyeyance of the lands to the defendant," and that the deed so tendered "is herewith filed and tendered to defendant," the obvious answer is that the plaintiff, having presented the deed itself with the petition (to keep good the tender), expressly invoked the judgment of the court upon its sufficiency. If the plaintiff had simply averred a tender of the reconveyance of the land, and the defendant had admitted it, there would have been force in the suggestion. As it is, the issue rests as upon the express admission of the defendant that the deed filed with the petition was tendered to him. How could he better raise the issue than to urge at the hearing, as he did, that the deed was not sufficient to pass title? But the plaintiff offered this deed in evidence, it was received without objection, and a true copy of it is marked " C," and made a part of the bill of exceptions. It is given in the foregoing statement of the case. It ought to be sufficient, however, to say that the plaintiff did not and does not make this question, but, on the contrary, all controversy is set at rest by the statement in the brief of plaintiff's counsel that "a true copy of the original deed tendered to the defendant will be found in the printed record in page twenty-five marked 'C.' This deed was deposited with the clerk, and, when the case was appealed, could not, for some time, be found, but was afterwards found, and put in evidence on the last trial of this case, without objection, but in argument to the court the defendant's counsel claimed that it was not the deed of the city, but that of Mr. S. J. Kintz."

As this deed must have entered into the consideration of the court below as one of the facts of the case, it is not easy to see how this court could review its action with the bill of exceptions silent upon this subject. This deed and its sufficiency were treated by the parties as involved in the issues, and it is now too late to contend that they were not in issue. Woodward *v.* Sloan, 27 Ohio St. 592. In this case it was held that where facts alleged in an answer are not denied in the reply, and the case proceeds to trial upon the evidence as if such facts were denied, without objection or exception until after the judgment of the court of common pleas is affirmed by the district court, the judgment will not be reversed on the ground that the answer was not denied in the reply.

2. As already stated, the right of the city to ask a specific performance, and hence the disposition of this case, rests upon SPECIFIC PER- the validity of this deed, or its sufficiency to pass FORMANCE—DUTY OF COURT AS TO to Shawhan a good, marketable title to the land. DECREEING. The duty of a court to decree specific performance of a contract cannot be determined by any iron rule, but depends upon the peculiar facts and equitable considerations of each case, and rests in the sound discretion of the court, guided and regulated, so far as may be, in the exercise of that discretion by precedent and established practice. Port Clinton R. R. Co. *v.* Cleveland & T. R. R. Co., 13 Ohio St. 549; Williard *v.* Tayloe, 8 Wall. 557; Waters *v.* Howard, 1 Md. Ch. 112; Ewing *v.* Beauchamp, 6 B. Mon. 426; 3 Pars. Cont. *352; 2 Story, Eq., § 724; 3 Pom. Eq. 446.

If a contract for the conveyance of real estate is in all respects fair and free from ambiguity, and its execution accord- SAME—CON- ing to the prayer of the vendor will vest a market- TRACT TO CON- VEY REAL ES- able title in the purchaser, it is as much a matter TATE. of course for a court of equity to decree specific performance of it as it is for a court of law to award damages for its breach. St. Paul Division *v.* Brown, 9 Minn. 151 (Gil. 141); King *v.* Hamilton, 4 Pet. 311; Greenaway *v.* Adams, 12 Ves. Jr. 395; 3 Pom. Eq. § 1404; 5 Waite, Ac. & Def. 765. If, however, the specific performance of a contract would be harsh and oppressive, or would leave the purchaser with a doubtful and unmarketable title, the court, in the exercise of its discretion, will refuse to decree its performance, but leave the parties to their legal remedies. The rule is fundamental that the purchaser will not be compelled to accept a doubt ful title. Ludlow *v.* O'Neil, 29 Ohio St. 182; Wilson *v.* Tappan, 6 Ohio, 172; Richmond *v.* Gray, 3 Allen, 27; Watts *v.* Waddle, 1 McLean, 200; Bates *v.* Delavan, 5 Paige, Ch. 299; Fry, Spec. Perf. § 576 *et seq.;* Powell *v.* Conant, 33 Mich. 396; Vreeland *v.* Blauvelt, 23 N. J. Eq. 483; Stapylton *v.* Scott, 16 Ves. Jr. 272; Willcox *v.* Bellaers, 13 Eng. Ch. (1 Turn. & R.) 495; Adams, Eq. *84. The reason of this rule applies with equal force where the doubt proceeds from the form of the conveyance tendered, as from the title of the vendor. The effect upon the title of the purchaser is the same in either case.

3. The foregoing considerations invite inquiry into the form and effect of the deed by which the city of Tiffin undertook to convey this land to Shawhan. There is no general statute in this State directing the form or manner DEEDS OF COR-of execution of deeds by corporations. "The PORATIONS— HOW EXECUTED. mode in which at common law corporations aggregate execute deeds is by affixing thereto their corporate seal. 1 Bl. Comm. 475; 1 Pars. Cont. 140, 141; 3 Sugd. Vend. & Pur. 353; Ang. & A. Corp. 268; [Clark *v.* Farmers' W. Manuf'g Co.] 15 Wend. 258." Scott J., in Sheehan *v.* Davis, 17 Ohio St. 581. This proposition is also strongly supported by the following authorities, relating chiefly to the subject of conveyances by public corporations; De Zeng *v.* Beekman, 2 Hill, 489; Kinzie *v.* Trustees of Chicago, 2 Scam. 187; City of San Antonio *v.* Gould, 34 Tex. 77. It is said, in this case, by Walker, J.: "A broad distinction is kept up through the authorities between trading and municipal corporations; the former are permitted to do many things in the way of simple contracts without the common seal of the corporation, which municipal corporations are not allowed to do."

At common law, the signature of a corporation is its corporate seal. Doe *v.* Hogg, 4 Bos. & P. 306; Gordon *v.* Preston, 1 Watts, 385; Frankfort Bank *v.* Anderson, 3 A. K. Marsh. 932; Beckwith *v.* Windsor Manuf'g Co., 14 Conn. 594. Regarding the form of conveyances by municipal corporations, it is said by Dillon (Mun. Corp. § 578): "Conveyances of real estate should, in general, be executed in the corporate name and under the corporate seal." In the case at bar, the deed is neither in the corporate name of the city nor under its corporate seal. The granting clause of the deed is in these words: "Now, therefore, I, Sylvester J. Kintz, city clerk of the city of Tiffin, by virtue of the powers in me vested by said ordinance, and in pursuance thereof, do hereby give, grant, bargain, sell, and convey unto the said Rezin W. Shawhan, his heirs and assigns forever, the lands and tenements described as follows," etc. The deed is signed by "Sylvester J. Kintz, city clerk, city of Tiffin," who affixes his own private scroll-seal, and the seal of the "city clerk of Tiffin, Ohio."

It is maintained, however, in behalf of the city, that, as the statutes do not prescribe the form of conveyance by the

city, it was competent for the city, by its council, to prescribe by ordinance how the conveyance should be made.
Section 4 of the ordinance relied upon directs "that the city
clerk of said city is hereby authorized and directed to make,
execute, and deliver . . . a proper deed of conveyance,
under the corporate seal of said city." Whether the city
could lawfully invest her clerk with power to make a con·
veyance under her corporate seal is a question which we are
not called upon to determine. It would seem, however, to
be a question of sufficient doubt to call for the application o
the rule already announced, and justify the court below in
refusing to compel the defendant to accept the deed tendered
him.

By immemorial usage, if not, indeed, by our statutes, the
mayor of a municipal corporation is its chief administrative
DUTIES   of and executive officer. 1 Dill. Mun. Corp. 208.
MAYOR CONSID-
ERED.   To him is confided the custody and use of its corporate seal. Rev. St. § 1745 provide that the mayor "shall
be furnished by council with the corporate seal of the corporation, in the centre of which shall be the words 'mayor
of the city of ——,' or 'mayor of the village of ——,' as
the case may be." Section 1746 provides that the mayor
"shall sign all commissions, licenses, and permits granted by
authority of the council, or authorized by this title, and such
other instruments as, by law or ordinance, may require his
certificate." Section 1764 provides that "the city council
shall cause to be provided for the clerk's office a seal, in the
centre of which shall be the name of the corporation, and
around the margin the words 'city clerk,' or, in case of a
village, the words 'corporation clerk;' which shall be affixed
to all transcripts, orders, certificates, or other papers which
it may be necessary or proper to anthenticate." The respective functions of the mayor and clerk, in these respects,
would seem to be clearly defined by these provisions. To
the mayor is confided the "corporate seal of the corporation;" to the clerk, the seal of his office. To the mayor is
confided the execution of such writings as the corporation
may be called upon to issue; to the clerk, the authentication
of such papers as may require it. We cannot suppose that
it was ever intended or contemplated that the use of the
mayor's seal, which is the corporate seal, should be intrusted

to the clerk, who is provided with a seal peculiar to his office.

If, however, we should go to the extreme of holding that it was competent for the council to authorize the city clerk to execute a conveyance in behalf of the city, under its corporate seal, we encounter another principle which suggests grave doubt of the validity of this conveyance. It is that the execution of a power to convey land by public officers must be in strict pursuance of the power, or no title is conveyed. Osborne *v.* Tunis, 25 N. J. Laws, 634.

The authority conferred upon the city clerk by the ordinance was to execute "a proper deed of conveyance under the corporate seal of said city." Even this authority, doubtful at best, was not pursued by the clerk. While too great nicety and formality ought not to be exacted in the execution of title-deeds, yet the highest considerations of public policy demand that the certainty and stability of the tenures by which our people hold their lands be not placed in peril by encouraging and enforcing forms and modes of conveyance so doubtful and equivocal as that now called in question. When the sufficiency of this deed was challenged, as counsel for plaintiff informs us it was, it was not too late for the plaintiff to supply a valid deed ; but it saw fit to rest its case upon the deed tendered, and invoked the action of the court upon its case as made.

This deed is worse than doubtful. It is invalid, and ineffectual to pass the title of these lands from the city of Tiffin to Shawhan. The court below very properly exercised its discretion in refusing to compel its acceptance by the defendant. Whether the city is concluded by this judgment from still tendering a sufficient deed and demanding performance of defendant, we are not called upon to determine.

City clerk's deed held invalid.

Judgment affirmed.

McILVAINE, C. J. (dissenting).—It appears to me that the judgment of the District Court should be reversed. The action was to enforce the specific performance of a contract brought by the city of Tiffin against Shawhan. The city had purchased from Shawhan a tract of land, had paid the purchase-money, and received a conveyance. By the con-

tract of sale Shawhan had stipulated to repay the purchase
money, with interest, to the city upon the reconveyance to him of said lands before the first of July, 1875.
Before the expiration of the time limited, the city determined
to reconvey the land and insist on the repayment of the
money.   The city, having given notice to Shawhan of its
determination, at the request of Shawhan, and for his benefit,
delayed the reconveyance of the land and the repayment of
the money until April 1, 1876.

The defendant by his answer admitted the making of the
contract, but denied that the time for reconveyance of the
land or repayment of the money was delayed until April 1,
1876, at his request.   The answer further set forth "that in
and by terms of said contract, as set forth in said petition,
the said city of Tiffin, Ohio, had the option to reconvey said
property to this defendant, and insist on the repayment of
said sum of money."   But this defendant avers "that the
city of Tiffin did not at or prior to the said first day of July,
1875, or within a reasonable time thereafter, offer or tender
to this defendant a reconveyance of said property, or seek to
enforce the said contract, and not until the —— day of April,
1876, when said property had largely decreased in value."

By an amendment to the answer the defendant averred
certain new matter which need not be here stated.   These
averments were denied by reply.   On the trial of the cause
in the District Court, where it had been taken by appeal, the
equities of the case were found for defendant, and judgment
accordingly.   The testimony is all set forth in a bill of exceptions.

It is evident from the record that the finding and judgment in the court below was founded on the ground that the
original purchase by the city was for an unauthorized purpose, and therefore the relief prayed for in the petition could
not be granted in this action.   The case was dismissed without prejudice to another form of action.

On consideration of the case in this court, I understand
that the court is unanimous in the conclusion that the testimony clearly shows that the delay in tendering a reconveyance of the land to Shawhan until April 1, 1876, was at his
request, and also that the issue made by the amendment to
defendant's answer, and the reply thereto, was wholly im-

material. Upon consideration of these questions the judgment below was clearly erroneous. There appears, however, in the bill of exceptions a copy of the deed purporting to be a reconveyance of the land to Shawhan, delivered by the city to Shawhan, on April 1, 1876. This deed does not purport to be a conveyance by the city to Shawhan, but a conveyance by one Kintz, who executed the same as city clerk. The seal of the city is not attached to the deed, but the seal of the city clerk is attached.

For the purposes of this case I concede that such deed would not be sufficient to transfer the title from the city to Shawhan, and was not such a deed as the city was bound to tender. The city clerk had been duly authorized to execute a proper and sufficient deed of the city; but admitting that he had failed to do so, as far as the record shows, my point is that the judgment should, nevertheless, be reversed for errors heretofore stated. The court, however, sustains it, solely on the ground that the deed, of which this purports to be a copy, was not sufficient to reconvey the title from the city to Shawhan. Under the state of the ISSUES STATED. pleadings set forth in this record, there was no issue as to the fact of reconveyance. The plaintiff had averred the tender of a sufficient deed of reconveyance on the first of April, 1876. The defendant had admitted the averment to be true. The plaintiff was not called upon to offer any proof. No such question of fact was raised by the pleadings. No such question, outside pleadings, was submitted to the court below, or passed upon by the court. True, a copy of the supposed deed is found in the bill of exceptions. But it has no legal significance there. It is said that it was offered by the plaintiff in error; at least, there was no objection to it. Suppose it be so, that does not give it legal significance. I may suppose that the history of the United States was found in a bill of exceptions, offered by the plaintiff, or without his objection; such exhibit does not change the law or the legal effect of the issue.

In my opinion, the judgment should not be affirmed on the ground stated. The judgment of the District Court is now conclusive between the parties. No opportunity is now given to the plaintiff to show that a proper and legal conveyance was tendered the defendant, as he has admitted was done. If the defendant desires to rely on this defence, no opportunity is given the plaintiff to correct the mistake if it be one. I think the case should have been sent back for further proceedings.

JOHNSON, J., concurred in the dissent.

WHAT CONSTITUTES A VALID EXECUTION OF A DEED BY A CORPORATION.—In the absence of statutory provisions, the only formalities necessary to the valid execution of a deed by a corporation are sealing with the corporate seal and delivery. It is usual to sign the name of the corporation. Ang. & Ames Corp., § 225; Flint *v.* Clinton Co., 12 N. H. 430, 433, But it is not necessary that the name of the corporation should be signed. Ang. & Ames Corp., § 225; Cooch *v.* Goodman, 2 Q. B. 580; Osborne *v.* Tunis, 1 Dutch. (N. J.) 633, 661. In some States a signing of the corporate name is required by statute. Isham *v.* Bennington Iron Co., 19 Vt. 251, 252.

A DELIVERY NOT NECESSARY TO THE VALIDITY OF A DEED OF A CORPORATION.—It is said that a delivery of a deed by a corporation is not necessary to its valid execution. The deed is said to be perfected by affixing the corporate seal, unless it affirmatively appears that it was the intention of the corporation that the deed should not take effect at and from the time of sealing. Angell & Ames Corp., § 227 (and cases cited).

A SEALING BY A CORPORATION WITH A SEAL NOT ITS ORDINARY CORPORATE SEAL IS VALID.—A corporation, like an individual, may, in the absence of statutory provisions to the contrary, adopt any seal it sees fit with which to seal its deed. Mill Dam Foundry *v.* Hovey, 21 Pick. 417, 428; Tenney *v.* Lumber Company, 43 N. H. 343, 354; Phillips *v.* Coffee, 17 Ill. 154.

Where the deed is proved to have been signed by one who was an agent of the corporation at the time, and the corporate seal attached, the authority of the agent signing to affix the seal is presumed in the absence of evidence to the contrary. Flint *v.* Clinton Co., *supra;* Eyster *v.* Gaff, 2 Colo. T. 228; Blackshire *v.* Iowa Homestead Co., 39 Iowa, 624; Morris *v.* Keil, 20 Minn. 531; Ang. & Ames Corp., § 224.

Even where the seal attached is not proved to be the corporate seal, proof of the signature of the officer or agent purporting to affix the seal or proof of the signature of the officer or agent of the corporation opposite whose name the seal is attached, is presumptive evidence that the seal is the corporate seal. Mill Dam Foundry *v.* Hovey, *supra*; Flint *v.* Clinton Co., *supra*.

Where the deed is not signed or the seal attested by an officer or agent of the corporation, or the signature of such officer or agent is not proved, the seal of the corporation must be proved. Foster *v.* Shaw, 7 Serg. & R. (Pa.) 156; Jackson *v.* Pratt, 10 John (N. Y.) 381; Den *v.* Vreelandt, 2 Hals. (N. J.) 352; Morris *v.* Thompson, 8 T. R. 303; Bank of England *v.* Chambers, 4 Ad. & E. 412; Farmers and Mechanics' Turnp. Co. *v.* McCullough, 25 Pa. St. 303. It seems that where the deed purports to be sealed with the corporate seal, the seal may be proved by one who knows the impression of the corporate seal. Foster *v.* Shaw, *supra.*

In an action of covenant for rent, the defendant asked for a nonsuit on the ground that the plaintiff, the city council of Charleston, had not executed the lease. The attestation clause of the lease was as follows: "In witness whereof, the said parties to these presents have hereunto set their hands and seals, this 17th day of June, 1844, and the said the city council of Charleston have hereto set their corporate seal attested by the mayor.

her

" Jane x Moorhead. [L.S.]

mark

" J· Schnierlie, Mayor. [L.S.]"

The deed was admitted in evidence without objection by defendant, but defendant afterward moved for a nonsuit on the ground that the corporate seal was not proved. It was *held* that the lease having been proved by the subscribing witnesses, without objection, and purporting to be attested by the mayor and common seal, there was evidence to lay the case before a jury, and the nonsuit was properly overruled. City Council *v.* Moorhead, 2 Rich. (S. C.), 430.

AN AGENT OF THE CORPORATION TO AFFIX THE CORPORATE SEAL NEED NOT BE APPOINTED BY SEALED INSTRUMENT.—" The common-law rule, with regard to natural persons, that an agent, to bind his principal by deed, must be empowered by deed himself. cannot, in the nature of things, be applied to corporations aggregate. These beings of mere legal existence, and their board, as such, are, literally speaking, incapable of personal act. They direct or assent by vote; but their most immediate mode of action must be by agents. If the corporation or its representative, the board, can assent primarily by vote alone to say that it could constitute an agent to make a deed only by deed would be to say that it could constitute no such agent whatever; for, after all, who could seal the power of attorney but one empowered by vote?" Hopkins *v.* Gallatin Turnpike Co., 4 Hump. (Tenn.) 403. See also Beckwith *v.* Windsor Mfg. Co., 14 Conn. 603; Burr *v.* McDonald, 3 Gratt. (Va.) 215; Morawetz Priv. Corp., § 168.

A DEED SEALED BY AN AUTHORIZED OFFICER OR AGENT OF THE CORPORATION WITH THE PRIVATE SEAL OF SUCH OFFICER IS NOT THE DEED OF THE CORPORATION.—In order that a deed may be that of the corporation, the corporate seal, or a seal adopted by and for the corporation, must be affixed by some duly authorized officer or agent. If such duly authorized officer affixes, not the regular corporate seal or one adopted for the occasion, but his own private seal, the deed will not be the deed of the corporation. Colburn *v.* Ellenwood, 4 N. H. 99; Damon *v.* Granby, 2 Pick. (Mass.), 345; Mitchell *v.* St. Andrew's Bay Land Co., 4 Fla. 200; Bank of Metropolis *v.* Guttschlick, 14 Pet. (U. S. Supr. Ct.) 19; Regents of Univ. *v.* Detroit, etc., Soc., 12 Mich. 138.

In Brinley *v.* Mann, 2 Cush. (Mass.) 337, the deed was as follows: "Know all men by these presents, that the New England Silk Company, a corporation legally established by C. C., their treasurer, etc.

"In witness whereof, I, the said C. C., in behalf of said company, and as their treasurer, have hereunto set my hand and seal, this," etc. (Signed and sealed.) "C. C., treasurer of New England Silk Co."

It was *held* that this instrument was not the deed of the corporation, because not sealed in the name of the corporation and with the corporate seal.

In Tenney *v.* Lumber Company, 43 N. H. 343, the deed was as follows: "Know all by these presents, that we, the E. W. Lumber Co., a firm doing business under an act of incorporation, etc.

"In witness whereof we have hereunto set our hands and seals, etc.

[Seal]   "D. C. F., President of E. W. Lumber Co.
[Seal]   "E. S. C., Treasurer of E. W. Lumber Co."

It was *held* that the concluding clause "in witness whereof," etc., must be construed as the language of the company, "we, the company, set our seals," in order to give effect to the intention of the parties, that the instrument in question was to be the deed of the corporation. See also Mill Dam Foundry *v.* Hovey, *supra.*

STRONG

v.

DISTRICT OF COLUMBIA.

(Advance Case, District of Columbia.   Oct. 5, 1885.)

When under a stipulation referees certify and return into court, with their award, all findings of law and fact, and also all the evidence, the court may set aside the award for patent mistakes of law or fact, but will not set it aside for error in fact, unless the finding of fact is clearly contrary to the weight of evidence.

Promises by individual members of a municipal board to pay existing debts of the board, made at different times and places, and without that joint official deliberation for which the law provides, are not binding upon the municipality.

A contracted with a municipal board to do certain works. The terms of the contract provided for monthly payments as the work progressed, but, the municipality being unable to make these payments, the contractor was advised by certain members of the Board acting as individuals to raise the necessary funds to proceed with the work on his own notes of hand, secured by certificates issued to him by the Auditor of the Board. This was accordingly done, and the certificates pledged were indorsed by A in blank, and delivered to pledgees. A also sold a large number of the certificates outright. These certificates were all paid by the municipal corporation. A sought to recover of the corporation the difference between the face value of the pledged certificates and the amount for which they were pledged. *Held*, that A, having by indorsement and delivery of possession, invested pledgees with apparent authority to collect the certificates, it was his duty to notify the makers of the certificates of any reasons why the certificates should not be paid to the holders thereof, and that, in absence of such notification, the makers were justified in paying the amount of the certificates to said holders.

Where there were numerous items in an award, and the evidence in relation to them was voluminous, it was held that, some of the items being wrongly allowed, the court would not undertake to revise the whole award and give judgment for the proper amount, but would vacate the entire award.

ACTION at law to recover for work done during the years 1872-73, under a number of written contracts executed by the Board of Public Works of the District of Columbia, and also for work claimed to have been done outside of these contracts, but arising therefrom, which work was performed under written or verbal orders from members of the Board of Public Works or some of its officers. The declaration contained substantially the common counts; the defendant pleaded a general denial and several special pleas, among which was one of payment. After issue joined and several ineffectual trials, the action was referred by a stipulation of the parties to three referees. By virtue of this stipulation the case was heard by the referees, and an award made and filed in accordance therewith in favor of the plaintiff for the sum of $234,798.48.

From such of the findings of fact by the referees as are material to the case, it appears that the contracts sued on were ten in number and were all substantially the same in character, being printed forms containing blank spaces filled in with the specific terms agreed upon between the parties. A material provision of all these contracts was that partial payments in monthly instalments should be made as the work progressed. The Board of Public Works, however, in many cases failed to make these monthly payments; whereupon Strong notified them that he would be compelled to suspend the work unless this part of the contract was complied with. Certain members of the Board, with the knowledge of all the others and without objection on the part of any, promised the plaintiff that if he would continue the prosecution of the work with money borrowed on his own notes, secured by pledges of certificates, issued to him by the Auditor of the Board of Public Works, the Board would seasonably provide money for the payment of his notes. The plaintiff thereupon borrowed on his own notes, so secured, large sums of money. When these notes matured, the Board failed to provide the money to meet them, and in consequence the pledgees sold the hypothecated certificates for about fifty cents on the dollar. These certificates, whenever the plaintiff found it necessary to hypothecate them, were indorsed by him or by his constituted attorneys in blank. In some instances they were sold outright by the plaintiff so indorsed. On the 20th of June, 1874, long after these certificates had passed, in the manner indicated, out of Strong's possession, Congress passed an Act, 18 Stat. at L., 126, ch. 337, creating what was called a Board of Audit, which was directed to examine and audit certain suspended and floating debts of the District of Columbia and the Board of Public Works specified in the Act, among which was " the debt purporting to be evidenced and ascertained by certificates of the Auditor of the Board of Public Works," to which class belonged the certificates which had been issued to Strong. The 7th section of the act then authorizes the issuing of what are known as 3.65 bonds of the District, and gives authority to the sinking fund commissioners " to exchange said bonds at par for like sums of any class of indebtedness in the preceding section of this act named."

A great many of the certificates which had been hypothecated or sold by Strong or by persons assuming to act as his attorneys, were thereupon presented by the holders to the Board of Audit ; and the Board without notice, it was claimed, to the plaintiff, issued to such holders certificates, called certificates of the Board of Audit, for like amounts with interest, which latter certificates were subsequently taken up by the District with the 3.65 bonds, as provided for by the Act of Congress. It also appears that on the 18th day of December, 1873, the plaintiff published the following advertisement in the *Evening Star*, a daily newspaper circulated in the District of Columbia :

Special Notice.

All persons are cautioned and notified that I have forbidden the Auditor and Treasurer of the Board of Public Works from paying certificates issued to me for work done, as certain parties holding my scrip have illegal possession of them. SAMUEL STRONG.

And again on the 9th of January, 1874, he published in the same newspaper the following:

Special Notice.

All persons holding my notes, bonds, or evidence of debt of any description whatsover, with collateral security for the same, in water bonds of the District of Columbia, bonds or certificates of the Board of Public Works, or any other securities as collateral for the payment thereof, are hereby notified and required to present the same without unnecessary delay to the Hon. Peter Campbell, Stock Broker, No. 1423 Penna. Ave., Washington, D. C., who will pay these claims on presentation and take up the securities. SAMUEL STRONG.

The referees here found, as matter of law, that, wherever Strong had made an absolute sale or assignment of these certificates, a payment to or settlement by the District authorities with the assignees was, in the absence of proof of other facts, binding upon Strong; but if, on the other hand, the proof showed a pledge of the certificates by Strong, the payment in whole or in part by the District to the pledgee, accompanied by a transfer of the certificate to the District, would not defeat a recovery by Strong from the District of the amount called for by the certificate less the amount realized by him when he pledged it. To the latter part of this finding, as well as to numerous other findings, the defendant excepted; and the case, coming on upon a motion to affirm the award, was certified by the Circuit Court to the General Term, to be there heard in the first instance.

Benjamin F. Butler, William A. Cook, Frank T. Browning and *O. D. Barrett* for plaintiff.

Francis Miller and *Henry E. Davis* for the District of Columbia.

MERRICK, J.—These cases come before this court, in the first instance, certified from the Circuit Court upon exceptions taken to the award of referees.

The reference stipulated that the referees should make

separate findings of law and of fact, and should, together with their award, and as part of it, certify and return all the evidence, and all their findings of law and of fact, into the Circuit Court.

The evidence and the findings of law and of fact are, therefore, all brought into court for revision. Now the power of POWER OF COURT a court, when all the facts and the law are brought IN REVIEWING AWARD. before it on the face of the award, plainly is to review and set aside the award if it can be successfully challenged for any patent mistake of law or fact apparent upon the face of the proceedings. The court will, of course, observe the same hesitation to disturb the findings of fact upon evidence which it would observe were there a motion for new trial after the verdict of a jury, and will not disturb such findings unless they be unsupported by evidence, or be so far opposed to the great preponderance of evidence as to leave the court free from doubt that the referees have erred in their conclusions of fact. The rules governing courts in such predicament are nowhere more clearly and concisely stated than in that admirable book, Adams's Equity, marginal pages 192 and 193.

Turning now to the exceptions in this case, the most important in principle and in the amount involved are taken to the dertermination of the referees, that the defendant is responsible to the plaintiff for the face value, less what is shown to have been realized by him, of all the certificates of the Auditor of the Board of Public Works which were issued to him for work done, and which he hypothecated with third parties by indorsement in blank of himself or his constituted attorneys, and which were, by the holders thereof. presented to and redeemed by the Board of Audit with 3.65 bonds, issued in virtue of the Act of June 20, 1874. So far as we can understand the somewhat confused findings, the referees base their conclusions in great part upon the tenth general finding of facts (p. 126 printed award), to the effect that the Board of Public Works having failed to make monthly payments according to contract, Strong notified the defendant that he would be compelled to suspend work if the monthly payments were not made; whereupon certain members of the Board of Public Works, with the knowledge of all the others and without objection on the part of any, promised that if he would continue his work by borrowing money on his own notes, secured by pledges of auditor's certificates, the Board would seasonably provide money for the payment of his notes; but they did not promise to make good all or any losses incurred from the sales of certificates at a sacrifice, in satisfaction of such pledges.

Now, assuming for the moment this finding to be accurate in point of fact, it is difficult to understand how such a promise to provide money to meet notes at maturity, or, in other words, to pay their already past due and dishonored debt at some newly designated period, could render the promisor liable in damages for not maintaining their own credit. The promise is, in substance and effect, an iteration of this existing or continuing obligation to pay an overdue debt, and nothing more nor less. But it is to be noted that the referees do not find any act or resolution of the board in their official character; and we are not aware of any authority or principle of justice for holding that unofficial statements by any or all the members of a public body, at different times and places, made without that joint official deliberation for which the law provides, can be binding upon the municipality. There is no record of any such action or conclusion of the members of the Board of Public Works. The testimony of Magruder, the treasurer. contradicts the conclusion of the referees; and the testimony of Shephard, the president, was not even taken upon the sub-ject. It would be of most dangerous, not to say fatal, tendency to sanction the notion that parol testimony of witnesses, were it clear and unqualified, could be admitted at the end of ten or twelve years to establish a contract of any kind by a municipal agency required by law to act within a very narrow range of power, and to keep a record of its public transactions. But to so loose an undertaking as the one now asserted (and which, moreover, was not within the scope of the delegated powers of the Board, however formally it might have been entered into), a court could attach no efficacy. But how stands the matter in other aspects of the referees' findings, so far as the rights and obligations of the District are involved? Samuel Strong was in need of money to prosecute large contracts which he deemed valuable to himself, and which, if you please, he was much urged to consummate. He

did what many other persons were doing to the extent of perhaps millions of dollars; he took the certificates of the auditor
for debts due by the District, and hypothecated them with
third parties, in some cases in proper person, in others through
attorneys and agents by him authorized, and delivered the
hypothecated certificates to his pledgees, indorsed, sometimes
in blank or with a printed power of attorney or assignment
over the signature, and threw them thus upon the public market. Floating side by side with such certificates, and with
precisely similar forms of indorsement, were other like certificates which he had sold out and out. He made no distinction in the forms of his indorsements, as a prudent man would
and ought to have done, between hypothecated certificates
and those he had sold absolutely. In this state of things, the
Act of June 20, 1874, was passed (18 Stat. at L., p. 126, ch.
337), reorganizing the whole structure of the District government. By the 6th section of that law, all and every of the
claims of Samuel Strong against the District derive their
efficacy, if they have any force at all. Without the vitalizing
influence of that statute, as this court has already adjudged
in 1 Mackey, 265, he would have no standing in court for any
purpose upon the claims advanced in this controversy. All
the world had constructive notice of the functions conferred
upon the Board of Audit by that law; and the Board was
required by it to give, and did give, notice to all persons having claims against the District to present them for liquidation,
and the Board was authorized to give to the claimants certificates of indebtment for their claims, which might be presented
and allowed after full investigation, which certificates were to
be exchanged at par for 3.65 bonds, by a sinking-fund commissioner. Now, Strong knew that his auditor's certificates
had been indorsed as above described, and were outstanding,
and might be presented to the Board of Audit for redemption,
as in fact they all were presented and redeemed in 3.63 bonds.

It became, then, his duty to see to it that the Board of
Audit should be in possession of any facts on which he might
rely as an objection to the redemption of the certificates in
NOTICE OF
TRANSFERROR'S
CLAIMS TO CER-
TIFICATES AS-
SIGNED.
favor of the possessors who, he knew, held through
himself or his attorneys *prima facie* title to them.
He did not do so; and not having done so, he was
guilty of laches, and must be held to have allowed their pay-

ment in that manner without objection. See Adams' Case, 17 Ct. Claims, 351.

But it is said that Strong gave notices by virtue of which the District is chargeable with knowledge of the infirmity of the title of his assignees, viz.: by his advertisements in the *Evening Star* of the 18th December, 1883, and January 9, 1874 (see 12th finding). And the 13th finding conveys the idea that the Board of Audit was not authorized to pay those who held Strong's hypothecated certificates without giving him notice in fact of their presentation.

SAME.— NOTICE BY AD-VERTISEMENT.

In Adams' Case, 17 Ct. Claims, 351, it was shown that the plaintiff had filed a protest with the Treasurer of the Board of Public Works, specifically claiming certain enumerated certificates which had been fraudulently disposed of by his pledgee; that notice was not filed with the Board, and what became of it did not appear. Yet it was held that in the absence of the fact of this specific notice being brought home to the knowledge of the Board of Audit, he was concluded from claiming those certificates, they having been redeemed and paid to the holders in 3.65 bonds by the Board of Audit. In that case it having been held, first, that it was the duty of the original owners to appear before the Board of Audit and there give notice of their claims; and, secondly, that a specific notice which had been given to the treasurer of the Board of Public Works, who was a member of that body, not brought home to the knowledge of the Board, was of no avail to preserve the equities of the original holder, it is vain to assert that the general notices of Strong, published in an evening paper, can signify anything. The decision in Adams' Case is adopted by the Supreme Court in Looney's Case, 113 U. S. 260. They there say that the nature and history of auditors' certificates, the so-called sewer certificates and other securities of the District, as well as the legislation of Congress relating to them, have been fully stated in opinions delivered by the Court of Claims, and need not be recapitulated, and then refer by name to Fendall's Case, Adams' Case, and Morgan's Case. The Court of Claims then having stated the nature of these certificates, and the effect, under the legislation of Congress, of their redemption, and the Supreme Court having unqualifiedly approved those cases, which contain explicit statements that,

by the indorsement in blank of the original holders, the possessors became clothed with an apparent ownership, which,
in the absence of explicit notice of the equities of the original
party, justified the Board of Audit in causing them to be
extinguished by an issue of 3.65 bonds to the possessor and
ostensible proprietor; and that unless the true owner did give
notice in fact to the Board of Audit he was guilty of laches,
and must be held to have consented to and allowed their payment in that manner,—the position taken by the referees that
Samuel Strong is not chargeable with the full face value of
all the auditor's certificates which he ever held, and which
have been liquidated with 3.65 bonds, is manifestly erroneous.
But long before those cases the Supreme Court had decided
in Cowdrey *v.* Vandenburgh, 101 U. S. 576, the principle
applicable to all choses in action, whether negotiable or non-
negotiable in the commercial sense, to wit: that when a party
makes a blank assignment he contemplates that the blanks
may be filled up, if necessary, by the holder, and that the
rights of innocent parties do not depend upon the actual
title or authority of the party with whom they deal directly,
but are derived from the act of the real owner, which pre-
cludes him from disputing, as against them, the existence of
the title or power which, through negligence or mistaken con
fidence, he caused or allowed to appear to be vested in the
party making the conveyance thereof.   It is further to be
considered that this case is not a dispute between the first
owner and any assignee, but it is a dispute between the
creditor and his debtor, which debtor by and through a means
and apparent authority furnished to him by the creditor himself, and after a public notice warning him and all others to
produce their claims, if any, before a lawful agency for
liquidation, has been induced to pay the demand in full.

To allow him, under such circumstances, to be paid over
again would be gross injustice to an innocent public.

The errors into which the referees fell upon this question,
being patent on the face of their award, permeating nearly all
of the claims, and the consequence of them being an allowance
of largely more than double of what the plaintiff could recover
upon all his claims together, were there no mistake of law or
fact in any other matter, the court would be compelled to set
aside the award.

Besides this fatal defect, and making every allowance for liberty of judgment in doubtful matters to the referees, there is an eminent probability that, with respect to some large allowances to which exception was taken, the referees have fallen into error.

Multitudinous as are the items in dispute between the parties, and voluminous as is the evidence, this court cannot undertake to discharge the duties of an accountant, comparing all the items of complicated transactions, and then striking the exact balance. Without so doing we could suggest no exact basis of settlement, even were the right of a court to cut down an award and adjust the final balance clear, a question on which we express no opinion. Being therefore unable to indicate an exact and definite result, we are satisfied, after mature consideration, that it would not be appropriate to designate those eminently probable miscarriages to which allusion is made; possible prejudices might arise to one or other of the parties from such expression, and we are not satisfied that an identification of those questionable allowances would result in promoting any settlement of the controversy. We are the more induced to this course from the fact that, after all the investigations which have taken place, the skilled professional advisers of the parties have before them all the elements to enable them, upon a careful review of the case, to approximate at least a result which will accomplish substantial justice, and terminate by private convention between themselves a protracted and vexatious litigation. The court will give an order vacating and annulling the whole award.

MEMBERS OF A MUNICIPAL BOARD CANNOT BIND THE CORPORATION BY THEIR INDIVIDUAL ACTS, EVEN THOUGH A MAJORITY JOIN IN OR RATIFY THE ACTS.—Members of a municipal board have as individuals no authority to act for the municipal corporation. This is true though the majority of the individuals composing the board join in or ratify the act. The board must act as a body or unit. It can only act at meetings regularly called. Thus in the case of McCortle *v.* Bates, 29 Ohio St. 419, the majority of the members of a town school board signed a writing ordering certain school supplies, and promising to ratify the contract at a meeting of the board to be called for the purpose. The supplies were duly delivered, but at the special meeting the board refused to ratify the contract.

It was held that the members of the board had no authority to act ex-

9 Cor. Cas.—37

cept at a board meeting, and that the contract to ratify was void as against public policy. The language of the court is instructive: "The board is constituted by statute a body politic and corporate in law, and as such is invested with certain corporate powers, and charged with the performance of certain public duties. These powers are to be exercised and these duties discharged in the mode prescribed by law. The members composing the board have no power to act as a board except when together in session. They then act as a body or unit. The statute requires the clerk to record, in a book to be provided for that purpose, all their official proceedings."

In the case of Jefferson County *v.* Slagle, the county commissioners had contracted with one D to build a court-house. D made a contract with the plaintiff to supply him with brick. After the plaintiff had delivered part of the brick called for by his contract, he refused to deliver the rest on the ground that D had not paid for the bricks delivered as agreed.

Two of the county commissioners thereupon went to the plaintiff and told him to proceed with the delivery of the bricks and that they would pay him. The law provided that two county commissioners should form a board for the transaction of business, and, when convened in pursuance of notice or according to adjournment, should be competent to perform the duties appertaining to their office. It did not appear that the other county commissioners were consulted with or notified beforehand of the contract made with plaintiff, or that such contract was being contemplated. The question was submitted to the jury whether the two commissioners acted in their official capacity in promising to pay for the bricks, or merely as individuals, and the jury found that they acted in their official character. This verdict was sustained by the Supreme Court on review of the case. Jefferson County *v.* Slagle, 66 Pa. St. 202.

AT A MEETING OF A PUBLIC OR MUNICIPAL BOARD A MAJORITY OF THE MEMBERS MAY ACT FOR THE BOARD.—When a power is submitted to three or more persons under an agreement of individuals, and no other provision is made in the agreement, all the persons to exercise the power must not only meet together, but all must agree in the result, or else nothing can be done by them. The People *v.* Walker, 23 Barb. (N. Y.) 304. But where a number of persons are entrusted with a power, not of mere private confidence, but in some respects of a general nature, it is not necessary that all the members should concur in the result, or even that all should meet. If all members are duly notified of a meeting and a majority attend, a majority of the entire number may act for the whole. People *v.* Walker, *supra* (citing The King *v.* Miller, 6 T. R. 269); Inhabitants of Plymouth *v.* County Commissioners of Plymouth, 16 Gray (Mass.), 341; People *ex rel.* McSpedon *et al. v.* Board of Supervisors, 18 How. Pr. (N. Y.) 152; Louk *v.* Woods, 15 Ill. 256; Withnell *v.* Gartham, 6 T. R. 388; Blucket *v.* Blizard, 9 Barn. & C. 851. In Johnson *v.* Dodd, 56 N. Y. 76, it seems to have been held that all must meet and confer, but that the majority had the power to act. See also In the Matter of Building the Thirty-fourth Street Sewer, 31 How. Pr. (N. Y.) 42.

In Gildersleeve *v.* Board of Education, 17 Abb. Pr. R. (N. Y.) 201, a statute providing that "whenever any duty or authority is confided by law to three or more persons, and whenever three or more persons are authorized or required by law to perform any act, such act may be done, and such power, authority, or duty may be exercised and performed by a majority of such persons or officers upon a meeting of all the persons or officers so entrusted or empowered, unless special provision is otherwise made." It was held that "the interpretation to be put upon this provision in its application to bodies entrusted with the management of matters of public concern is that when all the members of the body are notified that a meeting is to be held, and a majority of the whole number attend, the majority so attending may organize and legally proceed to the transaction of business. . . . If all have been duly notified, it is, within the meaning of the statute, 'a meeting of all the persons;' and if a majority of the whole number attend, it is competent for that majority to do any act or exercise any power confided by law to the body collectively."

THERE CAN BE NO MEETING OF A JUDICIAL OR QUASI-JUDICIAL BOARD OR BODY UNLESS ALL THE MEMBERS ARE PRESENT. — When the public duties imposed upon a board are judicial in their nature, the entire board must meet and confer, but the majority can decide or take final action. People *v.* Walker, *supra ;* Grindley *v.* Barker, 1 Bos. & Pull. 236. Both parties are entitled to the presence of all the judges, and to have the benefits of the consultation of each with every other. All must therefore meet together and consult, but a majority may decide.

Where all members of a judicial board meet, and a matter is brought before the board for it to take action upon, and the minority, being unable to agree with the majority, withdraw from the meeting before any action is taken in the matter, the majority may lawfully act in their absence in regard to such matter. *Ex parte* Rogers, 7 Cow. (N. Y.) 526. The court, in their opinion, say : "The commissioner, one of the three appraisers, dissents, and declares himself absent, and not a member of the board. He had assumed the trust delegated to him by the legislature, and had been actively engaged in its execution as a member for a long time. After a full investigation he had, it is to be presumed, joined in carrying on the deliberations of the board from time to time till the eve of the final decision. Can his simple declaration of absence at that point of time subvert his character as a member of the appraising body? We are warranted in saying his counsel had been bestowed, and that the other members had heard and appreciated his advice ; because every officer is presumed to have done his duty. Such advice is the object of the rule which requires all to associate, but at the same time allows a majority to decide. After so full a compliance with the spirit of the rule, we cannot admit that this desertion of the board should have the effect to invalidate the assessment. It is no more in effect than a ceasing to confer farther on the question, a point to which every discussion must come when the arguments for and against are exhausted."

But where two of three assessors revised the assessment list without notice to the third, and without his taking part in their deliberations, it was held that the revision was invalid. *In re* Beekman, 31 How. Pr. R. (N. Y.) 16.

A BOARD OR BODY CANNOT MEET AND PROCEED TO TRANSACT BUSINESS UNTIL ALL ITS MEMBERS HAVE BEEN APPOINTED. — Where the law provides for a board of a definite number of members, the board is not legally constituted until all its members are chosen and have duly qualified; consequently a majority of the members cannot proceed to the transaction of business before the minority have been chosen and have qualified. Schenck *v.* Peay, 1 Woolw. (U. S. C. Ct.) 175. But see, *contra,* Hartshorn *v.* Schoff, 58 N. H. 197. In this case the validity of an act of a board of three fence commissioners was in question. All were present at the hearing, made the decision, and signed the report; but only two of them took the oath prescribed by the statute. It was held that, as by statute a majority was empowered to decide, the decision of the two commissioners would have been binding if the third commissioner had not taken part in it; and that the fact that he did so take part in the decision did not invalidate it.

TO CONSTITUTE A MEETING OF A JOINT BODY COMPOSED OF TWO OR MORE DEFINITE BODIES, A MAJORITY OF EACH BODY MUST BE PRESENT.—To constitute a valid meeting for the transaction of business of a joint body composed of two or more definite bodies, it is necessary that a majority of each of the separate bodies should be present. Gildersleeve *v.* Board of Education, 17 Abb. Pr. R. (N. Y.) 201; King *v.* Bower, 1 Barn. & Cr. 492. But when the meeting has once been organized the identity of the component bodies is lost, and the vote of the majority of the persons present controls, even though one of the bodies should leave before the vote is taken. Gildersleeve *v.* Board of Education, *supra;* Whiteside *v.* People, 26 Wend. 634.

SCALLAY

v.

COUNTY OF BUTTE.

(Advance Case, California. July 30, 1885.)

§§ 4000, 4001, 4003, and 4046 of the Political Code of California confer upon the board of supervisors of a county the authority to retain lawyers to collect debts and other property of the county; but, in the exercise of· that power, they have no right to delegate to others the power to determine whether to commence a suit or not; the matter of the selection of attorneys to prosecute the suit; nor to abdicate the control of the suit in the matter of compromise or settlement of the suit. These powers are conferred upon the board of supervisors as a public trust and cannot be vicariously exercised.

APPEAL from a judgment of the superior court of Butte

county, entered in favor of the defendant. The opinion states the facts.

Wm. Pierson and *H. C. Newhall* for the appellant.

I. S. Belcher, John C. Gray, Chas. F. Lott, L. C. Granger and *A. F. Jones* for the respondent.

MCKEE, J.—In the year 1876 Butte county was the owner and holder of two hundred railroad bonds of the California Northern R. R. Co., secured by mortgage, the principal and interest of which had become due and payable; ꜰᴀᴄᴛꜱ. but the company would not pay and the county was desirous of collecting them. Under those circumstances, two persons—W. S. Watson and William Corcoran—proposed to the board of supervisors of the county that they would collect them, without attorney's fees, expenses, or costs to the county, for fifty cents on the dollar. The board accepted the proposal, and on the third of October, 1876, a written contract to that effect was drawn and signed by the chairman of the board, in the name of the county, and by Watson and Corcoran; and the contract, thus signed, was ratified by the board.

By the terms of the contract, the bonds were to be delivered to Watson and Corcoran for collection; they were to commence, within sixty days, "proceedings," or "negotiations," or "a proper suit," for their collection, and "prosecute the matter without any unnecessary delay," without costs or charges, or attorney's fees, and when collected, retain to their own use fifty per cent of the amount collected "in full payment of themselves, their agents, attorneys and employees employed or engaged in the matter." It was also "mutually understood and agreed that either of the parties thereto may compromise the matter of paying said bonds with said railroad company, upon such terms and conditions as they may deem just and equitable, but no compromise so made shall be final or binding without the express written consent of the parties hereto."

On the second of December, 1875, foreclosure proceedings upon the bonds and mortgage were commenced against the railroad company. These were continued for about seven years without other result than the recovery of a final judgment for the principal and interest due upon the bonds, but for the execution of this judgment, so far as it appears from

the complaint, no steps were taken; and under these circumstances the board of supervisors of the county, on the fifteenth
of May, 1883, compromised and settled with the railroad company, without the consent, written or otherwise, of Watson
and Corcoran, and received from the company twenty thousand dollars, which it accepted in full satisfaction of the bonds
and release of the mortgage.   It is alleged that " when this
settlement was made there was due and payable on said bonds
the sum of forty-seven thousand and fifty-eight dollars and
eighty cents, which could·and would have been collected and
received by the county but for the unauthorized compromise
and settlement by the board."   Five months after· this settlement, Watson and Corcoran assigned the contract to the
plaintiff and appellant, who presented a claim to the board of
supervisors for twenty-three thousand three hundred and
twenty-nine dollars and forty cents, due upon said contract.
The claim was rejected, and hence this suit.   The answer of
the county to the complaint is that the contract was *ultra vires.*

When the contract was made the powers of the several
counties of the State, as defined by the legislature, were contained in the following sections of the political code:

" Sec. 4000.   Every county is a body politic and corporate,
and as such has the powers specified in this code, or in special
statutes, and such powers as are necessarily implied from
those expressed.

·" Sec. 4001.   Its powers can only be exercised by the board
of supervisors, or by agents and officers acting under their
authority or authority of law.

" Sec. 4003.   It has power: ·

" 1.   To sue and be sued.

" 3.   To make such contracts, and purchase and hold such
personal property as may be necessary to the exercise of its
powers.

" 4.   To make such orders for the disposition or use of
property as the interests of its inhabitants require."

And the board of supervisors, as agents of the county, were
clothed with the following jurisdictions and powers:

"Sec. 4046.   The boards of supervisors, in their respective counties, have jurisdiction and power, under such limitations and restrictions as are prescribed by law.

" 8.   To purchase, receive by donation, or lease, any real or personal property necessary for the use of the county, preserve, take care of, manage and control the same.

" 10. To sell at public auction at the court house door, after thirty days' previous notice . . . to the highest bidder for cash, any property, real or personal, belonging to the county.

" 15. To direct and control the prosecution and defense of all suits to which the county is a party.

" 26. To do and perform all other acts and things required by law, not in this title enumerated, or which may be necessary to the full discharge of the duties of the chief executive authority of the county government," etc., etc.

These provisions constituted the charter of the county upon the subjects to which they relate; and for the declared purposes and objects within its jurisdiction, the board could exercise the powers expressly granted to it, and those which were necessarily or fairly implied in or incident to them.

Railroad bonds belonging to a county are property, upon which the county may sue, and about which the board of supervisors may make such orders as it may deem RIGHTS OF COUNTY best for the interests of the county, with reference OWNER OF RAILWAY BONDS. to the use or disposition of the same, in the mode prescribed for the exercise of its powers. No orders were made for the sale of the bonds in the mode prescribed by subdivision 10 of section 4046, *supra.* The contract was for their collection by negotiations or other proceedings, or by suit. No question is made as to the power of the county to sue. Such a power implies the power to employ an agent to commence and prosecute a suit, unless the law itself has provided for the county a law officer whose duty it is to commence and prosecute suits for the county. Such an officer has been provided in the district attorney, whose duty it is. as the legal adviser of the county . . . " to defend all suits brought against . . . his county, and prosecute . . . all actions for the recovery of debts, fines, penalties, and forfeitures accruing to . . . his county ;" and to collect and receipt for the same in his official capacity. Subs. 3, 4, sec. 4256, political code.

In Hornblower *v.* Duden, 35 Cal. 660, it was held, upon the authority of Smith *v.* The Mayor of Sacramento, 13 Id. 533, that, while the power to employ other counsel than the district attorney to commence and prosecute suits for the county was not expressly conferred on the board of supervisors, it

was obviously embraced in the general power to do and perform all such other acts and things as may be strictly necessary to the full discharge of the powers and jurisdiction conferred on the board and in the power to control the prosecution and defense of all suits to which the county is a party.

Accepting that as a correct rendition of the powers conferred on the board of supervisors in respect to the prosecution and defence of suits to which the county may be a party,
POWER   OF the contract under consideration is not of that
COUNTY TO AU-
THORIZE PERSONS character. The plaintiff does not allege that his
TO COLLECT ITS
CLAIMS.   assignors were attorneys or counselors at law, or
that they, or the board of supervisors, contracted for legal
services to be rendered by them in connection with or independent of the district attorney. The subject matter of the
action was the collection of choses in action which belonged
to the county. Without obtaining any order or instructions
from the board to sue, the contracting parties agreed "to
commence a proper suit, or proceeding, or negotiation, for the
collection of the amount due upon said bonds, within sixty
days from date, and to faithfully and diligently prosecute the
same until a final judgment or settlement, without any cost
or charge to the county ; . . . and to accept in full for all services to be rendered by them, or attorneys they may employ
in the matter. the sum of fifty per cent upon each and every
dollar so collected by them of the amounts due upon said
bonds," etc.

It may be conceded that the board of supervisors had
power to contract for the collection of the property of the
county ; but in the exercise of that power it had no authority
to delegate to others, whom it employed for that purpose, the
power to determine whether to commence a suit in the name
of the county and to select and employ attorneys to commence
and prosecute such a suit ; nor to abdicate its control of the
prosecution of such a suit, or to make its compromise or settlement dependent upon the written consent of strangers.
The commencement of a lawsuit, the selection and employment of attorneys to commence and prosecute it, and the
compromise and settlement of the same are acts which involve
the exercise of judgment and discretion ; and it is well settled,
that powers conferred upon a municipal corporation to do
such acts can not be delegated to others. Such powers are

in the nature of public trusts conferred upon the corporation for the public benefit, and cannot be vicariously exercised. Cooley's Const. Lim. 204. Hence the contract in suit was *ultra vires;* and the court below sustained the demurrer.

·Judgment affirmed.

ROSS, J., and MCKINSTRY, J., concurred.

GOODWIN

v.

BATH.

(*Advance Case, Maine. August 6, 1885.*)

The holder of an interest coupon, severed from the bond and which by mistake is for a larger sum than that named as interest in the, bond, cannot recover the sum named in the coupon without proof that he, or some one under whom he claims, acquired the same before maturity and without notice of the error.

ACTION on an interest coupon. The opinion states the case.

Wilbur F. Lunt for plaintiff.

Francis Adams for defendant.

EMERY, J.—The writing declared upon in this suit is a coupon for the forty-fourth instalment of inter- FACTS. est upon a bond for $100 issued by the defendant city. It is not the original contract for the interest. The original, fundamental undertaking to pay the interest is found in the bond itself. The bond expresses the original real contract for both principal and interest. The coupon is an incident of the bond. It is of the nature of a check or ticket for the interest. It is issued rather for convenience than to express the original obligation to pay interest. It is designed to pass from hand to hand, like a baggage check, and the lawful holder is entitled to the interest it represents. When taken up it is a convenient voucher for the officer paying the interest. It represents that interest NATURE OF promised in the bond, and no other, nor different COUPON. interest. Arents *v.* Commonwealth, 18 Gratt. 764; City *v.*

Lamson, 9 Wall. 482; McCoy *v.* Washington County, 3 Wall.
Jr.; s. c., 7 Am. Law. Reg. 196, cited in 4 Myers' Fred.
Dec. 876.

So clearly is the coupon an incident of the bond, and not
an original independent undertaking, that actions upon it,
though it be without seal, are not barred by any lapse of
time, short of that required to bar an action upon the bond
itself. The coupon draws its life from the bond, lives as
long as the bond, and dies with the bond. Clark *v.* Iowa
City, 20 Wall. 583.

In this case the city of Bath was authorized to issue its obligations, " with coupons for interest attached, payable semi-
annually." Special Laws of 1860, chap. 450, § 2. In this
$100 bond to which the coupon was attached, the stipulation
was to pay six per cent interest, which would make the
forty-fourth instalment, one for $3 only. At the time of the
issue of this bond the statute against usury was in force.
The city could not lawfully stipulate in the bond for more
interest, nor lawfully attach to the bond a coupon for more.
The sum of $3, the amount of the instalment promised in the
bond, is what the lawful holder of the coupon is entitled to,
and is as much as the city was authorized to pay, or to promise to pay.

The plaintiff, however, urges that, whatever may be the
nature of the coupon while attached to the bond,
when it is separated from the bond it becomes a
separate and a negotiable instrument. This coupon was separated from the bond when purchased
by the plaintiff, and he claims that he, as the holder of the separated coupon, is not affected by any mistakes or
excesses of authority in the issue, but can recover the sum
named in the coupon, whatever was the sum promised in the
bond.

RECOVERY ON
COUPON LIMITED
TO THE AMOUNT
SPECIFIED IN THE
BOND TO BE PAID
AS INTEREST—
BONA - FIDE
HOLDER.

The case as made up by the mutual admissions, without any
objection to their legal admissibility, shows that there was not
a full consideration for such a coupon, and that the coupon
was issued by mistake for a sum larger than that authorized
by law and by the terms of the bond. Such facts legally
appearing, it is incumbent on the holder, if he would avoid
them, to show that he, or some prior holder whose rights he
has succeeded to, acquired the coupon in good faith, before

maturity, and without notice of the true state of affairs. Roberts *v.* Lane, 64 Me. 111 ; s. c., 18 Am. Rep. 242. Does the case show this? The bond with coupon attached was delivered to the Androscoggin Railroad Company, by whom it was put on the market. That company, holding both bond and coupon, must be held to have known the discrepancy, and to have known the true amount of the forty-fourth instalment of interest. Every subsequent holder of both bond and coupon would be chargeable with similar notice. There is no evidence of any separate ownership of coupon or bond until the plaintiff acquired the coupon. There is a presumption that there was no such severance, and that the holder of the coupon was also the owner of the bond. McCoy *v.* Washington Co., 3 Wall. Jr. 381 ; Deming *v.* Houlton, 64 Me. 261 ; s. c., 18 Am. Rep. 253. The plaintiff, the first one shown to have a separate ownership of the coupon, acquired it after maturity, on January 10th. From the facts stated, there is no evidence or presumption that the plaintiff or any prior holder acquired the coupon both before maturity and without notice. Whatever be the negotiable nature or immunities of the coupon, the plaintiff is not in a situation to invoke them. The coupon upon its face shows that it was a ticket for the forty-fourth instalment of interest due on bond No. 77. which instalment was $3. There is in the writ a general *omnibus* money count, broad enough to include the plaintiff's claim for that instalment. He cannot recover the amount named in the coupon. He only claims interest upon the instalment from the date of his demand, January 15.

Judgment for plaintiff for $3, with interest from January 10, 1883.

STATE OF KANSAS

v.

SCHOOL DISTRICT NO. 3, CHAUTAUQUA CO.

(Advance Case, Kansas. October 9, 1885.)

Where an objection is made to the introduction of evidence at the trial on the ground that the petition does not state facts constituting a cause of action, the averments of the petition should be liberally construed in support of the petition.

Where a petition includes several causes of action, an objection to the introduction of evidence on the ground that the petition states no cause of action should be overruled if any of the causes of action included are well stated.

It is well settled that a Statute of Limitations will not run against the State or sovereign authority, unless the statute to that effect is so strong as to be utterly unavoidable.

As to whether the Statute of Limitations would run against the State, when the State procured the debt or claim after the statute had commenced to run, *quære.*

The statute authorizing school districts to issue bonds provided that the bonds should specify on their face *the purpose for which they were issued.* Certain school-district bonds specified on their face that they were issued in pursuance of this statute, but did not specify the purpose for which they were issued. *Held,* that inasmuch as the statute in question only authorized the issuance of bonds for a certain purpose specified in the statute, the reference on the face of the bonds to the statute was a sufficient specification of the purposes for which the bonds were issued.

Where the bonds appear on their face to be regular, and issued by proper authority, it is for the defence to aver and prove that anything was done or omitted in reference to the execution of the bonds that would render them invalid.

ERROR from Chautauqua county.

This was an action brought by the State of Kansas against school district No. 3, Chautauqua county, Kansas, to recover on 7 school-district bonds and 35 accompanying coupons. The petition contained a separate count and a separate statement of a cause of action upon each of the 7 bonds and on each of the 35 coupons. The statement of the cause of action upon the first bond reads as follows:

"That on the first day of January, 1873, at Peru, in the county of Howard and State of Kansas, school district No. 135, county of Howard, State of Kansas, the same being then a school district duly organized and existing under the laws of the State of Kansas, and acting as such, and by J. O. Greytrax, director; Albert Kees, clerk, and J. M. Brown, treasurer of said district, the same having been duly elected, appointed, qualified, and acting as such officers, made and issued its certain bond, dated on said day at said place, whereby, for value received, it promised, on the first day of June, A.D. 1875, to pay to A. B. Close, or bearer, two hundred dollars, at the banking-house of W. N. Coler & Co., in the city of New York, with interest at the rate of ten per cent per annum, payable annually on the first day of June of each year, according to divers coupons thereto attached, which bond, in order to distinguish it from others of like character, was marked ' No. one.' A copy of said bond is hereto attached and made part hereof. That on the sixteenth day of January, 1873, said bond was duly registered in the office of the county clerk of said Howard county, Kansas.

" And said plaintiff further says that, in pursuance of an act of the legislature of the State of Kansas entitled ' An act to divide the county of Howard, and to errect the territory thereof into the counties of Chautauqua and Elk, to provide for the due organization of said counties, the filling of vacancies in offices, for the proper division of the property and indebtedness of Howard county, and in regard to the taxes and records thereof,' approved March 3, 1875, the territory embraced in school district No. 135 of Howard county, Kansas, became, and still is, a part of Chautauqua county, Kansas. Thereupon, said Chautauqua county being organized in pursuance of the act of the legislature aforesaid, the county superintendent of said Chautauqua county proceeded to and did change the name of said school district No. 135, Howard county, to said defendant, school district No. 3, Chautauqua county, State of Kansas; that said school district No. 3 of Chautauqua county lies wholly within the boundaries of the former school district No. 135 of Howard county, Kansas, and includes within its borders all the inhabitants of school district No. 135, Howard county, and is the same corporate entity as school district No. 135, Howard county, Kansas. And plaintiff further says that school district No. 135, Howard county, Kansas, is wholly merged in and become a part of said school district No. 3 of Chautauqua county, State of Kansas, which has succeeded to and become possessed of all the property, rights, and privileges formerly enjoyed by said school district No. 135, Howard county ; that, before said bond by its terms became due and payable, the said bond came to, and for value became the property of, this plaintiff, the same having been sold and delivered for a valuable consideration to the commissioners of the permanent school fund of the State of Kansas for this plaintiff, who therefore became, and ever since has been, and still is, the true and lawful owner and holder thereof; that when said bond

by its terms became due and payable the same was duly presented at the place of payment therein mentioned and payment demanded, but refused because said defendant had not,
nor had said school district No. 135, Howard county, nor did
either of said districts, ever have funds at said place; that
the said plaintiff has often applied to said defendant to pay
the said bond, but it has refused to do so, notwithstanding it
is justly indebted thereon to the plaintiff in the full sum of
two hundred dollars, which it claims, with interest at the
rate of ten per cent per annum from the first day of June,
A.D. 1875."

The statement of the cause of action upon each of the other
bonds is precisely the same as the statement of the cause of
action upon the first bond, except that such statements show
that the bonds were numbered consecutively from one to
seven, and became due in successive years from June 1, 1875,
to June 1, 1881. The statement of the cause of action upon
each of the coupons is precisely the same as the statement of
the cause of action upon the bonds, except that clauses with
reference to the coupons are added. A copy of each of the
bonds and of each of the coupons is attached to the petition
and made a part thereof, and a part of the statement of the
cause of action to which it properly belongs. The first bond
reads as follows:

No. 1. $200

UNITED STATES OF AMERICA, STATE OF KANSAS.

District School Bond of School-District No. 135, Howard County:

Know all men by these presents, that school district No.
135, county of Howard, State of Kansas, is indebted unto
A. B. Close, or bearer, in the sum of two hundred dollars,
lawful money of the United States, to be paid on the first day
of June, A.D. 1875, at the banking-house of W. N. Coler & Co.,
in the city of New York, with interest at the rate of ten per
cent per annum, payable annually on the first day of June of
each year, on presentation of the annexed coupons, as the
same becomes due. This bond is issued in pursuance of an
act of the legislature of the State of Kansas entitled " An act
to enable school districts in the State of Kansas to issue

bonds," approved February 26, 1866, and acts amendatory and supplemental thereto.

In testimony whereof, this bond has been issued, signed by the director, countersigned by the clerk, and registered by the treasurer of said district.

Dated at Peru, County of Howard, State of Kansas, this first day of January, 1873.   J. O. GREYTRAX, Director.

Countersigned: ALBERT KEES, Clerk.

Registered by J. M. BROWN, Treasurer.

Indorsed: No. 1. $200. State of Kansas. Registered school bond of school district No. 135, Howard county. Ten per cent interest, payable annually on the first day of June, at the banking-house of W. N. Coler & Co., New York. Matures June 1, 1875.

Each of the other bonds is the same as this, except as to number and date of maturity. The first coupon attached to the first bond reads as follows:

School district No. 135, county of Howard, Kansas, will pay to bearer on the first day of June, 1874, twenty-eight and 33-100 dollars, at the banking-honse of W. N. Coler & Co., in the city of New York, being one year's interest on bond numbered one.   J. O. GREYTRAX, Treas.

ALBERT KEES, Clerk.

Each of the other coupons is the same as this, except as to number and date of maturity.

The defendant answered to the plaintiff's petition, setting up five separate defences, and the plaintiff replied to this answer by filing a general denial. Upon the issues made up by these pleadings the action came on for trial before the court without a jury, and the plaintiff, to maintain the issues on his part, put a witness on the stand and asked him a question; whereupon the defendant objected to the introduction of any evidence under the petition, upon the ground that the same did not state facts sufficient to constitute a cause of action against the defendant, and the court sustained the defendant's objection and dismissed the plaintiff's action; to all of which the plaintiff duly excepted, and now brings the case to this court for review.

W. A. Johnston for the State.

C. J. Peckham and *M. B. Light* for defendant in error.

VALENTINE, J.—The only ruling of the court below com-
PRACTICE—QUES-TIONING SUFFI-CIENCY OF PETI-TION ON APPEAL. plained of in this case is the sustaining of an objection made by the defendant to the introduction of
any evidence under the plaintiff's petition, upon
the ground that the petition did not state facts sufficient to
constitute a cause of action against the defendant, and the
dismissal of the plaintiff's action upon the same ground.
Preliminarily, we would say that such an objection is not
favored by courts, and that where the sufficiency of the
petition is raised for the first time, and only by such an objection, the courts will construe the allegations of the petition
very liberally for the purpose of sustaining the petition, if it
can reasonably be sustained. Barkley *v.* State, 15 Kan. 99,
107; Mitchell *v.* Milhoan, 11 Kan. 617, 625, 626, and cases
there cited. Also in this case, besides the direct allegations
contained in the body of the petition, copies of the bonds and
BONDS AND COU-PONS HELD PART OF PETITION. coupons sued on were attached to and made a part
of the petition; and, therefore, in construing the
allegations of the petition, the contents of the bonds and
coupons, as contained in such copies, must also be considered as a part of the petition. Budd *v.* Kramer, 14 Kan.
101, 102 *et seq.* See, also, Reed *v.* Arnold, 10 Kan. 103;
Campbell *v.* Blanke, 13 Kan. 62; Andrews *v.* Alcorn, 13 Kan.
351. Besides, section 123 of the Civil Code provides, among
other things, that "in an action, counter-claim, or set-off,
founded upon an account, promissory note, bill of exchange,
or other instrument, for the unconditional payment of money
only, it shall be sufficient for a party to give a copy of the
account or instrument, with all credits and the indorsements
thereon, and to state that there is due to him on such account
or instrument from the adverse party a specified sum, which
he claims, with interest."

The first objection made by the defendant to the plaintiff's
LIMITATION. petition is that a portion of the 42 causes of action
set forth therein is barred by the five-years statute of limitations contained in the first subdivision of section 18 of the
Civil Code. But this objection can certainly avail nothing;
for if any one of the several causes of action set forth in the
plaintiff's petition is good, the court below should not have
sustained the objection of the defendant to the introduction
of all evidence under the petition, and should not have dis-

missed the plaintiff's action. The action was commenced on December 18, 1882, and at least 14 of the several causes of action set forth in the plaintiff's petition accrued within less than five years prior to that time. These causes of action cannot therefore be considered as having being barred by any statute of limitations when this action was commenced. But are any of the causes of action set forth in the plaintiff's petition barred by any statute of limitations? Now, it is universally held by courts that no statute of limitations will run against the State or the sovereign authority unless the statute itself expressly so provides, or unless the implica- $\text{\tiny SAME — AGAINST}$ tions of the statute to that effect are so strong as to $\text{\tiny STATE.}$ be utterly unavoidable. It requires no citations of authorities to sustain this proposition. Even where there is a doubt as to whether the State was intended to be included within the provisions of the statute, the doubt must be solved in favor of the State and the State held not to be included. Des Moines Co. *v.* Harker, 34 Iowa, 84, and cases there cited. And even where the State holds the claim or debt sued on as the assignee or transferee of some individual person, still the statute of limitations will not run against the State where such statute has not commenced to run before the State obtained the claim or debt. U. S. *v.* White, 2 Hill, 59.

We need not decide the question whether the statute would continue to run, and to run against the State, where the State procured the claim or debt after the statute had commenced to run, for no such question is involved in this case. We think that no statute of limitations has so run against the State in the present case as to bar any of the causes of action set forth in the plaintiff's petition.

The next question urged by the defendant against the plaintiff's petition is that the bonds set forth therein and sued on do not state, as required by statute, the purpose $\text{\tiny WHETHER BONDS}$ for which they were issued. The bonds were $\text{\tiny SHOW PURPOSE FOR WHICH}$ issued under section 1 of an act entitled "An act $\text{\tiny BONDS WERE ISSUED.}$ to enable school districts in the State of Kansas to issue bonds," approved February 26, 1866, as amended by section 1, chapter 95, of the Laws of 1872; and that section provides, among other things, that "they [the bonds] shall specify on their face the date, amount, for what purpose issued, to whom, the time they run, and the rate of interest," while the bonds in the present case do not in terms specify for what purpose they were issued. We think, however, under the present circumstances, and as the question is now presented, that the bonds are sufficient in this respect. It must be remembered that the question has been raised only by an objection to the introduction of evidence under the petition. It must also now be considered that the bonds were issued in good faith; that the school district received ample compensation for them, and that the State of Kansas is an innocent and *bona fide* purchaser of them; for nothing appears to the contrary in the petition, and all the allegations of the petition would tend to indicate this. We have stated that the bonds do not in terms specify upon their face the purpose for which they were issued; but we think they do in effect. The bonds specify on their face that they were "issued in pursuance of an act of the legislature of the State of Kansas entitled 'An act to enable school-districts in the State of Kansas to issue bonds,' approved February 26, 1866, and acts amendatory and supplemental thereto." Now, under that act bonds could be issued only for one purpose, that of providing a school-house for the district, either by erecting or purchasing the same. It is true that it was not necessary that the bonds should recite the act under which they were issued, and it was necessary that they should recite the purpose for which they were issued; but as the bonds did recite the act under which they were issued, and as that act authorizes bonds to be issued only for one purpose, the bonds do in effect recite the purpose for which they were issued.

The next point made by the defendant is "that none of the several counts of said petition allege or show that the conditions precedent, or any of them, had been complied with when said bonds were made and executed." We think the petition is sufficient. It alleges that the school district made and issued the bonds; that it made and issued them by its proper officers, for value received; and copies of the bonds are given and made a part of the petition, which shows that the bonds were issued in pursuance of the said act of the legislature of 1866, and the acts amendatory and supplemental thereto; and we think the bonds are valid upon their face. See section 123, Civil Code, above cited. Presumptively the school district and its officers acted in good faith and according to law, and the officers did their duty; and if anything was done or omitted that would render the bonds invalid, it is for the defendant to set the same up in its answer as a defence. In this connection we would cite the case of Mosher *v.* Independent School District of Steamboat Rock, 42 Iowa, 632.

The fourth and last objection made by the defendant to the plaintiff's petition is " that none of the several counts of said petition allege or show that the conditions precedent to the sale of said bonds had been complied with when said bonds were negotiated and sold, or that they were sold at a price fixed by the district, as required by law." What has been said with reference to the last preceding objection may be said with reference to this. The petition alleges that the bonds were made and issued by the school district and its officers for value received, and the copies of the bonds show that they were made and issued in pursuance of the statute in such cases made and provided, and presumptively they were made and issued in accordance with law. It was not necessary for the plaintiff to state in his petition the amount of the consideration for which the bonds were issued, or the prices fixed by the qualified electors of the district for the sale of the bonds. When the bonds were issued they passed from the district and beyond its control, and into other hands, and presumptively they were valid; but if for some reason they were not valid, it devolves upon the defendant to allege and prove their invalidity. The petition certainly does not show they were invalid, but, on the contrary, shows that they were valid.

The judgment of the court below will be reversed and cause remanded for further proceedings.

HORTON, C. J., concurring. JOHNSTON, J., having been of counsel, did not sit.

STATUTES OF LIMITATION DO NOT APPLY TO THE STATE OR SOVEREIGNTY UNLESS IT IS ESPECIALLY PROVIDED THAT THEY SHALL APPLY TO IT.—Unless the State is especially included in the operation of a Statute of Limitation, such statute will not apply to the State. This is equally true of Statutes of Limitation barring the right of entry to lands after a certain period of adverse possession, and of statutes taking away the right of action on personal claims unless brought within the prescribed period. That statutes tolling the right of entry after a certain period of adverse possession do not apply to lands owned by the State, see Brinsfield *v.* Carter, 2 Ga. 143; Wright *v.* Swan, 6 Port. (Ala.) 84;

Doe *v.* Townsley's Heirs, 16 Ala. 239; Troutman *v.* May, 33 Pa. St. 455; Wallace's Lessee *v.* Miner, 6 Ohio, 366; Harlock *v.* Jackson, 3 Brev. (S. C.) 254; State *v.* Arledge, 2 Bailey (S. C.), 401; Lindsey *v.* Miller, 6 Pet. (U. S.) 666; Wilson *v.* Hudson, 8 Yerg. (Tenn.) 398; Levasser *v.* Washburn, 11 Gratt. (Va.) 572; Kirschner *v.* Western & Atlantic R. R. Co., 67 Ga. 760; Glaze *v.* Western & Atlantic R. R. Co., 67 Ga. 761.

That statutes taking away the right of action on personal claims or demands, unless brought within the prescribed time, do not apply to claims or demands of the State, see Ware *v.* Green, 37 Ala. 494; State *v.* Joiner, 23 Miss. 500; Swearinger *v.* United States, 11 G. & J. (Md.) 373 (judgment recovered by U. S.); People *v.* Gilbert, 18 John (N. Y.), 227; Nimmo's Executor *v.* Commonwealth (judgment), 4 H. & M. (Va.) 57; Parks *v.* State, 7 Mo. 194 (surety on bond); McKeehan *v.* Commonwealth, 3 Pa. St. 151; Commonwealth *v.* Hutchinson, 10 Pa. St. 466 (taxes); Commonwealth *v.* Baldwin, 1 Watts (Pa.), 54 (judgment lien); State Treasurer *v.* Weeks, 4 Vt. 215 (tort); *In re* Life Association of America, 12 Mo. App. 40 (period fixed by court, under provisions of statute, within which to present claims against an insolvent company).

THE STATE MUST BE NAMED IN EXPRESS WORDS IN THE STATUTE IF IT IS TO APPLY TO THE STATE.—The State must, it would seem, be named expressly in the Statute of Limitations, or the statute will not apply to it. If there is the slightest doubt as to whether the statute was intended to apply to the State or not, it will be held not to apply. County of Des Moines *v.* Harker, 34 Iowa, 84; Josselyn *v.* Stone, 28 Miss. 753, 763; People *v.* Gilbert, 18 Johns (N. Y.), 227; United States *v.* Hoar, 2 Mason (U. S. C. Ct.), 311, 314. This is a rule of construction, and the reason of it is well stated by Judge Story in the case of United States *v.* Hoar, *supra*. "Where the Government is not expressly or by necessary implication included, it ought to be clear from the nature of the mischief to be redressed, or the language used, that the Government itself was in contemplation of the Legislature, before a court of law would be authorized to put such an interpretation upon any statute. In general, acts of the Legislature are meant to regulate and direct the acts and rights of citizens; and in most cases the reasoning applicable to them applies with very different, and often contrary, force to the Government itself. It appears to me, therefore, to be a safe rule founded in the principles of the common law, that the general words of a statute ought not to include the Government, or affect its rights, unless that construction be clear and indisputable upon the text of the act."

In the County of Des Moines *v.* Harker *supra*, the Statute of Limitations provided that it should be "applicable to all actions brought by or against *all bodies, corporate or politic*, except when otherwise expressly provided." It was held that even this provision was not explicit enough to include the State within the operation of the statute. The court say: "There are subjects to which this statute can be applied, in all its language and force, without including the State. The Legislature does not, when prescribing a rule for the State, call it a 'body politic and corporate.' It is not probable such a designation can be found in the entire history of our legislation. Even if there was a doubt if the State was to be included in the language of the statute, that doubt should be resolved in favor of the State."

In the case of Commonwealth *v.* Johnson, 6 Pa. St. 136, suit was brought by the Commonwealth on the official bond of a prothonotary, for a breach in failing to pay over to the State treasurer, taxes levied on fees received by the prothonotary. The bond was filed in pursuance of the provisions of the act imposing the tax, which provided that prothonotaries should give bond conditioned for the payment by them of all taxes levied on them by virtue of the act, and that the effect, rights, and remedies of said bond should be governed by the provisions of a former act relating to sheriffs' and coroners' bonds. This former act provided that coroners and sheriffs should give bonds conditioned for the faithful performance of official duties, prescribed the form of the bond, and further provided that no suit should be sustained by any court on such bond unless brought within five years from its date. It was held that the reference in the statute relating to prothonotaries' bonds to the statute relating to sheriffs' bonds was not enough to incorporate in the former statute the limitation clause contained in the latter. The court say: "The principle deducible from all the cases, English and American, is that the Legislature shall not be taken to have postponed the public right to that of an individual, unless such an intent be manifested by express word or irresistible implication, and this principle is peculiarly applicable to a plea of the Statute of Limitations interposed to bar a public claim. I am not aware of any judicial construction of the act of 1803 (that relating to sheriffs' and coroners' bonds) in reference to this principle. If, however, it be admitted that its clause of limitation would operate to bar a suit by the commonwealth, it is by no means clear that the Legislature intended to engraft this quality upon the act of 1830 (relating to prothonotaries' bonds) by the use of the words 'effect, rights, and remedies of said bond.' Full operation may be given to these terms by referring them to the object of the bonds contemplated by the act, the right to be secured thereby, and the peculiar form of remedy afforded by the old act, without making them a conduit for infusing into the late statute a doctrine at least partially destructive of the remedy. When we recollect that this would be introductory of a new feature unknown to prior and subsequent legislation had in reference to the official bonds of these officers, . . . and that it is in violation of the long recognized axiom that the public right cannot be destroyed or compromised by the neglect of the public agent, nothing short of language clearly and explicitly pointing to a legislative intent in conformity with the construction demanded by these defendants would justify our sanction of it."

WHERE THE STATE ACQUIRES TITLE AFTER THE STATUTE HAS BEGUN TO RUN, THE STATUTE WILL CONTINUE TO RUN AGAINST THE STATE.— Where the State takes as assignee of a claim on which the statute has begun to run, it is said that the acquiring of title by the State will not stop the running of the statute. Wood Lim. of Actions, p. 92, citing United States *v.* White, 2 Hill (N. Y.), 59. In that case a promissory note was assigned to the United States before it was due. The court say that if the statute had begun to run against the note while in the hands of the assignee, it would continue to run against the United States; but that not having begun to run against the assignee, it never began to run against the United States.

LIEBMAN

v.

CITY AND COUNTY OF SAN FRANCISCO.

(*Advance Case, California. August* 24, 1885.)

By an act of the Legislature of the State of California, passed April 1, 1872, to open and establish a public street, to be named Montgomery Avenue, in the city and county of San Francisco, it was provided that the value of land taken for the improvement, the damage to improvements thereon or adjacent thereto, and all other expenses incidental to the proceedings, should be deemed the cost of opening the avenue, and should be assessed upon property in a certain specified district, by a board of public works to be created for that purpose. This board was to consist of the mayor, the tax-collector, and the surveyor of the city and county of San Francisco; and the improvement was not to be commenced until the owners of a majority of the frontage of the property to bear the burden of the improvement, should petition the mayor of the city and county of San Francisco, in writing, to have the improvement undertaken. The board was thereupon to organize and proceed to prepare a report showing the value of the land to be taken, and damage and benefits to property. This report was to be open for inspection by all persons interested, and was to be subject to revision by the county court as to matters shown in the report. *Held* (approving and following the decision of the supreme court of California in the case of Mulligan *v.* Smith, 59 Cal. 206), that as only matters appearing in the report could be called in question in the county court, an order of that court confirming the report did not estop the city and county of San Francisco from setting up as a defence that the petition for the opening of Montgomery Avenue was not signed by the owners of a majority in frontage of the property to bear the burden of the improvement, the facts as to the petition not being included in the report.

A municipal corporation is estopped to deny the truth of recitals contained in municipal bonds, to the effect that all acts and formalities necessary to the validity of the bond have been complied with, where such recitals are made by duly authorized officers of the municipality, but not otherwise.

Where the board of public works, described in the first paragraph of the head-note, were, after the confirmation of their report, to issue bonds to pay for the improvement, and were to raise enough money by assessment each year to pay the interest on the bonds and to create a sinking fund for the payment of the principal; and it was, moreover, especially provided that the city and county of San Francisco should in no event be liable for the payment of the bonds or any part of them; *held*, that the board of public works provided for in the statute was not an agency of the municipal corporation in the improvement of Montgomery Avenue, but that it acted as agent of the State; that the fact that the title to Montgomery Avenue, when completed and paid for, was to vest in the city and county of San Francisco did not indicate that the board was the agent of the municipality; and that the bonds issued by the board gave rise to no liability on the part of said city and county of San Francisco.

BEFORE FIELD, circuit justice, and SAWYER, circuit judge.
D. L. Delmas, A. L. Rhodes, and *J. P. Hoge* for the plaintiff.
Garber, Thornton & Bishop for the defendant.

FIELD, C. J.—This is an action against the city and county of San Francisco to compel the payment of twenty   FACTS. coupons for interest, each amounting to thirty dollars, attached to certain instruments designated in the pleadings as Montgomery Avenue bonds. The plaintiff prays for judgment that the coupons are valid obligations of the city and county; that there is due by it upon each of them the sum of thirty dollars, with interest from the date of its maturity at the rate of seven per cent per annum; that the city and county pay the amount thus adjudged due from the special tax to be annually levied, assessed, and collected for that purpose, pursuant to the act of the legislature of April 1, 1872; and that the plaintiff recover against it for the costs of this action.

The validity of the bonds to which the coupons are attached, and, of course, the validity of the coupons also, depends upon that act, and the compliance in their issue with its requirements. The object of the act was to open and establish a public street in the city and county of San Francisco, to be called Montgomery Avenue, and to take private lands therefor. It described a strip of land by metes and bounds, and declared that it was taken and dedicated for such street, and that, when paid for, the title thereto should vest in the city and county for that purpose, as the title of other public streets was vested. It provided that the value of the property taken, the damages to improvements thereon or adjacent thereto, and all other expenses incidental to the proceeding should be considered the cost of the opening of the avenue, and should be assessed upon lands within a described district in proportion to the benefits accruing therefrom, to be ascertained by a board of public works created for that purpose. That board was to consist of the mayor, the tax-collector, and the surveyor of the city and county of San Francisco; and whenever the owners of a majority in frontage of the property which was to bear the burden of the improvement, as they 'were named in the last preceding annual assessment roll for the State, city, and county taxes, should petition the mayor of the city and county, in writing, for the opening of the avenue according to the provisions of . the act, the board was to proceed to organize by the election of a president, and then to the performance of its prescribed duties. It was, among other things, to ascertain and report the cash value of the land taken ; and the damages caused to the property along the line and within the course of the avenue; also, the benefits accruing from its opening to the lots within the prescribed district.

The report was to remain at the office of the board for thirty days for the inspection of parties interested, and notice that it was thus open for inspection was to be published for twenty days in two daily papers in the city and county. Any person interested who was aggrieved by the action of the board, as shown in its report, might, within the thirty days, apply by petition to the county court, setting forth his interest in the proceedings, and his objections thereto, for an order on the board to file with the court its report, with such other documents or data as might be pertinent thereto, which were used by it in preparing the report. And the court was authorized to hear the petition, and the board could appear in response to it, and testimony could be taken in the matter. After hearing and consideration, it was in the discretion of the court to approve and confirm the report, or to refer it back to the board, with directions to alter or modify it in specified particulars. From the order of the county court, an appeal could be taken to the supreme court of the State, to review the matters complained of. Upon the final confirmation of the report, the board was required to prepare and issue bonds, in sums of not less than one thousand dollars each, for the amount necessary to pay and discharge all the damages, costs, and expenses incurred. These bonds were to be known and designated as the Montgomery Avenue bonds, and made payable in thirty years from their date, and to bear interest at the rate of six per cent per annum, payable semi-annually at the office of the treasurer of the city and county. Coupons for the interest were to be attached to each bond. The bonds were to be signed by all the members of the board, and its seal was to be affixed to each. The coupons were to be signed by the president.

Any person to whom damages for lands were awarded, upon tendering to the board a satisfactory deed of convey-ance of the property to the city and county, was entitled to have bonds issued to him equal to the amount awarded. The act also provided for the assessment and levy of an anual tax upon the property benefited, for the payment of interest upon the bonds, and to create a sinking fund for the redemp-tion of the principal, the assessment to be "adjusted and dis-tributed according to the enhanced values" of the respective parcels of land, as fixed in the final report of the board.

But the act declared that the city and county of San Fran-cisco should not, in any event whatever, be liable for the payment of the bonds, nor any part thereof, and that any per-son purchasing them, or otherwise becoming the owner of any bond or bonds, accepted the same upon that express stip-ulation and understanding.

The following is a copy of one of the bonds and coupons issued under the act. The others are similar in form, differ-ing from each other only in their number.

STATE OF   CALIFORNIA

BOARD OF PUBLIC WORKS

City and county (Number 205) San Francisco.

(Vignette.)

$1,000.   MONTGOMERY AVENUE BOND. $1,000.

In Conformity

with an act passed by the people of the State of California, represented in senate and assembly, entitled an act to open and establish a public street in the city and county of San Francisco to be called Montgomery Avenue, and to take pri-vate lands therefor, approved April 1, 1879, the treasurer of the city and county of San Francisco, State of California, will pay at his office in said city and county, to the holder hereof, one thousand dollars in United States gold coin, with interest at the rate of six per cent per annum, payable semiannually in like gold coin, upon surrender of the corresponding coupons, and that the principal sum is redeemable within thirty years from the date of these presents.

It being understood and agreed that this bond may be redeemed by said treasurer as provided in said above-mentioned act of the legislature of the state of California.

In witness whereof the mayor, the tax-collector, and city and county surveyor of said city and county of San Francisco, composing a board of public works, have respectively signed these presents, and the president of the board of public works has signed the annexed coupons as of the first day of January, 1873.

{ Seal of the Board of public works. }

WILLIAM ALVORD,
President of the board of public works and mayor of the city and county of San Francisco.

ALEXANDER AUSTIN,
Tax-collector and member of said board of public works.

RICHARD H. STRETCH,
City and county surveyor and member of said board of public works.

$30. Board of Public Works. Coupon No. 15.
Montgomery M. A. B. Av. Bond. } The treasurer of the city and county of San Francisco will pay bearer, at his office, thirty dollars, six months' interest.
On bond No. 612. } { Due 1st January, 1881.

WM. ALVORD,
President of board of public works.

From this brief statement of the act of April 1, 1872, three things distinctly appear: 1st, that the petition of the owners of a majority in frontage of the property to be charged with the cost of the improvement was essential to the validity of all subsequent proceedings taken for the opening of the avenue, including, of course, the issue of the bonds; 2d, that in no event could the city and county be held liable on the bonds, and necessarily, therefore, not on the coupons attached; and, 3d, that every person purchasing or becoming the owner of any bond took the same on that express stipulation and understanding.

The act in question was before the supreme court of the State, and the subject of exhaustive consideration RULINGS OF in Mulligan *v.* Smith, 59 Cal. 206. That was an STATE COURT UPON STATUTE. action of ejectment to recover land claimed by the plaintiff under a deed executed to him upon a sale of the premises for the non-payment of a tax levied thereon to raise a fund to pay the interest on the bonds. In the lower court, evidence was introduced which tended to show that the petition to the mayor, which was the essential initiatory step to the proceedings for opening the avenue, had not been signed by the owners of a majority in frontage of the property to be charged, as shown by the names on the assessment roll of the previous year; and the court found that such was the fact. In the supreme court, it was contended, as it had been in the court below, that evidence to impeach the correctness of the petition in this respect was inadmissible; and, also, that as the petition was sufficient on its face, and had been accepted by the mayor as sufficient, the defendant was estopped from questioning its validity, or the validity of the proceedings under it; and, also, that such estoppel followed from the judgment of the county court confirming the report of the board. But the supreme court held the evidence admissible, and that the defendant was not estopped from showing the insufficiency of the petition, either by the action of the mayor in accepting it, or the judgment of the county court; that whilst it might be true that the mayor was called upon in the first instance to decide upon the sufficiency of the petition, there was nothing in the statute which made his determination conclusive, and precluded an inquiry into its validity whenever the proceedings under it came up for judicial consideration. In no part of the statute, said the court, did it appear that provision was made for notice to the property-owners of the proceedings authorized to be taken before the mayor, or by the board, or in the county court. Neither the mayor nor the board was required to give notice of any kind until the board had completed the report of its work. And the

604 LIEBMAN v. CITY AND COUNTY OF SAN FRANCISCO.

notice then required was one of a general nature by publication, and was only that the report was open for inspection. Though any property-owner aggrieved by the action or de-·termination of the board, as shown in its report, could have made his objections to the county court, they could not extend to the character or sufficiency of the petition. "Nowhere in the statute," said the court, "is the petition made part of the report, or of the data or documents used in making it. Nor is it anywhere required that the board or the mayor shall return it to the court or file it there or elsewhere. The court had, therefore, no jurisdiction of the petition; no power to adjudge upon its execution, and it could not assume jurisdiction of it or by its judgment decide upon its sufficiency and validity so as to conclude the defendant." These conclusions of the court were concurred in by all its members, and sustained in separate opinions of marked ability and learning by three of them. All agreed that evidence to show the defect in the petition, in not being signed by owners of a majority in frontage of the property to be charged, was admissible, and that the defect existing invalidated all the subsequent proceedings. "When, therefore," said the court, "the legislature prescribed that a petition from the owners of a majority in frontage of the property to be charged with the cost of the improvement was necessary to set the machinery of the statute in motion, no step could be taken under the provisions of the statute until the requisite petition was presented. It was the first authorized movement to be made in the opening of the avenue. When taken, officers, who were to constitute and organize a board of public works, were authorized to organize. Until it was taken, they had no such authority. They could not legally act at all; or, if they acted, their proceedings would be unauthorized and void. The presentation of the petition required by the statute was, therefore, essential."

The authorities cited in the several opinions show that similar conclusions have been reached by the highest courts of other States in analogous cases. Indeed, the rule is fundamental that where private property is to be taken for a PETITION MUST public improvement upon the petition of a majority PRECEDE AP- PROPRIATION OF of those who are to bear its burden, the petition PRIVATE PROP- ERTY. of such a majority must be made before proceedings for the appropriation of the property can be had. This is a condition which must be strictly followed. A failure to comply with it will vitiate all subsequent proceedings. No one, indeed, would contend that proceedings had, in such cases, without the petition of any of the owners, would be valid; and a petition of a less number of the owners than that designated by the statute would be equally ineffectual. If one less than the required number may be omitted, so may all. Nor is the rule at all affected by the doctrine that in a certain class of cases evidence of such compliance is conclusively found in the action of officers required to consider and determine that fact. That doctrine, as we shall presently see, only applies to estop the obligors of a bond, and can have no bearing or consideration in the present case, where the bonds, to which the coupons in controversy are attached, are neither in form nor in law the obligations of the city and county.

The construction given by the supreme court of the State to the act of April 1, 1872, if not absolutely binding upon the judges of the Federal courts, in cases arising under it, is certainly not to be disregarded and rejected, except STATE CONSTRUC-
for the most cogent and persuasive reasons, such FOLLOWED.
as would leave little doubt of the error of the State court. Conflicts between State and Federal tribunals in the interpretation of State statutes are always to be avoided if possible. The Federal courts will, therefore, follow the exposition of the State courts unless it conflicts with or impairs the efficiency of some principle of the Federal constitution, or of a Federal statute, or a rule of commercial or general law. In this case, there is no such conflict or impairment. No principle of Federal law is invaded, or rule of commercial or general law disregarded. The construction given is one we should unhesitatingly adopt had the supreme court, the legitimate expounder of State statutes, never spoken on the subject.

There was, it is true, an intimation by one of the judges, in his opinion in Mulligan *v.* Smith, that in an action upon the bonds, that being an action upon contract, a different rule might exist, and that an estoppel might arise against the defendant. It was, however, only an intimation to mark a possible distinction in the proofs required in the two forms of action. No question as to the effect of the bonds as evidence was before the court. And it is plain that if, to recover in the ejectment, it was essential to establish the validity of the proceedings leading to the levy of the tax to pay the interest on the bonds, it must be essential to establish the validity of the proceedings leading to the issue of the bonds themselves, and, of course, the sufficiency of the petition upon which the proceedings were founded, unless such sufficiency is, from the character of the instruments, and the recitals in them, to be conclusively presumed. In the ejectment case, a comparison of the petition with the assessment roll of the previous year disclosed the fact that a number less than the majority of the owners in frontage, as shown by the names on the assessment roll, appeared on the petition. The subsequent proceedings were, therefore, from this defect, wholly unauthorized. The essential initiative to them had never been taken.

The question here is, assuming that an action will lie against the city and county on the coupons, will the sufficiency of the petition be presumed; or, what will amount to the same thing, will the defendant be estopped from denying its sufficiency so as to allow the admission in evidence of the coupons, without other proof than the production of the bonds to which they were attached.

ACTION ON COUPONS—WHETHER CITY ESTOPPED TO DENY SUFFICIENCY OF PETITION.

There are numerous cases where municipal bonds have been authorized by statute upon a vote of a majority of the citizens of a city, county, town, or other locality, and officers designated to ascertain and report as to the vote taken and issue the bonds. When, in such cases, the bonds refer to the statute, and recite a compliance with its provisions, and have passed, for a valid consideration, into the hands of *bona fide* purchasers, without notice of any defect in the proceedings, the obligors have been held to be estopped from denying the correctness of the recitals. The doctrine on this subject is well stated by the supreme court of the United States in the recent case of Pana *v.* Bowler, 107 U. S. 539. " This court," is the language used, " has again and again decided that if a municipal body has lawful power to issue bonds or other negotiable securities, dependent only upon the adoption of certian preliminary proceedings, such as a popular election of the constituent body, the holder in good faith has the right to assume that such preliminary proceedings have taken place if the fact be certified on the face of the bonds by the authorities whose primary duty it is to ascertain it."

This doctrine is not accepted in many of the State courts, and has in some instances met with earnest dissent from judges of the supreme court. It must, however, be conceded that it is the settled doctrine of that court; but to its application the recitals must clearly import a compliance with the statute under which the bonds were issued. If fairly construed they are consistent with any other interpretation; they will not estop the municipal corporation in whose name they are made from showing that they were issued without authority of law. School District *v.* Stone, 106 U. S. 186; Supervisors of Carroll County *v.* Smith, 11 U. S. 556. And the recitals when full will estop only the obligors of the bonds; they cannot estop others who are not parties to them; they cannot affect strangers to the transaction. In both particulars the alleged recitals in the avenue bonds are inoperative to create any estoppel against the city and county. There is no statement of any fact in the clause called a recital. The clause is a mere caption to an order or promise of the board of public works that the treasurer of the city and county of San Francisco will pay to the holder the sum of one thousand dollars. " In conformity with the act," the title of which is given, says the instrument, "the treasurer will pay." Read in connection with what follows, it imports that the treasurer will pay the amount designated in accordance with the act,—that is, out of the fund to be provided by it,—and that the holder can look to no other source of payment. There is nothing in the clause which would reach the petition and import that it had conformed to the requirements of the statute. But the fact which disposes of this question of recitals and any alleged effect attributed to them in the present case is that the so-called bonds, to which the coupons in controversy were attached, are not obligations of the city and county. They are not executed by it, or under its seal, or by its agents or officers, but by certain parties constituting the board of public works. The fact that certain officers of the city and county are made members of the board to appraise the property taken and the injuries and benefits caused by the opening of the avenue does not constitute them agents of the city and county, and render their work as such board the work of the city and county; no more than if they were constituted a board to establish a university, and prescribe the studies to be pursued in it, would make them the agents of the municipality for that purpose. Agents can only exercise the powers of their principals; they cannot lawfully exceed them. Here the city and county as a municipality is not authorized to open the avenue, to appraise the value of the property taken, or the amount of injuries received by or benefits conferred upon the owners of property along the line of the avenue, or to sign and issue its bonds to the parties injured. In all these matters the board acts independently of the municipality. It is made the agent of the State to carry out a public improvement directed by its statute, and not the agent of the city and county.

The foundation upon which the doctrine of estoppel from recitals in municipal bonds rests is that the officers signing the bonds and inserting the recitals are agents of the municipality, and authorized to bind it by their acts and representations. The principle which gives rise to the estoppel, as well stated by the defendant's counsel, is that it would be inequitable to permit a municipal corporation to take advantage of the falsity of solemn declarations of such agents within the scope of their authority. But if the officers making the recitals are not such agents, there is no room for the doctrine of estoppel. Their recitals, on no conceivable principle, can in such cases bind the corporation.

It follows that if any action can be maintained upon the coupons against any defendant, the validity of the proceedings upon which the bonds were issued must be established by affirmative proof of the sufficiency of the petition, which was the essential initiative to them.

SUFFICIENCY OF PETITION MUST BE AFFIRMATIVELY ASSUMED.

But the question is not before us, whether an action can be maintained against any other party; it is enough that we are of opinion that the present action cannot be maintained against the city and county of San Francisco. The plaintiff asks for judgment that the coupons are valid obligations of the city and county; that there is due, by the city and county, upon each of the coupons, thirty dollars, with interest; that the city and county pay the amount thus adjudged due out of the special tax to be levied under the act, and that the plaintiff recover his costs of the action. Such judgment could not be rendered upon the facts stated in the complaint. The statute to which the complaint refers, and upon which, alone, the judgment is sought, declares, in express terms, " that the city and county shall not, in any event whatever, be liable for the payment of the bonds, nor any part thereof," and " that any person purchasing said bonds, or otherwise becoming the owner of any bond or bonds, accepts the same on that express stipulation and understanding."

As already stated, the so-called bonds, which, in fact, are only orders or promises of the board of public works that the treasurer will pay to the holder the amounts designated, cannot be the foundation of any liability of the city and county, and that such liability is sought to be charged appears from the prayer for judgment, although the discharge of that liability is to be had out of funds to be raised by the special tax for which the act provided.

The asserted ground of the action is that it is essential to establish the validity of the bonds, as a preliminary to an application for a *mandamus* to levy the special tax. Counsel assume that the validity of the bonds issued by one party can be determined in an action against another in no way named in them, nor liable for their payment. We do not so understand the law. We have not met with any adjudged case to that purport. On the contrary, we have always supposed that the party actually liable on a bond must have his day in court, in person or by his representative, before a judgment determining its validity as against him or his estate could be regarded as having any binding force. Such liability cannot be vicariously imputed to him or charged upon his estate. If the action be to charge particular property of which there is no representative, there is a defect in the law which the legislature, and not the courts, must supply.

It is true that in the enforcement of bonds of municipal bodies, which are to be paid from funds raised by taxation, general or special, the validity of the bonds must first be established by the judgment of the court,—that is, the demand against the municipality on the bonds must be first carried into judgment; then a *mandamus* will issue, which is in the nature of an execution. It is the executory process for the enforcement of the judgment recovered. It can only issue to command the corporation against which the judgment is rendered, or its representatives or officers, to levy the tax prayed, just as an execution on an ordinary money judgment can only be issued against the property of the judgment debtor. Whether, when the judgment against the municipality is rendered, the writ is to direct a general or a special tax upon all or a portion of the property within its limits or only upon a particular class of property, real or personal, will depend upon the directions of the statute providing for the payment of the indebtedness created. The judgment, however, must, in all cases, be against the corporation to which, or to whose representatives or officers, the writ is directed. It is the liability of the corporation established by the judgment which is to be discharged by the levy of the tax prayed, and not the liability of any other body.

The several cases cited by counsel in support of their contention in no respect militate against these views, but, on the contrary, illustrate and confirm them. In all of them the bonds were issued in the name, or were in law the obligations, of the municipality against which the judgment was prayed, though in some of them the funds for the payment of the judgment were to be collected by a special tax upon the property of a particular district. It would serve no useful purpose to comment at length upon the cases in verification of this statement. Every one who may take an interest in the subject will find, upon examination of them, its correctness sustained.

One of the counsel of the plaintiff indulges in his brief in some strictures upon the action of the city and county of San Francisco with respect to these bonds, characterizing it as "dishonest and dishonorable repudiation." The accusation falls harmless in the face of the statute under which the bonds were issued, declaring that the city and county "shall not, in any event whatever, be liable for the payment of the bonds, nor any part thereof," and "that any person purchasing said bonds or otherwise becoming the owner of any bond or bonds accepts the same upon this express stipulation and understanding." Nor can the legislators of the city and county be subjected to any just imputations of a want of regard to the honor and credit of the municipality in refusing to order the levy of a tax to pay the interest on the bonds, so long as the judgment of the highest tribunal of the State, the constitutional expounder of its laws, remains unreversed, declaring that the proceedings on which the bonds were issued were taken in disregard of the conditions imposed by the legislature, and, therefore, were absolutely null and void. If property of citizens has been taken and is retained for an avenue of the city without compensation, upon proceedings not warranted by law, some other remedy must be sought by the parties injured than such as consists in affirming the validity of those proceedings in face of the judgment of that tribunal.

It follows from the views expressed that no recovery can be had upon the facts disclosed in the complaint; and the motion of the defendant to exclude all evidence in support of its allegations must be granted; and it is so ordered.

SAWYER, C. J.—This case having been regularly called for trial, the plaintiff offered in evidence the bonds and coupons set out in the complaint, to the introduction of which the defendant objected, on the ground that the complaint does not state a case sufficient to justify the introduction of any evidence whatever; or, in other words, that the   FACTS. facts stated in the complaint do not make a case which entitles the complainant to any judgment or relief against the defendant, or upon which the defendant is in any respect liable to be sued. The counsel of both parties treated the objection as, in effect, a demurrer to the complaint, on the ground that the facts set out, taken as true, do not constitute a cause of action, and they argued the question very elaborately on that hypothesis.

The first question that meets us at the threshold of the discussion is whether the defendant—the municipal corporation, the city and county of San Francisco—is, in any sense, the obligor on the bonds, or whatever the instruments in suit may be properly termed; or whether it is in any way a party to the transaction out of which these instruments arose, in such sense as to cast any liability or duty upon the municipality in its corporate capacity.

In my judgment, the instruments sued on are not bonds of the city and county of San Francisco; and the city and county of San Francisco, in its corporate capacity, does not stand in any such relation to these obligations as renders the corporation liable to be sued upon them for any purpose.

The act under which the instruments sued on purport to have been issued is not an amendment to the city charter, CERTAIN OFFI- and it does not purport to enlarge the powers or CERS, HELD AGENTS OF STATE, duties of the corporation, or of its officers in their NOT OF MUNICI- PALITY. capacity of officers or agents of the corporation. It does not confer any authority whatever upon the corporation to do any act, in its corporate capacity, or impose any duty or obligation upon the municipality relating to the opening and dedication to public use of Montgomery Avenue. The corporation is not authorized to do the acts necessary to the opening and dedication of the street to the public use contemplated by the act, or required to see that the costs of the work, upon completion, shall be collected or paid; in short, the corporation, as such, is neither required nor authorized to perform any act in relation to the opening · and dedication of the avenue, or in relation to payment therefor, when accomplished. Clearly, it seems to me, the State has undertaken to do this work through the instrumentalities chosen by itself, of which instrumentalities the corporation called the city and county of San Francisco is not one. Some of the officers of the city, it is true, are designated as instrumentalities for carrying out the scheme provided for; but in carrying it out they do not act by virtue of any authority derived under the charter of the corporation, or any act amendatory of the charter, or enlarging its powers, or under the authority of the corporation, but they act solely by authority of the act in question, independently of any act of the corporation, their designation by their official titles being only *descriptio personarum* to indicate the particular parties chosen for the work.

The act describes a specific tract of territory within the city and county of San Francisco by metes and bounds, and then declares that "it is hereby taken and dedicated for an open and public street, and, when paid for as hereinafter provided, the title thereto shall vest in the said city and county for such purposes forever, as the title of other public streets in said city and county now is vested." This, with a provision for subsequent improvement and care, is the only one in the whole act in which the city and county, in its corporate capacity, is brought into any relations with the improvement contemplated; and this relation only commences after the work of dedication and opening is fully completed, and paid for, by the agencies and in the manner appointed by the act. The expenses of dedication to public use and opening the avenue are to be paid for by assessments on a district of land specifically described and designated by the act as benefited by the improvement. The board of public works provided for is not a board of public works of the city and county of San Francisco, with powers derived under the charter of the city, or any act enlarging those powers, or acting by authority of the corporation or its charter. It is not one of the branches of the municipal government.

This board is a special board of public works created by the statute, without any reference to the powers and duties of the corporation, to carry out this particular improvement undertaken by the State, without reference to any action of the corporation, and without consulting its pleasure. It is, it is true, composed of three persons, who are also officers of the corporation, and their official name is used to designate the individuals who are to constitute the board. But their individual names might just as well have been used, or any other three persons having no connection with the corporate government might have been appointed to perform precisely the same acts; and had this been done, there would be just as good ground for considering them agents of the corporation, and not instrumentalities employed by the State itself to carry out its purposes, as there is, now, to consider the board as an agent of the municipality, and not an instrumentality of the State. Doubtless, the legislature might have enlarged the powers of the corporation, or conferred the authority, or imposed the duty, upon it to perform the contemplated work; but it did not see fit to do so. " The mayor, tax-collector, and city and county surveyor" of the city and county of San Francisco—that is to say, the persons who for the time being filled those offices—are " created a board of public works, within the meaning and intent of this act, and as such board are hereby authorized, empowered, and directed to perform all and singular the duties herein enjoined upon the board of public works as herein provided." A salary of two thousand dollars per annum is allowed to each for his services in such board, payable out of the "Montgomery Avenue Fund," to be assessed upon the property benefited, as a part of the expenses of the opening of the avenue. Section 25 provides that "the board of public works shall provide itself with an official seal, which shall be used to verify such acts of the board as are herein described to be done, under the seal of the board; thus, apparently making it an independent corporation, or quasi-corporation, for the purposes of the act.

Section 8 requires the board, at the proper stage of proceedings, to prepare and issue bonds for an amount in the aggregate " necessary to pay and discharge all said damages, costs, and expenses." "Said bonds shall be known and designated as ' Montgomery Avenue bonds,' and the bonds shall signed by all the members ' of the board,' and the seal thereof shall be affixed to each bond." There is nothing to authorize the issue of bonds by or in the name of the municipal corporation. They are to be issued by the board specially created for the purpose, under its own seal, provided for by the act, and not under the seal of the municipal corporation, and not signed by the mayor as mayor or agent of the city. Under section 11, a fund sufficient for the purpose of payment of coupons and redemption of the bonds is to be levied, assessed, and collected in the same manner as other taxes in said city or county are levied, assessed, and collected upon lands within the district supposed and determined by the act itself to be benefited. Thus, the same machinery and instrumentalities used for collecting other State as well as city taxes are adopted for assessing and collecting the special tax provided for the purposes of the act. The moneys so collected are to be paid, not into the treasury of the city and county as a part of its corporate funds, but to the treasurer of the city and county personally designated for the purpose, and is " to constitute the Montgomery Avenue fund," " to be paid out by said treasurer only in payment of the coupons attached to said bonds," . . . and " in redeeming the bonds issued in pursuance of the provisions of this act."

The fund thus provided is set apart for this specific purpose, having no connection with the funds of the municipality, under the sole charge and management of the board of public works, and the person who happens, for the time being, to be treasurer. The municipal corporation, as such, has no power or authority over it—nothing whatever to do with it. Nor has the board of supervisors, the legislative and governing body of the corporation. It is under the exclusive authority and control of the agents of the State, especially designated by the act, to carry out the will and purpose of the State as manifested by the act.

As if not enough to declare its purpose to make the improvement, to designate its own instrumentalities, and point out the mode of executing its will, leaving nothing to be done on the part of the corporation, or of its legislative and governing body, and to carefully avoid bringing the corporation or its legislative body into any relations whatever with the work; and as if to cut off all possibility of doubt upon the subject, it was expressly provided in the last section but one of the act " that the city and county of San Francisco shall not, in any event whatever, be liable for the payment of the bonds, nor any part thereof, provided to be issued under this act; and any person purchasing said bonds, or otherwise becoming the owner of any bond or bonds, accepts the same upon that express stipulation and understanding." Thus the statute in no provision authorizes the city and county of San Francisco, in its corporate capacity, or by the board of supervisors, its legislative and controlling body, or otherwise, to do anything in the matter of opening and dedicating to public use Montgomery Avenue, or to meddle with the funds provided for the purpose, or to assume any obligation or responsibility in the matter. The act imposes no obligation or duty upon the corporation or upon its controlling body, nor does it even confer any power to act, in any manner, in regard to the work of opening Montgomery Avenue, while, on the contrary, it expressly provides that it " shall not, in any event whatever, be liable for the payment of the bonds, nor any part thereof, provided to be issued under this act; and any person purchasing said bonds, or otherwise becoming the owner of any bond or bonds, accepts the same apon that express stipulation and understanding." Thus the statute in no provision authorizes the city and county of San Francisco, in its corporate capacity, or by the board of supervisors, its legislative and controlling body, or otherwise, to do anything in the matter of opening and dedicating to public use Montgomery Avenue, or to meddle with the funds provided for the purpose, or to assume any obligation. or responsibility in the matter. The act imposes no obligation or duty upon the corporation or upon its controlling body, nor does it even confer any power to act, in any manner, in regard to the work of opening Montgomery Avenue; while, on the contrary, it expressly provides that it "shall not, in any event whatever, be liable for the payment of the bonds, nor any part thereof, provided to be issued under this act."

The act does not authorize the issue of any bonds of the corporation, and the board of public works must have so understood the statute, for it did not, in fact, issue any such bonds. The instruments, set out in the complaint neither in substance, in form, nor in law, can be regarded as bonds of the city and county of San Francisco. They do not purport, upon their face, to be such, and there was no authority in the board to make them such. The only provisions in the whole act which bring the municipal corporation, in its corporate capacity, into any relations with the opening of the avenue are the provisions in sections 1 and 16 relating to its disposition, after the work is both done and paid for, as provided in the act—after the will of the State has been carried out, and the purpose of the act fully accomplished. The provision of section 1 is that the land described "taken and dedicated for an open public street," "when paid for, as hereinafter provided, the title hereto shall vest in said city and county for such purposes forever, as the title of other public streets in said city and county is vested." Thus, after opening and dedicating the avenue to public use, and paying for it, in the manner provided, which was the task assumed to be performed by the State, the street is donated to the city; and until all this is fully accomplished, the city, in its corporate capacity, has nothing at all to do with the matter. And then, as a consideration for opening and dedicating the land for the avenue, procuring and vesting the title in the city and county, section 16 imposes an obligation on the corporation to thereafter sewer, grade, sidewalk, plank, or pave the avenue, as in the case of other streets already dedicated to public use. The provision is, "The said Montgomery Avenue, when opened, shall be sewered, graded, sidewalked, and planked and paved by the municipal authorities in accordance with the rules, regulations, statutes, and ordinances applicable to the other public streets of the city and county of San Francisco.

Thus the State assumes the duty and work of dedicating and opening Montgomery Avenue, and providing for payment by a fund assessed upon the property determined by itself to be specially benefited by the improvement, and, when its task is fully accomplished, turns the avenue over to the municipal corporation, to be thereafter improved under its direction and authority in the same manner as other public streets are improved, in pursuance of the powers conferred on it by its charter. And, nntil the avenue was thus opened, and turned over to the municipality, the city and county, through its legislative controlling body, or otherwise, had no corporate control over or relation to the matter, and had nothing to do with it.

These bonds were issued in connection with that portion of the work assumed by and carried on exclusively by the State, and under its direction, and with which the corporation had no concern.

The board of public works, and other parties designated by the Montgomery Avenue act to perform the duties therein indicated, performed such duties solely by authority of that act. The duties were not performed by virtue of any authority of the municipal charter, or of any other act conferring power or authority upon the municipal corporation. The consent of the corporation was in no way obtained or asked. The acts were solely performed in pursuance of the express direct command of the statute itself, wholly irrespective of the will or the charter powers of the corporation. They were not performed in the exercise of corporate powers, and they were in no sense corporate acts. The authorities are numerous establishing the proposition that parties so acting by express direction of the statute, without the authority of the municipal corporation, and not acting by virtue of the powers conferred on the corporation by its charter, do not act as officers or agents of the corporation, and the corporation not being the principal, their acts are not the acts of the corporation; they are but the agencies employed by the directing power for the accomplishment of its own purposes.

The following are some of the authorities establishing this self-evident proposition, and it will be sufficient to cite the cases without analyzing or commenting upon them in detail: Sheboygan County *v.* Parker, 3 Wall. 96; Horton *v.* Town of Thompson, 71 N. Y. 521; Board of Park Commissioners *v.* Detroit, 28 Mich. 244–5; People, etc., *v.* Chicago, 51 Ill. 17; Hoagloud *v.* Sacramento, 52 Cal. 149; Tone *v.* Mayor, 70 N. Y. 165; N. Y. & B. S. M. & L. Co. *v.* Brooklyn, 71 N. Y. 584. In Horton *v.* Town of Thompson, *supra*, the court said: " In the present case no action on the part of the town in its corporate capacity, or on the part of any of its officers, was required by the act, or was taken. The money was to be borrowed and the bonds issued by commissioners to be appointed in the manner prescribed by the law. These commissioners were in no sense town officers, nor did they represent the town." P. 521.

The strongest case cited in opposition to the views expressed, and to support the position that the opening of Montgomery Avenue was a municipal and not a State undertaking for which the municipal corporation is liable, is that of Sage *v.* City of Brooklyn, 89 N. Y. 189. But there were several clauses in the statute involved in that case, upon which the court relied, and rested its decision, that are wholly wanting in the Montgomery Avenue case. " Thus," says the chief justice, who delivered the opinion of the majority of the court, " by the third section it is declared that the lands 'shall be deemed to have been taken by the city of Brooklyn for public use.'" Id. 197. " That the improvement of Sackett Street was regarded by the legislature of the State as a city and not a State improvement, also plainly appears from the supplementary act, chapter 592, Laws of 1873. The park commissioners were, by that act, authorized and directed to improve Sackett Street by grading, paving, planting shade-trees, constructing carriage-ways, etc.; and by the fourth section the city was required to issue its bonds for the purpose of raising money to pay the expenses of the improvement, and the money collected on assessments was directed to be paid to the commissioners of the sinking fund, for the redemption of the bonds." Id. 198. Thus, by the express terms of the statute, the land was "deemed to be taken by the city," and the city was expressly made primarily liable, and required to issue its own bonds, and reimburse itself from assessments on the property benefited. There is nothing of this kind in the Montgomery Avenue act, and nothing even looking in that direction. So, also, referring to section 16, of another act, as applicable, the chief justice says: "The direction of section 16, that the comptroller shall pay the land damages, is absolute and unqualified. It is not a direction to pay them out of the assessments when collected, or out of any particular fund." Id. 199. Again: "The city, under that atatute (supplemental act of 1873), was required, primarily, to advance the necessary fund. The provision in the act of 1873 furnishes a strong inference, in favor of the claim, that the legislature, by incorporating section 16 of the charter into the act of 1868, intended to impose upon the city the duty, either primary or ultimate, of paying the landowners." Id. 200. On these, and other similar provisions, the decision was rested. Yet, in the face of these strong provisions of the statutes, showing that the acts in question were intended to be municipal, and not State acts, and expressly imposing the liability on the city, those two able judges, of long service and ripe experience, Earl and Rapallo, dissented, in a clear and cogent opinion, and held the work to be a State and not a municipal work, for which the corporation was not liable. Said Mr. Justice Earl in the case: "The land was taken and appropriated by the direct act of the legislature, and, by the same act, the park commissioners were appointed to enter upon the land and make the improvement. They were not agents of the city, but State agents. They were not officers of the city, and, in what they did, they did not represent the city, and had no authority in any way to bind it, and could in no way make it responsible for these awards. They had the precise authority conferred upon them by the act, and no other; and the liability of the city for their acts, or for the land taken or awards made, is not so much as hinted at by the act."

"For the position that the park commissioners were not agents of the city for whose acts the city could be made responsible, the cases of Maxmilian *v.* The Mayor, 62 N. Y. 160; Tone *v.* The Mayor, 70 Id. 157; and New York and

Brooklyn Sawmill and Lumber Co. *v.* The City of Brooklyn, 71 Id. 580, are abundant authority. The general rule, as deduced from these cases, is that a municipality is not liable for the acts or omissions of an officer in respect to a duty specifically imposed upon him which is not connected with his duties as agent of the corporation, and that such a corporation is only liable for the acts or omissions of officers in the performance of duties imposed upon the principal."—Id., 204.

But, conceding the case to be well decided, the court, in its decision, rested upon express provisions of the statute making the city of Brooklyn responsible, and the case now in hand is entirely different. There is no such provision in the Montgomery Avenue act. That act is, absolutely, barren of any such or similar provisions.

The other cases apparently most confidently relied on to show the liability of the city are Jordan *v.* Cass County, 3 Dill. 185, and Davenport *v.* County of Dodge, 105 U. S. 238. The bonds in the former case were issued by the county in the name of the county, by express direction of the statute. In the latter case the bonds were issued by the county commissioners, the governing body of the county, in pursuance of an express provision of the statute, for a precinct indebtedness. It was held by the supreme court, following the construction adopted by the supreme court of Nebraska, that the county was liable upon the bonds, under the statute authorizing the issue of county bonds, for the precinct indebtedness, but it was held that the indebtedness was to be satisfied out of funds collected from the precinct. In Meath *v.* Phillips County, 108 U. S. 555, the supreme court, referring to this case and the case of Cass County *v.* Johnson, said: "In the case of Cass County, the law provided in terms for an issue of bonds in the name of the county; and in that of the county of Davenport we construed the law to be, in effect, the same. Consequently there were, in those cases, obligations of counties, payable out of special funds." These cases are, therefore, entirely different from the case under consideration. On the contrary, the case of Meath *v.* Phillips County just cited is decisive in favor of the proposition maintained in this opinion—that where the State, or some other district or organization, employs certain officers, desig-

nated by their official names, of a city or county, in pursuance of the statute, as agents or instrumentalities for accomplishing their own proper purposes, such officers, in performing the acts thus required, do not act as officers or agents
of such city or county, but as agents or instrumentalities of
the State, or other district or organization for which the services required by the statutes are performed. 108 U. S. 554–5.

It is clear to my mind, both upon principle and authority,
that the city and county of San Francisco is not, in substance or in form, an obligor on, or party in any CITY OF SAN FRANCISCO HELD
sense to, the bonds and coupons sued on; that un- NOT LIABLE ON BONDS.
der the Montgomery Avenue act it could not have been legally made an obligor on, or party to, the bonds issued in
pursuance of the act; and that, in its corporate capacity, it
has no relation to those bonds, and no duties to perform in
connection therewith. The duties to be performed, whatever they may be, in connection with the bonds and coupons
in suit, by parties who are also officers of the city and county
of San Francisco, are, in my judgment, to be performed by
them, under the provisions of the statute, as agencies or instrumentalities of the State, and not as agents or officers of
the city. It follows, necessarily, that the city and county of
San Francisco, in its corporate character, is in no respect
chargeable with any liability of any kind upon the instruments sued on.

There being no liability of any kind, and no duty to perform by the municipality, in its corporate capacity, in relation
to said instruments, no action or judgment can be rendered
in the case that could avail anything as a foundation for proceeding by *mandamus* to compel the assessment and collection of a fund for the payment of the coupons and ultimate
redemption of the obligations in question. For that, or any
other purpose looking to the collection of the money claimed
to ﾠbe due, the action might just as properly be brought
against the city of Oakland as against the city and county
of San Francisco.

The property-holders of the district liable to be assessed,
under the Montgomery Avenue act, with respect to their
lands and the indebtedness in question do not, JUDGMENT
under the act, stand in any respect in privity with AGAINST CITY NOT BINDING ON
the corporation, the city and county of San Fran- PROPERTY-HOLDERS.

cisco; and, in relation to the instruments in suit, the municipality does not represent either the owners or the lands. Any judgment against the city in this action could not bind or conclude the owners or their property, neither being in any sense parties, or privies to parties, to the suit. The judgment, under such circumstances, could not afford any valid or legal foundation for proceedings by *mandamus* against the parties charged with the duty of assessing and collecting the Montgomery Avenue bond tax; for in that capacity they are not officers, agents, or instrumentalities of the municipal corporation, and they are not in privity with it. A *mandamus* in the national courts is in the nature of process to execute a valid judgment; and it must be against the judgment debtor or obligor, or some one representing the judgment debtor or obligor. A proceeding by *mandamus* against the parties charged with assessing and collecting the tax in question, based upon a judgment in this case, would be very much like proceeding by an execution against B to satisfy a judgment against A, between whom there is no legal relation whatever affected by or affecting the judgment.

If the views expressed are sound, the complaint presents no cause of action against defendant, and the facts alleged and offered to be proved are wholly immaterial.

It would be but a waste of time to occupy the attention of the court in taking testimony which cannot prove or tend to prove any valid cause of action. The complaint is wholly insufficient and the pleadings present no material issue. For the reasons stated in this opinion and in the opinion of the presiding justice, in which I concur, the objection to the introduction of the evidence offered must be sustained.

WHEN PUBLIC AGENCIES APPOINTED TO EXERCISE PUBLIC DUTIES WITHIN THE LIMITS OF A MUNICIPALITY ARE NOT AGENCIES OF THE MUNICIPALITY.—In the principal case it was held that the board of public works for the opening of Montgomery avenue was a separate agency created by the State to act for the State independently of the municipal corporation of the city and county of San Francisco. The opening of the avenue in question being clearly an appropriate exercise of the powers of the sovereignty, the State had the right and power to employ either the agency of the municipal corporation in opening the street, or it could establish an independent special agency for that purpose. It does not, however, follow that because a special agency has been created by statute to exercise some public function or duty, that such special agency is the independent agency of the State. It may well happen that the State may create the agency to exercise the public function or duty as the agency of the municipal corporation; and whether such agency is to be regarded as the agency of the State or that of the municipal corporation is often one of great difficulty. In the case of Maxilian *v.* Mayor, etc., of the City of New York, 62 N. Y. 160, it was held that the Commissioners of Public Charities and Correction, a body created by statute and vested with the control, management, and direction, over all real and personal property of the alms-house, etc., with power of appointment and removal of inferior officers, and to require of the supervisors of the county the levy by tax of such moneys as should be needed by them, and of control of the poor, etc., was an agency of the State and not of the municipal corporation, though it exercised its jurisdiction wholly within the limits of the corporation, and though the commissioners were appointed by the mayor. The decision was based on the fact that the functions exercised by the board were not exercised for the benefit or interest of the municipal corporation as such, and that said functions were purely governmental in their character.

In Tone *v.* Mayor, etc., of the city of New York, 70 N. Y., 157, a board created by statute to revise and correct assessment lists in the city of New York, and composed of the comptroller, counsel to the corporation, and recorder of said city, was said not to be an agency of the municipal corporation. The court say: " In the discharge of their duties, the members of that board acted as independent public officers, engaged in the public service. They were not selected by the corporation, and it could not control their acts. Their powers were clearly defined by the legislature, and were not what might properly be called corporate powers, and they were not to be exercised for the peculiar benefit of the corporation in its local or special interest, but for the public good, in obedience to the mandate of the legislature."

In New York and Brooklyn Saw-mill and Lumber Company *v.* City of Brooklyn, a statute entitled " An act to provide for the assessment and collection of the costs of the improvement of the Gowanus canal in the city of Brooklyn, and for the reconstruction of the docks in the said improvement which have become sunk and unfit for use," it was provided that the common council of the city of Brooklyn should cause to be repaired or rebuilt, at the expense of the city, the docks constructed by the commissioners, where the same had sunk and become unfit for use. The plaintiff claimed that by reason of this act it became the duty of the city of Brooklyn to rebuild the docks on his land which had sunk, and sued the city for omitting to do so. It was held that the common council acted, in regard to the rebuilding of the sunken docks, as the agent of the State and not as that of the corporation of Brooklyn, and, consequently, that the city was not liable for their omission to rebuild the docks. The fact that the repairs were to be made at the expense of the city of Brooklyn was deemed immaterial. New York and Brooklyn Saw-mill and Lumber Company *v.* City of Brooklyn, 71 N. Y. 580.

In Meath *v.* Phillips County, 108 U. S. 553, an act of a State legislature was passed to provide for the reclaiming of overflowed lands by the construction of levees, and for this purpose such lands were divided into levee districts, and levee inspectors were appointed. Provision was made for the taxation of lands to be benefited, said tax to be collected in the same manner as county taxes. Payment of expenses of the work was to be made by means of drafts drawn by the levee inspectors on the levee treasurer. It was held that the levee inspectors were not agents of the county, and that the county was therefore not liable on drafts drawn by the levee inspectors.

In the case of Sage *v.* City of Brooklyn, 89 N. Y. 189, the commissioners of Prospect Park were directed by statute to open, grade, and improve Sackett Street, and to apply in court, on notice given to the city counsel, for the appointment of commissioners to estimate the expense of the improvement and to assess the same upon a district to be fixed by the park commissioners. The State took the lands required for widening Sackett Street, by direct legislative enactment, gave the park commissioners the initiation of proceedings for opening the street, and gave them the control of the street when completed. The majority of the court held that the improvement in question was a municipal as distinguished from a State improvement, that the park commissioners acted as agents of the city and not as agents of the State direct. The following extract from the opinion of the court will show the line of reasoning adopted by the majority : " A municipal corporation is the creature of the State, deriving its public faculties and political powers from the legislature. The legislature may, in place of remitting the question to the discretion of the city authorities, prescribe what local improvements shall be made, and create special agencies for their execution. It is not required to commit their execution to the ordinary representatives of the municipal body; and it may charge the expense of such improvement upon the locality. It does not, therefore, go far towards establishing the claim that a street improvement within a city is a State and not a municipal work, to show that it was directed by the legislature, and that its execution was committed to special agents appointed by the legislative act. In the case of Sackett street, the improvement was not one in which the State at large was specially interested, nor did the State assume the burden of the expense. The people at large were interested in the same sense and no other, in which they are interested in the opening of every highway within the State. But the improvement was peculiarly for the local convenience and advantage of the city of Brooklyn. When the act of 1868 was passed (providing for the improvement in question) Sackett Street was designated on the commissioners' map of the city as one of the city streets. The improvemeat to be made was limited territorially to the city. The unusual width of the proposed avenue was fixed, as may be inferred, not because the accommodation of public travel required so wide a street, but because it was supposed that a wide avenue, set with trees and otherwise improved, would enhance the beauty and attractiveness of the city, and promote the pleasure and comfort of its citizens. The improvement was, as we have said, a part of the park system, and it was with great propriety placed under the control of the park commissioners."

THE STATE MAY EMPOWER A MUNICIPAL CORPORATION TO ACT AS ITS SPECIAL AGENT IN THE EXERCISE OF A SPECIAL PUBLIC DUTY OR FUNCTION.—Where the State wishes to exercise some public function, or perform some act of sovereignty through a special agency, it may, instead of appointing or creating a special agency for the purpose, employ as its agent a municipal corporation already in existence. In such a case, if the State by statute provides for a liability on the part of such agent, contractual or otherwise, this liability will not be a municipal liability. Thus in Jordan *v.* Cass County, 3 Dill. (U. S. C. Ct.) 185, it was held that a statute relating to the furnishing of aid by townships to the building of railroads, which provided for the holding of a township election to decide whether such aid should be furnished or not, and, in case it was voted to furnish the aid, provided that the county court should make the subscription voted in behalf of the township, and, if so voted, should issue in payment of such subscriptions bonds in the name of the county, created the county the agent of the State in regard to the issuing of the bonds, and that judgment could be recovered against the county, as the special agent of the State created to issue the bonds and to be liable on them ; but that the liability of the county was not a municipal liability to be paid out of the general funds of the county, but only a special liability to be paid out of the township funds provided to be raised by special tax through the county machinery for taxation. Accord, see Davenport *v.* County of Dodge, 105 U. S. 237.

THE STATE CANNOT APPOINT OFFICERS OR AGENTS WHO ARE TO HAVE CHARGE OF LOCAL MUNICIPAL AFFAIRS. — Where the State wishes to exercise some public funtion, or perform some act of sovereignty through the agency of the municipal corporation, but by means of special agents or officers who are to act as agents of the corporation, it must leave the appointment of the agents to the municipal corporation, especially if such agents are to have authority to spend corporate funds or pledge the corporate credit. To allow the State to control or regulate property or rights of a municipal corporation by agents selected by itself would encroach on the vested rights of the municipal corporation.

In the case of Board of Park Commissioners *v.* Common Council of Detroit, 28 Mich. 228, by an act of legislature of 1871 certain commissioners were created to propose a plan for a park for the city of Detroit, the plan to be submitted to the vote of a citizens' meeting. Commissioners were duly appointed under this act, and their appointment was ratified by the city. Subsequently the legislature enlarged the powers of the commissioners, giving them power to locate the site of a park or boulevard, to expend a certain sum to be furnished by the city council in the purchase of land, and to condemn land for the park or boulevard. It was held that this act was unconstitutional as placing municipal rights and property at the disposal of an independent agency not appointed by the municipal corporation.

In Sheboygan Co. *v.* Parker, 3 Wall. (U. S.) 93, an act to authorize the county of Sheboygan to aid in the construction of a railroad appointed several persons to act as commissioners, and directed a vote of the people

9 Cor. Cas.—40

of the county to be taken as to whether or not they would have a sub-scription "in pursuance of the act." It was held that the commissioners were lawful agents of the people for the special purpose for which they were appointed, and, though nominated by the legislature, they could not act without the assent of the citizens of the county, ascertained in the manner directed by law; and that, having so acted, the county could not now repudiate their acts.

AUTHORITY TO SELL BONDS AT PAR DOES NOT AUTHORIZE SALE FOR LESS THAN PAR.—It is well settled that the agents, officers, or city council of a municipality cannot bind the corporation by any contract not within the scope of its powers.

The act of May 9, 1879, authorized, *inter alia,* the councils of any city of the second class, of which Pittsburgh was one, by ordinance, to make, execute, and negotiate its bonds, to be known as "improvement bonds," to an amount not exceeding $6,000,000, the proceeds thereof to be used in paying or retiring bonds previously issued by the city for the pur-pose of improving the streets and avenues thereof, and also temporary loan bonds issued to meet the interest on said street bonds, and for no other purposes whatever. . . . The third section of the act declares "they shall be sold at not less than par, with accrued interest, but the said coun-cils may allow a reasonable compensation for the sale or negotiation of the said bonds."

On the 27th of January, 1880, the city of Pittsburgh passed an ordinance authorizing an issue of bonds, substantially in the words of the act of 1879, and declared they should not be sold at lest than par and accrued interest ; but provided that the finance committee or sub-committee there-of might allow a reasonable compensation for the negotiation, sale, or exchange thereof.

Said sub-committee entered into several contracts with the appellants, and, each failing of their object, a final agreement was entered into which stipulated and declared that "the city of Pittsburgh sells at par and accrued interest " to the appellants the whole $6,000,000 of bonds which it was authorized to issue, and allows them a commission of one per cent on all bonds purchased or exchanged by them under the agreement.

On a bill being filed by citizens and taxpayers of the city to enjoin against the performance of the contract, *held,* that practically and substan-tially the transaction was an agreement to sell the bonds to the appellants for less than par and accrued interest, and, being unauthorized by the statute, was illegal and void. Whelen's Appeal, Supreme Court of Penn-sylvania, October, 1885.

EAMES v. SAVAGE.

SAME v. BICKFORD.

(Advance Case, Maine. March 20, 1885.)

Executions upon judgment against towns, may be levied upon the goods and chattels of the inhabitants. The statute of Maine authorizing this process is not in conflict with the fourteenth amendment, United States Constitution.

Strout & Holmes and *J. J. Parlin* for plaintiff.
D. D. Stewart and *A. H. Ware* for defendant.

EMERY, J.—The plaintiff was an inhabitant of the town of Embden, at the time Sarah J· Savage began suit, and   FACTS. recovered judgment against that town in this court. The execution upon that judgment was issued, and was levied upon the plaintiff's goods, pursuant to R. S. of 1871, chap. 84, § 29, now R. S., chap. 84, § 30, which expressly provides that executions against towns shall be issued against the goods and chattels of the inhabitants thereof, and shall be levied upon such goods and chattels. The plaintiff, however, claims that the statute is forbidden, and made null by the last clause of section 6 of the Maine Bill of Rights, which declares that a person accused shall not "be deprived of his life, liberty, property or privileges but by the judgment of his peers, or by the law of the land," and also by that clause in section 1 of the fourteenth amendment to the Constitution of the United States, which declares that no State shall "deprive any person of life, liberty, or property without due process of law."

The presumption is the other way, in favor of the validity of the statute, and it is a presumption of great strength. All the judges and writers agree upon this. Chief Justice Marshall, in Fletcher v. Peck, 6 Cranch, 87, says that STATUTE PRE-SUMED CONSTITU-TIONAL. to overturn this presumption the judges must be convinced, and "the conviction must be clear and strong." Judge Washington, in Ogden v. Saunders, 12 Wheat. 270, declared, that if he rested his opinion on no other ground than a doubt, that alone would be a satisfactory vindication of an opinion in favor of the constitutionality of a statute. Chief Justice Mellen, in Lunt's Case, 6 Me. 413, said, " the court will never pronounce a statute to be otherwise (than constitutional), unless in a case where the point is free from all doubt." This strong presumption is to be constantly borne in mind in considering the question here presented.

The statute itself in this case has existed for half a century, since February 27, 1833, but it introduced no new principle COLLECTION, or rule in the jurisprudence of this State. It FROM INHABI- TANTS, OF JUDG merely affirmed a well-known custom or law MENT AGAINST TOWN. that had long before existed. The practice of bringing suits against a political division or municipal organization and collecting the judgment, from the individuals composing it, is believed to have existed in England and to have been brought thence to New England. Actions against " the hundred," were known as far back as Edw. I. stat. 13, Edw. I. chap. 2 ; 3 Comyn's Dig., " Hundred," chap. 2. As " the hundred" had no property, except that of individuals, the judgments must have been collected from the individuals. In Russell *v.* Men of Devon, 2 T. R. 667, Lord Kenyon said, that indictments against counties were sanctioned by the common law, though they would be levied on the men of the county. In Atty.-Gen. *v.* Exeter, 2 Russ. 45, the chancellor said : " If the fee farm was charged on the whole place called Exeter, he who was entitled to the rent might have demanded it from any one who had a part of, or in the city, leaving the person who was thus called on, to obtain contributions from the other inhabitants as best he could." In New England the practice obtained from the earliest times, without any statute. " About the year 1790, one Gatehill was imprisoned on an execution against the town of Marblehead for a debt the town owed." 5 Dane's Abr., chap. 143, art. 5, §§ 10 and 11, page 158. Mr. Dane as early as his Abridgment, said the practice was justified " by immemorial usage." Ibid. Such an imprisonment so soon after the revolution, when the principles of liberty were so freshly vindicated, would never have been permitted had it not then been a familiar practice. The practice has been regarded as settled law in Massachusetts, and has been repeatedly alluded to in the opinions of the courts, as sanctioned by immemorial usage. Riddle *v.* Proprietors on Merrimac River, 7 Mass. 187 ; Sch.

Dist. *v.* Wood, 13 Id. 198; Brewer *v.* New Gloucester, 14 Id.
216; Marcy *v.* Clark, 17 Id. 330, 335; Merchants' Bank *v.* Cook,
4 Pick. 414; Chase *v.* Merrimack Bank, 19 Id. 568; Gaskill *v.*
Dudley, 6 Metc. 546; Hill *v.* Boston, 122 Mass. 344; s. c.,
23 Am. Rep. 332. The constitutionality of the law does not
seem to have been really questioned, till the case of Chase *v.*
Bank, 19 Pick. 568, as late as 1837, and its constitutionality
was there said to be so well established as not to be an open
question. The people of Maine, while a part of Massachusetts,
were familiar with the law and the practice. The Maine
courts have repeatedly recognized it as long established, and
as in harmony with the State Constitution. Adams *v.* Wiscasset Bank, 1 Me. 361; Fernald *v.* Lewis, 6 Id. 264; Baileyville *v.* Lowell, 20 Id. 178, 181; Spencer *v.* Brighton, 49 Id.
326; Hayford *v.* Everett, 68 Id. 507. Its constitutionality does
not seem to have been questioned by the profession till
Shurtleff *v.* Wiscasset, 74 Me. 130. In Connecticut, also, the
antiquity and constitutionality of the law have been repeatedly affirmed. Burs *v.* Botsford, 3 Day, 159; Beardsley *v.*
Smith, 16 Conn. 368.

That a statute, or rule or law or custom has so long existed,
unquestioned, and has been so often invoked, and universally
approved, and has become ingrained like this, in the jurisprudence of State, is a strong, if not conclusive reason for
pronouncing it constitutional, and a part of the "law of the
land." State *v.* Allen, 2 McCord, 525; Sears *v.* Cottrell, 5
Mich. 251.

The plaintiff urges that such a method of enforcing executions against towns arose out of the early theory that all the
inhabitants were parties to the suit, and could INHABITANTS LI-
appear personally and be heard. It is claimed ABLE ALTHOUGH
NOT PARTIES TO
that when New England towns were first formed, SUIT.
they did not have their present corporate character; that
they were an aggregation of individuals, generally owning
a large amount of territory in common, and with common
rights and common liabilities in respect thereto. These
individuals would necessarily be parties in any suit affecting their common liabilities, and execution must have
issued against them as individuals. In the progress of
time, such inhabitants were by statute made "bodies politic
and corporate." Massachusetts Laws of 1786. Though

they continued to be sued by the name of "the inhabitants of the town of ———," the individuals no longer appeared in court, but the defence was conducted by the town as a unit, through its officers. The argument is, that the town having been made a corporation, and the individual inhabitants debarred from defending personally, he is entitled to his day in court, through some appropriate mesne process, before final process of execution can issue against his private property. It is claimed that a method of enforcing judgments against the inhabitants, which might not have been unjust, when such inhabitants were really parties, has become so, and therefore unconstitutional, since such inhabitants can defend only through a corporate organization. Towns are not, however, full corporations. They have no capital stock, and no shares. They are only *quasi* corporations, created solely for political and municipal purposes, and given a *quasi* corporate character for convenience only. They remain still an aggregation of individuals, dwelling within certain territorial limits, and under the direct jurisdiction of the legislature. But legislatures in creating purely private corporations have an unquestioned power to prescribe the personal liability of a stockholder therein for corporate debts, and the method of enforcing it. They can limit this liability to the amount of his stock, or to his proportionate share, or can make him liable without limit. Morawetz on Corp. § 606 *et seq.;* Pollard *v.* Bailey, 20 Wall. 520; Hawthorne *v.* Calef, 2 Id. 10. The common method of enforcement is by first recovering judgment against the corporation, and then bringing some specified process against the stockholder. But under such proceedings against him, the stockholder cannot question the judgment against the corporation except for fraud. He is bound by such judgment until reversed. Morawetz on Corp. § 619; Marsh *v.* Burrough, 1 Woods, 470; Milliken *v.* Whitehouse, 49 Me. 527. The proceedings against the person alleged to be stockholder are to establish the fact that he is a stockholder, within the statute liability. In some instances, the statutes have permitted a judgment creditor of a corporation to determine for himself at his peril (of course indemnifying the officer), what persons are stockholders, liable for the debt, and to levy the execution directly on the prop-

Marginal notes: STATUS OF TOWNS AS CORPORATIONS. — PERSONAL LIABILITY OF MEMBERS OF CORPORATIONS.

erty of such persons without any intermediate process. The question of liability as stockholder would then be tried in a suit against the officer. This latter mode of enforcement, though perhaps harsher than the other, has been repeatedly held to be constitutional, and we do not know of any case holding otherwise. Morawetz on Corp. §§ 618, 619, and notes ; Leland *v.* Marsh, 16 Mass. 391 ; Marsy *v.* Clark, 17 Id. 330; Stedman *v.* Eveleth, 6 Metc. 115, 124, 125 ; Gray *v.* Coffin, 9 Cush. 205 ; Holyoke Bank *v.* Goodman Paper Co., Id. 576. See, also, Merrill *v.* Suffolk Bank, 31 Me. 57 ; Came *v.* Bridgham, 39 Id. 35. In Penniman's Case, 103 U. S. 714, the statute of Rhode Island authorized the arrest of a stockholder on an execution against the corporation. The constitution, ality of the statute was directly affirmed by the State court, and was assumed without question by the United States supreme court. The principle is analogous to that which permits a creditor holding an execution against A without first instituting any process to determine their ownership. If B's goods be taken, he has a remedy against the officer, or can successfully resist him. A is not injured in either event. If the person whose goods are sought to be taken on an execution against a corporation is liable as stockholder for the debt, he is not injured thereby. If he is not liable he has the same rights and remedies as B.

But the plaintiff urges, that whatever may have been the adjudications heretofore, upon this method of enforcing a judgment against a municipal or other corporation, by levying upon the property of any member, it is LEVY ON PROPERTY OF LIABILITY OF TOWN: DUE PROCESS OF LAW. now forbidden by that clause of the fourteenth amendment to the United States Constitution already quoted. He claims that "due process of law," as there used, requires a notice to him personally and an opportunity for him to be heard in court, before execution issue against his property. The general proposition would be that "due process of law" means judicial process with *judex, actor* and *res.* This proposition may seem to be supported by some general remarks of judges, and writers, but no case in point is cited, nor, indeed, any direct assertion.

The phrase "due process of law" in the United States Constitution, and in the Constitutions of many of the States, and the phrase "law of the land," in the Constitutions of others of the

States, including Maine, have long had the same meaning. 2
Coke's Inst. 50, 51. English political history is full of the
strife between the crown and the people, the crown seeking
to enlarge its irresponsible prerogatives, and the people insisting on fixed and certain laws. The Magna Charta, and the
various Bills of Rights, in which these phrases were used,
were demanded from the kings, as safeguards against arbitrary
action, against partial or unequal decrees. The barons and
people insisted on general laws, *legum terræ*, on uniformity,
"due process of law." They insisted on law, however harsh,
as better security than the prerogative, however indulgent.
These phrases did not mean merciful, not even just laws, but
they did mean equal and general laws, fixed and certain. The
solicitude was to preserve the property of the subject from
inundation of the prerogative. Broom's Const. Law, 228.
The English colonies in America were familiar with the conflict between customary law and arbitrary prerogative, and
claimed the protection of those charters. When they came
to form independent governments, they sought to guard
against arbitrary or unequal governmental action, by inserting
the same phrases in their Constitutions. They insisted that
all proceedings against the individual or his property should
be uniform, and by general law. They put the same limitation upon the Federal Government in the fifth constitutional
amendment. In commenting on these phrases, Mr. Cooley
cites with approval the language of Mr. Justice Johnson in
Bank of Columbia *v.* Okely, 4 Wheat. 235: "As the words
from Magna Charta, incorporated into the Constitution of
Maryland, after volumes spoken and written with a view to
their exposition, the good sense of mankind has settled down
to this, that they were intended to secure the individual from
the arbitrary exercise of the powers of government unrestrained by the established principles of private rights and
distributive justice." Cooley on Const. Law. 335. Judge
Green, in Bank *v.* Cooper, 2 Yerger, 599 (24 Am. Dec. 523),
said: "By law of the land is meant a general and public law,
operating equally on every individual in the community." He
also said that such was the opinion of the distinguished Judge
Catron and of Lord Coke.

Chief Justice Hemphill, in Janes *v.* Reynolds, 2 Texas, 251,
said: "The terms 'law of the land' . . . are now in their most

usual acceptation regarded as public laws, binding upon all the members of the community under their circumstances, and not partial or private laws." O'Neal, J., in State *v.* Simmons, 2 Spear, 767, said: "The words mean the common law, and the statute law existing in the State at the time of the adoption of the Constitution." But it has been expressly decided, that due process of law does not always mean judicial process. The individual's property is often taken for taxes without his being first warned and heard, and it is nowhere contended now that such summary process is not due process of law. It is the fixed, certain process, applicable to all, and not partial, nor unequal. McMillen *v.* Anderson, 95 U. S. 37. Mr. Justice Miller in the opinion said: "By summary is not meant arbitrary, or unequal, or illegal. It (the collection of the tax) must, under our Constitution, be lawfully done."

But that does not mean, nor does the phrase "due process of law" mean, by a judicial proceeding.

In Murray *v.* Hoboken Land Co., 18 How. 272, a warrant of distress was issued by the solicitor of the treasury against the collector of New York, upon a certificate of the first comptroller, that the collector was indebted to the treasury. The collector had not been notified nor heard so far as appears. The statute authorizing such a process was held constitutional. Judge Curtis, on page 276, said: "The Constitution contains no description of those processes which it was intended to allow or forbid. It does not even declare what the principles are to be applied to ascertain whether it be due process." See, also, Davidson *v.* New Orleans, 96 U. S. 97; Walker *v.* Sauvinet, 92 Id. 90. It does not follow that every statute is the "law of the land," nor that every process authorized by a legislature is "due process of law." It must not offend against "the established principles of private rights and distributive justice." This statute does not. It does not transfer A's property to B. It only makes A's property liable to be taken for a debt he, in common with others, owes to B. A can save his property by paying the judgment against his town, which judgment binds him and all the other inhabitants, and is a judgment he and each of the others ought to pay. Whether he pays or lets his property be sold, he can recover full damages of the town, and have the same final process for the collection of his debt. In the end he only pays his ratable share of the common debt. The statute is general, and is uniform in its application, to every town, and every inhabitant. It may not be in theoretical harmony with other methods of procedure, but it accomplishes its laudable purpose of compelling towns to pay their debts, without doing any injustice. Towns really obtain credit at low rates of interest upon the strength of it, and to now pronounce it void would destroy this credit, would work widespread disaster among those who have so confidently invested their savings in loans to towns.

The words " due process of law" in the fourteenth amendment do not have any enlarged nor different meaning from that heretofore ascribed to them. The amendment does not make Federal law, and Federal process of law, the law of the land and due process of law in each State. Whatever was due process of law in any State before the amendment, is due process of law in that State since the amendment. Before the amendment, the final determination of the question whether a State statute was according to the law of the land, rested with the courts of the State. Since the amendment, it rests with the supreme court of the United States. It is through this operation of the amendment, that the citizen receives additional protection against unequal and partial laws.

The United States supreme court considering and determining such a question, will look mainly at the fundamental law, and general jurisprudence of the State. If the statute or process is found to be of ancient origin, to have been fully acquiesced in, to be general in its character, and impartial in its application, and interwoven with the business of the people, that court will not pronounce against it because it is anomalous or has not been adopted elsewhere. The plaintiff cites Rees *v.* Watertown, 19 Wall. 107, and Meriwether *v.* Garrett, 102 U. S. 472, not as decisive or applicable authorities, but for some general observations in the opinions upon, 'due process of law." In neither case was there a comparison of a State statute with the fourteenth amendment, and in both cases—19 Wall. 122 and 102 U. S. 519—the New England method of enforcing judgments against municipalities is expressly noticed as an exception to the application of the general observations quoted by plaintiff, and is not even incidentally condemned. Elsewhere in the opinions of the same court, this method has been alluded to as actual, existing and binding law, and nowhere has it, even by implication, been declared contrary to the New England law of the land, or the fourteenth amendment. Riggs *v.* Johnson County, 6 Wall. 191 ; Supervisor *v.* Rogers, 7 Id. 180 ; Barkley *v.* Levee Commissioners, 93 U. S. 265.

The statute in question must be held to be constitutional, and unaffected by the fourteenth amendment.

Judgment for the defendant in each case.

PETERS, C. J., WALTON, DANFORTH, LIBBEY and FOSTER, JJ., concurred.

ENFORCEMENT OF JUDGMENTS AGAINST MUNICIPALITY BY EXECUTION ON INHABITANTS.—In Horner *v.* Coffey, 25 Miss. 434, a town was incorporated with the usual powers of contracting, suing and being sued, and levying taxes. A judgment was recovered against the corporation, on which execution was returned *nulla bona*. The corporation refused to levy a tax to pay the judgment, and thereupon the creditor issued another execution, and levied upon the private property of the inhabitants. The court restrained the proceedings, holding that in the absence of express provision private property could not be taken for corporate debts. The same doctrines are held in Alabama. Miller *v.* McWilliams, 50 Ala. 427. There the court observes : " The authority that contracts the debt should attend to its liquidation. After the amount of the liability is fixed by judgment against the corporation, and execution issued on such judgment is returned ' no property found,' then it becomes the duty of the corporate government to levy and collect such a tax as may be necessary to discharge the judgment thus existing. If they fail to do this, *mandamus* is the proper remedy."

The following cases will show that the decision in the principal case is well-settled law in New England : Beardsley *v.* Smith, 16 Conn. 368 ; Burs *v.* Botsford, 3 Day (Conn.) 159 ; Hawkes *v.* Kennebec, 7 Mass. 461 ; Chase *v.* Merrimack Bank, 19 Pick. (Mass.) 564 ; Gaskill *v.* Dudley 6 Met. (Mass.) 546 ; Riddle *v.* Proprietors on Merrimac River, 7 Mass. 187 ; School District *v.* Wood, 13 Mass. 198 ; Brewer *v.* New Gloucester, 14 Mass. 216 ; Marsy *v.* Clark, 17 Mass. 330 ; Merchants' Bank *v.* Cook, 4 Pick. 414 ; Hill *v.* Boston, 122 Mass. 349 ; Adams *v.* Wiscasset Bank, 1 Me. 361 ; Fernald *v.* Lewis, 6 Me. 264 ; Baileyville *v.* Lowell, 20 Me. 178 ; Spencer *v.* Brighton, 49 Me. 326 ; Hayford *v.* Everett, 68 Me. 507 ; Shurtleff *v.* Wiscasset, 74 Me. 130.

In Hill *v.* Boston, 122 Mass. 349, the court observes : " By the common law of Massachusetts and of other New England States, derived from immemorial usage, the estate of any inhabitant of a county, town, territorial parish or school district, is liable to be taken on execution of a judgment against the corporation. . . . In this Commonwealth, payment of such a judgment has never been compelled by *mandamus* against the corporation, as in other parts of the United States."

TOWN OF ONTARIO
v.
HILL *et al.*

(*Advance Case, New York. June 9, 1885.*)

Bonds issued by a town for the construction of a railroad under an act authorizing the same, upon consent being obtained of a majority of the taxpayers, are void unless such consent has actually been given. The affidavits of the assessors certifying that such consent had been obtained, and upon which the bonds were authorized to be issued, are not conclusive as against the town, and in an action brought upon the bonds the town may show that consent of a majority of the taxpayers had not been given.

But no action will lie on behalf of the town against the commissioners for damages sustained by the wrongful issuing of the bonds. The verified certificate of the assessors, made in conformity with the act, is a justification of and protection to the commissioners, acting in good faith, in issuing the bonds.

THIS action was brought against the defendants to recover damages sustained by the plaintiff by reason of their official misconduct as railroad commissioners, in issuing the bonds of the town of Ontario to the amount of $85,000 in aid of the construction of " The Lake Ontario Shore Railroad," under chapter 241 of the Laws of 1869. The defendants were appointed commissioners December 24, 1870. In May, 1871, they subscribed for $85,000 of the stock of the road at par, and agreed to pay therefor in the bonds of the town. In September, 1871, they issued $51,000 of the bonds, and $34,000 thereof on or before July, 1873. Prior to the commencement of the action suits had been brought in the United States court in favor of holders of bonds issued by the commissioners, against the town of Ontario, and judgment recovered thereon, and collected of the town, which judgments, with interest thereon to the time of the trial of this action, amounted to $17,710.05.

The second section of the act of 1869 makes it lawful for commissioners appointed under the first section to borrow money on the credit of the town, city, or village, not exceeding twenty per cent of the assessed valuation of its property according to the last assessment-roll, and to execute bonds therefor, but subject to the condition and prohibition that no debt shall be contracted or bonds issued, until the written consent "shall first have been obtained of persons owning more than one half of the taxable property assessed and appearing upon the last assessment-roll of such town, incorporated village, or city, and a majority of the taxpayers as appears by such assessment-rolls respectively, and which fact shall be proved by the affidavits of the assessors, or a majority of them, of such towns," etc., and it is made the duty of the assessors to make such affidavits. The section further provides that when the consent shall have been obtained, the affidavit, consent and a copy of the assessment-roll shall be filed, and that the same shall be evidence of the facts therein contained and certified in any court of the State, and before any judge or justice thereof. Prior to August 30, 1870, the defendants, acting as citizens, and having at that time no official relation to the town, procured consents to the bonding of the town and presented them on that day to the board of assessors, and the assessors thereupon made the affidavit provided for in section 2 of the act, and the affidavit, consent and assessment-rolls were filed as provided therein.

In August, 1871, after the defendants had been appointed commissioners and after they had subscribed to the stock of the railroad, but before they had issued the bonds, an action was brought by two taxpayers of the town, on behalf of themselves and others against these defendants as railroad commissioners, and other parties, to restrain the issuing of the bonds, and in the complaint which was sworn to, it was charged that a sufficient number of consents had not been obtained. In September, 1871, the suit was withdrawn as the result of an arrangement between the plaintiffs therein and the railroad company to reduce the town subscription to the stock from $107,000, as originally contemplated, to $85,000. The question whether the requisite number of consents to issuing the bonds had been obtained was litigated on the trial of the present action. It was substantially conceded that the requisite amount of property was represented by the consenters. But upon an analysis being made of the contents of the assessment-roll, and the consents, and after a minute and careful examination instituted by witnesses, and after going through a process of addition and subtraction in respect to the names on the assessment-roll, and a deduction from the consents of names improperly there, it was made to appear that a few less than a majority of the taxpayers had signed the consents. The official misconduct charged in the complaint is, in substance, that the commissioners issued the bonds, knowing that the majority of taxpayers had not consented, and that they procured the assessor to make the affidavit by false representations that the consents contained such majority. The trial judge directed a verdict for the plaintiff for $17,710.35, and refused to submit the question as to the good faith of the defendants. Other facts appear in the opinion.

W. F. Cogswell for appellant.

Chas. H. Roys for respondent.

ANDREWS, J.—The question of the invalidity of town bonds issued under circumstances similar to those in this case is not an open one in this State. The evidence, upon a careful analysis, discloses that, although the signatures to the consent exceed in number one half of the names on the assessment-roll, nevertheless when they are sifted, and only such names are counted as were legally entitled to be reckoned, there are of qualified signers something less than a majority of those whose names are upon the assessment-roll of 1869. There was a failure, therefore, to comply with the funda-

CONSENT OF TAX-PAYERS ESSEN-TIAL TO CREA-TION OF BONDED DEBT. mental condition of the bonding acts, that a certain proportion of taxpayers, as specified in the particular act, should consent to the bond-

ing before a debt should be created or bonds be issued. The act of 1869 does not substitute the affidavit of the assessors, therein provided for, in place of the fact of consent, or make it conclusive evidence of the performance of the condition. The town bonding acts have usually contained some provision for a verification of the fact of consent by the affidavit of assessors or other persons.

The act, chapter 375 of the Laws of 1852, which came under the consideration of this court in Starin *v.* Town of Genoa, 23 N. Y. 440, requires that the supervisor and commissioners

AUTHORITIES AS TO ASSESSORS' AFFIDAVITS OF CONSENT, AND CONCLUSIVENESS THEREOF. who, under that act, were charged with the duty of obtaining the consent, or some one or more of them, should make an affidavit, to be attached to the consent and to be filed, to the

effect that the persons assenting comprised two thirds of the resident taxpayers on the previous assessment-roll, but there was no provision making the affidavit evidence. The court held that in an action on this bond the affidavit was not competent evidence of the fact certified, and that the plaintiff was bound to prove affirmatively by competent common-law evidence that the required number of taxpayers had consented.

The act of 1869, under which the bonds in this case were issued, is broader than the act of 1852, considered in the Starin Case. It declares that the fact that the requisite consent had been obtained, should be provèd by the affidavit of the assessors, and that the affidavit, consent and a copy of the assessment-roll should be filed, and they are made evidence in any court, or before any judge, of the facts therein contained.

A similar provision in the act, chapter 398 of the Laws of 1866, was construed by this court. Cagwin *v.* Town of Hancock, 84 N. Y. 532. The action in that case was brought against the town to recover the amount of interest coupons on town bonds issued under the act, which the plaintiff had purchased for full value from a holder of bonds, who was also a purchaser for value. The action was defended on the ground that the requisite number of taxpayers had not consented to the bonding, and the trial court sustained the defence. The judgment was reversed by the general term on the ground that the affidavit of the assessor made in conformity with the terms of the act, before the bonds were issued, was conclusive of the fact therein stated, in favor of a *bona fide* holder of the securities. This court reversed the judgment of the general term and affirmed the judgment of the trial court on the ground that by the true construction of the act the affidavit was made *prima facie* evidence only of the fact certified, and that the defendant was not precluded thereby from showing that in truth and fact the requisite consent had not been obtained, and further that there could be no *bona fide* holding of bonds issued without consent in fact, which would preclude the town from contesting their validity.

These cases, considered in connection with the proof in this case. establish the proposition that the bonds issued by the defendants never had a legal inception, and were void. The town could have successfully defended against them in the courts of the State, and it would be no answer to the defence that the bonds were held by purchasers for value without actual notice of the defect in the authority of the commissioners. The town has been compelled to pay a portion of the bonds, pursuant to judgments obtained in the courts of the United States, in opposition to the rule and principle established in the courts of this State. But conceding, as we must upon the evidence, that the bonds were issued by the defendants without authority, in the sense that they were issued without the requisite consent having in fact been obtained, so as to make them valid obligations of the town, it does not follow that the defendants, in issuing the bonds, were guilty of official misconduct. The second section of the act of 1869 prescribes a rule of conduct and judgment for the government of the commissioners in determining the question whether the requisite consent of taxpayers, in number and in respect of property, has been obtained, so as to justify them in performing the executive and ministerial act of executing and delivering the bonds. They, of course, are bound to act in good faith and without fraud, but so acting, the verified certificate of the assessors, made in conformity with the act, is a complete justification of and protection to them in issuing the bonds, whatever the abstract truth may be, and whether or not the requisite majority of taxpayers have consented. The act is incapable of any other reasonable construction. The commissioners are authorized to issue the bonds upon the consent of the majority of taxpayers, representing a majority of the taxable property appearing on the assessment-roll. But they are not charged with the duty of procuring the consent or of ascertaining the fact of consent by inquiry, or the examination of witnesses, or from a comparison of the assessment with the consent.

The second section prohibits commissioners from contracting any debt, unless the specified consent shall first have been obtained, and then follows the clause, "and which fact shall be proved by the affidavits of the assessors," etc., thus plainly making the affidavits the evidence upon which the commissioners are to act in determining whether the requisite consent has been given. The affidavit protects the commissioners acting in good faith, because the legislature manifestly so intended. It does not protect the bondholders, because the assessors and commissioners are mere agencies to bind the town on the precedent condition of actual consent, the performance of which purchasers must ascertain at their peril, and while the affidavit of the assessors and the act of the commissioners afford some assurance of the regularity and validity of the proceedings, they are, as to third persons, the assertions of special public agents, which do not bind the town.

The town is not, however, remediless in case the assessors, contrary to the fact, certify that the requisite consent has been obtained, or, in case the commissioners, acting upon the certificate, issue the bonds. The proceedings may be reviewed on *certiorari*, People, *ex rel.* Yawger, *v.* Allen, 52 N. Y. 538; People, *ex rel.* Haines, *v.* Smith, 45 Id. 772; the town may bring an equitable action to cancel the bonds and restrain their transfer, Town of Springport *v.* Teutonia Sav. Bank, 75 Id. 397; s. c., 84 Id. 403; or it may await the bringing of an action to enforce the bonds and defend on the ground of their invalidity. Starin *v.* Town of Genoa, and Cagwin *v.* Town of Hancock, *supra*.

The trial court directed a verdict for the plaintiff for the amount of the judgments recovered and collected of the town, with interest, and refused to submit the question of the good faith of the defendants to the jury. We are of opinion that this direction was erroneous. If there was any evidence of bad faith on the part of the defendants in issuing the bonds, it was, to say the least, far from being conclusive. The defendants testified that they believed that the requisite number of taxpayers had consented, and issued the bonds in good faith, relying upon the affidavit of the assessors. It is claimed that they had notice from the complainant in the action brought by Gales and others in 1871, that the majority had not consented. It is true that this was charged in the complaint in that action, but the plaintiffs discontinued the action soon after its commencement upon a settlement between the plaintiffs and the railroad company, which assumed that bonds to some amount had been authorized, and the issue of consent or non-consent was not tried. The defendants were not bound to accept the statement of the plaintiffs in that action, as against the affidavits of the assessors. So also the fact that a paper purporting to be a revocation of consent on the part of certain taxpayers was, in 1870, served on one of

9 Cor. Cas.—41

the persons who was subsequently appointed a commissioner, did not tend to show fraud on the part of the commissioner in acting upon the certificate of the assessors.

The general course of adjudication in this State up to 1873 was adverse to the right of a consenting taxpayer afterward to revoke or withdraw his consent. *In re* Town of Greene, 38 How. 515; People, *ex rel.* Hoag, *v.* Peck, 4 Lans. 528; People, *ex rel.* Sayre, *v.* Franklin, 5 Id. 129. The contrary rule was first declared in People, *ex rel.* Irwin, *v.* Sawyer, 52 N. Y. 296, decided in 1873.

The claim that the defendants induced the assessors to make the affidavit, by the false representation that a majority had consented, was controverted on the trial. The affidavit was made before the defendants had been appointed commissioners, and if what took place at that time tended to show that their subsequent action as commissioners was not in good faith, it was a matter for the jury.

The same is true in respect to the claim that the defendants knew that the affidavit was made without an actual comparison by the assessors of the consent with the assessment-roll, and if this was known to them, it would not establish that they knew the affidavit was false.

We are of opinion that the plaintiff failed to maintain his action on the merits, and that the verdict was improperly directed. This conclusion renders it unnecessary to consider the other questions in the case.

The order of the general term should be affirmed, and judgment absolute entered for the defendants on the stipulation.

All concur.

MORSE

v.

CITY OF WORCESTER.

(*Advance Case, Massachusetts. June 29, 1885.*)

When the legislature authorizes a city or town to construct sewers, or to use a natural stream as a sewer, it is not to be assumed that it intends that it may be done in such a way as to create a nuisance, unless this is the necessary result of the powers granted; and if it is practicable to do the work authorized without creating a nuisance, it is to be presumed that the legislature intended it should be done so. This, however, does not imply the duty of the city to adopt an extensive system of purification independent of the construction of the sewers, or require the taking of large tracts of land not authorized by statute for that purpose.

BILL in equity praying that the defendant may be required to abate a nuisance, caused by the emptying its sewers into Mill brook, and adopt reasonable and proper precautions and methods for the purification of the waters discharged from Mill brook into Blackstone river. The defendant demurred to the bill. The case was heard by a single justice and reserved for the consideration of the full court upon the bill and demurrer.

R. M. Morse, Jr., and *J. Hopkins* for plaintiff.
E. R. Hoar and *F. P. Goulding* for defendant.

MORTON, C. J.—The statute of 1867, chap. 106, authorized the city of Worcester to fix the boundaries of several brooks, named therein, one of which is Mill brook, an actual stream emptying into the Blackstone river, and to alter, change, widen, straighten, and deepen the channels of said brooks and remove obstructions therefrom, and to use and appropriate such brooks, cover them, frame, and inclose them, FACTS. in retaining walls, so far as they shall adjudge necessary for purposes of sewerage, drainage, and the public health. The bill alleges that the city, acting under this statute, has changed, widened, and deepened the channel of Mill brook and now uses it for the purpose of the sewerage and drainage of the city, having constructed a great number of sewers and drains emptying into it; that the whole sewage of the city is discharged into it and through it into the Blackstone river; that a nuisance is thereby created, by which the plaintiff, who is the owner of a mill-site on the Blackstone river, is greatly injured; that the city could and should have so constructed said sewers and drains, and should have so properly purified the sewage passing through them, as not to create a nuisance; and that it " carelessly, negligently, and unnecessarily so constructed said sewers and drains, and carelessly, negligently, and unnecessarily so destroyed the waters therefrom, and so negligently omitted to take reasonable and proper precautions and methods in the construction of said sewers and drains and purification of said waters," that the nuisance complained of is created.

The defendant demurs to the bill and, therefore, for the purposes of this hearing, we must take all the facts alleged to be true. The question of the rights and duties of the city in the use of Mill brook as a sewer has been before this court in several previous cases. Merrifield *v.* Worcester, 110 Mass. 216; Washburn & Moen Manufacturing Co. *v.* Worcester, 116 Id. 458.

When the legislature authorized a city or town to construct sewers, or to use a natural stream as a sewer, it is not to be assumed that it intends to authorize the city or town so to construct its sewers, or so to use the stream, as to create a nuisance, unless this is the necessary result of the powers granted. On the contrary, if it is practicable to do the work authorized without creating a nuisance, it is to be presumed that the legislature intended that it should be so done. This principle has been recognized and applied in many cases. Haskell *v.* New Bedford, 108 Mass. 208; Brayton *v.* Fall River, 113 Id. 218; Boston Rolling Mills *v.* Cambridge, 117 Id. 396; Stainton *v.* Metropolitan Board of Works, 23 Beav. 225; Mersey Docks Trustees *v.* Gibbs, L. R., 1 H. of L. 93; Atty.-Gen. *v.* Colney Hatch Lunatic Asylum, L. R., 4 Ch. 147; Atty.-Gen. *v.* Leeds Corporation, L. R., 5 Ch. 583.

The English cases we have cited were decided under statutes differing from ours, but they are instructive for their statements and discussions of the general principles applying in such cases, irrespective of the particular provisions of their statutes. In the case at bar, the legislature authorized the city of Worcester to use Mill brook as a sewer; by necessary implication the statute authorized it to empty its sewage into Blackstone river, but we cannot presume that it was the intention of the legislature to exempt the city from the obligation to use due care in the construction and management of its works, so as not to cause any unnecessary, injurious consequences to the rights of others. If it is practicable to use any methods of constructing the sewer, and, as a part of the construction, of purifying the sewer at its mouth, at an expense which is reasonable, having regard to the nature of the work and the magnitude and importance of the interests involved, it is the duty of the city to adopt such methods. The bill alleges negligence in constructing the sewer and in failing to use reasonable caution to purify the sewage. Negligence in this, as in most other cases, is largely a question of degree. If the plaintiff shows that in constructing the sewer, or in adapting the brook to its use as a sewer, the defendant did the work in an improper manner, his bill can be maintained. So, if he proves that the defendant, in constructing the sewer, could have adopted, at an expense which is reasonable, a system of cesspools, or some other methods of purification, at the mouth of the brook, it may be that his bill can be maintained. We cannot say, in advance, that some such methods may not be practicable and within the duty of the defendant, to use reasonable precautions, in doing the work authorized by the statute, to prevent a nuisance. The allegations of the bill are so broad that the demurrer cannot be sustained. The question whether, upon the existing facts and conditions, the defendant has been guilty of any negligence, cannot be determined until such facts are developed by the evidence at the hearing. This is all that is necessary for the decision of this case.

But to prevent misunderstanding we add, that, if the only mode of preventing the pollution of the river is found to be by the adoption of an extensive system of purification, independent of the construction of the sewer, requiring AUTHORITY TO CONVERT BROOK the taking of large tracts of land, we must not be INTO A SEWER LIMITED: EMIN- understood as implying that it is within the duty ENT DOMAIN. or the power of the defendant to do this. The power to convert the brook into a sewer carries, by implication, the power to expend money for any plan of work which is an incident or part of the main work authorized by the statute; but it would seem that the statute does not give the defendant power to take lands or expend money for an independent system of sewage purification. If such system is rendered necessary by the construction of the sewer, the remedy must be sought from the legislature, which can best adjust and settle the conflicting rights aud interests of the public and the riparian owners upon the river. The bill further alleges, as an independent ground of relief, that the defendant has, within six years past, changed the outlet or mouth of Mill river, so that it empties into the river at a point much nearer the plaintiff's mill than the original mouth was. We are of opinion that this was within the power given by the statute to alter and change the channels of the brooks. This power embraced the whole brook, and gave the right to make a change in its mouth as well as in any other part of the brook. Woodward *v.* Worcester, 121 Mass. 245. There are no allegations to show that the city, before doing this, had exhausted its powers under the statute, or that for any reason the act was illegal.

Demurrer overruled.

CITY OF ATCHISON *et al. v.* STATE *ex rel.* TUFTS.

DILGERT *et al. v.* SAME.

ATCHISON NAT. BANK *v.* SAME.

(Advance Case, Kansas. November 7, 1885.)

Where a city, without authority of law, caused a tax to be levied and extended upon the tax-roll for the purpose of creating a fund with which to pay certain bonds theretofore issued and delivered in payment of bridges that had been built therein, and after the tax-roll had come to the hands of the county treasurer for the collection of the taxes, a number of the taxpayers of the city voluntarily paid the illegal tax thus levied. *Held,* that the public has no such interest in the money thus paid as will authorize the State to interfere and to maintain an action in the name of the State, enjoining the treasurer from paying out the money so received by him, and from disbursing it in· accordance with the will of those who paid the same.

ERROR from Atchison county.

Action for injunction brought in the district court of Atchison county on December 31, 1884, in the name of the State of Kansas, on the relation of James F. Tufts, acting county attorney of Atchison county, Kansas, against the city of Atchison, Charles J· Drury, as city treasurer of the city of Atchison, Dilgert & Wagner, John Peterson, James A. Loper, county treasurer of Atchison county, Kansas, and the Atchison National Bank. Demurrer sustained. Exceptions, and petition in error. The opinion sufficiently shows the facts.

Everest & Waggener and *Smith & Solomon* for plaintiffs in error.

Coates & Bird for defendant in error.

JOHNSTON, J.—On April 24, 1884, the city council of the city of Atchison enacted an ordinance appropriating $25,000 with which to build certain bridges in the city, and as there was no money in the treasury for that purpose, it was therein provided that the proposition of issuing the bonds   FACTS. of the city in the amount of $25,000, to be used in payment of the bridges, and the levy of a special tax to pay such bonds, should be submitted to the qualified voters of the city for their ratification or rejection. In accordance with the provisions of the ordinance, the election was held on the fourteenth day of May, 1884, and upon the canvass of the vote by the proper authorities it was found and declared that the proposition had been carried. The city then entered into contracts with the defendants Dilgert & Wagner and John Peterson for the construction of the bridges, and issued and delivered the bonds that had been voted in payment therefor. Afterwards the city levied, and caused to be extended upon the tax-roll a special tax of eight mills on the dollar of the taxable property of the city, for the purpose of paying the bridge bonds. The county treasurer obtained the possession of the tax-roll and proceeded to collect this tax, and had collected a considerable amount thereof, when, on December 31, 1884, this action was brought in the name of the State of Kansas by the acting county attorney of Atchison county. It was alleged by the plaintiff that the bonds issued for the building of the bridges were for many reasons unauthorized by law, and that the tax levied for the payment of the bonds was illegal and void ; and the plaintiff prayed the court to enjoin the disbursement of the money collected, or to be collected, upon such levy. To this extent a temporary injunction was granted, and upon the exceptions to the refusal of the court to vacate the temporary injunction, and to the ruling of the court upon the demurrers to plaintiff's petition filed by defendants, they come here by their several petitions in error, and raise the question that the State of Kansas has no special interest in the subject-matter of the controversy, and therefore cannot maintain this action.

In the determination of this question we must assume the truth of all proper allegations in plaintiff's petition, and for the purposes of this case we will assume, but not decide, that the tax in question, a portion of which has been collected, is excessive, illegal, and void. It is to be noticed that the contention in the case is in regard to the disposition of the money arising from the alleged illegal levy. The plaintiff does not seek to stay the hand of any of the officers in the further collection of the tax, but only asked what the district court granted, namely: that the defendants be "enjoined from demanding payment of, or receiving, taxes heretofore collected, or that may be hereafter collected, on account of said levy of taxes for special bridge fund, the same being a tax of eight mills on the dollar, for the year 1884, and enjoined from paying out any of the money by them hereafter received on tax levy of the city of Atchison of what is known as the 'special bridge fund tax.'" Conceding, then, that the tax is illegal, what interest has the State of Kansas in the controversy? If private rights and private interests only are involved, then the State cannot maintain the action. It can only be brought by the party who is beneficially or INTEREST OF specially interested in the subject-matter. This is STATE IN FUNDS DERIVED FROM ILLEGAL TAXES. not a case to prevent a corporation or its officers from violating the law, or from abusing the powers conferred upon it by the law. The bonds alleged to be unauthorized and illegal have long since been executed and delivered. The bridges, for the payment of which the bonds were issued, have been built and paid for by the city. The levy of taxes said to be illegal has been made and extended upon the tax-roll, and, so far as the city is concerned, it has consummated what are alleged to be illegal and unauthorized acts. It seems to us that the community at large had no special interest in the relief prayed for, and was not concerned as to the disposition of the fund which certain individuals had voluntarily paid in to be applied in payment of these bonds. There is a striking analogy between this case and that of State *v.* McLaughlin, 15 Kan. 228. There certain bonds alleged to be illegal had been issued by a school district, and a levy had been made to pay them off, and the proceedings had advanced so far that the county treasurer had possession of the tax-roll and was proceeding to collect, with the other taxes, the tax for the payment of the bonds, when the State interfered, upon the relation of the attorney-general, and asked that the county treasurer be enjoined from taking any further proceedings in the collection of that tax. In speaking of the right of the State to sue, the court remarked that—

" It is obvious that this interference on the part of the State is unnecessary for the protection of any rights. It is not a case where, but for the intervention of the State, an irremediable wrong would be perpetrated. Conceding the bonds to be void, each and every taxpayer has ample protection by an action of injunction. Nor is a multiplicity of suits necessary. The tax, as a tax being illegal, all the taxpayers may unite in a single. action. Hudson *v.* Commissioners Atchison Co., 12 Kan. 140. It is apparent, too, that no action of the corporation, the school district, is sought to be prevented. . . . It is obvious that the State, as a State, has no direct interest in this controversy, any more than a controversy between individuals. The payment of these bonds may be illegal, but their payment works no greater wrong to the State than the payment by a single individual of an illegal debt. The single individual may, if he chooses, by appealing to the ordinary proceedings of the law, protect himself against such illegal payment. So may the many taxpayers."

Here the complaint is not made by the city nor by the taxpayers. Probably for the purpose of showing an interest in the public, the plaintiff alleges that some of the taxpayers are in doubt about the legality of the tax, and are questioning and refusing to pay the same. If this be true, and they desire to prevent its collection, their remedy is ample and complete, as shown by the decision in State *v.* McLaughlin, *supra.* A taxpayer, or many taxpayers united, may maintain such an action. In such a case the action would be between parties actually and specially interested. A multiplicity of suits could thereby be avoided, and the exact questions sought to be raised in this case could be fully determined. The point made that the county may be embarrassed by reason of the objection to the tax, and the failure of the taxpayers to pay the same, and the probable lack of bidders at the tax-sale thereafter to be held, is without force in this proceeding. It appears that the special bridge fund tax is separate and distinct from all other levies, and the taxpayer can therefore distinguish, if he chooses, the legal from the illegal tax. But, more than that, the plaintiff does not desire, or at least is not asking, to restrain further proceedings in the collection of the tax. In fact, by the petition of the plaintiff, it is assumed and evidently intended that the county treasurer shall continue to collect the tax, and shall sell the property, if necessary to accomplish that end. He asks that the county treasurer shall hold and not pay out the money hereafter collected under such levy. As heretofore stated, the real controversy in the case is in regard to the disposition of the money which parties have voluntarily paid or may pay to the county treasurer for a specific purpose. It is true that the plaintiff, in connection with the prayer to restrain the disbursement of the money, asks that the bonds be declared void ; but it is admitted that they have been already issued and delivered, and it is conceded that there is authority in the city to issue bridge bonds, and while the bonds may not have been issued in conformity with such authority, yet it does not appear from the allegations of the petition that they are void in the hands of those holding them. This question, like the others, can be determined in an action between parties interested. However, this was not the real object of the proceeding, but, as stated in the argument of the plaintiff in this court, it is an action to prevent the illegal payment of money, and was not brought to prevent the collection of the taxes. The plaintiff argues the case upon the theory that the money in controversy is a public fund, and therefore its application is a matter of public concern ; but if the levy was made without authority of law, as the plaintiff alleges, the money which the taxpayers choose to pay thereunder does not constitute public revenue. Under that theory there was no legal obligation resting upon the taxpayers to pay the money, and that which they did pay does not constitute a public fund in which the community at large has any interest. Its disposition is a matter of private interest between the holder of the bonds and the taxpayers of the city. So that in no view which can be taken of the case can we say that there is such a public interest as will authorize the State to interfere or to maintain the action. State *v.* McLaughlin, *supra;* Ewing *v.* Board Ed. Jefferson City, 72 Mo. 436 ; Attorney-General *v.* Salem, 103 Mass. 138; People *v.* Clark, 53 Barb. 171 ; Attorney-

General *v.* Burrell, 31 Mich. 25 ; People *v.* Booth, 32 N. Y. 397.

Indeed, it would seem from the showing made by the plaintiff that even the taxpayers could not maintain an action to recover from the county treasurer the money RECOVERY OF which they have paid. It appears to have been a TAXES VOLUNTARILY PAID. free and voluntary act upon their part, and it has been settled by the repeated decisions of this court that money thus voluntarily paid cannot be recovered back by the individual paying the same. Phillips *v.* Jefferson Co. 5 Kan. 412 ; Wabaunsee Co. *v.* Walker, 8. Kan 431 ; Kansas Pac. Ry. Co. *v.* Commissioners Wyandotte Co., 16 Kan. 587 ; Sapp *v.* Commissioners Brown Co., 20 Kan. 243 ; Thimes *v.* Stumpff, 33 Kan. ——.

If the action brought by the plaintiff could be maintained, the peculiar dilemma is presented of inferentially authorizing the defendant James A. Loper to receive all moneys which persons choose to pay on account of the bridge bonds, and after its receipt to lock the same up in his hands so that it cannot be applied in payment of the bonds, as intended by those who contributed it, and cannot be applied or paid out by him on any account nor for any purpose. The citizens of Atchison may, if they see fit, absolutely donate their money to the city or to any individual, and no reason is seen why they cannot, if they desire to do so, contribute their money to be applied upon the bonds issued in payment of the bridges that have been constructed in the city. It would seem in such a case that the defendant Loper would be regarded as a trustee for the individuals paying the same, and it would therefore be his duty to apply the money so received in accordance with the will of those for whom he was acting. However that may be, we are satisfied that the public has no such interest in the controversy as will authorize the plaintiff to maintain this action ; and therefore the judgment of the district court will be reversed, and the cause remanded for further proceedings.

All the justices concurring.

TOWN OF BURLINGTON
v.
SCHWARZMAN.

(52 *Connecticut*, 181.)

Where a public way is obstructed by a fence set across the travelled path, though easily removable, and a continuance of such obstruction is threatened, an injunction will lie against the party making the obstruction.

The liability of a town for an injury received by a traveller from such obstruction gives it a sufficient interest to make ft a proper party to bring a suit for the injunction.

SUIT for an injunction against the obstruction of a highway. Facts found and injunction granted. Appeal by defendants. The opinion states the facts.

W. W. Perry for appellant.

E. Johnson and *S. O. Prentice* for appellees.

LOOMIS, J.—This is an appeal from a judgment of the Court of Common Pleas restraining the defendant, by injunction, from fencing in and obstructing a public highway.

The first ground of appeal is that the town is not the proper party plaintiff. It is contended that highways are RIGHT OF TOWN TO ENJOIN NUISANCE IN HIGHWAY. mere public easements which belong to the general rather than the local public, and, therefore, that the town, as such, has no interest sufficient to maintain the suit. The defendant fortifies this position by the following citation from High on Injunctions, § 756: "The simplest and most generally accepted test in determining whether one is a proper party complainant to a bill for an injunction is whether he possesses a legal or equitable interest in the subject-matter of the controversy." This would seem to be in point, but it would have more weight as applicable to the case at bar, were it not that the section immediately preceding in the same treatise says: "The corporate authorities of a town are proper parties to enjoin a public nuisance. Thus, the erection of buildings upon a public square which has been dedicated as such to the use of the inhabitants of a town constitutes a public nuisance which may be enjoined by the corporate authorities." It is obvious that the test mentioned was never intended for universal application. It needs, at least, this qualification, that where the threatened act is one involving corporate responsibility, the town so responsible may resort to this preventive remedy by injunction, upon the same principle as if the legal or equitable title to the subject-matter was in the town; or, perhaps, the rule given by the learned author needs no other qualification than such a liberal construction of the terms " legal or equitable interest" as would include corporate responsibility.

But the defendant also applies to the case another test, which, he argues, is fatal to the plaintiff's right to bring the suit. This is found in section 783 of Wood on RIGHT TO BRING SUIT AT LAW FOR Nuisances. It is there stated that " unless the NUISANCE NOT NECESSARY TO MAINTENANCE OF party injuriously affected could maintain an action BILL FOR INJUNCTION. at law, he cannot maintain a bill for an injunction." This cannot be necessarily the case, for the jurisdiction of a court of equity is far more extensive than that of a court of law. It is the very fact that a court of law cannot afford ample redress for all injuries, or even any redress for some, that called courts of equity into existence; hence, when a right is violated, even though it is a merely equitable right, which a court of law could not redress, equity will interfere.

Our conclusion is that the liability of the town to pay damages in case a person is injured by the obstruction is a sufficient interest to enable it to appear as plaintiff NUISANCE—IN- TEREST OF TOWN in a complaint in equity to prevent the threatened obstruction; and if this position needs further confirmation it may be found in the cases of City of New Haven *v.* Sargent, 38 Conn. 50; Derby *v.* Alling, 40 Conn. 410; Trustees of Watertown *v.* Cowen, 4 Paige, 510; and Mayor, etc., of London *v.* Bolt, 5 Ves. 129.

2. The defendant's next claim is that if the plaintiff is the proper party no case is shown for equitable relief. The facts upon which the claim is based are the temporary TEMPORARY, RE- MOVABLE OB- character of the obstruction, the fact that it might STRUCTION OF HIGHWAY—IN- have been removed easily, even by a traveller, and JUNCTION. that a public prosecution might have been instituted or a civil action brought by one injured against the defendant.

The defendant cites in support of the proposition Bunnell's Appeal, 69 Penn. St. 62. It is said in the opinion

" that where a mere wall of stone and timber was built across the road—a mere barricade temporary in character and easily and inexpensively removed—a remedy by injunction should be refused." This isolated passage comes fully up to the claim made in this case, but the actual decision falls far short of it; which was, not that an injunction should be permanently refused, but only temporarily, till after a trial at law; for the opinion proceeds immediately to say, " This is not the ordinary case, which was evidently in the mind of the learned judge" (referring to the court below that had granted the injunction), " of an old and long-known road. . . . But here the facts that the road was never opened throughout its entire length, . . . that the surveys lately made had no reliable beginning or ending point, and that the route has been disputed many years, are all reasons to lead a chancellor to doubt, and to send the case to a jury; while the obstruction complained of is but an unimportant barricade made to contest the right, and not a permanent or valuable erection or likely to produce irreparable injury." All these elements of doubt rendered it very proper to send the case to a jury for trial before determining the question as to an injunction.

It is quite possible that the Pennsylvania courts would go to the length indicated in the passage from the opinion relied upon by the defendant, for it must be conceded that there is considerable contrariety of decision in regard to the nature of the threatened act or exigency which will constitute such an irreparable injury as to justify the remedy by injunction. But as this branch of equity has been administered in this State, we cannot doubt that the facts of the case at bar lay an adequate foundation for an injunction.

Were the way merely a private one, thus wrongfully obstructed and threatened, we think our courts would not hesitate to enforce the remedy upon the ground of preventing a recurring grievance and a multiplicity of suits. But its being a public way and the act a public nuisance makes the case, in our judgment, vastly stronger; many people are exposed to great annoyance and injury and may have occasion to bring many suits. Moreover, the act complained of is one that denies the existence and defeats all the purposes of a public highway. Consequently the injury to the highway as such may well be termed irreparable. All remedies other than by injunction would be tardy, uncertain, and imperfect; that would be speedy, complete, and every way effective. As to the remedy by injunction, we like the reasoning of Breese, C. J., in giving the opinion of the court in Craig v. The People, 47 Ill. 496; although it refers to a more important highway than the one now in question, yet the underlying principle as to the nature of the remedy would be the same in both cases. The judge says: "It is true an action at law would lie against these appellants, should they obstruct the road. . . . But this remedy . . . would not only be tardy, but wholly inadequate. Intercourse between settled portions of the county and the county seat would be almost wholly interrupted, the citizens put to great inconvenience, and injuries inflicted which though in particular cases might be trifling, yet in the aggregate would be too grievous to be borne. It would be a monstrous public nuisance, to prevent which full power is lodged in a court of chancery by calling into exercise its restraining power. With that powerful arm the whole wrong can be at once grasped and the injury prevented."

3. The only remaining question is, whether the court erred in holding that the road in question was a public highway by dedication. The finding places this part of the case beyond the realm of doubt and renders discussion unnecessary. It shows the existence of every essential element of a complete dedication by the owner as and for a public highway, and a corresponding acceptance on the part of the public by an unquestioned and uninterrupted use for the period of thirty-two years. It is also found that the way thus used is required by common convenience and necessity.

There was no error in the judgment complained of.

In this opinion the other judges concurred.

CIRCLEVILLE

v.

NEUDING.

(41 *Ohio St.* 465.)

Where a city contracted for the construction of a cistern eighteen feet wide and twenty feet deep in a street, and before the cistern was completed a horse fell into it and was killed, for want of sufficient protection around and over the excavation to guard animals in the proper use of the street from danger,

Held, That the city was liable for the loss of the horse, although it did not reserve or exercise any control or direction over the manner of doing the work, except to see that it was done according to specifications which were a part of the contract.

ERROR to District Court of Pickaway County.

The city of Circleville on the 20th day of December, 1881, made a contract with one Peter Barndt to construct a public cistern for the city in one of its streets, according to plans and specifications adopted by the city council. Barndt agreed to furnish all materials and do all the labor in the construction of the cistern for a given price agreed upon by him and the city council. The cistern was eighteen feet in diameter and twenty feet deep. After the excavation for the cistern had been made and the wall built up about ten feet, and while the work was temporarily suspended, a mare, the property of the defendant in error, who lived within a few rods of the cistern, being at large accidentally on the street, fell into the cistern and was so injured that she died soon afterwards. The cistern was left by the workmen without a fence around it, but it was covered partly with three-inch plank and partly with one-inch pine boards. The covering of the excavation was not much raised above the level of the street, and at the time of the accident there was about eight inches of snow upon this covering. A trial in the common pleas resulted in a verdict and judgment for the plaintiff. This judgment was affirmed in the district court, and the defendant below files his petition in error to reverse this judgment.

Adolph Goldfrederick and *I. N. Abernethy* for plaintiff in error.

Samuel W. Courtright and *Festus Walters* for defendant in error.

McCAULEY, J.—It is contended on behalf of the city that it is not liable for the loss of the horse, because the cistern was in process of construction by an independent contractor when the injury occurred. The relation between the city and Barndt was clearly that of employer and independent contractor, and the rule is generally that for injuries occurring in the progress of work carried on by parties in that relation the contractor alone is liable. But this liability is limited to those injuries which are collateral to the work to be performed, and which arise from the negligence or wrongful act of the contractor or his agents or servants. Where, however, the work to be performed is necessarily dangerous, or the obligation rests upon the employer to keep the subject of the work in a safe condition, the rule has no application. This distinction has been taken in this State in a number of cases. Carman *v.* Railroad Co., 4 Ohio St. 399; Tiffin *v.* McCormack, 34 Id. 638; Hughes *v.* Railway Co., 39 Id. 461; and elsewhere, in McCafferty *v.* Railroad Co., 61 N. Y. 178; Prentiss *v.* Boston, 112 Mass. 43; Baltimore *v.* O'Donnell, 53 Md. 110; Logansport *v.* Dick, 70 Ind. 65; Crawfordsville *v.* Smith, 79 Id. 308; Robbins *v.* Chicago, 4 Wall. 657.

In this case, the cistern contracted for was to be built in a street, and to be eighteen feet wide and twenty feet deep. Such an excavation in a street, unless protected to guard persons and animals using the street from falling into it, was necessarily dangerous. The city was under the statutory obligation at the time of the accident to keep its streets open, in repair, and free from nuisance, and it could not cast this duty upon a contractor, so as to relieve itself from liability to one who should receive an injury. It is primarily liable for an injury resulting from such dangerous place in a street. If it has required the contractor to assume the risk of such damage, it may have a remedy against him. But the public in the use of the streets may rely upon the legal obligation of the city to keep them free from danger-

9 Cor. Cas.—42

ous places; or, if such places become necessary to be made in the course of an improvement or work necessary or proper for the city to do, that it shall so guard them that no injury shall result in the ordinary use of the street.

Judgment affirmed.

WHITCHER
v.
CITY OF SOMERVILLE.

(138 *Massachusetts,* 454.)

If a portion of a highway in a city is lowered for the purpose of having a railroad pass over it by means of a bridge, such portion is not included in the "approaches" to the bridge, within the meaning of the Pub. Sts. c. 112, § 128, so as to render the railroad corporation liable for an injury caused by a defect therein, and to exonerate the city from liability.

TORT for injuries to the plaintiff's horse, carriage, and harness, caused by a defect in Washington Street, in the defendant city.

S. C. Darling for defendant.
J. Bennett for plaintiff.

C. ALLEN, J.—A bridge under a highway, within the meaning of the Pub. Sts. c. 112, § 128, is a bridge for travellers to use as a part of the highway, crossing the railroad over the level thereof. Cambridge *v.* Charlestown Branch Railroad, 7 Met. 70, 72; Sawyer *v.* Northfield, 7 Cush. 490; Titcomb *v.* Fitchburg Railroad, 12 Allen, 254; White *v.* Quincy, 97 Mass. 430; Rev. Sts. c. 39, § 72; Gen. Sts. c. 63, § 61; St. 1874, c. 372, § 95.

In the present case, the railroad crossed the highway, over the level thereof, by means of the bridge, and the highway was lowered for the purpose of having the railroad pass over it. The only question is, whether that portion of the highway which was so lowered is included in the approaches to the bridge, within the meaning of the Pub. Sts. c. 112, § 128, so that the railroad company is liable for an accident happening thereon, and the city exonerated.

The approaches to a bridge are the ways at the ends of it, which are a part of the bridge itself, or are appendages to it. This was quite plain under the St. of 1846, c. 271, § 1. By the common law, the duty to keep a bridge in repair carried with it the duty to keep in repair, as a part of the bridge, the highway at each end of it for a space of three hundred feet. The King *v.* West Riding of York, 7 East, 588; s. c., in House of Lords, 5 Taunt. 284. This limit of space has not been adopted in this Commonwealth, but the highways at the ends of a bridge have been recognized as, and called, the approaches to it, in several decisions. Commonwealth *v.* Deerfield, 6 Allen, 449, 455; Titcomb *v.* Fitchburg Railroad, 12 Allen, 259; Rouse *v.* Somerville, 130 Mass. 361. This was the meaning in the St. of 1846, c. 271, § 1, and, when taken with the context, is the meaning in the Pub. Sts. c. 112, § 128. As the bridge in the present case was not a part of the highway, but was a part of the railroad track, and crossed the highway over the level thereof, the approaches to it did not include any part of the highway, and the city was not relieved of its liability to keep in repair that portion of the highway where the accident happened.

Exceptions overruled.

THE CITY OF BLOOMINGTON

v.

SHROCK.

(110 *Illinois*, 219.)

The weight of current authority is decidedly against the admission of scientific books in evidence before a jury, and against allowing them to be read from to contradict an expert, generally. When, however, an expert assumes to base his opinion upon the work of a particular author, that work may be read in evidence to contradict him.

Where a witness was examined as an expert, and gave evidence tending to prove that a party had been guilty of negligence after a fall, in omitting proper care to avoid an abortion, but did not quote from or make any reference to any medical books on the subject, the court allowed counsel, on cross-examination, to ask him if he was acquainted with Playfair and Bedford (treatises on midwifery), and upon his responding in the affirmative, and that they were standard authorities on such questions, the court allowed counsel to read at length from each of those authors, consecutively, and then inquire of the witness whether he agreed with the authors as to the parts so read. *Held*, that it was error to allow the reading from the books and the questions to be propounded to the witness as to his agreeing with the authors.

Since medical or other scientific books are not admissible as original evidence, it follows they are not admissible on cross-examination, when their introduction is not for the direct contradiction of something asserted by the witness, but simply to prove a different theory.

APPEAL from the Appellate Court for the Third District. Heard in that court on appeal from the Circuit Court of McLean county ; the Hon Owen T. Reeves, Judge, presiding.

Mr. John T. Lillard for appellant.

Messrs. Fifer & Phillips for appellee.

SCHOLFIELD, J—This was an action on the case for negligence by appellee against appellant. Appellee, a married woman, was violently thrown down while walking along a sidewalk adjacent to one of appellant's streets, by reason of a FACTS. defect in the sidewalk, and thereby received injuries which, she claimed, resulted in causing her to have an abortion. It was contended by appellant, upon the trial, that she was guilty of such contributory negligence as to bar her right to recover, in omitting proper care and caution to avoid the abortion,—and this was the most important question upon the trial, although there were other questions of minor consideration contested.

Dr. Luce was called and examined as a witness on behalf of appellant, as an expert, and gave evidence tending to prove that appellee was guilty of negligence in the respect contended by appellant. He quoted from and made reference to no book; but upon his cross-examination, counsel for appellee inquired of him whether he was acquainted with Playfair and Bedford (treatises on midwifery), and upon his responding in the affirmative, and that they were standard authorities on questions of this character, counsel proceeded to read at length from each of these authors, consecutively, and then inquired of the witness whether he agreed with the authors as to the parts so read. This was objected to by the counsel for appellant, but allowed by the court, and the witness was required to make answer.

The weight of current authority is decidedly against the admission of scientific books in evidence before a ADMISSION OF SCIENTIFIC BOOKS AS EVIDENCE. jury, although in some States they are admissible. 1 Greenleaf on Evidence, sec. 440, and note; Wharton on Evidence, sec. 665; Rogers on Expert Testimony, secs. 168, 169 *et seq.*, and cases cited in notes. And the weight of current authority is also against allowing such treatises to be read from, to contradict an expert, generally. See authorities *supra*, and Commonwealth *v.* Sturtevant, 117 Mass. 122; Davis *v.* The State, 38 Md. 15; The State *v.* O'Brien, 7 R. I. 336. Where, however, an expert assumes to base his opinion upon the work of a particular author, that work may be read in evidence to contradict him. This was, in effect, our ruling in Connecticut Mutual Life Ins. Co. *v.* Ellis, Admr., 89 Ill. 516; and it was expressly so ruled in Pinney *v.* Cahill, 48 Mich. 584; City of Ripon *v.* Bristol, 30 Wis. 614, and Huffman *v.* Click, 77 N. C. 55. See, also, Marshall *v.* Brown, 50 Mich. 148; Rogers on Expert Testimony, sec. 181.

But counsel for appellee insist the ruling of the court below is in exact conformity with the ruling of this court in Connecticut Mutual Life Ins. Co. *v.* Ellis, Admr., *supra*. This is a misapprehension. In that case the witness stated "that he had read text-books that he might be able to state why he diagnosed the case as *delirium tremens;*" and it was held "not unfair to the witness to call his attention to the definitions given in the books of that particular disease, and asking him whether he concurred in the definitions." And it was said: "That is, in no just sense, reading books to the jury as evidence, or for the purpose of contradicting the witness." The source of his professed knowledge was given, and it was allowed to show that he was mistaken, by resorting to that source. In the present case, it has been seen, the course pursued was entirely different. The witness based no opinion which he gave upon the authority of books, and they were only brought in to impair his evidence on cross-examination.

Where a witness says a thing or a theory is so because a book says so, and the book, on being produced, is discovered to say directly to the contrary, there is a direct contradiction which anybody can understand. But where a witness simply gives his opinion as to the proper treatment of a given disease or injury, and a book is produced recommending a different treatment, at most the repugnance is not of fact, but of theory; and any number of additional books expressing different theories would obviously be quite as competent as the first. But since the books are not admissible as original evidence in such cases, it must follow that they are not admissible on cross-examination, where their introduction is not for the direct contradiction of something asserted by the witness, but simply to prove a contrary theory.

We think the court erred in admitting this evidence, and for that error the judgment is reversed and the cause remanded.

Judgment reversed.

EXTRACTS FROM PROFESSIONAL OR SCIENTIFIC WORKS ARE NOT ADMISSIBLE AS OPINION EVIDENCE, OR IN SUPPORT OF OPINION EVIDENCE. —It is settled in most jurisdictions that where the issue involves or depends upon facts of a scientific or professional character, extracts from scientific or professional standard works are not admissible in evidence, (*a*) either independently—Collier *v.* Simpson, 5 Car. & P. 73; Commonwealth *v.* Wilson, 1 Gray (Mass.), 337—or·(*b*) in support of or in connection with expert testimony—Commonwealth *v.* Sturtevant, 117 Mass. 122; Davis *v.* State, 38 Md. 15, 36; Boyle *v.* State, 57 Wis. 472. For a full discussion of of this subject see Rogers on Expert Testimony, §§ 168 *et seq.*, where it is shown that professional or scientific books are held not admissible as evidence in England, Indiana, Maine, Maryland, Massachusetts, Michigan, North Carolina, Rhode Island, and Wisconsin; that there are dicta to the same effect in California and New Hampshire; and that Alabama and Iowa are the only jurisdictions where such books are held admissible.

MEDICAL OR OTHER PROFESSIONAL WORKS MAY BE READ FROM ON CROSS-EXAMINATION FOR THE PURPOSE OF BREAKING DOWN AN EXPERT WITNESS.—But although a professional book cannot be received in evidence, the better reasoning and authority both seem to indicate that such books may be read from in the course of the cross-examination of an expert witness for the purpose of breaking down his testimony. Thus in Pinney *v.* Cahill, 48 Mich. 584, a veterinary surgeon had on direct examination testified that a horse had died from the effects of overfeeding while hot, which would produce colic. On cross-examination the witness said that colic was caused by overfeeding when the animal was too warm, that all works of good authority spoke of it, and that Dr. Dodd's "Modern Horse Doctor" was a work of that kind. The defendant then offered to show from this work of Dr. Dodd, where the author treats of colic, the passage following: "In nine cases out of ten, colic is the result of impaired digestive organs." This evidence was admitted over objection and exception, and was held to have been properly admissible for the purpose of disparaging the opinion of the witness. So in Huffman *v.* Click, 77 N. C.

55, 58, the court say : "The medical expert himself may cite standard authorities in his profession as sustaining his views, and then they may be put in evidence by the opposing side to discredit him, but he cannot read them either as evidence or argument, nor can the counsel offering them." Again in City of Ripon *v.* Bittel, 30 Wis. 614, the court say: "The record does not inform us what the purpose or object of the offer of the treatise was. Counsel suggest that it may have been to expose or discredit the medical witnesses examined as experts, who, founding their opinions upon the same treatise, recognized as standard authority, had testified that the books laid down such and such particular conclusions, when in truth and fact the books did not do so, and the witnesses were mistaken. Counsel asks if, under such circumstances, the books would not be admissible as in the nature of impeaching evidence, or to show that the experts were in error. We cannot say that the admission would be improper, and so must overrule the objection."

On the other hand, it was held in Davis *v.* State, 38 Md. 15, that "medical books are not admissible in evidence, either for the purpose of sustaining or contradicting the opinion of a witness." And the same view seems to have been taken in State *v.* O'Brien, 7 R. I. 336, 338.

On principle it would seem that extracts from professional or scientific works are clearly admissible to discredit an expert witness, after a proper foundation has been laid for their admission. The grounds on which an expert witness bases his opinion are always relevant and material to the issue. Steph. Dig. Evid., art. 54; Dickinson *v.* Fitchburg, 13 Gray (Mass.) 546, 557. They may be inquired into on the direct examination or on the cross-examination. Rogers Expert Testimony, § 32. If the expert witness, in answer to an interrogatory, states that he bases his opinion on a professional or scientific work, this answer is material to the issue, and if the work cited does not support the opinion given, this fact may be shown to shake the credit of the witness by destroying one of the grounds on which his opinion was based. The objection to admitting such evidence in lieu of or in support of opinion evidence—namely, that it is hearsay and unsworn—has no application here, since the extracts are read, not in support of the opinions they set forth, but merely to show that they furnish no foundation for the opinion given by the witness.

WHAT FOUNDATION MUST BE LAID BEFORE EXPERT WITNESS MAY BE DISCREDITED BY EXTRACTS FROM PROFESSIONAL OR SCIENTIFIC WORKS.—It seems clear that an expert witness cannot be discredited in the manner before indicated, until he has been asked the source or foundation of his opinion, and has stated it to be based wholly or in part on professional or scientific books. In the principal case the witness was not asked the foundation of his opinion, but counsel proceeded to confront him with extracts from standard works, and asked him if he agreed with the authors as to the parts read. *Non constat* that the witness based his opinion on any books, and hence clearly the evidence offered had no tendency to shake the grounds of that opinion.

It would seem that if witness has based his opinion wholly or in part on "all the works of good authority" on a given subject, he may be discredited by reading from any work recognized by witness as a work of good authority. Pinney *v.* Cahill, *supra.*

HAYES
v.
CITY OF CAMBRIDGE.

(138 *Massachusetts*, 461.)

In an action against a city for personal injuries occasioned by stepping into a hole in a street crossing, caused by an accumulation of snow and ice, the defendant introduced evidence tending to show that, on certain days previously to the accident, there had been two very heavy snowstorms ; and also introduced evidence tending to show the length of the streets it had to clear, and their condition after the storms, the amount of labor it had to do on its streets, the amount it did, and the expenses incurred, and the time and labor involved. The plaintiff then offered in evidence an ordinance of the city providing that the tenant, occupant, or abutting owner of land should, within twenty-four hours after a fall of snow, clear the sidewalks in front of his premises, under a certain penalty. This evidence was excluded. *Held,* that the plaintiff had no ground of exception.

W. E. Russell for plaintiff.
J. W. Hammond for defendant.

MORTON, C. J.—The plaintiff was injured, on February 7, 1882, by stepping into a hole in a street crossing, caused by an accumulation of snow and ice. At the second trial, after the ꜰᴀᴄᴛꜱ.   decision reported in 136 Mass. 402, the defendant introduced evidence tending to show that on January 31, and on February 4 and 5, there had been two very heavy snowstorms ; and also evidence tending to show the length of the streets it had to clear, and their condition after the storms, the amount of labor it had to do on its streets, the amount it did, and the expenses incurred and the time and labor involved, with a view of showing that the defect which caused the injury could not have been remedied by reasonable care and diligence on its part. Pub. Sts. c. 52, § 18. Rooney *v.* Randolph, 128 Mass. 580 ; Hayes *v.* Cambridge, 136 Mass. 402.

The plaintiff offered in evidence an ordinance of the city which provides that the tenant, occupant, or abutting owner of land shall, within twenty-four hours after a fall of snow, clear the sidewalks in front of his premises, under a penalty of not less than two nor more than twenty dollars. The court excluded the evidence, and the plaintiff excepted.

The duty of clearing the streets and making them safe and convenient for travellers is primarily upon the city. CITY'S DUTY TO CLEAR STREETS. The ordinance, if valid, does not excuse it from this duty, nor exempt it from liability for defects. If abutters, or others, after the snow-storm of February 5, did in fact remove the snow from the sidewalks, and thus relieve the city of a part of the work which it was its duty to perform, this would be competent evidence. But the plaintiff did not offer to prove this. Mere proof of the existence of the ordinance would not aid the jury, but would tend to mislead them to decide the case upon speculation and conjecture rather upon facts proved.

Proof of the ordinance is not proof that work was done by the abutters under it; and, as the offer of the ordinance was not accompanied by any offer to prove that any sidewalks were in fact cleared under it, we think the Superior Court rightly rejected it.

Exceptions overruled.

SPRAGUE

v.

BRISTOL.

(Advance Case, New Hampshire. July 31, 1885.)

In an action for injuries to a traveller on the highway, evidence that the plaintiff's agent had directed her horse, which she was driving at the time of the accident, to be shod in a way to remedy the fault of stumbling is admissible.

CASE for injuries upon a highway. Trial by a referee, who returned a general finding for the defendant, with a statement of several exceptions taken by the plaintiff to his rulings at the trial, one of which was as follows:

The defendant claimed that the plaintiff's horse had the habit of stumbling, and that the accident was caused by his stu m bling, and not by any defect in the highway. It appearing, in fact, that the plaintiff's husband was her agent for the purpose of getting the horse shod, and that the horse was shod as a stumbling horse, the defendant was permitted to put in evidence, in connection therewith, that · on one occasion the plaintiff's husband directed the blacksmith to shoe the horse so as to prevent stumbling; and that on another occasion he directed the blacksmith to pare the horse's hoofs down, because he was a "stumbling old cuss."

The other exceptions appear in the opinion of the court.

Chase & Streeter, Bingham, Mitchell & Bachellor, Dearborn, Barnard & Barnard, Pike & Parsons for plaintiff.

Fling & Chase and *W. S. Ladd* for defendant.

CLARK, J.—1. The evidence tending to show that the witness has made statements inconsistent with his testimony at the trial was competent and relevant as affecting the credit of the witness.

2. There was no error of law in receiving evidence of the plaintiff's habit of driving in places similar to the place of the EVIDENCE— accident. State *v.* Railroad, 52 N. H. 528; State HABIT OF DRIV- ING. *v.* Railroad, 58 Id. 410; Plummer *v.* Ossipee, 59 Id. 55; Aldrich *v.* Monroe, 60 Id. 118.

3. Evidence that the plaintiff was driving rapidly before reaching the place of the accident tended directly to contradict her testimony that she drove slowly.

4. Upon the question of the condition of the highway at the place of the accident, evidence that travellers had encountered no difficulty in passing was competent as tending to show that the highway was suitable for the public travel.

5. Upon the question whether the plaintiff's horse was a stumbler, and whether the plaintiff knew it, it was competent to show that the horse was shod as a stumbler; as it would EVIDENCE— be competent to show that he was shod in a pecu- WHETHER HORSE A STUMB- liar manner to prevent interfering, if it was a ques- LER. tion whether he was addicted to that fault. It was also competent and material to show that the horse was shod as a stumbler by direction of the plaintiff, and for this purpose it was competent to show that it was done by direction of the plaintiff's agent who was charged with the duty of getting the horse shod. "Whatever is done by an

agent in reference to the business in which he is at the time employed, and within the scope of his authority, is said or done by the principal, and may be proved, as well in a criminal as a civil case, in all respects as if the principal were the actor and the speaker." Cliquot's Champagne, 3 Wall. 114; Burnside *v.* G. T. Ry. 47 N. H. 554. In this case the declarations of the agent were competent, not as admissions of the plaintiff, but as showing that the shoeing was by the direction of the plaintiff's agent, and that the direction was emphatic and not a mere casual or frivolous remark ; and the fact that the horse was shod as a stumbler by direction of the plaintiff's agent was an evidentiary fact tending to prove that the horse was in fact a stumbler and that the plaintiff knew it.

6. This exception is frivolous. The plaintiff, having inquired of the witness the price at which he sold the horse, could not object to the question being answered correctly.

Exceptions overruled.

ALLEN, J., did not sit ; the others concurred.

INDEX.

NOTE.—The mode of citing the American and English Corporation Cases is as follows:

9 Am. & Eng. Corp. Cas.

The index contains references to the decisions and to the notes. References to the decisions are to the pages upon which the cases begin. References to the notes are to the pages upon which the propositions stated in the index are found.

ABANDONMENT.
Of municipal powers. See PUBLIC WORKS, BOARD OF.
Of school property. See DEED; SCHOOLS.

ABUSE OF PROCESS.
See ARREST.

ACCEPTANCE.
Of town line: committee's report, and recording thereof, fixes line finally, in absence of fraud misconduct. Town of Suffield v. Town of E. Granby (Conn.). 1.

ADJOURNMENT.
See SCHOOLS.

ADMISSION TO OFFICE.
See OFFICE AND OFFICER.

ADVANCES.
By trustee. See TRUSTS.

ADVERSE POSSESSION.
See STATUTE OF LIMITATIONS.

AGENCY.
Authority of agent: seal, corporate, agent to affix need not be appointed under seal. 567 n.
Authority to sell bonds at par does not authorize sale for less than par. 626 n.
Municipal boards and members thereof as agents for municipality. See MUNICIPAL CORPORATIONS.

AGENCY—*Continued.*

Public agents. See also MUNICIPAL CORPORATIONS.

Public agents appointed to exercise public duties within the limits of a municipality, not agencies of the municipality, when. 622 *n.*

AGGRAVATION OF DAMAGES.

See DAMAGES.

ANNEXATION.

Of territory to municipality: payment of previous debts. See TAXES.

APPEAL BOND.

Contribution and subrogation between original sureties on instrument in suit and sureties on appeal bond: doctrine stated. Briggs *v.* Hinton *et al.* (Tenn.). 159.

Contribution and subrogation between surety on appeal bond and surety on the original debt. 168 *n.*

County auditor not required to give, when appealing case in official capacity. Scheerer *v.* Edgar (Cal.). 153.

APPEALABLE ORDER.

Order for jury trial on issue not of right triable by jury, is appealable (*e.g.*, on issue whether petition for election has proper signatures). Dutten *v.* Village of Hanover (Ohio). 30.

APPEALS AND APPELLATE PROCEDURE.

See APPEAL BOND.

Appellate court can give judgment only against parties before it. In suit on official bond it cannot give judgment against sureties not before it. Briggs *v.* Hinton *et al.* (Tenn.). 159.

Payment of judgment in trial court no estoppel against attacking judgment in appellate court against party not before that court. Briggs *v.* Hinton *et al.* (Tenn.). 159.

Presumptions on appeal: compensation paid to secretary of board of health presumed properly made, in absence of proof *contra.* Waller *v.* Wood (Ind.). 231.

Record, what contained in: motion must be embodied in bill of exceptions. Washington Ice Co. *v.* Lay (Ind.). 375.

Record, what contained in: motion to dismiss an appeal, *held* not part of. Washington Ice Co. *v.* Lay (Ind.). 375.

APPEARANCE.

Waiver of notice: appearance without objection is (which objection must be raised in some form 'incorporated in the record). Washington Ice Co. *v.* Lay (Ind.). 375.

APPOINTMENT.

Election and appointment different methods of filling an office. (Ohio Const. art. ii. § 27.) State *v.* Constantine (Ohio). 33

BAIL BOND.

Subrogation between sureties on, and sureties on original debt. 168 *n.*

BAILMENT.

See PUBLIC MONEY.

BALLOT.

See ELECTIONS; SCHOOLS.

Devices and marks upon: statutes prohibiting. 17 *n.*

Form and size of: regulation of, by statute. 16 *n.*

Form of: requirements as to length and other minor points cannot be disregarded; ballot not complying therewith cannot be counted. Reynolds *v.* Snow (Cal.). 14.

BEQUESTS.

See COUNTY BOARD; WILLS.

BILL OF ATTAINDER.

See ATTAINDER; CONSTITUTIONAL LAW.

BOARDS.

See APPROPRIATE DESCRIPTIVE TITLES.

BOARD OF HEALTH.

See HEALTH, BOARD OF.

BOARD OF SUPERVISORS.

See COUNTY BOARD.

BOND.

See APPEAL BOND; OFFICIAL BOND; RAILWAY BOND; SCHOOL BOND.

Licensee of municipality (*e.g.,* liquor seller) may be required to give bond to obey ordinances. *In re* Schneider (Oreg.). 548.

—— Such bond may exceed in amount the fine which city is authorized to impose, but must not be for unreasonable amount. *Id.*

Suit on: no breach assigned; defendant entitled to oyer and to rule on plaintiff to assign breach of condition. Defendant allowed under general issue. Machiasport *v.* Small (Me.). 179.

BOUNDARY.

See TOWN LINE.

Municipal: fixed by whom. 4 *n.*

Town line: location of, by committee, accepted and recorded, final in absence of fraud or misconduct. Town of Suffield *v.* Town of East Granby (Conn.). 1·

BRIBERY.

Disqualification for exercise of elective franchise under Const. 1875, art. viii. § 3. Washington *v.* State (Ala.). 7.

BRIDGE.

Highway, bridge is part of. Whitcher *v.* Somerville (Mass.). 658.

BURDEN OF PROOF.

Suit on collector's bond, plea of performance: plaintiff has burden of showing either actual collection or duty and legal authority to collect certain moneys before defendant has burden of proving performance in respect thereto. Machiasport v. Small (Me.). 179.

. —— On such proof by plaintiff, defendant has burden of adducing evidence in support of his plea. Machiasport v. Small (Me). 179.

CEMETERIES.

Exemption of, from taxation. 435 *n.*

CERTIORARI.

See HIGHWAY.

Common-law writ, to review judicial action of boards; court limited to questions of jurisdiction. People v. Board of Fire Comm'rs of New York (N.Y.) 76.

Municipal bonds: validity of issue of reviewable, by certiorari. Ontario v. Hill (N.Y.). 636.

Statutory extension of force of writ so as to open record to see whether "rule of law" has been violated; or if there is "absence of evidence" to sustain ruling of board; effect of. People v. Board of Fire Comm'rs of New York (N.Y.). 76.

When writ will lie. 78 *n.*

CHARITIES.

See WILLS.

COMMITTEE.

On town line: report of, accepted by court and recorded, fixes lines finally in absence of fraud or misconduct. Town of Suffield v. Town of E. Granby (Conn.). 1.

School committee. See SCHOOLS.

COMPENSATION.

See EMINENT DOMAIN; FEES; PUBLIC WORKS, BOARD OF.

CONDITION.

Deed in fee of land "to be used for school purposes and no other," *held* to be not upon condition. Barker *et. al.* v. Barrows (Tex.). 208.

CONCEALED WEAPONS.

Arrest for carrying, *held* authorized without warrant. State v. Turpen (Ohio). 128.

CONSTITUTIONAL LAW.

Abatement of nuisance. See NUISANCE.

Annexation of territory to municipality: payment of previous debts. See TAXES.

Compensation of official short-hand reporters: Act allowing judge in whose court they serve to determine, is constitutional. Smith v. Strother (Cal.). 234.

CONSTITUTIONAL LAW—*Continued.*

Constitutional provisions as to fees and salaries considered. See FEES AND SALARIES.

Contested election: provision as to. See ELECTIONS.

Ditches for county purposes: statutes authorizing, *held* constitutional. Zimmerman *v.* Canfield *et al.* and Zimmerman *v.* Prickett *et al.* (Ohio.) 382.

" Due process of law" as used in XIVth Amendment has no different meaning from that formerly ascribed to it. Eames *v.* Savage (Me.). 627. ·

Elections. See ELECTIONS.

Elections: regulation of—law for, constitutional. See ELECTIONS; SUFFRAGE.

Eminent domain, constitutional questions involved in. See EMINENT DOMAIN.

Ex post facto law: act annexing penalty against officer taking illegal fees and making bondsmen liable for penalty applies to bonds executed before law took effect. State *v.* Stevens (Ind.). 184.

Ex post facto law: Alabama constitution of 1875, art. vii. § 3, making conviction of felony a disqualification for exercise of elective franchise, acts upon convictions prior thereto. Washington *v.* State (Ala.). 7.

—— Such provision not an *ex post facto* law, nor a provision in nature of bill of attainder within prohibition of Federal Constitution. Washington *v.* State (Ala.). 7.

Jeopardy: exemplary damages where defendant is punishable criminally—relation of, to doctrine of no second jeopardizing. State *v.* Stevens (Ind.). 184.

Jeopardy: penalty for taking illegal official fees of five times amount taken is not a second jeopardizing. State *v.* Stevens (Ind.). 184.

Jury and jury trial: right to. See JURY AND JURY TRIAL.

Legislature: powers of. See LEGISLATURE.

Liquor laws: constitutionality of. See INTOXICATING LIQUORS.

Police power. See INTOXICATING LIQUORS; NUISANCE.

Statutes: passage of; amendments to bills pending need not be read three times. People *v.* Thompson (Cal.). 47.

Statutes: special act granting corporate power void. State *v.* Constantine (Ohio). 33.

Suffrage a privilege rather than a right, and exclusively within control of State, subject to Fifteenth Amendment of U. S. Constitution. Washington *v.* State (Ala.). 7.

Suffrage: conviction of felony a disqualification for exercise of elective franchise under Constitution of 1875, art. viil. § 3. Washington *v.* State (Ala.). 7.

Taxation : constitutional questions involved in. See TAXES.

U. S. Constitution: Fifteenth Amendment of, is sole restriction upon power of State to regulate suffrage within it borders. Washington *v.* State (Ala.). 7.

U. S. Constitution: Fourteenth Amendment of; application of, to police power. See NUISANCE.

U. S. Constitution: Fourteenth Amendment of; execution against municipality: statute authorizing levy upon goods and chattels of inhabitants, not in conflict with Fourteenth Amendment. Eames *v.* Savage (Me.). 627.

CONTRACTS.

See COVENANTS RUNNING WITH LAND: SPECIFIC PERFORMANCE.

Municipality: contracts of. See MUNICIPAL CORPORATIONS.

Prisoners' labor in county jail: contract for; county commissioners have control of. County of Bristol *v.* Gray (Mass.). 228.

Stipulation by municipalities as to taxes, on annexation. See TAXES.

CONTRIBUTION.

See SURETIES.

CORPORATIONS.

See MUNICIPAL CORPORATIONS.

Corporate Seal. See SEAL.

Cumulative voting in private corporations. 41 *n.*

Deed by corporation. See DEED.

CORRECTION, HOUSE OF.

See PRISONERS.

COSTS.

See FEES.

COUNTY.

See COUNTY BOARD; TITLES OF COUNTY OFFICERS; ELECTIONS.

Railway bonds: rights of county as owner of, considered. Scallay *v.* Butte County (Cal.). 580.

COUNTY BOARD.

See COUNTY COMMISSIONERS.

Auditing of claims by: averment of, *held* sufficient to show compliance with statute. Jones *v.* Morgan (Cal.). 287.

Contract by, to pay district-attorney for work within scope of his official duties would be void: otherwise of contract to attend to case after his term expired. Jones *v.* Morgan (Cal.). 287.

Delegation of power: power to sue, employ counsel, and settle suit cannot be delegated. Scallay *v.* Butte County (Cal.). 580.

Highways: powers of board over. See HIGHWAY.

Sheriff's compensation for provisions furnished prisoners determinable by, subject to review in courts. Fulkerth *v.* County of Stanislaus (Cal.). 222.

Suits: power to sue and to employ counsel conferred on county boards in California. Scallay *v.* Butte County (Cal.). 580.

——— Such power cannot be delegated, nor can discretion as to beginning or settling suits. Scallay *v.* Butte County (Cal.). 580.

COUNTY CLERK.

Compensation: statute authorizing him to receive, and fixing amount, and authorizing county commissioners to pay, necessary. Noble *v.* Board of Comm'rs of Wayne Co. (Ind.). 241.

DEMURRER.

Surplusage will not vitiate demurrer. Miller *v.* White River School Township (Ind.). 144.

DEPUTY.

Contribution and subrogation between sureties on sheriff's bond held for default of deputy sheriff, and sureties on deputy's bond. Briggs *v.* Hinton *et al.* (Tenn.). 159.

DEVISE.

See COUNTY BOARD; WILLS.

DISTRICT ATTORNEY.

County board's contract to pay district attorney for work within scope of his official duties would be void: otherwise of contract to attend to case after his term expired. Jones *v.* Morgan (Cal.). 287.

DITCH.

See IMPROVEMENTS, ASSESSMENTS FOR.

County ditches: statutes authorizing, *held* constitutional. Zimmerman *v.* Canfield *et al.* and Zimmerman *v.* Prickett *et al.* (Ohio). 382.

DRAINAGE.

See IMPROVEMENTS, ASSESSMENTS FOR.

EASEMENT.

Trespasser cannot assert public easement, as against owner of soil, where. Furley *v.* Mississippi and Rum River Boom Co. (Minn.) 353.

ELECTION.

See BALLOT; SCHOOLS; SUFFRAGE.

Appointment and election of officers: different modes of filling office. (Ohio Const. art. ii. § 27.) State *v.* Constantine (Ohio). 33.

By school committee. See SCHOOLS.

Candidate in first district *held* entitled to have certain votes cast in second district counted for him, where all circumstances show that they were intended for him. Inglis *v.* Shepherd (Cal.). 54.

Contest as to, triable, in Missouri, only in courts, except as to governor and lieutenant-governor. State *v.* John (Mo.). 238.

Cumulative voting, constitutionality of statutes providing for. 39 *n.*

Cumulative voting not authorized by Ohio constitution: statute attempting to establish it void. State *v.* Constantine (Ohio). 33

Election must conform to constitutional requirements to be valid. State *v.* Constantine (Ohio). 33.

Elector entitled to vote for a candidate for each office to be filled at the election. State *v.* Constantine (Ohio). 33.

Elector's right to vote for all officers: statute providing for election of four members of police board at one election, but denying elector the right to vote for more than two, is in conflict with Ohio Constitution, art. *v.* State *v.* Constantine (Ohio). 33.

EMINENT DOMAIN—_Continued._

Access: injury to, must be compensated. Cohen *v.* City of Cleveland (Ohio). 405.

Damages to property, by preventing access, cutting off light and air, and by jarring, as by a viaduct in front of and above, recoverable. Cohen *v.* City of Cleveland (Ohio). 405.

Ditch for county purposes: compensation for property taken for, may be out of county treasury. Zimmerman *v.* Canfield *et al.* and Zimmerman *v.* Prickett *et al.* (Ohio). 382.

Ditches for county purposes: statutes authorizing, *held* constitutional. Zimmerman *v.* Canfield *et al.* and Zimmermau *v.* Prickett *et al.* (Ohio). 382.

Ditch: view of proposed ditch by county commissioners, to determine need for, is exercise of political and not judicial function: notice to landowner not necessary. Zimmerman *v.* Canfield *et al.* and Zimmerman *v.* Prickett *et al.* (Ohio). 382.

Improvements, assessment for, of benefits in reduction of damages by taking, constitutional. Genet *v.* City of Brooklyn (N.Y.). 395.

Light, obstruction of, must be compensated. Cohen *v.* City of Cleveland (Ohio). 405.

Municipality can condemn lands beyond its borders only by express grant of power. Houghton Common Council *v.* Huron Copper Mining Co. (Mich.). 315.

Nuisance, abatement of, by eminent domain considered. 314 *n.*

Political function: view by county commissioners to determine need for proposed ditch is exercise of, and not of judicial function: notice thereof to property-owner not necessary. Zimmerman *v.* Canfield *et al.* and Zimmerman *v.* Prickett *et al.* (Ohio). 382.

Private ways: constitutionality of statutes authorizing opening of, by eminent domain. 367 *n.*

Several tracts, taking of, necessary to complete use of, each: all must be condemned in same proceeding. Washington Ice Co *v.* Lay (Mich.). 375.

"Taking for public use," note on. 412 *n.*

Viaduct: damage to property by viaduct recoverable though no property is taken, and though viaduct is a lawful structure. Cohen *v.* City of Cleveland (Ohio). 405.

Vibration and jarring of property elements of damage to be compensated. Cohen *v.* City of Cleveland (Ohio). 405.

View of line of proposed ditch by county commissioners, to determine need thereof, under statute directing, such view is exercise of *political* and not *judicial* function, notice of such action to property-owner unnecessary. Zimmerman *v.* Canfield *et al.* and Zimmerman *v.* Prickett *et al.* (Ohio). 382.

ENTRY, WRIT OF.

Bar of statute of limitations held to have intervened on peculiar facts. Barker *et al. v.* Barrows (Mass.). 208.

Title tried by, in Massachusetts: grant by deed of fee "to be used for school purposes and no other" is not upon condition. Barker *et al. v.* Barrows (Mass.). 208.

ESTOPPEL.

Payment of judgment in trial court no estoppel against attacking judgment in appellate court against party not before that court. Briggs *v.* Hinton (Tenn.). 159.

Purchaser at tax sale not estopped from obtaining tax deed by allowing property to be assessed against former owner, and subsequent taxes to be paid by him (*semble*); so of municipality buying for taxes. Berry *v.* Bickford (N.H.). 470.

EVIDENCE.

Appendices of printed official reports held admissible as evidence. Milford *v.* Greenbush (Me.). 71.

Highway, injury to one driving upon; evidence that plaintiff had directed the horse shod in a way to avoid a habit of stumbling, admissible for defendant. Sprague *v.* Bristol (N.H.). 665.

Objection to on ground that petition does not state cause of action; petition liberally construed. Kansas *v.* School District (Kan.). 567.

Such objection overruled if any cause of action is well stated in petition. Kansas *v.* School District (Kan.). 587.

Official character: proof of. 69 *n.*

Scientific books cannot be read to contradict expert, except where he has based his opinion upon work of a particular author when that work may be read to contradict him. Bloomington *v.* Shrock (Ill.). 659.

Scientific books generally not admissible, either directly or to contradict an expert; but where expert assumes to base opinion on work of a particular author, that work may be read to contradict him. Bloomington *v.* Shrock (Ill.). 659.

Scientific books are not admissible as opinion evidence or in support thereof, but are, in contradiction of expert. 662 *n.*

Scientific books: what foundation necessary for admission of. 663 *n.*

EXECUTION.

Municipality: execution against may (in Maine) be levied upon the goods and chattels of the inhabitants; statute authorizing such proceeding not in conflict with U. S. Court, XIVth Amendment. Eames *v.* Savage (Me.). 627.

Official bond: judgment on, for amount of penalty; execution for amount of loss; reference proper to ascertain amount of loss. Machiasport *v.* Small (Me.). 179.

EXEMPLARY DAMAGES.

See DAMAGES.

EX POST FACTO LAW.

See CONSTITUTIONAL LAW.

Alabama constitution of 1875, art. vii. §3, making conviction of felony a disqualification for exercise of elective franchise acts upon convictions prior thereto. Washington *v.* State (Ala.). 7.

Such provision not an *ex post facto* law, nor a provision in nature of bill of attainder within prohibition of Federal Constitution. Washington *v.* State (Ala.). 7.

EXTRAS.

See FEES.

FEES AND SALARIES.

Assessors' compensation fixed *per* list, *held* to mean each *list* taken by him, whether it contained property or not. Harrison *v.* Commonwealth (Ky.). 247.

Attorney appointed by court to defend poor person cannot recover fees from the county or State. Johnson *v.* Whiteside Co. (Ill.) 281.

Auditing of claim for: averment of, *held* sufficient to show compliance with statute. Jones *v.* Morgan (Cal.). 287.

Auditor required by statute to complete unfinished work of assessor: such statute *held* no authority to county board to vote auditor additional compensation for such services. Vandercook *v.* Williams (Ind.). 254.

Changing compensation of patrolmen and policemen: acts providing for, *held* constitutional. Mangam *v.* City of Brooklyn (N. Y.). 292.

Changing fees and percentages: constitutional provision against (N. Y. Const. art. iii. § 18), *held* to apply only to officers not receiving fixed and certain salaries. Mangam *v.* City of Brooklyn (N. Y.). 292.

Changing salary of municipal officers. 272 *n.*

Common law: generally no compensation for municipal officers at. 267 *n.*

Compensation of municipal officers: requisites for: constitutional office: statute or ordinance authorizing payment: due qualification of officer by bond, oath, etc., and title to the office. 267 *n.*

Compensation of municipal officers: usually none at common law. 267 *n.*

Compensation of municipal officers: who liable for. 279 *n.*

Contract by county board to pay district-attorney for work within his official duties, would be void: otherwise of contract to attend to case after his term expired. Jones *v.* Morgan (Cal.). 287.

County clerk: statutory authority necessary, authorizing him to receive, fixing amount, and authorizing county commissioners to pay. Noble *v.* Board of Comm'rs of Wayne Co. (Ind.) 241.

County-commissioners' salaries in Massachusetts are in full of compensation for their services, including travelling expenses. County of Bristol *v.* Gray (Mass.). 228.

County treasurer: compensation of, determinable by county board in certain counties. Supervisors of Seneca Co. *v.* Allen (N. Y.). 262.

Discovery of property owned by city: compensation for. 262 *n.*

Duties imposed upon officer by law to which no compensation is attached must be performed gratuitously. Board of Comm'rs of Carroll Co. *v.* Gresham (Ind.). 224.

Expenses of county commissioners for travelling are, in Massachusetts, covered by their salaries: no extra allowances made therefor. County of Bristol *v.* Gray (Mass.). 228.

Extra compensation for extra services. 273 *n.*

Forfeiture of salary. 280 *n.*

Gross sum in compensation for services of officer authorized by statute, "and no more," *held* that such sum is in full for all services performed by him, including services in completing the duties of other officers. Vandercook *v.* Williams (Ind.). 254.

FEES AND SALARIES—*Continued.*

Health, board of: compensation of secretary of, discretionary with county commissioners: no appeal from their order. Waller *v.* Wood (Ind.). 231.

Illegal fees: taking under color of official authority; averment of, *held* sufficient. State *v.* Nevin (Ind.). 184.

Illegal official fees: penalty for illegal taking of five times amount of such fees taken does not put defendant twice in jeopardy. State *v.* Nevin (Ind.). 184.

Invalidity of contract for compensating officers discovering and assessing property by a *percentum* on the taxes derived therefrom will not invalidate such taxes. Vandercook *v.* Williams (Ind.). 254.

Listers of town property: fees of, determinable by the town. Barnes *v.* Town of Bakersfield (Vt.). 246.

Mandamus to obtain: right to office not triable on. State *v.* John (Mo.). 238.

Physician as secretary of county commissioners as board of health entitled to compensation to be determined by county commissioners. Waller *v.* Wood (Ind.). 231.

Possession and title to office (*de facto* and *de jure*) considered respectively as affecting right to compensation. 267 *n.*

Prima-facie holder to office must be recognized as entitled to compensation until title to office settled. State *v.* John (Mo.). 238.

Short-hand reporters (official): act allowing judge in whose court they serve to determine their compensation, is constitutional. Smith *v.* Strothers (Cal.). 234.

Specific approbation by law of public money cannot be dispensed with, even for payment of official fees, which officers might have deducted before paying money into public treasury. State *ex rel.* Graham *v.* Babcock (Neb.). 152.

Statutory allowance of, intended as full compensation for service. Further allowance for duties to which no fees are annexed is unauthorized (*e.g.*, allowance to sheriff for care of prisoners and insane persons). Board of Comm'rs of Carroll Co. *v.* Gresham (Ind.). 224.

Statutory authority necessary as to county clerk, authorizing him to receive, fixing amount, and authorizing county commissioners to pay. Noble *v.* Board of Comm'rs of Wayne Co. (Ind.). 241.

Tax sale: compensation of officers for making, does not depend on validity of sale. Aldrich *v.* Picard (Tenn.). 243.

Tax sale, fee of clerk for making, in Tennessee, determined. Aldrich *v.* Picard (Tenn.). 243.

FELONY.

Disqualification for exercise of elective franchise under Const. 1875, art. viii, § 3. Washington *v.* State (Ala.). 7.

FIRE ESCAPE.

Ordinance regulating *held* too vague in terms to sustain criminal prosecution for its violation. Maker *v.* Slater Mill and Powder Co. (R. I.). 515.

FORFEITURE.

See PENALTIES.

FRAUD.

Town line: location of, may be vitiated by fraud or misconduct. Town of Suffield *v.* Town of E. Granby (Conn.). 1.

HEALTH, BOARD OF.

Compensation of secretary of, discretionary with county commissioners: no appeal from their order. Waller *v.* Wood (Ind.). 231.

County commissioners are, in Indiana. Waller *v.* Wood (Ind.). 231.

Physician employed as secretary by county commissioners acting as, entitled to compensation, to be determined by county commissioners. Waller *v.* Wood (Ind.). 231.

HIGHWAY.

See also PRIVATE WAYS; STREETS.

Bridge is part of. Whitcher *v.* Somerville (Mass.). 658.

Declaration of purpose of road by deed, that it should be "open to use of public at large for all manner of purposes in all respects as a common turnpike road," but subject to payment of tolls, not a dedication. Austerberry *v.* Corporation of Oldham (Eng. Ch. D.). 323.

Dedication for public use. 353 *n.*

Dedication with reservation of right to charge tolls, impossible except by legislative permission. (*Semble.*) Austerberry *v.* Corporation of Oldham (Eng. Ch. D.). 323.

Existence of, once established, continues till terminated in manner known to law. Refusal of county board to locate a highway where one already exists does not vacate such existing highway. Washington Ice Co. *v.* Lay (Ind.). 375.

Injury to one driving upon; evidence that plaintiff had directed the horse shod in a way to avoid habit of stumbling, admissible for defendant. Sprague *v.* Bristol (N. H.). 665.

Obstruction by easily removable fence is a nuisance which will be prevented by injunction, where continuance is threatened. Town's liability for injuries therefrom gives it interest sufficient to enable it to maintain bill. Burlington *v.* Schwarzman (Conn.). 652.

Opening of, by county board final : questions of public and private use are concluded by their decision. Washington Ice Co. *v.* Lay (Ind.). 375.

Opening of : petition and proposed order for, laid over : new proceedings begun : vote ordering was as asked by first petition : proceedings *held* regular, and to afford no ground on *certiorari* for order to quash. Cornell *v.* Mayor and Aldermen of New Bedford (Mass.). 371.

Petition for : requirement of signatures of freeholders is not a requirement that the fact of freeholding by signers shall appear on face of petition. Washington Ice Co. *v.* Lay (Ind.). 375.

Petition to county board for : board are judges of sufficiency of petition : objections not taken before the board are waived. Washington Ice Co. *v.* Lay (Ind.). 375.

Variance, slight of petition, and evidence, as to location of highway, *held* not fatal. Washington Ice Co. *v.* Lay (Ind.). 375.

IDIOTS.

Elective franchise; idiots prohibited to exercise. Washington *v.* State (Ala.). 7.

ILLEGAL FEES.

See FEES AND SALARIES.

IMPRISONMENT.

Fine upon summary conviction.

IMPROVEMENTS, ASSESSMENTS FOR.

Assessments for, are exercise of legislative right of taxation : whose determination is final. Genet *v.* City of Brooklyn (N. Y.). 395.

Benefit assessed in payment of damages for taking, is just compensation for land taken. Genet *v.* City of Brooklyn (N. Y.). 395.

Constitutionality : benefits, assessment of, in reduction of damages by taking, constitutional. Genet *v.* City of Brooklyn (N. Y.). 395.

—— So though fixing of district for assessment is by one body, and assessment of benefit is by another body: and though entire cost of a great improvement is laid on district so fixed. Genet *v.* City of Brooklyn (N. Y.). 395.

—— So though aliquot part of entire cost of improvement (proportioned to its size in relation to that of the whole district) is assessed as benefit upon a tract, irrespective of actual benefit. Genet *v.* City of Brooklyn (N. Y.). 395.

Damages and benefits: each tract treated separately as a unit: no set-off of or consolidation of damages and benefits to several tracts owned by same person. Genet *v.* City of Brooklyn (N. Y.). 395.

Damages by improvement to be compensated. See EMINENT DOMAIN.

Damages to property not abutting on improvement, recoverable, but need not be sought in the assessment proceedings. Cohen *v.* City of Cleveland (Ohio.). 405.

Exemption from taxes: whether it extends to special assessments for improvements. 438 *n.*

Laying out of improvement must precede assessment, and must be sufficient to acquaint land-owners with nature and extent of improvement. Town of Leominster *v.* Conant (Mass.). 390.

Laying out of improvement: no previous notice necessary. Town of Leominster *v.* Conant (Mass.). 390.

Notice not necessary to precede laying out of improvement. Town of Leominster *v.* Conant (Mass.). 390.

Particular improvement built: then general plan for improvements adopted, including the particular improvement, before assessment made therefor, and increasing assessment of land-owners beyond share of such first improvement: proceedings *held* valid. Town 'of Leominster *v.* Conant (Mass.). 390.

Report of assessment committee: order of county court confirming does not estop defense to assessment of defect in petition for improvement: *e.g.*, lack of signatures. Liebman *v.* San Francisco (Cal.). 598.

Sewer: laying out must precede assessment for: must be certain to degree sufficient to acquaint parties assessed with nature and extent of the improvement. Town of Leominster *v.* Conant (Mass:). 390.

Street opening: part of lot taken for: assessment upon residue proper: liability of public limited to excess of award of damages over amount of benefit. Genet *v.* City of Brooklyn (N. Y.). 395.

INDEPENDENT CONTRACTOR.

Liability of, for injuries from negligence in work, limited to injuries collateral to work. Circleville v. Neuding (Ohio). 656.

INDUSTRIAL SCHOOL.

Commitment of minor to: act authorizing justice of peace to make, for offence of which he has jurisdiction only to recognize with sureties is contrary to bill of rights. State v. Ray (N. H.). 135.

Commitment to a penal sentence. State v. Ray (N. H.). 135.

Magistrate's commitment to, would not bar sentence to prison for same offence; therefore, sentence to industrial school is illegal. State v. Ray (N. H.). 135.

Penal and reformatory character of. State v. Ray (N. H.) 135.

INJUNCTION.

Constitutional right to equal protection of laws; deprivation of, would be an irreparable injury and is ground for injunction. Barthet v. New Orleans (U. S. C. C. La.). 509.

—— So of attempted deprivation of constitutional right secured by XIVth Amendment, *e.g.*, by ordinance forbidding maintenance of slaughter-house without council's permission, after it was located in compliance with former ordinance. Barthet v. New Orleans (U. S. C. C.). 509.

—— Above opinion strongly disapproved in note. 514 *n.*

Nuisance as ground for. See NUISANCE.

Opening of street by municipality for what evidence showed to be a private use, restrained by injunction. Pells v. Boswell (Ont.). 358.

Obstruction of highway by easily removable fence prevented by injunction, where continuance threatened. Burlington v. Schwarzman (Conn.). 652.

—— Town's liability for injuries therefrom gives it interest, sufficient to enable it to maintain bill. Burlington v. Schwarzman (Conn.). 652.

Taxes: injunction against levy or collection of. See TAXES.

Tax on exempt property: collection of, restrained by injunction. Galveston Wharf Co. v. City of Galveston (Tex.). 422.

INJUNCTION BOND.

Subrogation between sureties on, and sureties on original debt. 168 *n.*

INSTRUCTIONS TO JURY.

See JURY AND JURY TRIAL.

INTEREST.

Interest coupons on municipal bonds: See MUNICIPAL BONDS.

Judgment against defaulting county treasurer should bear interest from first of year succeeding default. Simmons v. County of Jackson (Tex.). 199.

School fund: interest-bearing notes for; county treasurer and bondsmen liable for such interest in Texas. Simmons v. County of Jackson (Tex.). 199.

Taxes: interest payable on when. See TAXES.

INTOXICATING LIQUORS.

"Bar-room or drinking shop" is a place where the business of selling liquor to be drank on the premises is carried on. *In re* Schneider (Oreg.). 548.

College, towns, and villages : act authorizing such towns to provide against evils of sale of intoxicating liquors not an unconstitutional classification of towns and not unconstitutional. Bronson *v*. Oberlin (Ohio). 529.

College towns and villages not authorized by such act to prohibit sale of liquor within their limits. Bronson *v*. Oberlin (Ohio). 529.

Delegation to villages of power to regulate sale of liquor held not unconstitutional under Ohio constitution. Bronson *v*. Oberlin (Ohio). 529.

License:

Bond may be required of licensee to obey ordinances. *In re* Schneider (Oreg.). 548.

Such bond may exceed in amount the fine which city is authorized to impose, but must not be unreasonable in amount. *In re* Schneider (Oreg.). 548.

Bond calling for observance of "all other ordinances" construed to mean all other ordinances relating to drinking shops. *In re* Schneider (Oreg.). 548.

Ohio "Scott law" required tenant to obtain landlord's written consent to sell liquor on the premises in order to make sale valid. This in effect required a license, and violated constitutional provision that no license to traffic in intoxicating liquors shall hereafter be granted. Butzman *v*. Whitbeck (Ohio). 535.

Ohio Scott law, so far as providing for a lien on real estate occupied by tenant dealing in liquors, for assessment against dealer, is in effect a license law and unconstitutional. Butzman *v*. Whitbeck (Ohio). 535.

Whether law is a license law is determined by its operation and effect and not from its form and words. Butzman *v*. Whitbeck (Ohio). 535.

Ordinance prohibiting sale or gift of, with proviso for sale by druggists for medicinal and mechanical purposes, without provision for written permit to druggists, is a general permission to all druggists to sell for such purposes. Moore *v*. People (Ill.). 524.

JEOPARDY.

See CONSTITUTIONAL LAW.

JUDGMENTS.

Claim under is taxable as personalty. Cameron *v*. Cappeller (Ohio). 438.

—— So though judgment is *held* open by writ of error. Id.

Collateral attack: an action on official bond of clerk of court to recover penalty 'for an illegal fee taxed as costs and included in judgment does not attack the judgment collaterally. State *v*. Stevens (Ind.). 184.

Collateral attack: payment of judgment in trial court no estoppel against attacking judgment in appellate court against party not before that court. Briggs *v*. Hinton *et al*. (Tenn.) 159.

Interest on judgment against defaulting county treasurer should bear interest from first of year succeeding default. Simmons *et al. v*. County of Jackson (Tex.). 199.

Municipality: execution on judgment against, may be levied upon goods and chattels of inhabitants; statute authorizing such levy not in conflict with XIVth Amendment of U. S. Constitution. Eames *v*. Savage (Me.). 627.

JUDGMENTS—*Continued.*

Official bond: judgment for amount of penalty; execution for amount of loss; reference proper to ascertain amount of loss. Machiasport *v.* Small (Me.). 179.

JUDICIAL DISTRICT.

See ELECTIONS.

JUDICIAL NOTICE.

Of journals of legislature. People *v.* Thompson (Cal.). 47.

JURISDICTION.

See CERTIORARI; JUSTICE OF PEACE.

JURY AND JURY TRIAL.

Challenge to array sustainable where jury in eminent-domain proceeding are all taken from one township, and that one is affected by the improvement. Houghton Common Council *v.* Huron Copper Mining Co. (Mich.) 315.

Election, petition for: in *mandamus* proceedings issue whether petition has proper signatures is not one of right triable by jury. Dutten *v.* Village of Hanover (Ohio). 30.

Fine upon summary conviction, without jury, enforcible by imprisonment, for violation of police regulation, or for immoral practice, is not an invasion of constitutional right to jury trial (Ohio Const. art. i. §§ 5, 17), nor is statute providing therefor unconstitutional. Inwood *v.* State (Ohio). 520.

Instruction directing a verdict: when improper. Miller *v.* White River School Township (Ind.). 144.

Instruction to find specially on special issues of fact should be granted when asked. Miller *v.* White River School Township (Ind.). 144.

—— Where court may properly direct a verdict, failure so to instruct is harmless error. Id.

Mandamus proceedings: jury trial in. 33 *n.*

Verdict, direction of, by court improper, when. Miller *v.* White River School Township (Ind.). 144.

JUSTICE OF PEACE.

Commitment by, for offence as to which justice's jurisdiction is not to hear and determine, but only to recognize with sureties: statute authorizing such commitment contrary to bill of rights. State *v.* Ray (N. H.). 135.

KNOWLEDGE OF LAW.

Knowledge of unconstitutionality of statute not presumed. People *v.* Thompson (Cal.). 47.

Power of: ratification of illegal expenditure by municipality and authorization of tax to cover such expense is beyond legislative power. Carlton *v.* Newman (Me.). 454.

LAND CONTRACT.

See SPECIFIC PERFORMANCE.

LANDLORD AND TENANT.

Covenant running with land : burden of, in covenants not involving a grant, never runs with land at law, except as between landlord and tenant. Austerberry *v.* Corporation of Oldham (Eng. Ch. D.). 323.

Intoxicating liquor: act requiring tenant to procure landlord's written consent to sell liquor on the premises, in order to make sale lawful, required a license, and violated constitutional 'provision against licensing liquor traffic. Butzman *v.* Whitbeck (Ohio). 535.

Lessees of school lands taxable for their interest therein. Bentley *v.* Barton (Ohio). 440.

LARCENY.

Disqualification for exercise of elective franchise under Const. 1875, art. viii. § 3. Washington *v.* State (Ala.). 7.

LAYING ON TABLE.

See PARLIAMENTARY LAW.

LEGISLATURE.

Legislative control over devises to municipal corporations. 116 *n.*

LIBERTY.

See ARREST; NUISANCE.

LICENSE.

· Liquor license. See Intoxicating Liquors.

LIMITATIONS, STATUTE OF.

Action on official bond to recover penalty for taking illegal fee is governed by provision of statute of limitations for action on official bonds, and not by provision for penalties. State *v.* Stevens (Ind.). 184.

State: doctrine that statute does not run against; statutes expressly running against; note on. 595 *n.*

State, statute does not run against, except when expressly so provided. Kansas *v.* School District (Kan.). 587.

—— Quære, where State acquired a claim or debt after statute began to run against it. Kansas *v.* School District (Kan.). 587.

Writ of entry: bar of statute *held* to have intervened against, on peculiar facts. Barker *et al. v.* Barrows (Mass.). 208.

LIQUOR LAWS.

See· INTOXICATING LIQUORS.

LUNATICS.

Elective franchise: lunatics prohibited to exercise. Washington *v.* State (Ala.). 7.

9 Cor. Cas.—44

MAJORITY.

Majority of official board may exercise powers of board. People *v.* Police
Commissioners (N. Y.). 73.

MALFEASANCE IN OFFICE.

Disqualification for exercise of elective franchise under Const. 1875, art. viii.
§ 3. Washington *v.* State (Ala.). 7.

MANDAMUS.

Applicant for, must show clear legal right to the relief sought. Klokke *v.*
Stanley (Ill.). 465.

Auditing of claims : averment of, in petition, *held* sufficient to show compliance
with statute. Jones *v.* Morgan (Cal.). 287.

Auditor of public accounts compellable by, to issue warrant for public money
in proper case. State *ex. rel.* Mainx. *v* Turpen (Ohio). 119.

Election: *mandamus* to compel council to order; issue whether petition for,
had proper number of signatures is not an issue of right triable by jury.
Dutten *v.* Village of Hanover (Ohio). 30.

Fruitless exercise of power not indulged; *mandamus* not granted where it
would be of no avail to petitioner. Klokke *v.* Stanley (Ill.). 465.

Jury trial in *mandamus* proceedings: right to. 33 *n.*

Mistakes or omissions of petitioner not corrected by *mandamus.* Klokke *v.*
Stanley (Ill.). 465.

Power to issue not fruitlessly exercised; *mandamus* not granted where it would
be of no avail to petitioner. Klokke *v.* Stanley (Ill.). 465.

Right to office not determinable on *mandamus* to compel payment of salary.
State *v.* John (Mo.). 238.

Second tax deed under same certificate of purchase as prior deed is not compellable from county clerk by holder of first deed, where he has filed with
the clerk more perfect evidence of compliance with law as to notice of purchase. Klokke *v.* Stanley (Ill.). 465.

—— But where first tax deed is inoperative, through a mistake by clerk in
execution thereof, he is compellable by *mandamus* to correct the mistake,
and he may correct it without compulsion. Klokke *v.* Stanley (Ill.). 465.

To compel officer to perform his duty; his honest doubts as to extent of his
duty no reason for not issuing writ. State *v.* Turpen (Ohio). 119.

MANUFACTURER.

Ice-packer is not. Knickerbocker Ice Co. *v.* People (N. Y.). 418

Pork-packer taxable as. Engle *v.* Sohn & Co. (Ohio). 413.

Who is, and who is not. 421 *n.*

MINOR.

Elective franchise: minors prohibited to exercise. Washington *v.* State (Ala.). 7.

MINORITY REPRESENTATION.

See ELECTIONS.

MISTAKE.

Tax deed: mistake in by clerk in executing it, rendering it inoperative, correction of is compellable by *mandamus*, and clerk may correct it without compulsion. Klokke *v.* Stanley (Ill.). 465.

MUNICIPAL BONDS.

See also SCHOOL BONDS.

Authority to sell bonds at par does not authorize sale for less than par. 626 *n.*

Estoppel against municipality by recitals: recitals of conformity to law 'in all respects necessary to give validity to bond, work estoppel, where made by duly authorized officers of the municipality; otherwise not. Liebman *v.* San Francisco (Cal.). 598.

Estoppel: municipality not estopped by affidavits of its officers, to effect that lawful conditions for issuing bonds exist; *e.g.*, that consent of majority of taxpayers has been obtained. Ontario *v.* Hill (N. Y.). 636.

Interest coupon, severed from bond, being for a larger sum than bond names as interest, holder must show purchase for value without notice of the error, before maturity, to recover the sum named in coupon. Goodwin *v.* Bath (Me.). 585.

Issue of, grounds for, and validity of, reviewable by *certiorari* or in equity. Ontario *v.* Hill (N. Y.). 636.

Railway aid bonds: under Act authorizing same upon consent obtained of majority of taxpayers, bonds are void unless such consent has actually been given. Ontario *v.* Hill (N. Y.). 636.

—— Affidavits by town officers that such consent has been obtained not conclusive upon town. Ontario *v.* Hill (N. Y.). 636.

—— No action will lie on behalf of town against commissioners for damages sustained by wrongful issue of bonds. Assessors' certificate, duly made, is a justification to commissioners in issuing the bonds. Ontario *v.* Hill (N. Y.). 636.

MUNICIPAL BOUNDARIES.

Fixed by whom. 4 *n.*

MUNICIPAL CORPORATIONS.

See COUNTY COMMISSIONERS; TOWNS.

Agency:

Public agencies appointed to exercise public duties within the limits of a municipality, not agents of the municipality, when. 622 *n.*

State cannot appoint officers or agents who are to have charge of local municipal affairs. 625 *n.*

State may empower municipality to act as its special agent in the exercise of a special public duty or function. 625 *n.*

Amendment of record: authority to keep record includes authority to amend it at subsequent date. Town of Leominster *v.* Conant (Mass.). 390.

Annexation of territory to municipality: payment of previous debts. See TAXES.

Boards: meeting of; when all members must be present. 579 *n.*

—— Majorities; powers of. 579 *n.*

MUNICIPAL CORPORATIONS—*Continued.*

Bonds of. See MUNICIPAL BONDS; PUBLIC DEBT.

Bond: city may take from persons in business it is authorized to license and regulate, *e.g.*, liquor-selling, to obey ordinances. *In re* Schneider (Oreg.). 548.

—— Such bond may exceed in penalty amount of fine which city is authorized to impose, but must not be unreasonable in amount. *In re* Schneider (Oreg.). 548.

Bond calling for observance of "all other ordinances" construed to mean all other ordinances relating to drinking-shops. *In re* Schneider (Oreg.). 548.

Certificates of indebtedness; pledge of. See PLEDGE.

Change of organization: school property, how affected. Board of Education *v.* Board of Education (Ohio). 211.

Charter power: "to license and regulate drinking-shops;" power authorizes municipality to take bonds from keepers of such places to observe ordinances. Bond with larger penalty than pecuniary limit of fine which municipality can impose is valid. *In re* Schneider (Oreg.). 548.

—— Bond must not be for unreasonable amount. *In re* Schneider (Oreg.). 548.

—— Such bond, calling for observance of "all other ordinances of said city," construed to mean all other ordinances relating to drinking-shops. *In re* Schneider (Oreg.). 548.

Contracts: promises by individual members of municipal board to pay existing debts of the board without any joint action not binding on municipality. Strong *v.* District of Columbia (D. C.). 568.

Council proceedings on petition and order to open highway: two sets of proceedings, first laid over, second begun; order then made in first proceedings *held* regular, and on *certiorari* to show no ground for order to quash. Cornell *v.* Mayor and Aldermen of New Bedford (Mass.). 371.

Deed by municipality. See DEED.

Devises to municipal corporations. 114 *n.*

—— Legislative control over. 116 *n.*

Election on surrender of municipal powers : petition for. In *mandamus* proceeding, issue whether petition has proper signature is not one of right triable by jury. Dutten *v.* Village of Hanover (Ohio). 30.

Election, petition for : duty of council to see that it has proper signatures. Dutten *v.* Village of Hanover (Ohio). 30.

Election, petition for : signers may withdraw their names while petition is under consideration by municipal council; if such withdrawals reduce signatures below necessary number, petition must be denied. Dutten *v.* Village of Hanover (Ohio). 30.

Eminent domain exercisable by, beyond its own borders only by express grant of power. Haughton Common Council *v.* Huron Copper Mining Co. (Mich.). 315.

Execution against doctrine that it is enforceable by levy upon inhabitants' property. Eames *v.* Savage (Me.). 627.

Execution against may, in Maine, be levied upon the goods and chattels of the inhabitants: statute authorizing such levy not in conflict with XIVth Amendment of U. S. Constitution. Eames *v.* Savage (Me.). 627.

Individual promises of members of municipal board not binding on corporation. Strong *v.* District of Columbia (D. C.). 568.

MUNICIPAL CORPORATIONS—*Continued.*

Individual promises or acts of members of board cannot bind corporation, though majority of members join in or ratify same. 577 *n.*

Instrumentalities of government: municipalities are, for levying taxes: lien of their taxes is of same rank with those of State and county taxes. Justice *v.* Logansport (Ind.). 451.

Meeting of municipal board: majority may act for board. 578 *n.*

Negligent construction of cistern in street: city liable for injury resulting from lack of guard. Circleville *v.* Neuding (Ohio). 656.

Nuisances, power to abate, considered. 314 *n.*

Officers. See, under MUNICIPAL CORPORATIONS, *Agency;* and see AGENCY.

Ordinances. See ORDINANCES.

Record: authority of selectmen to keep, includes authority to amend same at subsequent date. Town of Leominster *v.* Conant (Mass.). 390.

Seal of municipality. See SEAL.

Sewer: authority to construct not presumed an authority to create a nuisance unless that is the necessary result; if the work can be done without, the intention that it should be so done is presumed. But if extensive purifying works would be necessary, it will not be implied that the end was to be so obtained. Morse *v.* Worcester (Mass.). 642.

Sidewalks: duty of city to clear. Hayes *v.* Cambridge (Mass.). 664.

Sidewalks: suit for injury caused by snow upon; ordinance requiring owners and tenants to remove snow held inadmissible in suit against city. Hayes *v.* Cambridge (Mass.). 664.

Street lowered in order to be crossed by railway bridge: such lowered portion is not part of "approach" to bridge within statute thereon. Whitcher *v.* Somerville (Mass.). 658.

Street: negligent construction of cistern in: city liable from injury from lack of guard. Circleville *v.* Neuding (Ohio). 656.

Taxation of municipal property. See TAXES.

Taxes: municipal property not taxable. 434 *n.*

Taxes of liens of, are of equal rank with those of State and county taxes. Justice *v.* Logansport (Ind.). 451.

NEGLIGENCE.

Independent contractor's liability for injuries from negligent conduct of work limited to injuries collateral to the work. Circleville *v.* Neuding (Ohio). 656.

Municipality liable for injury from lack of guard around cistern in construction in street. Circleville *v.* Neuding (Ohio). 656.

Street: negligent construction of cistern in; city liable for injury from lack of guard. Circleville *v.* Neuding (Ohio). 656.

NOTICE.

See COUNTY COMMISSIONERS.

By municipal body of intention to purchase lands, *held* not to extend to purchase for children's home. State *ex rel.* Manix *v.* Turpen (Ohio). 119.

NUISANCE.

Abatement by attempted exercise of eminent domain: such acts are beyond power of council, and city is not answerable therefor. Cavanagh *v.* City of Boston (Mass.). 311.

NUISANCE—*Continued.*

Abatement of: appropriation of private property for, by municipality without owner's consent and without enabling act, unconstitutional. Cavanagh *v.* City of Boston (Mass.). 311.

Abatement of, by exercise of eminent domain considered. 314 *n.*

Authority to construct sewer, not presumed an authority to create a nuisance, unless that is the necessary result; if the work can be done without, the intention that it should be so done is presumed. But if extensive purifying works would be necessary, it will not be implied that the end was to be so attained. Morse *v.* Worcester (Mass.). 642.

Dangerous and noxious forms of industry, trade, and property: regulation and inhibition of, by statute considered. 499 *n.*

Equal protection of laws; secured by Fourteenth Amendment of U. S. Constitution; application of, to laws affecting nuisances. Barthet *v.* New Orleans (U. S. C. C. La.). 509.

—— Deprivation of such constitutional right would be an irreparable injury and is ground for injunction. Id.

—— So slaughter-house ordinance *held* to deprive owner of slaughter-house of equal protection of laws, and to be unconstitutional. Id.

—— Above decision strongly disapproved. 514 *n.*

Highway: obstruction of, by easily removable fence prevented by injunction, where continuance threatened. Burlington *v.* Schwarzman (Conn.). 652.

—— Town's liability for injuries therefrom gives it sufficient interest to maintain bill. Burlington *v.* Schwarzman (Conn.). 652.

Highway: obstruction of, by fence is. Burlington *v.* Schwarzman (Conn.). 652.

Municipal power to abate: note on. 314 *n.*

Noxious trades: regulation and inhibition of, by statute considered. 499 *n.*

Oleomargarine: absolute prohibition of manufacture of, unconstitutional under U. S. Const., Fourteenth Amendment, and N. Y. Const., art. 1, §§ 1, 6. P. *v.* Marx (N. Y.). 491.

Oleomargarine: prohibition and regulation of manufacture of, by statute considered. 499 *n.*

Ordinance prescribing place for slaughter-houses: purchase and erection of slaughter-house there by complainant; amendmet to ordinance forbidding maintenance of slaughter-house there except by permission of city council; amendment *held* unconstitutional under U. S. Const., Fourteenth Amendment, securing.

Power to abate: act conferring upon municipality or taxing district is not a taxing of property or service for public use without compensation. Theilan *v.* Porter (Tenn.). 486.

U. S. Const., Fourteenth Amendment, secures to every citizen a right to follow any lawful industry. Absolute prohibition of any such industry, *e.g.*, manufacture of oleomargarine, is unconstitutional. So also under N. Y. Const., art. i. §§ 1, 6. P. *v.* Marx (N. Y.). 491.

OATH.

Judge of election of school trustees cannot administer oath to school trustees. State *v.* Horton *et al.* (Nev.). 65.

Of office: act requiring oath "to be indorsed on certificate of appointment"

OFFICIAL REPORTS.

Appendices to, *held* admissible in evidence. Milford *v.* Greenbush (Me.). 17.

OLEOMARGARINE.

See NUISANCE.

ORDINANCES.

Intoxicating liquors: ordinances in relation to. See also INTOXICATING LIQUORS.

Intoxicating liquors: ordinance prohibiting sale or gift of, with proviso for sale by druggists for medicinal and mechanical purposes, without provision for written permit to druggists, is a general permit to all druggists to sell for such purposes. Moore *v.* P. (Ill.). 524.

Ordinance regulating fire-escape *held* too vague in terms to sustain criminal prosecution for its violation. Maker *v.* Slater Mill and Powder Co. (R. I.). 515.

"Quarter" in provision for license fee payable five days from beginning of each quarter means quarter of year, and is not ambiguous. *In re* Schneider (Oreg.). 548.

PARLIAMENTARY LAW.

"Laying on table till next meeting" does not prevent council from taking the matter up at a meeting after such "next meeting." Cornell *v.* Mayor and Aldermen of New Bedford (Mass.). 371.

PAUPER.

Attorney appointed to defend poor person cannot recover fees from the county or State. Johnson *et al. v.* Whiteside Co. (Ill.). 281.

Settlement of, in a town, may be admitted by the town, by vote. West Bridgewater *v.* Wareham (Mass.). 483.

Settlement of: votes of town in town meeting held to contain admissions that pauper had a settlement therein. West Bridgewater *v.* Wareham (Mass.). 483.

PENALTIES.

See OFFICIAL.

Action on official bond to recover penalty for taking illegal fee is governed by provision of statute of limitations for actions on official bonds, and not by provision for penalties. State *v.* Stevens (Ind.). 184.

Fine imposed on summary conviction, without jury, enforceable by imprisonment, not a violation of right to jury trial. Inwood *v.* State (Ohio). 520.

Repeal of statute imposing, is a remission of the penalty. It cannot be collected thereafter. So delinquent taxpayer may redeem from sale prior to repeal without tendering penalty in addition to redemption money. Snell *v.* Campbell (N. H.). 472.

PETITION.

For election. See ELECTIONS.

For election: signers may withdraw their names before petition is acted on by municipal authorities; if such withdrawals reduce signatures below necessary number, petition must be denied. Dutten *v.* Village of Hanover (Ohio). 30.

PLAT.

Dedication for street by, complete upon conveyance of lots with reference to plat, though plat be not properly certified for record. Hurley *v.* Mississippi and Rum River Boom Co. (Minn.). 353.

Lots fronting on line of continuation of street: implication that street does so continue, though not so marked on plat, and conveyance *held* to extend to line of centre of such street produced. Hurley *v.* Mississippi and Rum River Boom Co. (Minn.). 353.

Open, unmarked space on plat: dedication of, a question determinable by acts *in pais,* user, etc. Hurley *v.* Mississippi and Rum River Boom Co. (Minn.). 353.

PLEADING AND PRACTICE.

See BURDEN OF PROOF; DEMURRER.

Bond, suit on: no breach assigned: defendant is entitled to oyer, and to rule on plaintiff to assign breach of condition; defence allowed under general issue. Machiasport *v.* Small (Me.). 179.

Illegal fees: taken under color of official authority; averment of, *held* sufficient. State *v.* Stevens (Ind.). 184.

Objection to evidence for plaintiff, on ground that petition does not state cause of action: petition liberally construed. Kansas *v.* School District (Kan.). 587.

—— Such objection overruled if any cause of action is well stated in petition. Kansas *v.* School District (Kan.). 587.

PLEDGE.

Pledge of municipal certificates of indebtedness confers authority on pledgee to receive payment. Pledgor must notify municipality of any reasons for withholding payment. Strong *v.* District ot Columbia (D. C.). 568.

POLICE.

Majority of police board may exercise powers of board, *e.g.,* may pass on charge against police-officer. People *v.* Police Commissioners (N. Y.). 73.

Tax-assessors are not local police; their term not measured by that of local police. Dibble *v.* Merrman *et al.* (Conn.). 96.

POLICE POWER.

See NUISANCE.

Fire-escape ordinance held too vague in terms to sustain criminal prosecution for its violation. Maker *v.* Slater Mill and Powder Co. (R. I.). 515.

Ordinances enacted as exercise of. See ORDINANCES.

POLITICAL PARTY.

Membership of, cannot be made test of eligibility for office (Mich.). 18 and 29 *n*.

PRESIDING OFFICER.

Moderator, resignation of. See Town Meeting.

PRISONERS.

Employment of, in county jail: county commissioners control, in Massachusetts. County of Bristol *v.* Gray (Mass.). 228.

Products of their labor in county jail: master who employs them to dispose thereof: allowance to him for expense thereof proper. County of Bristol *v.* Gray (Mass.). 228.

Rules for government of: county commissioners to make, in Massachusetts. County of Bristol *v.* Gray (Mass.). 228.

Sheriff responsible for safe-keeping of. County of Bristol *v.* Gray (Mass.). 228.

Supplies for: county commissioners responsible for, in Massachusetts. County of Bristol *v.* Gray (Mass.). 228.

PRIVATE WAYS.

Eminent domain: statutes authorizing exercise of, for opening: constitutionality of such acts considered. 367 *n*.

PUBLIC DEBT.

Annexation of territory to municipality: payment of previous debts. See Taxes.

PUBLIC MONEY.

See County Treasurer.

Embezzlement of, a disqualification for exercise of elective franchise under Const. 1875, art. viii. § 3. Washington *v.* State (Ala.). 7.

Public officers intrusted with public money, and required to give bonds for faithful discharge of official duties, are not mere bailees of the money, required only to exercise ordinary care and diligence; they are liable for money stolen without their fault or negligence. State *v.* Nevin (Nev.). 171.

Specific appropriation by law, when required by constitution, cannot be dispensed with, in plainest case of public indebtedness, *e.g.*, fees to public officers who might have deducted their fees before paying money into public treasury. State *ex rel.* Graham *v.* Babcock (Neb.). 152.

Suit on collector's bond: plea of performance; plaintiff has burden of showing either actual collection or duty and legal authority to collect certain moneys, before defendant has burden of proving performance in respect thereto. Machiasport *v.* Small (Me.). 179.

—— On such proof by plaintiff, defendant has burden of adducing evidence in support of his plea. Machiasport *v.* Small (Me.). 179.

Warrant for, not invalid because it fails to direct collector how to dispose of money when received. Town of Leominster *v.* Conant (Mass.). 390.

PUBLIC WORKS, BOARD OF.

Public use the paramount object of public works. Temporary lease of public
works, when needed for public use, valid; but is subject to public right of
resumption. State *ex rel.* Fanger *v.* Board of Public Works (Ohio). 213.
—— Board cannot lawfully part with such power to resume. State *ex rel.*
Fanger *v.* Board of Public Works (Ohio). 213.
Water-power, surplus leased: power of board to resume direct use of, when
necessary. State *ex rel. v.* Board of Public Works (Ohio). 213.
Water-power, surplus leased: provision that public shall pay for private improvements on resumption of water-power invalid. State *ex rel.*, Fanger
v. Board of Public Works (Ohio). 213.

PUNITIVE DAMAGES.
See DAMAGES.

PURCHASE FOR VALUE WITHOUT NOTICE.

Covenant to repair: purchaser taking, with notice of covenant not running with
the land at law, not bound in equity by same. So of covenant to repair
road. Austerberry *v.* Corporation of Oldham (Eng. Ch. D.). 323.
Interest coupon, severed from bond, being for a larger sum than bond names
as interest: holder must show purchase for value without notice of the
error before maturity, to recover the sum named in coupon. Goodwin *v.*
Bath (Me.). 585.

QUO WARRANTO.

Election case: record of declared election not conclusive in. State *ex rel.*
Libbey *v.* Megin (N. H.). 68.

RAILWAY BONDS.

County, rights of, as owner of railway bonds considered. Scallay *v.* Butte
County (Cal.). 580.

RECONSIDERATION.
Of vote by school committee. See SCHOOLS.

RECORD.

Municipal: authority of municipal officers to keep, includes authority to amend
at subsequent date. Town of Leominster *v.* Conant (Mass.). 390.
Of town line: location of town line becomes final by acceptance and recording
of committee's report, in absence of fraud or misconduct. Town of Suffield
v. Town of E. Granby (Conn.). 1.

REFERENCE.

Award containing voluminous items, with mistakes as to some: court will not
revise award, and give judgment for proper amount, but will vacate entire
award. Strong *v.* District of Columbia (D.C.). 568.
Official bond. judgment on, for amount of penalty; execution for amount of
loss; reference proper to ascertain amount of loss. Machiasport *v.* Small
(Me.). 179.

REFERENCE—*Continued.*

Report of referees under stipulation, certifying all findings of law and fact, and all the evidence may be set aside for patent mistakes of law or fact. Strong *v.* District of Columbia (D.C.). 568.

—— Mistake of fact must be clear, or finding clearly against weight of evidence, or report will not be set aside. Strong *v.* District of Columbia (D.C.). 568.

REGISTRATION.

See ELECTIONS.

RELATION.

Sureties' liability on official bond executed after entry into office: no relation of liability without appropriate words. State *v.* Polk *et al.* (Tenn.). 154.

REPAIRS.

Covenant for: purchaser taking, with notice of, which does not run with land at law, not bound by same in equity. So of covenant to repair road. Austerberry *v.* Corporation of Oldham (Eng. Ch. D.). 323.

RES ADJUDICATA.

County Commissioners' judgment is, on matters within their jurisdiction. State *ex rel. v.* Board of Com'rs of Washington Co. (Ind.). 98.

Injunction suit to prevent execution of tax deed and vacate sale, *held res adjudicata* by previous suit by complainant and others to test validity of tax. Snell *v.* Campbell (U. S. C. C., Iowa). 472.

Special assessment: confirmation of, does not conclude defence to assessment, of defect in petition for improvement, *e.g.*, lack of signatures. Liebman *v.* San Francisco (Cal.). 598.

RESIGNATION.

Sheriff's resignation creates a vacancy *eo instanti*. Chowning *v.* Boger (Tex.). 91.

ROAD.

Covenant to repair: purchaser taking, with notice of covenant to repair, which does not run with land at law, not bound in equity by same. Austerberry *v.* Corporation of Oldham (Eng. Ch. D.). 323.

RULES.

Prisoners: county commissioners to make rules for government of. County of Bristol *v.* Gray (Mass.). 228.

SALARIES.

See FEES AND SALARIES.

SCHOOLS.

Act vesting control of property in new village-school authorities, but saving vested rights, held to save management of high-school to former township school board. Board of Education v. Board of Education (Ohio). 211.

Committee on schools: vote of, appointing superintendent; committee may reconsider at same meeting, before it is communicated to appointee, and appoint another person. Wood v. Cutter *et al.* (Mass.). 203.

Contracts for schools: formalities required in making school contracts *held* not to extend to certain contracts for supplies. Miller v. White River School Township (Ind.). 144.

County commissioners may take gifts for educational purposes, though not custodians of school fund. Christy v. Commissioners of Ashtabula Co. (Ohio). 105.

Funds: appropriation by mistake by county court of permanent funds instead of available funds; county treasurer liable for safe-keeping of such funds so coming to his hands. Simons v. County of Jackson (Tex.). 199.

Funds: county treasurer's bond (in Texas) renders him and his sureties liable for misappropriation of school funds of any kind or description, without reference to their sources. Simons v. County of Jackson (Tex.). 199.

Municipal officers erecting a school-house can lawfully expend no more money than is voted for the purpose. Carlton v. Newman (Me.). 454.

—— Nor if more than this sum is expended can the legislature authorize the excess to be taxed upon the polls and estates of the district. Carlton v. Newman (Me.). 454.

Property of schools: how affected by change of municipal organization. Board of Education v. Board of Education (Ohio). 211.

Trustees of schools: judge of election of school trustees cannot administer oath to school trustees. State *ex rel.* Atty.-Gen'l v. Horton *et al.* (Nev.). 65.

Trustee's power to contract debts. Miller v. White River School Township (Ind.). 144.

Trustee of schools, advancing money to pay teachers' wages, may recover same from township, Keifer v. Troy School Township (Ind.). 205.

Trustee of schools has power to bind school corporation by purchase of supplies, and to give valid corporate note therefor. Miller v. White River School Township (Ind.). 144.

SCHOOL BONDS.

Purpose of, to be specified on face: bonds referring on face to statute which states their purpose *held* a sufficient specification. Kansas v. School District (Kan.). 587.

SCHOOL LANDS.

Taxation of: school lands conferred on State by United States are taxable (*i.e.*, private interest therein) after sale or lease thereof, in absence of special exemption. Bentley v. Barton (Ohio). 440.

SEAL.

See also DEED.

Agent to affix corporate seal need not be appointed under seal. 567 *n*.

SEAL—*Continued.*

Deed of corporation was at common law executed by affixing corporate seal. Tiffin (City) *v.* Shawhan (Ohio). 556.

—— So of municipal corporation. Tiffin (City) *v.* Shawhan (Ohio). 556.

—— Where corporate seal, *e.g.*, of municipality, is by law committed to custody of one officer, *quære* whether municipality can empower another officer to make a valid deed. Tiffin (City) *v.* Shawhan (Ohio). 556.

Deed sealed by authorized officer or agent of a corporation with his private seal is not the deed of the corporation. 567 *n.*

Sealing by corporation by seal not its ordinary seal binding on corporation. 566 *n.*

SET-OFF.

Benefits of improvement against damages. See IMPROVEMENTS, ASSESSMENTS FOR.

SEWER.

See IMPROVEMENTS, ASSESSMENTS FOR.

Authority to construct, not presumed an authority to create a nuisance unless that is the necessary result; if the work can be done without, the intention that it should be so done is presumed. But if extensive purifying works would be necessary, it will not be implied that the end was to be so obtained. Morse *v.* Worcester (Mass.). 642.

SHERIFF.

See PRISONERS.

Compensation for provisions for prisoners, sheriff entitled to. Fulkerth *v.* County of Stanislaus (Cal.). 222.

Compensation determinable by county board subject to review in courts. Fulkerth *v.* County of Stanislaus (Cal.). 222.

Resignation of sheriff makes vacancy *eo instanti.* Chowning *v.* Boger (Tex.). 91.

Safe-keeping of prisoners: sheriff is responsible for. County of Bristol *v.* Gray (Mass.). 228.

Statutory fees of, intended as full compensation for all duties; further allowance for duties to which no fees are attached is unauthorized (*e.g.*, allowance to sheriff for care of prisoners and insane persons). Board of Comm'rs of Carroll Co. *v.* Gresham (Ind.). 224.

SIDEWALKS.

See MUNICIPAL CORPORATIONS.

SINKING FUND.

See SCHOOLS.

SLAUGHTER-HOUSE.

See NUISANCE.

SPECIFIC PERFORMANCE.

Land contract not specifically enforced where title which purchaser would acquire would be doubtful and unmarketable. Tiffin (City) *v.* Shawhan (Ohio). 556.

STATE.

Suffrage within, for State offices, a privilege exclusively within control of State, subject to Fifteenth Amendment to U. S. Constitution. Washington *v.* State (Ala.). 7.

STATE TREASURER.

Official bond of, is joint and several. State *v.* Polk (Tenn.). 154.

—— But if bond is accepted which binds his sureties only for aliquot parts of the penalty, they cannot be charged for more. State *v.* Polk (Tenn.). 154.

STATUTE.

Construction of: all of a statute to be read together. Justice *v.* Logansport (Ind.). 451.

STATUTE OF LIMITATIONS.

See LIMITATIONS, STATUTE OF.

STREETS.

See HIGHWAY; PLAT.

Dedication of: by plat, complete on conveyance of lots with reference to plat, though plat be not properly certified for record, and lots *held* to go to centre of such street as extended. Hurley *v.* Mississippi and Rum River Boom Co. (Minn.). 353.

Opening of, by assessment for improvements. See IMPROVEMENTS, ASSESSMENT FOR.

Public use: streets must be for; ordinance for opening *held* on peculiar facts to be shown to be for private use, and injunction against opening of such street granted. Pells *v.* Boswell (Ont.). 358.

Trespasser cannot assert public easement as against owner of soil, when. Hurley *v.* Mississippi and Rum River Boom Co. (Minn.). 353.

SUBROGATION.

See SURETIES.

SUFFRAGE.

See ELECTIONS.

A privilege rather than a right, and exclusively within regulation of State, subject to Fifteenth Amendment of U. S. Constitution. Washington *v.* State (Ala.). 7.

Crime as ground for disfranchisement. 12 *n.*

Disqualification for: Const. 1875, art. viii. § 3, disqualifies persons convicted of treason, embezzlement of public funds, malfeasance in office, larceny, bri-

SUFFRAGE—*Continued.*

bery, or other felony, and acts upon persons previously convicted. Washington *v.* State (Ala.). 7.

Idiots, lunatics, and minors ptohibited to exercise elective franchise. Washington *v.* State (Ala.). 7.

SUPERVISORS.

See COUNTY BOARD; and also see COUNTY COMMISSIONERS.

SUPPLIES.

Prisoners: county commissioners responsible for supplies for. County of Bristol *v.* Gray (Mass.). 228.

SURETIES.

See OFFICIAL BONDS.

Contribution and subrogation between original sureties on instrument in suit and sureties on appeal bond: doctrine stated. Briggs *v.* Hinton *et al.* (Tenn.). 159.

Contribution from co-sureties not allowed for payment by surety which he was not bound to pay. Briggs *v.* Hinton *et al.* (Tenn.). 159.

Subrogation between surety on bond to stay legal proceedings and surety on the original debt. 168 *n.*

Subrogation of sureties on bond given to release person or property of debtor and sureties on original debt. 169 *n.*

SURPLUSAGE.

Demurrer not vitiated by. Miller *v.* White River School Township (Ind.). 144.

TABLE.

Laying matter on. See PARLIAMENTARY LAW.

TAXES.

See EMINENT DOMAIN; IMPROVEMENTS, ASSESSMENTS FOR.

Abatement of tax: non-abatement no evidence of payment. Milford *v.* Greenbush (Me.). 71.

Annexation of territory to city: statutory provision for payment of previous debt of such territory by taxes levied upon property of such territory alone, *held* to continue existence of previous organization of such territory for purpose of paying such debt. City of Cleveland *v.* Heisley (Ohio). 444.

—— City organization may properly be used to levy such taxes, but debt does not become city debt. City of Cleveland *v.* Heisley (Ohio). 444.

—— Stipulation for annexation *held* to provide for payment of previous debt of annexed territory in accordance with such statute. City of Cleveland *v.* Heisley (Ohio). 444.

—— Levy of tax in such manner to amount above constitutional limit in relation to value, avoids such tax, same as if laid by original organization of such annexed territory. Stipulation for payment of debt by taxation in such man

TAXES—*Continued.*

Interest on unpaid taxes. distinct vote fixing date when taxes are payable, ..cessary. Snow *v.* Weeks (Me.). 462.

Invalidity of contract for compensating officers discovering and assessing property by a *per centum* on the taxes derived therefrom, will not invalidate such taxes. Vandercook *v.* Williams (Ind.). 254.

Judgment. claim under is taxable, as personalty, though held open by writ of error. Cameron *v.* Cappeller *et al.* (Ohio). 438.

—— Should be listed at true and not at nominal value. Cameron *v.* Cappeller *et al.* (Ohio). 438

Lessee of school lands taxable in respect of such property as "property of lessee." Bently *v.* Barton (Ohio). 440.

Levy cannot exceed limits fixed by statute or constitution. 450 *n.*

Liens of municipal taxes: lien of, is of same rank with those of State and county taxes. Justice *v.* Logansport (Ind.). 451.

Lien of : priority: no priority between State, county, and municipal taxes, when property is of sufficient value to pay all ; where not the first valid tax sale exhausting value will divest the lien of other taxes. Justice *v.* Logansport (Ind.). 451.

Listers of town property : fees of, determinable by the town. Barnes *v.* Town of Bakersfield (Vt.)., 246.

List of personalty : judgment claim held open by writ of error should be listed: omission should be corrected by auditor. Cameron *v.* Cappeller (Ohio). 438.

"Manufacturer" and "merchant," as taxable classes, considered. Engle *v.* Sohn & Co. (Ohio). 413.

Manufacturers : who are and who are not. 421 *n.*

Municipal property not subject to, in absence of controlling statute or constitutional provision. Galveston Wharf Co. *v.* Galveston (Tex.). 422.

Municipal property not taxable. 434 *n.*

Municipal taxes: liens of are of same rank with those of State and county taxes. Justice *v.* Logansport (Ind.). 457.

Penalty for non payment: repeal of statute imposing is a remission of the penalty. It cannot be collected thereafter, and delinquent taxpayer may redeem from sale prior to repeal without tendering penalty in addition to redemption money. Snell *v.* Campbell (N. H.). 472.

Pork-packer taxable as "manufacturer." Engle *v.* Sohn & Co. (Ohio). 413.

School lands conferred on State by United States are taxable (*i.e.*, private interest therein) after sale or lease thereof in absence of special exemption. Bently *v.* Barton (Ohio). 440.

Tax deed : purchaser not estopped from obtaining deed by allowing property to be assessed against former owner, and subsequent taxes to be paid by him (*semble*). So of municipality buying for taxes. Berry *v.* Bickford (N. H.). 470.

Tax deed: second tax deed under same certificate of purchase as prior deed is not compellable from county clerk by holder of first deed where he has filed with the clerk more perfect evidence of compliance with law as to notice of purchase. Klokke *v.* Stanley (Ill.). 465.

—— But when first tax deed is inoperative through a mistake by clerk in execution thereof, he is compellable by *mandamus* to correct the mistake,

TAXES—*Continued.*

and he may correct the same without compulsion. Klokke *v.* Stanl~y (Ill.). 465.

Tax in aid of railroad: validity of raised, but disposed of as *res adjudicata.* Snell *v.* Campbell (N. H.). 472.

Unauthorized taxes voluntarily paid: application of same for such unauthorized purpose will not be prevented by injunction on behalf of State. State has not interest sufficient to maintain bill. Atchison *v.* State (Kan.). 646.

Voluntarily paid taxes cannot be recovered by taxpayer. Atchison *v.* State (Kan.). 646.

Voluntary payment of unauthorized taxes: application of same for such unauthorized purpose will not be prevented by injunction on behalf of State. State has not sufficient interest to maintain bill. Atchison *v.* State (Kan.). 646.

TAX SALE.

Compensation of officers for making, does not depend on validity of. Aldrich *v.* Picard (Tenn.). 243.

Fee of clerk for making, in Tennessee, determined. Aldrich *v.* Picard (Tenn.). 243.

Municipality may be a purchaser at. Berry *v.* Bickford (N. H.). 470.

TOWNS.

See MUNICIPAL CORPORATIONS.

Highways: interest of town in. See HIGHWAYS.

Liability to be called on in damages for injuries to travellers from obstruction of highway gives town interest to maintain bill to enjoin obstruction. (Conn.). 652.

TOWN LINE.

Location of, by committee, accepted and recorded, final in absence of fraud or misconduct. Town of Suffield *v.* Town of E. Granby (Conn.). 1.

TOWN MEETING.

Appointment of town clerk, though invalid, *held* to enable him to make a valid town record. Attorney-General *v.* Crocker (Mass.). 57.

Check list in voting, use of. Attorney-General *v.* Crocker (Mass.). 57.

Moderator, resignation of, and election of successor. Attorney-General *v.* Crocker *et al.* (Mass.). 57.

TREASON.

Disqualification for exercise of elective franchise under Const. 1875, art. viii. § 3. Washington *v.* State (Ala.). 7.

TRUSTS.

See SCHOOLS.

Trustee of schools advancing money to pay teacher's wages may recover same from township. Keifer *v.* Troy School Township (Ind.). 205.

VACANCY.

Resignation of sheriff creates vacancy *eo instanti*. Chowning *v.* Boger (Tex.). 91.

VARIANCE.

Highway: petition and evidence as to location of; slight variance in, *held* not fatal. Washington Ice Co. *v.* Lay (Ind.) 375.

VENDORS AND PURCHASERS.

Rescission of purchase by county commissioners: when power lost. State *ex rel. v.* Turpen (Ohio). 119.

VIADUCT.

Damage to property by, recoverable, though viaduct is a lawful structure. Cohen *v.* City of Cleveland (Ohio). 405.

VILLAGE.

Annexation of, to other municipality: payment of previous debts. See TAXES.

VOLUNTARY PAYMENT.

See TAXES.

VOTE.

See SUFFRAGE.

WARRANT FOR PUBLIC MONEY.

See PUBLIC MONEY.

WATER-POWER.

See PUBLIC WORKS, BOARD OF.

WHARF.

City wharf held put to public use and to be exempt from taxation. Galveston Wharf Co. *v.* City of Galveston (Tex.). 422.

—— Charge of reasonable fee for use of such wharf does not change its public character. Galveston Wharf Co. *v.* City of Galveston (Tex.). 422.

WILLS.

Gifts to county by will for any lawful public purpose, affecting body of county, lawful and valid. Christy *v.* Commissioners of Ashtabula Co. (Ohio). 105.

Devises to municipal corporations. 114 *n.*

—— Legislative control over. 116 *n.*

Lightning Source UK Ltd.
Milton Keynes UK
UKHW011207240219
337912UK00010B/509/P